Quantitative Methods for Business Decisions

SECOND EDITION

Quantitative Methods for Business Decisions

SECOND EDITION

LAWRENCE L. LAPIN

San José State University

Harcourt Brace Jovanovich, Inc.

New York   San Diego   Chicago   San Francisco   Atlanta
London   Sydney   Toronto

To my brothers,
Charles and Robert

Printed in the United States of America
Library of Congress Catalog Card Number: 80-84576
ISBN: 0-15-574319-8

Preface

My goal in writing *Quantitative Methods for Business Decisions* has been to provide as complete a treatment as possible of basic management science methodology. The Second Edition expands this topical coverage to include several new subjects: forecasting, the assignment problem, Vogel's approximation (for transportation problems), and integer programming and the branch-and-bound method. This book is written for college students who have only an algebra background. Even more important, it is designed to provide a feeling for the variety and power of management science tools, to alleviate apprehension of the subject, and to enable students to recognize on-the-job situations where management science methodology can be successfully employed.

This book is more intuitive than most. I have treated difficult topics "with kid gloves," so that discussions devoted to this material are longer than those in some other books. Explanations are richly illustrated with relevant and interesting examples to provide more meaningful and *easier* learning experiences than in briefer books. The Second Edition now includes an entirely new chapter on linear programming applications and problem formulation (Chapter 10). Chapter 11 thoroughly describes in nonmathematical terms the underlying rationale of the simplex method, so that the student can learn why—as well as how—this method works. Because many instructors may wish to omit the more advanced simplex concepts, such as artificial variables, these more difficult

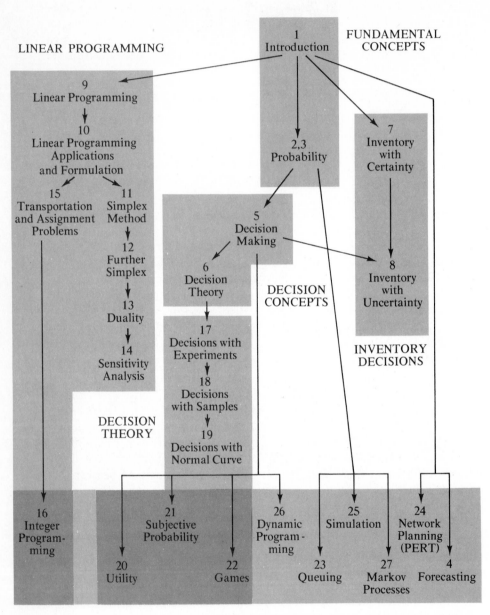

LINEAR PROGRAMMING

FUNDAMENTAL
CONCEPTS

1
Introduction

9
Linear Programming

10
Linear Programming
Applications
and Formulation

15
Transportation
and Assignment
Problems

11
Simplex
Method

12
Further
Simplex

13
Duality

14
Sensitivity
Analysis

2,3
Probability

7
Inventory
with
Certainty

5
Decision
Making

6
Decision
Theory

DECISION
CONCEPTS

8
Inventory
with
Uncertainty

INVENTORY
DECISIONS

17
Decisions with
Experiments

18
Decisions
with Samples

19
Decisions with
Normal Curve

DECISION
THEORY

16
Integer
Program-
ming

21
Subjective
Probability

26
Dynamic
Program-
ming

25
Simulation

24
Network
Planning
(PERT)

20
Utility

22
Games

23
Queuing

27
Markov
Processes

4
Forecasting

SPECIAL TOPICS

topics are now grouped in a second optional simplex chapter (Chapter 12). Chapter 24 discusses network planning (PERT or CPM) in a broad context, including management implications, milestone and activity scheduling, time–cost trade-off, and (in an appendix to the chapter) probabilistic aspects. Chapter 25 introduces Monte Carlo simulation as a simple substitute for the stopwatch observation of an actual system operation. Highly intuitive decision trees are used extensively throughout to explain a variety of concepts.

This book also highlights the limitations and pitfalls associated with various mathematical models and algorithms. For example, some basic models, such as the EOQ model used in inventory decisions and the simple queuing formulas, are based on assumptions that rarely apply in real life. Wherever practical, alternative approaches such as Monte Carlo simulation are indicated and fully described. Traditional probabilistic PERT assumptions are accompanied by a critical analysis of their applicability. The severe limitations on the use of Markovian decision models are also noted.

Because hand calculations are required (a difficulty encountered in any quantitative methods course), I have designed the problem material to minimize computational chores and to emphasize concepts and formulation. Coverage of the computer is provided wherever appropriate, although specific programs are not described in detail—a subject properly covered elsewhere.

As the tinted areas in the preface figure indicate, the overall design of the book is modular to provide maximum flexibility for adaptation to the requirements of a particular course. All or portions of any part of these subject groupings may be used in constructing a one- or two-quarter or a one- or two-semester quantitative methods course. For example, Chapters 2 and 3 may be bypassed by students who have had a prior course in statistics or by instructors who teach a purely deterministic course (a viable possibility with this book). The specific sequencing constraints to be followed are also shown in the figure.

The chapters on probability (or some prior knowledge of this subject) serve as the prerequisite to all the stochastic material. Much of the book follows directly from Chapter 5, which examines the basic concepts of decision making and how to cope with uncertainty, and applies expected value and decision tree analysis to general problem solving. After reading Chapter 5, students should be able to handle any of the special topics and to pursue decision theory in detail.

The book has been thoroughly class-tested several times in a variety of different courses, which has resulted in the culling, revising, and grading of the problem material. In general, the problems are broken into several distinct parts to make the student's job easier and to permit the instructor added flexibility in making assignments. As an added bonus, brief answers to selected problems are provided in the back of the book, so that students can check their own work.

The *Instructor's Manual* contains specific recommendations for various course designs and teaching suggestions and provides detailed solutions to the nearly 400 problems in the text. As an additional aid to the instructor, a set of more than 150 solved problems of slight to moderate difficulty for supplementary homework or examinations is available to adopters (from the publisher). A comprehensive bibliography is included in the back of the book for students who wish to pursue a particular topic in greater detail.

I wish to thank my colleagues who were instrumental in helping me shape the manuscript: C. Randall Byers of the University of Idaho, Ross Lanser of San José State University, Don McBrien of Boston University, Zeb Vancura of the University of Santa Clara, and William D. Whisler of the California State University at Hayward. I also wish to acknowledge the valuable assistance of my students, and to extend special mention to Erika Heider, who helped find errors and assisted in preparing the *Instructor's Manual*.

LAWRENCE L. LAPIN

Contents

13   DUALITY IN LINEAR PROGRAMMING   301

14   SENSITIVITY ANALYSIS IN LINEAR PROGRAMMING   321

15   THE TRANSPORTATION AND ASSIGNMENT PROBLEMS   347

25 SIMULATION 637

26 DYNAMIC PROGRAMMING 671

Quantitative Methods for Business Decisions

SECOND EDITION

1

Introduction to Quantitative Methods for Decision Making

A quiet revolution has taken place in managerial decision making over the past several years—a revolution that is largely due to the successful implementation of *quantitative methods* and the widespread use of computers. The list of the types of business problems that these procedures can be employed to solve grows daily. Examples of successful applications can be found in literally every functional area—from marketing to production, from finance to personnel—and in all major industries. Indeed, quantitative methods can be applied to decision making in general and can be used by individuals or groups, in education, in the professions, and in every type of organization, including governments and nonprofit foundations.

QUANTITATIVE METHODS: A CONTINUING STORY OF SUCCESS   1-1

A few short case histories will demonstrate how useful quantitative methods have been in solving a variety of actual problems.

Managing Research and Development

In the late 1950s, the U.S. Navy was faced with the monumental task of equipping its nuclear submarine fleet with Polaris ballistic missiles. The ships and missiles were designed and built over a period of several years, with the objective of reaching operational capability as soon as possible. A new quantitative method called PERT (Program Evaluation and Review Technique) was used to establish schedules and coordinate and control the efforts of hundreds of contractors. PERT has been credited with the fact that the Polaris program was implemented more than one year earlier than anticipated.

Determining the Number of Bank Tellers

All of us have spent a great deal of time waiting in line at banks. Quantitative methods have been applied in this and a variety of similar situations to find the proper balance between customer annoyance and inconvenience resulting from waiting and the bank's operational efficiency. One result has been a major change in how customers are served. Today, the individual lines that used to form before teller windows are being replaced by a single line that feeds customers to all the open windows. Now customers do not feel guilty if they engage in a time-consuming transaction, such as buying money orders, and they can conduct their business in private.

Banks often use quantitative analysis to decide how many tellers are needed at various times during the week, so that employee workloads can be balanced and customers spend a tolerable amount of time waiting in line. One bank now opens ten windows on Friday afternoons, but only three during slow periods, such as on Tuesday mornings. Previously, five tellers worked at all times. The new policy provides further advantages in that part-time employees can fill in during rush hours and tellers no longer stand at their windows with nothing to do for long periods of time. The bank's customers are satisfied, too; business has improved considerably, and there have been far fewer defections to competing banks since the new system was employed.

Locating Warehouses

A chemical company that produces fertilizers and pesticides employed quantitative methods to determine where to locate its warehouses. The resulting sites minimized the combined annual cost of transportation, storage, and handling. This was achieved by treating all the customers in each of several hundred sales territories as a single demand center. Figure 1-1 is a schematic representation of the distribution system to these centers, showing how each

PLANTS WAREHOUSES DEMAND CENTERS

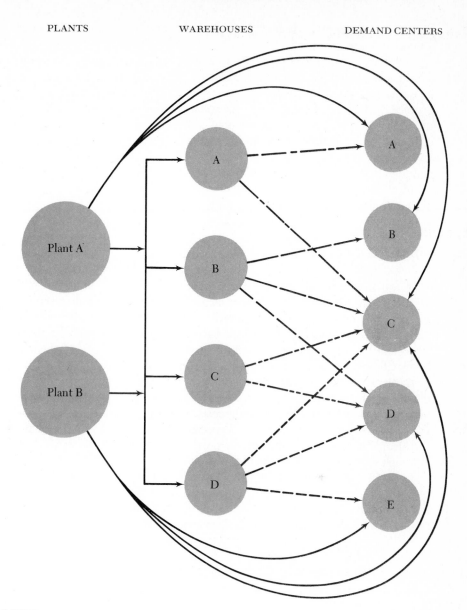

FIGURE 1-1
A schematic representation of a distribution system.

center can be supplied directly from a plant, a regional warehouse, or both a plant and a warehouse.

Possible solutions ranged from having no warehouses (all customers would receive shipments directly from the plants) to having one warehouse in the largest town or city in each territory; both of these alternatives were prohibitively costly. Selecting an in-between solution was a major task because of the astronomical number of possible combinations. First, a screening procedure eliminated all but the most attractive plans. Then each alternative siting plan was evaluated thoroughly by a lengthy computer program that determined the minimum-cost distribution pattern for the indicated warehouse locations. The final solution provided a plan capable of saving several million dollars annually compared with the former operation.

Designing an Oil-Tanker Port Facility

An international oil company committed several hundred million dollars to the construction of a port facility in the Persian Gulf to service oil tankers. Various alternative configurations of loading and storage components were considered, and the potential capacities ranged from miniscule to huge. A host of variables affected the design evaluation, and many of them were uncertain due to long construction lead times. Such factors included future world demands for petroleum, reserve level in fields supplying the port, and the size and characteristics of the oil tanker fleet. Other variables included oil prices and all kinds of operating costs. Political ramifications also had to be considered. (At the time, major oil-producing nations were not nationalizing petroleum production, forming cartels, or embargoing consumer countries—although such contingencies had been allowed for.)

Each alternative port facility was constructed and run "on paper" for a number of years to determine a statistical pattern for future profits. Through this computer simulation, the design was selected that provided the greatest rate of return on invested capital at an acceptable level of risk.

Deployment of Fire-Fighting Companies

A recent study was conducted in New York City to determine how many fire companies the city needed, where they should be located, and how they should be dispatched to alarms.* Traditionally, the nearest available five companies (three engines and two ladders) were dispatched to each alarm, and more units were on call. A more flexible plan was evaluated that varied

---

* Ignall, E. J. et al., "Improving the Deployment of New York City Fire Companies," *Interfaces* (February 1975), pp. 48–61.

the number of companies sent to any given alarm, depending on the nature of the call, to prevent the depletion of nearby units and make them available for future calls.

A simulation of this adaptive procedure indicated that faster response times could be achieved and workloads could be substantially lowered at the same time. Further study identified imbalances in levels of service between various regions within the city, which indicated how companies should be reallocated. When the results were implemented, six companies were eliminated and total annual savings to the city exceeded $5 million per year.

Advantages of Recycling Paper

Paper production and consumption has become increasingly excessive. Close to 100 million tons of virgin pulp is processed each year in the United States, but many of our paper needs can be satisfied by using recycled paper. Figure 1-2 shows how waste recovery provides secondary pulp that can be used in making new paper. A study was made to determine how much paper could be recycled and what could be done to increase the amounts so treated.

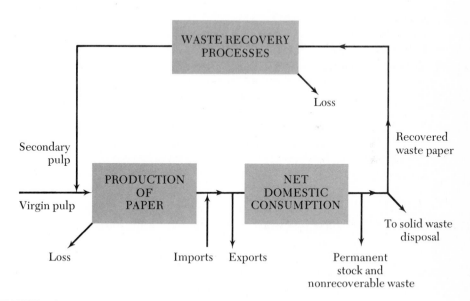

FIGURE 1-2
Paper production and consumption system.

SOURCE: Glassey, C.R., and V.K. Gupta, "A Linear Programming Analysis of Paper Recycling," *Management Science* (December 1974), p. 393.

The basic data for the study were developed from the chemical processes used in making various types of paper. Information relating to how and what quantity of each paper type is consumed was also used. A mathematical procedure based on one of the quantitative methods described in this book was then applied to the problem. The results indicate that waste recovery methods can cut virgin pulp requirements almost in half. Allowing for the cost of collecting and processing waste paper, the net savings throughout the economy would still be substantial.

Investing in Satellite Communications Systems

Satellites have become an increasingly important element in worldwide communications. In 1971, the RCA Corporation decided to enter the satellite business for the private sector.* Due to new technological needs and the nature of the uncertainties involved, previous planning methods could not be used to establish an overall strategy for this new communications business. A variety of options were considered in three areas. The technical alternatives included type of satellite, kind of launch vehicle, and the equipment for and the location of ground stations. Hardware choices included the following alternatives:

Satellite	Capacity	Weight
Spinner	12 transponders	1,500 lb
Spinner	24 transponders	2,800–3,300 lb
Three-axis stabilized	12 transponders	1,500 lb
Three-axis stabilized	24 transponders	2,000 lb

Launch Vehicle	Synchronous Orbit Payload Capability
Thor Delta 2914	1,550 lb
Thor Delta 3914	2,000 lb
Atlas Centaur	4,000 lb

Decisions also had to be made regarding the types of service to provide (for example, television and several kinds of voice transmission). Finally, a number of financial alternatives were available.

A study team formed to evaluate the various alternatives and to recommend the optimal strategy. Various types of quantitative methods in many different areas of application were employed. Alternatives were compared across operational and financial lines in terms of a variety of goals. A best strategy was determined and eventually adopted by RCA management. One

* Nigam, A.K., "Analysis for a Satellite Communications System," *Interfaces* (February 1975), pp. 37–47.

TABLE 1-1
Party Identification by Electoral Loyalty of Party Registration (Sample Results)

	Electoral Loyalty to Party of Registration		
Party Identification	Loyal Democrats	Defectors	Loyal Republicans
Strong Republicans	1%	5%	43%
Weak Republicans	1	8	36
Independents	25	51	21
Weak Democrats	33	33	—
Strong Democrats	40	6	—

benefit of this effort was a greater level of cooperation between corporate staff analysts and line management.

Planning Political Campaign Strategies

A candidate running for high political office must spend a great deal of money campaigning to win the election. One interesting application of quantitative methods occurred during a U.S. Senatorial race. A candidate wished to select target precincts for various activities, such as registration drives, candidate appearances, mailings, and door-to-door canvassing. Geographical segments of the electorate where a small gain could swing the district had to be separated from areas with such high loyalty that campaign efforts would be wasted. To achieve this, voters were divided into more precise categories (shown in Table 1-1) than were available on voter registration rolls. By using quantitative methods to identify the important characteristics of small geographical units throughout the state, the candidate was able to concentrate campaign expenditures on the few that would be most profitable.

MANAGEMENT SCIENCE AND OPERATIONS RESEARCH   1-2

This book is largely concerned with the specific techniques used in the cases just described and similar situations. These quantitative methods can be broadly categorized as techniques of *management science*—a field melding portions of business, economics, statistics, mathematics, and other disciplines into a pragmatic effort to help managers make decisions. As an area of study, these quantitative methods are often identified as *operations research*. Regardless of the label used, the techniques of management science and operations research are concerned with selecting the best alternative course of action whenever mathematics can be helpful in reaching a decision. Many problem situations can be structured so that the possible choices can be ranked on a numerical scale. Common rankings are *profit* or *cost*. In such cases, an *optimal solution* is the one that yields the maximum profit or minimum cost. Other yardsticks may apply in some applications, so that an optimal solution might be the most effective alternative in terms, of time, reliability, or one of many kinds of measures. The particular quantitative method for finding the best solution is sometimes called a *mathematical optimization procedure*.

1-3   HISTORY OF QUANTITATIVE METHODS

The beginnings of operations research can be traced to World War II, when the United States and Great Britain employed mathematicians and physicists to analyze military operations. The need for new thinking was created by the accelerating technological development of weapon systems and by the terrific pressures of modern warfare. Radar and sonar were just coming into use, and long-range, high-altitude bombing required the efficient operation of sophisticated equipment. Operations-research groups were established to determine the most effective deployment and operation of these sophisticated systems. Notable success was achieved in solving a number of problems, especially in the vital area of antisubmarine warfare.

After the war, many of those involved in military operations research retained their interest in analyzing decision making in peacetime endeavors and developed new techniques that could be directly applied to business problems. Corporations patterned operations-research groups after their military predecessors. Schools of business and engineering began to offer graduate programs in operations research, and the field evolved into a complete academic discipline, fostering further applications and theoretical developments. Concurrently, the wide-scale availability of digital computers, which were also being improved constantly, allowed the newly developed techniques to be applied quickly to large-scale optimization problems that had previously been beyond human ability to solve.

1-4   PROCEDURES AND APPLICATIONS

As presently conceived, operations research is concerned with using available resources to find optimal courses of action. In its most general scope, the field is functional in nature, so that interdisciplinary teams (which sometimes include such disparate persons as historians, sociologists, and psychologists) are often used to attack decision-making problems. In this book, we will view operations research in terms of the tools historically associated with it, as they are applied to managerial decision making.

Waiting Lines and Inventory Control

Operations-research methods have been cataloged by type of application and procedure. One of the earliest applications—the analysis of *waiting lines*—predates modern operations research by several decades and has given rise to an area of mathematics referred to as *queuing theory*. It has been used in a variety of operational decisions and in helping to design facilities. Successful applications range from determining the number of supermarket check stands to deciding the size of a parking lot. Quantitative methods have also been developed in the areas of *inventory control* and *equipment replacement*. Businesses have subsequently saved annual costs amounting to billions of dollars just by improving their inventory management.

Linear and Mathematical Programming

The most well-known operations-research procedure is *linear programming*—a mathematical optimization tool that has been used to solve a tremendous variety of decision-making problems requiring the allocation of scarce resources. Today, linear programming is used in oil refineries to determine how gasolines should be blended and in similar applications throughout the chemical industry. Linear programming is also used to determine how goods should be transported. Even the successful tactics employed by the Israeli Air Force in bombing missions during the 1967 Six-Day War were reputedly based in large part on linear programming techniques. (Several times the usual number of sorties were flown by each aircraft, multiplying the effective number of available bombers.)

Related resource-allocation methods include the more general *mathematical programming*, which extends beyond linear programming to a much wider class of problem situations. For decisions that must be made at several successive points in time, such as budgetary investment decisions, *dynamic programming* may be used. Another important tool, mentioned earlier, is PERT; the Polaris program experience shows that this technique has proved useful in controlling large, long-run projects.

Decision Theory and Simulation

The list of operations-research procedures and applications is still growing.

Although the two fields are often confused and their borders may overlap, management science is somewhat broader in concept than operations research.

Management science encompasses a variety of quantitative methods from older disciplines, especially economics, statistics, and industrial engineering, as well as from newer ones, such as cybernetics, systems analysis, organization theory, and the computer and information sciences. Management science relies heavily on *statistical decision theory*—itself an amalgam of statistics, economics, and psychology. The concepts of *game theory*, which is the province of mathematicians and economists, are also included in management science. Both management science and operations research use elements of the stochastic processes employed in *probability theory*; important applications to business problems may be expressed as *Markov processes*. Another powerful tool—*Monte Carlo simulation* (used in the oil-tanker port facility study described earlier)—is essentially a form of statistical sampling that is usually carried out on a computer.

1-5   MODELS AND DECISION MAKING

Every decision-making situation involves *alternatives*. Quantitative methods are used to select the alternative that best satisfies the decision maker's goals. Identifying the possible alternatives and goals is an important task. Once the alternatives are identified, a problem can be quantitatively analyzed by comparing the alternatives in terms of how well they meet the decision maker's objectives. We have already noted that various yardsticks are used for comparison; the classical gauge in business is *profit* or *cost*, although we will encounter others as well.

The Mathematical Model: Parameters and Variables

The first step in applying quantitative methods is generally to express the problem mathematically. Such a formulation is called a *mathematical model*. All mathematical models consist of *variables* and constant terms, which are sometimes referred to as *parameters*. The variables and parameters are usually linked together by algebraic expressions that reflect the decision maker's goals and any special limitations on the kinds of alternatives to be considered.

As an example, we will consider a simple inventory problem where the decision maker's goal is to determine the quantity of items to order periodically so that total operating cost is minimized. A simple mathematical model takes the form

Total annual cost = Ordering cost + Holding cost + Procurement cost and the objective can be expressed as

$$\text{Minimize:}\quad \text{Total annual cost} = \left(\frac{A}{Q}\right)k + hc\left(\frac{Q}{2}\right) + Ac$$

where Q is the order quantity and the single decision variable for this particular problem. The variable Q can assume many different alternative values, such as $0, 1, 2, 3, \ldots, 100, 101 \ldots$. The parameters are

A = annual number of items demanded

k = cost of placing an order

h = annual cost per dollar value for holding items in inventory

c = unit cost of procuring an item

These parameters may be set at any levels that apply to a given situation, so that the same model applies regardless of the levels established for the parameters. This particular model will be explained in further detail in Chapter 7.

Constraints and Feasible Solutions

Sometimes a mathematical model incorporates *constraints* that place special limitations on the problem variables. These constraints are often expressed algebraically. For example, suppose that the storage facilities can accommodate only 300 units at a time. This constraint could be expressed as

$$Q \le 300$$

which would then become an integral part of the model formulation. This restriction disallows any order quantity greater than 300, such as $Q = 350$ units. In effect, this constraint separates the alternatives into two groups: *feasible solutions* (values of Q not exceeding 300 units) and *infeasible solutions* (values of Q exceeding 300 units).

Optimal Solutions

Quantitative methods are also employed to solve the problem; that is, to find the value of the variable that meets the requirements of the mathematical model. For our inventory model, we must find the optimal value for the variable

Q. Here, the *optimal solution* can be found from

$$Q = \sqrt{\frac{2Ak}{hc}}$$

which is derived from mathematical analysis. To illustrate, suppose that each order costs \$4 to place, the annual demand is 1,000 units, it costs \$.20 per year for each dollar value of items held in inventory, and these items may be procured from the supplier for \$1 each. Substituting the values $k = 4$, $A = 1,000$, $h = .20$, and $c = 1$ into the above expression, the minimum-cost order quantity is

$$Q = \sqrt{\frac{2(1000)4}{.20(1)}} = \sqrt{40,000} = 200 \text{ units}$$

Algorithms and Model Types

The solution procedure we just used to solve our inventory problem is an example of an *algorithm*. Algorithms often are simple formulas, but they can also be very complex and involve a series of required steps. Sometimes a mathematical model will exhibit certain undesirable features or be so complex or large that it is impractical to arrive at a solution purely by mathematical reasoning. In such cases, it may be impossible to construct an algorithm that results in a truly optimal solution. In such instances, it is still possible to apply quantitative methods to reach a reasonably satisfactory problem solution.

In this book, we will consider two basic classes of models. The simplest model, like the inventory order-quantity model here, involves no uncertainty. These models contain certain (known and fixed) constants throughout their formulation and are referred to as *deterministic models*. It is more difficult to solve problems that involve one or more uncertain quantities. In these cases, probability must be considered and *stochastic models* may be used.

1-6 THE IMPORTANCE OF STUDYING QUANTITATIVE METHODS

The purpose of this book is not to make you an expert in quantitative methods. Its goal is to familiarize you with the more important tools of quantitative methods and to expose you to a wide variety of successful applications. No great skill in mathematics is required.

Three main advantages can be gained from exposure to quantitative methods. First, it should increase your confidence as a decision maker, largely because you will see how vast and varied the problems are that can be solved through the application of quantitative methods. Second, a study of quantitative methods creates problem-solving skills that will be extremely helpful when you encounter an unsolved problem, whether or not you are directly responsible for finding the answer. A final advantage will be your ability to cope with decisions, as a manager, as an employee or in your personal life.

Some knowledge of quantitative methods is especially crucial to the modern manager. An effective manager must make good choices, and the ability to know where, when, and how to use quantitative methods to make optimal decisions gives managers a definite advantage. This doesn't mean that an effective manager must be mathematically skilled or must personally develop models and solutions. There are a tremendous number of opportunities for the layman to do exactly that, but experts can be hired to perform the more demanding tasks. However, it is important to know enough about this subject to guide those high-powered analysts (who too often stray into a mathematical "never-never land"). As a bare minimum, any exposure to quantitative methods will teach future managers to ask the right questions and to recognize when outside help may be useful.

2
Probability Concepts

Probability plays a special role in all our lives, because we use it to measure uncertainty. We are continually faced with decisions that lead to uncertain outcomes, and we rely on probability to help us choose our course of action. In business, probability is a pivotal factor in most significant decisions. A department store buyer will order large quantities of a new style that is predicted to sell well. A company will introduce a new product when the chance of its success seems high enough to outweigh the possibility of losses due to its failure. A new college graduate is hired when the probability of satisfactory performance is judged to be sufficiently high.

A *probability* is a numerical value that measures the uncertainty that a particular event will occur. The probability of an event ordinarily represents the *proportion of times under identical circumstances that the event can be expected to occur*. Such a long-run frequency of occurrence is referred to as an *objective probability*. In tossing a fair coin, the probability of obtaining a head is 1/2. This can be verified after tossing the coin many times and observing that a head appears about half of the time. However, a probability value is often subjective; that is, it is determined solely on the basis of personal judgment. *Subjective probabilities* are expressed for events that have no meaningful long-run frequency of occurrence. For example, an oil wildcatter may express his uncertainty about the presence of oil beneath a candidate drilling site in terms of a probability value such as 1/2. One attempt will be made at drilling on that site; since no two sites are identical, there are no other situations like the present one for which the frequency of oil strikes can be determined.

Several mathematicians initially studied probability more than 300 years ago in connection with gambling problems. Probability theory has since evolved into one of the most elegant and useful branches of mathematics. Today, devices ordinarily associated with gambling, such as dice and playing cards, are useful in illustrating how we find probabilities.

2-1 FUNDAMENTAL CONCEPTS

The Event

Uncertain outcomes are called *events*. A preliminary step in finding an event's probability is to identify all possible outcomes of the uncertain situation. In cataloging possible outcomes or events, it is convenient to discuss them in groupings or *sets*. A complete listing of events is called the *sample space*. Exactly one and only one event on this master list will occur.

The sample space for tossing a coin contains just two events—head and tail—which may be conveniently expressed in set notation as

$$\text{Sample space} = \{\text{head, tail}\}$$

Head and tail are the *elementary events* of the sample space. Only one of these events can occur.

As another illustration, consider the characteristics of a card drawn from a shuffled deck of 52 ordinary playing cards. Here the sample space is expressed as

$$\text{Sample space} = \{\text{ace of spades, deuce of spades, \ldots, king of diamonds}\}$$

It is convenient to represent the sample space pictorially as shown in Figure 2-1.

The elements in the sample space are the simplest outcomes or *elementary events*. We may also be interested in more complex outcomes. For example, consider the sample space for the outcome from tossing a six-sided die

$$\text{Sample space} = \{1, 2, 3, 4, 5, 6\}$$

where the elements represent the number of dots on the showing face. The outcome "an even-valued face" is a *composite event*, which occurs whenever any one of the elementary events 2, 4, or 6 results. Maintaining our set represen-

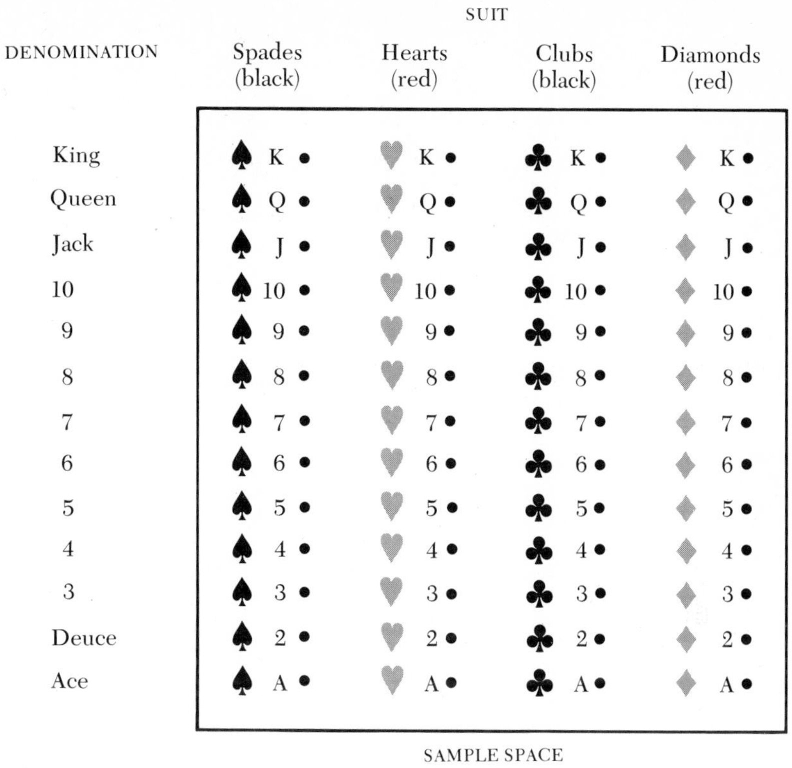

SUIT

DENOMINATION	Spades (black)	Hearts (red)	Clubs (black)	Diamonds (red)
King	♠ K ●	♥ K ●	♣ K ●	♦ K ●
Queen	♠ Q ●	♥ Q ●	♣ Q ●	♦ Q ●
Jack	♠ J ●	♥ J ●	♣ J ●	♦ J ●
10	♠ 10 ●	♥ 10 ●	♣ 10 ●	♦ 10 ●
9	♠ 9 ●	♥ 9 ●	♣ 9 ●	♦ 9 ●
8	♠ 8 ●	♥ 8 ●	♣ 8 ●	♦ 8 ●
7	♠ 7 ●	♥ 7 ●	♣ 7 ●	♦ 7 ●
6	♠ 6 ●	♥ 6 ●	♣ 6 ●	♦ 6 ●
5	♠ 5 ●	♥ 5 ●	♣ 5 ●	♦ 5 ●
4	♠ 4 ●	♥ 4 ●	♣ 4 ●	♦ 4 ●
3	♠ 3 ●	♥ 3 ●	♣ 3 ●	♦ 3 ●
Deuce	♠ 2 ●	♥ 2 ●	♣ 2 ●	♦ 2 ●
Ace	♠ A ●	♥ A ●	♣ A ●	♦ A ●

SAMPLE SPACE

FIGURE 2-1
Sample space describing a randomly selected playing card.

tation, the possible ways in which this event may occur are denoted by

$$\text{Even-valued face} = \{2, 4, 6\}$$

Such a partial listing is an *event set*. Note that an event set is a *subset* of the sample space: All of its elements also belong to the sample space. An event set for an elementary event, such as the king of spades, contains a single element:

$$\text{King of spades} = \{\text{king of spades}\}$$

Many composite events are possible for most uncertain situations. Figure 2-2 shows a few event sets that can be associated with drawing one card from a deck of 52 ordinary playing cards. Here, each event set is pictured as a grouping of those dots corresponding to the applicable elementary events.

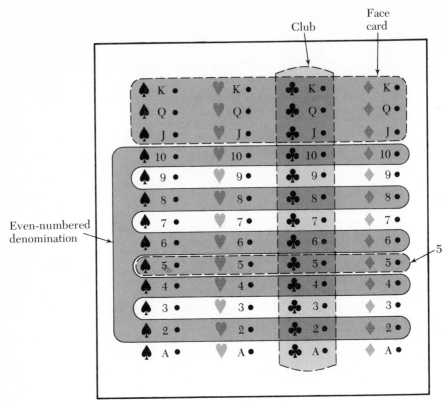

SAMPLE SPACE

FIGURE 2-2
Composite events for drawing a playing card.

The Basic Definition of Probability

Classically, the probability of an event is the relative frequency that it occurs when the identical situation is repeated a large number of times. This is denoted by the ratio of the number of times the event occurs to the number of times the circumstances are faced:

$$Pr[event] = \frac{\text{Number of times the event occurs}}{\text{Number of times the situation is repeated}}$$

This expression indicates that a probability is an empirically derived value that can be obtained only after repeated experimentation. In practice, actual experimentation is often unnecessary. The probability of an event such as obtaining a head in a coin toss can be determined by plausible reasoning about the types of outcomes that can be expected. Knowing that a coin has two sides, assuming that it is evenly balanced, and presuming that it is tossed with no bias toward any particular face, it is reasonable to expect a head to occur in about half of any number of tosses. Thus, we can deduce that

$$Pr[head] = \frac{1}{2}$$

When all elementary events are equally likely, we determine the probability of an event this way:

$$Pr[event] = \frac{\text{Number of elementary events in the event set}}{\text{Total number of equally likely elementary events}}$$

For example, since the event "even-valued face" resulting from a die toss occurs whenever any one of the 3 elementary events 2, 4, or 6 occurs and since we can reasonably assume that there are exactly 6 equally likely elementary events, or showing faces

$$Pr[\text{even-valued face}] = \frac{3}{6} = \frac{1}{2}$$

We can use this definition to find the probabilities of the other composite events shown in Figure 2-2 for drawing one card from a shuffled deck:

$$Pr[club] = \frac{13}{52} = \frac{1}{4}$$

$$Pr[\text{face card}] = \frac{12}{52} = \frac{3}{13}$$

$$Pr[5] = \frac{4}{52} = \frac{1}{13}$$

$$Pr\begin{bmatrix}\text{even-numbered} \\ \text{denomination}\end{bmatrix} = \frac{20}{52} = \frac{5}{13}$$

In each case, all cards (elementary events) are equally likely, so that each denominator is 52. The numerators are the sizes of the respective event sets.

If the elementary events are not all equally likely, probabilities must be estimated through experimentation. For example, if a die is shaved until it is asymmetrical, it becomes more likely to roll some sides than others. Logical reasoning cannot tell us what the probabilities are for the faces of a shaved die. These probabilities can be estimated only from actual results after many tosses of the die.

Certain and Uncertain Events

A probability will always be between 0 and 1, inclusively, because the numerator in the probability fraction can never be negative or larger than the denominator. If an event is certain to occur, the same value will appear in both the numerator and the denominator of the probability fraction, because the same events will result from all experiments with a frequency of 1. Thus

$$Pr[\text{certain event}] = 1$$

The event "the next President of the United States will be at least 35 years old" is a certain event and has a probability of 1, because the Constitution specifies that the minimum age of the President be 35. The event "food prices will rise, fall, or remain unchanged" is also certain and has a probability of 1.

At the other extreme, an impossible event's frequency ratio will always have a 0 in the numerator, because the event will occur in no experiment. Thus

$$Pr[\text{impossible event}] = 0$$

For example, the U.S. automobile industry is limited in its production capacity and cannot manufacture 50 million cars. This outcome for next year is impossible, and we can state that

$$Pr[\text{50 million cars manufactured}] = 0$$

2-2   EVENT RELATIONSHIPS

In computing probabilities, it is often helpful to examine the relationships between events. Several types of relationships are important. First, we will consider how events may be combined.

Some outcomes may be explained by the occurrence of more than one event. For example, obtaining *at least* two heads when tossing three coins is equivalent to obtaining exactly two heads *or* exactly three heads. Drawing the ace of spades may be stated more precisely as drawing a card that is both an ace and a spade. The basic event combinations important to probability are expressed in the logical connective sense of "or" and "and."

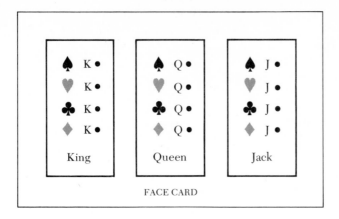

Face card = King *or* queen *or* jack

FIGURE 2-3
The union of three component events.

An outcome that occurs whenever any one of several more specific events happens is called the *union* of those events. This is expressed as

A or B

which represents the outcome when either event *A* occurs singly, event *B* occurs singly, or both *A* and *B* occur together. This relationship is important because probability computations can often be simplified by first looking at *A* and *B* separately. Figure 2-3 illustrates how the union of the events "king," "queen," and "jack" provides the event "face card."

An outcome that arises only when both *A* and *B* occur is referred to as the *intersection* of events *A* and *B*. We express this as

A and B

We sometimes refer to *A and B* as a *joint event*. Figure 2-4 illustrates this concept for three coin tosses, where the event "all heads" is portrayed as the intersection of the events "dime is head" and "all coins show same side."

Several events are *mutually exclusive* if the occurrence of any one event automatically precludes the occurrence of the others. Another way of saying this is that the joint occurrence of the events is itself an impossible event.

For example, the event of primary interest to a company considering its advertising budget is next year's anticipated sales. The number of possible events (sales figures) varies from a minimum of 0 to some maximum. Only one of these sales events will occur, so that the sales events are mutually exclusive.

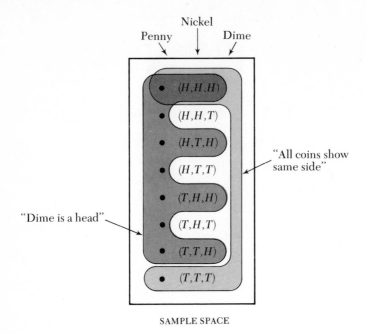

SAMPLE SPACE

FIGURE 2-4
The intersection of two events.

As another example, consider two possible events for a firm: bankruptcy and profit. These events are *not* mutually exclusive, since a business can earn a profit but still be forced into bankruptcy by the claims of impatient creditors.

A collection of events is *collectively exhaustive* if at least one of those events is bound to occur. For example, consider the following events describing the characteristics of a randomly chosen playing card:

red suit, black suit, spade

It is certain that one of these events will occur, because together they comprise all possibilities.

Two events exhibit *independence* when the probability of one is unaffected by the occurrence of the other. Consider the outcomes of two successive coin tosses. Assuming that one toss outcome has no influence on the other, we can conclude that obtaining a head on the second toss is independent of obtaining a head on the first toss, because the probability of a head is 1/2 whether a head or a tail is obtained first. But we cannot conclude that a randomly chosen person's education and income are independent events, since we know that education influences income levels. The probability of earning a high income is greater for a college graduate than for a high-school dropout.

THE ADDITION LAW 2-3

Several laws make it easier to determine probabilities. The *addition law* provides a convenient way to find the probability of *A or B:*

$$\Pr[A \text{ or } B] = \Pr[A] + \Pr[B] - \Pr[A \text{ and } B]$$

For a randomly chosen playing card, the addition law tells us that

$$\Pr[\text{ace } or \text{ heart}] = \Pr[\text{ace}] + \Pr[\text{heart}] - \Pr[\text{ace } and \text{ heart (ace of hearts)}]$$

$$= \frac{4}{52} + \frac{13}{52} - \frac{1}{52} = \frac{16}{52}$$

Note that the event sets for "ace" and "heart" in Figure 2-5 intersect at the ace

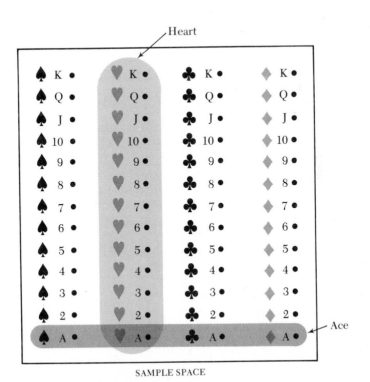

SAMPLE SPACE

FIGURE 2-5
The union of events "heart" and "ace" is the entire shaded area.

of hearts, so that the ace of hearts is included in both event sets. Therefore, the probability of obtaining the ace of hearts was subtracted from the sum of these probabilities.

The Addition Law for Mutually Exclusive Events

If A and B are mutually exclusive events, their joint occurrence is impossible and $\Pr[A \text{ and } B] = 0$. This allows us to simplify the addition law to

$$\Pr[A \text{ or } B] = \Pr[A] + \Pr[B]$$

This simplified law applies only when the components are mutually exclusive events.

To illustrate, suppose that the number of customers arriving at a barber-shop during the first 10 minutes it is open can be any value between 0 and 4, with the following probabilities:

Number of Persons	Probability
0	.1
1	.2
2	.3
3	.3
4	.1

We can apply the simplified addition law to obtain the probability that 2 or 3 persons arrive

$$\Pr[2 \text{ or } 3] = \Pr[2] + \Pr[3]$$
$$= .3 + .3 = .6$$

since the two event components are mutually exclusive,

The addition law applies for any number of components. For example, the probability that at least 1 person arrives may be expressed as

$$\Pr[\text{at least } 1] = \Pr[1 \text{ or } 2 \text{ or } 3 \text{ or } 4]$$
$$= \Pr[1] + \Pr[2] + \Pr[3] + \Pr[4]$$
$$= .2 + .3 + .3 + .1 = .9$$

Mutually Exclusive and Collectively Exhaustive Events

Many uncertain situations involve outcomes that are not only mutually exclusive but also collectively exhaustive. The following property of the addition law can be used *whenever the component events are both mutually exclusive and collectively exhaustive:*

$$\Pr[A \text{ or } B \text{ or } C] = \Pr[A] + \Pr[B] + \Pr[C] = 1$$

The probabilities of these components sum to 1 because the two properties guarantee that the complex outcome *A or B or C is certain.*

Application to Complementary Events

The addition law can be very useful in dealing with *complementary events* (opposites). The addition law provides

$$\Pr[A \text{ or not } A] = \Pr[A] + \Pr[\text{not } A] = 1$$

From this it follows that

$$\Pr[A] = 1 - \Pr[\text{not } A]$$

This principle is useful when the probability value of the event "not A" is easier to find than the probability value of A itself.

Now suppose we want to determine a faster way to compute the probability that at least 1 person arrives at the barbershop. "At least 1" means "some," and *the opposite of "some" is "none."* The complementary event is therefore "0 customers" and

$$\Pr[\text{at least } 1] = 1 - \Pr[0]$$
$$= 1 - .1 = .9$$

THE JOINT PROBABILITY TABLE AND CONDITIONAL PROBABILITY 2-4

The Joint Probability Table and Marginal Probabilities

We will now consider how probabilities can be obtained when several events occur simultaneously. The credit applicants of a department store are classified in terms of home ownership and job tenure. Suppose that one application is chosen by lottery from a total of 200 applications grouped into the four categories in Table 2-1. The letters *O, R, L,* and *M* will be used to simplify

TABLE 2-1
Number of Credit Applicants by Category

	On Present Job Two Years or Less (L)	On Present Job More Than Two Years (M)	Total
Owns Home (O)	20	40	60
Rents Home (R)	80	60	140
Total	100	100	200

the following discussion. Using the probability definition for equally likely events, we can determine the following probability values:

$$\Pr[O \ and \ L] = \frac{20}{200} = .10 \qquad \Pr[R \ and \ L] = \frac{80}{200} = .40$$

$$\Pr[O \ and \ M] = \frac{40}{200} = .20 \qquad \Pr[R \ and \ M] = \frac{60}{200} = .30$$

The marginal totals can be used to determine the probabilities that the applicant has the respective attributes. For instance, the probability that the applicant owns a home is $\Pr[O] = 60/200 = .30$. In a similar manner, we can find $\Pr[R]$, $\Pr[L]$, and $\Pr[M]$. Since only the numbers in the margins of Table 2-1 are needed to compute these probabilities, they are sometimes called *marginal probabilities*.

The *joint probability table* in Table 2-2 may prove helpful. The joint events represented by each cell in a joint probability table are mutually exclusive. Thus, the marginal probabilities can also be found by applying the addition law for mutually exclusive events. For example, the event O has two mutually exclusive

TABLE 2-2
Joint Probability Table for a Randomly Selected Application

	On Present Job Two Years or Less (L)	On Present Job More Than Two Years (M)	Marginal Probability
Owns Home (O)	.10	.20	.30
Rents Home (R)	.40	.30	.70
Marginal Probability	.50	.50	1.00

components: O *and* L; O *and* M. Using the appropriate values from Table 2-2, we can determine the probability that the applicant is a homeowner by

$$Pr[O] = Pr[(O \text{ } and \text{ } L) \text{ } or \text{ } (O \text{ } and \text{ } M)]$$
$$= Pr[O \text{ } and \text{ } L] + Pr[O \text{ } and \text{ } M]$$
$$= .10 + .20 = .30$$

Conditional Probability

The occurrence of one event can affect the probability of another event. We refer to probability values obtained under the stipulation that some events have occurred or will occur as *conditional probabilities*.

Conditional probability may be illustrated for the outcome of drawing a card from a fully shuffled deck. Suppose another person draws the card without letting you see it, but you catch a brief glimpse and know that it is a face card. The deck has only 12 face cards. What is the probability that the card is a king? Although the deck contains 4 kings, your answer is not 4/52, because the information you gained indicates that some of the 52 cards are impossible. The sample space has been restricted to the 12 face cards, and the only remaining uncertainty is which one of these 12 cards has been removed. In a sense, there is a new "sample space" in which the 12 face cards are the elementary events. Using basic concepts, we can determine that the probability of the card being a king is 4/12 = 1/3. Thus, we may state that the conditional probability of a king *given* face card is

$$Pr[\text{king} | \text{face card}] = \frac{4}{12} = \frac{1}{3}$$

where the vertical bar stands for "given."

Computing Conditional Probability from Joint Probability

We can use the joint probability of two events, when it is known, and the probability of the given event to compute conditional probabilities in the form of the following expression:

$$Pr[A|B] = \frac{Pr[A \text{ } and \text{ } B]}{Pr[B]}$$

Applying this property to our credit-applicant illustration, we can compute the conditional probability that the applicant owns a home given job tenure of more than two years as

$$Pr[O|M] = \frac{Pr[O \text{ and } M]}{Pr[M]} = \frac{.20}{.50} = .40$$

Note that we could have obtained the same result from the data in Table 2-1 by calculating the proportion of applicants on their present job more than two years who are also homeowners:

$$\frac{40}{40 + 60} = \frac{40}{100} = .40$$

Thus, we can see that *the conditional probability of A given B is the proportion of times that A occurs out of all the times that B occurs.* This explains why we divide the joint probability by the probability of the given event to obtain $Pr[A|B]$.

Independent Events

To further illustrate conditional probability, we may use the preceding property to recompute the probability of obtaining a king given a face card:

$$Pr[king|face] = \frac{Pr[king \text{ and } face]}{Pr[face]} = \frac{4/52}{12/52} = \frac{4}{12} = \frac{1}{3}$$

Note that in both illustrations the conditional probabilities differ from the corresponding probabilities when there are no stipulations, which we call *unconditional probabilities.* Thus

$$Pr[king|face] = \frac{1}{3} \neq \frac{1}{13} = Pr[king]$$

$$Pr[O|M] = .40 \neq .30 = Pr[O]$$

The unconditional and conditional probabilities do not always differ, but the comparative values may be used to establish independence, which exists when the probability of one event is unaffected by the occurrence of the other. In effect, *events are independent only when their conditional probabilities equal their respective unconditional probabilities.* Here, we see that the events "king" and "face" are not independent; likewise, O and M are dependent events.

Consider another example. For a randomly selected card, the events "ace" and "heart" are independent. To verify this, we compute

$$\Pr[\text{ace}] = \frac{4}{52} = \frac{1}{13}$$

which is equal to

$$\Pr[\text{ace}|\text{heart}] = \frac{1}{13}$$

THE MULTIPLICATION LAW   **2-5**

The *multiplication law* is used to find the probability of the joint occurrence of two or more events. The multiplication law is expressed as

$$\Pr[A \text{ and } B] = \Pr[A] \times \Pr[B|A]$$

The multiplication law may be extended to any number of components, such as for *A and B and C.*

We can apply the multiplication law to our credit applicant illustration. Recall that $\Pr[O|M] = .40$ and that $\Pr[M] = .50$. Multiplying these values, we obtain

$$\Pr[M \text{ and } O] = \Pr[M] \times \Pr[O|M] = .50(.40) = .20$$

This is the same joint probability value that we found earlier.

When the joint probabilities are already known, the multiplication law is not needed. But when only conditional and marginal probabilities are available, the joint probabilities can be obtained only by using the multiplication law.

Illustration: Automobile Accident Probabilities

A highway commissioner has found that one-half of all fatal automobile accidents in the state may be blamed on drunk drivers. Only 4 in 1,000 reported accidents have proved fatal, and 10% of all accidents in the state are attributed to drunk drivers. The commissioner wishes to summarize this information in a joint probability table related to future accidents. Assuming that the present pattern prevails, the joint probability that a reported accident will

TABLE 2-3
Joint Probability Table for the Cause and Type of Automobile Accident

	Fatal (F)	Nonfatal (not F)	Marginal Probability
Drunk Driver (D)	**.002**	**.098**	.100
Other Cause (O)	**.002**	**.898**	**.900**
Marginal Probability	.004	**.996**	1.000

be fatal (F) is

$$Pr[F] = \frac{4}{1,000} = .004$$

whereas the probability that a drunk driver (D) will cause the accident (fatal or not) is

$$Pr[D] = .10$$

and the conditional probability that a drunk driver will cause the accident given that it is fatal is

$$Pr[D|F] = .50$$

Table 2-3 is the joint probability table for the causes and the types of automobile accident. Only the numbers shown in regular type are directly provided from the data given here. The boldface probability values were obtained in the following manner.

The multiplication law provides the joint probability that a fatal accident will be caused by a drunk driver:

$$Pr[F \text{ and } D] = Pr[F] \times Pr[D|F]$$
$$= .004(.50) = .002$$

The marginal probabilities for the causes and the types of accidents must sum, respectively, to 1. It therefore follows that

$$Pr[O] = 1 - Pr[D] = 1 - .100 = .900$$
$$Pr[\text{not } F] = 1 - Pr[F] = 1 - .004 = .996$$

The remaining joint probabilities were found by using the fact that the joint probabilities in each row and column must sum to the respective marginal probability values.

THE PROBABILITY TREE DIAGRAM   2-6

It can be convenient to use a *probability tree diagram* to apply the multiplication law. To illustrate this concept, we will consider a situation commonly encountered in quality-control sampling. Suppose that a shipment of 100 parts contains exactly 5 defectives. This fact is unknown to the inspector, who must decide whether to accept or reject the entire shipment based on a sample of three items selected at random.

The various probabilities pertaining to the contents of the sample are diagrammed in the probability tree in Figure 2-6. There, the outcome of each successive sample observation is represented by a *branch*, and the probability of each outcome is indicated beside its branch. Since one of two complementary events can occur for each item observed, there are two branches for each item—one for a defective item (D) and one for a good item (G). There is a different

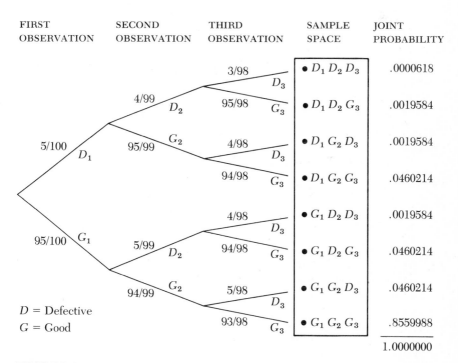

FIRST OBSERVATION	SECOND OBSERVATION	THIRD OBSERVATION	SAMPLE SPACE	JOINT PROBABILITY
		3/98 D_3	• $D_1 D_2 D_3$	.0000618
	4/99 D_2	95/98 G_3	• $D_1 D_2 G_3$	.0019584
5/100 D_1	95/99 G_2	4/98 D_3	• $D_1 G_2 D_3$	.0019584
		94/98 G_3	• $D_1 G_2 G_3$	.0460214
	5/99 D_2	4/98 D_3	• $G_1 D_2 D_3$	.0019584
95/100 G_1		94/98 G_3	• $G_1 D_2 G_3$	.0460214
	94/99 G_2	5/98 D_3	• $G_1 G_2 D_3$	.0460214
		93/98 G_3	• $G_1 G_2 G_3$	.8559988

D = Defective
G = Good

1.0000000

FIGURE 2-6
Probability tree for selecting a random sample of three items without replacement from a population of size 100.

branching point or *fork* for each observation. Two forks are required for the second item—a different fork for each possible attribute of the first observation. Because four distinct outcomes are possible for the quality of the earlier items, four forks are needed for the third observation. To distinguish the outcomes for each item, we use the subscripts 1, 2, and 3. For instance, D_1 means that the first item will be defective; G_2 means that the second item will be good. Altogether there are eight paths through the tree, each representing a different sample outcome. Each path leads to a different elementary event, so that the eight end positions provide the sample space for the final sample results.

The results of each selection are *not independent*, because each item is not replaced in the shipment after it is inspected. This means that the composition of the remainder of the shipment changes each time. The proportion of defective items remaining in the shipment increases or decreases, depending on the quality of the prior selection. Thus, if the first item proves to be defective, so that D_1 occurs, only 4 of the remaining 99 items can possibly be defective and the probability that the second item will be defective D_2 is 4/99. But if G_1 is the first event, then the probability that D_2 will occur is 5/99, because any one of the 5 remaining defective items can be chosen. These values are *conditional probabilities*, because there is a different chance that D_2 will occur in each case.

The joint probabilities for each elementary event can be found by multiplying the probability values for the branches on the path leading to a particular outcome. For instance, the multiplication law may be applied to find the probability that all three items in the sample are defective:

$$\Pr[D_1 \text{ and } D_2 \text{ and } D_3] = \Pr[D_1] \times \Pr[D_2|D_1] \times \Pr[D_3|D_1 \text{ and } D_2]$$

$$= \left(\frac{5}{100}\right)\left(\frac{4}{99}\right)\left(\frac{3}{98}\right)$$

$$= .0000618$$

The joint probabilities for all the other outcomes listed in the far-right column of Figure 2-6 were found in the same way.

2-7 THE MULTIPLICATION LAW FOR INDEPENDENT EVENTS

Recall that two events are independent if the probability of one event is unaffected by the occurrence of the other event. This means that the conditional and unconditional probabilities are identical. Thus

$$\Pr[A|B] = \Pr[A] \quad \text{and} \quad \Pr[B|A] = \Pr[B]$$

The multiplication law can then be simplified to the form

$$Pr[A \text{ and } B] = Pr[A] \times Pr[B]$$

only when A and B are independent events.

Earlier, we established that the events "ace" and "heart" are independent events for a randomly selected playing card. Thus

$$Pr[\text{ace } and \text{ heart}] = Pr[\text{ace}] \times Pr[\text{heart}]$$

$$= \frac{1}{13} \times \frac{1}{4} = \frac{1}{52}$$

To further illustrate, we will return to our quality-control situation. This time, instead of the user, let's consider the analogous problem faced by the supplier who continuously produces the parts. The production inspector wishes to use sample data to determine whether adjustments should be made in the plant machinery. Suppose that defectives actually occur 5% of the time (but the inspector does not know this). The probability tree in Figure 2-7 can be constructed for the random selection of three parts at separate times from the

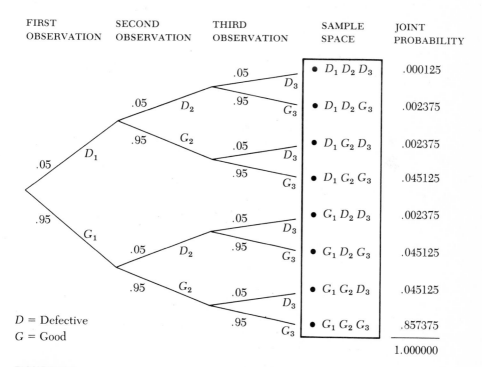

FIGURE 2-7

Probability tree for a random sample of three items from a production process.

production line. There, the successive events G_1 (first item is good), D_2 (second item is defective), D_3, and so on, for any tree path are independent, because errors in such continuous processes are generally erratic. Therefore, the characteristics of an earlier item will not influence the incidence of defective items in the future. The probability is therefore .05 for a defective item, regardless of the sequence in which it is chosen, and .95 for a good item. The conditional and unconditional probabilities are equal. The probability that all of the sample items will be defective is thus

$$Pr[D_1 \text{ and } D_2 \text{ and } D_3] = Pr[D_1] \times Pr[D_2] \times Pr[D_3]$$

$$= (.05)(.05)(.05)$$

$$= (.05)^3 = .000125$$

The trees in Figures 2-6 and 2-7 illustrate some important probability concepts. The tree in Figure 2-6 pertains to sampling *without replacement* from a small population of items; there, the successive events are dependent. The second tree represents the same situation for a population of unlimited size. A probability tree identical to Figure 2-7 also applies when sampling *with replacement* from a small population. Independence between successive events applies in either case. The latter two situations are analogous to a series of coin tosses and give rise to the very important binomial probability distribution, which we will discuss in Chapter 3.

2-8 COMMON ERRORS IN APPLYING PROBABILITY

Some of the most prevalent errors in determining probabilities result from the improper use of the laws of probability. Four common mistakes are listed here:

(1) Using the addition law to find the probability of the union of several events when they are *not* mutually exclusive, without correcting for the double counting of possible occurrences.

For example, a casualty-insurance underwriter might establish that the probabilities of a city experiencing one of the following natural disasters in the next decade are

tornado	.5
flood	.3
earthquake	.4

We cannot say that the probability of suffering one of these acts is $.5 + .3 + .4 = 1.2$. Clearly, two or more of these disasters may occur over a ten-year period, and some may occur more than once.

(2) Using the addition law when the multiplication law should be used, and conversely. Remember that *or* signifies addition and that *and* signifies multiplication.

For example, the probability of drawing a red face card is the same as the probability for the event "red *and* face." Recall that $Pr[red] = 26/52$ and that $Pr[face] = 12/52$. If we add these values, we obtain 38/52, which is a meaningless result. Since "red" and "face" are independent events

$$Pr[red \text{ } and \text{ } face] = \frac{26}{52} \times \frac{12}{52} = \frac{6}{52}$$

(3) Using the multiplication law for independent component events when the events are dependent.

This error occurs, for example, when replacement is mistakenly assumed in calculating the probability of obtaining a particular sample result. As we have seen, removing an item from a group changes the group's composition and therefore the probabilities that future selections will be of a certain type.

(4) Improperly identifying the complement of an event. For example, *the complement of "none" is "some,"* which may be expressed as "one or more" or as "at least one."

The following example, which actually happened, dramatically illustrates how ludicrous results may be obtained by applying the probability laws incorrectly.*

Trial by Probability—A Misapplication

An elderly woman was mugged in the suburb of a large city. A couple was convicted of the crime, although the evidence on which the prosecution rested its case was largely circumstantial. The multiplication law for independent events was used to demonstrate the extremely low probability that any specific couple could have committed the crime. The events (the characteristics witnesses ascribed to the couple) are listed below, with their assumed probabilities:

Characteristic Event	Assumed Probability
Drives yellow car	1/10
Interracial couple	1/1000
Blonde girl	1/4
Girl wears hair in ponytail	1/10
Man bearded	1/10
Man black	1/3

* For a detailed discussion, see "Trial by Mathematics," *Time* (April 26, 1968), p. 41.

These values were multiplied to obtain the probability that any specific couple, chosen at random from the city's population, would have all six characteristics:

$$\frac{1}{10} \times \frac{1}{1,000} \times \frac{1}{4} \times \frac{1}{10} \times \frac{1}{10} \times \frac{1}{3} = \frac{1}{12,000,000}$$

Since the defendants exhibited all six characteristics, the jury was mystified by the overwhelming strength of the probability argument and convicted them.

The Supreme Court of the state heard the appeal of one of the defendants. The defense attorneys, after obtaining some good advice on probability theory, attacked the prosecution's analysis on two points: (1) the rather dubiously assumed event probability values, and (2) the invalid assumption of independence implicit in using the multiplication law in this manner (examples: the proportion of black men having beards may be greater than the proportion of the population as a whole having beards; "interracial couple" and "black man" are definitely not independent events). The judge accepted the arguments of the defense and noted that the trial evidence was misleading on another score: A high probability that the defendants were the *only* such couple should really have been determined to demonstrate a strong case. Using the prosecution's original figures and its assumptions of independence, it can be demonstrated that the probability was large that at least one other couple in the area had the same characteristics.

2-9   REVISING PROBABILITIES USING BAYES' THEOREM

In this section, we will introduce a procedure whereby probabilities can be revised when new information is obtained. Revising probabilities is a familiar concept. For example, think how many times you have left home in the morning with no raincoat, only to look up and notice a menacing cloud cover which sends you back for some protection in case it rains. On first charging outdoors, you judged the probability of rain to be small. But the presence of clouds caused you to revise this probability significantly upward.

We need to be able to revise probabilities so that we can make better use of experimental information. We can accomplish this by applying a fundamental principle that follows immediately from the laws of probability we developed earlier in this chapter. This principle is referred to as *Bayes' Theorem*, which is named after the Reverend Thomas Bayes, who proposed in the eighteenth century that probabilities be revised in accordance with empirical findings.

Most information is not conclusive. Any empirical test can camouflage the truth. For instance, some potentially good students will perform poorly on college entrance examinations and some poor students will do well. A good example of how such information may be unreliable is illustrated by the geologist's seismic test. A seismic survey can deny the presence of oil in a field where it is already being produced and can confirm the presence of oil under a site already proved dry. Still, such imperfect findings can be valuable. An unfavorable test result can increase the chance of rejecting a poor prospect (college applicant or drilling lease) and a favorable result can enhance the likelihood of selecting a good one.

The information obtained will affect the probabilities of the events that determine the consequences of each act. We can revise the probabilities of these events upward or downward, depending on the evidence we obtain. Thus, the geologist increases the probability of finding oil after obtaining a favorable seismic survey analysis and decreases this probability after obtaining an unfavorable survey.

Bayes' Theorem

Consider a situation for which two uncertain events "E" and "not E" are possible. Suppose that $\Pr[E]$ and $\Pr[\text{not } E]$ have been obtained. These are referred to as *prior probabilities*, because they represent the chances of the events occurring *before* the results of the empirical investigation have been obtained. The investigation itself results in several possible outcomes, each statistically dependent on E. For any particular result, denoted by the letter R, the conditional probabilities $\Pr[R|E]$ and $\Pr[R|\text{not } E]$ are often available. The result itself serves to revise the probabilities of "E" and "not E" upward or downward. The values obtained are called *posterior probabilities*, since they apply *after* the outcome has been determined.

The posterior probability values are actually conditional probabilities of the form $\Pr[E|R]$, $\Pr[\text{not } E|R]$ that may be found according to

BAYES' THEOREM: **The posterior probability of event *E* for a particular result *R* of an empirical investigation can be found from**

$$\Pr[E|R] = \frac{\Pr[E]\Pr[R|E]}{\Pr[E]\Pr[R|E] + \Pr[\text{not } E]\Pr[R|\text{not } E]}$$

The principle underlying Bayes' Theorem is best explained in terms of the following example.

Crooked Die Cube Illustration

A box contains four fair dice and one crooked die containing a leaded weight which makes the six-face appear on two-thirds of all tosses. You are asked to select one die at random and toss it. If the crooked die cannot be distinguished from the fair dice and the result of your toss is a six-face, what is the probability that you tossed the crooked die?

The events in question are

$$C = \text{crooked die}$$

$$\text{not } C = \text{fair die}$$

The empirical investigation here is the toss itself, so

$$R = \text{six-face}$$

Since 1 out of 5 dice is crooked, the prior probabilities for the type of die tossed are

$$\Pr[C] = 1/5$$

$$\Pr[\text{not } C] = 4/5$$

You know that when the crooked die is tossed

$$\Pr[R|C] = 2/3$$

If the fair die is tossed, you know that one of the equally likely sides has a six-face, and

$$\Pr[R|\text{not } C] = 1/6$$

The posterior probability that the die you tossed is crooked is therefore

$$\Pr[C|R] = \frac{\Pr[C]\Pr[R|C]}{\Pr[C]\Pr[R|C] + \Pr[\text{not } C]\Pr[R|\text{not } C]}$$

$$= \frac{(1/5)(2/3)}{(1/5)(2/3) + (4/5)(1/6)}$$

$$= \frac{2/15}{4/15} = \frac{1}{2}$$

We can see that the probability of tossing the crooked die must be revised upward from the prior value of 1/5 (which applied when you had no information) to the posterior value of 1/2 now that you know the toss resulted in a six-face.

Posterior Probability as a Conditional Probability

Although it has a special interpretation, a posterior probability is merely a conditional probability when some relevant result is given, and it can be found in the same manner:

$$\begin{array}{c}\text{Posterior}\\\text{probability}\\\text{of event}\end{array} = \Pr[\text{event}\,|\,\text{result}] = \frac{\Pr[\text{event } and \text{ result}]}{\Pr[\text{result}]}$$

A straightforward procedure for calculating an event's posterior probability is first to find the joint probability that the event will occur with the given result and then to divide by the probability of that result. This is exactly what Bayes' Theorem accomplishes. The numerator is the joint probability found from applying the multiplication law. The denominator is the probability of obtaining the particular empirical result and is basically the sum of all the joint probabilities of the potential outcomes that might yield that result. In practice, Bayes' Theorem can be cumbersome to use, and the data may be provided in such a way that the posterior probabilities can be found more directly.

For example, if a statistics class contains just as many men as women, then the prior probability that an examination paper chosen at random will belong to a man (M) is 1/2. Now suppose that after the exams have been graded, 20% of the papers received a mark of "C or better" (C) *and* were written by men; a total of 60% of the exams were scored "C or better." If a randomly selected test sheet is graded "C," we have sufficient information to calculate the posterior probability that it was written by a man:

$$\Pr[M\,|\,C] = \frac{\Pr[M \text{ } and \text{ } C]}{\Pr[C]} = \frac{.20}{.60} = \frac{1}{3}$$

Here, the information about the grade given to the paper causes us to revise downward the probability that it was written by a man.

Typically, the probability values needed to make such a simple calculation are not immediately available. When we use evidence or empirical results to revise probabilities, our knowledge of the various events involved is usually structured so that some preliminary work is required to obtain the necessary probability values. It may be helpful to construct a joint probability table to accomplish this.

Posterior Probabilities in Jury Selection

A noted lawyer specializing in defending corporate clients in personal-injury suits thinks that a sympathetic jury is half the battle. A jury panel can be winnowed down to a largely sympathetic group by preemptory challenges. Since a potential juror's leaning in a particular case is usually concealed during the selection interview, superficial characteristics must be relied on in accepting or rejecting jury candidates. The lawyer has found that mature and stable

TABLE 2-4
Joint Probability Table Used to Illustrate Posterior Probability Calculation

	Older (O)	Younger (Y)	Marginal Probability
Sympathetic (S)	**.195**	**.105**	.300
Unsympathetic (U)	**.205**	**.495**	**.700**
Marginal Probability	.400	.600	1.000

persons, those who have "made it on their own," are most likely to be sympathetic to the defendant and that younger jurors tend to have a "social worker attitude" and to favor the plaintiff. From post-trial talks with jurors over the years, the lawyer has determined that 65% of the sympathetic jurors have been older persons. A special bar study has shown that only 30% of all jury panel members in that county are sympathetic to the defendant in a personal-injury suit.

Eleven jurors have been chosen in a negligence suit resulting from an elevator accident, and both lawyers have exhausted their challenges. Six of the potential jurors are younger and four are older. Based on alphabetical sequence, one of the ten will be the last juror.

The joint probability table concerning this last juror appears in Table 2-4. The probability values obtained directly from the data provided here are shown in lightface type. The boldface numbers were obtained from these data after first noting that

$$Pr[U] = 1 - Pr[S] = .70$$

The fact that we have been given the conditional probability

$$Pr[O|S] = .65$$

enables us to find the joint probability of obtaining an older, more sympathetic juror:

$$Pr[S \text{ and } O] = Pr[S] Pr[O|S] = .30(.65) = .195$$

The remaining values can be obtained from knowing this value and from the fact that the joint probabilities must sum to the respective marginal values.

The prior probability that a sympathetic juror will be obtained is only .30 (which is also the marginal probability of this event). If an older juror is chosen, the posterior probability that the juror will also be sympathetic is

$$Pr[S|O] = \frac{Pr[S \text{ and } O]}{Pr[O]} = \frac{.195}{.40} = .4875$$

This example shows how we can calculate posterior probabilities by relying on basic concepts, instead of using the complicated expression of Bayes' Theorem. Nevertheless, as Table 2-4 shows, essentially the same steps are required in either case.

PROBLEMS

2-1   A smoker has eight pipes, two of which are meerschaums. One of his meerschaums has a curved stem, and has a total of four curved-stem pipes. He asks his son to bring him the curved-stem meerschaum. The boy, not knowing rose briar from ivory nor calabash from hookah, selects a curved-stem pipe at random. What is the probability that the father will be given the pipe he wants?

2-2   A coin is tossed exactly three times in succession. The sample space takes the form shown in Figure 2-7. List the elements of the event set for each of the following events and then determine each event's probability:
(a) Exactly two heads appear in the three tosses.
(b) The same side does not appear twice in succession.
(c) The toss sequence ends with a head.
(d) An odd number of tails is obtained.

2-3   Determine the probabilities that:
(a) A man chosen randomly from a group of ten men is a doctor, if the group contains two doctors.
(b) A single raffle ticket will be drawn out of 10,000 tickets.
(c) A head will be obtained on one toss each of a dime and a penny. (First determine the sample space.)
(d) A number greater than 2 will be the value of the showing face from the toss of a six-sided die.

2-4   There are 100 members on a consumer testing panel: 40 women and 60 men. Of these, 15 of the women and 35 of the men are married. One panel member is chosen at random.
(a) Find the probabilities of the following outcomes:
   (1) Man   (2) Married man   (3) Woman
   (4) Married woman   (5) Married   (6) Unmarried man
   (7) Unmarried   (8) Unmarried woman
(b) Using your answers to (a), apply the addition law to find the probabilities of the following results:
   (1) Woman *or* unmarried   (2) Man *or* married
   (3) Woman *or* married   (4) Man *or* unmarried

2-5   An antique car parts supplier has determined the following probabilities for the number of annual orders for Locomobile fuel pumps:

Number of Orders	Probability
0	.3
1	.2
2	.1
3	.1
4	.1
5	.1
6	.1
7 or more	0
	Total 1.0

Find the probability that there will be:

(a) Less than 4 orders.   (b) Between 2 and 6 orders, inclusively.
(c) At least 1 order.   (d) Between 2 and 4 orders, inclusively.
(e) At the most 2 orders.

2-6   Events A, B, C are mutually exclusive and collectively exhaustive, each having a probability of 1/3. Find:

(a) $\Pr[A\ or\ B]$ (b) $\Pr[not\ C]$
(c) $\Pr[not\ (A\ or\ B)]$ (d) $\Pr[A\ or\ B\ or\ C]$
(e) $\Pr[not\ (A\ or\ B\ or\ C)]$

2-7   In conducting a check, an auditor randomly selects 5 accounts receivable out of 10 that are listed as outstanding. Only 4 of the 10 accounts have incorrect balances. The following probabilities apply for the number of incorrect accounts to be selected:

Number of Incorrect Accounts	Probability
0	1/42
1	10/42
2	20/42
3	10/42
4	1/42

Determine the probability that the number of incorrect accounts selected is:

(a) At least 2.   (b) At most 3.   (c) 1 or more.
(d) Greater than 2.   (e) Less than 4.   (f) 4 or less.

2-8   A group of 100 credit applicants can be divided into the following proportions:

	Renter	Homeowner
Married	15/100	50/100
Single	25/100	10/100

(a) If one applicant's file is selected at random, find the probabilities of the following events:

(1) renter (2) married (3) homeowner
(4) renter *or* married (5) renter *and* married (6) married *given* renter

(b) Are the events "married" and "renter" statistically independent? Substantiate your answer.

2-9 An employment agency specializing in clerical and secretarial help classifies candidates in terms of primary skills and years of experience. The skills are bookkeeping, switchboard, and stenography. (We will assume that no candidate is proficient in more than one of these.) Experience categories are less than one year, one to three years, and more than three years. There are 100 persons currently on file, and their skills and experience are summarized in the following table.

Experience	Skill			Total
	Bookkeeping	Switchboard	Stenography	
Less Than One Year	15		30	50
One to Three Years	5	10		20
More Than Three Years			10	
Total		30		100

One person's file is chosen at random. Determine:
(a) The missing numbers in the table.
(b) Pr[stenography *or* bookkeeping]
(c) Pr[stenography|more than three year's experience]
(d) Pr[bookkeeping *or* less than one year's experience]

2-10 An employment screening test is being evaluated by a company. Historically, 80% of all persons hired by the company have proved to be satisfactory (S); the rest have been unsatisfactory (U). During this evaluation, the screening examination scores are not used to make the final hiring decision. Altogether, 16% of the applicants score low (L) on the test; the remaining scores are high (H). However, only 10% of the satisfactory employees receive a low score. One employee is selected at random.

(a) For that employee, determine:
(1) $\Pr[S]$ (2) $\Pr[L]$ (3) $\Pr[L|S]$
(b) Construct a joint probability table for the performance quality and the test score of the selected employee.
(c) Use your answer to (b) to find the following probabilities:
(1) $\Pr[S|L]$ (2) $\Pr[L|U]$

2-11 A box contains 100 marbles; 60 are red and 40 are green. There are 30 striped marbles and 70 solid ones; 10 of the marbles have green stripes. One marble is chosen at random from the box.

(a) Construct a joint probability table summarizing the events describing the properties (color and solid or striped) of the selected marble. Include the marginal probabilities.

(b) Find Pr[marble is solid | marble is green].

(c) Is the event "marble is solid" independent of the event "marble is green"? Why?

2-12 You have drawn a card from a fully shuffled deck of 52 ordinary playing cards. Find:

(a) Pr[ace | red]   (b) Pr[ace of diamonds | red]

(c) Pr[diamond | red]   (d) Pr[face card | red]

2-13 A new family with two children of different ages has moved into the neighborhood. Suppose it is equally likely that either child is a boy or girl, so that the following situations are equally likely:

Youngest	Oldest	
boy	boy	(B, B)
boy	girl	(B, G)
girl	boy	(G, B)
girl	girl	(G, G)

(a) Find Pr[at least one girl].

(b) If you know there is at least one girl, what is the conditional probability that the family has exactly one boy?

(c) Given that at least one child is a girl, what is the conditional probability that the other child is a girl?

2-14 A company has employed two consumer testing panels of 100 persons each to evaluate product design. One person is chosen at random from each panel.

(a) Panel A is 50% men and 50% women; 70% of the panel members are married, and just as many men as women are married. Thus, any two sex and marital-status events are independent. Construct a joint probability table by first finding the marginal probabilities and then using the multiplication law to obtain the joint probabilities, which in this case may be expressed as the products of the two respective marginal probabilities.

(b) Panel B is also 50% men and 50% women, and 70% of the panel members are married. However, only 60% of the men are married, whereas 80% of the women are married. Thus, any two sex and marital-status events are dependent. This means that the product of the respective marginal probabilities does not equal the corresponding joint probability. Construct a joint probability table.

2-15 A fruit inspector accepts or rejects shipments of bananas after performing tests on a few sample bunches. He rejects 15% of all the shipments he inspects. Thus far, he has rejected 95% of all bad shipments inspected, and 10% of all shipments have ultimaltey proved to be bad.

(a) Using this experience as a basis, find the values of the following probabilities regarding the outcome of any particular shipment handled by this particular inspector: (1) Pr[reject], (2) Pr[bad], (3) Pr[reject | bad].

(b) Apply the multiplication law to the appropriate values you found in (a) to find Pr[reject *and* bad].

(c) Construct a joint probability table showing the joint and marginal probabilities for the inspector's actions (accept or reject) and the quality (good or bad) of the banana shipment.

2-16 An experiment is conducted using three boxes, each containing a mixture of 10 (R)ed and (W)hite marbles. The three boxes have the following compositions:

Box A	Box B	Box C
6 R	4 R	7 R
4 W	6 W	3 W

Two marbles are selected at random. The first is selected from Box A. If it is red, the second marble is to be taken from Box B; if the first marble is white, the second marble is to be taken from Box C. Using R_1 and W_1 to represent the color of the first marble and R_2 and W_2 to represent the color of the second marble:
(a) Find the following probabilities:
    (1) $\Pr[R_1]$ (2) $\Pr[W_1]$ (3) $\Pr[R_2|R_1]$
    (4) $\Pr[R_2|W_1]$ (5) $\Pr[W_2|R_1]$ (6) $\Pr[W_2|W_1]$
(b) Apply the multiplication law to your answers to (a) to determine the following joint probabilities:
    (1) $\Pr[R_1 \ and \ R_2]$ (2) $\Pr[R_1 \ and \ W_2]$
    (3) $\Pr[W_1 \ and \ R_2]$ (4) $\Pr[W_1 \ and \ W_2]$
(c) Determine the probabilities that:
    (1) One red and one white marble will be chosen.
    (2) Either two red or two white marbles will be chosen.

2-17 Of the ball bearings in a lot of 50, 10% are known to be overweight. Three bearings are randomly selected, one at a time, and weighed. Each bearing in turn is returned to the lot and given the same chance of being selected as the unweighed items. Construct a probability tree diagram for this situation. Then find the following probabilities describing the final results of the sampling procedure:
(a) No overweight items are selected.
(b) All the items selected are overweight.
(c) Exactly one ball bearing in the sample is overweight.

2-18 Repeat Exercise 2-17 if the successively weighed items are not replaced.

2-19 A new movie "Star Struck" has a prior probability of success of .20. Ruth Grist is going to review the film. She has liked 70% of all the successful films and has disliked 80% of all the unsuccessful films she has reviewed. Find the posterior probability that "Star Struck" will be a success if:
(a) Grist likes it.   (b) Grist dislikes it.

2-20 A local television weather reporter makes a daily forecast indicating the probability that it will rain tomorrow. On one particular evening, she announces an 80% chance of rain (E) the next day. The manager of the city golf courses has established a policy that he will water the greens only if the probability of rain is less than 90%. Using the local TV forecast as his prior probability, the manager also relies on his mother-in-law's rheumatism: historically, she gets a "rain pain" (R) on 90% of all days that are followed by rain, but she also gets a pain on 20% of the days that are not followed by rain. The following probabilities therefore apply:

$$\Pr[E] = .80 \qquad \Pr[R|E] = .90 \qquad \Pr[R|not \ E] = .20$$

(a) Assuming that the golf-course manager's mother-in-law is currently receiving pain signals, find the posterior probability that it will rain tomorrow. Should the manager water the greens?

(b) If the manager's mother-in-law feels just fine, what is the posterior probability of rain tomorrow?

2-21 From a given response to a question, a marketing researcher wishes to determine whether a randomly selected person will choose BriDent when next purchasing toothpaste. The question is designed to reveal whether or not the selected person recalls the name BriDent—an event we will denote by R. Previous testing has established that 99% of the people who bought BriDent previously recalled the name and that only 10% of the people who did not buy BriDent recalled this particular brand name. Since BriDent has cornered 30% of the toothpaste market, the researcher chooses .30 as the prior probability that the person selected will buy BriDent. Denoting this event by B gives us the following probabilities:

$$\Pr[B] = .30 \qquad \Pr[R|B] = .99 \qquad \Pr[R|\text{not } B] = .10$$

(a) If the person who is selected remembers BriDent, what is the posterior probability that BriDent will be purchased next?

(b) If the person who is selected does *not* remember BriDent, what is the posterior probability that BriDent will be purchased next?

2-22 An oil wildcatter has assigned a probability of .50 to striking oil on his property. He orders a seismic survey that has proved to be only 80% reliable in the past: Given oil, it predicts favorably 80% of the time; given no oil, it augurs unfavorably with a frequency of .8.

(a) Given a favorable seismic result, what is the probability of oil?

(b) Given an unfavorable seismic result, what is the probability of oil?

2-23 An employment screening test is being evaluated for possible inclusion in clerical services hiring decisions. Presently, only 50% of the persons hired for these positions perform satisfactorily. The test itself has been evaluated by outside consultants, who have given it an upside reliability of 90% (90% of all satisfactory employees will pass the test) and a downside reliability of only 80% (80% of all unsatisfactory employees will fail the test). One clerical applicant (acceptable in all other screening activities) is chosen at random. Find the following probabilities:

(a) The prior probability of satisfactory on-the-job performance if the applicant is hired.

(b) The posterior probability of satisfactory on-the-job performance if the applicant passes the screening test.

(c) The posterior probability of satisfactory on-the-job performance if the applicant is hired after failing the screening test.

3

Probability Distributions and Expected Value

Chapter 2 provided us with the fundamental concepts of probability. We are now ready to study some of the tools that are used to analyze business decisions when uncertainty is present. The outcomes of business decisions are often numerical, and the result to be achieved is usually expressed as a variable. Because the particular value is uncertain and determined by chance, we call it a random variable. The probabilities assigned to each possible value of this variable constitute a probability distribution.

For instance, alternative locations for a new plant can be compared in terms of profitability, which can be viewed as a random variable with a probability distribution. But to rank the attractiveness of each candidate plant site, we must obtain a single profit figure for each site. We will see how the expected level of profitability can be determined for each alternative by using the respective probability distribution to arrive at an "average" figure.

In this chapter, we will discuss random variables, probability distributions, and expected value. Finally, we will examine two specific probability distributions: the binomial distribution, which is one of the most commonly encountered distributions, and the normal distribution, which is the most important distribution whenever sample information is used to help analyze decisions.

3-1   THE RANDOM VARIABLE

A variable whose level is determined by chance is called a *random variable*. When a specific outcome is uncertain, it is treated as a variable. The random variable assumes actual numerical value only *after* all relevant outcomes are known. Many different kinds of random variables can be generated by a single situation.

An Illustration from Roulette

Roulette, the internationally popular casino game, vividly illustrates the relationship between elementary events and random variables. In roulette, the players commit themselves to particular bets. A wheel with 38 slots is then spun, and a ball is set in motion. Whatever slot the ball drops into determines the outcome. The sample space consists of the 38 slots; 36 slots (half red, half black) are numbered from 1 to 36, and two slots are green and are numbered 0 and 00.

There are several ways to place a roulette bet. For instance, a player may place a $1 bet on a particular number—say, 7. If the ball drops into the 7 slot, the player receives a $35 payoff;* otherwise, the player forfeits the bet. Another roulette gamble is to bet $1 on the red field. If the ball drops into a red slot, the player receives $1; the bet is lost if a black or green number appears. In either case, the sample space for the outcome of the spin of a roulette wheel is comprised of 38 equally likely elementary events.

For each player, the random variable of prime interest is the winnings. The 7-player's random variable has two values: +$35 (if 7 comes up) and −$1 (if the ball drops into any of the other slots). For the game, there are two distinctly different random variables, *depending on the type of gamble*.

In Figure 3-1, each of the roulette random variables is defined in terms of the same sample space. On each play, the values of the respective random variables are determined by the elementary event that occurs. The arrows in the figure match each elementary event to a particular point on a numerical scale, depending on the gamble chosen. Mathematically, a random variable is a function that we use to map the elementary events onto their corresponding points on the numerical scale.

---

* Since there are 38 equally likely slots, the probability of getting the 7 slot is 1/38. To be a fair gamble, the payoff should be 37 to 1, but the house does not pay on 0 or 00, giving it an edge and a built-in source of long-run profits.

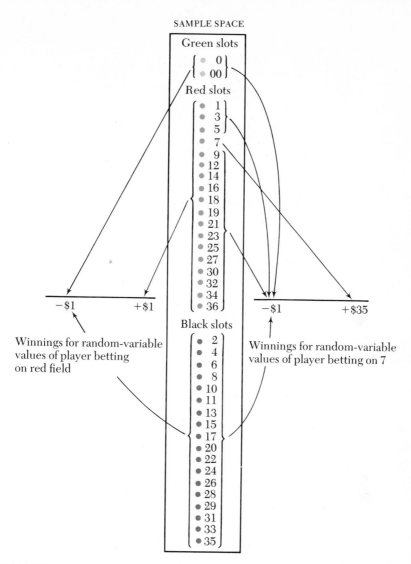

FIGURE 3-1
Portrayal of two different random variables for two types of roulette gambles.

The Probability Distribution

The random variable is a fundamental concept in applying probability theory to decision making. The relationship between the values of a random variable and their probabilities is summarized by the *probability distribution*.

Each possible value of a random variable corresponds to a particular composite event in the underlying sample space. We can use the procedures we learned in Chapter 2 to find the probabilities for each possible value. As an example, we'll consider the winnings from a roulette gamble again. The single-number bettor's winnings equal $35 whenever the event "the ball drops into the slot of the number played" occurs and equal $-\$1$ (the bettor loses $1) when the complementary event "some other slot receives the ball" occurs. Thus, 37 out of 38 possibilities are equally likely for this second event, and the probabilities of our random-variable values are equal to the probabilities of the corresponding events. In this instance

$$\Pr[\text{winnings} = \$35] \ = 1/38$$

$$\Pr[\text{winnings} = -\$1] = 37/38$$

Note that these probabilities sum to 1, which follows from the fact that possible random-variable values correspond directly to events that are *collectively exhaustive and mutually exclusive*. In roulette, the wager is either won or lost.

Many probability distributions can be expressed in terms of a table. Table 3-1 lists the possible rates of return from operating a new piece of equipment. Notice that the probabilities sum to 1. When there are too many possibilities to list conveniently in a table, an algebraic expression is used to describe the probability distribution.

TABLE 3-1
Rate-of-Return Probability Distribution

Possible Rate of Return	Probability
10%	.05
11	.10
12	.15
13	.17
14	.12
15	.08
16	.09
17	.06
18	.05
19	.05
20	.04
21	.04
Total	1.00

EXPECTED VALUE 3-2

When business decisions are made under uncertain conditions, a different random variable with its own probability distribution is usually arrived at for each possible choice. In comparing alternative budget decisions, a company president may be faced with a variety of choices with different rate-of-return probability distributions similar to the one in Table 3-1. It is hard to compare several tables. To facilitate the choice, each probability distribution is often summarized by a single "average" value. These summary numbers can then be used to rank the various alternatives.

This average can be computed directly from the probability distribution. The resulting figure, called the *expected value* of the random variable, is found by multiplying every possible value by its probability and summing all the products. The expected value is therefore a weighted average, with the probabilities serving as weights. Table 3-2 shows the expected-value calculation for the number of dots obtained in tossing a six-sided die.

The Meaning of Expected Value

The expected value has many uses. In a gambling game, it tells us what our long-run average losses per play will be. Sophisticated gamblers know that slot machines pay off poorly in relation to the actual odds and that the average loss per play will be less in roulette or dice games. In the early 1960s, the mathematician Edward Thorp caused quite a stir when he demonstrated that various betting strategies could be applied in playing the card game blackjack to produce positive expected winnings.*

We can illustrate the meaning of expected value by returning to our roulette example. The expected winnings from betting $1 on the 7 slot are

Winnings	Probability	Winnings × Probability
+ $35	1/38	+ $35/38
− $1	37/38	− $37/38
		− $2/38 = − $.053

---

* See Edward Thorp, *Beat the Dealer*, 2nd ed. (New York: Random House, 1966). Unlike other gambling games, bets in blackjack can be placed when the odds are in the player's favor, because the card deck may not be reshuffled after each stage of play. By significantly raising their bets at these times, players will make a profit on the average.

TABLE 3-2
Calculation of the Expected Value for a Die Toss

Number of Dots	Probability	Number × Probability
1	1/6	1/6
2	1/6	2/6
3	1/6	3/6
4	1/6	4/6
5	1/6	5/6
6	1/6	6/6
	1	21/6 = 3.5

Expected value = 3.5 dots

Thus, the expected winnings from a single gamble is a loss of 5.3 cents. This means that the gambler who keeps making $1 bets indefinitely will lose an average of 5.3 cents on each bet. Of course, an individual gamble will show either a gain of $35 or a loss of $1. But *on the average* the gambler will win $35 in only 1 out of every 38 gambles and will lose $1 in 37 out of every 38 gambles.

Note that in both illustrations, the expected values of the random variables themselves are not outcomes of the uncertain situation. It is impossible for 3.5 dots to show; the outcome must be a whole number (1, 2, 3, 4, 5, or 6). The roulette player will always be dealing in whole dollars. In either case, the expected value is only an average result. Although it is possible to obtain the expected value in some random experiments, there is no reason why the expected outcome should be a possible result in a single circumstance.

Because any decision that involves uncertainty may be viewed as a gambling situation, knowing the expected value can help us choose among alternative actions. But unlike a dice game, practical business decisions must often be made regarding nonrepeatable situations, such as the sales response to an advertising budget. In such cases, there is only one opportunity to "play." Here, uncertainty must be measured in terms of *subjective* probabilities. An expected value may still be calculated, but in these situations it represents an average of the decision maker's *convictions* about the outcomes. This is illustrated in Table 3-3, where the expected rate of return is calculated for the equipment we discussed earlier.

What does a 14.44% expected rate of return mean? In this instance, the future conditions that will produce a particular percentage return are not repeatable, and the given probabilities really express the decision maker's convictions that the respective percentages will result. Thus, the expected value calculated from these subjective probabilities expresses the decision maker's "average conviction" as to what the return will be.

TABLE 3-3
Calculation of the Expected Value for the Rate of Return

Possible Rate of Return	Probability	Rate × Probability
10%	.05	.50%
11	.10	1.10
12	.15	1.80
13	.17	2.21
14	.12	1.68
15	.08	1.20
16	.09	1.44
17	.06	1.02
18	.05	.90
19	.05	.95
20	.04	.80
21	.04	.84
	1.00	14.44%

Expected rate of return = 14.44%

The Variance of a Random Variable

The expected value measures the *central tendency* of a probability distribution. A second type of measure—*dispersion or variability*—summarizes the degree to which the possible random-variable values differ among themselves. To determine the dispersion, we use the *variance*, which expresses the average of the squared deviations of the individual values from their expected value or mean. This is analogous to a statistical variance. The variance for the number of dots obtained from a die toss is calculated in Table 3-4.

TABLE 3-4
Calculation of the Variance for a Die Toss

Number of Dots	Deviation: Number—3.5	(Number—3.5)^2	Probability	(Number—3.5)^2 × Probability
1	−2.5	6.25	1/6	6.25/6
2	−1.5	2.25	1/6	2.25/6
3	− .5	.25	1/6	.25/6
4	.5	.25	1/6	.25/6
5	1.5	2.25	1/6	2.25/6
6	2.5	6.25	1/6	6.25/6
				17.50/6

Variance = 17.50/6 = 2.917

Because the variance expresses dispersion in terms of original units squared (squared dots for a die), its square root is often used to measure dispersion. The resulting value is called the *standard deviation*. The standard deviation for the die toss outcome is

$$\sqrt{2.917} = 1.71 \text{ dots}$$

Both the expected value, or mean, and the variance can be useful in evaluating outcomes that are random variables. In making investment decisions, the variance is often used as a measure of risk. In analyzing stock portfolios, for example, each possible security combination may be portrayed in two dimensions: expected return and variance in returns.* The concept of variance is very important when decisions are made based on sample information. Later in this chapter, we will see how the normal distribution can be characterized in terms of two parameters—the mean and the variance (or standard deviation).

3-3   THE BINOMIAL DISTRIBUTION

In making decisions under uncertain conditions it is often necessary to use sample data. We are presently concerned with samples obtained from *qualitative* populations, so that each observation results in one of two complementary outcomes, such as liking or disliking a new package design. Here, we will discuss the *binomial distribution*, which is concerned with the *number of outcomes* in a particular category.

A Coin Tossing Illustration

An evenly balanced coin is tossed fairly five times. The corresponding probability tree diagram appears in Figure 3-2, where the sample space is also listed. Our initial problem is to find the probability for obtaining exactly two heads. Since each of the 32 outcomes is equally likely, the basic definition of probability allows us to find the answer by counting the number of elementary events involving two heads and dividing this result by the total number of equally likely elementary events. The sample space contains 32 elementary events, and Figure 3-2 shows that 10 of these are two-head outcomes. Thus, we can determine that

$$\Pr[\text{exactly two heads}] = 10/32$$

* See Harry M. Markowitz, *Portfolio Selection: Efficient Diversification of Investments* (New Haven: Yale University Press, 1959).

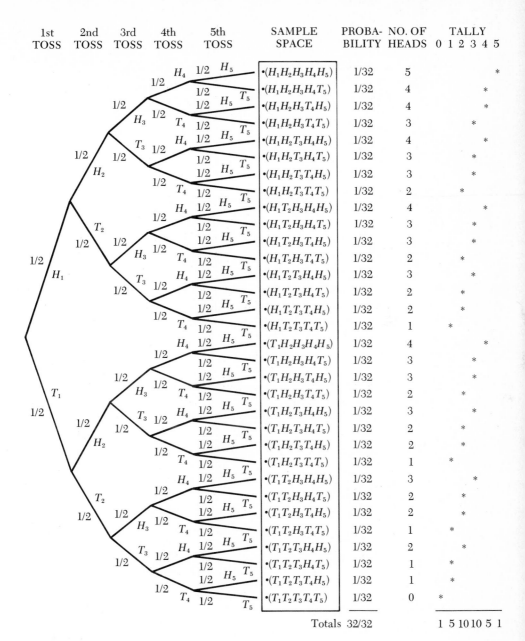

FIGURE 3-2
Probability tree diagram for five tosses of a fair coin.

As we saw in Chapter 2, it is impractical to list all possible outcomes unless there are only a few. For instance, if 10 tosses were to be considered, the list would contain 1,024 (2^{10}) entries. Before discussing a procedure to simplify finding such probabilities, it will be helpful to relate coin tossing to a similar class of situations.

The Bernoulli Process

A sequence of coin tosses is one example of a *Bernoulli process*. A great many circumstances fall into the same category: All involve a series of situations (such as tosses of a coin), which are referred to as *trials*. For each trial, *there are only two possible complementary outcomes*, such as head or tail. Usually one outcome is referred to as a *success*; the other, as a *failure*.

Examples include: single childbirths in a maternity hospital, where each birth is a trial resulting in a boy or girl; canning a vegetable, where each trial is a full can that is slightly overweight or underweight (cans of precisely correct weight are so improbable that we can ignore them); and keypunching numerical data, where each completed card is a trial that will either contain errors or be correct. In all these cases, only two opposite trial outcomes are considered.

What further distinguishes these situations as Bernoulli processes is that *the success probability remains constant* from trial to trial. The probability of obtaining a head is the same, regardless of which toss is considered; this is also true of the probability of delivering a boy for any successive birth in a maternity hospital, picking up an overweight can of vegetables, and receiving a correctly punched card each time. (The last condition would not hold if a keypuncher tires over time; then the probability could be larger that an earlier card would be correct than that a later card would be.)

A final characteristic of a Bernoulli process is that *successive trial outcomes must be independent events*. Like a fairly tossed coin, the probability for obtaining a success (head) must be independent of what occurred in previous trials (tosses). The births in a *single family* may violate this requirement if the parents use medical techniques to obtain a second child of the opposite sex of their first child. Or a keypuncher's errors may occur in batches due to fatigue, so that once an error is made it is more likely to be followed by another.

Sampling to determine the impact of advertising, voter preference, or response to drug treatment can all be classified as Bernoulli processes. To preserve the requirements of independence and constant probability of success, we ought to sample with replacement, thereby allowing each person the same chance of being selected each time and perhaps being chosen more than once. In each case, the probability of a trial success would be the proportion of persons in the respective population who would provide the desired response.

The Binomial Formula

When the trial outcomes result from a Bernoulli process, the number of successes is a random variable with a binomial distribution. The following expression, referred to as the *binomial formula,* can then be used to find the probability values:

$$\Pr[\text{successes} = r] = \frac{n!}{r!(n-r)!} P^r(1-P)^{n-r}$$

where n = number of trials achieved

$\quad P$ = trial success probability

$\quad r = 0, 1, \ldots, n$

We place an exclamation point after the quantity to denote factorial notation. A 5 factorial is

$$5! = 5 \times 4 \times 3 \times 2 \times 1 = 120$$

In general

$$n! = n \times (n-1) \times (n-2) \times \cdots \times 2 \times 1$$

with the following defined values

$$0! = 1$$

$$1! = 1$$

The binomial formula can be used to determine the probability found earlier for obtaining successes = 2 heads in $n = 5$ tosses of a fair coin. In this case, $P = \Pr[\text{head}] = 1/2$ and $1 - P = \Pr[\text{tail}] = 1/2$, so that

$$\Pr[\text{successes} = 2] = \frac{5!}{2!(5-2)!} \left(\frac{1}{2}\right)^2 \left(1 - \frac{1}{2}\right)^{5-2} = \frac{5!}{2!3!} \left(\frac{1}{2}\right)^2 \left(\frac{1}{2}\right)^3$$

$$= 10\left(\frac{1}{2}\right)^5 = \frac{10}{32}$$

The factorial terms in this product provide the number of outcomes involving exactly 2 heads, which is equal to 10 and represents the number of combinations of 2 particular tosses that may result in heads out of a total of 5 tosses. The product containing 1/2 represents the probability of obtaining any one of the 10 two-head sequences represented by the end positions on the probability tree diagram in Figure 3-2. Each of these positions is reached by traversing a particular path of 2 head and $5 - 2 = 3$ tail branches. Each of these probabilities can be obtained by applying the multiplication law. Since a 2-head result can occur in any one of 10 equally likely ways, the addition

TABLE 3-5
Binomial Distribution for the Number of Heads in Five Coin Tosses

Possible Number of Heads r	Pr[heads $= r$]		
0	$\dfrac{5!}{0!5!}\left(\dfrac{1}{2}\right)^{0}\left(\dfrac{1}{2}\right)^{5}$	$= \dfrac{1}{32} =$	.03125
1	$\dfrac{5!}{1!4!}\left(\dfrac{1}{2}\right)^{1}\left(\dfrac{1}{2}\right)^{4}$	$= \dfrac{5}{32} =$	.15625
2	$\dfrac{5!}{2!3!}\left(\dfrac{1}{2}\right)^{2}\left(\dfrac{1}{2}\right)^{3}$	$= \dfrac{10}{32} =$	.31250
3	$\dfrac{5!}{3!2!}\left(\dfrac{1}{2}\right)^{3}\left(\dfrac{1}{2}\right)^{2}$	$= \dfrac{10}{32} =$	.31250
4	$\dfrac{5!}{4!1!}\left(\dfrac{1}{2}\right)^{4}\left(\dfrac{1}{2}\right)^{1}$	$= \dfrac{5}{32} =$	.15625
5	$\dfrac{5!}{5!0!}\left(\dfrac{1}{2}\right)^{5}\left(\dfrac{1}{2}\right)^{0}$	$= \dfrac{1}{32} =$	.03125
		Total	1.00000

law of probability tells us to add 10 of the identical terms together or, more simply, to multiply by 10.

The entire binomial distribution corresponding to the number of heads resulting from $n = 5$ fair coin tosses appears in Table 3-5. There the probability values are found by applying the binomial formula to all possible r values.

We have already noted that different Bernoulli processes will have different probability values. But the number of successes resulting from each process is a random variable belonging to the binomial family. Note that the probabilities for all possible values of r depend on the value of P. Different sizes of n will result in a larger or smaller number of possible r values and will also affect each probability value.

Cumulative Probabilities

Using the binomial formula to calculate probabilities can be tedious and time consuming. Imagine the effort it would take to determine the probability of 17 successes in $n = 58$ trials when $P = .13$. We can simply find the probabilities we need from a table, but most tables provide only *cumulative probabilities*.

To illustrate this concept, consider the binomial probabilities in Table 3-6 provided for the number of aircraft departure delays at a major airport for

TABLE 3-6
Cumulative Probability Distribution for the Number
of Aircraft Departure Delays

(1) Number of Successes (Delays) r	(2) Pr[successes = r]	(3) Cumulative Probabilities Pr[successes ≤ r]
0	.0060	.0060
1	.0404	.0464
2	.1209	.1673
3	.2150	.3823
4	.2508	.6331
5	.2007	.8338
6	.1114	.9452
7	.0425	.9877
8	.0106	.9983
9	.0016	.9999
10	.0001	1.0000
	1.0000	

$n = 10$ departing flights on different dates. We will assume that a Bernoulli process applies and that the probability that any particular flight will be delayed is $P = .4$. The cumulative probabilities, which appear in column (3), were obtained by adding all the preceding entries for the values in column (2). Thus

$$\Pr[\text{successes} \le 0] = \Pr[\text{successes} = 0] = .0060$$

and

$$\Pr[\text{successes} \le 1] = \Pr[\text{successes} = 0] + \Pr[\text{successes} = 1]$$

$$= .0060 + .0404$$

$$= .0464$$

and

$$\Pr[\text{successes} \le 2] = \Pr[\text{successes} = 0] + \Pr[\text{successes} = 1]$$
$$+ \Pr[\text{successes} = 2]$$

$$= .0060 + .0404 + .1209$$

$$= .1673$$

The sign $\le$ means "less than or equal to," so that [successes ≤ 2] means either exactly 0, 1, or 2 successes. Table 3-6 is constructed cumulatively from the individual probability values, so that the values obtained constitute the *cumulative probability distribution* for the number of successes.

The individual probabilities are graphed as spikes in Figure 3-3(a). (No spike appears for 10 successes, since the probability for this outcome is too low to show.) The cumulative probability distribution appears in Figure 3-3(b). The cumulative probability value corresponding to any particular number is obtained from the *highest point* on the "stairway" directly above. For instance, the cumulative probability for 5 or fewer delays is .8338 (not .6331, which is associated with the lower "step"). Notice that the size of each step in (b) is the

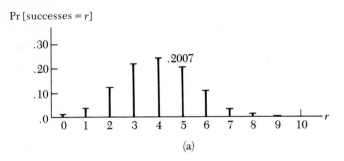

(a)

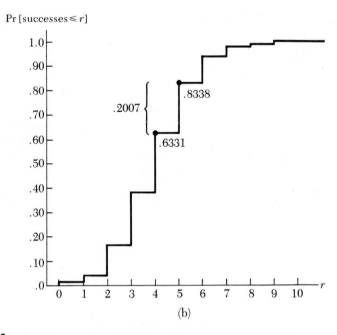

(b)

FIGURE 3-3

(a) Binomial probability mass function and (b) cumulative probability distribution function for the number of successes from a Bernoulli process with n = 10 and P = .4.

same as the height of the respective spike of the individual probability in (a). The underlying probability distribution may be obtained from the cumulative probability distribution by finding these step sizes. For example, to find the probability that there will be exactly 5 departure delays, we find the difference

$$\text{Pr}[\text{successes} = 5] = \text{Pr}[\text{successes} \leq 5] - \text{Pr}[\text{successes} \leq 4]$$

$$= .8338 - .6331 = .2007$$

Using Binomial Probability Tables

Appendix Table A provides the cumulative binomial probability values for various sizes of n (with separate tabulations for several P values). It is possible to use this table to compute probabilities for the number of successes in a variety of situations. To illustrate, suppose we wish to find probabilities regarding the number of $n = 100$ readers who will remember an aspirin advertisement that appears on the back cover of *Time*. We will assume that $P = .30$ is the underlying proportion of all readers who will remember the ad. We will use the portion of Appendix Table A that begins at $n = 100$.

(1) To obtain a result less than or equal to a particular value: The probability that 40 or fewer persons in the sample will remember the ad is a cumulative probability value that can be read directly from the table when $r = 40$ successes:

$$\text{Pr}[\text{successes} \leq 40] = .9875$$

(2) To obtain a result exactly equal to a single value: Recall that cumulative probabilities represent the sum of individual probability values and are portrayed graphically as a stairway (see Figure 3-3). A single-value probability may be obtained by determining the size of the step between two neighboring cumulative probabilities. For example, the probability that exactly 32 of the persons will remember the ad is

$$\text{Pr}[\text{successes} = 32] = \text{Pr}[\text{successes} \leq 32] - \text{Pr}[\text{successes} \leq 31]$$

$$= .7107 - .6331$$

$$= .0776$$

(3) To obtain a result strictly less than some value: The probability that fewer than 30 successes are achieved is the same as the probability that exactly 29 or less successes are obtained, or

$$\text{Pr}[\text{successes} < 30] = \text{Pr}[\text{successes} \leq 29] = .4623$$

(4) To obtain a result greater than or equal to some value: To find the probability that at least 20 of the readers will remember the ad, we look up the cumulative probability that 19 or less will remember and subtract this value from 1:

$$Pr[\text{successes} \geq 20] = 1 - Pr[\text{successes} \leq 19]$$
$$= 1 - .0089 = .9911$$

(5) **To obtain a result that lies between two values:** Suppose we want to find the probability that the number of successes will lie somewhere between 25 and 35, inclusively. Thus, we want to determine

$$Pr[25 \leq \text{successes} \leq 35]$$

In this case, we obtain the difference between two cumulative probabilities:

$$Pr[\text{successes} \leq 35] - Pr[\text{successes} \leq 24] = .8839 - .1136 = .7703$$

The Mean and Variance of the Binomial Distribution

The expected number of successes can be determined from probabilities obtained by using the binomial formula or a binomial distribution table for a particular n and P. Instead of multiplying these probabilities, by the respective number of successes and summing the products, however, a special feature of the binomial distribution enables us to arrive at the answer quickly. The following expression provides the expected number of successes:

$$\text{Expected successes} = nP$$

Thus, the expected number of aircraft delays when $n = 10$ and $P = .4$ is $10(.4) = 4$.

A similar expression provides the variance and the standard deviation:

$$\text{Variance} = nP(1 - P)$$
$$\text{Standard deviation} = \sqrt{nP(1 - P)}$$

In our aircraft delay example, the variance is $10(.4)(1 - .4) = 2.4$ and the standard deviation is $\sqrt{2.4} = 1.55$.

3-4 THE NORMAL DISTRIBUTION

The normal distribution plays a central role in sampling. It is used to describe frequency patterns for a great many phenomena, including the physical characteristics of both things and people, and is often used to express the

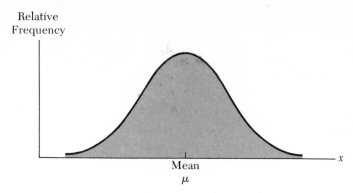

FIGURE 3-4
Frequency curve for the normal distribution.

probability distribution for times needed to complete work tasks, such as a bank teller's transaction or the installation of an automobile bumper.

The normal distribution applies to *continuous random variables,* such as times, weights, and diameters measured on a continuous scale. It is usually described in terms of a bell-shaped curve, as shown in Figure 3-4. There, x represents the possible values of the random variable, and the height of the curve represents the relative frequency at which the corresponding values occur. A particular normal distribution is specified by only two parameters: the *mean μ* (Greek lower case *mu*) and the *standard deviation σ* (Greek lower case *sigma*).* The location or center of the corresponding normal curve is determined by the mean, and its shape is established by the standard deviation. Figure 3-5 shows the curves for three different normal distributions.

Because the height of the normal curve above any point expresses its relative frequency, or proportional occurrence, the total area beneath the normal curve is 1. We can find the probabilities for various values of a normally distributed random variable by determining the *areas* under the applicable portions of its normal curve. These areas correspond to the proportion of times that the particular range of values will occur when identical conditions are repeated.

The areas under the normal curve are tied to the distance separating the points of interest from the mean. For example, the Stanford-Binet IQ test was designed so that the scores of persons taking it have a mean of $\mu = 100$ and a standard deviation of $\sigma = 16$. A feature of every normal curve is that

---

* Mathematically, this curve is called a *probability density function,* and its height may be determined from

$$f(x) = \frac{1}{\sqrt{2\pi\sigma^2}} \, e^{-[(x-\mu)^2/2\sigma^2]}$$

where $\pi = 3.1416$ and e is the base of natural logarithms (2.7183).

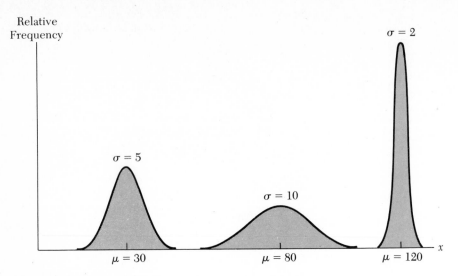

FIGURE 3-5
Three different normal distributions graphed on a common axis.

about 68% of the values will fall within ± 1 standard deviation from the mean. Thus, 68% of all people who take the Stanford–Binet test should achieve IQ scores within the range $\mu \pm 1\sigma$, or 100 ± 16, and their IQs should fall between 84 and 116. Likewise, about 95.5% of the test scores will fall within $\mu \pm 2\sigma$, or $100 \pm 2(16)$, reflecting IQs between 68 and 132. Approximately 99.7% of all scores should fall within $\mu \pm 3\sigma$, so that the IQs of practically all people lie between $100 - 3(16) = 52$ and $100 + 3(16) = 148$. Of course, higher or lower scores are possible; but, like geniuses, the extremes are rare. Theoretically, the tails of the normal curve never touch the axis, so that there is always some area, and hence probability, for any extreme set of values.

Finding Areas Under the Normal Curve

Before we can obtain the probability values of normally distributed random variables, we must find the appropriate area lying under the normal curve by using Appendix Table B.

How would you find the desired areas for the time a particular typesetter takes to compose 500 lines of standard type? We will assume that the population of times is normally distributed, with a mean of $\mu = 150$ minutes and a standard deviation of $\sigma = 30$ minutes. The time it takes to set any given 500 lines, such as the next 500 to be composed, represents a randomly chosen time from this population.

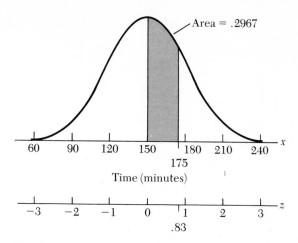

FIGURE 3-6
Determining the area under a normal curve.

The probability that it takes between 150 and 175 minutes to set 500 lines is represented by the shaded area under the normal curve in Figure 3-6. We know that the area beneath the normal curve between the mean and a certain point depends only on the number of standard deviations separating the two points. We see that 175 minutes is equivalent to a distance above the mean of .83 standard deviation. This figure is determined by observing that 175 minutes minus the mean of 150 minutes is equal to 25 minutes. Since the standard deviation is 30 minutes, 25 minutes is only $25/30 = .83$ of the standard deviation.

Appendix Table B has been constructed for the *standard normal curve*, which provides the area between the mean and a point above the mean at some specified distance measured in standard deviations. Because this distance will vary, it is treated as a variable and denoted by z. Sometimes the value of z is referred to as a *normal deviate*. The distance z that separates a possible normal random-variable value x from its mean can be determined from the following expression for the *normal deviate*:

$$z = \frac{x - \mu}{\sigma}$$

A negative value will be obtained for z when x is smaller than μ.

The first column of Appendix Table B lists values of z to the first decimal place. The second decimal place value is located at the head of one of the remaining 10 columns. The area under the curve between the mean and z

standard deviations is found at the intersection of the correct row and column. For example, when $z = .83$, we find the area of .2967 by reading the entry in the .8 row and the .03 column. The area under the normal curve for a completion time between 150 and 175 minutes is .2967, which represents the probability that it will take this long to set the next 500 lines of print.

Although Table B provides areas only between the mean and some point above it, we can also use this table to find areas encountered in other common probability situations, such as those shown in Figure 3-7. Each of these areas is described here.

Area (a) Between the Mean and Some Point Lying Below the Mean.   To find the probability that the completion time lies between 125 and 150 minutes, first we must calculate the normal deviate:

$$z = \frac{125 - 150}{30} = -.83$$

Here, z is negative because 125 is a point lying below the mean. Since the normal curve is symmetrical about the mean, this area must be the same as it would be for a positive value of z of the same magnitude (in this case .2967, as before). It is therefore unnecessary to tabulate areas for negative values of z. The area between the mean and a point lying below it will be equal to the area between the mean and a point the same distance above it.

Area (b) to the Left of a Value Above the Mean.   To find the probability that 500 lines can be set in 185 minutes or less, we must find the entire shaded area below 185. Here, we must consider the lower half of the normal curve separately. Since the entire area of the normal curve is 1, the area under the half to the left of 150 must be .5. The area between 150 and 185 is found from Table B, with $z = (185 - 150)/30 = 1.17$, to be .3790. The entire shaded portion is the sum of the two areas, or $.5000 + .3790 = .8790$.

Area (c) in Upper Tail.   To find the probability that the number of minutes required exceeds 195, first we must find the area between the mean and 195. The normal deviate $z = (195 - 150)/30 = 1.50$; the area from Table B is .4332. Since the area under the upper half of the normal curve is .5, we find the desired area above 195 by subtracting the unwanted portion, or $.5000 - .4332 = .0668$.

Area (d) in Lower Tail.   To find the probability that it will take 90 minutes or less to set the type, we follow two steps similar to those taken in (c). First, we find the area between 90 and 150. Using $z = (90 - 150)/30 = -2.00$, we obtain .4772 from Table B. Subtracting this value from .5 yields $.5000 - .4772 = .0228$.

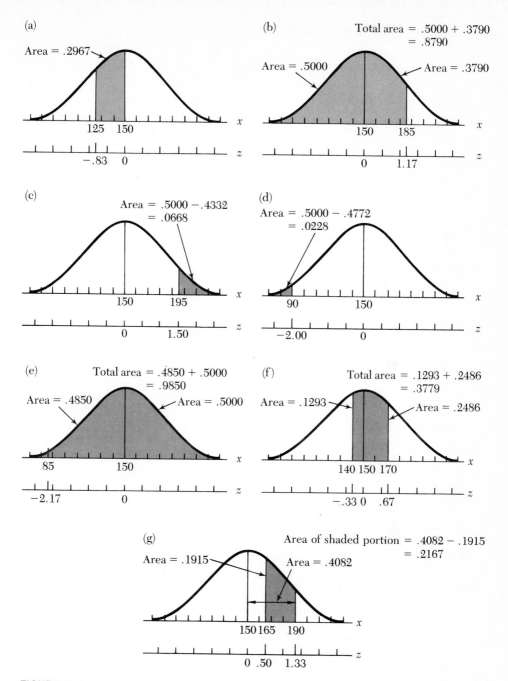

FIGURE 3-7
Various areas under the normal curve, where x = completion time in minutes and z = standard deviations.

Area (e) to the Right of a Value Below the Mean.   To find the probability that the completion time will be equal to or greater than 85 minutes, the area between 85 and the mean is added to the area to the right of the mean, which is .5. Here, we calculate $z = (85 - 150)/30 = -2.17$. Adding the area from Table B (.4850) to .5, gives us a combined area of $.4850 + .5000 = .9850$.

Area (f) Under Portion Overlapping the Mean.   To find the probability that it will take between 140 and 170 minutes to set the 500 lines, we simply add the portion of the shaded area that lies below the mean to the portion above it. The respective normal deviates are $z = (140 - 150)/30 = -.33$ and $z = (170 - 150)/30 = .67$. From Table B, the lower area is .1293 and the upper area is .2486, so that the combined area is $.1293 + .2486 = .3779$.

Area (g) between Two Values Lying Above or Below the Mean.   To   find the probability that the composition time is between 165 and 190 minutes, first we must determine the areas between the mean and each of these two values. The respective normal deviates are $z = (165 - 150)/30 = .50$ and $z = (190 - 150)/30 = 1.33$. From Table B, the area between the mean and 190 is .4082, and the area between the mean and 165 is .1915. Thus, the shaded area is found by subtracting the smaller area from the larger one; or $.4082 - .1915 = .2167$.

The normal curve represents values that lie on a continuous scale, such as height, weight, and time. The probability that a specific value, such as 129.40 minutes, will occur is 0 (the area under the normal curve covering a single point is 0). Thus, in finding a probability, it does not matter whether we use a "strict" inequality, such as the composition time is "less than" ($<$) 129.40 minutes, or an ordinary inequality, such as the time is "less than or equal to" ($\leq$) 129.40 minutes. Using $z = (129.40 - 150)/30 = -.69$, the area is the same in either case: $.5000 - .2549 = .2451$.

The Standard Normal Random Variable

The area under any normal curve can be found by using the standard normal curve. This curve provides the probability distribution for the *standard normal random variable*. In our typesetting illustration, we essentially transformed the original random variable X, the time required to set 500 lines, into the standard normal random variable whenever we used Table B to find areas. This transformation can be accomplished physically by shifting the center of the curve and then stretching or contracting it. To shift the original curve so that its center lies above the point $x = 0$, we subtract μ from each point on the x axis. Then the repositioned curve may be stretched or squeezed until the scale on the horizontal axis matches the scale for the standard normal distribu-

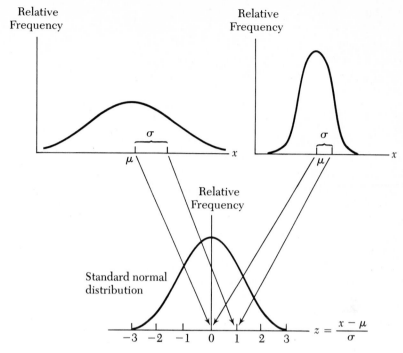

FIGURE 3-8

Illustration of the linear transformation of normal random variables into the standard normal distribution.

tion. If all the values of the random variable are divided by its standard deviation, the transformed curve will have the same shape as the standard normal curve in Figure 3-8. The net effect will always be the same, no matter what the values of μ and σ are. The horizontal scale may be either expanded or contracted. Fortunately, we do not need to physically transform the original random variable X into the standard normal random variable, because we can manipulate the possible values of X algebraically.

As an example, suppose the Sunflower Vegetable Oil Company supplies its customers from barrels that contain about 100 gallons apiece. The current stock of barrels fluctuates in carrying capacity, having a mean of $\mu = 100$ gallons and a standard deviation of $\sigma = .6$ gallon. Letting X represent the capacity of any particular barrel selected at random from barrels ready for shipment to a certain customer, we can determine the probability that $X \leq 99$ gallons. The normal deviate is

$$z = \frac{99 - 100}{.6} = -1.67$$

Thus, the applicable area under the normal curve lies 1.67 standard deviations below the mean. From Table B, the area under the standard normal curve between 0 and $z = 1.67$ is .4525. Because the normal curve is symmetrical, the area between $z = -1.67$ and 0 is also .4525. We wish to obtain the lower tail area, so we subtract .4525 from .5, yielding

$$\Pr[X \leq 99] = .5000 - .4525 = .0475$$

This tells us that about 5% of all barrels shipped will contain 99 gallons or less. To avoid possible ill will, management has decided to replace Sunflower's present barrels with a more uniform variety having a mean of $\mu = 100$ gallons and a standard deviation of $\sigma = .25$ gallon. The probability that a chosen new barrel will have a capacity of 99 gallons or less is

$$z = \frac{99 - 100}{.25} = -4.00$$

$$\Pr[X \leq 99] = .5000 - .49997 = .00003$$

Thus, on the average, a barrel containing 99 gallons or less will be shipped fewer than 3 times out of 100,000.

The Normal Distribution and Sampling

In several applications of quantitative methods, we use sample information to facilitate the final choice. Frequently, the value of the *sample mean* is the pivotal factor in making such a decision. It is therefore important to be able to compute probabilities for the possible values of the sample mean for a given situation. The normal distribution plays a critical role in establishing these probabilities.

We use a special symbol $\bar{X}$ to represent the *sample mean*, which is calculated from

$$\bar{X} = \frac{X_1 + X_2 + \cdots + X_n}{n}$$

This expression indicates that $\bar{X}$ is the arithmetic average of the n sample observations taken from a population or universe. We presume that the sample is selected randomly. Because the actual value of $\bar{X}$ cannot be known until after the sample has been selected, the sample mean must be treated like any other random variable until that time. The expected value of $\bar{X}$ is the mean μ of the population from which the sample is taken. The standard deviation σ of that population partly determines the variability in the possible levels of $\bar{X}$.

The *central limit theorem* of statistics states that *probabilities for the value of $\bar{X}$ may be closely approximated from the normal curve when the sample size is large.* This normal curve has a mean of μ and a standard deviation of $\sigma_{\bar{x}} = \sigma/\sqrt{n}$, reflecting the fact that $\bar{X}$ should exhibit less variability and cluster more tightly about its expected value μ than any single random observation. Thus, the normal curve can be a valuable analytical tool in a tremendous variety of decision-making situations involving samples.

To illustrate, suppose that $n = 100$ scores are chosen as a random sample from a population of IQ test scores having an unknown mean of μ and a standard deviation of $\sigma = 16$ points. The sample mean $\bar{X}$ is normally distributed with the same mean and has the standard deviation

$$\sigma_X = \frac{16}{\sqrt{100}} = \frac{16}{10} = 1.6$$

Assuming that the population mean IQ is $\mu = 100$, consider the following cases.

(1) The probability that $\bar{X}$ is less than or equal to 101.5:

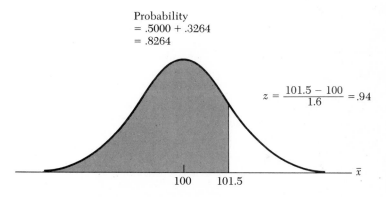

Probability
= .5000 + .3264
= .8264

$$z = \frac{101.5 - 100}{1.6} = .94$$

100   101.5

(2) The probability that $\bar{X}$ lies between 97 and 102:

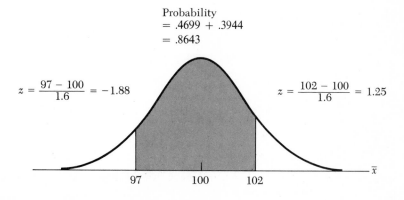

Probability
= .4699 + .3944
= .8643

$$z = \frac{97 - 100}{1.6} = -1.88$$

$$z = \frac{102 - 100}{1.6} = 1.25$$

97   100   102

(3) The probability that $\bar{X}$ is greater than 102.5:

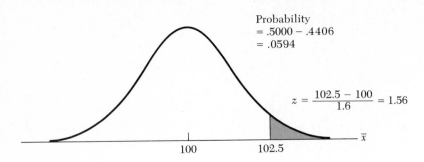

Probability
= .5000 − .4406
= .0594

$$z = \frac{102.5 - 100}{1.6} = 1.56$$

100   102.5

3-5   POISSON AND EXPONENTIAL DISTRIBUTIONS

Two other probability distributions play very important roles in management-science applications. One of these—the *Poisson distribution*—provides probabilities for the number of events that may occur over time. A related distribution—the *exponential distribution*—provides probabilities for the times between events. Both of these distributions are used extensively in queuing (waiting-line) analysis, where the events of interest are customer *arrivals* to the service facility being evaluated. Because we will use the Poisson and exponential distributions primarily in conjunction with queuing analysis, a detailed examination of these distributions will be reserved until Chapter 23.

PROBLEMS

3-1 From the following probability distributions for the receipts and expenses for a charity carnival, determine the probability distribution for the net proceeds (Receipts—Expenses), assuming that receipts and expenses are independent.

Receipts	Probability	Expenses	Probability
$30,000	1/3	$30,000	1/3
40,000	1/3	40,000	1/3
50,000	1/3	50,000	1/3
	1		1

3-2 A coin is tossed three times. Use the binomial formula to determine the probability distribution for the number of heads. Then calculate the expected number of heads.

3-3 Determine the probability distribution for the winnings of a roulette player who places a $1 bet on the red field. Then calculate the expected winnings and state the meaning of your answer in words.

3-4 In canasta, points are assigned to cards in the following manner: red three = 100; joker = 50; ace or deuce = 20; 8 through king = 10; 4 through 7 and black three = 5 points. A canasta deck is composed of two decks of ordinary playing cards, each containing 52 cards and 2 jokers. Determine the probability distribution for the point value of the first card dealt from a shuffled canasta deck.

3-5 An investor wishes to buy a stock to hold for one year in anticipation of capital gain. The choice has been narrowed down to High-Volatility Engineering and Stability Power. Both stocks currently sell for $100 per share and yield $5 dividends. The probability distributions for next year's price have been judgmentally assessed for each stock.

High-Volatility Engineering		Stability Power	
Price	Probability	Price	Probability
$ 25	.05	$ 95	.10
50	.07	100	.25
75	.10	105	.50
100	.05	110	.15
125	.10		1.00
150	.15		
175	.12		
200	.10		
225	.12		
250	.14		
	1.00		

(a) Determine the expected price of a share of each stock.

(b) Should the investor select the stock with the highest expected value? Explain your answer.

3-6 The point spread from tossing two fair dice is the difference between the number of dots showing on the top faces of the cubes. Determine the probability distribution for this random variable.

3-7 The number of persons arriving at a movie theater during any specified minute between 8 and 9 P.M. has the following probability distribution:

Persons	Probability
0	.4
1	.3
2	.2
3	.1
	1.0

Calculate the expected value and the variance for the number of persons arriving between 8:30 and 8:31 P.M.

3-8 Can each of the following situations be classified as a Bernoulli process? If not, state why.

(a) Childbirths in a hospital, the relevant events being the sex of each newborn child.

(b) The outcomes of successive rolls of a die, considering only the events "odd" or "even."

(c) A crooked gambler has rigged a roulette wheel so that whenever the player loses, a mechanism is released that gives the player better odds; when a player wins, the chance of winning on the next spin is somewhat smaller than before. Consider the outcomes of successive spins.

(d) The measuring mechanism on a paint mixer that determines how much dye to squirt into the mixture occasionally violates the required tolerances. The mechanism is highly reliable when it is new, but with use it continually wears, becoming less accurate. Consider the outcomes (within or not within tolerance) of successive mixings.

(e) A machine produces items that are sometimes too heavy or too wide to be used. The events of interest express the quality of each successive item in terms of both weight and width.

3-9 An evenly balanced coin is fairly tossed seven times.

(a) Use the binomial formula to determine the probabilities for obtaining: (1) exactly 2 heads; (2) exactly 4 heads; (3) no tails; (4) exactly 3 tails.

(b) What do you notice about your answers to (2) and (4)? Why is this so?

3-10 Suppose that the proportion of product users favoring a new brand is $P = .70$. A random sample of $n = 5$ users is chosen. Use the binomial formula to determine the probability that:

(a) Exactly 5 favor the new brand.   (b) 0 favor it.   (c) Exactly 3 favor it.

3-11 n parts are randomly chosen from a production process that yields 5% defectives. What is the expected proportion of defectives when (a) $n = 5$? (b) $n = 10$? (c) $n = 100$?

3-12 Use the probability values in Table 3-5 (page 58) to construct the cumulative probability distribution for the number of heads.

3-13 A fair coin is tossed 20 times in succession. Use Appendix Table A to determine the probability that the number of heads obtained is:

(a) Less than or equal to 8.   (b) Equal to 10.
(c) Less than 15.   (d) Greater than or equal to 12.
(e) Greater than 13.   (f) Between 8 and 14, inclusively.

3-14 The chief engineer in a chemical plant has established the policy that five sample vials be drawn from the final stage of a chemical process at random times over a four-hour period. If one or more vials (20% or more) contain impurities, all the settling tanks are cleaned. Find the probability that the tanks will have to be cleaned when the process is so clean that the probability for a dirty vial is: (a) $P = .01$; (b) $P = .05$; (c) $P = .20$; (d) $P = .50$. (*Hint:* Use the fact that Pr[at least 1 dirty vial] $= 1 - $ Pr[no dirty vials].)

3-15 A process produces defective parts at the rate of .05. If a random sample of five items is chosen, what is the probability that at least 80% of the sample will be defective?

3-16 A lopsided coin provides a 60% chance of a head on each toss. If the coin is tossed 20 times, find the probability that the number of heads obtained will be:
(a) Less than or equal to 8.   (b) Equal to 9.
(c) Less than 15.   (d) Greater than or equal to 12.
(e) Greater than 13.   (f) Between 8 and 14, inclusively.

3-17 A student marks an examination consisting of 50 true-or-false questions by tossing a coin. Assuming that one-half of the correct answers should be marked true, find the probability that the student will pass the examination by marking at least 60% of the answers correctly.

3-18 Errors in the measurement of the height of a weather satellite above a ground station are normally distributed with a mean of $\mu = 0$ and a standard deviation of $\sigma = 1$ mile. These errors will be negative if the measured altitude is too low and positive if the altitude is too high. Find the probability that for the next orbit the error will be:
(a) Between 0 and $+1.55$ miles.   (b) Between -2.45 and 0 miles.
(c) $+.75$ miles or less.   (d) Greater than $+.75$ miles.
(e) -1.25 miles or less.   (f) Greater than -1.25 miles.
(g) Between $+.10$ and $+.60$ miles. (h) Between $+1$ and $+2$ miles.

3-19 The lifetime of a particular model of a stereo cartridge is normally distributed with a mean of $\mu = 1,000$ hours and a standard deviation of $\sigma = 100$ hours. Find the probability that one of these cartridges will last:
(a) Between 1,000 and 1,150 hours.   (b) Between 950 and 1,000 hours.
(c) 930 hours or less.   (d) More than 1,250 hours.
(e) 870 hours or less.   (f) Longer than 780 hours.
(g) Between 700 and 1,200 hours.   (h) Between 750 and 850 hours.

3-20 A quality-control manager shuts down an automatic lathe for corrective maintenance whenever a sample of the parts it produces has an average diameter greater than 2.01 inches or smaller than 1.99 inches. The lathe is designed to produce parts with a mean diameter of 2.00 inches, and the sample averages have a standard deviation of .005 inches. Using the normal distribution:
(a) What is the probability that the quality-control manager will stop the process when the lathe is operating as designed, with $\mu = 2.00$ inches?
(b) If the lathe begins to produce parts that are too wide on the average, with $\mu = 2.02$ inches, what is the probability that the lathe will continue to operate?
(c) If an adjustment error causes the lathe to produce parts that on the average are too narrow, with $\mu = 1.99$ inches, what is the probability that the lathe will be stopped?

3-21 Assuming that an office supplier's accounts receivable have a mean time to payment of $\mu = 45$ days and that the standard deviation is $\sigma = 10$ days, find the probability that the mean of a sample of 100 payment times will lie between 43 and 47 days.

3-22 A machine used for filling jars of instant coffee is shut down for adjustment whenever a mean of 25 sample jars is more than $\frac{1}{2}$ ounce under or over the intended mean of 32 ounces for a perfectly adjusted machine. The filling process has a standard deviation of 1 ounce per jar.
(a) What is the probability that the machine will be shut down when it is perfectly adjusted?
(b) What is the probability that the machine will be shut down when it overfills each jar by an average of 1 ounce?

3-23 A random sample of size $n = 100$ job applicants is taken from a population of screening test scores having a mean of $\mu = 70$ and a standard deviation of $\sigma = 15$. Find the probability that the sample mean will lie:

(a) Below 74.   (b) Between 68 and 72.   (c) Above 73.

The test is revised whenever the sample mean score falls outside the 67 through 73 range. Find the probability that the test will *not* be revised when:

(d) $\mu = 69$ (e) $\mu = 70$ (f) $\mu = 71.5$

3-24 The operations manager of a port authority ordered an extensive study to determine the optimal number of toll booths to open during various times of the week. One unanticipated finding is that the mean time to collect a toll decreases as traffic becomes heavier. For example, on late Friday afternoon, collection times were found to have a mean of $\mu = 10$ seconds with a standard deviation of $\sigma = 2$ seconds. On less busy Wednesday mornings, the mean was $\mu = 12$ seconds and the standard deviation was $\sigma = 3$ seconds. A consistency check is now being made to determine whether the season of the year affects efficiency. Random samples of $n = 25$ cars are taken on Wednesday mornings and Friday afternoons. Assuming that these results are true population parameters:

(a) What is the probability that the Wednesday sample mean will differ by more than 1 second from the assumed mean?

(b) What is the same probability for Friday?

(c) Why do the probabilities you found in (a) and (b) differ?

4

Forecasting

Forecasting the future is a fundamental aspect of business decision making. *Future sales* is the most important variable in business forecasts. *Unit sales* establish levels for most business activities—from purchasing and production to marketing—and knowledge about sales is a prerequisite to the budgetary and planning process.

A variety of quantitative techniques have been developed to forecast future values. The underlying models can be classified into three broad categories:

(1) *Forecasting Using Past Data.* The historical patterns of a variable are identified and projected into the future. These patterns are obtained through extrapolation from time-series data.
(2) *Forecasting Using Causal Models.* A relationship is found between the unknown variable and one or more other known variables. The values of the known variables are then used to predict the value of the variable of interest.
(3) *Forecasting Using Judgment.* Quantitative representations are used to express judgments in terms of subjective probabilities. These methods can incorporate the forecaster's actual "batting average" and may provide a way to express collective judgments.

In Chapter 4, we will survey the forecasting methods commonly used in each of these three categories.

4-1   FORECASTING USING PAST DATA: TIME-SERIES ANALYSIS

A *time series* is best described in terms of a graph like the one in Figure 4-1, where the gross national product (GNP) of the United States is plotted against time for the period from 1929 to 1974. The graph shows that GNP has grown over the years, but that this growth has been erratic—faster in some years than in others. Wide swings are evident in the graph: The GNP declines during the Great Depression of the 1930s and then rises rapidly with the advent of World War II. One goal of *time-series analysis* is to identify the swings and fluctuations of a time series and then to sort them into various categories by the arithmetic manipulation of the numerical values obtained.

Several models can be used to characterize time series. The classical model used by economists provides the clearest explanation of the four com-

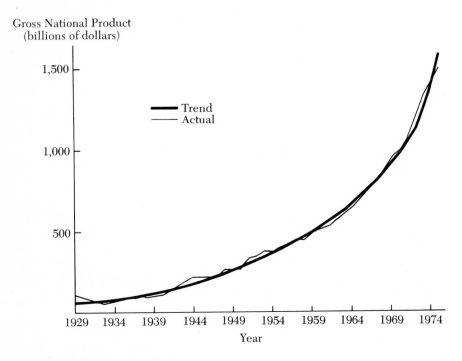

FIGURE 4-1

U.S. Gross National Product, 1929–1974.

SOURCE: *Economic Report of the President, 1970, 1976.*

ponents of time-series variation and how they relate to each other:

(1) Secular trend (T_t) (2) Cyclical movement (C_t)
(3) Seasonal fluctuation (S_t) (4) Irregular variation (I_t)

These components can be related to the forecast variable by mathematical equations. The forecast variable is denoted by the symbol Y_t, where the subscript t refers to a period of time. Examples of Y_t are annual sales, passenger miles flown by domestic airlines, and acre-feet of water supplied to a city.

Secular trend is defined as the long-range general movement in Y_t over an extended period of time. In this chapter, we will develop methods for isolating trend from other variational components in a time series. *Cyclical movement* in time-series data is characterized by wide swings—usually a year or more in duration—upward or downward from the secular trend. Cyclical movements are temporary in nature and are typified by alternating periods of economic expansion and contraction or recession. *Seasonal fluctuation* is a generally recurring upward and downward pattern of movement in Y_t, usually on an annual basis. A classic example of seasonal fluctuation is the household consumption of fossil fuels, such as oils, coal, or natural gas. *Irregular variations* are characterized by events that are completely unpredictable. These variations, sometimes referred to as *random factors*, can be the most perplexing to encounter in time-series analysis.

The Classical Time-Series Model

The classical time-series model originally used by economists combines the four components of time-series variation in the equation

$$Y_t = T_t \times C_t \times S_t \times I_t$$

This equation states that factors associated with each of these components can be multiplied together to provide the value of the forecast variable.

This model can be explained by means of a hypothetical time series—the sales Y_t of stereo speakers by the Speak E-Z Company. Figure 4-2 shows how the final time series (bottom graph) might be obtained by combining the four components. But only a hypothetical time series can be synthesized from the assumed characteristics of the four components. In actual applications, we may not know anything about T_t, C_t, S_t, or I_t. Usually, we begin with the raw time-series data and reverse the procedure, sifting the data to sort out and identify the components. We will discuss some examples of this technique in this chapter.

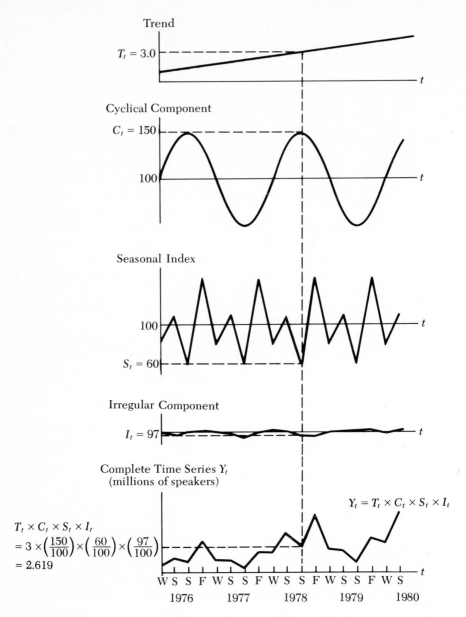

FIGURE 4-2
The construction of a complete time series for Speak E-Z sales, using individual components.

FORECASTING TREND USING REGRESSION   **4-2**

The secular trend component T_t of a time series may be the most valuable variable in making forecasts. Trend analysis focuses on finding the appropriate trend line or curve that provides the best fit to the historical scatter of Y_t over time.

Determining Trend Using Least Squares

As an example, we will consider the unit sales of Blitz Beer. Each year's sales are plotted as a point on the *scatter diagram* in Figure 4-3. The heavy line, representing trend, was constructed to minimize the sum of the squared deviations. These deviations are represented by the vertical segments connecting each point to the *trend line*.

The trend line is found by the *method of least squares*, according to the *regression equation*

$$\hat{Y} = a + bX$$

Here, $\hat{Y}$ represents the computed value of the *dependent variable* (the variable being forecast) of the time series, and X represents the *independent variable* (the time period). We use X instead of t, because it is simpler to express time relative to a base period.

The *regression coefficients* a and b are obtained from the equations

$$b = \frac{n\sum XY - (\sum X)(\sum Y)}{n\sum X^2 - (\sum X)^2}$$

$$a = \bar{Y} - b\bar{X}$$

where $\bar{Y}$ and $\bar{X}$ are the respective mean values. The individual X and Y values represent the time-series *raw data*. These data appear in Table 4-1, where the preliminary least-squares calculations are made.

The regression coefficients are calculated as

$$b = \frac{10(3,701.2) - 45(795.6)}{10(285) - 45^2} = 1.47$$

$$\bar{X} = 45/10 = 4.5 \quad \text{and} \quad \bar{Y} = 795.6/10 = 79.56$$

$$a = 79.56 - 1.47(4.5) = 72.95$$

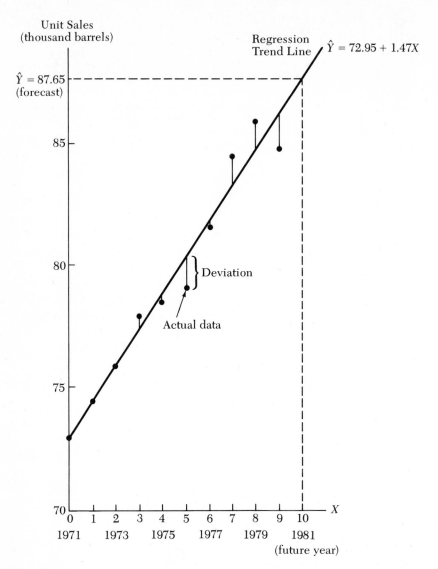

FIGURE 4-3
Least-squares regression line for trend in unit sales of Blitz Beer.

The regression equation for the trend line in Blitz Beer sales (in thousands of barrels) is therefore

$$\hat{Y} = 72.95 + 1.47X \qquad (X = 0 \text{ for } 1971)$$

This equation indicates that for 1971 the trend value is sales of 72.95 thousand barrels and that Y_t increases by 1.47 thousand barrels per year. Because the

TABLE 4-1

Computations for Fitting Least-Squares Trend Line to Blitz Beer Sales

Year	Year in Transformed Units X	Unit Sales (thousands of barrels) Y	XY	X^2
1971	0	72.9	0	0
1972	1	74.4	74.4	1
1973	2	75.9	151.8	4
1974	3	77.9	233.7	9
1975	4	78.6	314.4	16
1976	5	79.1	395.5	25
1977	6	81.7	490.2	36
1978	7	84.4	590.8	49
1979	8	85.9	687.2	64
1980	9	84.8	763.2	81
	$45 = \sum X$	$795.6 = \sum Y$	$3,701.2 = \sum XY$	$285 = \sum X^2$

calendar years have been transformed, it is important to indicate the base year: $X = 0$ for 1971.

Forecasting Trend

We can forecast Blitz Beer sales for 1981 on the basis of the trend line. To do this, we must use $X = 10$, because this year is $X = 1981 - 1971 = 10$ periods beyond the base year. From the trend equation, we can project that 1981 Blitz Beer sales will be

$$\hat{Y} = 72.95 + 1.47(10) = 87.65 \text{ thousand barrels}$$

The estimate of 87.65 is an *extrapolation*. Its validity depends on the assumption that the growth pattern of beer sales in the ensuing year will be similar to the growth pattern in the past.

FORECASTING USING SEASONAL INDEXES   **4-3**

In this section, we will examine a procedure for isolating seasonal fluctuations in time-series data. Identifying seasonal patterns is a necessary first step in short-range planning. The management of a firm whose business drops in May is not alarmed if it is only the beginning of an annual seasonal trough.

Likewise, government economists recognize that the Consumer Price Index will rise or fall in certain months solely due to the influence of seasonal factors, such as changing varieties of produce on the market. To monitor the performance of a business or an economy, it is useful to "deseasonalize" time-series data to determine whether a current drop or rise is greater than normal.

Ratio-to-Moving-Average Method

The *ratio-to-moving-average method* is widely used to isolate seasonal fluctuations. Beginning with the actual time series, the trend and cyclical elements are isolated together in what is referred to as a "smoothed" time series. The isolation of the long-term elements is accomplished by means of *four-quarter moving averages.*

In the context of the classical time-series model, the ratio-to-moving-average method is summarized by the expression

$$\frac{Y_t}{\text{Moving average}} = \frac{T_t \times C_t \times S_t \times I_t}{T_t \times C_t} = S_t \times I_t$$

The moving average provides both trend and cycle, so that $T_t \times C_t$ is obtained for each time period. Dividing Y_t by the moving average is therefore equivalent to canceling the $T_t \times C_t$ terms from the multiplicative model, so that only the seasonal and irregular components, expressed by $S_t \times I_t$, remain.

To illustrate this procedure, data for average weekly freight-car loadings are provided in Table 4-2. The original data are listed in column (2), and the moving totals for four successive quarters appear in column (3). For 1968, the quarterly figures are 508.0, 565.7, 549.7, and 543.7 thousands of carloads. The total of these four quarters is 2,167.1, which represents all of the carloading figures for 1968. This is not an annual total, however, because the original data are weekly averages. The entries in column (3) are positioned in the table to fall *between* the quarters. These numbers must be adjusted to arrive at a true value for each quarter.

To illustrate this procedure, we will consider the first two entries, 2,167.1 and 2,166.4, from column (3). Their sum, 4,333.5, represents two overlapping years of carloadings and appears in column (4) in the row for the summer quarter of 1968. Because three quarters have been counted twice, the value 4,333.5 represents a total of eight quarterly figures. The four-quarter moving average for the summer quarter of 1968 is obtained by dividing the sum 4,333.5 by 8. This yields 541.7, which is entered in column (5), where four-quarter moving averages have been similarly obtained for the remaining quarters.

The four-quarter moving averages from column (5) of Table 4-2 are graphed in Figure 4-4, along with the original time-series data. Note that two quarters at the beginning and end of the series are "lost."

TABLE 4-2

Ratio-to-Moving-Average Calculations for Average Weekly Carloadings

(1) Quarter	(2) Average Weekly Carloadings (thousands)	(3) Four- Quarter Moving Total	(4) Sum of Two Successive Four-Quarter Totals	(5) Four-Quarter Moving Average (4) ÷ 8	(6) Original as a Percentage of Moving Average [(2) ÷ (5)] × 100	(7) Seasonal Index
1968						
Winter	508.0					96.11
Spring	565.7	2,167.1				103.66
Summer	549.7	2,166.4	4,333.5	541.7	101.48	100.25
Fall	543.7	2,162.4	4,328.8	541.1	100.48	99.98
1969						
Winter	507.3	2,158.0	4,320.4	540.1	93.93	96.11
Spring	561.7	2,171.3	4,329.3	541.2	103.79	103.66
Summer	545.3	2,162.7	4,334.0	541.8	100.65	100.25
Fall	557.0	2,151.3	4,314.0	539.3	103.28	99.98
1970						
Winter	498.7	2,129.7	4,281.0	535.1	93.20	96.11
Spring	550.3	2,086.0	4,215.7	527.0	104.42	103.66
Summer	523.7	2,073.0	4,159.0	519.9	100.73	100.25
Fall	513.3	2,048.7	4,121.7	515.2	99.63	99.98
1971						
Winter	485.7	2,002.0	4,050.7	506.3	95.93	96.11
Spring	526.0	1,946.0	3,948.0	493.5	106.59	103.66
Summer	477.0	1,928.3	3,874.3	484.3	98.49	100.25
Fall	457.3	1,916.0	3,844.3	480.5	95.17	99.98
1972						
Winter	468.0	1,939.3	3,855.3	481.9	97.12	96.11
Spring	513.7	1,993.3	3,932.6	491.6	104.50	103.66
Summer	500.3	2,028.0	4,021.3	502.7	99.52	100.25
Fall	511.3	2,047.6	4,075.6	509.5	100.35	99.98
1973						
Winter	502.7	2,077.3	4,124.9	515.6	97.50	96.11
Spring	533.3	2,100.3	4,177.6	522.2	102.13	103.66
Summer	530.0	2,109.3	4,209.6	526.2	100.72	100.25
Fall	534.3	2,108.3	4,217.6	527.2	101.35	99.98
1974						
Winter	511.7	2,085.3	4,193.6	524.2	97.62	96.11
Spring	532.3	2,030.7	4,116.0	514.5	103.46	103.66
Summer	507.0					100.25
Fall	479.7					99.98

SOURCE OF DATA: *Moody's Transportation Manual*, 1975. Reproduced with permission of Moody's Investment Service.

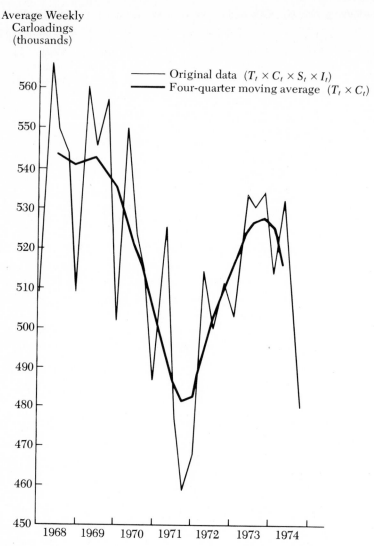

Average Weekly
Carloadings
(thousands)

——— Original data $(T_t \times C_t \times S_t \times I_t)$
━━━ Four-quarter moving average $(T_t \times C_t)$

FIGURE 4-4

Four-quarter moving averages and original data for average weekly carloadings.

If the series curve provided by the moving averages (the heavier line segments in the graph) represents only the trend and cyclical elements, then the fluctuations in the original data about this curve illustrate the seasonal and irregular components. The combination $S_t \times I_t$ can be obtained by dividing the original data by the corresponding four-quarter moving average. For

Summer 1968, the actual average weekly carloading value is 549.7 thousand. Dividing this number by the corresponding moving average of 541.7 and multiplying by 100 gives us the *percentage of moving average*

$$\frac{549.7}{541.7} \times 100 = 101.48$$

The percentages of moving averages for the remaining quarters, provided in column (6) of Table 4-2, are plotted in Figure 4-5. Note the repetitive nature of the oscillations, which are more or less regular from one time period to the next. The overall pattern is not precisely the same for all years, however, due to the irregular variation I_t. The remaining step in the ratio-to-moving-average method is to isolate a seasonal index completely by removing the irregular component.

　　The classical model assumes that short-term random influences will either increase or decrease the value of Y_t from its expected level for a particular quarter. If the summer quarters for several different years are considered, the irregular fluctuations will have a positive effect in some years and a negative influence in others. For the duration of the time series, we can assume that the average effect of random factors will be 0.

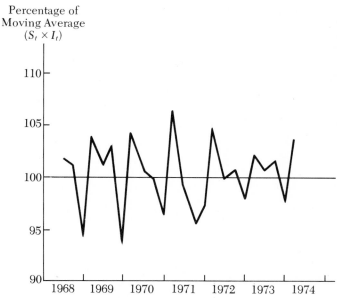

FIGURE 4-5

Original average weekly carloading data as percentage of four-quarter moving average.

TABLE 4-3
Calculation of Seasonal Indexes from the Percentage of
Moving-Average Values for Carloading Data in Table 4-2

		Quarter		
Year	Winter	Spring	Summer	Fall
1968			101.48	100.48
1969	93.93	103.79	100.65	103.28
1970	93.20	104.42	100.73	99.63
1971	95.93	106.59	98.49	95.17
1972	97.12	104.50	99.52	100.35
1973	97.50	102.13	100.72	101.35
1974	97.62	103.46		
Median	96.53	104.11	100.69	100.42

Sum of medians = 401.75

$$\text{Seasonal index} = \text{Median} \times \frac{400}{401.75}$$

| | = 96.11 | 103.66 | 100.25 | 99.98 |

We can isolate S_t by averaging the $S_t \times I_t$ values for the same season. This is illustrated in Table 4-3, where the percentage of moving average values from column (6) of Table 4-2 are grouped into the four seasonal categories. Note that the values for the winter quarter range from a low of 93.20 for 1970 to a high of 97.62 for 1974. The median will be used to represent the true seasonal factor. For winter, this value is 96.53, which is found by averaging the two middle values:

$$\frac{95.93 + 97.12}{2} = 96.53$$

(For an odd number of years, the median is simply the middle value itself.)

The successive medians for the remaining groups are 104.11, 100.69, and 100.42. From these medians, we can obtain a seasonal index for each quarter. The sum of the medians is 401.75. A further adjustment (multiplying each median by 400/401.75) is necessary for the seasonal indexes to sum to 400. For instance, the seasonal index for the winter quarter is 96.53(400/401.75) = 96.11.

Monthly Data

Because a quarter is too long a time period to provide an accurate seasonal index for many businesses, fluctuations are often predicted on the basis of a 12-month seasonal cycle instead. The general procedures illustrated for quarterly data can also be applied to monthly figures. First, 12-month moving totals are obtained and centered by finding the sum of two successive totals. The 12-month moving average is determined by dividing the centered totals by 24 (the number of monthly figures included). The percentage of moving average is then found by dividing the original monthly data by the respective moving averages. Seasonal indexes are obtained by grouping all the percentages for the same month in each year together to obtain 12 monthly groups. The median of each monthly group is then calculated, and the sum of the medians is determined. Finally, these medians are adjusted so that their sum is 1,200 (12 months per year × 100%).

Making the Forecast

Seasonal indexes are useful in making short-term forecasts. First, a trend over the annual period is determined, and then seasonal adjustments are made for each period within the year. For example, suppose the managers of a department store who wish to forecast monthly sales for the next calendar year determine the following trend equation:

$$\hat{Y} = 1,025,000 + 50,000X$$

where X is in months and $X = 0$ for January 15 of next year. Calculations of the monthly forecasts of department store sales are provided in Table 4-4. The

TABLE 4-4
Calculations of the Monthly Forecasts of Department Store Sales

(1)	(2)	(3)	(4)	(5)
			Monthly Sales Trend Level	Monthly Sales Forecast
Month	X	Seasonal Index	$\hat{Y}$	[(3) × (4)] ÷ 100
Jan.	0	56.7	$1,025,000	$ 581,175
Feb.	1	64.5	1,075,000	693,375
Mar.	2	62.1	1,125,000	698,625
Apr.	3	99.9	1,175,000	1,173,825
May	4	83.6	1,225,000	1,024,100
Jun.	5	67.4	1,275,000	859,350
Jul.	6	58.2	1,325,000	771,150
Aug.	7	100.1	1,375,000	1,376,375
Sep.	8	110.6	1,425,000	1,576,050
Oct.	9	137.7	1,475,000	2,031,075
Nov.	10	167.3	1,525,000	2,551,325
Dec.	11	191.9	1,575,000	3,022,425
		1,200.0		

12 monthly seasonal indexes appear in column (3), and the monthly sales trend levels are calculated in column (4) from the managers' trend equation. For January, the trend value of $1,025,000 is multiplied by 56.7% to obtain the forecast sales of $581,175. The sales forecasts for all 12 months are listed in column (5).

4-4   EXPONENTIAL SMOOTHING

Exponential smoothing is a popular forecasting procedure that offers two basic advantages: It simplifies forecasting calculations, and its data-storage requirements are small. Exponential smoothing produces self-correcting forecasts with built-in adjustments that regulate forecast values by increasing or decreasing them in the opposite direction of earlier errors, much like a thermostat.

Single-Parameter Exponential Smoothing

The basic exponential smoothing procedure provides the next period's forecast directly from the current period's actual and forecast values. This is summarized by the expression

$$F_{t+1} = \alpha Y_t + (1 - \alpha)F_t$$

where t is the current time period, F_{t+1} and F_t are the forecast values for the next period and the current period, respectively, and Y_t is the current actual value. α (the lower-case Greek letter alpha) is the *smoothing constant*—a chosen value lying between 0 and 1. Since only one smoothing constant is used, we refer to this procedure as *single-parameter exponential smoothing*.

To illustrate, we will suppose that actual sales of Blitz Beer in period 10 (October) were $Y_{10} = 5,240$ barrels and that $F_{10} = 5,061.6$ had been forecast earlier for this period. Using a smoothing constant of $\alpha = .20$, the forecast for period 11 (November) sales can be calculated as

$$F_{11} = .20(5,240) + (1 - .20)(5,061.6) = 5,097.3 \text{ barrels}$$

Elementary exponential smoothing is extremely simple, because only one number—last period's forecast—must be saved. But, in essence, the entire time series is embodied in that forecast. If we express F_t in terms of the preceding actual Y_{t-1} and forecast F_{t-1} values, then the equivalent expression for next period's forecast is

$$F_{t+1} = \alpha Y_t + \alpha(1 - \alpha)Y_{t-1} + (1 - \alpha)^2 F_{t-1}$$

Continuing this for several earlier periods shows us that all preceding Ys are reflected in the current forecast. The name for this procedure is derived from the successive weights α, $\alpha(1 - \alpha)$, $\alpha(1 - \alpha)^2$, $\alpha(1 - \alpha)^3, \ldots$, which *decrease exponentially*. Thus, the more current the actual value of the time series is, the greater its weight is. Progressively less forecasting weight is assigned to older Ys, and the oldest Ys are eventually wiped out. The forecasting procedure can be modified at any time by changing the value of α.

Table 4-5 provides the actual and forecast Blitz Beer sales for 20 periods when $\alpha = .20$. There, the actual sales figure for period 1 has been used for the initial forecast for period 2. (Eventually, the same Fs will be achieved in later time periods, regardless of the initial value.) The errors in this procedure are determined by subtracting the forecasts from their respective actual values. α should be set at a level that minimizes these errors. Often several trial periods are required to "tune" the smoothing constant to past data. Large α levels assign

TABLE 4-5

Forecast of Blitz Beer Sales

by Single-Parameter Exponential Smoothing ($\alpha = .20$)

Period t	Actual Sales Y_t	Forecast Sales F_t	Error $Y_t - F_t$
1	4,890	—	—
2	4,910	4,890.0	20.0
3	4,970	4,894.0	76.0
4	5,010	4,909.2	101.8
5	5,060	4,929.4	130.6
6	5,100	4,955.5	144.5
7	5,050	4,984.4	65.6
8	5,170	4,997.5	172.5
9	5,180	5,032.0	148.0
10	5,240	5,061.6	178.4
11	5,220	5,097.3	122.7
12	5,280	5,121.8	158.2
13	5,330	5,153.5	176.5
14	5,380	5,188.8	191.2
15	5,440	5,227.0	213.0
16	5,460	5,269.6	190.4
17	5,520	5,307.7	212.3
18	5,490	5,350.2	139.8
19	5,550	5,378.1	171.9
20	5,600	5,412.5	187.5

more weight to current values, whereas small α levels emphasize past data. By trial and error, an optimal level can be found for α that minimizes *variability* in forecasting errors.

Two-Parameter Exponential Smoothing

Note that the forecast sales for Blitz Beer are smaller than (lag behind) the actual sales. Whenever there is a pronounced upward trend in actual data (here, increasing sales), forecasts resulting from the single-parameter exponential smoothing procedure will be consistently low.

Two-parameter exponential smoothing eliminates such a lag by explicitly accounting for trend by using a second smoothing constant for the trend itself. A total of three equations are employed:

$$V_t = \alpha Y_t + (1 - \alpha)(V_{t-1} + b_{t-1}) \quad \text{(smooth the data)}$$

$$b_t = \gamma(V_t - V_{t-1}) + (1 - \gamma)b_{t-1} \quad \text{(smooth the trend)}$$

$$F_{t+1} = V_t + b_t \quad \text{(forecast)}$$

Here, V_t represents the smoothed value for period t. The difference between the current and the prior smoothed values provides the current trend: $V_t - V_{t-1}$. The second equation contains the *trend-smoothing constant* γ (the lower-case Greek letter gamma), which is used to obtain smoothed trend values, represented by b_t. The third equation provides the forecast.

Table 4-6 lists the forecasts of Blitz Beer sales when $\alpha = .20$ and $\gamma = .30$. (The initial smoothed-data value of $V_2 = 4,890$ is the actual sales for period 1. The first smoothed-trend value of $b_2 = 20$ is the difference in actual sales for periods 1 and 2.) As an illustration, to forecast period 8 sales, first we obtain the smoothed data value for period 7:

$$V_7 = .20Y_7 + (1 - .20)(V_6 + b_6)$$

$$= .20(5,050) + .80(5,045 + 35.7)$$

$$= 5,075 \text{ barrels}$$

Then we compute the smoothed trend value for period 7:

$$b_7 = .30(V_7 - V_6) + (1 - .30)b_6$$

$$= .30(5,075 - 5,045) + .70(35.7)$$

$$= 34.0$$

TABLE 4-6

Forecast of Blitz Beer Sales by Two-Parameter Exponential Smoothing
($\alpha = .20$ and $\gamma = .30$)

Period t	Actual Sales Y_t	Smoothed Data V_t	Smoothed Trend b_t	Forecast Sales F_t	Error $Y_t - F_t$
1	4,890	—	—	—	—
2	4,910	4,890	20.0	—	—
3	4,970	4,922	23.6	4,910.0	60.0
4	5,010	4,958	27.3	4,945.6	64.4
5	5,060	5,000	31.7	4,985.3	74.7
6	5,100	5,045	35.7	5,031.7	68.3
7	5,050	5,075	34.0	5,080.7	−30.7
8	5,170	5,121	37.6	5,109.0	61.0
9	5,180	5,163	38.9	5,158.6	21.4
10	5,240	5,210	41.3	5,201.9	38.1
11	5,220	5,245	39.4	5,251.3	−31.3
12	5,280	5,283	39.0	5,284.4	− 4.4
13	5,330	5,324	39.6	5,322.0	8.0
14	5,380	5,367	40.6	5,363.6	16.4
15	5,440	5,414	42.5	5,407.6	32.4
16	5,460	5,457	42.7	5,456.5	3.5
17	5,520	5,504	44.0	5,499.7	20.3
18	5,490	5,536	40.4	5,548.0	−58.0
19	5,550	5,571	38.8	5,576.4	−26.4
20	5,600	5,608	38.3	5,609.8	− 9.8

which indicates that sales were increasing at a rate of 34.0 barrels per period at that time. The forecast for period 8 is the sum of the preceding period's smoothed data and trend values:

$$F_8 = V_7 + b_7 = 5{,}075 + 34.0 = 5{,}109.0 \text{ barrels}$$

The forecasts that result from this procedure are close to the actual sales values. The current trend itself is readjusted for each period to coincide with the latest growth in the raw data.

Further Exponential Smoothing Procedures

A wide variety of exponential smoothing procedures can be used. One adjusts the smoothing constant α itself from period to period. Others consider nonlinear relationships between values. A somewhat more complicated procedure than the one just described involves three parameters and provides for *seasonal smoothing* in addition to trend smoothing.

4-5   FORECASTING USING CAUSAL MODELS: REGRESSION ANALYSIS

Thus far, we have discussed forecasting procedures based only on extrapolations from time-series data, and until this point, our conclusions have been somewhat tenuous. Such forecasts—especially long-range ones—can be severely in error, because they are based on historical patterns that will not necessarily continue in the future. Often the cause for such patterns cannot even be identified.

Sometimes we can achieve more satisfactory forecasts by using a causal model that explains the dependent forecast variable in terms of the level for one or more predictor variables (rather than simply in terms of a period of time). Ideal predictors *lead* (have values that are determined in advance of) the main variable. Thus, a student's success at college might be predicted from his or her high-school grade point average. Predictions of future growth in GNP might be based on today's prices, level of employment, and plant capacities. Or a product's sales forecast might be determied from its current share of the market and planned advertising expenditures.

Simple Regression

When one predictor variable is used, forecasts are obtained from a regression line. This procedure is referred to as *simple regression analysis*. To illustrate, we will forecast the monthly sales Y of Deuce Hardware Store outlets using floorspace X as the independent variable. Table 4-7 provides the pertinent data from a sample of 10 stores.

The *regression coefficients* are

$$b = \frac{n\sum XY - (\sum X)(\sum Y)}{n\sum X^2 - (\sum X)^2} = \frac{10(48,690) - 2,270(191)}{10(594,832) - (2,270)^2} = .067$$

$$\bar{X} = \frac{2,270}{10} = 227 \quad \text{and} \quad \bar{Y} = \frac{191}{10} = 19.1$$

$$a = \bar{Y} - b\bar{X} = 19.1 - .067(227) = 3.9$$

Thus, the *regression equation* is

$$\hat{Y} = 3.9 + .067X$$

This equation can be used to forecast the monthly sales of a new store of a particular size. For instance, the forecast monthly sales of a store with $X = 300$

TABLE 4-7
Deuce Hardware Store Data for Monthly Sales and Floorspace with Regression Calculations

Store	Monthly Sales (thousands of dollars) Y	Floorspace (square yards) X	XY	X^2
1	20	305	6,100	93,025
2	15	130	1,950	16,900
3	17	189	3,213	35,721
4	9	175	1,575	30,625
5	16	101	1,616	10,201
6	27	269	7,263	72,361
7	35	421	14,735	177,241
8	7	195	1,365	38,025
9	22	282	6,204	79,524
10	23	203	4,669	41,209
	$191 = \sum Y$	$2{,}270 = \sum X$	$48{,}690 = \sum XY$	$594{,}832 = \sum X^2$

square yards of floorspace is

$$\hat{Y} = 3.9 + .067(300) = 24.00, \text{ or } \$24{,}000$$

Multiple Regression

We will now expand the method of least squares so that it can be applied to *multiple regression analysis*, which includes several independent predictor variables. Multiple regression often improves forecasting accuracy.

The essential advantage of considering two or more independent variables is that it permits us to make greater use of the information that is available. For example, a regression line that expresses a new store's sales in terms of the population of the city it serves should yield a poorer sales forecast than an equation that also considers the median income, the number of nearby competitors, and the local unemployment rate. A plant manager should be able to predict the cost of processing a new order more precisely if, in addition to the size of the order, he considers the total volume of orders, the current manpower level, and the production capacity of available equipment. A marketing manager should be able to gauge the sales response to a magazine advertisement more accurately if, in addition to the magazine's circulation, she considers the demographical features of its readers, such as median age, median income, and proportion of urban readers.

Linear multiple regression analysis involves two or more independent variables. In the case of two independent variables, denoted by X_1 and X_2, the *estimated multiple regression equation* is

$$\hat{Y} = a + b_1 X_1 + b_2 X_2$$

Here, two independent variables and one dependent variable, or a total of three variables, are considered. The sample data will consist of three values for each sample unit observed, so that a scatter pattern of these observations will be three dimensional.

To explain how multiple regression data can be portrayed in three dimensions, we will draw an analogy using the walls and floor of a room. Letting a corner of the room represent the case when all three variables have values of 0, we can denote the data points by suspending marbles in space at various distances from the floor and the two walls. A marble's height above the floor can represent the value of Y for that observation. Its distance from the wall on the left then measures the observed value of X_1, and its distance from the wall on the right expresses the observed value of X_2. Figure 4-6 is a pictorial representation of a three-dimensional scatter for a hypothetical set of data.

The regression equation corresponds to a plane. This plane must be slanted in such a way that it provides the best least-squares fit to the sample data. The three-dimensional surface that results is referred to as the *regression plane*.

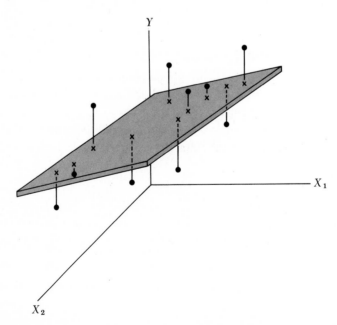

FIGURE 4-6
A regression plane for multiple regression, using three variables.

TABLE 4-8

Deuce Hardware Store Data for Monthly Sales, Floorspace, and Daily Advertising Expenditure

Store	Monthly Sales (thousands of dollars) Y	Floorspace (square yards) X_1	Daily Advertising Expenditure (dollars) X_2
1	20	305	35
2	15	130	98
3	17	189	83
4	9	175	76
5	16	101	93
6	27	269	77
7	35	421	44
8	7	195	57
9	22	282	31
10	23	203	92

Slanting this plane can be compared to determining how to position a pane of glass through the suspended marbles so that its incline approximates the incline of the pattern of the scatter.

The coefficients of the estimated regression plane can be determined by solving a set of three equations in three unknowns. These are referred to as the *normal equations*:

$$\sum Y = na + b_1 \sum X_1 + b_2 \sum X_2$$
$$\sum X_1 Y = a \sum X_1 + b_1 \sum X_1^2 + b_2 \sum X_1 X_2$$
$$\sum X_2 Y = a \sum X_2 + b_1 \sum X_1 X_2 + b_2 \sum X_2^2$$

We find a, b_1, and b_2 by calculating the required sums from the data for the various combinations of Y, X_1, and X_2 and then substituting these values into the normal equations, which are solved simultaneously. To illustrate, we will consider our Deuce Hardware Store example again. In addition to floorspace (now denoted by X_1), Table 4-8 includes a new independent variable—daily advertising expenditure, denoted by X_2.

The intermediate calculations required to solve the regression equation appear in Table 4-9, where the columns contain the individual variable values and the squared and product terms. We obtain the following normal equations:

$$191 = 10a + 2{,}270b_1 + 686b_2$$
$$48{,}690 = 2{,}270a + 594{,}832b_1 + 139{,}565b_2$$
$$12{,}569 = 686a + 139{,}565b_1 + 52{,}682b_2$$

TABLE 4-9
Intermediate Calculations for Obtaining Regression Coefficients

Y	X_1	X_2	X_1Y	X_2Y	X_1X_2	X_1^2	X_2^2
20	305	35	6,100	700	10,675	93,025	1,225
15	130	98	1,950	1,470	12,740	16,900	9,604
17	189	83	3,213	1,411	15,687	35,721	6,889
9	175	76	1,575	684	13,300	30,625	5,776
16	101	93	1,616	1,488	9,393	10,201	8,649
27	269	77	7,263	2,079	20,713	72,361	5,929
35	421	44	14,735	1,540	18,524	177,241	1,936
7	195	57	1,365	399	11,115	38,025	3,249
22	282	31	6,204	682	8,742	79,524	961
23	203	92	4,669	2,116	18,676	41,209	8,464
191	2,270	686	48,690	12,569	139,565	594,832	52,682
$= \sum Y$	$= \sum X_1$	$= \sum X_2$	$= \sum X_1Y$	$= \sum X_2Y$	$= \sum X_1X_2$	$= \sum X_1^2$	$= \sum X_2^2$

Solving these equations simultaneously for the unknowns a, b_1, b_2, we obtain

$$a = -23.074$$
$$b_1 = .1148$$
$$b_2 = .2349$$

The values of a, b_1, and b_2 provide the estimated multiple regression equation

$$\hat{Y} = -23.074 + .1148X_1 + .2349X_2$$

which can be used to forecast the sales of a particular store. Suppose a new store is to be built that will have 250 square yards of floorspace and spend \$75 in daily advertising, so that $X_1 = 250$ and $X_2 = 75$. The forecast sales level is then

$$\hat{Y} = -23.074 + .1148(250) + .2349(75) = 23.244, \text{ or } \$23,244$$

Comparison of Simple and Multiple Regression

Table 4-10 shows the Deuce Hardware sales forecasts made by applying both simple and multiple regression to the actual data. Note that multiple regression provides greater accuracy, because the forecasting errors tend to be smaller when this procedure is used. Including the second predictor variable (daily advertising expenditure) allows us to "explain" more variation in sales Y.

It is not clear whether including more variables generally reduces forecasting error. In some cases, adding independent variables can even confuse

TABLE 4-10
Comparison of Forecasting Errors
Using Simple and Multiple Regression

	Actual Data		Simple Regression		Multiple Regression	
			Forecast	Error	Forecast	Error
Y	X_1	X_2	$\hat{Y}$	$Y - \hat{Y}$	$\hat{Y}$	$Y - \hat{Y}$
20	305	35	24.3	− 4.3	20.2	− .2
15	130	98	12.6	2.4	14.9	.1
17	189	83	16.6	.4	18.1	− 1.1
9	175	76	15.6	− 6.6	14.9	− 5.9
16	101	93	10.7	5.3	10.4	5.6
27	269	77	21.9	5.1	25.9	1.1
35	421	44	32.1	2.9	35.6	− .6
7	195	57	17.0	− 10.0	12.7	− 5.7
22	282	31	22.8	− .8	16.6	5.4
23	203	92	17.5	5.5	21.8	1.2

the analysis. Independent variables must be chosen with care and must have some rational basis for affecting Y.

Further Considerations

We have barely scratched the surface of regression analysis. For example, we have entirely avoided an examination of nonlinear relationships. Forecasts made from the regression line or plane can be qualified in a statistical sense by means of confidence intervals. The procedures involved, however, are based on formidable theoretical assumptions that are too complex to discuss here. Regression analysis is often accompanied by *correlation analysis,* where the major concern is how strongly the variables are related. Advanced techniques, such as *stepwise multiple regression,* help determine not only the regression equation but also the particular predictor variables it is best to include. An area of statistics and economics called *econometrics* considers causal models in great depth and wide breadth. References dealing with this topic are provided in the Bibliography.

FORECASTING USING JUDGMENT   4-6

The third major forecasting technique is based on judgment. In a sense, all forecasting involves some judgment, even when data are extensively analyzed. But we can use judgment to make forecasts even when no data at all are available.

Until now, all of the forecasting methods we have discussed involve *point forecasts;* that is, they provide future predictions in the form of specific numerical values. Such forecasts are almost certain to be in error: The actual data will inevitably differ in some way from the forecasts; at best, the forecasts will be slightly above or below the actual values. It may therefore be more realistic to predict a *range of values.* An even better method might be to include future uncertainty by treating it as a random variable with a *probability distribution.* A detailed discussion of three methods of finding judgemental probability distributions will be reserved for Chapter 21.

In one popular prediction procedure called *Delphi forecasting,* individual judgments regarding future events are combined to express a collective opinion. Delphi forecasting has been successfully employed in predicting technological breakthroughs and scientific advancements. It has also been used to forecast long-range sales and profits.

Another judgmental application, *scenario projection,* is often employed in government and military planning. Here, detailed circumstances are used as stage settings to provide background for a future analysis that simulates reality. *Industrial* and *world dynamics* operate in the same vein. In these procedures, mathematical models are employed to make long-range predictions and to simulate future conditions.

There are many other types of forecasting methods too numerous to mention here. More detailed discussions of forecasting methods can be found in some of the references in the Bibliography.

PROBLEMS

4-1 Managers of the Variety Galore Store wish to forecast its sales for the next calendar year. The following components have been determined by the store accountant:

Quarter t	Trend T_t	Cyclical Component C_t	Seasonal Index S_t
Winter	$100,000	90	80
Spring	110,000	110	70
Summer	121,000	100	100
Fall	133,100	90	150

Use the multiplicative time-series model to determine the forecasts of sales Y_t for each quarter.

4-2 The sales data for Humpty Dumpty Toys, Inc., have been analyzed, and the trend, cyclical, seasonal, and irregular components have been determined for operations during the preceding four quarters. Supply the missing values in the following table, assuming that the time-series components are multiplicative.

Quarter t	Trend T_t	Cyclical Component (percentage) C_t	Seasonal Index (percentage) S_t	Irregular Component (percentage) I_t	Sales Y_t
Winter	$1,000,000	107	50	101	—
Spring	1,100,000	105	70	—	$ 820,000
Summer	1,200,000	105	—	98	987,840
Fall	1,300,000	—	200	97	2,622,880

4-3 The following amounts of annual electricity usage (in millions of kilowatt-hours) have been recorded for a region served by a certain utility company:

Year	Consumption	Year	Consumption
1970	205	1975	241
1971	206	1976	267
1972	223	1977	268
1973	234	1978	277
1974	231	1979	290

(a) Plot these time-series data on graph paper.
(b) Using the method of least squares, determine the equation for the estimated regression line $\hat{Y} = a + bX$, with X in years and $X = 0$ in 1970. Draw this line on your graph.
(c) What is the forecast consumption for 1980?

4-4 The following percentages of moving average values have been obtained for a dairy's ice cream sales:

		Quarter		
Year	Winter	Spring	Summer	Fall
1974	—	—	156	111
1975	49	92	137	109
1976	53	93	148	108
1977	52	91	162	104
1978	51	89	153	110
1979	51	90	151	112
1980	48	88		

Determine the seasonal index for each quarter.

4-5 The following quarterly sales data (in millions of dollars) were recorded for a certain men's clothing chain:

	1976	1977	1978	1979	1980
Winter	3.9	7.8	12.9	13.9	13.5
Spring	6.1	10.6	15.2	14.4	18.2
Summer	4.3	6.9	10.3	10.2	14.2
Fall	10.8	13.5	18.7	17.3	20.7

(a) Determine the four-quarter moving averages.
(b) Calculate the percentages of moving average values and use them to determine the seasonal indexes.

4-6 In arranging for short-term credit with its bank, the Make-Wave Corporation must project its cash needs on a monthly basis. To help management do this, seasonal indexes are to be developed from the following historical data pertaining to cash requirements (in hundreds of thousands of dollars):

	1976	1977	1978	1979	1980
Jan.	2.7	2.9	3.5	2.5	4.2
Feb.	5.4	6.4	7.3	8.1	9.6
Mar.	9.3	10.1	11.3	7.9	12.4
Apr.	2.4	4.1	3.8	5.2	6.2
May	6.1	7.8	8.1	9.2	8.7
Jun.	7.3	7.4	6.9	8.1	8.3
Jul.	6.5	5.5	6.5	7.6	6.6
Aug.	9.7	9.6	8.9	9.3	9.8
Sep.	13.4	13.5	14.3	15.8	16.3
Oct.	10.6	10.7	11.5	12.6	13.4
Nov.	5.1	4.8	6.5	7.2	6.9
Dec.	3.4	2.8	3.9	4.1	6.1

(a) Using 12-month moving averages, determine the seasonal index for each month by means of the ratio-to-moving-average method.
(b) Make-Wave's cash needs for the coming year are forecast to be $1,000,000 per month on the average. Using the seasonal indexes you calculated in (a), estimate the cash requirements for each month.

4-7 Use single-parameter exponential smoothing with $\alpha = .40$ to forecast sales levels for the actual data given in Table 4-5 (page 91).

4-8 Repeat Problem 4-7 with $\alpha = .50$.

4-9 Use two-parameter exponential smoothing with $\alpha = .30$ and $\gamma = .20$ to forecast sales levels for the actual data given in Table 4-6 (page 93).

4-10 A statistician for the Civil Aeronautics Board wishes to construct an equation relating destination distance to freight charge for a standard-sized crate. A random sample of 10 freight invoices provides the following data:

Distance (in hundreds of miles)	Charge (to nearest dollar)
14	68
23	105
9	40
17	79
10	81
22	95
5	31
12	72
6	45
16	93

(a) Plot a scatter diagram for these data.

(b) Using the method of least squares, construct the equation for the estimated regression line. Then plot the regression line on your scatter diagram.

4-11 A stereo-cartridge manufacturer wishes to conduct a regression analysis to estimate the average cartridge lifetime (in hours) at various record tracking forces X (in grams). The following regression equation has been obtained for a sample of $n = 100$ cartridges that were played at various tracking forces until they were worn out: $\hat{Y} = 1,300 - 200X$. Find the forecast lifetimes when (a) $X = 1$ gram; (b) $X = 2$ grams; and (c) $X = 3$ grams.

4-12 Suppose that a college admissions director relies on high-school GPA X_1 and IQ score X_2 to predict college GPA Y. Using the regression equation

$$\hat{Y} = .5 + .8X_1 + .003X_2$$

forecast the college GPA for each of the following students:

	(a)	(b)	(c)	(d)
High-School GPA	2.9	3.0	2.7	3.5
IQ Score	123	118	105	136

4-13 A record manufacturer uses special machines to press recording grooves onto blank disks from a die. Each die lasts for about 1,000 pressings. Due to the time constraints inherent in the record business, it is sometimes necessary to use several pressing machines simultaneously. Because each machine requires an expensive die disk and many production runs are completed before the useful lifetime of each die disk is exhausted, this increases production costs. For $n = 100$ production runs, the total manufacturing cost Y (in thousands of dollars) has been determined for the number of pressings made X_1 (in thousands) and the number of die disk required X_2. The following regression equation applies:

$$\hat{Y} = 1.082 + 1.2X_1 + .553X_2$$

Forecast the cost $\hat{Y}$ of each of the following production runs:

Run	Number of Pressings (thousands)	Number of Die Disks
(a)	15	5
(b)	20	3
(c)	15	4
(d)	100	10

4-14 Restaurant sales predictions are to be made from a regression equation based on total floorspace and number of employees. The following data have been obtained. for a sample of $n = 5$ restaurants:

Sales (thousands of dollars) Y	Floorspace (thousands of square feet) X_1	Number of Employees X_2
20	10	15
15	5	8
10	10	12
5	3	7
10	2	10

Construct and calculate the multiple regression equation for these data.

5

Basic Concepts of Decision Making

The central focus of this book is using quantitative methods in decision making. In Chapter 5, we will consider the structural properties of decisions in general. We will make a basic distinction between decision making under *certain conditions*, where no elements are left to chance, and decision making under *uncertainty*, where one or more random factors affect the outcome of a decision. By considering the common features shared by all decisions, we will set the stage for discussions related to decision-making situations with particular applications that require the use of more detailed quantitative methods.

CERTAINTY AND UNCERTAINTY IN DECISION MAKING 5-1

The least complex applications of decision theory are encountered when we make decisions under certain conditions. Perhaps the simplest example of *decision making under certainty* is selecting what clothes to wear. Although the possibilities are numerous, we all manage to make this choice quickly and with little effort. But not all decisions are this easy to make. Remember how hard it was to choose from among an assortment of candy bars when you were a child? And not all decisions made under certainty are as trivial as choosing the day's apparel.

When the outcomes are only partly determined by choice, the decision-making process takes on an added complexity. So that we can see what is involved in structuring a decision under uncertainty, we will consider the choice of whether to carry an umbrella or some other rain protection. Here, we are faced with two alternatives: carrying an ungainly item that can, in the event of rain, help to defer a cleaning bill or a cough, or challenging the elements with hands free and hoping not to be caught in the rain. Because the weather prediction may be inaccurate we are uncertain about whether it will rain. Yet faced with the needs of daily life, we must make a decision despite our uncertainty. This illustrates a common decision made under uncertainty: An action must be taken, even though its outcome is unknown and determined by chance.[*]

In this chapter, we will present a framework within which we can explain how and why particular choices are made. The decision we must make in coping with the weather illustrates the essential features of making any decision under uncertainty. We choose to carry an umbrella when the chance of rain seems uncomfortably high, and we choose not to carry it when rain seems unlikely. But two people will make two different choices occasionally. Is there always one correct decision? If so, then how can two persons make different choices? We can begin to answer these questions by identifying several key elements common to all decisions and then structuring them in a convenient form for analysis.

5-2   ELEMENTS OF DECISIONS

Every decision made under certainty exhibits two elements—*acts* and *outcomes*. The decision maker's choices are the acts. For example, when choosing among three television programs in the 9 P.M. time slot, each program represents a potential act. The outcomes can be characterized in terms of the enjoyment we may derive from each of the programs.

If the decision is made under uncertainty, a third element—*events*—exists. Continuing with our uncertainty about the rain, the acts are "carry an umbrella" and "leave the umbrella home." All decisions involve the selection of an act. But the outcomes resulting from each act are uncertain, because *an outcome*

---

[*] This class of decisions is often divided into two categories–decision making under *risk*, where outcome probabilities are known, and under *uncertainty* where outcome probabilities are unknown. We will make no distinction here, but will assume that probabilities may always be found somehow–either objectively, through long-run frequency, or subjectively.

TABLE 5-1
Decision Table for the Umbrella Decision

	Act	
Event	Carry Umbrella	Leave Umbrella Home
Rain	Stay dry	Get wet
No Rain	Carry unnecessary burden	Be dry and free

is determined partly by choice and partly by chance. For the act "carry an umbrella" there are two possible outcomes: (1) unnecessarily carting rain paraphernalia and (2) weathering a shower fully protected. For the other act, "leave the umbrella at home," the two outcomes are (1) getting wet unnecessarily and (2) remaining dry and unencumbered. Again, whether the first or second outcome occurs depends solely on the occurrence of rain. The outcome for any particular chosen act depends on which *event*, rain or no rain, occurs.

The Decision Table

To facilitate our analysis, we can summarize a decision problem by constructing a *decision table*, which indicates the relationship between pairs of decision elements. The decision table for the umbrella decision is provided in Table 5-1. Each row of the decision table corresponds to an event, and each column corresponds to an act. The outcomes appear as entries in the body of the table. There is a specific outcome for each event–act combination, reflecting the fact that the interplay between act and event determines the ultimate result.

Only the acts that the decision maker wishes to consider are included in this decision table. "Staying home" is another possible act, which we will exclude because it is not contemplated. The acts in Table 5-1 are mutually exclusive and collectively exhaustive, so that exactly one act will be chosen. The events in the table are also mutually exclusive and collectively exhaustive.

The Decision Tree Diagram

A decision problem can also be conveniently illustrated with a *decision tree diagram* like the one shown in Figure 5-1. It is especially convenient to portray decision problems in the form of decision trees when choices must be made at different times over an extended period of time. The decision tree diagram is similar to the probability tree diagrams we used in Chapters 2 and 3. The choice of acts is shown as a fork with a separate branch for each act. The

ACT   EVENT   OUTCOME

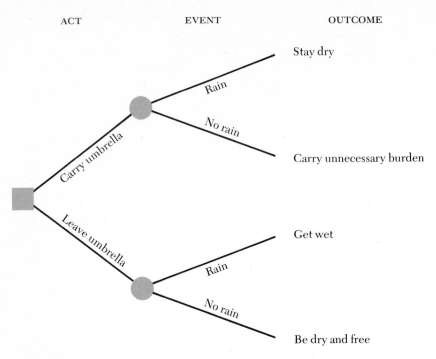

FIGURE 5-1
Decision tree diagram for the umbrella decision.

events are also represented by branches in separate forks. We distinguish between these two types of branching points, using squares for act-fork nodes and circles for event-fork nodes. A basic guideline for constructing a tree diagram is that the flow should be chronological from left to right. The acts are shown on the initial fork, because the decision must be made *before* the actual event is known. The events are therefore shown as branches in the second-stage forks. The outcome resulting from each event–act combination is shown as the end position of the corresponding path from the base of the tree.

5-3 RANKING THE ALTERNATIVES AND THE PAYOFF TABLE

In this chapter, we will consider how the choice of an act should be determined. We all cope with rain and manage to make umbrella decisions. But if we analyze the decision-making process we will be able to make better decisions.

TABLE 5-2
Payoff Table for a Gambling Decision

	Act	
Event	Gamble	Don't Gamble
Head	$1	$0
Tail	−$1	$0

Our analysis will focus on two measures: one for *uncertainty* and one for the comparative worth or *payoff* of the outcomes to the decision maker.

For now, we will consider examples with outcomes that have obvious payoffs, such as dollars. Every outcome—that is, every event–act combination—will have a payoff value. Since the payoffs that the decision maker actually receives after choosing a particular act are conditional on whichever event occurs, these payoffs are sometimes referred to as *conditional values*. These values can be conveniently arranged in a *payoff table*, or a *conditional value table*, as shown in Table 5-2 for a gambling decision. The decision is to choose one of two acts: "gamble" or "don't gamble." Regardless of the choice made, a coin will be tossed, which will result in one of two possible events: "head" or "tail." The possible outcomes correspond to the four event–act combinations. A wager of $1 will be made if the decision maker chooses to gamble and net winnings will be the payoff measure.

Objectives and Payoff Values

In determining appropriate payoffs, we will assume that the decision makers will choose to take action that will bring them closest to their objectives. Each outcome must somehow be ranked in terms of how close it is to the decision maker's goal. The payoff table should provide a meaningful basis for comparison and enhance the decision maker's ability to make a good choice.

For example, if a business decision maker's goal is to achieve a high level of profits, then a natural payoff would be the profit for each outcome. Profit is a valid measure for a limited set of objectives, but it is by no means the top concern of all business managers. The goal of the founder of a successful corporation may be to maintain personal control and the founder may consciously keep profits low so that the firm will not be attractive to other merger-minded entrepreneurs.

In general, decision making might involve different kinds of goals, each requiring a distinct payoff measure. Decision makers with different goals may

TABLE 5-3
**Payoffs for the Alternative Routes Relevant to the Goals
of Three Decision Makers**

	Payoff Measure		
	Mr. Snyder	Mr. Brown	Ms. Gold
Alternative Route	Time Savings (hours)	Fuel Savings (gallons)	Enjoyment (subjective rating)
Interstate 5	4	3	1
Highways 118 & 33	3	7	3
Highway 1	0	0	10

even select for payoffs dissimilar measures when considering the same set of alternatives. The following example illustrates how the best choice may be a different course of action for two decision makers.

Charles Snyder, Herman Brown, and Sylvia Gold wish to choose one of three routes from Los Angeles to San Francisco: (1) Interstate No. 5, which is a freeway nearly all the way and has a high minimum speed limit, (2) State Highways 118 and 33, which are fairly direct and have no minimum speed limit, and (3) State Highway 1, which winds along the Pacific coast and is slow and long but very beautiful. Mr. Snyder is a salesman who travels to San Francisco regularly; his goal is to reach his destination as quickly as possible. Mr. Brown is an economy "nut"; he wants to reach San Francisco as cheaply as possible. Ms. Gold is on vacation and loves to drive on hilly, winding, scenic roads; she wishes to select the route that provides the greatest driving pleasure.

The payoffs that each person would assign to the three routes appear in Table 5-3. Time savings, rather than the slowest route, is Mr. Snyder's payoff measure, so he chooses Interstate 5, which yields the greatest payoff of 4 hours. Mr. Brown likes to drive at a moderate speed to obtain maximum gasoline mileage, while taking the shortest route possible. His payoff measure is gasoline savings (based on the amount of gasoline required on the most expensive route), so he chooses the back roads, State Highways 118 and 33, to save 7 gallons of gas. Ms. Gold has rated the routes in terms of points of interest, types of scenery, and number of hills and curves. This rating serves as her payoff measure, so her best route is scenic State Highway 1, which rates 10.

We can conclude that *a payoff measure should be selected so that the payoff will rank outcomes by the degree to which they attain the decision maker's goals.* The goal dictates which payoff measures are valid.

Tippi-Toes: A Case Illustration

As a detailed example of a business decision made under uncertainty, we will consider a hypothetical toy manufacturer who must choose among four prototype designs for Tippi-Toes, a dancing ballerina doll that does pirouettes and bourrées. Each prototype represents a different technology for the moving parts, all powered by small, battery-operated motors. One prototype is a complete arrangement of gears and levers. The second is similar, with springs instead of levers. Another works on the principle of weights and pulleys. The movement of the fourth design is controlled pneumatically through a system of valves that open and close at the command of a small, solid-state computer housed in the head cavity. The dolls are identical in all functional aspects.

The choice of the movement design will be based solely on a comparison of the contributions to profits made by the four prototypes. The payoff table is provided in Table 5-4. The demand for Tippi-Toes is uncertain, but management feels that one of the following events will occur:

> Light demand (25,000 units)
> Moderate demand (100,000 units)
> Heavy demand (150,000 units)

The toy manufacturer in this example is considering only three possible levels of demand, which greatly simplifies our analysis. Demand does not have to be precisely 25,000 or 100,000 units, however. The problem could be analyzed at several hundred thousand possible levels of demand—say, from 0 to 500,000 dolls. The techniques we will develop here can be applied to a more detailed situation. Due to the computational requirements, the demand probability distribution could be approximated to the nearest 100, 1,000, or 10,000 units.

Our example has only four alternatives. In the practical, business decision-making environment, the number of possible alternatives can be quite large.

TABLE 5-4
Payoff Table for the Tippi-Toes Decision

Demand Event	Act (Choice of Movement)			
	Gears and Levers	Spring Action	Weights and Pulleys	Pneumatic
Light	$ 25,000	–$ 10,000	–$125,000	–$300,000
Moderate	400,000	440,000	400,000	300,000
Heavy	650,000	740,000	750,000	700,000

For instance, deciding what mix of toys to sell could easily involve trillions of alternatives. *The decision analysis should include only the alternatives that the decision maker wishes to consider.* When there is no compelling reason for choosing one of the alternatives, "doing nothing" should be an alternative. The search for attractive alternatives is essential to sound decision making. However, decision analysis cannot tell us what factors should and should not be considered, although it can be used to guide our selection.

5-4 REDUCING THE NUMBER OF ALTERNATIVES: INADMISSIBLE ACTS

Regardless of the decision-making process we ultimately employ to help us make a choice, an initial screening may be made to determine if there are any acts that will never be chosen. To illustrate this, consider the payoffs in Table 5-4. An interesting feature is exhibited by the payoffs of the "weights-and-pulleys" and the "pneumatic" acts: No matter which demand event occurs, the "weights-and-pulleys" act results in a greater payoff. If a light demand occurs, for instance, the payoff for weights and pulleys is $-\$125,000$, which is more favorable than the $-\$300,000$ payoff from the pneumatic movement. A similar finding results if we compare these two acts for the other possible demand events. Thus, the "weights-and-pulleys" movement will always be a superior choice to the pneumatic movement, so that we say that the first act *dominates* the second act. One act dominates another when it achieves a better or an equal payoff, no matter which events occur, and when it is strictly better for one or more events.

In general, whenever an act is dominated by another one, it is *inadmissible*. Thus, the pneumatic movement is an *inadmissible act*. The toy-manufacturer's decision can be simplified by eliminating pneumatic movement from further consideration. Removing the pneumatic act leaves us with the modified payoff table in Table 5-5.

TABLE 5-5
Modified Payoff Table for the Tippi-Toes Decision

Demand Event	Act (Choice of Movement)		
	Gears and Levers	Spring Action	Weights and Pulleys
Light	$ 25,000	-$ 10,000	-$125,000
Moderate	400,000	440,000	400,000
Heavy	650,000	740,000	750,000

A simple way to determine if an act is inadmissible is to see if every entry in its column in the payoff table is less than or equal to the corresponding entry in some other column. It is easy to verify that this is not true for the entries in Table 5-5, so the remaining movement acts must be retained. The acts that remain are called *admissible acts*.

MAXIMIZING EXPECTED PAYOFF: BAYES DECISION RULE   5-5

How does a decision maker choose an act? When there is no uncertainty, the answer is straightforward: Select the act that yields the highest payoff (although finding this particular optimal act can be very difficult when there are many alternatives). But when the events are uncertain, the act that yields the greatest payoff for one event may yield a lower payoff than a competing act for some other event.

Suppose that our toy manufacturer accepts the following probabilities for the demand for Tippi-Toes:

Light demand   .10
Moderate demand .70
Heavy demand   .20
                 ‾‾‾‾‾
                 1.00

We calculate the expected payoff for each act in Table 5-6 and find that the spring-action movement results in the maximum expected payoff of $455,000. Thus, using maximum expected payoff as a decision-making criterion, our toy manufacturer would select the spring-action movement for the Tippi-Toes doll.

TABLE 5-6
Calculation of Expected Payoffs for the Tippi-Toes Decision

Demand Event	Prob-ability	Gears and Levers		Spring Action		Weights and Pulleys	
		Payoff	Payoff × Probability	Payoff	Payoff × Probability	Payoff	Payoff × Probability
Light	.10	$ 25,000	$ 2,500	−$ 10,000	−$ 1,000	−$125,000	−$ 12,500
Moderate	.70	400,000	280,000	440,000	308,000	400,000	280,000
Heavy	.20	650,000	130,000	740,000	148,000	750,000	150,000
Expected payoff:			$412,500		$455,000		$417,500

The criterion of selecting the act with the maximum expected payoff is sometimes referred to as *Bayes decision rule*. This rule takes into account all the information about the chances of the various payoffs. But we will see that it is not a perfect device and can lead to a choice that is not actually the most desirable. However, we will also see that this criterion is a suitable basis for decision making under uncertainty when the payoff values are selected with great care.

5-6 DECISION TREE ANALYSIS

The decisions under uncertainty we have encountered thus far can be portrayed in terms of a payoff table. But some problems are too complex to be presented in a table. Difficulties arise when the same events do not apply for all acts. For example, a contractor might have to choose between bidding on a construction job for a dam or on one for an airport, not having sufficient resources to bid on both. Regardless of the job chosen, there is some probability (which may differ for the two projects) the contractor will win the job bid on. Separate sets of events and probabilities are required for each act.

Decisions must often be made at two or more points in time, with uncertain events occurring between decisions. Sometimes these problems can be analyzed in terms of a payoff table, but usually the earlier choice of the act will have a bearing on the type, quantity, and probabilities of later events. At best, this makes it cumbersome to attempt to force the decision into the limited confines of the rectangular arrangement of a payoff table.

The decision tree diagram we described earlier allows us to meaningfully arrange the elements of a complex decision problem without the restrictions of a tabular format. A further advantage of the decision tree is that it serves as an excellent management communication tool, because the tree clearly delineates every potential course of action and all possible outcomes.

Ponderosa Record Company: A Case Illustration

The president of Ponderosa Record Company, a small independent recording studio, has just signed a contract with a four-person rock group, called the Fluid Mechanics. A tape has been cut, and Ponderosa must decide whether or not to market the recording. If the record is to be test marketed, then a 5,000-record run will be made and promoted regionally; this may result in a later decision to distribute an additional 45,000 records nationally, for which a second pressing run will have to be made. If immediate national marketing is chosen, a pressing run of 50,000 records will be made. Regardless of the test-market results, the president may decide to enter the national market or decide not to.

A Ponderosa record is either a complete success or a failure in its market. A recording is successful if all records that are pressed are sold; the sales of a failure are practically nil. Success in a regional market does not guarantee success nationally, but it is a fairly reliable predictor.

The Decision Tree Diagram

The structure of the Ponderosa decision problem is presented in the decision tree diagram in Figure 5-2. Decisions are to be made at two different points in time, or stages. The immediate choice is to select one of two acts: "test market" or "don't test market." These acts are shown as branches on the initial fork at node a. If test marketing is chosen, then the result to be achieved in the test marketplace is uncertain. This is reflected by an event fork at node b, where the branches represent favorable and unfavorable outcomes. Regardless of which event occurs, a choice must be made between two new acts: "market nationally" or "abort." These acts occur at a later stage and are represented by a pair of act forks. Each fork corresponds to the two different conditions under which this decision may be made: At node c, when the test marketing is favorable, and at node d, when it is unfavorable. If national marketing is chosen at either node c or node d, the success or failure of the recording still remains unknown, and the possible events are reflected on the decision tree as branches on the terminal event forks at nodes f and g.

If the initial choice at decision point a is "don't test market," then a further choice must be made at the act fork represented by decision point e: "market nationally" or "abort." As before, node h reflects the two uncertain events that will arise from the choice to market nationally. The "abort" path leading from node e contains a "dummy" branch—a diagrammatical convenience that allows event and act forks of similar form to appear at the same stage of the problem and permits all paths to terminate at a common stage. Thus, all "abort" acts are followed by a dummy branch.

Every path from the base of the decision tree leads to a terminal position corresponding to a decision outcome. Each possible combination of acts and events, or each path, has a distinct outcome. For instance, O_1 represents the following sequence of events and acts: "test market," "favorable," "market nationally," "success."

The first step in analyzing the decision problem is to obtain a payoff for each outcome.

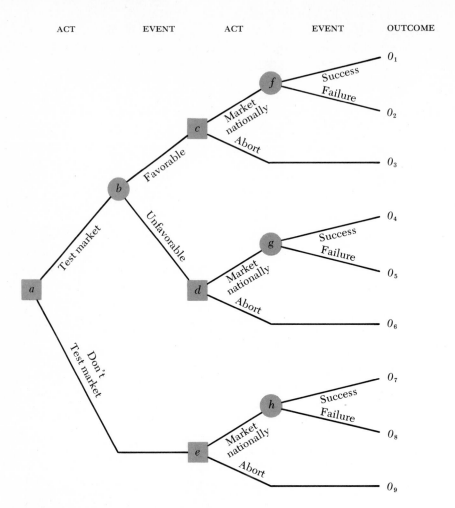

FIGURE 5-2
Decision tree diagram for the Ponderosa decision.

Determining the Payoffs

The contract with the Fluid Mechanics calls for a $5,000 payment to the group if records are produced. Ponderosa arranges with a record manufacturer to make its pressings. For each pressing run, there is a $5,000 fixed cost plus a $.75 fee for each record. Record jackets, handling, and distribution cost an additional $.25 per record. The total variable cost per record is therefore $1.00. Using these figures, we can calculate the immediate cash effect of each act in the decision tree in Figure 5-2. Some of these cash effects, or *partial cash flows*, are computed in Table 5-7.

TABLE 5-7
Some Partial Cash Flows Used in Determining the Payoff Values of Ponderosa's Outcomes

Act		Partial Cash Flow	
Test Market		−$ 5,000	(payment to group)
		− 5,000	(fixed cost of pressing)
		− 5,000	(variable costs of 5,000 records at $1.00)
	Total	−$15,000	
Don't Test Market		$0	
Market Nationally		−$ 5,000	(payment to group)
(without test)		− 5,000	(fixed cost of pressing)
		− 50,000	(variable costs of 50,000 records at $1.00)
	Total	−$60,000	
Abort		$0	

The negative cash flows indicate expenditures. The partial cash flows in Table 5-7 appear on the respective branches extending from decision points a and e of the decision tree in Figure 5-3. In a similar manner, we determine the partial cash flows for the acts at the forks at decision points c and d: −$50,000 to market nationally ($5,000 fixed pressing cost plus $1.00 each in variable costs for 45,000 records) and $0 to abort.

Ponderosa receives $2 for each record it sells through retail outlets. Since the events—"favorable" and "unfavorable," or "success" and "failure"—represent sales of all and no records, respectively, the partial cash flows may be obtained by multiplying the number of records sold by $2. The partial cash flows for the events at the fork at node b are therefore +$10,000 (for 5,000 records sold) and $0 (for no sales). The amounts for the events at nodes f and g are +$90,000 (for 45,000 records sold) and $0, whereas the amounts for the events at node h are +$100,000 and $0.

The payoff for each outcome may be obtained by adding the partial cash flows on the branches of the path leading to its terminal position. Thus, for O_1, we add the partial cash flows −$15,000, +$10,000, −$50,000, and +$90,000. The payoff for O_1 is therefore +$35,000. The payoffs calculated for each outcome are shown at the respective terminal positions of the decision tree in Figure 5-3.

Assigning Event Probabilities

Ponderosa's management wishes to choose the act that will yield the maximum expected payoff. But before this choice can be made, probability values must be assigned to the events in the decision structure. Suppose that

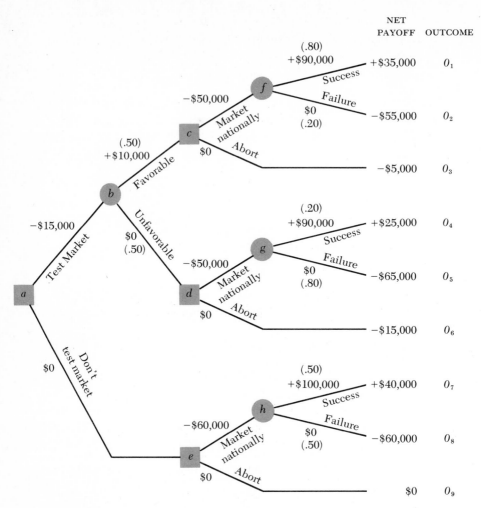

FIGURE 5-3

The Ponderosa decision tree diagram, showing partial cash flows and probabilities on branches with NET-CASH-FLOW payoffs at the terminal positions.

Ponderosa's president believes that the chance of favorably test marketing the recording is .50. The probability of unfavorably test marketing the recording is also .50. These probability values are placed in parentheses along the branches at node b in Figure 5-3. In assigning probability values to the success and failure events for national marketing, our decision maker is faced with three distinctly different situations. With no test marketing, the chance of national success is judged to be .50. Past favorable test marketing indicates that a record appeals to the regional segment of the market, so the chance of national success in this case is judged to be a much higher .80; this is a *conditional probability.* Similarly, unfavorable test marketing is a likely indication of national appeal, so the conditional probability of success is judged to be .20 in this case. The following probability values are placed on the branches for the event at the remaining forks in the decision tree diagram: .80 for success and .20 for failure at node f; .20 for success and .80 for failure at node g; and .50 for success and .50 for failure at node h. (It is just coincidental that the probability of national marketing success after unfavorable test marketing is .20, which is also the probability of national marketing failure after favorable test marketing. Our decision maker could have selected another value, such as .10.)

Backward Induction

We are now ready to analyze Ponderosa's decision. Our decision maker wishes to select an initial or immediate act at decision point a. The first act we will evaluate is "test market." What is the expected payoff for this act? Referring to Figure 5-3, we see that six outcomes, O_1 through O_6, may result from this choice. How can we translate the corresponding payoffs into an expected value? We cannot do this until we specify the intervening acts that will be chosen at nodes c and d. In general, *it is impossible to evaluate an immediate act without first considering all later decisions that result from this choice.*

Thus, to find the expected payoff for the "test market" act, our decision maker must first decide whether to market nationally or to abort if (1) test marketing proves favorable or (2) test marketing proves unfavorable. This illustrates an essential feature of analyzing multistage decisions: *Evaluations must be made in reverse of their natural chronological sequence.* Before deciding whether to test market, our decision maker must decide what to do if the test marketing is favorable or if it is unfavorable. The procedure for making such evaluations is called *backward induction.*

We can clarify this point by describing the procedure for our decision-making problem. For simplicity, the Ponderosa president's decision tree diagram is redrawn in Figure 5-4 without the partial cash flows.

Consider the act fork at decision point c. If the decision is to market nationally, then Ponderosa' president is faced with the event fork at node f. With a probability of .80, that marketing nationally will be a success, a net payoff of $+\$35,000$ will be achieved. The probability that marketing nationally will be a failure is .20, which leads to a net payoff of $-\$55,000$. The expected payoff for this event fork can therefore be calculated as

$$.80(+\$35,000) + .20(-\$55,000) = +\$17,000$$

The amount $+\$17,000$ is entered on the decision tree at node f, since this is the expected payoff for the act to market nationally. For convenience, we place the expected payoff for a sequence of acts or events above the applicable node.

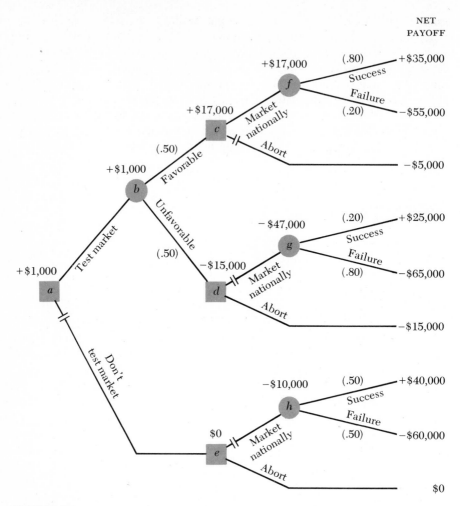

NET
PAYOFF

FIGURE 5-4
The Ponderosa decision tree diagram, showing backward induction analysis.

The act to abort at decision point *c* will lead to a certain payoff of − $5,000. Since the expected payoff for the act to market nationally (+$17,000) is larger than −$5,000, the choice to market nationally should be made over aborting. We may reflect on this future choice by *pruning* the branch from the tree that corresponds to the act "abort" at decision point *c*. This act merits no further consideration, since if decision point *c* is reached, the president will choose to market nationally. That is, if the decision maker initially decides to test market and the results turn out to be favorable, the president will choose to market nationally. Thus, +$17,000 is the expected payoff resulting from making the best choice at decision point c. We bring back the amount $+\$17,000$ and enter it on the diagram above the node at c.

As a rule of thumb in performing backward induction, ultimately all but one act will be eliminated at each decision point (except in the case of ties), so that all branches except those leading to the greatest expected payoff will be pruned. Only the *best single payoff* from the later stage is brought backward to the preceding decision point (square). *Branch pruning takes place only in act forks—never in event forks.* Instead, event forks (circles) involve an expected value calculation, so that an average payoff is always computed from the later stage values.

The available choices when test marketing results are unfavorable may be handled in the same way. First, we calculate the expected payoff at node g that arises from the act market nationally," or

$$.20(+\$25,000) + .80(-\$65,000) = -\$47,000$$

We place this figure on the decision tree diagram above node g. Since the act "abort" leads to a payoff of $-\$15,000$, which is larger than $-\$47,000$ the branch for the act to market nationally is pruned from the tree. The best choice when test marketing fails is to abort. We therefore bring back and enter the amount $-\$15,000$ on the diagram above the node at decision point d.

In a similar fashion, the expected payoff of the event fork at node h, when the initial choice is to market nationally, is determined as follows:

$$.50(+\$40,000) + .50(-\$60,000) = -\$10,000$$

At decision point e, the act "abort" is superior to the act "market nationally," and the latter branch is pruned from the tree. Our decision maker must now compare the acts at decision point a. The expected payoff from the act "test market" is still to be determined. This is the expected payoff for the event fork at node b, which has two event branches. The branch corresponding to success leads to a portion of the tree with an expected payoff of $+\$17,000$. The other branch leads to a later choice with an expected payoff of $-\$15,000$. We use these two amounts to calculate the expected payoff at node b:

$$.50(+\$17,000) + .50(-\$15,000) = +\$1,000$$

We enter the amount $+\$1,000$ on the diagram above node b.

Ponderosa's president is now in a position to compare the two acts at decision point a: "test market" and "don't test market." Since the expected payoff for test marketing ($+\$1,000$) is higher than the expected payoff for not testing ($\$0$), our decision maker should choose to test market. The expected payoff of $1,000 is brought back and placed above node *a*. The branch corresponding to "don't test market" is pruned, and our backward induction is complete.

A decision is indicated. Ponderosa's president should choose to test market the Fluid Mechanics' record. If the test marketing is favorable, then the president should market nationally; if the test marketing is unfavorable, then the president should abort the recording. This result is illustrated in Figure 5-4 by the unpruned branches that remain on the decision tree.

Additional Remarks

Choices that are made in later stages are not irrevocable, and this analysis does not preclude the fact that the decision maker's mind may change over time. New information may be received before the future decision must be made at node *c*, for instance, indicating a need to revise the probability of national success downward. If there is bad publicity about one of the Fluid Mechanics, for example, the expected payoff for national marketing might be smaller than the expected payoff for aborting. Possible changes in conditions do not invalidate the original backward induction analysis. In our example, *the choice to test market is the best decision that can be made based on the currently available information.*

The decision tree structure is suitable for analyzing decisions that extend over a long time period. It indicates the best course of action for the *current* decision. As time progresses, however, some uncertainties may be reduced and new ones may arise. Acts previously identified as optimal may turn out to be obviously poor choices, and brand new candidates may be determined. The relevant portion of the decision tree can be updated and revised prior to each new immediate decision. But each such decision is analyzed in the same general manner, using the best information available at the time a choice must be made.

Although a decision tree is analyzed by moving backward in time, the analysis is really forward-looking because it indicates the optimal course of action to take when future decision points are reached. The dollar amount brought backward to each node represents the best payoff the decision maker can expect to achieve if that position is reached at a later time. Regardless of what events have occurred, the optimal course of action for future choices is still indicated by the original analysis.

PROBLEMS

5-1   A young bachelor is deciding whether to spend his Christmas vacation at a ski resort or surfing in Hawaii. He must commit himself to one of these alternatives in the early fall, since reservations have to be made months in advance. He really enjoys skiing more than surfing. Unfortunately, he cannot be certain about December snow conditions, and his ski trip will be ruined if there is poor snow. The trip to Hawaii would be a sure bet. But if he must go there when the snow is good elsewhere, his trip will be somewhat spoiled by regrets that he did not make arrangements to spend his vacation skiing.

(a) Construct the bachelor's decision table.

(b) Draw his decision tree diagram.

5-2 Peggy Jones, the founder of a computer-programming services firm, wishes to expand the firm's activities into the manufacture of peripheral equipment. Funds must be raised to build and operate the necessary facilities. Three financing alternatives are available: (1) Issue additional common stock, (2) sell bonds, and (3) issue nonvoting preferred stock. A common stock issue will provide a strong financial base for future expansion through borrowing, but will considerably reduce Jones' percentage of ownership and control from its current 100%. New common stock will also divide future earnings into smaller amounts per share to existing shareholders. Bonds will allow existing shareholders to accrue all of the benefits of new earnings, but will also increase the risk of forced liquidation if the new venture proves unsuccessful. Preferred stockholders have no claims on the firm's assets, but will drastically reduce the rate of earnings participation on the part of existing common stockholders. Table 5-8 summarizes the forecast financial status of the firm if the manufacturing venture is successful.

    For each of the following goals, suggest an appropriate payoff measure. Then use this measure to identify the best and the worst alternative choices for financing in terms of the degree to which each *single* goal is met. Indicate any ties.

(a) Maintain a high percentage of control by Jones.

(b) Maximize the earnings of Jones' shares.

(c) Maximize the availability of short-term credit.

(d) Maximize the potential for cash dividends to Jones.

TABLE 5-8

	Financing Alternatives		
Possible Payoff Measure	Additional Common Stock	Bonds	Preferred Stock
1. Earnings after taxes and preferred dividends	$5,000,000	$3,500,000	$4,000,000
2. Common shares outstanding	1,000,000	500,000	500,000
3. Earnings per common share	$5.00	$7.00	$8.00
4. Jones' percentage of common ownership	50	100	100
5. Emergency line of credit	$1,000,000	$400,000	$500,000
6. Earnings available for common dividends	$5,000,000	$2,000,000	$4,000,000
7. Maximum possible dividends per share of common stock	$5.00	$4.00	$8.00

5-3 Consider the following payoff table:

		Act Payoff		
Event	Probability	A_1	A_2	A_3
E_1	.3	$10,000	$ 20,000	$ 5,000
E_2	.5	5,000	− 10,000	10,000
E_3	.2	15,000	10,000	10,000

Compute the expected payoffs for each act. According to the Bayes decision rule, which act should be chosen?

5-4 Identify any inadmissible acts in the following payoff table:

	Act				
Event	A_1	A_2	A_3	A_4	A_5
E_1	3	4	4	5	1
E_2	6	2	1	4	2
E_3	1	8	8	7	3

5-5 Recompute the expected payoffs for the Tippi-Toes decision in Table 5-5, assuming that the demand event probabilities are now:

Light demand	.20
Moderate demand	.50
Heavy demand	.30

According to the Bayes decision rule, which act should the toy manufacturer choose?

5-6 A new product is to be evaluated. The main decision to be made is whether or not to market the product, in which case it will be a success (probability = .40) or a failure. The net payoff for a successful product is $10 million; a failure would result in a − $5 million payoff. Construct a payoff table for the decision, and then find the expected payoffs. Should the product be marketed?

5-7 Suppose that the president of the Ponderosa Record Company uses the following probability values to analyze the decision about the Fluid Mechanics' recording.

Pr[national marketing success|favorable test marketing] = .9

Pr[national marketing failure|unfavorable test marketing] = .6

Pr[national marketing success] = .7

Pr[favorable test marketing] = .75

Repeat the decision tree analysis we used in this chapter to determine Ponderosa's optimal marketing strategy. Assume that all payoffs remain unchanged.

EXAMINATION
ACT   EVENT   ACT   EVENT   PAYOFF

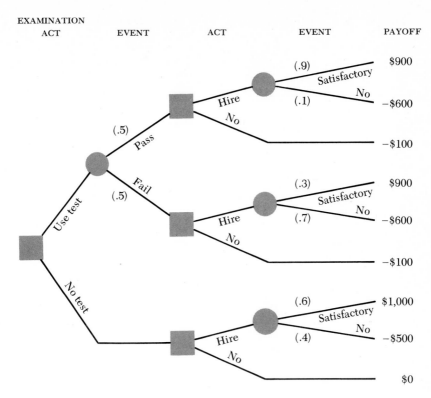

(.9) $900
Satisfactory
No
Hire   (.1)   −$600
No
(.5)
Pass   −$100

Fail   (.3) $900
(.5)   Satisfactory
No
Use test   Hire   (.7)   −$600
No
−$100

No test   (.6) $1,000
Satisfactory
No
Hire   (.4)   −$500
No
$0

FIGURE 5-5

5-8 The manager of an oil company's data-processing operations personally interviews applicants for jobs as keypunchers. Employees who are hired with no previous experience are placed in a one-month training program on a trial basis. Satisfactory employees are retained; all others are let go at the end of the month. Most of the people who have been let go in the past have been found to be lacking in aptitude. The manager is contemplating contracting the testing services of a personnel agency. For a fee the agency would administer a battery of aptitude tests. The manager has developed the decision tree in Figure 5-5 to help her make her hiring decisions. Perform backward induction analysis to determine the strategy or course of action that will maximize the manager's expected payoff.

5-9 Buzzy-B Toys must decide the course of action to follow in promoting a new whistling yo-yo. Initially, management must decide whether to market the yo-yo or to conduct a test marketing program first. After test marketing the yo-yo, management must decide whether to abandon or nationally distribute it.

A national success will increase profits by $500,000, and a failure will reduce profits by $100,000. Abandoning the product will not affect profits. The test marketing will cost Buzzy-B a further $10,000.

If no test marketing is conducted, the probability for a national success is judged to be .45. The assumed probability for a favorable test marketing result is .50.

The conditional probability for national success given favorable test marketing is .80; for national success given unfavorable test results it is .10.

Construct the decision tree diagram and perform backward induction analysis to determine the optimal course of action if a net change in profits is the expected payoff.

5-10 Spillsberry Foods must determine whether or not to market a new cake mix. Management must also decide whether to conduct a consumer test marketing program that would cost $25,000. If the mix is successful, Spillsberry's profits will increase by $1,000,000; if the mix fails, the company will lose $250,000. Not marketing the product will not affect profits. The cake mix is considered to have a 60% chance of success without testing. The assumed probability for a favorable test marketing result is 50%. Given a favorable test result, the chance of product success is judged to be 85%. However, if the test results are unfavorable, the probability for the product's success is judged to be only .35.

Construct a decision tree diagram that can be used to determine the optimal course of action that will provide the greatest expected payoff. Include the choice of whether or not to use the test. Perform backward induction analysis to determine which course of action maximizes the expected payoff.

5-11 A product manager for a soap manufacturer wishes to determine whether or not to market a new toothpaste. In addition, the manager can order a consumer testing program for $50,000. The present value of all future profits for a successful toothpaste is $1,000,000; The brand's failure would result in a net loss of $500,000. Not marketing the toothpaste will not affect profits. The manager judges that the toothpaste would have a 50–50 chance of success without testing. Customer testing will be either favorable (40% chance) or unfavorable. Given a favorable test result, the chance of product success is judged to be 80%. But for an unfavorable test result, the toothpaste's success probability is judged to be only 30%.

Construct the product manager's decision tree diagram. Perform backward induction analysis to determine which course of action provides the greatest expected profit.

5-12 The following two experiments with the product in Problem 5-6 have been proposed. (Both experiments cannot be used.)

Test market at a cost of $1 million. Results will be "favorable" (probability = .48) or "unfavorable." Given a favorable result, the probability for product success is .75. Given an unfavorable result, the probability for product success is only .08.

Attitude survey at a cost of $.5 million. Results will be "warm" (probability = .40) or "cold." Given a warm response, the probability for product success is .70. Given a cold response, the probability for success is only .20.

In addition to these choices, the main decision to market or not to market may be made without obtaining any further information.

Construct a decision tree diagram for this problem, indicating all of the probabilities and payoffs. Perform backward induction analysis to determine which course of action maximizes expected payoff. (Specify all choices that may then have to be made.)

5-13 A government official wishes to determine the most effective way to control crop damage from the gypsy moth. Three methods for attacking the pest are: (1) spray with DDT; (2) use a scent to lure and trap males, so that the remaining males must compete for mating with a much larger number of males that have been sterilized in a laboratory and then released; and (3) spray with a juvenile hormone that prevents the larvae from developing into adult moths.

The net improvement in current and future crop losses using DDT is 0, because it is assumed that DDT will never completely eradicate the moth.

If the scent-lure program is instituted, the probability that it will leave a low number of native males is .5, with a .5 chance that it will leave a high number. Once the scent-lure results are known, a later choice must then be made either to spray with DDT or to release sterile males. The cost of the scent lures is $5 million and the cost of sterilization is an additional $5 million. But if this two-phase program is successful, present and future crop savings will be $30 million. If scent lures leave a small native male population, there is a 90% chance for success using sterile males; otherwise, there is only a 10% chance for success using sterile males. A failure results in 0 crop savings.

The juvenile hormone must be synthesized at a cost of $3 million. There is only a .20 probability that the resulting product will work. If it does, the crop savings would be $50 million, because the gypsy moth would become extinct. If the hormone does not work, crop savings would be 0.

Construct a decision tree diagram for the official's decision. Using crop savings minus cost as the payoff measure (relative to using DDT, which has a payoff of 0), determine the course of action that will yield the maximum expected payoff.

6

Elements of Decision Theory

Modern analysis of decision making under uncertainty has its roots in the area of study called *statistical decision theory*. A primary focus of statistical decision theory is establishing systematic means for choosing an act, which is largely accomplished by using the payoff table introduced in Chapter 5. Various *decision-making criteria* may be employed in selecting the best act. The payoff measure itself is a key element in determining rules for decision making, and decision theory encompasses a variety of these measures.

We will begin our discussion of decision theory by examining some of the well-known criteria used in selecting a best act. Then we will describe *opportunity loss*—a payoff measure that enables us to assess the worth of the *information* that is obtained about uncertain events. Indeed, we use the adjective *statistical* because sampling is a rich source of such information.

For various reasons, we will also see that the Bayes decision rule, which helps the decision maker select the act with the maximum expected payoff, is the favored criterion. The theoretical concepts of decision making largely expand on this rule, since it is the only criterion that makes use of all the information at the disposal of the decision maker. When the proper payoff measure is used, the Bayes decision rule always leads to the most desirable choice. The device that makes this possible is the *utility payoff*, which measures a decision maker's preference. *Utility theory* is a special field within the broader context of decision theory.

This chapter surveys decision theory. In later chapters, we will consider more specialized topics. Chapter 17 examines how experimental information can be systematically incorporated into decision making. Chapters 18 and 19 are more statistical in nature; there, specific probability distribution structures are melded with decision-making concepts. Chapter 20 describes utility theory and outlines the practical details of obtaining and using utility values. Much of Chapter 21 is devoted to the practical problems of obtaining and using subjective probabilities. This topical grouping concludes in Chapter 22 with a discussion of *game theory*, where two or more persons independently determine outcomes, which helps to explain interactive decision making.

6-1   DECISION CRITERIA

The Maximin Payoff Criterion

No decision-making theory is complete until the decision maker has considered the various rules that might be used in selecting the most desirable act. We will begin with the simplest criterion, the *maximin payoff criterion*— a procedure that guarantees that the decision maker can do no worse than achieve the best of the poorest outcomes possible. As an illustration, we will use the payoff table given in Table 6-1, which presents the toy manufacturer's choices of movement for the Tippi-Toes doll.

Suppose that our toy manufacturer wishes to choose an act that will ensure a favorable outcome no matter what happens. This can be accomplished by taking a pessimistic viewpoint—that is determining the *worst* outcome for each act, regardless of the event. For the gears and levers movement, the lowest possible payoff is $25,000 when light demand occurs. The lowest payoff for the spring-action movement is a negative amount, −$10,000, also obtained when demand is light. For the weights and pulleys movement, the lowest

TABLE 6-1
Payoff Table for the Tippi-Toes Decision

Demand Event	Act (Choice of Movement)		
	Gears and Levers	Spring Action	Weights and Pulleys
Light	$ 25,000	−$ 10,000	−$125,000
Moderate	400,000	440,000	400,000
Heavy	650,000	740,000	750,000

TABLE 6-2
Determining the Maximin Payoff Act for the Tippi-Toes Decision

Demand Event	Act (Choice of Movement)		
	Gears and Levers	Spring Action	Weights and Pulleys
Light	$ 25,000	−$ 10,000	−$125,000
Moderate	400,000	440,000	400,000
Heavy	650,000	740,000	750,000
Column minimums	$ 25,000	−$ 10,000	−$125,000

Maximum of column minimums = $25,000
Maximin payoff act = Gears and levers

payoff is −$125,000, again when demand is light. By choosing the act that yields the largest lowest payoff, our decision maker can guarantee a minimum return that is the best of the poorest outcomes possible. In this case, a gear and levers movement for the doll will guarantee the toy manufacturer a payoff of at least $25,000.

The gears and levers movement is the act with the maximum of the minimum payoffs. A more concise statement would be to say that "Gears and levers is the *maximin payoff act.*" To show how the maximin payoff can be determined in general, we reconstruct the payoff table for the Tippi-Toes decision in Table 6-2.

In most decision-making illustrations so far, we have used profit as the measure of payoff. As we noted in Chapter 5, a variety of measures may be used to rank outcomes. In business applications, *cost* is often used for this purpose when the goal is to minimize operational cost and when revenues are not subject to chance. We can apply the maximin payoff criterion to a situation involving costs by reversing our rule and selecting the act with the minimum of the maximum costs. The comparable terminology for this rule would be *minimax cost.* This criterion is identical to the maximin profit in the sense that cost can be viewed as negative profit, so that what is minimized and maximized must be reversed. Either criterion leads to choosing the best of the poorest outcomes. To avoid confusion, we will always use maximin and minimax as adjectives connected to a noun such as profit or cost.

The suitability of the maximin payoff criterion depends on the nature of the decision to be made. Consider the decision problem in Table 6-3. In this situation, the maximin decision maker chooses A_1 over A_2. A_2 may be a better choice if the probability of E_2 is high enough, but the maximin decision maker is giving up an opportunity to gain $10,000 in order to avoid a possible loss of $1. To avoid losing $1, the decision maker chooses an act that will guarantee at least the maintenance of the status quo. We can envision circumstances in which A_1 would be the better choice, however. If our decision maker had only

Table 6-3
Determining the Maximin Payoff Act
for Hypothetical Decision A

Event	Act	
	A_1	A_2
E_1	$0	-$1
E_2	1	10,000

Column minimum $0   -$1
Maximum of column minimums = $0
Maximin payoff act = A_1

$1 and had to use it to pay a debt to a loan shark or lose his life, the payoffs would not realistically represent the true values the decision maker assigned to them.

Consider the situation represented by the payoffs given in Table 6-4. Here, the maximin payoff act is B_1. This would be the better choice for a decision maker who could not tolerate a loss of $10,000, no matter how unlikely it was. Few people would risk losing their businesses by choosing an act that could lead to bankruptcy unless the odds were extremely small. But an individual who could survive a loss of $10,000 would find B_2 a superior choice if the probability of E_2 were substantially lower than E_1.

Our examples illustrate a key deficiency of the maximin payoff: It is an extremely conservative decision criterion and can lead to some very bad decisions. Any alternative with a slightly larger risk is rejected in favor of a comparatively risk-free alternative, which may be far less attractive. Taken to a ludicrous extreme, a maximin payoff policy would force any firm out of business. No inventories would be stocked, because there would always be a possibility of unsold items. No new products would be introduced, because management could never be certain of their success. No credit would be granted, because there would always be some customer who did not pay.

TABLE 6-4
Payoff Table
for Hypothetical Decision B

Event	Act	
	B_1	B_2
E_1	$1	$10,000
E_2	-1	-10,000

Another major deficiency of the maximin payoff criterion exists if the probabilities of the various events are known. The maximin payoff is primarily suited to decision problems with unknown probabilities that cannot be reasonably assessed. As our illustrations indicate, it is usually in the extreme cases— the person hounded by loan sharks or the business that could go bankrupt— that the maximin payoff criterion leads to the best decision.

The Maximum Likelihood Criterion

Another rule that serves as a model for decision-making behavior is the *maximum likelihood criterion*, which focuses on the most likely event, to the exclusion of all others. Table 6-5 illustrates this criterion for the Tippi-Toes toy-manufacturer's decision analyzed previously.

For this decision, we can see that the highest probability is .70 for a moderate demand. The maximum likelihood criterion tells us to ignore the light and heavy demand events completely—in effect, to assume that they will not occur. This rule then tells us to choose the best act assuming that a moderate demand will occur. In this example, the *maximum likelihood act* is to use the spring-action doll movement, which provides the greatest profit of $440,000 for a moderate demand.

How suitable is the maximum likelihood criterion for decision making? Using it in this example does not permit us to consider the range of outcomes for the spring-action movement, from a $10,000 loss if a light demand occurs to a $740,000 profit if demand is heavy. We also ignore most of the other possible outcomes, including the best (selecting weights and pulleys when demand is heavy, which yields a $750,000 profit) and the worst (selecting weights and pulleys when demand is light, which leads to a $125,000 loss). In a sense, the maximum likelihood criterion would have us "play ostrich," ignoring much that might happen. Then why is it discussed here?

TABLE 6-5
Determining the Maximum Likelihood Act for the Tippi-Toes Decision

Demand Event	Probability	Act (Choice of Movement)		
		Gears and Levers	Spring Action	Weights and Pulleys
Light	.10	$ 25,000	−$ 10,000	−$125,000
Moderate	.70	400,000	440,000	400,000
Heavy	.20	650,000	740,000	750,000

Most likely event = Moderate demand
Maximum row payoff = $440,000
Maximum likelihood act = Spring action

We describe this criterion here primarily because it seems to be so prevalent in the decision-making behavior of individuals and businesses. It can also be used to explain certain anomalies that would otherwise be hard to rationalize. These quirks are epitomized by the so-called "hog cycle" in the raising and marketing of pigs, which is related to the more or less predictable two-year-long pork price movement from higher to lower levels and back to higher price levels again. Hog farmers have been blamed for this, since they expand their herds when prices are high, so that one year later the supply of mature hogs is excessive and prices are driven downward; then when prices are low, these same farmers reduce their herds, cutting the supply of marketable hogs, and next year's prices consequently rise.

Why don't the farmers break this cycle? It doesn't seem rational to be consistently wrong in timing hog production. One explanation is that the hog farmers use the maximum likelihood criterion. In their minds, the most likely, future market price is the current one—and we know that this has proved to be a very poor judgment. Given such a premise, the maximum likelihood act is to increase herd sizes when current prices are high and to decrease them when prices are low.

The Criterion of Insufficient Reason

Another criterion employed in decision-making problems is the *criterion of insufficient reason*. This criterion may be used when a decision maker has no information about the "event probabilities." In this case, no event may be regarded as more likely than another event, and all events are assigned equal probability values. Since the events are collectively exhaustive and mutually exclusive, the probability of each event must be

$$\frac{1}{\text{Number of events}}$$

Using these event probabilities, the act with the maximum expected payoff is chosen.

A major criticism of the criterion of insufficient reason is that, except in a few situations, some knowledge of the relative chances that events will occur is always available. When more realistic probabilities can be obtained, employing the Bayes decision rule will provide more valid results.

Bayes Decision Rule Is Preferred

The three decision-making criteria just discussed have obvious inadequacies. *None of them incorporates all of the information available to the decision maker.* Maximin payoff totally ignores event probabilities. Although it is argued

TABLE 6-6
Payoff Table for Hypothetical Decision C

Event	Probability	Act C_1		Act C_2	
		Payoff	Payoff × Probability	Payoff	Payoff × Probability
E_1	.5	− $1,000,000	− $ 500,000	$250,000	$125,000
E_2	.5	2,000,000	1,000,000	750,000	375,000
Expected payoff:			$ 500,000		$500,000

that this is a strength when probabilities cannot be easily determined, judgment can be used to arrive at acceptable probability values in all but a few circumstances.

The maximum likelihood criterion ignores all events but the most likely one, even if that event happens to be a lot less likely than the rest combined. (Among 20 events, for instance, the most likely event may have a probability of .10 leaving a .90 probability that one of the other 19 events will occur.)

The criterion of insufficient reason essentially asks us to ignore judgments and "willy nilly" assume that all events are equally likely. According to this criterion, even such events as "war" and "peace" and "prosperity" and "depression" have equal probabilities.

Bayes decision rule has become the central focus of statistical decision theory. This makes the greatest use of all available information and is the only criterion that allows us to extend decision theory to incorporate sampling or experimental information. The major deficiency of the Bayes decision rule occurs when alternatives involve different magnitudes of risk. To illustrate this point, we will consider the decision structure in Table 6-6. Acts C_1 and C_2 are equally attractive according to the maximum expected payoff criterion. Yet most decision makers would clearly prefer C_2, because it avoids the rather large risk of a $1,000,000 loss.

The paradox here may be resolved not by choosing another criterion, but by reconsidering the values chosen for the payoffs. The theory of utility presented in Chapter 21 will allow us to establish payoffs at values that express their true worth to the decision maker.

BAYES DECISION RULE AND UTILITY 6-2

We have presented a strong case for using expected values as the basis for decision making under uncertainty. As we have seen, a criterion based on expected values uses all the available probability data and assigns the proper weight to every outcome. The other decision-making criteria employ fewer structural elements from the decision. Expected values also provide us with a gauge for evaluating additional sources of information that can be used in decision making.

But when applied to *monetary* payoffs, the Bayes decision rule—maximizing expected profit and minimizing expected cost or loss—often leads to a less preferred choice.

Perhaps the best example of this occurs in casualty insurance decisions, where the choices are to buy or not to buy a policy. Most drivers have liability insurance for their cars, and most carry greater coverage than the legal minimum. We know that the policyholder's annual insurance costs exceed the expected loss from an accident. (This is because insurance companies must charge more than what they expect to pay in claims just to meet overhead costs and expenses.) But according to the Bayes decision rule, the best decision would be not to insure, because no insurance would have a greater expected monetary payoff (that is, the expected cost of no insurance is less than the cost of insurance). This course of action contradicts the true preference of most people.

Similar breakdowns of the Bayes decision rule occur whenever a person prefers a less risky alternative to one that involves considerable risk but actually has a greater expected monetary payoff. Since other decision-making criteria have serious defects, too, how should we objectively analyze decisions that involve great risk?

Fortunately, *decision theory accounts for attitudes toward risk by permitting an adjustment in the payoff values themselves.* This is accomplished by establishing a true-worth index called a *utility value* for every outcome. Thus, a decision may be analyzed using utilities instead of dollars or some other standard payoff measure.

In Chapter 21 we will describe the theory of utility and its application in great detail. One very important principle will be established there: *When the Bayes decision rule is applied to a decision-making problem with utility payoffs, it always indicates the most preferred course of action.* This makes that rule the theoretically perfect criterion for decision making, no matter how complex the decision happens to be.

6-3   DECISION MAKING USING STRATEGIES

One important aspect of decision making is the use of information that might be helpful in making a choice. In establishing an employment policy based on a screening test, an applicant's score is the basis for hiring or rejecting that person. Regardless of the score achieved, a person who is hired will ultimately perform satisfactorily or not. When receiving components for assembly, manufacturers generally take a random sample to decide whether to accept or reject a shipment; the actual quality of the entire shipment will be known only after this decision has been made. As a further example, consider the choice between adding a new product to the line or abandoning it. This decision might be based on the results of a marketing research study; the success or failure of the new product will be known only after it has actually been marketed.

All of these situations are decisions with two points of uncertainty. The first uncertainty is the kind of information obtained—the screening-test score, the number of defective sample items, or the results of the marketing research study. The second uncertainty concerns the ultimate outcome—the new employee's performance, the quality of the shipment, the new product's performance. Between these points in time, a decision has to be made. The chosen act depends on which particular event has just occurred.

It is possible to determine the best acts to select for each informational event in advance. The resulting decision rule is called a *strategy*. The ultimate decision is what particular strategy to select. We will show how this is done by means of a case illustration that involves sampling and inspection.

The Cannery Inspector: A Case Illustration

A cannery inspector monitors tests for mercury-contamination levels before authorizing shipments of canned tuna. The procedure is to randomly select two crates of canned fish from a shipment and determine the parts per million of mercury. The number of these crates R exceeding government contamination guidelines is determined. The inspector may then approve (A) or disapprove (D) the shipment. If approved, the shipment is sent to distributors who perform more detailed testing to determine whether the average mercury levels of the entire shipment are excessive (E) or tolerable (T). An excessively contaminated shipment is returned to the cannery. If the company inspector originally disapproves a shipment, the production batch is sent to the rendering department to be converted into pet food. At this time, it is determined whether the entire shipment actually contains excessive average levels of mercury.

The decision tree diagram for the cannery inspector's decision is provided in Figure 6-1. Eight strategies, S_1 through S_8, are identified in Table 6-7. A strategy must specify which act—"approve" or "disapprove"—should be chosen for each possible test result. From Table 6-7, we can see that strategy S_1 is a decision rule specifying that the shipment must be approved no matter what the number of excessively contaminated crates R happens to be. Strategy S_2 specifies approval if $R = 0$ or $R = 1$, but disapproval if $R = 2$. Eight strategies are possible because there are 2 choices for each of the 3 events and therefore $2^3 = 8$ distinct decision rules.

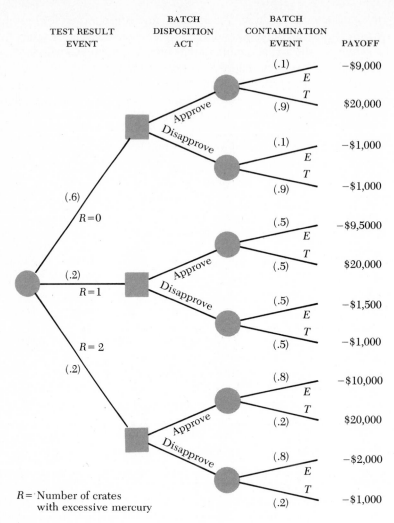

TEST RESULT
EVENT

BATCH
DISPOSITION
ACT

BATCH
CONTAMINATION
EVENT

PAYOFF

FIGURE 6-1
Decision tree diagram for the cannery inspector's problem.

A table can be constructed to indicate the payoff for each strategy-event combination. Such a payoff table, shown in Table 6-8, is identical in form to the payoff table for a single-stage decision, except that strategies are used in place of acts. Another difference is that there are uncertainties at two stages in the cannery decision: (1) how many excessively contaminated crates will be found in the sample and (2) whether the contamination level of the entire production batch will be found to be excessive or tolerable on the average. The six

TABLE 6-7
Strategies for the Cannery Inspector's Decision

	Strategy							
Test Result Event	S_1	S_2	S_3	S_4	S_5	S_6	S_7	S_8
$R = 0$	A	A	A	D	A	D	D	D
$R = 1$	A	A	D	A	D	A	D	D
$R = 2$	A	D	A	A	D	D	A	D

joint events are of the form $R = 0$ *and E, R = 2 and T*. The payoff values given in the table are the same as the payoff values on the decision tree in Figure 6-1 and correspond to the joint event that occurs for the specified strategy. Thus, if the joint event $R = 2$ *and E* occurs when S_1 is used, the payoff is -10 thousand dollars, since the inspector approves the shipment whenever $R = 2$, according to this particular strategy. If the inspector uses S_2, the same event indicates disapproval, and because the shipment contains excessive mercury, the payoff is -2 thousand dollars.

This strategy-selection decision can be analyzed by applying any of the various decision-making criteria we encountered earlier and then treating each strategy in the same way that an act is treated in a single-stage decision structure. However, we will continue to maximize expected payoff.

Extensive and Normal Form Analysis

The cannery strategy-selection decision can be analyzed using the Bayes decision rule and maximizing expected payoff either by (1) backward induction

TABLE 6-8
Payoff Table for the Cannery Inspector's Decision Using Strategies
(payoffs in thousands of dollars)

	Strategy							
Joint Event	S_1	S_2	S_3	S_4	S_5	S_6	S_7	S_8
$R = 0$ and E	-9	-9	-9	-1	-9	-1	-1	-1
$R = 0$ and T	20	20	20	-1	20	-1	-1	-1
$R = 1$ and E	-9.5	-9.5	-1.5	-9.5	-1.5	-9.5	-1.5	-1.5
$R = 1$ and T	20	20	-1	20	-1	20	-1	-1
$R = 2$ and E	-10	-2	-10	-10	-2	-2	-10	-2
$R = 2$ and T	20	-1	20	20	-1	-1	20	-1

on the decision tree or (2) direct computation from the values given in the payoff table to determine the strategy with the maximum expected payoff. *The two approaches will provide identical results.* When a decision tree is used, the procedure is called an *extensive form analysis.* When the analysis is based on the payoff table, it is referred to as *normal form analysis.*

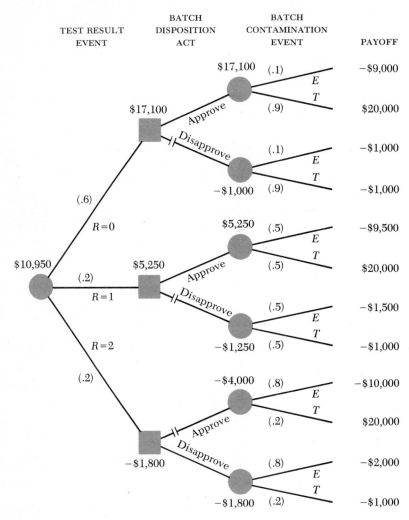

FIGURE 6-2
Extensive form analysis of the cannery inspector's problem, using the decision tree diagram.

Figure 6-2 illustrates extensive form analysis. The probability value determined for each event is shown on the corresponding branch of the decision tree. Backward induction indicates that the best procedure is to approve the shipment when $R = 0$ or $R = 1$ and to disapprove the shipment when $R = 2$. Referring to Table 6-7, we can see that this corresponds to strategy S_2.

The results of the normal form analysis for the cannery inspector's problem are shown in Table 6-9. There, we can see that strategy S_2 has a maximum expected payoff of 10.95 thousand dollars, which is the same result we obtained in extensive form analysis ($10,950). Indeed, every strategy listed in Table 6-7 can be represented by the unique pruned decision tree shown in Figure 6-3. Fortunately, extensive form analysis requires that we prune the tree just once. This makes decision tree analysis superior to payoff table analysis in terms of computational efficiency. It is not even necessary to catalog the various strategies in decision tree analysis. In backward induction, only the maximum expected payoffs need to be brought back to the earlier branching point.

Extensive form analysis using a decision tree is often the only possible approach, because the problem structure cannot be forced into the rectangular format of a payoff table. This is especially true of multistage problems that have two or more decision points, such as the Ponderosa Record Company problem diagrammed in Figure 5-4 (page 120). Only problems that result in a symmetrical decision tree like the one in Figure 6-2 can be analyzed either way in terms of expected payoff.

TABLE 6-9
Expected Payoff Calculations for the Cannery Inspector's Decision Using Strategies (payoffs in thousands of dollars)

(1) First-Stage Event Probability	(2) Second-Stage Event Probability	(3) Joint Probability (1) × (2)	(4) Payoff for S_2	(5) Payoff × Joint Probability (3) × (4)
$\Pr[R = 0] = .6$	$\Pr[E \mid R = 0] = .1$	.06	-9	$-.54$
$\Pr[R = 0] = .6$	$\Pr[T \mid R = 0] = .9$	.54	20	10.80
$\Pr[R = 1] = .2$	$\Pr[E \mid R = 1] = .5$	.10	-9.5	$-.95$
$\Pr[R = 1] = .2$	$\Pr[T \mid R = 1] = .5$	.10	20	2.00
$\Pr[R = 2] = .2$	$\Pr[E \mid R = 2] = .8$	.16	-2	$-.32$
$\Pr[R = 2] = .2$	$\Pr[T \mid R = 2] = .2$	.04	-1	$-.04$
			Expected payoff =	10.95

Strategy:	S_1	S_2	S_3	S_4	S_5	S_6	S_7	S_8
Expected payoff:	10.51	10.95	9.21	$-.35$	9.65	.09	-1.65	-1.21

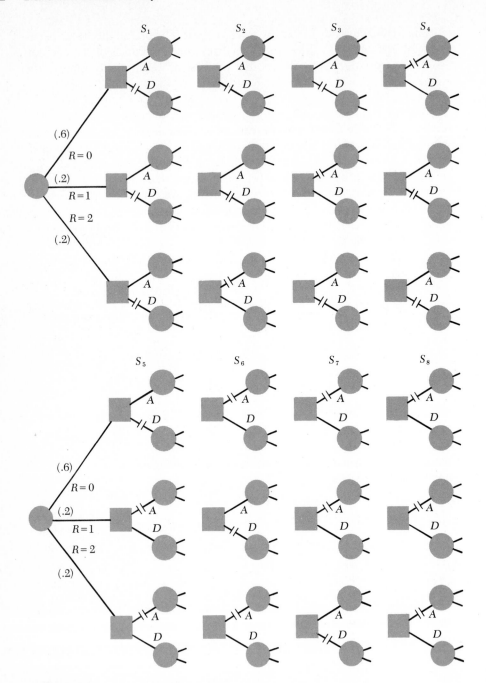

FIGURE 6-3
Pruned decision tree diagrams illustrating the eight strategies
for the cannery inspector's problem given in Table 6-7.

OPPORTUNITY LOSS AND THE EXPECTED VALUE OF PERFECT INFORMATION 6-4

Is it worthwhile to buy information that may help us choose the best act? Information is usually not free. Resources, for example, are required to take a sample or to administer a test. In this section, we will attempt to place a value on such information. To do this, we will introduce the concept of *opportunity loss*.

Opportunity Loss

Suppose that we view each possible outcome in terms of a measure that expresses the difference between the payoff for the chosen act and the best payoff that could have been achieved. This measure, referred to as an *opportunity loss*, is defined as the amount of payoff that is forgone by not selecting the act that has the greatest payoff for the event that actually occurs.

Table 6-10 shows how the opportunity losses are obtained for the payoffs for the toy manufacturer's doll-movement decision. To calculate the opportunity losses, the maximum payoff for each row is determined. Each payoff is then subtracted from its respective row maximum.

The *opportunity loss table* for the Tippi-Toes decision appears in Table 6-11. All opportunity loss values are non-negative, since they measure how much worse off the decision maker is made by choosing some act other than

TABLE 6-10
Determining the Opportunity Losses for the Tippi-Toes Decision

Demand Event	Payoff			Row Maximum
	Gears and Levers	Spring Action	Weights and Pulleys	
Light	$ 25,000	−$ 10,000	−$125,000	$ 25,000
Moderate	400,000	440,000	400,000	440,000
Heavy	650,000	740,000	750,000	750,000

Row maximum − Payoff = Opportunity loss
(thousands of dollars)

Light	25 − 25 = 0	25 − (−10) = 35	25 − (−125) = 150
Moderate	440 − 400 = 40	440 − 440 = 0	440 − 400 = 40
Heavy	750 − 650 = 100	750 − 740 = 10	750 − 750 = 0

TABLE 6-11
Opportunity Loss Table for the Tippi-Toes Decision

Demand Event	Act (Choice of Movement)		
	Gears and Levers	Spring Action	Weights and Pulleys
Light	$ 0	$35,000	$150,000
Moderate	40,000	0	40,000
Heavy	100,000	10,000	0

the best act for the event that occurs. Let us consider the meaning of the opportunity-loss values. For example, suppose that the gears and levers movement is chosen and that a light demand occurs. The opportunity loss is 0, because we can see from Table 6-10 that no better payoff than $25,000 (the row maximum) could have been achieved if another act had been chosen. But if the gears and levers movement is chosen and a heavy demand occurs, the opportunity loss is $100,000, because the weights and pulleys movement has the greatest payoff for a heavy demand ($750,000). Since the gears and levers movement has a payoff of only $650,000, the payoff difference $750,000 − $650,000 = $100,000 represents the additional payoff forgone by not selecting the act with the greatest payoff. It should be emphasized that the $100,000 opportunity loss is not a loss in the accounting sense because a net positive contribution of $650,000 to profits is obtained. Instead, the opportunity to achieve an additional $100,000 has been missed. We might say that the decision maker would have $100,000 in *regret* by not choosing weights and pulleys instead of gears and levers, should demand prove to be heavy.

Bayes Decision Rule and Opportunity Loss

We can calculate the expected opportunity loss for each act and then select the act that has the minimum loss. This is done in Table 6-12 for the Tippi-Toes decision. The minimum expected opportunity loss is $5,500 for the spring-action movement, which is the *minimum expected opportunity loss act* in this example.

In Chapter 5, we saw that the spring-action movement was also the maximum expected payoff act and was therefore the best choice according to the Bayes decision rule. Our new criterion leads us to the same choice. It can be mathematically established that this will always be so. Since either criterion will always lead to the same choice, we can say that the *Bayes decision rule is to select the act that has the maximum expected payoff or the minimum expected opportunity loss.*

TABLE 6-12

Calculation of Expected Opportunity Losses for the Tippi-Toes Decision

Demand Event	Probability	Gears and Levers		Spring Action		Weights and Pulleys	
		Loss	Loss × Probability	Loss	Loss × Probability	Loss	Loss × Probability
Light	.10	$ 0	$ 0	$35,000	$3,500	$150,000	$15,000
Moderate	.70	40,000	28,000	0	0	40,000	28,000
Heavy	.20	100,000	20,000	10,000	2,000	0	0
Expected opportunity loss:			$48,000		$5,500		$43,000

The Expected Value of Perfect Information

Until this point, our toy manufacturer has selected an act without the benefit of any information except that acquired through experience with other toys. But it is possible to secure better information about next season's demand through test marketing, from opinion and attitude surveys, or by obtaining inside information concerning competitors' plans. How much would the decision maker be willing to pay for additional information?

It is helpful to know the payoff that can be expected from securing improved information about the events. We will consider the extreme case when the decision maker can acquire *perfect information*. Using this information, the decision maker can guarantee the selection of the act that yields the greatest payoff for whatever event actually occurs. Because we wish to investigate the worth of such information *before* it is obtained, we will determine the *expected payoff with perfect information*.

To calculate the expected payoff with perfect information, we determine the highest payoff for each event. This is illustrated for the Tippi-Toes decision in Table 6-13. The maximum payoff for each demand level is determined by finding the largest payoff in each row. Thus, for a light demand, we find that choosing the gears and levers movement yields the largest payoff ($25,000). If perfect information indicated that light demand was certain to occur, our decision maker would choose this movement. Similarly, $440,000 is the maximum payoff possible for moderate demand, and this amount can be achieved only if the spring-action movement is chosen. Likewise, $750,000 is the maximum possible payoff when a heavy demand occurs, and this amount corresponds to a choice of the weights and pulleys movement. The last column of Table 6-13 shows the products of the maximum payoffs and their respective event probabilities. Summing these, we obtain $460,500 as the expected payoff with perfect

TABLE 6-13
Calculation of the Expected Payoff with Perfect Information for the Tippi-Toes Decision

Demand Event	Prob- ability	Act			With Perfect Information		
		Gears and Levers	Spring Action	Weights and Pulleys	Maximum Payoff	Chosen Act	Payoff × Probability
Light	.10	$ 25,000	−$ 10,000	−$125,000	$ 25,000	G/L	$ 2,500
Moderate	.70	400,000	440,000	400,000	440,000	S.A.	308,000
Heavy	.20	650,000	740,000	750,000	750,000	W/P	150,000
					Expected payoff with perfect information		= $460,500

information. This figure represents the average payoff if the toy manufacturer were faced with the same situation repeatedly and always selected the act that yielded the best payoff for the event indicated by the perfect information. Keep in mind that the $460,500 represents the expected payoff viewed from some point in time *before* the information becomes available. *After* the information has been obtained, exactly one of the payoffs, $25,000, $440,000, or $750,000, is bound to occur. When the information is actually obtained, the payoff is a certainty.

We can now answer the question regarding the worth of perfect information to the decision maker. As we have seen, the Bayes decision rule leads to the choice of the particular act that maximizes the expected payoff without regard to any additional information. Since this is the best act that our decision maker can select without any new information and since the expected payoff with perfect information is the average payoff that can be anticipated with the best possible information, the worth of perfect information to the decision maker is expressed by the difference between these two amounts. We call the resulting number the *expected value of perfect information*, which is conveniently represented by the abbreviation EVPI and may be expressed as

EVPI = Expected payoff with perfect information
      − Maximum expected payoff (with no information)

For the toy-manufacturer's decision, we obtain the FVPI by subtracting the maximum expected payoff of $455,000 (calculated in Table 5-6 on page 113) from the expected payoff with perfect information of $460,500:

EVPI = $460,500 − $455,000 = $5,500

In this case, the EVPI represents the greatest amount of money that the decision maker would be willing to pay to obtain perfect information about what the demand will be. Stated differently, $5,500 is the increase in the decision maker's expected payoff that can be attributed to perfect knowledge of demand. Both $455,000 and $460,500 are meaningless values *after* the perfect information is obtained. Thus, the EVPI of $5,500 can be interpreted only *before* the perfect information has become known.

EVPI and Opportunity Loss

Note that $5,500 is the same amount as the minimum expected opportunity loss calculated in Table 6-12. Thus, we can see that *the expected value of perfect information is equal to the expected opportunity loss for the optimal act.*

Therefore, we can calculate the expected value of perfect information by calculating the expected opportunity losses. The minimum loss is then the EVPI. Table 6-14 summarizes the relationships among expected payoff, expected opportunity loss, and expected value of perfect information for the toy manufacturer's decision. Note that for any act, the sum of the expected payoff and the expected opportunity loss is equal to the expected payoff with perfect information.

Since perfect information is nonexistent in most real-world decision making, why are we interested in the EVPI? Our answer is that it helps us to establish a limit on the worth of less-than-perfect information. For example, if a marketing research study aimed at predicting demand costs $6,000, which exceeds the EVPI by $500, then the study should not be conducted, regardless of its quality. We will investigate the concepts involved in decision making with experimental information further in Chapter 17.

TABLE 6-14

Relationships Among Expected Payoff, Expected Opportunity Loss, and EVPI for the Tippi-Toes Decision

	Gears and Levers	Spring Action	Weights and Pulleys
Expected payoff	$412,500	$455,000	$417,500
Expected opportunity loss	48,000	5,500	43,000
Expected payoff with perfect information	$460,500	$460,500	$460,500

Expected value of perfect information (EVPI) = $5,500   └─Optimal act

PROBLEMS

6-1 You have decided to participate in a gamble that offers the following monetary payoffs:

	Act	
Event	Choose Red	Choose Black
Red	$1	− $2
Black	− 1	100

(a) Which act is the maximin payoff act?

(b) Suppose that the probability of red is .99 and calculate the expected payoffs for each act. Which act is better according to the Bayes decision rule? Which act would you choose?

(c) Suppose that the probability of red is .5 and calculate the expected payoffs for each act. Which act has the maximum expected payoff? Which act would you choose?

(d) In view of your answers to (b) and (c), what is your opinion of the maximin payoff decision criterion in this case?

6-2 A decision maker must choose one of three acts. The payoff table and the event probabilities are provided below.

		Act		
Event	Probability	A_1	A_2	A_3
E_1	.3	$10	$15	$20
E_2	.4	15	20	15
E_3	.3	25	15	15

(a) Which act is the maximin payoff act?

(b) Which act is the maximum likelihood act?

(c) Calculate the expected payoffs. According to the Bayes decision rule, which act should be chosen?

6-3 A farmer intends to sign a contract to provide a cannery with his entire crop. He must choose to produce one of the following five vegetables: corn, tomatoes, beets, asparagus, or cauliflower. The farmer will plant his entire 1,000 acres with the selected crop. The yields of these vegetables will be affected by the weather to varying degrees. The following table indicates the approximate productivities for each vegetable in dry, moderate, and damp weather and also lists the price per bushel that the cannery has offered for each crop.

| Weather | (Approximate Yield (Bushels per Acre) | | | | |
	Corn	Tomatoes	Beets	Asparagus	Cauliflower
Dry	20	10	15	30	40
Moderate	35	20	20	25	40
Damp	40	10	30	20	40
Price per bushel	$1.00	$2.00	$1.50	$1.00	$.50

(a) Using the approximate total cash receipts when the crop is sold as a payoff measure, construct the payoff table for the farmer's decision.

(b) Identify any inadmissible acts and eliminate them from the payoff table.

(c) Which act is the maximin payoff act?

(d) Suppose that the following probabilities have been assigned to the types of weather and calculate the expected payoff for each act. Then identify the act that has the maximum expected payoff.

Weather	Probability
Dry	.3
Moderate	.5
Damp	.2

6-4 A newsdealer must decide how many copies of a particular magazine to stock in December. He will not stock less than the lowest possible demand or more than the highest possible demand. Each magazine costs him $.50 and sells for $1.00. At the end of the month the unsold magazines are thrown away. Three levels of monthly demand are equally likely: 10, 11, and 12. If demand exceeds stock, sales will equal stock.

(a) Using December profit as the payoff measure, construct the newsdealer's payoff table.

(b) According to the maximin criterion, how many copies should he stock?

(c) Which number of copies will provide the greatest expected payoff?

6-5 Use the payoff table below to construct an opportunity loss table.

| | | Act | | | | |
Event	Probability	A_1	A_2	A_3	A_4	A_5
E_1	.2	10	20	10	15	20
E_2	.2	− 5	10	− 5	10	− 5
E_3	.6	15	5	10	10	10

Compute the expected opportunity loss for each act. Which act yields the lowest expected opportunity loss?

6-6 Answer the following based on the payoff table below.

			Act	
Event	Probability	A_1	A_2	A_3
E_1	.3	10	20	30
E_2	.5	40	-10	20
E_3	.2	20	50	20

(a) What is the maximum expected payoff? To which act does this payoff correspond?
(b) What is the expected payoff with perfect information?
(c) Use your answers from (a) and (b) to calculate the expected value of perfect information.
(d) What is the minimum expected opportunity loss?
(e) What do you notice about your answers to (c) and (d)?

6-7 A product manager for a soap manufacturer wishes to determine whether or not to market a new toothpaste. The present value of all future profits from a successful toothpaste is $1,000,000, whereas failure of the brand would result in a net loss of $500,000. Not marketing the toothpaste would not affect profits. The manager has judged that the toothpaste would have a 50–50 chance of success.
(a) Construct the payoff table for this decision.
(b) Which act will maximize the expected payoff?
(c) Compute the decision maker's EVPI. What is the minimum expected opportunity loss?

6-8 B.F. Retread, a tire manufacturer, wishes to select one of three feasible prototype designs for a new longer-wearing radial tire. The costs of making the tires are:

Tire	Fixed Cost	Variable Cost per Unit
A	$ 60,000	$30
B	90,000	20
C	120,000	15

There are three levels of unit sales: 4,000 units, 7,000 units, and 10,000 units; the respective probabilities are .30, .50, and .20. The selling price will be $75 per tire.
(a) Construct the payoff table using total profit as the payoff measure.
(b) Determine the expected payoff for each act. According to Bayes decision rule, which is the best act?
(c) Calculate the EVPI.
(d) Complete the opportunity loss table and compute the expected opportunity losses.

6-9 An oil wildcatter must decide whether to drill on a candidate drilling site. His judgment leads him to conclude that there is a 50–50 chance of oil. If the wildcatter drills and strikes oil, his profit will be $200,000. But if the well turns out to be dry, his net loss will be $100,000.

(a) According to the Bayes decision rule, should the wildcatter drill or abandon the site?

(b) What is the wildcatter's EVPI?

(c) A seismologist offers to conduct a highly reliable seismic survey. The results could help the wildcatter make his decision. What is the most that the wildcatter would consider paying for such seismic information?

6-10 Suppose that the following probabilities apply to the cannery illustration in Section 6-3:

Test Result	Probability	Conditional Probabilities	
$R = 0$	.4	.2 (E)	.8 (T)
$R = 1$	.3	.6 (E)	.4 (T)
$R = 2$	.3	.9 (E)	.1 (T)

(a) Conduct a new extensive form analysis (using a corrected decision tree) to determine the strategy that maximizes expected payoff.

(b) Conduct a new normal form analysis (using corrected joint probabilities) to select the strategy that maximizes expected payoff.

6-11 A cannery manager classifies each truckload of apricots purchased under contract from local orchards as underripe, ripe, or overripe. The manager must then decide whether a particular truckload will be used for dried apricots (D) or for apricot preserves (P). A truckload of apricots used for preserves yields a profit of $6,000 if the fruit has a high sugar content, but only $4,000 if the sugar content is low (because costly extra sugar must be added). Regardless of sugar content, a truckload of dried apricots yields a profit of $5,000. In either case, the actual sugar content can be determined only during final processing.

The probabilities are .3 for an underripe truckload, .5 for a ripe one, and .2 for an overripe one. The following probabilities for sugar content have been established for given levels of ripeness:

Sugar Content	Underripe	Ripe	Overripe
Low	.9	.4	.2
High	.1	.6	.8
	1.0	1.0	1.0

(a) Construct the manager's decision tree diagram and perform an extensive form analysis to determine the maximum expected payoff strategy for disposing of a truckload of apricots.

(b) List the possible strategies for disposing of a truckload of apricots. Perform a normal form analysis to select the strategy that yields the greatest expected profit.

6-12 Suppose that the manager in Problem 6-7 wishes to implement a consumer testing program at a cost of $50,000. Consumer testing will be either favorable (a 40% chance) or unfavorable. Given a favorable test result, the chance of product success is judged to be 80%. For an unfavorable test result, the toothpaste's success probability is judged to be only 30%.

(a) Assuming that testing is used, construct a decision tree diagram. Then perform backward induction analysis to determine the optimal strategy to employ in using the test results.

(b) Identify the basic strategies involving the use of the results of the consumer testing program. Construct a payoff table with these strategies as the choices and the joint market outcomes and test results as the events. Then conduct a normal form analysis to determine which strategy maximizes expected payoff.

7

Inventory Decisions with Certain Factors

O ne area of business decision making in which quantitative methods have played a highly successful role in achieving cost savings is the area of inventory control. A primary reason for this success story is that inventories represent such a vast segment of total economic activity. In the United States alone, hundreds of billions of dollars are presently invested in inventories. Due to the sheer size of inventory investments, even minor improvements in controlling inventories can create large savings.

Two phenomena have contributed to improvements in controlling inventories. One has been the application of mathematical models and optimization techniques to achieve efficiencies. In Chapter 7, we will focus on these quantitative methods. A second source of savings has been the development of the digital computer with improved information processing and retrieval capabilities. Managers in complex organizations now have immediate access to all kinds of information relevant to inventories that was once impossible to obtain quickly. The closing of this information gap has dramatically reduced the need to maintain inventories. Many inventory systems are automated to the extent that even orders to replenish stock are issued by computer.

The central problem we face in making any decision involving physical storage is finding an efficient *inventory policy*. A key element in establishing such a policy is determining how many items should be stocked periodically and when replenishment should occur. It is convenient to refer to the number of items to be stocked as the *order quantity* and to the level of inventory when the requisition is made as the *order point*. For example, a family might always purchase two gallons of milk (the order quantity) and repurchase milk only when all of it has been drunk (so that order point is zero).

Our objective is to determine optimal inventory policies. In this chapter, we will consider the basic structure of inventory decisions and present some of the models that are applicable when all factors are certain. These models will serve to explain the essential concepts that are common to more advanced models. In Chapter 8, we consider inventory decisions made under uncertainty.

7-1   FACTORS INFLUENCING INVENTORY POLICY

The usual long-run objective of an inventory policy is to maximize profits or to minimize costs. In the simpler situations we will encounter in this chapter, these two goals coincide. The desired end result is ordinarily achieved by minimizing the average inventory cost over a short period of time, such as one year. Our initial models will all be based on minimizing *annual* cost.

Inventory Cost Components

In typical business situations, the various costs considered in evaluating inventory systems are

(1) Ordering and procurement costs for items to be stocked.
(2) Holding or carrying costs.
(3) Shortage costs.

Inventory ordering and procurement costs represent all expenses incurred in ordering or manufacturing items, including not only the acquisition costs but also the costs of transporting, collecting and sorting, and placing the items in storage. Also included in this category are any managerial and clerical costs associated with placing an order. These costs often vary with the size of the order; for example, this occurs when products are priced with quantity discounts. Ordering and procurement costs are of two kinds: a fixed portion for each order that is independent of the number of items stocked, and a variable portion for each order that is dependent on the number of items stocked. We will refer to the *fixed* portion as the *ordering costs* and to the *variable* portion as the *procurement costs*.

Inventory holding or *carrying costs* are the expenses incurred during the storage of items. This includes physical costs—the most common being the operation of warehouse facilities—as well as the costs of insurance and property taxes. Other cost components might be expenses arising from pilferage, spoilage, and obsolescence. A very important portion of inventory holding costs is the *opportunity cost* of those funds invested in inventory that might have been profitably used elsewhere. All such costs depend on *how many* items are stored and for *how long*. Such costs frequently can be 20–25% of the value of the items held in inventory.

Inventory shortage costs occur whenever there is a demand for items that are not currently in stock. For items that are usually backordered, such as a new car of a particular color with special options, shortage costs may have only a fixed component—the extra paperwork and managerial expenses incurred in processing the order. For shortages of more mundane items, such as a particular brand of paint, an additional variable cost component that depends on the *duration* of the shortage must be considered. This cost is largely due to the potential loss of customer goodwill that may be expected to increase in proportion to the length of the delay; such a decline in goodwill might be reflected in the loss of future business. In extreme cases of convenience products, such as cigarettes, or necessities, such as gasoline, there is no backordering at all. Under these circumstances, a shortage results in the loss of a sale. The minimum cost of a lost sale is the marginal profit that the item would have earned, but it can be larger due to the loss of goodwill.

In evaluating an inventory policy, some or all of these three types of costs might be considered. But it is very important that only *relevant costs* be used. These involve only those expenses that are in some way affected by the inventory policies themselves. Certain legitimate accounting costs may therefore be ignored. For instance, the rent on a warehouse would not be included as a carrying cost if the same facility were to be used regardless of the number of items stocked. Instead, the rent would properly be considered an overhead item, like the company president's salary. No proration of overhead items should be reflected in the inventory costs, unless these items somehow differ from policy to policy. But certain nonaccounting costs, such as the opportunity cost of invested capital and the loss of customer goodwill, are definitely relevant and should be incorporated into the evaluation.

The Nature of Demand and Supply

In typical business situations, demands occur erratically. The demands for most items also occur discretely; that is, a few items are demanded at a time. In this chapter, demands are assumed to occur *continuously* (as if each item is a cubic foot of natural gas fed into a heater that is always lighted—either from a pilot light or by the main flame) and *at the same rate over time* (as if the gas heater is always on full flame). As long as demand is predictable, such a simplifying assumption makes little difference in the inventory costs or in the particular policy that minimizes cost.

But one element does matter. Demands typically occur *randomly* over time, so that the overall level is generally uncertain. In this chapter, however, we will consider only cases in which the demand is *certain* and known in advance. These cases will prepare us for the discussion in Chapter 8, where uncertainty in demand will be explicitly considered.

How items are supplied is another important element in establishing inventory policies. Generally, this is handled in one of two ways. From the retailer's or the wholesaler's point of view, the only question is how long does it take to fill an order. This is the *lead time* that it will take to receive the units ordered. Like demand, lead time is often uncertain. Here, we will only consider *constant* lead times. This will greatly simplify the analysis and will allow us to analyze most problems without explicitly considering the lead time at all, as if inventories were instantaneously replenished. In Chapter 8, we will consider how the choice of policy is affected by uncertain lead times.

The method of supply differs for the manufacturer who must produce items for later sale. Here, replenishment cannot be instantaneous. Instead items must be added to the inventory at a rate equal to the speed at which they are produced.

7-2 THE ECONOMIC ORDER QUANTITY (EOQ) MODEL

The simplest inventory model involves one type of item that has a known and constant demand and that is resupplied instantaneously. No backordering of items is allowed. The problem objective is to select an inventory policy—that is, to choose the order quantity (which in turn establishes the time when an order must be placed)—in such a way that the annual inventory cost is minimized.

The Mathematical Model

The following parameters are used to establish a mathematical model for this problem:

k = cost per order

A = annual number of items demanded

c = unit cost of procuring an item

h = annual cost per dollar value of holding items in inventory

T = time between orders

The objective is to choose the number of items to order

$$Q = \text{Order quantity}$$

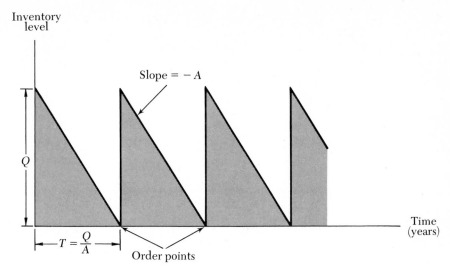

FIGURE 7-1
Inventory system for the simple economic order quantity model.

such that

Total annual cost = Ordering cost + Holding cost + Procurement cost

is minimized.

The features of this inventory system are illustrated in Figure 7-1, where the inventory level is plotted versus calendar time. This graph will help to explain the development of the mathematical model. Figure 7-1 tells us that Q items are replenished periodically, at which time a new *inventory cycle* begins and an old one ends. Each cycle has a duration of T years (some fraction of one year), which is determined by the order quantity Q. The length of time is equal to the proportion of the annual demand consumed in one inventory cycle, or

$$T = \frac{Q}{A}$$

The items are depleted at the rate of A units per year, so that the slanted line segments, each with a slope of $-A$, indicate the level of inventory at any given point in time. The sawtooth effect of the graph represents the sequence of inventory depletions and replenishments of successive inventory cycles. Because it costs something to hold items in inventory, there is no advantage to restocking until the inventory is zero. Thus, each inventory cycle can be pictured as a triangle of height Q and base T, with a new cycle or triangle beginning at the order point, where the leg of the preceding triangle touches the time axis.

To find a mathematical expression for the problem objective, we begin with the first cost component, the *annual ordering cost*, which is based on how many orders are placed each year. The number of annual orders depends on two factors: (1) the annual number of items demanded A, and (2) the order quantity Q. It follows that

$$\text{Number of annual orders} = \frac{A}{Q}$$

Multiplying this equation by the cost per order k, we obtain

$$\text{Annual ordering cost} = \left(\frac{A}{Q}\right)k$$

The second cost component, the *annual holding cost*, is based on the number of items placed in inventory and the duration they are held in inventory. Individually, some items will be sold immediately; others will be held until the inventory is restocked. However, we need to concern ourselves only with an average value. Since the inventory level in any cycle ranges from Q downward to zero and there is a constant rate of depletion, we have for any cycle

$$\text{Average inventory} = \frac{Q}{2}$$

This same quantity applies from cycle to cycle and therefore represents the *average inventory level* throughout the entire operating life of the inventory system.

It is realistic to base the holding cost on the value of the items held. This is certainly true of the opportunity cost of the invested capital and applies to other costs, such as insurance and property taxes, as well. (Physical storage costs are usually highly correlated with an item's value, too.) Here, we base the value of an item on its procurement cost. The cost of holding an item in inventory for one year is therefore the product of the annual holding cost per dollar h and the unit procurement cost c, or

$$\text{Annual holding cost of one item} = hc$$

We can now determine the annual holding cost of all the items involved by multiplying the above cost by the average inventory, or

$$\text{Annual holding cost} = hc\left(\frac{Q}{2}\right)$$

There is another way of looking at this annual cost component that will prove useful in discussing later models. Consider the *single-cycle holding cost*, which can be related to the area of one of the triangles in Figure 7-1. The single-cycle holding cost represents the average item-time (product years) for one inventory cycle, or

$$\text{Triangle area} = \frac{1}{2} \text{ base} \times \text{Height}$$

$$= \frac{1}{2} TQ$$

$$= \frac{1}{2}\left(\frac{Q}{A}\right)Q = \frac{Q^2}{2A}$$

The holding cost of a single cycle is the product of hc and this area, or $hc(Q^2/2A)$. Since there are A/Q inventory cycles in one year, the annual holding cost can be obtained by multiplying the single-cycle value by A/Q. Canceling terms yields $hc(Q/2)$, which is the expression we obtained earlier for the annual holding cost.

For the entire year, A items will be demanded, so that

$$\text{Annual procurement cost} = Ac$$

Adding together the three cost components, we find that

$$\text{Total annual cost} = \left(\frac{A}{Q}\right)k + hc\left(\frac{Q}{2}\right) + Ac$$

The problem objective is to select the value Q that minimizes this total annual cost.

However, we need to consider only relevant costs (which differ, depending on the inventory policy). We can therefore ignore the procurement cost Ac, since that expense will arise regardless of the value of Q. Equivalently, the objective for our simple inventory model is to

$$\text{Minimize } TC = \left(\frac{A}{Q}\right)k + hc\left(\frac{Q}{2}\right)$$

where TC is the total annual *relevant* cost.

Finding the Optimal Solution

The TC equation is a mathematical expression that we refer to as the *objective function*. The value of TC depends on the order quantity Q. The TC

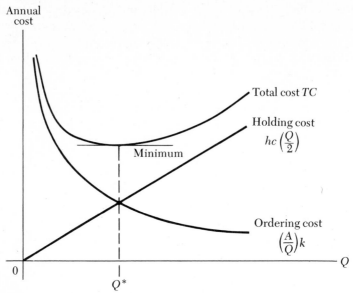

FIGURE 7-2
Graphical representation of inventory cost components.

expression is plotted in Figure 7-2, where the vertical axis indicates the annual cost and the horizontal axis represents the order quantity Q. The total annual relevant cost has two components: annual ordering cost and annual holding cost. Each of these components is also plotted in Figure 7-2. Since TC is the sum of ordering and holding costs, the height of the TC curve at any level of Q is the sum of the respective heights of the ordering-cost curve and the holding-cost line.

The annual ordering-cost curve has the geometric shape of a hyperbola. Recall that the cost of each order is an amount k, regardless of how many items are requested each time. Thus, very low levels of Q will involve a great number of orders throughout the year, and ordering costs will be huge. As Q becomes larger, fewer orders are required and the annual ordering cost declines as we move to the right on the ordering-cost curve. The annual holding cost is plotted as a straight line because this component is a constant multiple of the average inventory level. This line begins at the origin with zero holding cost at $Q = 0$, where no inventory is held. Each item is sold as demanded, so that the holding-cost line rises with constant slope as Q increases. This is because progressively larger order quantities raise the average inventory level, causing holding costs to rise proportionately.

The *optimal solution* to the objective function occurs at the point where total annual relevant cost is minimized. We denote the optimal order quantity by Q^*. This level corresponds to the *minimum-cost point* on the TC curve, where its slope is zero. The slope equation for a curve may be determined by using mathematical procedures. Once the equation for the slope has been found, it can be set equal to zero and algebraically solved to determine the corresponding order quantity.*

The equation for the *optimal order quantity* is

$$Q^* = \sqrt{\frac{2Ak}{hc}}$$

which is sometimes called the *economic order quantity*. This equation is often referred to as the *Wilson formula*, in honor of the man who first proposed it. Once Q^* has been obtained, the corresponding reorder time is automatically determined to be

$$T^* = \frac{Q^*}{A}$$

and a complete optimal inventory policy is thereby obtained which tells how much should be ordered and when each order should be placed. The total annual relevant cost of this policy can be determined by substituting the value of Q^* for Q in the TC equation.

Referring again to Figure 7-2, we can see that Q^* happens to be the order quantity at which holding cost is equal to ordering cost. The Wilson formula can be verified by setting the respective component cost equations equal to each other and algebraically solving for Q. Study of the Q^* formula allows us to draw some interesting conclusions. The economic (optimal) order quantity increases with the square root of the annual demand A instead of becoming proportional to it. Also, it is inversely proportional to the square root of the unit procurement cost c, indicating that all else being equal, fewer expensive items should be ordered than would be the case for cheaper items. Thus, the various *parameters k, A, c, and h* really serve to determine the optimal inventory policy, and widely different results may be obtained for different levels of these constants.

* To do this, we employ calculus. The first derivative of the objective function $TC(Q)$ is obtained and set equal to zero:

$$\frac{dTC(Q)}{dQ} = -\frac{A}{Q^2}k + \frac{hc}{2} = 0$$

Because $TC(Q)$ is convex from below, if we solve for Q, the minimum cost occurs when

$$Q = \sqrt{\frac{2Ak}{hc}}$$

A Retail-Sales Illustration

Suppose that a liquor store sells 5,200 cases of beer each year. For simplicity, we will assume that the beer is sold at a constant rate throughout the year. The net cost of each case to the store is $2. The wholesale supplier charges $10 for each delivery, regardless of how many cases have been ordered, and delivery always occurs the day after the order is placed. The owner's only working capital is tied up in inventory, and these funds have been borrowed from the local bank at a simple annual interest rate of 10%. In addition, the owner must pay a state franchise tax of 5% of the annual inventory value, and another 5% for theft insurance. All other operating costs are either fixed in nature or do not depend on the amounts of beer ordered.

The owner wishes to evaluate the present procedure of ordering 100 cases each week and to establish a better inventory policy that will minimize the annual costs of doing business in beer. The following constants apply:

$k = \$10$ per order

$A = 5,200$ cases per year

$c = \$2$ per case

$h = \$.20$ annual cost per dollar value of beer held in inventory

The present policy of ordering every week involves an order quantity of

$$Q = \frac{5,200}{52} = 100 \text{ cases}$$

The total annual relevant cost of this policy is

$$TC = \left(\frac{A}{Q}\right)k + hc\left(\frac{Q}{2}\right)$$

$$= \left(\frac{5,200}{100}\right)10 + .20(2)\left(\frac{100}{2}\right)$$

$$= 520 + 20$$

$$= 540 \text{ dollars per year}$$

Note that the annual ordering cost of $520 is much larger than the annual $20 holding cost. These two cost components should be the same to achieve an optimal inventory policy.

To establish the optimal inventory policy, first we use the Wilson formula to determine the economic order quantity

$$Q^* = \sqrt{\frac{2Ak}{hc}}$$

$$= \sqrt{\frac{2(5,200)10}{.20(2)}} = \sqrt{260,000}$$

$$= 509.9, \text{ or } 510 \text{ cases of beer}$$

The optimal time between orders is

$$T^* = \frac{510}{5,200} = .098 \text{ years}$$

which can be converted to once every $365(.098) = 35.8$, or 36 days. The optimal inventory policy is therefore to order 510 cases of beer every 36 days. The resulting total annual relevant cost is

$$TC = \left(\frac{5,200}{510}\right)10 + .20(2)\left(\frac{510}{2}\right)$$

$$= 101.96 + 102.00$$

$$= 203.96 \text{ dollars per year}$$

(The two cost components differ by $.04 because we rounded the value of Q^* to the nearest whole number.) Thus, more than $300 in annual beer costs alone can be saved by switching to the optimal inventory policy.

The Effect of Parameter Values on the Solution

To show how greatly the solution depends on the parameter values, we will consider the retail store's inventory policy for fine domestic wine. Suppose that only 1,000 cases of this wine are sold anually at a net cost of $20 per case. The liquor store is located in San Francisco, and the owner—who prides himself on the caliber of his product—makes periodic trips through the Napa Valley to pick up orders at various wineries. He always rents a large truck and travels a fixed route; the cost is a flat $100 per trip. The holding costs are the same as they are for beer. Thus

$k = \$100$ per order

$A = 1,000$ cases per year

$c = \$20$ per case

$h = \$.20$ annual cost per dollar value of wine held in inventory

The optimal inventory policy (again, assuming a known, constant demand rate and a predictable lead time for inventory replenishment) is

$$Q^* = \sqrt{\frac{2(1,000)100}{.20(20)}} = \sqrt{50,000}$$

$$= 223.6, \text{ or } 224 \text{ cases of wine}$$

$$T^* = \frac{224}{1,000} = .224 \text{ years, or approximately 82 days}$$

The total annual relevant cost is

$$TC = \left(\frac{1,000}{224}\right)100 + .20(20)\left(\frac{224}{2}\right)$$

$$= 894.43 \text{ dollars per year}$$

Notice the difference between the results for wine and beer.

Some Limitations of the Model

Applying economic order quantity analysis to two different items is only valid under special conditions. Here, we must assume that beer and wine have independent demands and that the storage capacity is sufficient to handle any contemplated quantities of each product. If beer and wine must compete for limited space or if there is a constraint on the amount of working capital that can be tied up in inventories, then the products must be analyzed jointly and the mathematics can become quite complicated.

7-3 OPTIMAL INVENTORY POLICY WITH BACKORDERING

The simple inventory model we have just described assumes that backordering is not possible. We will now consider how items can be sold even after the inventory has been exhausted. Such a situation could apply when buying automobile tires, for example; a retailer might not have the exact size in current stock but might be willing to place a special order to satisfy a customer. An inventory system that permits backordering is summarized in Figure 7-3. As before, Q represents the order quantity. Since sales may be made even after the on-hand inventory reaches the zero level, it may be desirable to use part of each

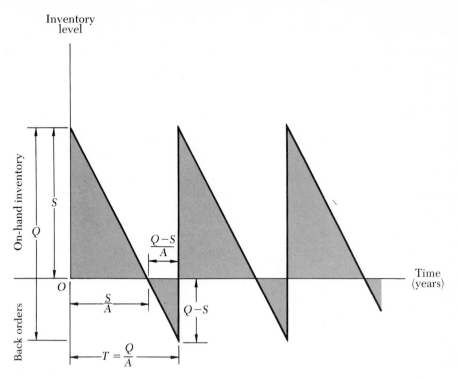

FIGURE 7-3
An inventory system when backordering is allowed.

successive order to fill backordered items. The *order level* is represented by S; this quantity is the on-hand inventory position at the beginning of each inventory cycle. The optimal inventory policy must specify the values of both Q and S that minimize total annual cost.

The Two-Phase Inventory Cycle

Each inventory cycle is now represented by two phases. The initial phase occurs when all demands can be filled from current on-hand inventory and is represented by the large triangles of height S in Figure 7-3. This quantity is the initial inventory level after filling those demands shorted in the previous cycle. The duration of the first phase is that fraction of one year that it takes to deplete S items from on-hand inventory, or S/A. The second phase of this inventory cycle is represented by the small inverted triangle; its height is $Q - S$, the number of items that are backordered, and its base is the duration of time it takes for these backorders to accumulate $(Q - S)/A$.

Expressions for Holding and Shortage Costs

We will now assume that a shortage cost applies and that, like a holding cost, this cost depends on how many items are short and on the amount of time that each shortage lasts. Such a penalty, represented by p, arises largely from loss of goodwill. (An additional fixed shortage penalty that is based only on the number of items short is sometimes applied, but for simplicity, that second penalty is not included here.)

Thus, we can now express total annual relevant cost

$$TC = \text{Ordering cost} + \text{Holding cost} + \text{Shortage cost}$$

The expression for ordering cost is the same as it was in our earlier model. The expression for holding cost is different, since only a portion of the entire order is ever stored and this cost is applied only in the first phase of the inventory cycle. The single-cycle cost is obtained by multiplying hc by the area of the first large triangle, or

$$hc \times \text{First area} = hc\left[\frac{1}{2} S\left(\frac{S}{A}\right)\right]$$

$$= \frac{hcS^2}{2A}$$

This result is then converted to the annual holding cost by multiplying by the number of orders per year A/Q and canceling terms, so that

$$\text{Annual holding cost} = \frac{hcS^2}{2Q}$$

To obtain the expression for shortage cost, we again consider what happens in a single cycle. The penalty p is applied to the average item-time short. Multiplying p by the area of the second small triangle in Figure 7-3 gives us the single-cycle shortage cost

$$p \times \text{Second area} = p\left(\frac{1}{2}\right)\left[\left(\frac{Q-S}{A}\right)(Q-S)\right]$$

$$= \frac{p(Q-S)^2}{2A}$$

This result is then converted to the annual shortage cost by multiplying by the number of inventory cycles per year A/Q and canceling terms, so that

$$\text{Annual shortage cost} = \frac{p(Q-S)^2}{2Q}$$

The New Model

The total annual relevant cost can be expressed as

$$TC = \left(\frac{A}{Q}\right)k + \frac{hcS^2}{2Q} + \frac{p(Q - S)^2}{2Q}$$

The problem objective is to find the values of Q and S that minimize TC. The following expressions may be used to calculate the optimal values:*

$$Q^* = \sqrt{\frac{2Ak}{hc}} \sqrt{\frac{p + hc}{p}}$$

$$S^* = \sqrt{\frac{2Ak}{hc}} \sqrt{\frac{p}{p + hc}}$$

The time between orders is

$$T^* = \frac{Q^*}{A}$$

Returning to our earlier example, beer is a convenience product that cannot be backordered (customers will always buy it elsewhere rather than wait). However, wine customers are connoisseurs who are willing to order out-of-stock items. Nevertheless, the store owner will incur some penalty if there is a shortage of wine.

Suppose that every day that a customer must wait for a favorite wine costs the store a penny per case; this means that the annual penalty is $p = \$3.65$ per case. Using the same constants for wine as before ($k = \$100$, $A = 1,000$, $c = \$20$, and $h = \$.20$), we can establish the optimal inventory policy:

$$Q^* = \sqrt{\frac{2(1,000)100}{.20(20)}} \sqrt{\frac{3.65 + .20(20)}{3.65}} = 324$$

$$S^* = \sqrt{\frac{2(1,000)100}{.20(20)}} \sqrt{\frac{3.65}{3.65 + .20(20)}} = 154$$

and

$$T^* = \frac{324}{1,000} = .324 \text{ years, or approximately 118 days}$$

* It can be established that the function $TC(Q, S)$ is convex over the ranges being considered. These equations are derived by setting the partial derivatives with respect to Q and S equal to zero and solving them algebraically.

The optimal inventory policy is to order 324 cases of wine every 118 days. Only 154 of these cases will be stored in inventory; the remaining $Q^* - S^* = 170$ cases will be used to satisfy outstanding backorders. The total annual relevant cost of this policy is

$$TC = \left(\frac{1,000}{324}\right)100 + \frac{.20(20)(154)^2}{2(324)} + \frac{3.65(170)^2}{2(324)}$$

$$= 617.82 \text{ dollars per year}$$

Note that this cost is smaller than the optimal cost of $894.43 when no back-ordering was allowed. This is because fewer orders are placed when backordering is permitted, so that the average on-hand inventory level is lower. Although shortage costs now exist, these costs are lower than the combined cost reduction for ordering and holding items.

7-4 INVENTORY POLICY FOR LOST SALES

As we have already noted, items like convenience products cannot be backordered. When a demand for such an item cannot be met from on-hand inventory, a sale is lost. It is possible to extend the model we have developed with backordering to accommodate this special case. However, a complete analysis of the case of lost sales is merely a mathematical exercise. If an inventory system is to be in operation at all, it can be shown that the basic economic order quality model should be used, so that no shortages leading to lost sales should be allowed.

Remember that in this chapter we have been dealing with certain, constant demands and predictable lead times for replenishment. We know that many successful retail establishments occasionally run out of convenience items like cigarettes and lose some sales. But these businesses are faced with uncertain demands. Stores would never run out of convenience items if demands could be precisely predicted and lead times never varied.

7-5 ECONOMIC PRODUCTION-QUANTITY MODEL

In the models presented thus far, orders have been filled instantaneously. Identical results are obtained when the lead time is constant, so that all items arrive at some future date that is fixed when the order is placed. We will now consider the special case encountered when a manufacturer can supply demanded items either from inventory or from current production. Since production itself requires some time, the replenishment of inventory items is not instantaneous. We will assume that production, like demand, occurs at some known and constant rate of B items per year. We will further assume that no backorders are allowed and that the production rate exceeds the demand rate, or $B > A$.

The Production Phase

Figure 7-4 illustrates such an inventory system. Each inventory cycle consists of two phases, depending on whether or not production is occurring. The *production phase* is represented by the upward-sloping triangle on the left. Although the total amount produced is Q, a portion of the items produced is siphoned off to customers before it can be stored, so that the maximum inventory build-up is

$$\text{Maximum inventory} = Q\left(\frac{B - A}{B}\right)$$

at which point production stops. The net accumulation of on-hand inventory occurs at the rate of $B - A$ units; the duration of the production phase is T_1.

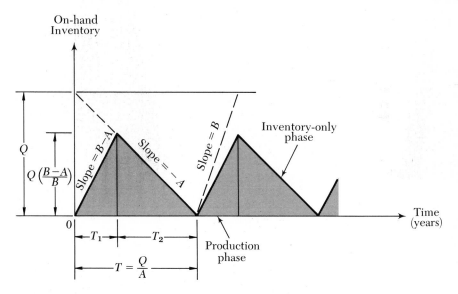

FIGURE 7-4
The production and inventory system when items are produced at a uniform rate.

The *demand-only phase*, represented by the downward-sloping triangle, then begins. During this stage, all demands are filled from inventory until the stock is totally depleted; the duration of the demand-only phase is T_2. The respective phase durations are

$$T_1 = \frac{Q}{B}$$

$$T_2 = T - T_1 = \frac{Q}{A} - \frac{Q}{B}$$

$$= Q\left(\frac{B-A}{AB}\right)$$

The Complete Model

In place of the usual ordering cost k, we now substitute the fixed cost of making a production run. This quantity is referred to as a *set-up cost* or a *start-up cost*. Like the ordering cost, the annual set-up cost is exactly the same as before:

$$\text{Annual set-up cost} = \left(\frac{A}{Q}\right)k$$

The inventory holding cost per cycle is hc multiplied by the average area under the combined triangle (which is the sum of the areas for the two smaller triangles), or

$$hc\left[\frac{1}{2}T_1Q\left(\frac{B-A}{B}\right) + \frac{1}{2}T_2Q\left(\frac{B-A}{B}\right)\right] = hc\left[\frac{Q^2(B-A)}{2B^2} + \frac{Q^2(B-A)^2}{2AB^2}\right]$$

$$= hc\frac{Q^2}{2A}\left(\frac{B-A}{B}\right)$$

Multiplying this result by the number of inventory cycles per year A/Q, we obtain

$$\text{Annual holding cost} = hc\left(\frac{Q}{2}\right)\left(\frac{B-A}{B}\right)$$

The total annual relevant cost is therefore

$$TC = \left(\frac{A}{Q}\right)k + hc\left(\frac{Q}{2}\right)\left(\frac{B-A}{B}\right)$$

which differs only slightly from this cost in the simple EOQ model. The minimum-cost production (order) quantity, often referred to as the *economic production quantity*, is found from

$$Q^* = \sqrt{\frac{2Ak}{hc}} \sqrt{\frac{B}{B-A}}$$

To illustrate, we will consider a manufacturer whose product demand is $A = 100,000$ units per year. Assume that the product can be produced at the rate of $B = 200,000$ units per year. Each production run costs $k = \$5,000$ to set up, and the variable production cost of each item is $c = \$10$. The annual cost per dollar value of holding items in inventory is $h = \$.20$.

The optimal production run is of size

$$Q^* = \sqrt{\frac{2(100,000)5,000}{.20(10)}} \sqrt{\frac{200,000}{200,000 - 100,000}}$$

$$= 31,623 \text{ items}$$

and each production run lasts

$$T_1^* = \frac{Q^*}{B} = \frac{31,623}{200,000} = .158 \text{ years, or approximately 58 days}$$

A new production run occurs every

$$T^* = \frac{Q^*}{A} = \frac{31,623}{100,000} = .316 \text{ years, or approximately 115 days}$$

The total annual relevant cost of the this production plan is

$$TC = \left(\frac{100,000}{31,623}\right)5,000 + .20(10)\left(\frac{31,623}{2}\right)\left(\frac{200,000 - 100,000}{200,000}\right)$$

$$= 15,811 + 15,812$$

$$= 31,623 \text{ dollars per year}$$

ADDITIONAL REMARKS 7-6

The EOQ (economic order quantity) models discussed in this chapter have been purposely simplified. More complex models are available. For instance, a second shortage penalty that does not depend on the duration of a backorder is sometimes included in more general representations. The models described here can be expanded to include several different types of items. These more advanced models consider constraints that might reflect limitations on storage space or on the dollar investment in inventory. Slight extensions of the basic EOQ models also permit the treatment of quantity discounts.

Perhaps the greatest deficiency of the simple EOQ models is that they do not reflect that uncertainties exist. Few real-life inventory systems are based on predictable, constant demands. Yet the models presented in this chapter set the stage for our examination of inventory policy formulation under uncertainty in Chapter 8. There we will see that the basic Wilson formula can often provide a solution that is very close to optimal, even though many of the assumptions on which it is based are not strictly true.

PROBLEMS

7-1   A department sells 1,000 waterbeds per year. The beds cost $400 each, and it costs $2,000 to place an order with the supplier. The annual cost per dollar value of holding items in inventory is $.25. Find the economic waterbed order quantity. How often should orders be placed?

7-2   Albers, Crumbly, and Itch sells mosquito repellents all over the world. Demand for the Malabug brand is 10,000 bottles per year. The African supplier charges AC&I $2 per bottle, and the fixed cost of placing an order for Malabug is $100. AC&I targets a 15% annual rate of return on working-capital funds. The physical storage cost of Malabug is fixed.
   (a) Determine the optimal order quantity and inventory cycle duration for Malabug.
   (b) How many orders should be placed each year?
   (c) Find the total annual relevant inventory cost of Malabug.

7-3   A car-parts wholesaler supplies 20 batteries to various service stations on each weekday. Batteries are purchased from the manufacturer in lots of 100 for $1,000 per lot. Multiple and fractional lots can be ordered at any time, and all orders are filled the next day. Each order placed with the manufacturer incurs a $50-handling charge and a $200 per-lot freight charge. The incremental cost is $.50 per year to store a battery in inventory. The wholesaler finances inventory investments by paying its holding company $1\frac{1}{2}\%$ monthly for borrowed funds.
   (a) Determine the values of k, A, c, and h.
   (b) How many batteries should be ordered, and how often should orders be placed to minimize total annual inventory cost?

7-4   Suppose that the store in Problem 7-2 can backorder Malabug when it is out of stock But since most customers are simply itching to go backpacking and may have to delay their departure to wait to purchase the repellant, there is a penalty of $10 per year in lost goodwill for every bottle short.
   (a) Determine the optimal order quantity, inventory level, and time between orders. What proportion of the time is Malabug out of stock?
   (b) Compute the total annual relevant inventory cost of the policy you found in (a). Is this cost larger or smaller than your answer to Problem 7-2(c)? Do you think

the same conclusion would be reached if the annual shortage penalty were $1,000 per bottle?

7-5 A hardware store periodically buys 10-penny size nails. The supplier will deliver any quantity of a particular order size for a charge of $1 plus $.20 per pound. It costs the store $.15 per dollar value of inventory items stored for one year. A total of 600 pounds of 10-penny nails are sold each year.

(a) How many pounds of nails should be ordered, and how often should orders be placed to minimize total annual inventory cost?

(b) Suppose that the hardware store has patient customers who will backorder 10-penny nails when they are out of stock. The annual cost of each pound of nails short is $.01. Determine the optimal order quantity. How many nails will have been backordered when each new shipment arrives?

7-6 The manufacturer of the nails in Problem 7-5 makes them at an annual rate of 400 tons, even though only 300 tons are demanded per year. The unit cost of manufacturing is $100 per ton, and it costs an additional $30 to set up a production run. The annual holding cost of the nails is $.20 per dollar value.

(a) What is the optimal number of tons that should be manufactured in a single production run? How often should the nails be produced? How long will a production run last?

(b) What is the manufacturer's total annual relevant inventory and production cost using the optimal policy you found in (a)?

7-7 The headquarters office for a large conglomerate buys 1,000 reams of stationery every two months at a cost of $5 per ream. Paper usage is uniform and constant over time. The cost of placing an order with the supplier is $50. Assume that the present inventory policy is optimal, so that it minimizes annual stationery inventory cost. How many reams will be demanded in one year? What annual cost per dollar value of holding items in inventory is implicit under the present policy?

7-8 Suppose that it costs the office in Problem 7-7 $2 to hold a ream of paper in inventory for one year.

(a) What is the annual cost per dollar value of holding items in inventory?

(b) Suppose that the policy of ordering 1,000 reams every two months must be reevaluated because shortages are now allowed. Assuming an annual penalty of $10 per ream short, determine the optimal order quantity and inventory level. How often should orders be placed?

7-9 The manufacturer of Snail Hail, a garden mollusk pesticide, distributes its product from a plant warehouse. The plant has the capacity to produce 1,000 tons per year at a variable cost of $100 per ton. However, only 200 tons of Snail Hail are sold annually. The cost of setting up a production run is $2,000. The net cost of holding the highly volatile Snail Hail in inventory is $.40 per dollar value per year.

(a) Find the economic production quantity.

(b) How long is each inventory cycle?

(c) What is the duration of a production run for Snail Hail?

7-10 Ace Widgets Supply distributes two products—Regular and Deluxe widgets—throughout the Midwest. The demands for the two items are independent; a total of 2,000 Regular and 4,000 Deluxe items are sold every year. The Regular items cost Ace $10 each; the Deluxe models cost twice as much. Ace's annual holding cost is $.25 for each dollar invested in inventory. The ordering cost is $100 per batch for each item. The Regular item may be ordered only when a Deluxe order is placed, but Regular widgets can be ordered less frequently than Deluxe widgets.

(a) Find the optimal order quantities of each item. What is the total annual relevant inventory cost in each case?

(b) If a maximum of $10,000 can be invested in inventory at any given time, will the quantities you found in (a) still be possible?

(c) Ace's warehouse can store a maximum of only 1,000 items. Are the quantities you found in (a) still possible?

(d) Suppose that the Regular and the Deluxe models must be ordered at the same time and that each order costs $200. Treating combinations of 1 Regular and 2 Deluxe units as a single item, determine the economic order quantity and the corresponding total annual relevant cost. Will this procedure be less costly than the one in (a)? Explain.

7-11 Mrs. Moo's is a self-sufficient dairy; all feed grasses are grown on the premises. To rejuvenate the grass and trigger growth, periodic fertilizing is necessary. The dairy herd eats full-grown grass at the rate of 5,000 acres per year. Each fertilizing costs $100 to set up and requires $50 worth of chemicals per acre to create full growth. It takes a fertilized acre one-tenth of a year to reach maturity. There are 1,000 acres of grassland at Mrs. Moo's. The dairy finances its chemical purchases through the local bank at a 10% annual interest rate.

(a) Determine the number of acres that should be fertilized in each application, how often fertilization should take place, and how many applications should be made each year.

(b) Do you think that it is totally satisfactory to apply the EOQ model to this problem? Explain.

7-12 A large vending-machine operator must establish a policy for periodically restocking its candy machines and collecting the coins deposited by customers. The total labor cost of restocking a machine is $7, most of which is due to travel time. Each machine can hold quite a lot of candy, so the machines do not need to be filled to capacity. All machines are identical, and each satisfies a demand of 5,000 candy bars per year. Candy bars cost $.10 each and are sold for $.25. The firm's annual opportunity cost of working capital is 20%. A significant aspect in establishing a policy is that all those quarters are uselessly locked up in coin boxes, so that the quicker retrieval of these funds translates directly into smaller working-capital requirements.

(a) Determine the values of c and h. (Assume that the same cost of working capital applies to the value of the candy and to the value of the coins. Also assume that the average inventory of candy bars is the same as the average inventory of quarters.)

(b) Determine the restocking quantity that minimizes total annual cost. How often should the machines be restocked?

8

Inventory Decisions with Uncertain Factors

Most inventory decisions must be made under uncertain conditions, so that one or more quantities must be represented by random variables having probability distributions. Real-world demands are usually not constant and uniform, and probabilities should be used to represent them. Mathematical models involving probability are often referred to as *stochastic models*. In situations that do not involve uncertainty, such as the ones we discussed in Chapter 7, the analytical procedures employ *deterministic models*.

Deterministic models are limited in scope and can be applied only approximately to most real-world decision-making problems. They do, however, provide points of departure for developing more realistic methods of analysis. It is easier to cope with uncertainty when an analytical framework has already been established by means of deterministic models. But making the leap from certainty into the world of uncertainty presents new difficulties. We encountered some of these in chapters 5 and 6 when we evaluated various decision-making criteria under uncertain conditions.

Inventory models involving probability are generally based on the Bayes decision rule. The optimal inventory policy is found by considering *expected* profits or costs, so that the best we can do is to maximize or minimize long-run "average" profits or costs. Thus, even an optimal policy can lead to a range of outcomes from poor to excellent. The actual result is determined largely by luck. Such a lack of determinism on the part of the decision maker is an unavoidable burden we face whenever we attempt to cope with uncertainty.

8-1   A SIMPLE INVENTORY DECISION: THE *PLAYBOY* PROBLEM

To set the stage for analyzing inventory decisions from explicit mathematical models, we will begin by treating the choice of inventory policy like any other decision to be made under uncertainty. First, we will establish a payoff measure that ranks alternatives in terms of how well they meet the decision maker's goals. Then we will identify the alternative inventory policies and use them, together with uncertain demand events, to construct a payoff table. Next, we will obtain probability values for each possible demand level, apply the Bayes decision rule, and choose the inventory policy that provides the best expected payoff. At this point, the optimal decision will be indicated.

The Nature of Uncertain Demand

As an illustration, consider the problem a small drugstore faces in trying to determine how many copies of various magazines to order. In particular, the drugstore owner wants to estimate how many copies of the October issue of *Playboy* to stock. Assume that past demand has provided a history of customer interest in this product and that the owner knows the frequencies of the various demand levels, which serve to establish probabilities for demand in future months.

Demand is a totally distinct notion from *sales*. A retailer can only sell a product if it is in stock or if a customer is willing to order and wait for it. *Playboy* is not an item that customers will order (except by subscription); if they do not see it on the shelf, no sale can be made. Yet, the desire to buy a copy of *Playboy* is a demand. Thus, we might define the demand for an item as the *intent to buy* it. Such a demand will result in either a sale or the loss of a potential sale (when the item is not in stock).

Suppose that the drugstore owner has determined the following probability distribution for the demand for the October issue of *Playboy*.

Copies Demanded	Probability
$D = 20$	.2
$D = 21$	.4
$D = 22$	.3
$D = 23$	.1

Alternative order quantities must be considered. Obviously, *Playboy* is a profitable item to include on the magazine rack, so the owner will not want to stock less than the minimum demand (if any issues are stocked at all, which is another

TABLE 8-1
Payoff Table for the *Playboy* Problem

Demand Event	Order Quantity Act			
	$Q = 20$	$Q = 21$	$Q = 22$	$Q = 23$
$D = 20$	$18.00	$16.60	$15.20	$13.80
$D = 21$	$18.00	$18.90	$17.50	$16.10
$D = 22$	$18.00	$18.90	$19.80	$18.40
$D = 23$	$18.00	$18.90	$19.80	$20.70

question entirely). Also, there is no advantage to stocking more than the maximum demand. Thus, any order quantity below $Q = 20$ or above $Q = 23$ copies is an inadmissible act (20 copies must always be more profitable than 19 or less copies, stocking 23 copies is clearly superior to ordering 24).

Maximizing Expected Payoff

Playboy is purchased directly from the local distributor at an assumed price of $1.60 and sells for $2.50 per copy. Unsold copies are returned at the end of the month for a $.20 credit. We assume the drugstore owner's goal is long-run profit maximization, so that the payoff table in Table 8-1 has been constructed using monthly *Playboy* profit as the payoff measure. In calculating the profits for each act and event combination, we assume whenever Q is greater than D, that $Q - D$ unsold *Playboys* will be returned for the $.20 credit. Also, when Q is smaller than D, we assume that the excess demand is not filled and the disappointed customer must buy the October *Playboy* elsewhere. No penalty is considered for being short.

We assume that the owner will choose the value of Q that maximizes expected profit. Table 8-2 shows the calculations involved. The optimal order

TABLE 8-2
Expected Payoffs for the *Playboy* Problem

Demand Event	Probability	Payoff × Probability			
		$Q = 20$	$Q = 21$	$Q = 22$	$Q = 23$
$D = 20$	.2	$ 3.60	$ 3.32	$ 3.04	$ 2.76
$D = 21$	.4	7.20	7.56	7.00	6.44
$D = 22$	.3	5.40	5.67	5.94	5.52
$D = 23$	.1	1.80	1.89	1.98	1.07
Expected payoffs:		$18.00	$18.44	$17.96	$16.79
			Maximum		

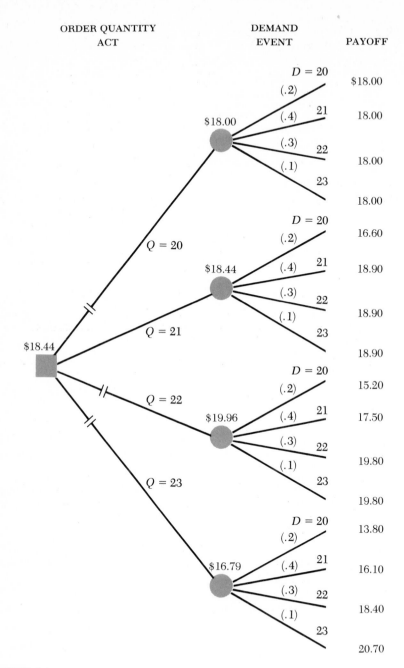

ORDER QUANTITY   DEMAND
ACT   EVENT   PAYOFF

FIGURE 8-1
Decision tree diagram for the *Playboy* problem.

quantity is $Q = 21$ *Playboy*s. This same decision could be analyzed in terms of a decision tree diagram. Figure 8-1 illustrates the applicable decision tree, where backward induction leads to the identical result.

MARGINAL ANALYSIS: THE NEWSBOY PROBLEM   **8-2**

We analyzed the *Playboy* problem using only the basic concepts of decision making under uncertainty. This problem typifies inventory policy decisions when the demand for a product is uncertain and its lifetime is limited, so that a single time period applies. Such a perishable product is epitomized by the daily newspaper, which has an effective demand lasting only one day. A news vendor has one opportunity to decide how many copies of today's *Wall Street Journal* to stock. An entire class of inventory decisions of identical structure is referred to as the *newsboy problem*.

It is convenient to develop a mathematical model to solve this type of problem. Although analysis using a payoff table or a decision tree is effective for small-scale problems like our *Playboy* example, a large number of alternatives or possible events makes these procedures impractical.

The Mathematical Model

In its simplest form, the objective of the newsboy problem is to decide how many items Q should be stocked at the beginning of the inventory cycle. The uncertain demand D expresses the number of items that customers will require during this period. Two types of outcomes may occur. If demand is less than or equal to the order quantity, sales will equal the quantity demanded; if demand is greater than the initial stock, sales will equal the order quantity:

$$\text{Sales} = \begin{cases} D \text{ if } D \le Q \\ Q \text{ if } D > Q \end{cases}$$

Three cost elements are considered:

$c =$ Unit procurement cost

$h =$ Additional cost of each item held at the end of the inventory cycle

$p =$ Penalty for each item short

For the present, we will assume that there is no fixed ordering cost. The unit holding cost ordinarily represents the disposal cost of the unsold items in the ending inventory. If these items have any further limited economic use, h represents the unit disposal cost minus the salvage value (so that h can be negative). The shortage penalty for each item demanded beyond the quantity stocked includes the value of the loss of customer goodwill. In addition, p reflects the *lost revenue* from missing a sale; the reason for this is explained in the following discussion.

As we did in the *Playboy* problem, we will assume that the news vendor's objective is to maximize expected profit or to minimize expected cost for the inventory period. This can be achieved only when revenue is assumed to be independent of inventory policy, which is not strictly true when the potential for lost sales exists. For example, if the news vendor pays $.20 for each paper and sells it for $.25, then the revenue consists of $.25 times the demand minus $.25 times the unfilled demand if shortages arise. We can ignore the former, since it is unaffected by inventory policy. But the latter is the revenue lost due to shortages and must be treated as a cost of unfilled demand. The full $.25 (not just the $.05 gross profit) must therefore be included in the shortage penalty, along with any other amounts identified in that category, such as the loss of goodwill. In effect, the shortage penalty p itself can be considered lost revenue. Viewed differently, the revenue lost due to shortages would be identical to the out-of-pocket cost the news vendor would incur if shortages had to be filled by purchasing papers from another dealer at the full $.25 retail price.

To obtain the expected cost, we will assume that probabilities $\Pr[D = d]$ for possible levels of demand d are available in tabular form. (It is convenient to use capital D to denote the actual but unknown demand and lower-case d to represent any one of the many possible demands.) For an order quantity of Q when demand is d, the total cost is

$$TC = cQ + \begin{cases} h(Q - d) & \text{if } d \leq Q \\ p(d - Q) & \text{if } d > Q \end{cases}$$

Note that the procurement cost c applies to the ordered quantity Q and not to the demand. The unit holding cost h applies only to the surplus items procured beyond the amount demanded, represented by the difference $Q - d$. The shortage penalty p applies only to the deficit in available items below the actual demand, which is denoted by the the quantity $d - Q$. The *total expected cost* TEC is found by applying the appropriate probability weights and summing over all possibilities, or

$$TEC(Q) = cQ + \sum_{d=0}^{Q} h(Q - d)\Pr[D = d] + \sum_{d > Q} p(d - Q)\Pr[D = d]$$

Note that the total expected cost depends on what value of Q is chosen.

Finding the Optimal Solution Through Marginal Analysis

To facilitate our explanation of how to find the optimal order quantity that minimizes total expected cost, we will develop the news vendor's problem. We already know that the unit procurement cost $c = \$.20$ and the shortage penalty $p = \$.25$. Although reprocessors sometimes buy unsold newspapers, the cyclical demand for paper salvage is down and they are not buying now. Unsold papers must be hauled to the dump at a cost of $h = \$.01$ each. The probability distribution in Table 8-3 is assumed to apply for daily demand. This table provides the cumulative probabilities for demand and the calculation of expected demand, which is equal to 49.50 papers.

The optimal solution could be obtained by calculating a payoff table with 11 events (one for each possible demand) and 11 order quantity acts. Using cost as the payoff measure, we could then find the expected cost of each value of Q by multiplying the respective column values by the probabilities for d and summing. The optimal Q would have the smallest expected cost. However, it is simpler to follow another approach called *marginal analysis*.

Marginal analysis is based on *convexity*—a mathematical property of expressions of the form $TEC(Q)$. In principle, any mathematical expression is convex when its value decreases steadily at a progressively slower rate for

TABLE 8-3
Probability Distribution Data for the Newsboy Problem

(1) Possible Demand d	(2) Probability $\Pr[D = d]$	(3) Cumulative Probability $\Pr[D \leq d]$	(4) Demand × Probability
45	.05	.05	2.25
46	.06	.11	2.76
47	.09	.20	4.23
48	.12	.32	5.76
49	.17	.49	8.33
50	.20	.69	10.00
51	.12	.81	6.12
52	.08	.89	4.16
53	.06	.95	3.18
54	.04	.99	2.16
55	.01	1.00	.55
	1.00		Expected demand = 49.50

increasing levels of the independent variable until a minimum is achieved, after which values of the expression increase steadily at an increasing rate. This means that $TEC(Q)$ achieves its minimum value at the lowest level of Q that is followed by an increase in total expected cost. This feature is illustrated in Figure 8-2.

We can find the smallest order quantity that is followed by an increase in total expected cost by considering all of the differences between successive $TECs$:

$$\text{Difference} = TEC(Q + 1) - TEC(Q)$$

The smallest Q having a non-negative difference is optimal.

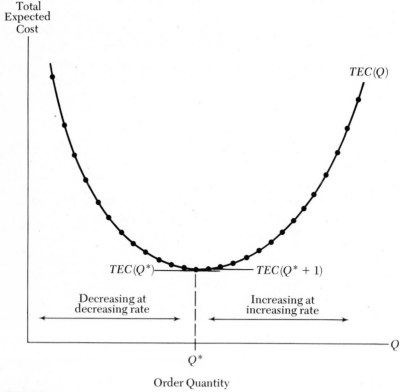

Order Quantity

FIGURE 8-2

The convexity principle in marginal analysis.

A mathematical analysis shows that the successive total cost difference is*

$$\text{Difference} = c + h \Pr[D \le Q] - p(1 - \Pr[D \le Q])$$

which must be greater than or equal to zero. Notice that this expression involves only the unit cost constants and the cumulative probability that demand falls at or below the order quantity. The condition for the optimal order quantity is established by setting the total expected cost difference greater than or equal to zero and rearranging terms.

The optimal order quantity Q^* is the smallest level of Q such that

$$\frac{p - c}{p + h} \le \Pr[D \le Q]$$

This tells us that we need to calculate only the ratio $(p - c)/(p + h)$, using the constants given for the problem, and establish the cumulative probability for demand. The smallest demand with a cumulative probability that exceeds this ratio is equal to the order quantity that minimizes total expected cost.

Returning to the news vendor example, we can calculate the ratio

$$\frac{p - c}{p + h} = \frac{.25 - .20}{.25 + .01} = .192$$

From column (3) of Table 8-3, we can see that the smallest cumulative demand probability that exceeds this value is .20, which applies when the demand is for 47 papers. Thus, $Q^* = 47$, and the news vendor will minimize expected cost by stocking exactly 47 papers. The total expected cost of this inventory policy is calculated in Table 8-4 to be $TEC(47) = \$10.0666$. Notice that this optimal order quantity is less than the expected demand of 49.50. Depending on the values for c, h, and p, Q^* may lie above or below the expected demand.

---

* The difference in *holding costs only* is

$$\sum_{d=0}^{Q+1} h[(Q + 1) - d] \Pr[D = d] - \sum_{d=0}^{Q} h(Q - d) \Pr[D = d] = h \Pr[D \le Q]$$

Likewise, the difference in *shortage costs only* is

$$\sum_{d>Q+1} p[d - (Q + 1)]\Pr[D = d] - \sum_{d>Q} p(d - Q)\Pr[D = d] = -p(1 - \Pr[D \le Q])$$

Combining these results with the fact that ordering $Q + 1$ items involves one unit of further procurement (an expenditure of c) gives us the above expression.

TABLE 8-4

Total Expected Cost Calculation for the News Vendor's Optimal Inventory Policy ($Q^* = 47$)

Possible Demand d	Probability $Pr[D = d]$	Holding Cost $.01(47 - d)$	Shortage Cost $.25(d - 47)$	Cost × Probability
45	.05	$.02	—	$.0010
46	.06	.01	—	.0006
47	.09	0	—	0
48	.12	—	$ .25	.0300
49	.17	—	.50	.0850
50	.20	—	.75	.1500
51	.12	—	1.00	.1200
52	.08	—	1.25	.1000
53	.06	—	1.50	.0900
54	.04	—	1.75	.0700
55	.01	—	2.00	.0200
	1.00			$.6666

$$cQ = \$.20(47) = \$9.40$$
$$TEC(47) = \$9.40 + \$.6666 = \$10.0666$$

The Impact of Cost Elements on Total Expected Cost

The shortage penalty p is perhaps the most elusive cost element in inventory decisions because it is difficult to quantify the loss of goodwill. For this reason, it may be desirable to analyze the inventory decision for a range of levels of p. Such optional additional work is referred to as *sensitivity analysis,* because it tells us just how sensitive the optimal solution is to variations in the value assumed for the parameter constant. Table 8-5 shows the total expected costs for the newsboy problem when p is .25, .30, .35, .40, or .45, with $c = .20$ and $h = .01$. Notice that within each row, at each level of Q, the $TECs$ increase as p increases (except in the last row, where Q is equal to the maximum possible demand and shortages are impossible). This is because a greater shortage penalty can only increase total inventory cost.

It is interesting to see how Q^* changes as p is increased. When p is raised from .25 to .30, the optimal order quantity jumps from $Q^* = 47$ to $Q^* = 49$ and remains at that level through $p = .40$. At $p = .45$, the optimal order quantity jumps again to $Q^* = 50$. Thus, we can see that when shortage penalties are more severe, larger order quantities (larger levels of Q^*) are required to minimize total expected costs.

Similar conclusions may be drawn about the other cost parameters. In general, TEC will increase as either c or h increases, but the relationship to Q^* will differ. Since the optimal order quantity is determined by the ratio

TABLE 8-5
Total Expected Costs for the Newsboy Problem at Several Levels for the Shortage Penalty

Order Quantity Q	Total Expected Cost $TEC(Q)$				
	$p = .25$	$p = .30$	$p = .35$	$p = .40$	$p = .45$
45	$10.1250	$10.3500	$10.5750	$10.8000	$11.0250
46	10.0880	10.2655	10.4430	10.6205	10.7980
47	10.0666*	10.1996	10.3326	10.4656	10.5986
48	10.0686	10.1616	10.2546	10.3476	10.4406
49	10.1018	10.1608*	10.2198*	10.2788*	10.3378
50	10.1792	10.2127	10.2462	10.2797	10.3132*
51	10.3086	10.3266	10.3446	10.3626	10.3806
52	10.4692	10.4777	10.4862	10.4947	10.5032
53	10.6506	10.6536	10.6566	10.6596	10.6626
54	10.8476	10.8481	10.8486	10.8491	10.8496
55	11.0550	11.0550	11.0550	11.0550	11.0550
$\dfrac{p-c}{p+h}$	.192	.323	.417	.488	.543
Q^*	47	49	49	49	50

$(p - c)/(p + h)$ and the cumulative probability for demand, Q^* increases as the ratio increases. Thus, holding p and h fixed, a reduction in c will make the numerator larger and increase Q^*, whereas the reverse is true for an increase in c. This reflects the fact that a smaller procurement cost makes it less painful to hold unsold items. Increasing the level of h will increase the denominator, thereby reducing the ratio, and lowering the level of Q^*, whereas a reduction in h will increase Q^*. Thus, everything else being equal, the more expensive it is to dispose of unsold items, the lower the order quantity should be.

CONTINUOUS PROBABILITY DISTRIBUTION FOR DEMAND: THE CHRISTMAS TREE PROBLEM 8-3

When the number of possible demands is large—as it would be when hundreds or thousands of units are sold daily—it is usually convenient to use a continuous approximation for the demand probability distribution. The single-period models discussed thus far can be adapted to continuous probability distributions. As was true for the discrete probabilities applicable in these earlier models, the order level depends only on the cumulative probability for demand. However, there is one change: Q^* is chosen so that the ratio is exactly equal to the cumulative probability that demand lies at or below that level. *When demand is a continuous random variable, the optimal order quantity Q^* is that level of Q where*

$$\frac{p - c}{p + h} = \Pr[D \leq Q]$$

Suppose that the demand for Christmas trees experienced by a particular Gotham City seller is approximately normally distributed with a mean of $\mu = 2{,}000$ trees and a standard deviation of $\sigma = 500$ trees. The trees sell for an average of $10 and cost $3 each. The city license requires that all unsold trees be converted into mulch pulp, which is donated to the Gotham City Parks Department; the cost of pulverization averages $.50 per tree. There is no loss of goodwill from shortages, and the seller has already committed funds to any fixed costs involved. How many trees should be ordered from Canadian suppliers to minimize inventory costs (and thereby maximize profits)?

The applicable cost constants (in dollars) are

$$c = 3 \qquad h = .50 \qquad p = 10$$

The following ratio applies:

$$\frac{p - c}{p + h} = \frac{10 - 3}{10 + .50} = .67$$

This ratio establishes the cumulative demand probability that determines Q^*, or

$$\Pr[D \leq Q] = .67$$

Figure 8-3 will help to explain how the value of Q^* is obtained. The shaded area under the normal curve for Christmas tree demand is equal to the cumulative probability of .67. The portion of this area that is above the mean is equal to .17, which corresponds to a normal deviate value of $z = .44$ (see Appendix Table B). This expresses the number of standard deviations that Q^* lies beyond the mean, so that

$$Q^* = \mu + z\sigma$$

Substituting $\mu = 2{,}000$ and $\sigma = 500$ trees into this equation, we obtain

$$Q^* = 2{,}000 + .44(500) = 2{,}220 \text{ trees}$$

The Gotham City seller should order 2,220 Christmas trees.

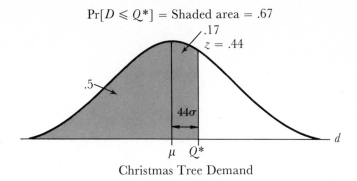

Christmas Tree Demand

FIGURE 8-3
The normal curve used to establish Q^*.

MULTI-PERIOD INVENTORY POLICIES 8-4

Until this point, we have discussed only single-period inventory problems. These models generally apply to perishable items that can be ordered only once and that cannot be held in inventory to satisfy demands occurring in another period. It is far more common, however, to encounter the problem of establishing an inventory policy for items that can be stored over several time periods and that can be reordered with considerable flexibility.

We began our initial discussion of inventory decisions in Chapter 7 with what we may now refer to as *multi-period inventory* policies. At this point, we must begin to cope with uncertainties. The two major uncertain variables encountered in inventory decisions are *demand* and *lead time* required to fill orders.

The mathematical procedures for analyzing multi-period inventory decisions under uncertainty fall into two categories. *Continuous review models* assume that a continuous monitorship of inventory positions takes place, so that decision rules regarding replenishment are based on the current inventory position. These models give rise to (r, Q) policies, and orders are triggered whenever the current inventory position falls below the *reorder point r*, at which point Q items are ordered.

Figure 8-4 illustrates the behavior of an inventory system when demand and lead time are uncertain. Notice that inventory depletion occurs erratically due to the varying intensities of demand. Orders are placed whenever the inventory position falls below r. But continued variations in demand and unpredictable lead times cause shortages to occur in some periods and not in others.

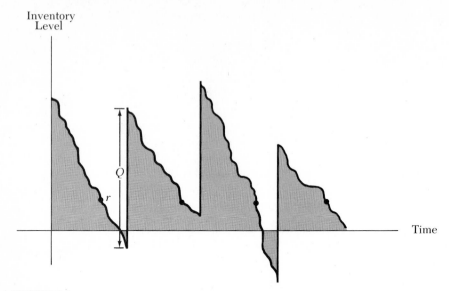

FIGURE 8-4
Inventory system using (r, Q) policy with uncertain demand and lead time.

This erratic behavior results in varying cycle durations and beginning inventory positions.

The other category of multi-period inventory decisions involves *periodic review models*. These models apply when circumstances permit a physical count of the inventory items to be made only once every week, month, quarter, or year. In such inventory systems, the current inventory position remains unknown between inventory tallies. Periodic review models differ considerably from the (r, Q) type of model that we will consider in this chapter.

Here, we will present two simple continuous review models that may be employed to find the optimal multi-period inventory policy. Our models are only approximately correct, although the solutions they provide are usually as adequate as more complex formulations. We will consider only the case in which *short items are backordered* and no sales are lost due to shortages. (Although only a minor adjustment in these models is required to consider the case of lost sales, a detailed discussion of this application is beyond the scope of this book.)

The EOQ Model for Uncertain Demand

Because several time periods are involved in a multi-period inventory decision, we will return to the problem objective we established in Chapter 7 of minimizing total annual relevant cost. Since demands and lead times are now uncertain, we minimize *expected cost*, which is the sum of the following expected values:

Annual ordering cost
Annual holding cost
Annual shortage cost

Although demand is no longer presumed to be certain, we will assume that the mean annual demand rate applies uniformly over time. We use the symbol

A = Mean annual demand rate

(The *mean* demand rate is constant, but demands can vary from period to period.) If Q items are ordered each time at a cost of k per order, it then follows that

$$\text{Expected annual ordering cost} = \left(\frac{A}{Q}\right)k$$

which was true for the earlier models described in Chapter 7.

The actual demand D over any interval of time is uncertain and must be specified in terms of a probability distribution. Instead of focusing on some fixed calendar period like a day, week, or month, our model will consider the level of demand during the lead time for filling an order. For this purpose, we will employ *the probability distribution of lead-time demand*, which we will distinguish from the earlier single-period distributions by a subscript L:

Probability of d units demanded in lead time = $\text{Pr}_L[D = d]$

This distribution reflects two uncertainties: one regarding the demands themselves and one surrounding the duration of the lead time. Our model will focus on the expected value of D:

μ = Mean lead-time demand

Each inventory cycle begins when an order arrives. Stock is then depleted until it falls below the reorder point r, which is assumed to exceed μ, and a new order is placed. Continued depletion occurs until the order arrives. Any items short are then provided from the incoming shipment. The expected level of inventory just before the order arrives is $r - \mu$, so that the subsequent cycle begins with an expected inventory of $Q + r - \mu$ items. Because the mean rate of depletion is uniform, the average inventory level during a cycle must be the average of these quantities. Thus

$$\text{Expected average cycle inventory} = \frac{1}{2}[(Q + r - \mu) + r - \mu]$$

$$= \frac{Q}{2} + r - \mu$$

As we did in the EOQ models described in Chapter 7, we let h represent the annual cost per dollar value of holding items in inventory. From this, it follows that

$$\text{Expected annual holding cost} = hc\left[\frac{Q}{2} + r - \mu\right]$$

The most complicated part of the EOQ model for uncertain demand involves the shortage cost component. The shortage cost depends on the number of items backordered in each cycle, which is a random variable due to the uncertain lead-time demand. Since items are only backordered when lead-time demand exceeds the reorder point r, we can determine the expected number of backorders per inventory cycle

$$B(r) = \sum_{d > r} (d - r) \, \text{Pr}_L[D = d]$$

Multiplying $B(r)$ by the expected number of cycles per year A/Q and the penalty p for each item short, we obtain

$$\text{Expected annual shortage cost} = p\left(\frac{A}{Q}\right) B(r)$$

In keeping with the single-cycle models employed in this chapter, we let p represent the cost of each item short, regardless of how long it is backordered. This parameter therefore differs from its counterpart in the backordering model we examined in Chapter 7, where the penalty applied to the duration of the shortage as well. Since backordering occurs, no lost sales revenue is included in p.

The total annual expected cost can be expressed as

$$TEC(r, Q) = \left(\frac{A}{Q}\right) k + hc\left[\frac{Q}{2} + r - \mu\right] + p\left(\frac{A}{Q}\right) B(r)$$

Our objective is to find the values of Q and r that minimize this expression.

The following procedure permits us to determine the optimal levels of these variables:

(1) For a given order quantity Q, the optimal reorder point r is the *smallest* quantity having a cumulative lead-time demand probability such that

$$1 - \frac{hcQ}{pA} \leq \Pr_L[D \leq r]$$

(2) For a given reorder point r, the optimal order quantity is found from

$$Q = \sqrt{\frac{2A[k + pB(r)]}{hc}}$$

To solve for either r or Q, the value of the other variable must be known. Before we can begin, a seed value must be obtained for one of these variables. This value is then used to determine the level of the second variable, which in turn is used to refine the value of the first variable. This procedure continues— using the last Q to obtain the next r and that r to obtain the next Q—until no values change.

A good starting or seed value can be obtained by using the Wilson formula from Chapter 7 for the economic order quantity when no backordering is allowed:

$$Q_1 = \sqrt{\frac{2Ak}{hc}}$$

The subscript 1 simply indicates that this is the first attempt to determine the value of the order quantity.

A Stationery Store Illustration

Suppose that a stationery store stocks carbon typewriter ribbons. The demands and lead times are uncertain, but historical experience indicates that the lead-time demand distribution in Table 8-6 applies. The mean annual demand is 1,500 ribbons per year; the cost of placing an order is $5; each ribbon has a wholesale price of $1.50; the store finances its working capital through bank loans at a rate of 12% per annum; and the store incurs an estimated

TABLE 8-6
Lead-Time Demand Probability Distribution for Carbon Typewriter Ribbons

Possible Demand d	Probability $\Pr_L[D = d]$	Demand × Probability	Cumulative Probability $\Pr_L[D \leq d]$
0	.01	0	.01
1	.07	.07	.08
2	.16	.32	.24
3	.20	.60	.44
4	.19	.76	.63
5	.16	.80	.79
6	.10	.60	.89
7	.06	.42	.95
8	.03	.24	.98
9	.01	.09	.99
10	.01	.10	1.00
	1.00	$\mu = 4.00$	

penalty in future profits of \$.50 for each ribbon short and backordered. Thus, we have the following parameters:

$$A = 1,500$$
$$k = \$5$$
$$c = \$1.50$$
$$h = \$.12$$
$$p = \$.50$$

and the mean lead-time demand is computed in Table 8-6 as $\mu = 4$.

The starting value of the order quantity is

$$Q_1 = \sqrt{\frac{2(1,500)5}{.12(1.5)}} = 289$$

Using the value $Q = 289$ in step (1), we compute

$$1 - \frac{hcQ}{pA} = 1 - \frac{.12(1.5)289}{.5(1,500)} = .93$$

The smallest cumulative probability greater than or equal to this value in Table 8-6 is

$$\Pr_L[D \leq 7] = .95$$

so that the reorder point is $r = 7$ ribbons.

Using $r = 7$ in step (2), first we must evaluate the corresponding expected number of backorders per cycle $B(r) = B(7)$. This quantity is computed as follows:

Demand d	Probability $Pr_L[D = d]$	Difference $d - r = d - 7$	Difference × Probability
8	.03	1	.03
9	.01	2	.02
10	.01	3	.03
			$B(7) = .08$

Substituting $B(7) = .08$ into the expression for Q gives us

$$Q = \sqrt{\frac{2(1,500)[5 + .5(.08)]}{.12(1.5)}} = 290$$

Since this result differs from the initial value of $Q = 289$, we must continue the procedure with a second *iteration*.

Returning to step (1), we use $Q = 290$ to recompute the reorder point. First, we find

$$1 - \frac{hcQ}{pA} = 1 - \frac{.12(1.5)290}{.5(1,500)} = .93$$

which is identical to the cumulative probability indicated for $r = 7$ that we found before. The reorder point does not change. Thus, the values in the optimal (r, Q) policy are

$$r = 7 \quad \text{and} \quad Q^* = 290$$

so that $Q^* = 290$ ribbons should be ordered whenever the current inventory falls below $r = 7$. The total annual expected cost of this policy is

$$TEC = \left(\frac{1,500}{290}\right)5 + .12(1.5)\left[\frac{290}{2} + 7 - 4\right] + .50\left(\frac{1,500}{290}\right)(.08)$$

$$= 25.86 + 26.64 + .21$$

$$= 52.71 \text{ dollars}$$

Notice that the Wilson formula for the simple inventory model provides an order quantity of $Q_1 = 289$, which is very close to the final optimal solution of $Q^* = 290$. Although the starting and final values will not always be so close (this depends on the various parameter values and on the lead-time demand distribution), this illustration shows that sometimes the simple inventory model works quite well—even though it assumes that demand is certain and constant.

The expected inventory on-hand when an order arrives is called the *safety stock*. This is the difference between the reorder point and mean lead time, or

$$\text{Safety stock} = r - \mu$$

In this illustration, the safety stock is $7 - 4 = 3$ ribbons. On the average, when the optimal (7, 290) policy is employed, 3 ribbons will be on hand when any order arrives.

8-5 THE EOQ MODEL FOR NORMALLY DISTRIBUTED DEMAND

When large inventory systems are comprised of many units or when a product such as gasoline is sold in divisable quantities, it is convenient to represent lead-time demand with a continuous probability distribution. Only slight modifications are required to use the preceding model to find the optimal (r, Q) policy when lead time is normally distributed.

The primary change is the way in which the expected number of backorders per cycle $B(r)$ is computed. This is somewhat complicated due to the nature of continuous random variables. To illustrate the principles involved, we will consider Figure 8-5, where the normal curve for lead-time demand is super-

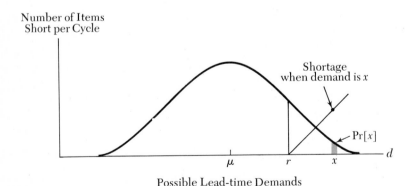

Possible Lead-time Demands

FIGURE 8-5
Graphical explanation of a normal loss function.

imposed on a graph relating number of items short to possible demands. The line rising at a 45° angle with a slope of 1 indicates that each unit demanded beyond the recorder point is a shortage and must be backordered.

The Normal Loss Function

Recall that the *area* under the normal curve provides the probability values. By dividing the area in the upper tail beyond r into small intervals, we can see how the desired expected value can be computed. If the area corresponding to each interval is multiplied by the shortage at a representative demand for that interval, as illustrated at point x in Figure 8-5, and then summed, the resulting value approximates the expected number of backorders. Fortunately, it is not necessary to make this approximation, since a table has been constructed for this purpose. Thus, we compute

$$B(r) = \sigma L\left(\frac{r - \mu}{\sigma}\right)$$

where

μ = mean lead-time demand

σ = standard deviation in lead-time demand

L is the *normal loss function*, and its values are listed in Appendix Table C.*

A Gasoline Refinery Illustration

We can illustrate this normal demand model with an example of how to find the optimal inventory policy for unleaded gasoline at an oil refinery. Due to the varying availability of crude-oil and other petroleum processing requirements, the starting time for processing a batch of unleaded gasoline is unpredictable. The lead time is the period from the point that an order is issued until the unleaded gasoline product begins to flow into the holding tanks. We will assume that the demand while this is happening is normally distributed with a mean of $\mu = 200{,}000$ liters and a standard deviation of $\sigma = 20{,}000$ liters. When the unleaded tanks are empty, trucks scheduled to deliver that fuel are dispatched with other gasolines, and the unleaded customers receive their backorders later via a special delivery.

---

* This function is ordinarily used in calculating expected opportunity losses, which accounts for its name. These applications will be discussed in Chapter 19.

The mean annual demand rate for unleaded fuel from this refinery is $A = 40$ million liters per year. The fixed cost of a production run is $k = \$1,000$, and the wholesale value of this gasoline is $c = \$.40$ per liter. The annual opportunity cost per dollar value of funds tied up in inventory is $h = \$.20$. From the refinery's point of view, the only shortage cost for backordering fuel is the expense of the special delivery, which exceeds regular costs by $p = \$.05$ per liter. (For simplicity, we will assume that the production rate is so much greater than the inventory depletion rate that the savings in holding costs while simultaneously filling and emptying the holding tanks are too small to be significant.)

First Iteration. The first step in finding the optimal order quantity is to determine a starting value

$$Q_1 = \sqrt{\frac{2(40,000,000)(1,000)}{.20(.40)}} = 1,000,000 \text{ liters}$$

We then use this value of Q to calculate

$$1 - \frac{hcQ}{pA} = 1 - \frac{.20(.40)(1,000,000)}{.05(40,000,000)} = .96$$

The reorder point r is the lead-time demand with a cumulative probability *equal* to this result (since the distribution is continuous). This corresponds to a *normal deviate* z for the area under the standard normal curve. We choose the normal deviate with the area between the mean and z that is closest to $.96 - .5 = .46$. Reading Appendix Table B in reverse, we obtain $z = 1.75$. This means that the reorder point r lies $z = 1.75$ standard deviations above the mean lead-time demand. Thus

$$r = \mu + z\sigma$$
$$= 200,000 + 1.75(20,000)$$
$$= 235,000 \text{ liters}$$

This figure is then used to calculate Q, again by following step (2) on page 191. This requires computing the expected number of backorders in an inventory cycle $B(r)$. For $r = 235,000$ liters

$$B(235,000) = (20,000)L\left(\frac{235,000 - 200,000}{20,000}\right)$$
$$= (20,000)L(1.75)$$

From Appendix Table C, we find that $L(1.75) = .01617$, so that

$$B(235,000) = (20,000)(.01617) = 323.4$$

Substituting this value and the other parameter values into the equation for Q gives us the improved order quantity value

$$Q = \sqrt{\frac{2(40,000,000)[1,000 + .05(323.4)]}{.20(.40)}} = 1,008,050 \text{ liters}$$

Since this value differs from the starting value of $Q_1 = 1,000,000$, a further iteration is required.

Second Iteration. We repeat step (1), using the improved order quantity to calculate

$$1 - \frac{hcQ}{pA} = 1 - \frac{.20(.40)(1,008,050)}{.05(40,000,000)} = .9597$$

The closest normal deviate corresponding to .9597 is $z = 1.75$, which is identical to the normal deviate in the first iteration. *No further steps are required*, since the value of r, and therefore of Q, do not change.

The optimal policy is

$$Q^* = 1,008,050 \text{ liters}$$

$$r = 235,000 \text{ liters}$$

ANALYTIC AND NUMERICAL SOLUTION METHODS   8-6

Methods for analyzing multi-period inventory decisions can be quite complex. These methods may be divided into two categories. *Analytic methods* solve the model mathematically, giving precise answers that lead to truly optimal inventory policies. All of the procedures we have described thus far are analytic methods. Unfortunately, we have found that the problem situations to which a particular mathematical model can be applied are severely limited. Often, the representation of the inventory system itself must be simplified or slightly changed to make an existing model fit the situation. This can lead to decidedly inferior solutions despite the mathematical perfection of the analytic method.

To avoid this pitfall, complex inventory systems are often evaluated by *numerical methods*. Strict optimization is not the goal of a numerical method; instead, a reasonably good inventory policy is sought. A numerical solution can be obtained essentially by a "trial-and-error" process or by making suitable approximations. Two types of numerical methods are primarily employed. One of these methods embodies *heuristic procedures* and might be called an "optimal-seeking" approach. Under such a policy, a starting solution is obtained and successively improved through minor modifications until further improvements are hard to make.

When uncertainty is present, *Monte Carlo simulation* is a very satisfactory numerical solution procedure. (Chapter 25 is devoted entirely to this topic.) Usually performed with the assistance of a digital computer, Monte Carlo simulation evaluates alternatives "on paper" through exhaustive trial-and-error operations. Various combinations of (r, Q) policies can be evaluated by applying each one to an inventory decision over a very long time frame of, say, 100 years. The (r, Q) policy that yields the minimum average cost is then chosen for actual use. Simulation can be used to tackle highly complex problems that are too intractable to solve realistically any other way.

PROBLEMS

8-1   The Green Thumb roadside fruit and vegetable stand must order its cherries from a nearby orchard before they are picked. Green Thumb's seasonal cherry demand has the following probability distribution:

Possible Demand	Probability
$D = 100$ boxes	.15
$D = 150$	.20
$D = 200$	.30
$D = 250$	.20
$D = 300$	.15

Green Thumbs buys its cherries for $2 a box and sells them for $3 a box. Unsold, over-ripe cherries are picked up for disposal by a hog farmer, who charges $.10 for each box. Green Thumb must determine how many boxes to order so that expected profit is maximized. Construct the payoff table, and determine which quantity of cherries should be ordered.

8-2   Construct the cumulative probability distribution for Green Thumb's cherry demand. Then use the newsboy-problem approach to determine the optimal number of cherries to order to minimize total expected cost.

8-3   A news vendor must decide how many copies of *The Daily Planet* he should order. Each paper sells for a dime and costs a nickel. Unsold papers are sold for a penny and then converted into fireplace logs. The news vendor believes that any quantity between 51 and 70 papers, inclusively, is equally likely to be demanded. There is no goodwill lost due to unfilled demands.

(a) How many *Daily Planets* should be ordered to minimize total expected daily cost?

(b) What is the total expected daily cost of the optimal inventory policy?

(c) What is the news vendor's maximum expected daily profit from selling *Daily Planets*?

8-4 A baker must decide how many dozen donuts to bake. Leftovers are ordinarily sold the next day, but she is closing her shop today to take a vacation. Daily demand has the following probability distribution:

Dozen Donuts	Probability
5	.10
10	.15
15	.30
20	.20
25	.15
30	.10

Donuts cost $.50 per dozen to make, and they sell for $1 per dozen. Before closing the shop, the baker plans to throw away any unsold donuts. How many donuts should be baked?

8-5 The captain of a tramp steamer picks up a load of cocoa beans whenever he travels to West Africa. He always sells them to a candymaker in Rotterdam for twice what he paid for them. The candymaker buys only what she needs, and the captain must dispose of any excess beans at less than cost to a cocoa dealer who also resides in Rotterdam. The present African price is 2 guilders per kilogram, and the Dutch cocoa dealer buys the beans for 1.50 guilders per kilogram. The candymaker's demand probability distribution is

Demand	Probability
100 kg	.05
200	.12
300	.18
400	.25
500	.22
600	.09
700	.09

How many kilograms of cocoa beans should the captain take on?

8-6 Horatio Dull is a college professor who supplements his paltry salary each year by selling Christmas trees—a venture that has been immensely successful in the past. He must order his trees in October for delivery in early December. His net cost for each tree is $5, and the trees sell for an average of $15. On those occasions when there have been unsold trees, Horatio has managed to dispose of every excess tree on Christmas Eve for a price of $.50. Having built up a loyal clientele, Dull values any goodwill lost for each tree short at $20. Demand for his trees has been established as approximately normally distributed, with a mean of $\mu = 5,000$ trees and a standard deviation of $\sigma = 1,000$. How many trees should Professor Dull order to minimize total expected cost?

8-7   Miller's Moth Balls are stocked by a pesticide supply house. The annual demand is 1,000 boxes. Due to uncertain deliveries and customer requirements, the following distribution applies for lead-time demand:

Boxes	Probability
11	.10
12	.25
13	.30
14	.20
15	.15

(a) Determine the mean value and the cumulative probability distribution for the lead-time demand.
(b) Each box of moth balls costs $1, and the ordering charge is $10, regardless of the quantity ordered. Assuming an annual holding cost of $.20 per dollar value and a goodwill loss of $1 per box short, find the optimal order quantity and reorder point.

8-8   Sylvester's Bootery caters to customers who cannot obtain the more specialized shoe sizes anywhere else. An optimal policy is sought for stocking size $8\frac{1}{2}$ EEE men's wingtip shoes, which cost Sylvester $20 a pair. The manufacturer charges a flat $10 for each size and style that is special ordered, regardless of quantity. When it is out of stock, all customers will backorder this shoe. But they will usually reheel and resole their present shoes while waiting, so Sylvester loses some amount of future profits, which he estimates to be $5 for each pair short. He finances his inventory with a bank loan at a 10% annual interest rate. The following lead-time demand probabilities apply:

Demand	Probability
5	.1
6	.2
7	.3
8	.2
9	.1
10	.1

Sylvester sells an average of 100 size $8\frac{1}{2}$ EEE pairs of wingtip shoes each year.
(a) Determine the mean lead-time demand.
(b) Find the optimal levels for the order quantity and the reorder point.
(c) What is the safety stock level?
(d) Determine the expected annual inventory cost for this particular store.

8-9   The cost data given in Problem 8-8 apply for Sylvester's size 10 AA shoes, which are rarer. An average of only 50 pairs of these shoes are sold per year. The following lead-time demand distribution applies

Demand	Probability
8	.05
9	.13
10	.21
11	.36
12	.11
13	.07
14	.04
15	.03

Answer (a)–(d) in Problem 8-8 for this shoe.

8-10 Suppose that the oil refinery discussed on pages 195–97 experiences identical costs for its leaded or regular gasoline, which has a mean annual demand of 100 million liters and a normally distributed lead-time demand of 500,000 liters with a standard deviation of 100,000 liters.

Determine the optimal order quantity and reorder point.

8-11 A chemical manufacturer periodically formulates batches of SX-100. There is a set-up cost of $500 for each production run, and the variable cost is $5 per gallon. Each dollar invested in inventory costs $.20 per year, and each backordered gallon represents a loss of $.25. Annual demand is for 100,000 gallons. Assuming that the lead-time demand is normally distributed, with a mean of $\mu = 5,000$ gallons and a standard deviation of $\sigma = 1,000$ gallons, find the optimal order (production) quantity and reorder point.

9

Linear Programming

In Chapter 9, we will consider perhaps the most successful quantitative procedure currently used to facilitate the process of making business decisions. The collection of tools referred to as *linear programming* has a wide variety of applications. It is used by oil companies to determine the best mixture of ingredients for blending gasoline. It has successfully served in the development of optimal schedules for transportation, production, and construction. And it has been applied in such diverse areas as finance and advertising. Without doubt, linear programming has had the widest impact of all modern quantitative methods. Billions of dollars in annual cost savings have been attributed to it alone.

What is linear programming? The use of the word "programming" here should not be confused with the written instructions to a computer called "programs." In the present context, we speak of programming as a form of planning that involves the economic allocation of scarce resources to meet all of the basic requirements. Thus, *programming establishes a plan that efficiently applies all factors toward the achievement of the desired objective.* For example, a linear program will tell a refinery manager the precise number of gallons of various petroleum distillates to use in blending a batch of gasoline with a certain octane rating. Moreover, the plan will achieve this in such a way that costs are minimized and the ultimate automobile exhaust meets environmental pollution limits.

By linear programming we mean that the ultimate plan is obtained by employing a mathematical procedure that involves *linear relationships*; that is, the entire problem can be expressed in terms of straight lines, planes, or analogous geometrical figures. There can be no curved surfaces in any graphical representation of the problem. The mathematical model expressing the problem relates all requirements and management's goals by means of algebraic expressions representing straight lines.

Although we will be restricted to linear situations in this textbook, similar allocation models and procedures exist for more general relationships. Quadratic, convex, and stochastic programming are included under the umbrella of mathematical programming. Each approach is similar to linear programming but involves mathematics beyond the scope of this text. In Chapter 16, linear procedures will be extended to *integer programming*. A further procedure, *dynamic programming*, involves planning decisions over time; this topic will be discussed in Chapter 26.

9-1 THE REDWOOD FURNITURE PROBLEM

The Redwood Furniture Company manufactures tables and chairs as part of its line of patio furniture. Table 9-1 shows the resources consumed and the unit profits for each product. For simplicity, we will assume that only two resources are consumed in manufacturing the patio furniture: wood (300 board feet in inventory), and labor (110 hours available). The owner wishes to determine how many tables and chairs should be made to maximize the total profits from patio furniture.

Linear programming is not essential to establishing such a production plan. After all, it is a recent technique that has been widely used for only the last 30 years, and people have been making furniture for several thousand years. Without any knowledge of linear programming, the owner might decide to make as many chairs as possible, since chairs are more profitable than tables. Altogether, there is enough labor to produce exactly 11 chairs, and the owner's

TABLE 9-1

Data for the Redwood Furniture Problem

Resource	UNIT REQUIREMENTS Table	Chair	Amount Available
Wood (board feet)	30	20	300
Labor (hours)	5	10	110
Unit profit	$6	$8	

profit would be $88. But this plan would leave 80 board feet of wood unused. Would it be more profitable for the owner to make some tables and fewer chairs? If so, how many of each item should be produced? Which brings us back to where we began. Linear programming will tell the owner of Redwood Furniture the exact number of tables and chairs that will *maximize profit*.

FORMULATING THE LINEAR PROGRAM   9-2

We will begin by treating the number of tables and the number of chairs as unknown quantities, or *variables*. We will then express the problem algebraically, using the following symbols:

$$X_T = \text{number of tables made}$$

$$X_C = \text{number of chairs made}$$

Our usual convention will be to represent a problem's essential variables in terms of X, with subscripts taken directly from the variable's description. Thus, using X_T ("X sub T") to represent the number of tables, where T is the first letter in the word "table," eases our task of abstracting the problem to a *mathematical model*. Occasionally, we will use letters other than X and numbers to represent subscripts.

Each resource places limitations on the values of X_T and X_C. In the case of wood, any production plan must meet the requirement that

Wood for tables + Wood for chairs ≤ Available wood

This *constraint* tells us that the amount of wood used cannot exceed the amount of wood that is available. Note that this constraint does not require that every single foot of wood be used, but only that we do not use more wood than there is. This is why we use the "less than or equal to" symbol ≤. It would be less flexible, and therefore less desirable, to be unduly restrictive and require the use of all wood, which is what using = in this constraint would indicate.

The wood constraint is referred to as an *inequality*. It is convenient to express this inequality in terms of the quantity variables for tables and chairs in the following equivalent form:

$$30X_T + 20X_C \le 300 \quad \text{(wood)}$$

The first term on the left side ($30X_T$) expresses the total amount of wood to be used in the manufacture of tables and is found by multiplying the 30 board feet of wood required for each table by the number of tables X_T. Similarly, since each chair requires 20 board feet, $20X_C$ represents the total amount of wood that will be used in the manufacture of chairs.

An analogous constraint pertains to the labor resource:

$$5X_T + 10X_C \leq 110 \quad \text{(labor)}$$

As before, this simply says that the total quantity of labor expended on either tables or chairs cannot exceed the 110 units available. Together, these two constraint inequalities establish limits for the values of X_T and X_C.

The profit objective may also be stated algebraically. Denoting total profit by P, we relate this to the variables by

$$P = 6X_T + 8X_C$$

since total profit consists of the profit derived from selling tables at $6 each plus the profit derived from selling chairs at $8 each. Thus, $6X_T$ is the profit earned by making and selling tables, and $8X_C$ is the corresponding profit from making chairs. Remember that the owner wants to achieve the greatest possible profit, or to maximize P. We can incorporate this objective directly into the mathematical model by writing the profit equation as

$$\text{Maximize} \quad P = 6X_T + 8X_C \quad \text{(objective)}$$

In this form, the profit expression provides the *objective function*.

Before proceeding, we should note that there are two fundamental types of objective functions, depending on the goal. Instead of maximizing profit, in some problems our goal is to minimize cost. In such situations, the objective function would take the form "minimize C," where C represents the unknown cost variable.

We are now ready to incorporate all of these expressions into a single mathematical model, which will prescribe exactly what is to be done within the resource limitations. The model itself, referred to as a *linear program*, is

Letting	$X_T =$ number of tables made
	$X_C =$ number of tables made
Maximize	$P = 6X_T + 8X_C$ (objective)
Subject to	$30X_T + 20X_C \leq 300$ (wood)
	$5X_T + 10X_C \leq 110$ (labor)
where	$X_T, X_C \geq 0$ (non-negativity)

This linear program identifies the variables and specifies the problem objective, subject to the constraints that limit what may be done.

The linear program includes further limitations that we have not previously encountered. The *non-negativity conditions* state that the variables cannot assume negative values. Although a negative quantity of tables or chairs makes no sense at all, without these prescriptions it would be mathematically possible to obtain a solution such as ($X_T = -10$, $X_C = 16$) with a profit of $68. Obviously, this solution is impossible, because it implies the absurdity of disassembling 10 tables, retrieving all the wood and labor used to manufacture them, and channeling both the "saved" resources into the production of more chairs than could have been made with the original wood and labor!

THE GRAPHICAL SOLUTION METHOD   **9-3**

A linear program is only a mathematical *formulation.* It merely sets up the problem. We still don't know how many tables and chairs should be made. This answer is provided by the *solution* to the linear program.

Several different approaches or *algorithms* might be used to solve this problem. In this book, we will consider a variety of algorithms for solving linear programs. For simple linear problems, the easiest procedure is the *graphical method.*

We begin by constructing a graph that represents the linear program in two dimensions—one for the number of tables X_T, and the other for the number of chairs X_C. We use a ruler to make a heavy horizontal line for the X_T axis and a heavy vertical line for the X_C axis on a piece of graph paper, as shown in Figure 9-1. For convenience, we place tick marks every five squares along the respective axes and label these in increments of 5, starting at 0 in each case. Any point in this two-dimensional space corresponds to a production quantity combination or plan for tables and chairs.

The *origin* is the point where the two axes cross and can be represented in terms of its coordinates along the respective axes ($X_T = 0$, $X_C = 0$). The coordinates for point A ($X_T = 2$, $X_C = 12$) represent its distance of 2 units along the X_T axis and its height of 12 units along the X_C axis. This same point represents a production plan for 2 tables and 12 chairs.

Plotting Constraint Lines

Our next step is to plot the constraints on the graph. We begin with the wood constraint

$$30X_T + 20X_C \leq 300 \quad \text{(wood)}$$

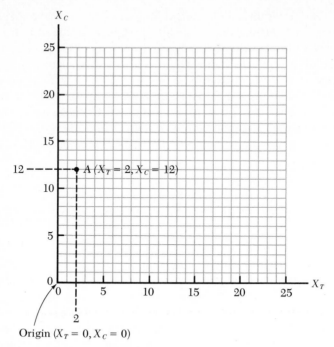

FIGURE 9-1
Linear programming axes constructed on graph paper.

Temporarily, we will consider the special case where the left side of this expression (wood used) is precisely equal to the right side (wood available), which gives us the wood *equation*

$$30X_T + 20X_C = 300 \quad \text{(wood)}$$

When plotted on our graph, this equality will be linear. It is therefore referred to as the wood *constraint line*. All points falling on this line represent combinations of table and chair quantities that consume the exact amount of wood that is available.

In constructing this wood constraint line, we apply the geometrical principle that any line can be defined by two points. These can then be connected by positioning a straightedge beside both points and drawing the connecting line.

Generally, it is simplest to locate the two points where the line cuts the respective axes. First, consider the X_T axis. The intersection point on the horizontal axis is called the *horizontal intercept*. Since it will have no vertical height, one of its coordinates will be $X_C = 0$. Plugging this value of X_C into the wood equation gives us

$$30X_T + 20(0) = 300$$

Since $20 \times 0 = 0$, we may ignore the second term on the left, so that we have

$$30X_T = 300$$

Dividing both sides of this equation by 30, we obtain

$$X_T = 300/30 = 10$$

Thus, the remaining coordinate for the horizontal intercept is $X_T = 10$. In a similar way, we obtain the *vertical intercept* by setting $X_T = 0$ and solving the wood equation for X_C:

$$30(0) + 20X_C = 300$$

$$X_C = 300/20 = 15$$

We then plot these intercepts in Figure 9-2 and draw the wood constraint line to connect them. (For clarity, the grid squares have been omitted in this figure.)

The wood constraint line represents all possible production plans that call for the consumption of the entire 300 board feet of available wood. This is true for the vertical intercept ($X_T = 0$, $X_C = 15$), which corresponds to 0 tables and 15 chairs, and for the horizontal intercept ($X_T = 10$, $X_C = 0$), which corresponds to 10 tables and 0 chairs. For any other point on the wood constraint line, such as point A ($X_T = 2$, $X_C = 12$) or point B ($X_T = 5$, $X_C = 7\frac{1}{2}$), exactly 300 board feet of wood are used. Note that it is possible to have fractional quantities in linear programming; coordinates do not have to be whole numbers.

Finding the Valid Side of the Constraint Line

Of course, the original wood constraint does not require us to use all of the available wood. We must reconsider the inequality $\leq$ that we temporarily discarded so that we could work with the wood equation. Actually, an inequality relationship can be incorporated in a linear graph. Any inequality allows all of the points that fall on one side of the constraint line to be valid. But which side is the valid side?

A simple check is to evaluate a point that does not fall on the line itself. If that point satisfies the constraint, then all points on the same side of the line are valid; if it does not, then all points on the other side of the line are valid. The simplest point to evaluate is the origin. If ($X_T = 0$, $X_C = 0$) satisfies the original wood constraint, then every point on the same side of the wood line

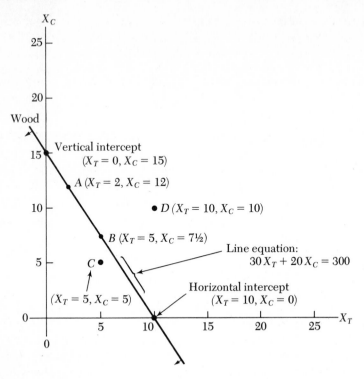

FIGURE 9-2
Plotting the wood constraint line for the Redwood Furniture problem.

will also satisfy it. To check this, we plug the origin's coordinates into the original wood inequality, so that

$$30(0) + 20(0) \le 300$$

and obtain

$$0 \le 300$$

which is a true statement. Now we know that the origin is valid and that all points lying on the same side—below and to the left of the line—apply. We indicate the valid side by attaching small arrows to the constraint line, as shown in Figure 9-2. (Keep in mind that the origin happens to be valid for this particular constraint. In a different situation, the origin might not satisfy the constraint and the side opposite of the line would be the valid side.)

To show that other points on the same side of the line in Figure 9-2 satisfy the constraint, we consider point C ($X_T = 5$, $X_C = 5$). This production plan consumes $30(5) + 20(5) = 250$ board feet of wood, which is less than the available 300 board feet. Point C is a valid point. However, point D ($X_T = 10$, $X_C = 10$), which lies above the wood line, is *infeasible*, since it would consume $30(10) + 20(10) = 500$ board feet of wood, which is more than the existing amount of 300 board feet.

The Feasible Solution Region

The entire procedure that we followed to determine the wood constraint must now be duplicated for the labor constraint. The labor equation (again ignoring the $\leq$) is

$$5X_T + 10X_C = 110 \quad \text{(labor)}$$

The horizontal intercept is $X_T = 110/5 = 22$, and the vertical intercept is $X_C = 110/10 = 11$. The labor line and the wood line are plotted on the same graph in Figure 9-3. The valid side of the labor line includes the origin (doing nothing meets the labor constraint).

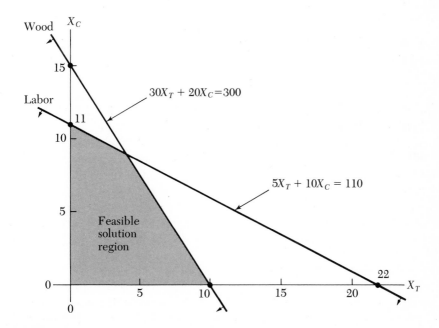

FIGURE 9-3
A complete graph of the Redwood Furniture problem constraints, showing the feasible solution region.

Any workable production plan must simultaneously satisfy these wood and labor constraints. Any such plan is called a *feasible solution*. The feasible solutions correspond to the points that lie on the valid sides of both constraint lines, or within the shaded area in Figure 9-3, which is called the *feasible solution region*. Since the non-negativity conditions do not permit negative levels of either X_T or X_C, the feasible solution region is bounded not only by the two constraint lines but also by the vertical and horizontal axes.

The Most Attractive Corner

The Redwood Furniture Company could produce the number of tables and chairs that corresponds to any point in the feasible solution region, since all of these solutions are possible. However, the owner's objective is to maximize total profit, as expressed by the equation

$$P = 6X_T + 8X_C$$

To complete the graphical solution method, we must therefore incorporate profit in our graph.

Because P itself is unknown, various values of profit must be considered. If $P = 48$, for example, the objective function may be written as

$$48 = 6X_T + 8X_C$$

which we recognize as the equation for a straight line. This *profit line* has intercepts of $X_T = 48/6 = 8$ and $X_C = 48/8 = 6$ and is plotted in Figure 9-4 as a dashed line to distinguish it from the constraint lines we found earlier. Of course, we could plot a similar line for any other value of P, such as 47, 49, or 53. We chose $P = 48$ because it is evenly divisible by both unit profits, so that the $P = 48$ profit line is easy to construct.

Each point that lies on the $P = 48$ profit line and that also lies inside the feasible solution region corresponds to a production plan yielding a profit of exactly $48. But we need to know if we can do better and, if so, what the best possible profit is. Let's see what happens if we consider a larger profit, such as $P = 72$ (again a value that is evenly divisible by $6 and $8). The corresponding profit line has been plotted as a second dashed line in Figure 9-4. Notice that the $P = 72$ profit line lies above the $P = 48$ profit line. All feasible points on the $P = 72$ profit line will yield the larger profit of $72.

Note that these two profit lines are *parallel*. This is characteristic of any linear program and of any value of P. This property of parallel profit lines is all that we need to know to find the maximum profit. Together, the two profit lines in our graph indicate the *direction of increasing profit* shown by the large arrow in Figure 9-4.

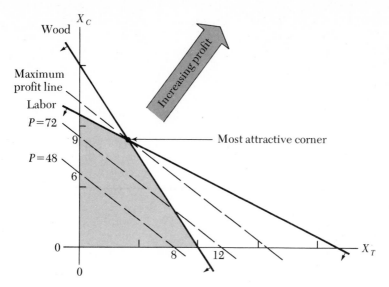

FIGURE 9-4
**Finding the direction of increasing profit and the most attractive corner
for the Redwood Furniture problem.**

Now we can begin to put the solution to our problem together. We still don't know the maximum P, but we do know that as larger possible values of P are considered, the profit lines we plot will be parallel to the first two lines and will lie above them. But there is a limit to how large P can become, because we are only interested in determining the maximum profit that can be achieved by a feasible production plan. By positioning a straightedge parallel to the original two profit lines in Figure 9-4 and sliding it in the direction of increasing profit, we can see by a visual inspection of the graph that the highest allowable profit line must just touch the corner of the feasible solution region where the wood and labor constraint lines intersect. Any higher profit line will lie outside the feasible solution region. We refer to the highest allowable point as the *most attractive corner*. A third dashed profit line passes through this corner in Figure 9-4. We must now determine what value of P this *maximum profit line* represents.

Finding the Optimal Solution

The most attractive corner provides us with the production plan that will yield the maximum possible profit. We refer to this plan as the *optimal solution*. Mathematically, the coordinates of the most attractive corner are determined by simultaneously solving the wood and labor equations with two unknowns:

$$30X_T + 20X_C = 300 \quad \text{(wood)}$$

$$5X_T + 10X_C = 110 \quad \text{(labor)}$$

The simplest procedure is to use the method of elimination. We do this by subtracting a multiple of one equation from the other equation in such a way that one of the variables has a coefficient of 0 in the resulting equation difference. The value of the remaining unknown can then be found directly. We can eliminate X_C from the equation difference if we multiply the labor equation by 2 and subtract the result from the wood equation:

$$
\begin{array}{ll}
30X_T + 20X_C = 300 & \text{(wood)} \\
-2(5X_T + 10X_C = 110) & \text{(labor)} \\
\hline
20X_T + 0X_C = 80 &
\end{array}
$$

Thus

$$X_T = 80/20 = 4 \text{ tables}$$

Substituting this value into either of the constraint equations, we can solve for the value of X_C. Using the wood equation

$$30(4) + 20X_C = 300$$

$$20X_C = 300 - 30(4) = 300 - 120 = 180$$

so that

$$X_C = 180/20 = 9 \text{ chairs}$$

The optimal solution to the Redwood Furniture linear program is therefore

$$X_T = 4 \text{ tables}$$

$$X_C = 9 \text{ chairs}$$

and the profit obtained is calculated by substituting these numbers into the objective function:

$$P = 6(4) + 8(9) = 96 \text{ dollars}$$

Figure 9-5 illustrates the profit line that corresponds to $P = 96$. Notice that this line touches the most attractive corner, confirming our earlier conclusion

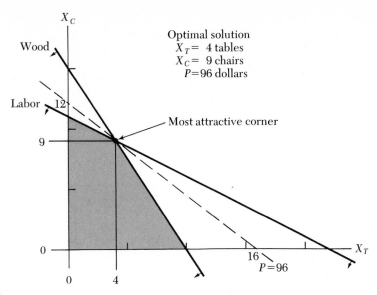

FIGURE 9-5
The optimal solution for the Redwood Furniture problem.

that the profit line that passes through this point will represent the maximum profit.

It is logical to observe that it might be simpler to read the coordinates of the most attractive corner and obtain the optimal solution directly. Just reading the graph would certainly save us a lot of algebraic calculations. *For this problem*, this would be true. But if the optimal solution were, say, $X_T = 4\frac{1}{32}$ and $X_C = 8\frac{15}{16}$, the thickness of the pencil lead used to draw the lines would not allow us to read the graph accurately enough to obtain the answer given by the algebraic solution. The graph should enable us to tell *by visual inspection* where the most attractive corner lies. Even a graph that is quickly sketched by hand, without graph paper, may suffice. But only by solving algebraically can we be sure that we have found the precise optimal solution.

A SUMMARY OF THE PROCEDURE 9-4

The steps in solving a linear program can now be summarized.

(1) Formulate the linear program. A proper formulation begins with a definition of the variables that clearly describes how the symbols apply. The rest is algebraic calculation. First, the objective function (maximize P or minimize C) is stated in an equation, followed by the expressions for the constraints. No formulation is complete without a final statement of non-negativity conditions, if they apply.

(2) Construct a graph and plot the constraint lines. Ordinarily, this involves locating two points and connecting them. The points are usually the horizontal and vertical intercepts found from each constraint equation. But we will see that for certain constraints, a different pair of points must be found to draw these lines.

(3) Determine the valid side for each inequality constraint. The simplest approach is to see whether the origin (the point of "doing nothing") satisfies the constraint by plugging its coordinates $(0, 0)$ into the inequality. If it does, then all points on the origin's side of the line are valid, and the rest are infeasible. If the origin does not satisfy the constraint, then the valid points lie on the side of the line that is opposite the origin. The *two exceptions* to this rule of thumb will be discussed shortly.

(4) Identify the feasible solution region. This region will be indicated by the group of points on the graph that are valid for all constraints collectively. These points correspond to feasible plans. Ordinarily, the feasible solution region is a contiguous area lying in the positive quadrant, since the non-negativity conditions preclude negative variable values.

(5) Plot two objective function lines and determine the direction of improvement. When profit maximization is the goal, two P lines will tell us the direction of increasing P. Two lines are necessary because the direction cannot always be predicted from a single line. The two P lines do not have to intersect the feasible solution region to indicate the direction of increasing P. When the goal is to minimize cost, two C lines are plotted. In this case, the direction of improvement is a decrease in C.

(6) Find the most attractive corner by visual inspection. This corner will be the last point in the feasible solution region touched by the P or C line that is formed by sliding a straightedge in the direction of improvement while holding it parallel to the two original objective lines.

(7) Determine the optimal solution by algebraically calculating coordinates of the most attractive corner. The optimal solution is often represented by the intersection of two constraint lines. However, it might also be denoted by the coordinates of a corner point formed by the horizontal or vertical intercept of one constraint equation. When this is the case, the algebraic calculations have already been performed and the optimal solution can be read directly from the coordinates shown on the graph without error. *A common mistake made by beginning linear programming students is to assume that the most attractive corner must be the corner where the two constraint lines cross.* If this were so, we would never need to construct a graph. Furthermore, there can be three or more constraint lines (as there would have been in our furniture problem if machine time had been included as a third resource). Only the graph can indicate which intersection is the most attractive corner.

(8) Determine the value of the objective function for the optimal solution. This is found by substituting the optimal variable values into the P or C equation. No solution is complete until the maximum value of P or the minimum value of C is stated.

COST MINIMIZATION: A FEED-MIX PROBLEM   9-5

We will now consider a simplified problem that might be faced by a seed packager—determining the number of pounds of two types of seeds that should be mixed to formulate the wheat portion of a batch of wild bird seed. Table 9-2 shows the nutritional content of two seed types—buckwheat and sunflower wheat—along with the minimum required pounds of fat and protein. In addition, there is a maximum limit of 1,500 pounds of roughage. Unlimited quantities of either seed type can be purchased at the costs indicated. The packager's goal is to minimize the total cost of satisfying the nutritional requirements of the bird-seed mix.

The linear program for this problem can be formulated as follows:

Letting X_B = pounds of buckwheat in mixture

X_S = pounds of sunflower wheat in mixture

Minimize $C = .18X_B + .10X_S$

Subject to $.04X_B + .06X_S \geq 480$ (fat)

$.12X_B + .10X_S \geq 1{,}200$ (protein)

$.10X_B + .15X_S \leq 1{,}500$ (roughage)

where $X_B, X_S \geq 0$

TABLE 9-2
Data for the Feed-Mix Problem

Nutritional Item	PROPORTIONAL CONTENT		Total Requirement
	Buckwheat	Sunflower Wheat	
Fat	.04	.06	$\geq$ 480 lb
Protein	.12	.10	$\geq 1{,}200$
Roughage	.10	.15	$\leq 1{,}500$
Cost per pound	$.18	$.10	

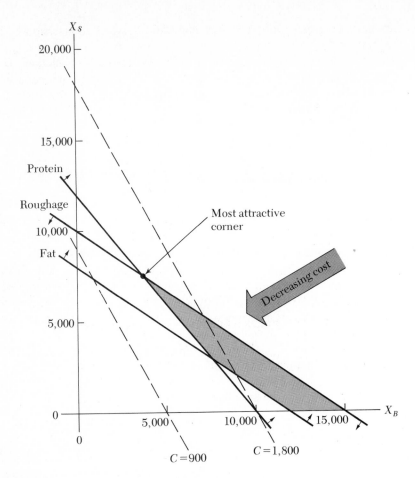

FIGURE 9-6
The graphical solution for the feed-mix problem.

The fat and protein constraints are represented by ≥ (greater than or equal to) inequalities because minimum quantities of each have been established, and the total pounds of fat or protein (provided on the left sides of the respective inequalities) must be at least as large as these quantities. The roughage constraint is a ≤ (less than or equal to) inequality, since total mixture roughage (again represented on the left side) cannot exceed 1,500 pounds.

Figure 9-6 is a graphical representation of the feed-mix problem. Notice that the valid sides of the fat and protein constraints are opposite to the origin side (0 pounds of both seed types will satisfy neither constraint). Cost lines for $C = 1,800$ and $C = 900$ dollars have been plotted. (Even though the $C = 900$ cost line lies outside the feasible solution region, the direction of decreasing cost is readily determined.) The most attractive corner occurs at the intersection of the protein and roughage constraint lines.

Solving the protein and roughage equations simultaneously, we can determine the optimal solution:

$$
\begin{array}{rl}
.12X_B + .10X_S = 1,200 & \text{(protein)} \\
-\frac{2}{3}(.10X_B + .15X_S = 1,500) & \text{(roughage)} \\
\hline
.0533X_B + \quad 0X_S = \quad 200 &
\end{array}
$$

$$X_B = 200/.0533 = 3,752.345 \text{ pounds}$$

Plugging the value of X_B into the protein equation, we can then find the value of X_S:

$$.12(3,752.345) + .10X_S = 1,200$$

$$.10X_S = 1,200 - .12(3,752.345) = 1,200 - 450.281 = 749.719$$

$$X_S = 749.719/.10 = 7,497.19 \text{ pounds}$$

The optimal solution (rounded) to the feed-mix problem is therefore

$$X_B = 3,752.35 \text{ pounds}$$
$$X_S = 7,497.19 \text{ pounds}$$

and the minimum cost is

$$C = .18(3,752.35) + .10(7,497.19) = 1,425.14 \text{ dollars}$$

SPECIAL PROBLEMS IN CONSTRUCTING LINES 9-6

Earlier, we indicated that most constraint lines may be constructed by connecting the horizontal and vertical intercepts. Even though we generally restrict solutions to the positive quadrant, there is no reason why one of these intercepts cannot be negative. Consider the line

$$-5X_1 + 3X_2 = 15$$

which is graphed as line A in Figure 9-7. Notice that the horizontal intercept is *negative*:

$$X_1 = 15/-5 = -3$$

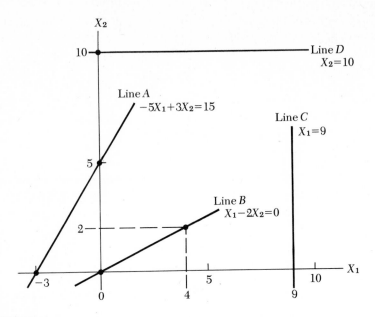

FIGURE 9-7
Examples of special types of lines.

The equation for line B in Figure 9-7 is

$$X_1 - 2X_2 = 0$$

Both the vertical and horizontal intercepts for this equation occur at the *origin*. Since the intercept method yields a single point in this case, a second point must be found. The choice of this second point is arbitrary. We can plug the value of $X_2 = 2$ into the equation to obtain the other coordinate:

$$X_1 - 2(2) = 0$$
$$X_1 = 0 - [-2(2)] = 0 - (-4) = 4$$

Connecting the origin with the point ($X_1 = 4$, $X_2 = 2$) will then give us the required line.

A third type of line has only one intercept. These lines are either horizontal or vertical and have equations of the form

$$X_1 = 9 \quad \text{(line } C\text{)}$$
$$X_2 = 10 \quad \text{(line } D\text{)}$$

where only one variable appears in the equation. For $X_1 = 9$, the value of X_1 is restricted to exactly 9, regardless of the value of X_2, which can be any quantity whatsoever. This relationship is illustrated in Figure 9-7 by line C, a vertical line perpendicular to the X_1 axis and parallel to the X_2 axis. For the equation $X_2 = 10$, line D is plotted as a horizontal line perpendicular to the X_2 axis at a height of 10 units. For that matter, the axes themselves can be represented in terms of the equations $X_2 = 0$ (for the horizontal axis) and $X_1 = 0$ (for the vertical axis).

MIXTURE CONSTRAINTS   9-7

A line that passes through the origin generally applies to a special type of restriction called a *mixture constraint*. Such a constraint arises in manufacturing applications when some products must be made in a fixed ratio to other products. The Redwood Furniture problem can be modified slightly to incorporate a mixture constraint.

Ordinarily, Redwood's tables and chairs are sold in sets of 4 chairs and 1 table. However, there is an occasional need for extra chairs. Thus, Redwood wishes to make at least 4 chairs for every table, which means that the number of chairs must be at least as large as the number of tables multiplied by 4. This adds a further mixture constraint of the form

$$4 \times \text{Number of tables} \leq \text{Number of chairs}$$

to the problem. Expressed in terms of the variable symbols used in the previous Redwood problem, this constraint tells us that

$$4X_T \leq X_C \quad \text{(mixture)}$$

For convenience, all variables are usually collected on the left side of the inequality. Subtracting X_C from both sides, we obtain

$$4X_T - X_C \leq 0 \quad \text{(mixture)}$$

Temporarily ignoring the inequality gives us the equation for the mixture constraint line

$$4X_T - X_C = 0 \quad \text{(mixture)}$$

which is the expression for a line that passes through the origin.

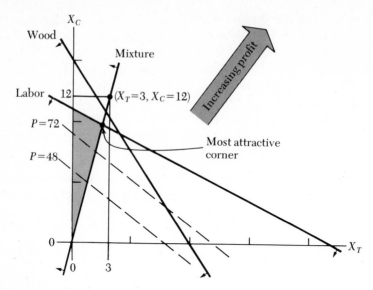

FIGURE 9-8
The graphical solution of the Redwood Furniture problem
expanded to include a mixture constraint.

The graph for the expanded Redwood Furniture problem is provided in Figure 9-8. (The original wood and labor constraints are replotted here.) The mixture constraint line is found by connecting the origin with the point ($X_T = 3$, $X_C = 12$), since when 3 tables are made, $3 \times 4 = 12$ chairs must be produced.

Finding the valid side of the mixture constraint line is a little complicated. Since the line passes through the origin, we cannot use the origin for this purpose. Instead, we must evaluate some point that does not lie on the line. Any such point will do, so we will choose ($X_T = 10$, $X_C = 15$). Substituting these coordinates into the mixture inequality gives us

$$4(10) - 15 \leq 0$$

$$25 \leq 0$$

which is certainly not true. Thus, the valid side of the mixture constraint line lies opposite this point.

The feasible solution region obtained by including the mixture constraint is smaller than the feasible solution region for the original Redwood Furniture problem in Figure 9-3. (Additional constraints ordinarily reduce the number of possible solutions. Why?) Visual inspection indicates that the most attractive corner for this new linear program lies at the intersection of the mixture and labor constraint lines. The simultaneous solution of these equations provides the optimal solution:

$$X_T = 22/9 \ \ = 2\tfrac{4}{9} \text{ tables}$$

$$X_C = 88/9 \ \ = 9\tfrac{7}{9} \text{ chairs}$$

$$P = 836/9 = 92\tfrac{8}{9} \text{ dollars}$$

Remember that linear programming may produce fractional solutions. We can view the extra $\tfrac{4}{9}$ table and $\tfrac{7}{9}$ chair as work-in-progress inventory items.

One interesting feature of this solution is that there is leftover wood. The total amount of wood consumed is

$$30(22/9) + 20(88/9) = 268\tfrac{8}{9} \text{ board feet}$$

leaving $300 - 268\tfrac{8}{9} = 31\tfrac{1}{9}$ board feet of wood in inventory. The unused portion of an inventoried resource is called *slack*. We will explore the concept of slack extensively in Chapter 11.

EQUALITY CONSTRAINTS   9-8

Thus far, all of the constraints we have encountered have been expressed as inequalities. As we have seen, inequalities produce valid points that lie to one side of a bisected plane. Under some circumstances, however, constraints may take the form of a strict equality. They are then called *equality constraints*. For example, suppose that Redwood Furniture sells all of its tables and chairs only in sets and that *exactly* 4 chairs are required for each table. The basic constraint would have no $<$ inequality in it and would be expressed directly by the equation for the line

$$4X_T - X_C = 0 \quad \text{(revised mixture)}$$

Figure 9-9 is a graph of the linear program that reflects this further amendment. Notice that *there is no valid side of the mixture line:* Valid points must lie exactly on the line. The feasible solution region consists of that *line segment* of the mixture constraint that also satisfies the remaining resource constraints. In general, when there is one equality constraint, the feasible points will lie on a line segment, but there are no other basic changes in the linear programming steps.

When there is more than one equality constraint, the procedure becomes ridiculously simple. Suppose that Redwood wishes to produce 2 tables because exactly this number can be sold. In this case, the *demand constraint* would be

$$X_T = 2 \quad \text{(demand)}$$

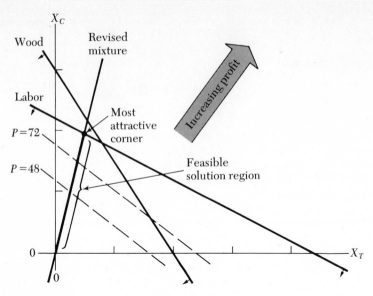

FIGURE 9-9
The graphical solution of the Redwood Furniture problem amended
to incorporate an equality mixture constraint.

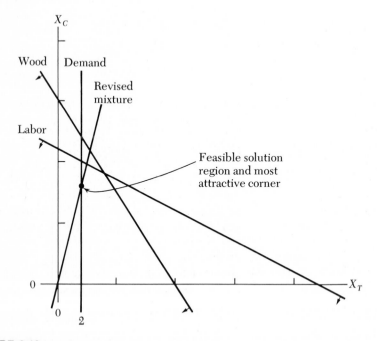

FIGURE 9-10
The graphical solution of the Redwood Furniture problem restricted
by two equality constraints.

Figure 9-10 is a graph of this more restricted linear program. The demand constraint is plotted as a vertical line intersecting the X_T axis at 2. Notice that *the feasible solution region consists of the single point* where the two equality constraints intersect. The most attractive corner is the same point! In this case, the optimal solution is $X_T = 2$ tables and $X_C = 8$ chairs, with a profit line of $P = 76$ dollars.

MULTIPLE OPTIMAL SOLUTIONS 9-9

Until now, we have examined linear programs with unique optimal solutions corresponding to the most attractive corner. Although the solution to a linear program is generally represented by a corner point of the feasible solution region, more than one corner can be equally most attractive. As an example, consider the following linear program:

$$\text{Maximize} \quad P = 10X_1 + 12X_2$$

Subject to
$$5X_1 + 6X_2 \leq 60 \quad \text{(resource } A)$$
$$8X_1 + 4X_2 \leq 72 \quad \text{(resource } B)$$
$$3X_1 + 5X_2 \leq 45 \quad \text{(resource } C)$$

where
$$X_1, X_2 \geq 0$$

This problem is graphed in Figure 9-11. Visual inspection indicates that there are two candidates for the most attractive corner: the intersection of the A and C lines at point (1) or the intersection of the A and B lines at point (2). To resolve this potential ambiguity, we must determine which point is the last one touched by the highest P line. A visual analysis is not precise enough, because if we slide a straightedge in the direction of increasing P, it is impossible to make a distinction between the two corner points. Alternatively, we can simultaneously solve the respective equation pairs for both points and choose the one with the greatest P. Doing this, we obtain

	(1)	(2)
	$X_1 = 4\frac{2}{7}$	$X_1 = 6\frac{6}{7}$
	$X_2 = 6\frac{3}{7}$	$X_2 = 4\frac{2}{7}$
	$P = 120$	$P = 120$

which both yield the same profit. This means that both points are equally attractive, and we have *two most attractive corners*. Thus, both of these solutions are optimal, and the maximum profit is $P = 120$.

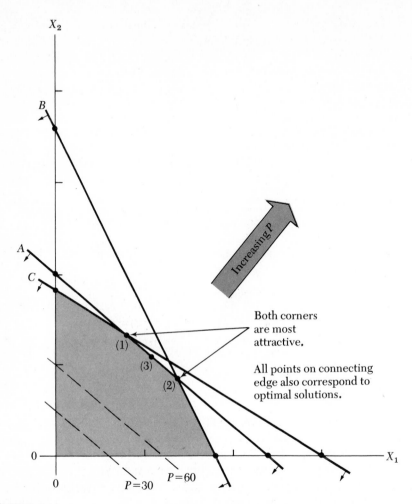

FIGURE 9-11
The graphical solution to a problem having multiple optimal solutions.

Why did we obtain two most attractive corners? The answer is because *the objective function line is parallel to one of the constraint lines*, so that the maximum P line must coincide with that constraint. This can be verified visually in Figure 9-11, where the $P = 30$ and $P = 60$ profit lineas are parallel to the resource A constraint line. It is possible to prove mathematically that all P lines are parallel to that line by comparing their equations:

$$P = 10X_1 + 12X_2 \quad \text{(objective)}$$

$$5X_1 + 6X_2 = 60 \quad \text{(resource } A)$$

Notice that the coefficients of the variables in the resource equation exhibit a constant ratio to the respective coefficients in the P equation. The X_1 terms are 10 and 5, so that the ratio is $10/5 = 2$; this same ratio result $12/6 = 2$ applies to X_2. Thus, the coefficients in the P equation are exactly *twice* the value of the coefficients in the resource A equation. Whenever all of the coefficients in one equation are the same multiple of their counterparts in another equation, the two lines must be parallel.

Whenever more than one corner provides the optimal solution, all points on the connecting edge will also correspond to optimal solutions. For example, consider point (3), which is midway on the optimal edge in Figure 9-11, with coordinates $(X_1 = 5\frac{4}{7}, X_2 = 5\frac{5}{14})$. The maximum profit for this solution is also

$$P = 10(5\tfrac{4}{7}) + 12(5\tfrac{5}{14}) = 120$$

Any other point on the *most attractive edge* will also represent an optimal with a profit of $P = 120$, reflecting the fact that the maximum P line must coincide with this edge.

CONCLUDING REMARKS 9-10

In this chapter, we have considered the essential features of linear programming. But we have only scratched the surface of this subject. By nature, the graphical solution method is limited to problems that contain two variables, since our graphs can only represent two dimensions. It would be possible for us to extend this analysis to three variables, using three-dimensional graphs, but to do so would be cumbersome. When four or more variables are involved, entirely different algorithms must be used. In Chapter 11, we will consider the most generally used solution procedure in linear programming—the *simplex method*. In later chapters, more efficient special-purpose algorithms will be described.

PROBLEMS

9-1 Labeling the horizontal axis X_1 and the vertical axis X_2, plot the following lines on a graph:
(a) $X_1 + X_2 = 5$ (b) $2X_1 + 3X_2 = 18$
(c) $-3X_1 + 6X_2 = 24$ (d) $X_1 = 12$
(e) $X_2 = 9$ (f) $X_1 - 2X_2 = 0$

9-2 Solve each of the following equation pairs simultaneously:
(a) $X_1 + X_2 = 10$ (b) $2X_1 + 3X_2 = 6$
    $X_1 - X_2 = 5$ $X_2 = 1$

(c) $8X_1 + 7X_2 = 10$ (d) $4X_1 + 4X_2 = 12$
$4X_1 + 5X_2 = 8$ $5X_1 + 3X_2 = 6$

9-3 Use the graphical procedure to determine the optimal solution to the linear program

Maximize $P = 5X_A + 6X_B$
Subject to $3X_A + 2X_B \le 12$ (resource W)
             $2X_A + 3X_B \le 12$ (resource Y)
where $X_A, X_B \ge 0$

9-4 Use the graphical procedure to determine the optimal solution to the linear program

Minimize $C = .5X_A + .3X_B$
Subject to $X_A + 2X_B \ge 10$ (restriction Y)
             $X_A + X_B \ge 8$ (restriction Z)
where $X_A, X_B \ge 0$

9-5 Use the graphical procedure to determine the optimal solution to the linear program

Maximize $P = 2X_1 - 3X_2$
Subject to $4X_1 + 5X_2 \le 40$ (resource A)
             $2X_1 + 6X_2 \le 24$ (resource B)
             $3X_1 - 3X_2 \ge 6$ (mixture)
             $X_1 \ge 4$ (demand)
where $X_1, X_2 \ge 0$

9-6 Consider the following linear program:

Maximize $P = 2X_1 + 4X_2$
Subject to $4X_1 + 8X_2 \le 48$
             $8X_1 + 4X_2 \ge 48$
             $X_2 \le 5$
where $X_1, X_2 \ge 0$

(a) Plot the constraint lines on a graph. Then determine the feasible solution region and plot two profit lines. Indicate the direction of increasing profit.
(b) How many attractive corners are there? Find the optimal solution that corresponds to each corner you find.
(c) Plot point ($X_1 = 8$, $X_2 = 2$) on your graph. What profit level corresponds to this point? What can you conclude about this point?

9-7 Not all linear programs can be solved. Consider the following problem:

Maximize $P = 2X_1$
Subject to $X_1 + X_2 \le 5$
             $X_2 \ge 6$
where $X_1, X_2 \ge 0$

This problem is *infeasible*. Attempt to solve it graphically and briefly state any difficulties you encounter.

9-8   Ace Widgets makes two models of its ubiquitous product—regular and deluxe. Both models are assembled from an identical frame. The regular model differs from the deluxe model only in terms of the finish work, which takes 5 hours of labor on the regular version and 8 hours on the deluxe model. In planning the current month's production, Ace's foreman finds that only 12 frames and 80 hours of finishing labor are available. The supply of all other required materials and labor is unlimited. Any number of widgets can be sold at a profit: $10 per regular widget, and $15 per deluxe widget. The foreman wants to produce quantities of the two models that will maximize company profits.
(a) Formulate the foreman's problem as a linear program.
(b) Solve the linear program graphically.

9-9   The marketing manager of Hops Brewery must determine how many television spots and magazine ads to pruchase within an advertising budget of $100,000. Each spot is expected to increase sales by 30,000 cans, whereas each magazine ad will account for 100,000 cans in sales. Hops' gross profit on sales is $.10 per can. One television spot costs $2,000; each magazine ad requires an expenditure of $5,000. To have a balanced marketing program, the advertising budget must involve no more than $70,000 in magazine ads and no more than $50,000 in television spots.
(a) Determine the net increase in beer profits for each television spot and magazine ad (that reflects their respective costs).
(b) Assuming that Hops' management wishes to maximize the net increase in beer profits, formulate the marketing manager's decision as a linear program.
(c) Solve the linear program graphically.

9-10 Mildred's Tool and Die shop must provide exactly 10 experimental bits to a pneumatic drill company. The bits can be shaped either by forging or by machining. Both procedures involve a final milling stage, but the forged bits require more milling because they are not as smooth initially. In either case, only one bit can be shaped at a time using either process, and the order must be filled within two working days. The following table summarizes the restrictions.

Process	HOURS PER ITEM		Total Hours Available
	Forged	Machined	
Forging	3	—	15
Machining	—	2	16
Milling	2	4/3	16
Unit profit	$12	$9	

Assuming that the proprietor, Ms. Mildred Riveter, wishes to maximize profits, formulate a linear program specifying the number of bits that should be shaped using each process in order to maximize total profits. Then solve this problem graphically.

9-11 Cee's Candy Company mixes its Rainbow Box from two basic confections—chocolates and pastels. To meet its packaging requirements and to reflect changing ingredient costs, the company runs a linear program periodically to determine the number of pounds of each type of candy to put into the mix. The costs and requirements for a one-pound box are provided below.

Item	PROPORTION OF CANDY WEIGHT		Minimum Mix Requirement
	Chocolates	Pastels	
Nuts	.15	.05	.10 lb
Soft centers	.50	1.00	.60
Hard centers	.50	0.00	.20
Total weight	1.00	1.00	1.00
Cost per pound	$4.00	$1.00	

Nuts are included in some candies of both types (hard and soft centers). The total weight restriction guarantees that boxes contain at least 1 pound of candy.

(a) Formulate Cee's linear program, and then solve it graphically to determine the optimal weights of chocolates and pastels to put in a Rainbow Box. Assume that each box must contain exactly 1 pound.

(b) Suppose that the total weight restriction is relaxed, so that *at least* 1 pound of candy must be included in each box. Find the new most attractive corner and the optimal solution.

9-12 Tubby Tucker is on a very strict diet and is allowed a bonus on Saturday night if he remains on his diet throughout the week. The bonus must contain less than 200 mg sodium (Na) and no more than 60 g carbohydrate (CHO). Tubby wants to consume as many calories as he can within these constraints. He has selected apple pie a la mode, for which the following data apply:

	Calories	Na	CHO
Piece of pie	100	120	15
Scoop of ice cream	140	40	15

Formulate Tubby's decision as a linear program and then solve it graphically. How much pie and ice cream will Tubby eat?

10

Linear Programming Applications and Problem Formulation

L inear programming is perhaps the most successful quantitative method, as evidenced by its widespread use at virtually all levels of business and in every major industry. It is well-accepted and is used in most functional areas—particularly finance, management, marketing, and production. Linear programming has an excellent track record for achieving operational efficiencies and cost savings. In Chapter 10, we will examine a variety of linear programming applications. The problem descriptions will also illustrate a variety of ways to formulate linear programs.

FINANCE APPLICATION: PORTFOLIO SELECTION 10-1

Portfolio managers use linear programming and its extensions to determine what investments to make. As an illustration, we will consider an income portfolio to be made up of bonds from six different corporations. The manager must choose the amounts to invest in each security, with

$$X_i = \text{size of investment in company } i \text{ bonds}$$

Here, i represents any one of the six companies: $A, B, C, D, E,$ or F. The objective is to choose the values of the X's that will maximize total interest income. The following yields apply:

Bond	Current Interest Yield
A	8.5%
B	9.0
C	10.0
D	9.5
E	8.5
F	9.0

The objective function can be expressed as

Maximize $\quad P = .085X_A + .090X_B + .100X_C + .095X_D + .085X_E + .090X_F$

The initial portfolio investment will be $100,000, so that the individual bond purchases must sum to this amount:

$$X_A + X_B + X_C + X_D + X_E + X_F = 100,000 \quad \text{(funds)}$$

It is usually wise to diversify investments. Public investment funds are often diversified because limitations are usually placed on the proportion of the portfolio that may be applied to any particular issue. We will assume that our manager cannot place more than 25% of the invested funds in any single bond. The diversification constraint that applies to bond A is therefore

$$X_A \leq 25,000 \quad \text{(diversification limit for bond } A)$$

Identical constraints are applicable to $X_B, X_C, X_D, X_E,$ and X_F.
The following redemption dates and bond ratings apply:

Bond	Scheduled Redemption	Quality Rating
A	1991	excellent
B	2005	very good
C	1989	fair
D	1988	good
E	1995	excellent
F	2000	very good

Investment policy is that at least one-half of the funds be placed in longer maturity (post 1990) issues. This requirement provides the maturity constraint

$$X_A + X_B + X_E + X_F \geq 50,000 \quad \text{(maturity)}$$

It is also investment policy that no more than 30% of all funds be placed in bonds rated in categories lower than "very good." This requirement is represented by the quality constraint

$$X_C + X_D \leq 30,000 \quad \text{(quality)}$$

Non-negativity conditions ordinarily apply to the variables in portfolio selection. The optimal solution to this linear program is

$$X_A = 20,000 \qquad X_D = 5,000$$

$$X_B = 25,000 \qquad X_E = 0$$

$$X_C = 25,000 \qquad X_F = 25,000$$

$$P = 9,175$$

Notice that none of bond E is purchased—a plausible result considering its low yield of 8.5%. But more money must be invested in bond F at 9% than in bond D at 9.5%. This is largely due to maturity and quality differences. Collectively, several linear programming constraints may provide surprising—even perplexing—results. Linear programming has been used extensively by many mutual funds and other large financial institutions to facilitate portfolio selections.

MANAGEMENT APPLICATION: SHIPMENT SCHEDULING 10-2

A large category of linear programs arises from the need to control distribution costs. A typical problem is faced by a multiplant manufacturer who must schedule shipments to several regional warehouses. As an illustration, we will consider the operations of a sporting goods company that makes skis in three plants throughout the world. The plants supply four company-owned warehouses that distribute the skis directly to ski shops. Depending on which mode is cheaper, the product is air-freighted or trucked from the plants to the warehouses. Table 10-1 provides the various point-to-point costs of shipping a pair of skis. The monthly capacities of the plants in terms of the number of pairs of skis that can be made are

Plant	Capacity
Juarez	100
Seoul	300
Tel Aviv	200
Total	600

TABLE 10-1
The Shipping Costs Per Pair of Skis

	To Warehouse			
From Plants	Frankfurt	New York	Phoenix	Yokohama
Juarez	$19	$ 7	$ 3	$21
Seoul	15	21	18	6
Tel Aviv	11	14	15	22

and warehouse demand requirements for next month are

Warehouse	Demand
Frankfurt	150
New York	100
Phoenix	200
Yokohama	150
Total	600

To determine how many pairs of skis should be shipped from each plant to the various warehouses, the shipping schedule shown in Table 10-2 is constructed. The numbers of pairs of skis sent via each route are unknown and are represented as variables by the letter X with the appropriate subscripts. In general, we will adopt the convention

$$X_{ij} = \text{quantity shipped from plant } i \text{ to warehouse } j$$

where each possible i or j may be represented by a number $(1, 2, 3, 4, \ldots)$ or a letter $(A, B, C, D, \ldots)$ corresponding to the identity of the respective plant or warehouse.

TABLE 10-2
The Shipment Schedule for Skis

	To Warehouse				Plant Capacity
From Plants	F	N	P	Y	
J	X_{JF}	X_{JN}	X_{JP}	X_{JY}	100
S	X_{SF}	X_{SN}	X_{SP}	X_{SY}	300
T	X_{TF}	X_{TN}	X_{TP}	X_{TY}	200
Warehouse Demand	150	100	200	150	600

The Xs are to be chosen so that total shipping cost is minimized. The total cost over each route is the shipping cost per pair of skis multiplied by the quantity shipped. From Juarez to Frankfurt, this cost would be $19X_{JF}$. Summing the values from all routes, our problem objective is to

$$
\begin{aligned}
\text{Minimize} \quad C = \quad & 19X_{JF} + 7X_{JN} + 3X_{JP} + 21X_{JY} \\
& + 15X_{SF} + 21X_{SN} + 18X_{SP} + 6X_{SY} \\
& + 11X_{TF} + 14X_{TN} + 15X_{TP} + 22X_{TY}
\end{aligned}
$$

The problem involves two kinds of constraints. One set applies to the plants and specifies that *the total number of units shipped from each plant must equal that plant's capacity*. The three plant-capacity constraints for this problem are

$$
\begin{aligned}
X_{JF} + X_{JN} + X_{JP} + X_{JY} &= 100 \quad \text{(Juarez capacity)} \\
X_{SF} + X_{SN} + X_{SP} + X_{SY} &= 300 \quad \text{(Seoul capacity)} \\
X_{TF} + X_{TN} + X_{TP} + X_{TY} &= 200 \quad \text{(Tel Aviv capacity)}
\end{aligned}
$$

Analogously, every warehouse must meet a second set of constraints, so that *the total number of units shipped to each warehouse must equal that warehouse's demand*. The four warehouse demand constraints for our problem are expressed explicitly as

$$
\begin{aligned}
X_{JF} + X_{SF} + X_{TF} &= 150 \quad \text{(Frankfurt demand)} \\
X_{JN} + X_{SN} + X_{TN} &= 100 \quad \text{(New York demand)} \\
X_{JP} + X_{SP} + X_{TP} &= 200 \quad \text{(Phoenix demand)} \\
X_{JY} + X_{SY} + X_{TY} &= 150 \quad \text{(Yokohama demand)}
\end{aligned}
$$

Finally, we include the non-negativity conditions

$$
\text{where} \quad \text{all } X_{ij}\text{'s} \geq 0
$$

Our example illustrates a class of linear programming situations that are referred to as *transportation problems*. In Chapter 15, we will learn how such problems are solved using the *transportation method*. The optimal solution to this problem (which will be discussed in detail in Chapter 15) is

$$
\begin{array}{llll}
X_{JF} = 0 & X_{JN} = 0 & X_{JP} = 100 & X_{JY} = 0 \\
X_{SF} = 50 & X_{SN} = 0 & X_{SP} = 100 & X_{SY} = 150 \\
X_{TF} = 100 & X_{TN} = 100 & X_{TP} = 0 & X_{TY} = 0
\end{array}
$$

$$
C = 6,250
$$

This solution provides the most economical plan. Some of the results are obvious—for example, that Seoul (Korea) supply Yokahama (Japan) but not New York. It seems a little odd that Seoul supplies Phoenix, but its demand outstrips Juarez's capacity and the Korean supplier must take up the slack. When the number of sources and destinations is great, linear programming solutions may involve a great number of unobvious shipping assignments. Cost savings in transportation can be huge. Many companies of moderate size have saved millions of dollars in freight charges by using linear programming to schedule shipments.

10-3 MANAGEMENT APPLICATION: ASSIGNING PERSONNEL

Linear programming is widely used to assign workers to specific jobs. As an example, we will consider a small machine shop, where each worker operates different pieces of equipment at varying skill levels. The following average times apply to each item processed by the shop:

| Individual | Time Required to Complete One Job | | |
	Drilling	Grinding	Lathe
Ann	5 min	10 min	10 min
Bud	10	5	15
Chuck	15	15	10

Management wishes to assign operators to jobs so that the total time required to process one item is minimized.

As in shipment scheduling, it is convenient to designate the variables with double subscripts. In this case

$$X_{ij} = \text{fraction of time individual } i \text{ is assigned to job } j$$

Notice that we have $3 \times 3 = 9$ variables (the number of individuals multiplied by the number of jobs). The objective function is to

$$\text{Minimize} \quad C = \quad 5X_{AD} + 10X_{AG} + 10X_{AL}$$
$$+ 10X_{BD} + 5X_{BG} + 15X_{BL}$$
$$+ 15X_{CD} + 15X_{CG} + 10X_{CL}$$

One set of constraints applies to the availability of the operators, thereby ensuring that every individual is fully occupied:

$$X_{AD} + X_{AG} + X_{AL} = 1 \quad \text{(Ann's availability)}$$

$$X_{BD} + X_{BG} + X_{BL} = 1 \quad \text{(Bud's availability)}$$

$$X_{CD} + X_{CG} + X_{CL} = 1 \quad \text{(Chuck's availability)}$$

Another set of constraints applies to the jobs, each of which requires a complete assignment:

$$X_{AD} + X_{BD} + X_{CD} = 1 \quad \text{(drill-press requirement)}$$

$$X_{AG} + X_{BG} + X_{CG} = 1 \quad \text{(grinder requirement)}$$

$$X_{AL} + X_{BL} + X_{CL} = 1 \quad \text{(lathe requirement)}$$

Of course, non-negativity is a condition for all variables.

Our example is a linear programming representation of the broad class of problems called *assignment problem*, which will also be examined in detail in Chapter 15. The optimal solution to this problem is

$$X_{AD} = 1 \qquad\qquad X_{CL} = 1$$

$$X_{BG} = 1 \qquad \text{all other } X\text{'s} = 0$$

$$C = 20$$

MARKETING APPLICATION: BUDGETING ADVERTISING EXPENDITURES 10-4

Linear programming can be employed in establishing advertising budgets to designate a firm's level of expenditures for each media, such as television, radio, billboards, and magazines. Linear programming can even be used to determine how much space or time should be allocated to each medium, as the following example illustrates.

The owner of Real Reels, a fishing equipment manufacturing company, wishes to determine how many quarter-page ads to place in *Playboy*, *True*, and *Esquire*. The following variables apply:

$$X_P = \text{number of ads in } Playboy$$

$$X_T = \text{number of ads in } True$$

$$X_E = \text{number of ads in } Esquire$$

The goal is to maximize total product exposure to significant buyers of expensive fishing gear. Exposure in any particular magazine is the number of ads placed multiplied by the number of significant buyers. The following data apply:

	Playboy	True	Esquire
Readers	10 million	6 million	4 million
Significant buyers	10%	15%	7%
Cost per ad	$10,000	$5,000	$6,000

The exposure for a *Playboy* ad is $.10 \times 10,000,000 = 1,000,000$. It will be convenient to express everything in millions. Letting P represent total exposure, the objective function is to

$$\text{Maximize} \quad P = 1X_P + .9X_T + .28X_E$$

Real has budgeted a maximum of $100,000 for the ads. The owner has already determined that no more than 5 ads should be placed in *True* and that at least 2 ads apiece should be placed in *Playboy* and *Esquire*. The problem constraints are

$$10,000X_P + 5,000X_T + 6,000X_E \leq 100,000 \quad \text{(budget)}$$
$$1X_T \leq 5 \quad \text{(maximum \textit{True} ads)}$$
$$1X_P \geq 2 \quad \text{(minimum \textit{Playboy} ads)}$$
$$1X_E \geq 2 \quad \text{(minimum \textit{Esquire} ads)}$$
$$\text{where} \quad X_P, X_T, X_E \geq 0$$

The optimal solution to this problem is

$$X_P = 6.3 \qquad X_T = 5 \qquad X_E = 2$$
$$P = 11.36 \text{ million}$$

Notice that this solution involves a fractional amount for the *Playboy* ads. Remember that linear programming permits this. Fractional solutions may not be troublesome when quantities are large. In Chapter 16, we will examine *integer programming*, where variables are restricted to whole numbers.

The example here only partially illustrates the power of linear programming in advertising decision making. Many more magazines and media types can be considered simultaneously and several time periods can even be incorporated in a linear programming problem. Various demographic characteristics in the target audiences, such as reader ages and earnings, can also be included.

Constraints may result in more or less emphasis on certain groups of people. Advertising problems involving thousands of variables with hundreds of constraints have been solved by using the linear programming approach.

PRODUCTION APPLICATION: LIQUID BLENDING 10-5

Many products, from toothpaste to gasoline, are blended from a variety of raw ingredients. The processes involved are often highly flexible because these products must meet various restrictions, such as limited ingredient availability and minimum product demand. Managers can apply linear programming to determine the particular blend of ingredients that will meet all constraints and still maximize total profit.

As an illustration, we will consider an aftershave and a cologne that are both made of essentially the same three active ingredients: oil, rinse, and stabilizer. As before, it is convenient to define the variables using double subscript notation, so that

$$X_{ij} = \text{quantity of ingredient } i \text{ used in blending product } j$$

The letters O, R, and S will be used to denote the respective ingredients; A and C, the products.

We will begin this particular formulation by defining the constraints that pertain to liquid availabilities (in liters):

$$X_{OA} + X_{OC} \leq 2,000 \quad \text{(oil)}$$
$$X_{RA} + X_{RC} \leq 500 \quad \text{(rinse)}$$
$$X_{SA} + X_{SC} \leq 1,000 \quad \text{(stabilizer)}$$

The left-hand sides of these inequalities represent the total quantities of the respective ingredients; the right-hand sides indicate the current inventory levels.

A second set of constraints pertains to product demands in liters of active ingredients:

$$X_{OA} + X_{RA} + X_{SA} \geq 1,500 \quad \text{(aftershave demand)}$$
$$X_{OC} + X_{RC} + X_{SC} \geq 500 \quad \text{(cologne demand)}$$

Here, the left-hand sides represent the total volumes of active liquid ingredients in the present production run of the respective product, and the right-hand sides indicate the minimum volumes required to meet the product demands.

A final set of constraints pertains to the proportional content of the ingredients in each product. For example, at least 30% of the volume of cologne must be emulsions. The oil is 50% emulsions, the rinse is 100%, and the stabilizer is only 10%. The emulsion requirement can therefore be summarized as

$$\frac{.50X_{OC} + 1.00X_{RC} + .10X_{SC}}{X_{OC} + X_{RC} + X_{SC}} \geq .30 \quad \text{(emulsions in cologne)}$$

where the numerator expresses the total emulsion volume of the cologne ingredients and the denominator indicates the total volume of the cologne. This ratio must be at least .30.

A similar restriction applies to the aftershave, which must contain more than 20% evaporative agents. The rinse is 25% evaporatives, the stabilizer is 50%, and the oil contains none. The evaporative requirement is summarized as

$$\frac{.25X_{RA} + .50X_{SA}}{X_{OA} + X_{RA} + X_{SA}} \geq .20 \quad \text{(evaporatives in aftershave)}$$

These two proportional content constraints are ordinarily rearranged by multiplying both sides of the inequality by the denominator, canceling, and then collecting X terms on the left-hand side:

$$.20X_{OC} + .70X_{RC} - .20X_{SC} \geq 0 \quad \text{(emulsions in cologne)}$$

$$-.20X_{OA} + .05X_{RA} + .30X_{SA} \geq 0 \quad \text{(evaporatives in aftershave)}$$

Of course, all Xs must be non-negative. The objective is to maximize total profit. We begin to express this by considering total sales. The value per liter of active ingredients is $10 for aftershave and $20 for cologne. This gives us total sales of

$$10(X_{OA} + X_{RA} + X_{SA}) + 20(X_{OC} + X_{RC} + X_{SC})$$

Ingredient costs are $2 per liter of oil, $30 per liter of rinse, and $4 per liter of stabilizer. Total cost is therefore expressed as

$$2(X_{OA} + X_{OC}) + 30(X_{RA} + X_{RC}) + 4(X_{SA} + X_{SC})$$

By subtracting total cost from total revenue and collecting and rearranging terms, we obtain the objective function

$$\text{Maximize} \quad P = 8X_{OA} - 20X_{RA} + 6X_{SA} + 18X_{OC} - 10X_{RC} + 16X_{SC}$$

The optimal solution to this problem is

$$X_{OA} = 220 \qquad X_{OC} = 1,780$$

$$X_{RA} = 280 \qquad X_{RC} = 0$$

$$X_{SA} = 1,000 \qquad X_{SC} = 0$$

$$P = 34,200$$

Linear programming is used extensively by oil and chemical companies. Managers at many large oil refineries routinely employ linear programs in operational planning. One refinery makes a daily computer run to solve a linear program that indicates the day's gasoline blending plan. Shifts in ingredient availabilities and costs and slight variations in ingredient composition require frequent planning, and linear programming has proved to be a very valuable tool in accomplishing this task.

PRODUCTION APPLICATION: PRODUCT-MIX SELECTION 10-6

The Redwood Furniture problem we described in Chapter 9 provides an example of an extensive linear programming application—product-mix selection. Linear programming can generate periodic production plans that indicate in detail the particular quantities of various items that are most profitable. This can be done in such a way that the customer demands for each product are met. All resources used in manufacturing—raw materials, labor, supplies, and facilities—can be explicitly accounted for to ensure that limitations are satisfied by a feasible production plan that employs these resources most efficiently. Special interrelationships between two or more products—for example, the requirement that at least four chairs must be manufactured for each table—may also be reflected as constraints in the linear program.

PRODUCTION APPLICATION: THE DIET PROBLEM 10-7

In Chapter 9, we also described a feed-mix problem, where our objective was to choose the quantities of the various ingredients used in mixing animal feed that would minimize cost and, at the same time, meet minimum nutritional requirements without exceeding the maximum limits on certain contents, such as water and inert substances. That is an example of a broad class of linear programs that are referred to as diet problems. Diet problems that include human as well as animal food products are a very common linear programming application. For example, the ingredients in frankfurters may vary depending on availability and cost. One large meat packer reportedly solves a diet problem daily by formulating the current production plan for making its hot dogs. In Chapter 12, we will discover how the diet problem is applied in making Persian sausage.

PROBLEMS

The following problems all involve too many variables to be solved graphically and are to be *formulated only*.

10-1 Rott Irony manufactures four types of light fixtures. A fancy lamp yields a profit of $100, takes 10 hours of labor and 2 hours of machine time, and requires 10 ft^2 of sheet metal. An ornate lamp yields a profit of $150, takes 8 hours of labor and 3 hours of machine time, and requires 20 ft^2 of metal. The plain and rococo lamps each yield a $200 profit and involve 1 hour of machine time. However, the rococo lamp requires 20 hours of labor and 30 ft^2 of metal, and the plain lamp requires 10 hours of labor and 15 ft^2 of metal. Rott must produce at least twice as many plain lamps as rococo ones. Only 1,000 hours of labor and 200 hours of machine time are available, and 5,000 ft^2 of sheet metal are in inventory. Rott wishes to determine how many of each type of lamp to make to maximize total profits. Formulate this problem as a linear program.

10-2 Quicker Oats must determine how much of its $200,000 advertising and promotional budget should be spent in the following mediums: television, radio, magazines, and prize promotion. Each dollar spent on television advertising increases sales $10; both radio and magazine ads result in one-half that return, and prize promotion returns $20 in sales for each dollar invested. Television advertising cannot exceed one-half of the total budget, and total radio advertising must be at least 20% of total TV advertising. At least $20,000 must be spent on magazine ads, and no more than $25,000 can be spent on the prize promotion. Management's objective is to maximize the total increase in Quicker's sales volume. Formulate the decision as a linear program.

10-3 CompuQuick must determine which of its computer facilities should process client company payrolls. Based on the complexity and size of the payroll and on processing speed, data-transmission requirements, and volumes of input and output, the following costs apply:

Facility	Company Payroll		
	Blitz Beer	Waysafe Markets	Quicker Oats
Arizona	$500	$750	$400
California	600	500	300
Illinois	700	600	300

Each facility has the capacity to process only one payroll. CompuQuick wishes to minimize its total data-processing costs. Formulate this problem as a linear program.

10-4 A portfolio manager wishes to invest $100,000 of current receipts in order to maximize total annual interest income. She has narrowed her choices to a municipal bond yielding 6%, an industrial bond yielding 8%, Treasury bills at 10%, and certificates of deposit (CDs) at 9%. For safety, at least one-half of the funds must be placed in bonds. For liquidity, at least 25% of the funds must be invested in CDs. Due to volatile Fed policies, no more than 20% of the portfolio can be in Treasury bills. Tax-sheltering considerations dictate that at least 30% of the investment must be in municipal bonds. Formulate this problem as a linear program.

10-5 A meat packer wishes to determine the quantity of ingredients to use in making each pound of sausage at a minimum cost. The available ingredients and their costs are provided in the following table:

Pound of Ingredient	Cost	Protein	Fat	Water
Hog bellies	$.30	3 oz	7 oz	6 oz
Tripe	.20	5	4	7
Beef	.70	4	2	10
Pork	.60	3	4	9
Chicken	.45	3	5	8

The meat packer is faced with some restrictions in doing this. Not more than 10% of the sausage weight can composed of hog bellies and tripe, chicken cannot exceed 25% of the total content, and at least 30% of the sausage must consist of beef. In addition, a minimum of 3 ounces of protein must be present in each pound of sausage. Furthermore, each pound of sausage *may* contain a maximum of 4 ounces of fat and *must* contain a maximum of 8 ounces of water. Formulate the decision as a linear program.

10-6 The Bugoff Chemical Company manufacturers three pesticides—Ant-Can't, Boll-Toll, and Caterpillar-Chiller—at respective profits of $5, $6, and $7 per gallon. Bugoff must decide what quantities of each pesticide to produce. Regardless of brand, each gallon requires 100 milligrams (.1 gram) of catalyst. Every gallon of Ant-Can't and Caterpillar-Chiller requires 1/10 gallon of malathion, and each gallon of Boll-Toll and Caterpillar-Chiller must contain 2/10 gallon of parathion. Seasonal requirements dictate that the quantity of Ant-Can't may exceed the quantity of Boll-Toll by no more than 500 gallons. The available ingredients are 1,000 grams of catalyst, 1,000 gallons of malathion, and 2,000 gallons of parathion, Bugoff wishes to produce the most profitable quantities of each pesticide. Formulate this problem as a linear program.

10-7 Returning to the liquid blending example described in Section 10-5, formulate each of the following constraints in a form suitable for incorporation into the original linear program.

(a) The proportion of alcohol in cologne cannot exceed 50% of the total volume. The oil contains no alcohol, but the rinse is 50% alcohol and the stabilizer is 20% alcohol.

(b) The volume of skin-bracing agents in the aftershave cannot exceed 30%. These agents comprise 10% of the oil, 20% of the rinse, and 20% of the stabilizer.

10-8 Druids' Drayage hauls rock from two quarries to three tombstone masons. The manager, H. Priest, wishes to minimize total shipping costs in such a way that every quarry operates precisely at full capacity and each mason receives exactly the number of stones demanded. The following unit shipping costs and quantity requirements apply to tombstones:

| | To Mason | | | Quarry |
From Quarry	Cedrick	Dunstan	Eldred	Capacity
Abinger	£10	£ 15	£ 8	100
Barnesly	12	9	10	200
Mason demand	50	150	100	300

A linear program can be used to establish a shipping schedule that indicates how many tombstones should be supplied from each quarry to the various masons. A quarry can service any number of masons, and any mason can receive shipments from one or more quarries. Formulate this problem as a linear program.

10-9 ChipMont manufactures silicon wafer circuits for use in microprocessors. Computer makers presently buy ChipMont's entire production of the following types of silicon chips: central processing unit (CPU), integrated circuit, and core memory. The following data apply:

| | Chip Types | | | Available |
Item	CPU	Integrated	Memory	Maximums
Silicon	.005	.02	.01	10,000 sheets
Sorting labor	.2	.5	.1	200,000 minutes
Chemical wash	.10	.40	.15	400,000 hours
Profit per wafer	$.25	$.40	$.15	

ChipMont must decide how many of each chip to manufacture. The number of integrated circuits must be at least as large as the combined total for the other two types of wafers.
(a) Formulate ChipMont's decision as a linear program.
(b) One possible production plan is to make 50,000 CPU's, 300,000 integrated circuits, and 200,000 core memories. Place these quantities in each of your linear programming constraints to verify that this plan is feasible. Then find the corresponding profit.

10-10 Conformity Systems has three employees, a clerk, a typist, and a stenographer. Each employee will be assigned exactly one of the following tasks: filing, bookkeeping, or report preparation. The manager wishes to assign workers to jobs so that total cost is minimized. The costs for each possible employee–job assignment are provided in the following table:

| | Job | | |
Employee	Filing	Bookkeeping	Reports
Clerk	$20	$25	$35
Typist	25	20	30
Stenographer	30	25	25

Treating each possible employee–job assignment as a separate variable, formulate this problem as a linear program.

10-11 Blitz Beer has allotted $10,000 for radio advertising in Gotham City and must determine the placement of spot ads that will maximize increased sales. Top-40 stations attract a heavier beer-drinking audience than golden-oldie stations do, but top-40 stations also charge more for each spot. The following data apply:

Station	Cost per Spot	Sales Increase per Spot	Spots Available	Format
KBAT	$100	$300	30	top-40
WJOK	50	120	unlimited	golden-oldie
WROB	75	.150	unlimited	golden-oldie
KPOW	150	400	40	top-40

At least 25% of the spots must be placed with golden-oldie stations. Formulate Blitz's problem as a linear program.

10-12 Horrible Harry's, a chain of self-service gas stations, must determine how to blend its hybrid petroleum products—gasahol and petrolmeth. Both products are blended from 90-octane unleaded gasoline. Ethyl alcohol, the only gasahol additive, cannot exceed 10% of the final product's volume. Petrolmeth may contain both ethyl and methyl alcohols, but these combined ingredients must not exceed 30% of the final product's volume. The octane ratings are 120 for ethyl alcohol and 110 for methyl alcohol. Final product octane ratings must equal the average octane ratings for the ingredients by volume. Gasahol must have an octane rating of at least 91, and petrolmeth must have a rating of at least 93. There are 20,000 gallons of gasoline presently available for blending, at a cost of $1.00 per gallon. Up to 5,000 gallons of methyl alcohol can be acquired for $.50 per gallon, and 3,000 gallons of ethyl alcohol are available at $1.50 per gallon. The demands are at least 10,000 gallons for gasahol and 5,000 gallons for petrolmeth. Horrible Harry's must meet all of the above requirements at minimum cost. Formulate this problem as a linear program.

10-13 Geo-Pet is the managing partner in a variety of oil-exploration ventures. It must decide its level of dollar investment in the five ventures described in the following table:

Joint Venture	Expected Return	Minimum Investment	Primary Product
Athabasca Tar Sands (Canada)	100%	$100,000	crude
Kern County (U.S.)	30	none	crude
Louisiana Miocene Trend (U.S.)	50	50,000	gas
Persian Gulf (Arabia)	150	none	crude
West Texas (U.S.)	75	100,000	gas

Geo-Pet wishes to maximize its expected rate of return on a maximum total investment of $700,000 and still meet the dollar minimums given here. At least $300,000 must be placed in gas-producing investments, and no more than one-half of the total amount can be invested outside the United States. Formulate this problem as a linear program.

10-14 Ace Widgets manufactures products in plant A at a cost of $10 each and products in plant B at a cost of $11 each. The products are shipped to warehouses at a cost of $.01 per mile. The following distances apply:

	Distance to		
From	C	D	E
A	100	200	300
B	200	100	200

Plant A can manufacture 1,000 units; plant B has the capacity to manufacture only 500 units. Warehouse demands are 500 units for each. Ace Widgets must determine a manufacturing and shipping schedule that will meet these exact limitations at the least total cost. Formulate Ace's problem as a linear program.

10-15 Shale–Bituminous Processors use gasification and pressurization to make low-sulfur and high-sulfur crude oil. The two processes require different mixtures of coal and shale solids. A batch processed by gasification requires an input of 1 ton of coal and 2 tons of shale to yield 100 gallons of low-sulfur crude and 200 gallons of high-sulfur crude. Under pressurization, each batch requires 2 tons of coal and 1 ton of shale to provide 150 gallons of low-sulfur crude and 100 gallons of high-sulfur crude.

The refinery manager wishes to determine how many batches should be converted to crude oil under each process to maximize total profits when supplying an order for 10,000 gallons of low-sulfur and 5,000 gallons of high-sulfur crudes. Available tonnages for filling this order are 100 tons of coal and 150 tons of shale. The costs of the solids per ton are $20 for coal and $25 for shale. The processor receives $.50 per gallon for low-sulfur crude and $.30 for high-sulfur crude.

(a) If 10 batches are processed under gasification and 20 batches are processed under pressurization, determine how many
  (1) tons of coal are used.
  (2) tons of shale are used.
  (3) gallons of low-sulfur crude are produced.
  (4) gallons of high-sulfur crude are produced.
(b) Determine the profit per batch converted under each process.
(c) Formulate the processor's problem as a linear program.

10-16 Backpackers' Budget Shoppe is concocting a package to sell under the label "Hiker's Daily Dried Gruel." Designed only with nutritional value and ease of preparation in mind, each kilogram of the mix must meet the nutritional requirements provided in the following table:

Nutrient	NUTRITIONAL VALUE OF INGREDIENT PER KILOGRAM					Minimum Requirement
	Corn Meal	Beans	Spinach	Peanuts	Milk	
Calories	4,000	3,000	250	2,000	2,000	4,000
Protein	100	200	25	100	100	100 g
Iron	12	100	30	8	2	12 g
Vitamin A	4,000	1,000	50,000	5,000	13,000	5,000 units
Thiamine	2	6	1.5	1.5	1	2 mg
Riboflavin	1	5	3	1	6	3 mg
Niacin	12	25	8	80	3	20 mg
Ascorbic acid	0	0	500	0	15	100 mg
Cost per kilogram	$.50	$.75	$1.25	$.75	$1.50	

Formulate a linear program that determines the minimum-cost ingredient weights that satisfy these nutritional requirements.

11

The Simplex Method in Linear Programming

We are now ready to tackle linear programs that are impossible to solve by the graphical method because they contain too many variables to plot on a two-dimensional graph. An algebraic procedure—the *simplex method*—works on all linear programs, regardless of the number of variables. With the aid of a high-speed digital computer, the simplex method can be used to solve problems with thousands of variables and ten times that number of constraints. Indeed, without the simplex method, linear programming would be little more than a mathematical curiosity that could describe problems algebraically but could not solve any problem that had more than two or three variables.

The word simplex was *not* formed by adding the ubiquitous suffix *-ex* to the word simple (as in Kleenex and Memorex). *Simplex* is a legitimate term in the language of mathematics that represents the simplest object in an n-dimensional space connecting $n + 1$ points. In one dimension, a simplex is a line segment connecting two points. In two dimensions, a simplex is a triangle formed by joining three points. A three-dimensional simplex is a four-sided pyramid having just four corners. Such geometrical objects, extended to higher dimensions, are used to explain how and why the *simplex method* works. Although the procedure itself is quite simple to master, the mathematical arguments justifying this procedure are fairly complex.

Even though its underlying concepts are geometrical, the simplex algorithm itself is fundamentally an algebraic procedure. George B. Dantzig developed the algorithm after World War II and, with other mathematicians, has since extended and expanded it in a variety of ways. Like the graphical method, the simplex algorithm finds the most attractive corner of the feasible solution region, thereby solving the linear program. Ordinarily, the region itself exists in a higher dimensional space that can be imagined but not pictured. An underlying theoretical concept of the simplex method is that *any problem having a solution at all must have an optimal solution that corresponds to a corner point.*

This means that we need to evaluate only the corner points. Although finding and evaluating corners would seem to be child's play, remember that they are not pictured, so we cannot see them. Furthermore, the number of corners associated with even a moderately large linear program can be huge. For example, solving a 10-product planning problem with 10 resource constraints would involve nearly 200,000 corners. In our lifetimes, the biggest, fastest computer could not evaluate the trillions and trillions of corners in a problem just 10 times that size. A second feature of the simplex method incorporates a reliable search through the formidable thicket of corners to rapidly find the most attractive one. Based on *economic analysis*, this searching procedure is so efficient that only about 20 corners are evaluated in the 10-product case just mentioned.

In conclusion, the simplex method embodies geometry, but it combines algebra with economic principles to solve linear programs. Simplex is really an odyssey in *n*-dimensional space where you visit a few corner points on a multifaceted "gem stone" you can't see. Each time you stop, you perform a small analysis to find out where you should stop next; your journey ends at the most attractive corner.

11-1 BASIC SIMPLEX CONCEPTS

To introduce the simplex method, we will continue our Redwood Furniture problem, using the data repeated in Table 11-1. As before, X_T and X_C represent the number of tables and chairs. The linear program is

$$\text{Maximize} \quad P = 6X_T + 8X_C \quad \text{(objective)}$$

$$\text{Subject to} \quad 30X_T + 20X_C \le 300 \quad \text{(wood)}$$

$$5X_T + 10X_C \le 110 \quad \text{(labor)}$$

$$\text{where} \quad X_T, X_C \ge 0$$

TABLE 11-1
Data for the Redwood Furniture Problem

Resource	UNIT REQUIREMENTS		Amount Available
	Table	Chair	
Wood (board feet)	30	20	300
Labor (hours)	5	10	110
Unit profit	$6	$8	

Slack Variables

We will now solve this problem algebraically. Our first step is to acknowledge the existence of *slack*, which represents unused resources. We define the following *slack variables*:

$$X_W = \text{amount of unused wood}$$

$$X_L = \text{amount of unused labor}$$

(The original problem variables X_T and X_C are sometimes called *main variables* to distinguish them from the slacks.) Each slack variable is incorporated into the original constraints. In the case of wood, we may equivalently express the constraint as

Wood used in tables or chairs + Unused wood = Available wood

By adding the quantities of wood on the left side, this constraint tells us "what we use plus what we don't use must equal what we start with." The meaning of the constraint is the same as before. Stated algebraically, our revised wood constraint is

$$30X_T + 20X_C + X_W = 300 \quad \text{(wood)}$$

which is equivalent to the original expression. Adding the slack variable converts an inequality into an equality. The X_W term bridges the gap, taking up the slack between the less than ($<$) and the equal ($=$) signs.

In the same way, we can convert the labor constraint into the equality

$$5X_T + 10X_C + X_L = 110 \quad \text{(labor)}$$

Notice that the unused wood X_W appears only in the wood constraint equation and that the unused labor X_L appears only in the labor constraint equation.

Slack variables have a two-fold purpose. First, and most importantly, adding the slack variables allows us to convert inequalities into equalities, thereby converting the linear program into a form that is amenable to algebraic solution. It is mathematically easier to analyze equalities than inequalities. Second, slack variables permit us to make a more comprehensive economic interpretation of a solution than would otherwise be possible.

Expressing the Linear Program in Terms of Slacks

Incorporating the slack variables into the entire linear program formulation, we have

$$\text{Maximize} \quad P = 6X_T + 8X_C + 0X_W + 0X_L \quad \text{(objective)}$$
$$\text{Subject to} \quad 30X_T + 20X_C + 1X_W + 0X_L = 300 \quad \text{(wood)}$$
$$5X_T + 10X_C + 0X_W + 1X_L = 110 \quad \text{(labor)}$$
$$\text{where} \quad X_T, X_C, X_W, X_L \geq 0$$

X_W and X_L appear in the objective equation with coefficients of zero, reflecting the fact that unused resources contribute nothing to profit (or to cost) but remain assets in inventory. The non-negativity conditions apply to X_W and X_L as well as to X_T and X_C. Slack variables cannot be negative. (If they were, it would mean that more of the resource than was originally available could be consumed, which would remove the limitation of the original constraint.)

For later convenience, X_W and X_L appear in their respective constraint equations with coefficients of 1. X_L also has a coefficient of zero in the wood constraint, and X_W similarly appears with a coefficient of zero in the labor constraint. This in no way distorts the original relationships, since a term appearing with a coefficient of zero is mathematically equivalent to being absent. This arrangement merely makes it easier for us to keep track of the problem.

Algebraic Solution

The feasible solution region to the new problem cannot be graphed, because we now have four variables and our problem is four-dimensional. Our algebraic system contains two constraint equations with four unknowns:

$$30X_T + 20X_C + 1X_W + 0X_L = 300$$
$$5X_T + 10X_C + 0X_W + 1X_L = 110$$

We learned how to solve two equations with two unknowns in Chapter 9 when we found the coordinates for the most attractive corner. But here *we have more unknowns than equations.* How do we find the solution?

Let's take a slight detour and consider the problem of finding values for x and y that satisfy the equation

$$2x + 4y = 12$$

Here, we must solve one equation with two unknowns. We recognize that this equation represents a line in the xy plane; we can even graph it. But here we are faced with essentially the same dilemma presented in the preceding linear program.

What's the answer? The line itself is the answer! But what are the x and y values? An infinite number of pairs of x and y values satisfy the equation, each pair being the coordinates of some point on the line.

To find any one solution, we must fix the value of x or y and then solve for the other variable. For example, if we

$$\text{set } x = 3$$

then we have

$$2(3) + 4y = 12$$

$$4y = 12 - 2(3) = 12 - 6 = 6$$

and

$$y = \tfrac{6}{4} = 1\tfrac{1}{2}$$

Thus, $(x = 3, y = 1\tfrac{1}{2})$ is one pair of coordinates. For any other arbitrary value of x, we can obtain a unique y. Likewise, for any arbitrary value of y, we can find a unique x. These ambiguous solutions are the best we can achieve.

Continuing with our detour, consider the equations

$$2x + 4y + 3z = 12$$

$$3x + 2y + 1z = 6$$

Here again, we have more unknowns than equations. In a three-dimensional graph, each equation represents a plane and the solution is the intersection of the planes. (Imagine two sheets of paper held at different angles and crossed.) The solution is a line again! As before, we can only obtain numerical values of x, y, and z that satisfy both equations by arbitrarily establishing the value of one variable and then solving for the others. For example, if we

$$\text{set } y = 1$$

then we have

$$2x + 4(1) + 3z = 12 \quad \text{or} \quad 2x + 3z = 8$$

$$3x + 2(1) + 1z = 6 \quad \text{or} \quad 3x + 1z = 4$$

and, solving for x and z, we obtain

$$x = \tfrac{4}{7} \qquad y = 1 \qquad z = 2\tfrac{2}{7}$$

From our detour, we can draw the following conclusion: *Whenever the number of variables exceeds the number of equations, the values of the extra variables must be arbitrarily set.*

The Variable Mix

In our Redwood Furniture problem, there are two more variables than equations. The values of these extra variables must be fixed before the equations can be solved algebraically. Part of our problem is deciding which variables are assigned arbitrary values and which variables are "free" to be solved for algebraically. We must also determine what arbitrary values to use.

We will refer to the variables that must be solved for algebraically as the *variable mix.* As we have seen, their values can be found only after the other variables have been fixed at some arbitrary level. The fixed-valued variables are identified as not being in the variable mix. Table 11-2 shows all of the possible combinations of variable-mix and nonmix variables for the Redwood Furniture problem. In each of the six cases, two complementary pairs of variables are involved.

We have noted that an essential feature of simplex is to evaluate corner points only. *Such a corner point is the algebraic solution to the constraint equations when the nonmix variables have been arbitrarily* set at 0. This fact considerably simplifies finding solutions and allows us to greatly streamline the overall simplex method.

Each of the six variable-mix pairs in Table 11-2 for the Redwood Furniture problem provides a different corner point solution. All of these corner points are graphed in Figure 11-1. The solutions for corner points A, B, C, and D follow.

TABLE 11-2

Possible Variable-Mix Combinations and Their Algebraic Solutions for the Redwood Furniture Problem

Corner Point	Variable Mix (free variables)	Nonmix Variables (arbitrarily set at 0)	X_T	X_C	X_W	X_L	P
A	$X_W X_L$	$X_T X_C$	0	0	300	110	$ 0
B	$X_W X_C$	$X_T X_L$	0	11	80	0	88
C	$X_L X_T$	$X_C X_W$	10	0	0	60	60
D	$X_T X_C$	$X_W X_L$	4	9	0	0	96
E	$X_L X_C$	$X_W X_T$	0	15	0	−40	infeasible
F	$X_W X_T$	$X_L X_C$	22	0	−360	0	infeasible

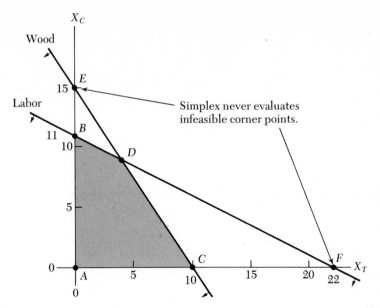

FIGURE 11-1
Possible corner points for the Redwood Furniture problem.

Corner point A:
 Set $X_T = 0$, $X_C = 0$

$$30(0) + 20(0) + 1X_W + 0X_L = 300$$
$$5(0) + 10(0) + 0X_W + 1X_L = 110$$

getting
$$1X_W \qquad\qquad = 300$$
$$1X_L = 110$$

Solution: $X_T = 0$, $X_C = 0$, $X_W = 300$, $X_L = 110$
 Profit: $P = 6(0) + 8(0) + 0(300) + 0(110) = 0$

Corner point B:
 Set $X_T = 0$, $X_L = 0$

$$30(0) + 20X_C + 1X_W + 0(0) = 300$$
$$5(0) + 10X_C + 0X_W + 1(0) = 110$$

getting
$$20X_C + X_W = 300$$
$$10X_C \qquad = 110$$

Solution: $X_T = 0$, $X_C = 11$, $X_W = 80$, $X_L = 0$
 Profit: $P = 6(0) + 8(11) + 0(80) + 0(0) = 88$

Corner point C:
  Set $X_C = 0$, $X_W = 0$

$$30X_T + 20(0) + 1(0) + 0X_L = 300$$
$$5X_T + 10(0) + 0(0) + 1X_L = 110$$

getting

$$30X_T \qquad\qquad = 300$$
$$5X_T + 1X_L = 110$$

Solution: $X_T = 10$, $X_C = 0$, $X_W = 0$, $X_L = 60$

  Profit: $P = 6(10) + 8(0) + 0(0) + 0(60) = 60$

Corner point D:
  Set $X_W = 0$, $X_L = 0$

$$30X_T + 20X_C + 1(0) + 0(0) = 300$$
$$5X_T + 10X_C + 0(0) + 1(0) = 110$$

getting

$$30X_T + 20X_C = 300$$
$$5X_T + 10X_C = 110$$

Solution: $X_T = 4$, $X_C = 9$, $X_W = 0$, $X_L = 0$

  Profit: $P = 6(4) + 8(9) + 0(0) + 0(0) = 96$

Only corner points A, B, C, and D are feasible. Point E is infeasible because it violates the labor constraint (the algebraic solution leads to a negative quantity for X_L), and point F is infeasible because it violates the wood constraint.

Before we continue, let's put our current example into its proper context. We are only illustrating the *concepts* of the simplex method here. We have not yet describe the algorithm steps. Furthermore, it is never necessary to perform all of these calculations to solve a simple problem for which a graphical solution can be achieved. Resolving the Redwood Furniture problem algebraically here just makes it easier for us to understand what is happening. Ordinarily, *simplex will only be used when there are too many main variables in the original inequality formulation to be depicted on a graph.* Also keep in mind that if we include slack variables, our present problem is four-dimensional, and we cannot construct a graph that directly incorporates slacks. In Figure 11-1, points on the constraint line represent zero slack for that particular resource; a feasible point off the line has an amount of positive slack that cannot be directly read from the graph.

Before describing the simplex algorithm in detail, a few more points will prove helpful. Suppose that we can identify all of the corner points in a linear program (as we did in Table 11-2). Then why can't we simply evaluate all of the feasible corner points algebraically and pick the one with the largest P? In our example, the most attractive corner is point D, with a profit of $96. After all, no graph is needed to list all of the combinations of variables mixes, and we know that each variable-mix pair must correspond to a particular corner.

There are two reasons why we do not follow this procedure. First, as we noted earlier, the number of corners can be astronomical for a moderately sized problem, and even if we want to, it may be impossible to consider them all. Second, each corner-point evaluation requires a lengthy algebraic solution. To obtain each corner-point solution for a 10-constraint linear program, 10 equations with 10 unknowns must be solved—a horrendous task without some simplifying procedure. Simplex eliminates both of these difficulties.

THE SIMPLEX METHOD 11-2

Simplex ordinarily begins at the corner that represents "doing nothing," where the variable mix is composed only of slack variables. It then moves to the neighboring corner point that improves the solution at the greatest rate. It continues to move progressively from neighboring corner to neighboring corner, making the greatest possible improvement in the solution on each successive move. When no more improvements can be made in the solution, the most attractive corner has been found. As we have noted, this method usually results in evaluating only a tiny fraction of all of the corner points in a linear program; a huge number of corner points are simply skipped. Simplex also reduces the task of algebraically solving for the unknowns at a cornerpoint to a few simple arithmetic steps.

The Simplex Tableau

For convenience, we will again express the latest Redwood Furniture linear program:

Maximize $P = 6X_T + 8X_C + 0X_W + 0X_L$ (objective)

Subject to $30X_T + 20X_C + 1X_W + 0X_L = 300$ (wood)

$5X_T + 10X_C + 0X_W + 1X_L = 110$ (labor)

where $X_T, X_C, X_W, X_L \geq 0$ (non-negativity)

All of this information is incorporated into Table 11-3, which is referred to as a *simplex tableau*. Along the top of the central portion of the tableau, we list the problem variables in their original order of appearance in the formulated constraint equations. In the top margin, we list the corresponding per-unit

TABLE 11-3

The Redwood Furniture Simplex Tableau

UNIT PROFIT		6	8	0	0	
Var. Mix		X_T	X_C	X_W	X_L	Sol.
X_W		30	20	1	0	300
X_L		5	10	0	1	110

profits from the objective equation. The first row in the body of the tableau consists of the coefficients in the first constraint equation in their original order of appearance; the numbers in the second row are reproduced from the second constraint equation. In essence, these two rows supply the same information that the original equations provide; *they are streamlined and equivalent versions of the original constraint equations.*

The variable-mix column of the tableau lists the slack variables X_W and X_L; we will solve for these variables. All variables that are not listed in this column are categorized as nonmix variables and are assumed to be arbitrarily fixed at zero. Thus, X_T and X_C are presently set at zero. The solution column lists the values of the variable mix: $X_W = 300$ and $X_L = 110$. This tells us that all of the available wood and labor are unused. The amounts are precisely what would be left from the original equations after zeroing out X_T and X_C:

$$30(0) + 20(0) + 1X_W + 0X_L = 300 \quad \text{or} \quad X_W = 300$$
$$5(0) + 10(0) + 0X_W + 1X_L = 110 \quad \text{or} \quad X_L = 110$$

The rows of the simplex tableau simultaneously provide us with two pieces of information:

(1) Each row is written in a new form that preserves the original constraint equation.
(2) The rows indicate the variable mix for the corner point being evaluated. The variable-mix values appear in the solution column; all nonmix variables are assumed to have a value of zero.

The values in the body of the tableau represent the original constraint coefficients and are sometimes referred to as *exchange coefficients,* because they indicate how many units of the variable listed on the left must be given up to accommodate a unit increase in the variable listed at the top of the tableau. Thus, the value 30 in the X_W row and the X_T column indicates that 30 board feet of unused wood may be exchanged for one table. We can also see that

UNIT PROFIT		6	8	0	0		
	Var. Mix	X_T	X_C	X_W	X_L	Sol.	
0	X_W	30	20	1	0	300	Exchange
0	X_L	5	10	0	1	110	coefficients
	Sac.	0	0	0	0	0	←—Current P
	Imp.	6	8	0	0	—	

TABLE 11-4
An Expanded Simplex Tableau for the Redwood Furniture Problem

exactly 20 units of wood must be provided to produce one chair. Similarly, 5 hours of unused labor must be given up to produce one table, and 10 hours must be given up to produce one chair. These are the same figures we used at the outset in Table 11-1. The exchange coefficients are 0 or 1 for the mix variables and are not very meaningful. They indicate, for example, that 1 board foot of unused wood may be traded for 1 more board foot and that no unused wood is required to accommodate more unused labor.

The simplex tableau for the Redwood Furniture problem is expanded in Table 11-4. In the left margin, we list the per-unit profits for the mix variables. For the slack variables X_W and X_L, per-unit profits are zero. Below the heavy rule are two special rows where economic data are compiled that tell us which corner point to evaluate next. Values in the *sacrifice row* tell us what we will lose in per-unit profits by making a change. The *improvement row* indicates the per-unit change in profits that will result from making that same change.

The sacrifice entry for each column is determined by making the following computation:

Unit sacrifice = Unit profit column × Exchange coefficient column

The result of this calculation is a *vector product*, because the terms in the unit-profit and exchange-coefficient columns constitute *vectors*. First, each pair of values is multiplied together; then the sum of these products is obtained. For example, in the X_T column, we have

Unit Profit Column × X_T Column

$$0 \times 30 = 0$$
$$0 \times 5 = \underline{0}$$
$$\text{Sacrifice for } X_T = 0$$

The first product (0×30) is the unit profit of unused wood multiplied by the amount needed to make one table; this is the reduction in unused wood profit required to produce one table. The second product (0×5) is the unused labor profit that must be given up to make that table. Together, these products constitute the profit that must be sacrificed by the mix variables to accommodate a unit increase in tables.

This computation can also be made for the solution column. The entry obtained, which is $P = 0$ in Table 11-4, is the current value of the objective function.

Since the unit-profit column for the current variable mix (the slack variables) consists of zeros, all of the sacrifice terms result in product sums of zero. This concept seems obvious now—we give up no profit to make tables or chairs if the unused resource has no profit to begin with—but it will prove crucial later.

The entries in the improvement row are found by subtracting each sacrifice term from the corresponding unit profit listed at the top of the tableau:

$$\text{Unit improvement} = \text{Unit profit} - \text{Unit sacrifice}$$

In the tableau in Table 11-4, all of the improvement terms are identical to the unit profits, since all the sacrifices are zero.

Summary of the Simplex Method

Before we examine the simplex algorithm, it will be helpful to summarize the required steps in the simplex method.

(1) **Formulate the linear program.** Add slack variables to the problem, eliminating any inequality constraints. Construct the initial simplex tableau, using slack variables in the starting variable mix.

(2) **Find the sacrifice and improvement rows.**

(3) **Apply the entry criterion.** Find the current nonmix variable that increasing from zero will improve the objective at the greatest rate, breaking any ties arbitrarily. This variable is the *entering variable*. Mark the top of its column with an arrow pointing down. If no improvement can be found, the optimal solution is represented by the present tableau.

(4) **Apply the exit criterion.** Use the current tableau's exchange coefficient values from the column of the entering variable to calculate the following *exchange ratio* for each row:

$$\frac{\text{Solution value}}{\text{Exchange coefficient}}$$

Ignoring ratios with zero or negative denominators, find the smallest *non-negative* exchange ratio,* again breaking ties arbitrarily. The mix variable for the row of this ratio is the *exiting variable*. Mark this varible's row with an arrow pointing left.

(5) Construct a new simplex tableau. Replace the variable-mix label of the exiting variable with that of the entering variable. All other variable-mix labels remain the same. Also, change the unit-profit (unit-cost) column value to correspond to the newly entered mix variable. Then recompute the variable-mix row values to obtain a new set of exchange coefficients. (This procedure is illustrated in the Redwood Furniture example.)

(6) Go back to step (2).

Thus far in our Redwood Furniture example, we have completed steps (1) and (2). We must now determine the *entering variable* through economic analysis by applying the *entry criterion* in step (3). In our profit-maximization problem, we accomplish this by finding the largest positive value in the improvement row. Referring to Table 11-5. we can see that 8 in the X_C column is the largest per-unit improvement. This means that we can improve the current solution by $8 per unit for each chair made. Increasing the value of the X_C variable from zero (remember, X_C is a nonmix variable and all such variables equal zero) to some positive quantity is the best change to make. (Another change—increasing tables—has a smaller per-unit improvement of only $6.) Thus, X_C is the entering variable. We indicate this on the simplex tableau by placing a small arrow pointing downward just to the right of the X_C column. In step (4), we find the *exiting variable*. As the name implies, one variable will enter the mix and replace

TABLE 11-5
Simplex Tableau Showing Entering and Exiting Variables and Pivot Element

UNIT PROFIT		6	8	0	0		
	Var. Mix	X_T	X_C	X_W	X_L	Sol.	Exchange ratios:
0	X_W	30	20 ↓	1	0	300	300/20 = 15
0	X_L ←	5	(10)	0	1	110	110/10 = 11*
	Sac.	0	0	0	0		0	* Smallest non-negative ratio
	Imp.	6	8	0	0		—

Greatest per-unit improvement

* A divisor of zero results in an infinitely large ratio (and is treated as such, even when the numerator is 0, too). If all divisors are zero or negative, the problem is *unbounded*. This special case is discussed on page 289.

another, which *exits* from the variable mix and assumes a nonmix status. Such an exchange of variables is referred to as a *pivot operation*. Simplex involves a sequence of such pivots. In each case, the pivot identifies the next corner point to be evaluated. The current variable mix differs by only one variable from the subsequent variable mix created by the pivot. The two corresponding corners are often called *neighbors*.

At this point, we want to increase our entering variable X_C as much as possible from zero. Dividing the solution value by the corresponding exchange coefficient in the X_C column, we obtain

$$300/20 = 15 \quad \text{for the } X_W \text{ row}$$

$$110/10 = 11 \quad \text{for the } X_L \text{ row}$$

These *exchange ratios* tell us how many chairs Redwood can make by trading away all of the current level of the respective mix variable. By trading 300 board feet of unused wood, Redwood can produce 15 chairs, because one chair can be exchanged at the rate of 20 board feet. Likewise, by trading all 110 hours of unused labor at an exchange rate of 10 hours per chair, Redwood can produce 11 chairs.

The *exit criterion* requires that we find the smallest ratio; here, it is 11. This value limits the number of chairs that can result from the exchange. It is impossible to make more than 11 chairs because all of the available labor will be used to produce that quantity. The exiting variable is therefore X_L, so that X_C will replace X_L in the variable mix. X_W will remain in the mix, since labor will be depleted before wood and some unused wood will still remain once the exchange is made. We indicate that unused labor exits the variable mix by placing a small arrow pointing toward the X_L in Table 11-5.

The circled value in the X_C column and the X_L row is called the *pivot element*. This value is used to evaluate the new corner point represented by exchanging X_C and X_L. The evaluation is achieved by means of a *new* simplex tableau.

Constructing the New Simplex Tableau

We must construct a new simplex tableau that provides the solution values for the new corner point. Each mix-variable row must also represent an equation, and together these equations must preserve the underlying constraint relationships. We begin with the constraint equations

$$30X_T + 20X_C + 1X_W + 0X_L = 300 \quad \text{(old } X_W \text{ row)}$$

$$5X_T + 10X_C + 0X_W + 1X_L = 110 \quad \text{(old } X_L \text{ row)}$$

$$\underset{\text{Set at 0}}{\uparrow \qquad \uparrow}$$

Since X_C is to replace X_L, we want to transform the second equation so that X_C will have a coefficient of 1. Dividing both sides of the second equation by 10 gives us

$$\left(\frac{5}{10}\right)X_T + \left(\frac{10}{10}\right)X_C + \left(\frac{0}{10}\right)X_W + \left(\frac{1}{10}\right)X_L = \frac{110}{10}$$

and provides us with the equivalent expression

$$\tfrac{1}{2}X_T + 1X_C + 0X_W + \tfrac{1}{10}X_L = 11 \qquad \text{(new } X_C \text{ row)}$$

which we will refer to as the new X_C row. If X_T and X_L are set at zero, this equation directly provides the solution $X_C = 11$.

Now consider the two equations

$$30X_T + 20X_C + 1X_W + 0X_L = 300 \qquad \text{(old } X_W \text{ row)}$$
$$\tfrac{1}{2}X_T + 1X_C + 0X_W + \tfrac{1}{10}X_L = 11 \qquad \text{(new } X_C \text{ row)}$$

The variable X_C can be eliminated from the first equation, so that X_C will appear in only one equation. Then $X_C = 11$ is a solution value that satisfies both equations. Subtracting 20 times the second equation from the first, we obtain

$$
\begin{array}{r}
30X_T + 20X_C + 1X_W + 0X_L = 300 \\
-20(\tfrac{1}{2}X_T + 1X_C + 0X_W + \tfrac{1}{10}X_L = 11) \\
\hline
20X_T + 0X_C + 1X_W - 2X_L = 80 \qquad \text{(new } X_W \text{ row)}
\end{array}
$$

We will refer to the equation for this difference as the new X_W row, since it provides the solution $X_W = 80$ when the nonmix variables are set at zero ($X_T = 0$, $X_L = 0$). This reflects the fact that when 11 chairs—each requiring 20 board feet of wood—are made, exactly $300 - 11(20) = 80$ board feet will remain unused.

Our two new constraint equations are then

$$20X_T + 0X_C + 1X_W - 2X_L = 80 \qquad \text{(new } X_W \text{ row)}$$
$$\tfrac{1}{2}X_T + 1X_C + 0X_W + \tfrac{1}{10}X_L = 11 \qquad \text{(new } X_C \text{ row)}$$

Set at zero

Since we obtained each equation by dividing both sides of an original constraint equation by a constant or by subtracting equal amounts from both sides of an original constraint equation, the two new equations preserve the problem constraints.

The beauty of the simplex method is that we don't have to perform all of these steps to obtain these new equations. We can work directly from the previous tableau to determine the values for the new tableau. This procedure can be summarized as follows:

(a) Divide all values in the row of the exiting variable by the pivot element. (Such calculations can be easily made in your head.) Place the answers in the *same position* in the new tableau. Label this row with the symbol of the newly entered variable.

(b) To obtain each of the remaining rows, find the value in that row in the old tableau that is also in the pivot element column. Then multiply the first number in the new row found in step (a) by this quantity and *subtract* that product from the old value in the first position. The result is the first term in the new row. Repeat this process for all positions in the new row, including the solution position. Then repeat this process for all the remaining rows until the tableau is complete. The variable-mix labels on these rows will be the same as they were in the old table.

TABLE 11-6

Constructing the New Simplex Tableau

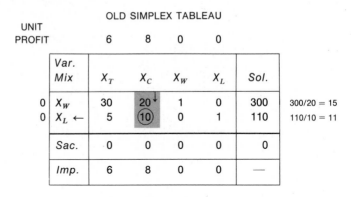

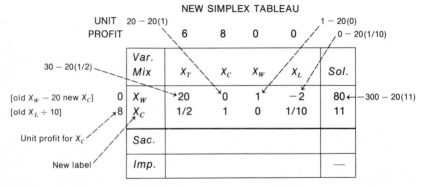

(c) Place the appropriate unit profits (costs) for the mix variables in the left margin.

Applying this procedure to the simplex tableau in Table 11-5 results in the second tableau provided in Table 11-6 for the Redwood Furniture problem. Every term in the new X_C row is found by dividing the respective old X_L row value by 10 (the pivot element). The new X_W row values are found by successively subtracting from the old X_W row the product of 20 (the old X_W row value in the pivot-element column) multiplied by the new X_C row value for that column position. Notice that the new tableau is exactly what we would obtain if we transferred the coefficients from the equations on page 263. Also notice that this procedure yields *column* values for each mix variable with a 1 where the variable's row and column intersect and a *zero* everywhere else. This feature ensures that the underlying equations will provide solution values when the nonmix variables are zeroed out.

Finding the Optimal Solution

We have now completed the final simplex step (5) for the Redwood Furniture problem. At this point, according to the procedure, we return to step (2) and begin a new iteration with a new tableau and variable mix. Each iteration repeats the earlier ones, using new values.

We must also find the per-unit sacrifice and improvement values for the new simplex tableau, which is given in Table 11-7. But before we perform the calculations to obtain these values, let's assess the exchange coefficients in the X_T column. The value in the X_W row is 20, which indicates that Redwood must give up a net amount of 20 board feet of unused wood to make one table— not the 30 board feet specified in the original problem statement. Where are

TABLE 11-7

Final Version of the Second Simplex Tableau

UNIT PROFIT		6	8	0	0		
	Var. Mix	X_T	X_C	X_W	X_L	Sol.	
0	X_W	20	0	1	−2	80	
8	X_C	1/2	1	0	1/10	11	
	Sac.	4	8	0	8/10	88 ←	Current P
	Imp.	2	0	0	−8/10	—	

the missing 10 board feet? The second number in that column, 1/2, tells us that Redwood must also relinquish one-half of a chair to produce one table. This happens because some labor currently being spent on chairs must be diverted to that table. That one-half chair returns 5 hours of labor as well as the missing 10 board feet of wood to Redwood.

The exchange coefficients in the X_L column tell a similar story. To increase X_L by one unit—that is, to increase unused labor by one hour—we must trade $-2X_W$. In other words, if one hour of labor is *taken away* (which is what increasing unused resource means), Redwood must give up -2 board feet of unused wood; that is, Redwood gets back $+2$ board feet of unused wood (so that it uses 2 feet less than before). The net changes in unused resources correspond to the requirements for a fraction of a chair (1/10, to be exact) that must be relinquished if X_L is increased by one hour (remember, it takes 10 hours to make a whole chair). This is why the second exchange coefficient in the X_C row is 1/10.

The per-unit profits for X_W and X_C are \$0 and \$8. The per-unit sacrifice for X_T is therefore

$$
\begin{array}{ccc}
\text{Unit profit} & \times & \text{Exchange coefficient} \\
\hline
0 & \times & 20 & = 0 \\
8 & \times & 1/2 & = 4 \\
& & \overline{\text{Sacrifice for } X_T = 4}
\end{array}
$$

This represents the \$4 profit forgone by giving up the 1/2 chair to accommodate one table. For X_L, we obtain

$$
\begin{array}{ccc}
\text{Unit profit} & \times & \text{Exchange coefficient} \\
\hline
0 & \times & -2 & = 0 \\
8 & \times & 1/10 & = 8/10 \\
& & \overline{\text{Sacrifice for } X_L = 8/10}
\end{array}
$$

which is the \$8/10 profit (one-tenth of \$8) lost by giving up the 1/10 of a chair that cannot be made if unused labor is increased by one hour. The value computed in the solution column is

$$
\begin{array}{r}
0 \times 80 = \ \ 0 \\
8 \times 11 = 88 \\
\hline
88
\end{array}
$$

which is the \$88 profit represented by the current variable-mix solution.

The solution for the new variable mix may be read directly from Table 11-7 as

$$X_T = 0, \ X_C = 11, \ X_W = 80, \ X_L = 0; \ P = 88$$

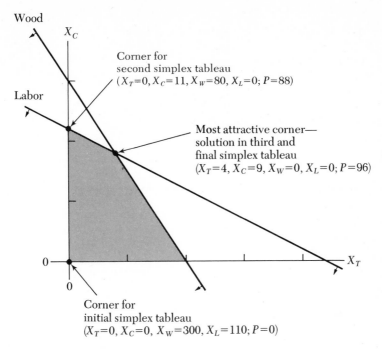

Wood

X_C

Corner for
second simplex tableau
$(X_T=0, X_C=11, X_W=80, X_L=0; P=88)$

Labor

Most attractive corner—
solution in third and
final simplex tableau
$(X_T=4, X_C=9, X_W=0, X_L=0; P=96)$

X_T

0

0

Corner for
initial simplex tableau
$(X_T=0, X_C=0, X_W=300, X_L=110; P=0)$

FIGURE 11-2
Graphical illustration of successive corners evaluated in simplex.

X_T and X_L are not in the mix and must therefore be zero. Figure 11-2 summarizes our current situation. We have now reached a second corner of the
feasible solution region that must be evaluated further. For this purpose, we
must determine the possible per-unit profit improvements from increasing each
of the nonmix variables.

The values in the per-unit improvement row of the latest simplex tableau,
shown again as the top tableau in Table 11-8, are found by subtracting the
sacrifice values from the profits listed in the top margin. We can see that only
one value is positive (the 2 in the X_T column). This indicates that increasing
X_T will result in a net increase in profits of $2 per unit. Redwood does not
receive the full profit of $6 on each table, because for every table made, we
must "steal" back resources that could be used to make one-half a chair, thereby
losing $4 of chair profit. Thus, Redwood receives a profit of only $6 – $4 = $2
per table.

Our entering variable is X_T. According to the exit criterion, we see that
the smallest exchange ratio applies to X_W, which limits table production more
(Redwood would run out of unused wood before giving back all chairs). This
exchange will result in 4 tables and no unused wood, so that the exiting variable

TABLE 11-8

Constructing the Third Tableau from the Second Tableau

	UNIT PROFIT	6	8	0	0		
	Var. Mix	X_T	X_C	X_W	X_L	Sol.	Exchange ratios:
0	X_W ←	(20) ↓	0	1	−2	80	80/20 = 4*
8	X_C	1/2	1	0	1/10	11	11/(1/2) = 22
	Sac.	4	8	0	8/10	88	*Smallest non-negative ratio
	Imp.	2	0	0	−8/10	—	
[old X_W ÷ 20] 6	X_T	1	0	1/20	−1/10	4	
[old X_C − 1/2 new X_T] 8	X_C	0	1	−1/40	3/20	9	
	Sac.	6	8	1/10	6/10	96	
	Imp.	0	0	−1/10	−6/10	—	

No per-unit improvement is positive;
no further improvement is possible.

is X_W. The present pivot element occurs where the X_W row and X_T column intersect and has a value of 20.

The new (third) simplex tableau, constructed by transforming the second tableau, appears as the bottom tableau in Table 11-8. This tableau provides the solution

$$X_T = 4, X_C = 9, X_W = 0, X_L = 0; P = 96$$

which we know (from our earlier graphical analysis in Chapter 10) is the optimal solution. Simplex tells us that this must be the stopping point, since none of the per-unit improvement row values is positive. No further improvement is possible.

11-3 THE COMPUTATIONAL ASPECTS OF SIMPLEX

The only real thinking involved in solving a linear programming problem occurs during the formulation phase. Once the initial tableau has been satisfactorily completed, the rest is simple arithmetic. However, simplex calculations can require a substantial amount of time. They are particularly onerous when we must determine the new tableau's exchange coefficients, since fractions such as 5/3, 2/17, and 23/31 often occur. It may be helpful to keep computations in fractional form throughout the process to avoid errors due to rounding. Making side calculations on scratch paper, with the aid of a calculator, can be helpful.

Hand Computations and Locating Errors

For example, suppose that we must subtract $4/7 \times 6/21$ from 5. We would perform the calculation

$$5 - \left(\frac{4}{7}\right)\left(\frac{6}{21}\right) = 5 - \frac{24}{147}$$

and convert the difference to fractions that have the same denominator:

$$5\left(\frac{147}{147}\right) - \frac{24}{147} = \frac{735 - 24}{147} = \frac{711}{147}$$

We can then attempt to reduce the resulting fraction to the form with the lowest common denominator by dividing 711 by factors that comprise the denominator (21, 7, and 3) to see if a whole number results. In this case, $711/3 = 237$ exactly, and we obtain the more elementary fraction 237/49. Although this is equal to 4 and 41/49, it is preferable to enter the basic fraction 237/49 in the new tableau.

It is easy to make errors in arithmetic when performing simplex computations by hand. Unfortunately, just one mistake can ruin every calculation that follows. These checks can be made to catch obvious errors:

(1) The solution-column values can never be negative. If one value is negative, an error has been made somewhere, and no further steps should be taken until it has been corrected.
(2) The mix-variable columns should contain a single 1 in the proper row and a zero everywhere else, except the sacrifice row.
(3) The new P or C should be at least as good as the preceding one. If it is not, an error has been made.
(4) If any set of solution values violates the original problem's constraints, an error has been made.

Hand computation is not only error-prone, but it is also quite time-consuming. A good arithmetician could spend a day or two solving a 10-row, 20-column simplex problem by hand. The same person would require more than a week to find the answer to a simplex problem represented by a tableau with twice as many rows and columns.

Using the Computer

The computational difficulties in simplex would preclude the use of linear programming in many applications if it were not for high-speed digital computers. The computer eliminates the errors that are so inevitable in hand calculations and completes these calculation much more quickly. Today, it is routine to use a computer to solve problems that involve thousands of variables and constraints. In business, a linear program is rarely completely solved by hand. In modern linear programming applications, the human element is concentrated on the conceptual areas of problem formulation.

Computer programs for use in solving linear programs are widely available. It is no longer necessary to write a computer program from scratch. Most college computer centers and time-sharing systems have library programs that can be used to solve large problems. Computer advisors should be able to explain how to arrange the input data and how to interpret the computer printouts. It is therefore best to solve with the assistance of a computer any linear programming problem that requires more than nominal hand calculations.

11-4 APPLYING SIMPLEX WHEN GRAPHING IS IMPOSSIBLE

Simplex was developed to solve realistic problems that ordinarily have too many variables to be solved graphically. We can illustrate this with the following linear program, which involves five main variables and two constraints.

$$\text{Maximize} \quad P = 5X_1 + 4X_2 + 4X_3 + 1X_4 + 2X_5$$

Subject to
$$1X_1 + 2X_2 \qquad\qquad + 4X_5 \le 30 \quad (\text{resource } A)$$
$$4X_1 \qquad + 8X_3 + 5X_4 \qquad\quad \le 40 \quad (\text{resource } B)$$

where
$$\text{all } X\text{'s} \ge 0$$

As slack variables, we use X_A and X_B to denote the unused quantities of the respective resources. In presimplex equation form, this linear program can be expressed as shown on the top of page 271.

Maximize $P = 5X_1 + 4X_2 + 4X_3 + 1X_4 + 2X_5 + 0X_A + 0X_B$

Subject to $1X_1 + 2X_2 + 0X_3 + 0X_4 + 4X_5 + 1X_A + 0X_B = 30$ (resource A)

                  $4X_1 + 0X_2 + 8X_3 + 5X_4 + 0X_5 + 0X_A + 1X_B = 40$ (resource B)

where   all X's ≥ 0

Table 11-9 summarizes the entire simplex procedure. The first tableau involves a starting solution of "doing nothing," and the slack variables are in the starting variable mix. The entering variable is X_1 (because it has the greatest per-unit improvement of 5), which replaces the exiting variable X_B (because it has the smaller exchange ratio of 10).

The values in the second tableau are calculated first by dividing the old X_B row entries from the first tableau by 4 (the pivot element in the first tableau). This results in the new X_1 row. Because the old X_A row has a 1 in the entering column, we can calculate the new X_A row values by subtracting 1 multiplied by the new X_1 row values from the old X_A row values.

TABLE 11-9

Simplex Tableaus for a Linear Programming Problem That Cannot Be Graphed

	UNIT PROFIT	5	4	4	1	2	0	0	
	Var. Mix	X_1	X_2	X_3	X_4	X_5	X_A	X_B	Sol.
0 X_A		1	2	0	0	4	1	0	30	30/1 = 30
0 X_B		④	0	8	5	0	0	1	40	40/4 = 10*
	Sac.	0	0	0	0	0	0	0	0
	Imp.	5	4	4	1	2	0	0	—

[old X_A − 1 new X_1]   0 X_A
[old X_B ÷ 4]   5 X_1

	Var. Mix	X_1	X_2	X_3	X_4	X_5	X_A	X_B	Sol.
0 X_A		0	②	−2	−5/4	4	1	−1/4	20	20/2 = 10*
5 X_1		1	0	2	5/4	0	0	1/4	10	10/0 (ignore)
	Sac.	5	0	10	25/4	0	0	5/4	50
	Imp.	0	4	−6	−21/4	2	0	−5/4	—

[old X_A ÷ 2]   4 X_2
[old X_1 − 0 new X_2]   5 X_1

	Var. Mix	X_1	X_2	X_3	X_4	X_5	X_A	X_B	Sol.
4 X_2		0	1	−1	−5/8	2	1/2	−1/8	10
5 X_1		1	0	2	5/4	0	0	1/4	10
	Sac.	5	4	6	15/4	8	2	3/4	90
	Imp.	0	0	−2	−11/4	−4	−2	−3/4	—

The entering variable for the second tableau is X_2. This replaces the exiting variable X_A. (The exchange ratio of 10/0 found for the X_1 row is ignored because the divisor is zero.)

The new X_2 values in the third tableau are found by dividing the old X_A values from the second tableau by 2 (the pivot element found there). The new X_1 row values are the same as the X_1 row values in the second tableau because there is a zero in the X_1 position of the entering variable column.

No improvement is possible from the third tableau, and the following solution is obtained:

$$X_1 = 10 \qquad X_4 = 0 \qquad X_A = 0$$

$$X_2 = 10 \qquad X_5 = 0 \qquad X_B = 0$$

$$X_3 = \;\; 0$$

$$P = 90$$

11-5 SHORTCUTS IN CONSTRUCTING SIMPLEX TABLEAUS

A variety of shortcuts can be taken when making simplex computations. The following rules of thumb always apply:

(1) In constructing the new tableau from the old tableau, only the columns for the nonmix and exiting variables change. The columns for any variable remaining in the variable mix can therefore be incorporated directly into the new tableau.
(2) To simplify calculations, wherever a zero is found in the pivot *column*, that *row* in the body of the tableau is repeated in the next tableau without change. Wherever a zero is found in the pivot *row*, that *column* in the body of the tableau is repeated in the next tableau without change.
(3) The newly entered mix variable column will contain a zero everywhere, except that a 1 will appear in the same position as the pivot element in the preceding tableau and the per-unit profit or cost for this variable will appear in the sacrifice row.

11-6 SPECIAL SIMPLEX CONSIDERATIONS

We have just described the simplex algorithm in detail. The same steps are followed regardless of the number of variables or constraints involved. But we must consider several further aspects before our discussion is complete.

Like the graphical technique, the simplex method can be applied to either profit-maximization or cost-minimization problems. Only a slight procedural modification is required when minimizing C. Costs are substituted for profits. As we will see in Chapter 12, we must reinterpret the improvement row of the simplex tableau to coincide with this change in the problem objective, which will cause a minor change in the application of the entry criterion.

All of the simplex constraints we have encountered in this chapter involve the ≤ (less than or equal to) constraint, which is the natural orientation when considering resource limitations. Sometimes it is necessary to manipulate a constraint expression to obtain the proper orientation. For example, suppose that a mixture requirement for Redwood Furniture is that a minimum of 4 chairs be made for each table, so that the number of chairs must be ≥ (greater than or equal to) 4 times the number of tables. Algebraically, this requirement is

$$X_C \geq 4X_T \quad \text{(mixture)}$$

If we subtract $4X_T$ from both sides of this constraint, we obtain an inequality that has the wrong orientation:

$$X_C - 4X_T \geq 0 \quad \text{(wrong orientation)}$$

By changing all signs, the direction of the inequality can be reversed, giving us a mathematically equivalent expression that has the proper orientation:

$$-X_C + 4X_T \leq 0 \quad \text{(proper orientation)}$$

It is not always possible to reverse inequality orientations this way without creating difficulties. (If the constant term were not zero, then this type of change would result in a negative right-hand side, which simplex cannot handle.) Chapter 12 tells how to deal with constraints of the ≥ or = form.

PROBLEMS

11-1 Express the following linear programming constraints in equation form, using an appropriate slack variable:
(a) $2X_1 + 3X_2 \leq 12$ (wood)
(b) $4X_A + 2X_B \leq 20$ (labor)
(c) $3X_1 - 2X_2 \leq 3$ (byproduct)
(d) $X_1 + 2X_2 + 3X_3 \leq 100$ (machine time)

11-2 Reformulate the following linear program, incorporating the slack variables X_A, X_B, and X_C into the respective constraints. The modified objective equation will include the slack variables, and each constraint will be represented by an equation instead of an inequality. Then construct only the initial simplex tableau. Position all marginal values and label all rows and columns, but do not compute the sacrifice and improvement values.

$$\begin{aligned}
\text{Maximize} \quad & P = 20X_1 + 40X_2 + 60X_3 \\
\text{Subject to} \quad & 2X_1 + 3X_2 \leq 20 \quad \text{(resource } A) \\
& 4X_2 + 5X_3 \leq 30 \quad \text{(resource } B) \\
& X_1 + 2X_2 + X_3 \leq 50 \quad \text{(resource } C) \\
\text{where} \quad & X_1, X_2, X_3 \geq 0
\end{aligned}$$

11-3 Consider the following simplex tableau:

UNIT PROFIT		5	7	9	7	8	
	Var. Mix	X_1	X_2	X_3	X_4	X_5	Sol.
9	X_3	−2	0	1	2	1	6
7	X_2	3	1	0	−3	2	3
	Sac.						
	Imp.						—

(a) Find the sacrifice and improvement row values.
(b) Find the entering variable and the exiting variable and identify the pivot element.

11-4 Consider the following simplex tableau:

UNIT PROFIT		5	3	4	5	0	
	Var. Mix	X_1	X_2	X_3	X_4	X_5	Sol.
5	X_4	−2	0	0	1	0	1.5
4	X_3	1	0	1	0	−1	2.5
3	X_2	3	1	0	0	2	3.0
	Sac.	3	3	4	5	2	26.5
	Imp.	2	0	0	0	−2	—

The entering variable is X_1 and the exiting variable is X_2. Construct the next simplex tableau.

11-5 Consider the following simplex tableau:

UNIT PROFIT		3	2	1	0	0	
	Var. Mix	X_1	X_2	X_3	X_4	X_5	Sol.
0	X_4	0	2	1	1	0	10
0	X_5	0	−3	2	0	1	15
3	X_1	1	1	0	0	0	20
	Sac.						
	Imp.						—

(a) Find the sacrifice and improvement row values.

(b) Find the entering and exiting variables and identify the pivot element.

(c) Construct the next simplex tableau.

11-6 For the linear program

Maximize $P = 100X_1 + 200X_2 + 150X_3$

Subject to $5X_1 + 20X_2 + 30X_3 \le 60$ (resource A)

$10X_1 + 20X_2 + 50X_3 \le 100$ (resource B)

where $X_1, X_2, X_3 \ge 0$

the following final simplex tableau applies, where X_A and X_B are the slack variables for the first and second constraints, respectively.

UNIT PROFIT		100	200	150	0	0	
	Var. Mix	X_1	X_2	X_3	X_A	X_B	Sol.
100	X_1	1	0	4	−1/5	1/5	8
200	X_2	0	1	1/2	1/10	−1/20	1
	Sac.	100	200	500	0	10	1,000
	Imp.	0	0	−350	0	−10	—

Use the data provided in this tableau to determine the optimal values of all five variables and the maximum possible profit.

11-7 Consider the linear program

Maximize $P = 2X_1 + 3X_2$

Subject to $3X_1 + 2X_2 \le 6$ (resource A)

$X_1 \qquad \le 5$ (resource B)

$X_2 \le 4$ (resource C)

where $X_1, X_2 \ge 0$

(a) Solve this problem graphically.

(b) Reformulate this problem in an equation form that is suitable for the simplex method.

(c) Resolve the problem using the simplex procedure.

11-8 Consider the linear program

Maximize $P = 5X_A + 6X_B$

Subject to $3X_A + 2X_B \le 12$ (resource 1)

$2X_A + 3X_B \le 12$ (resource 2)

where $X_A, X_B \ge$

(a) Solve this problem graphically.

(b) Reformulate this problem in equation form suitable for simplex.

(c) Solve the problem again using the simplex procedure.

11-9 The manager of Ace Widgets must decide how many regular and deluxe models to produce. It requires 5 hours of finishing labor and 1 frame to produce the regular model and 8 hours and 1 frame to produce the deluxe widget. Only 12 frames and

80 hours of labor are available. The unit profits are $10 for the regular model and $15 for the deluxe widget.

(a) Formulate the linear program for this problem and then solve it graphically.

(b) Reformulate the problem in an equation form that is suitable for the simplex method.

(c) Solve the problem again using the simplex procedure.

11-10 Reconsider the Hops Brewery advertising decision in Problem 9-9 (page 229), where no more than the budgeted $100,000 is to be spent on television spots (costing $2,000 each) and magazine ads (costing $5,000 each). The net profit to Hops is $1,000 per television spot and $5,000 per magazine ad. Maximum allowable expenditures are $50,000 for television spots and $70,000 for magazine ads.

(a) Formulate the linear program. Then solve it graphically.

(b) Reformulate the problem in an equation form suitable for simplex.

(c) Solve the problem again using the simplex procedure.

11-11 The following linear program applies for the Piney Woods Furniture Company, which makes tables (T), chairs (C), and bookcases (B):

$$\text{Maximize} \quad P = 20X_T + 15X_C + 15X_B$$
$$\text{Subject to} \quad 10X_T + 3X_C + 10X_B \le 100 \quad \text{(wood)}$$
$$5X_T + 5X_C + 5X_B \le 60 \quad \text{(labor)}$$
$$\text{where} \quad X_T, X_C, X_B \ge 0$$

Apply the simplex method to determine how many of each item should be made.

11-12 Sammy Love sells three types of candied apples on the street corner—butterscotch, cinnamon, and peppermint. In making today's batch, Sammy is limited only by the amounts of sugar and gelatin, since all other ingredients are in good supply. Each butterscotch apple requires 1 cup of sugar; each cinnamon or peppermint apple requires $\frac{1}{2}$ cup of sugar. Cinnamon apples require 2 ounces of gelatin; peppermint apples, 1 ounce; and butterscotch apples, none. Only 200 cups of sugar and 100 ounces of gelatin are available.

Sammy makes a profit of $.10 on each butterscotch apple, $.15 on each cinnamon apple, and $.20 on each peppermint apple. He always sells his entire stock.

(a) Formulate Sammy's linear program.

(b) Identify any slack variables required to solve this problem using the simplex method.

(c) Apply the simplex procedure to determine how many candied apples of each type Sammy should make.

11-13 Use the simplex method to determine how many of each type of lamp Rott Irony should manufacture in Problem 10-1 (page 242). (Hint: Make sure all of the constraints are of the $\le$ form before introducing the slack variables.)

11-14 Referring to Problem 10-6 (page 243), use the simplex method to determine what quantities of the respective pesticides the Bugoff Chemical Co. should produce. (Hint: Make sure all of the constraints are of the $\le$ form before introducing the slacks.)

11-15 Referring to Problem 10-9 (page 244), use the simplex method to determine how many of each type of silicon chip ChipMont should manufacture. (Hint: Make sure all of the constraints are of the $\le$ form before introducing the slacks.)

12

Further Simplex Method Considerations

The applications of the simplex method we described in Chapter 11 were limited to profit-maximization problems with constraints of the ≤ form. We are now ready to consider more general problems with constraints involving ≥ or = relations. These applications will require us to use some new auxiliary variables that play an analogous role to the slack variable we have already encountered. By including cost-minimization problems in this chapter, we will also expand the scope of the problems that can be solved using the simplex method. Chapter 12 concludes with a discussion of the special difficulties encountered in linear programming.

SURPLUS AND ARTIFICIAL VARIABLES: THE BIG-M METHOD 12-1

Suppose that we slightly modify our original Redwood Furniture problem to include a third product—benches—and that we represent the quantity of benches by the variable X_B. This increases the number of dimensions for the problem beyond our capability to draw a simple graph, thereby making the use of the simplex method essential. Suppose that each bench requires 25 board feet of wood and 7 hours of labor and is sold for a profit of $7. To further complicate the problem, we will assume that at least 2 benches must be made to satisfy outstanding orders, which creates a third "demand" constraint. The basic linear program is

$$\text{Maximize} \quad P = 6X_T + 8X_C + 7X_B \quad \text{(objective)}$$

$$\text{Subject to} \quad 30X_T + 20X_C + 25X_B \leq 300 \quad \text{(wood)}$$

$$5X_T + 10X_C + 7X_B \leq 110 \quad \text{(labor)}$$

$$X_B \geq 2 \quad \text{(demand)}$$

$$\text{where} \quad X_T, X_C, X_B \geq 0$$

The new demand constraint must be converted into an equality. This presents a special problem, because the inequality points to the right. Since the value on the left can be larger than the minimum requirement of 2 benches, we can express any extra quantity beyond 2 as *surplus* benches. Thus, the demand constraint can be equivalently stated

$$\text{Number of benches} - \text{Surplus benches} = 2$$

Or, if we let X_D represent the surplus benches beyond the demand requirement, this constraint becomes

$$X_B - X_D = 2 \quad \text{(demand)}$$

We refer to X_D as a *surplus variable*. Surplus variables are analogous to slack variables, in that they allow us to express linear programs in the equation form required by simplex. Surplus variables also have an economic connotation. Like any simplex variable, X_D must be non-negative. (A negative surplus has no meaning here.)

Our demand constraint has one further inadequacy. Zeroing out X_B leaves us with $0 - X_D = 2$, or $X_D = -2$, so that X_D would begin as a negative value, which is not allowed. Thus, our demand constraint cannot serve as a starting simplex row in its present form, and X_D cannot be part of the *initial* variable mix. In fact, *surplus variables can never be in the initial variable mix.*

To begin the simplex procedure we introduce the *artificial variable*—a quantity that has no meaningful economic interpretation. It is merely a temporary expedient. We generally use the letter a, with an appropriate subscript, to identify this type of variable. In our problem, a_D will represent the artificial variable. This is added to the left side of the demand constraint equation, providing

$$X_B - X_D + a_D = 2 \quad \text{(demand)}$$

This expression in no way distorts the underlying production requirement *as long as a_D ultimately assumes a value of zero*. To guarantee that $a_D = 0$ (so that it is not in the final variable mix), we must make it highly unprofitable to do otherwise. We therefore assign a very large negative per-unit profit to a_D. For this purpose, we use the letter M (for mammoth) to represent a huge number and assign a per-unit profit of $-M$ to a_D.

Employing the slack variables X_W and X_L as before and noting that, like slacks, surplus variables contribute nothing to profit (or cost), we obtain the expanded linear program in a form suitable for beginning the simplex procedure:

Maximize

$$P = 6X_T + 8X_C + 7X_B + 0X_W + 0X_L + 0X_D - Ma_D \quad \text{(objective)}$$

Subject to

$$30X_T + 20X_C + 25X_B + 1X_W + 0X_L + 0X_D + 0a_D = 300 \quad \text{(wood)}$$
$$5X_T + 10X_C + 7X_B + 0X_W + 1X_L + 0X_D + 0a_D = 110 \quad \text{(labor)}$$
$$0X_T + 0X_C + 1X_B + 0X_W + 0X_L - 1X_D + 1a_D = 2 \quad \text{(demand)}$$

where $\qquad\qquad X_T, X_C, X_B, X_W, X_L, X_D, a_D \geq 0$

As before, we list all variables in all equations. Those variables not in the original constraint equations appear with coefficients of zero.

The initial simplex tableau for this problem is provided in Table 12-1. The variable mix consists of the slack variables and the artificial variable. Notice that the columns of these variables contain a 1 in their row and zeros elsewhere. The initial solution is $X_T = X_C = X_B = X_D = 0$, $X_W = 300$, $X_L = 110$, $a_D = 2$, and $P = -2M$ (a very poor profit indeed). Also notice that the sacrifice and improvement rows contain M terms.

The entering variable is X_B, since it shows the largest profit improvement of $7 + M$ dollars per unit. The exit criterion indicates that a maximum of $2X_B$ can be traded in the variable mix for a_D, the exiting variable. The remaining iterations of the simplex method are provided in Table 12-2.

TABLE 12-1
Initial Simplex Tableau for the Expanded Redwood Furniture Problem

UNIT PROFIT		6	8	7	0	0	0	$-M$		
	Var. Mix	X_T	X_C	X_B	X_W	X_L	X_D	a_D	Sol.	
0	X_W	30	20	25↓	1	0	0	0	300	300/25 = 12
0	X_L	5	10	7	0	1	0	0	110	110/7 = 15.71
$-M$	a_D ←	0	0	①	0	0	-1	1	2	2/1 = 2*
	Sac.	0	0	$-M$	0	0	M	$-M$	$-2M$	
	Imp.	6	8	$7+M$	0	0	$-M$	0	—	

TABLE 12-2

Tableaus for the Remaining Iterations of the Expanded Redwood Furniture Problem

	UNIT PROFIT		6	8	7	0	0	0	-M		
		Var. Mix	X_T	X_C	X_B	X_W	X_L	X_D	a_D	Sol.	
[old X_W - 25 new X_B]	0	X_W	30	20↓	0	1	0	25	-25	250	250/20 = 12.5
[old X_L - 7 new X_B]	0	X_L ←	5	⑩	0	0	1	7	-7	96	96/10 = 9.6*
[old a_D ÷ 1]	7	X_B	0	0	1	0	0	-1	1	2	2/0 = ∞
		Sac.	0	0	7	0	0	-7	7	14	
		Imp.	6	8	0	0	0	7	-M - 7	—	

[old X_W - 20 new X_C]	0	X_W ←	⑳↓	0	0	1	-2	11	-11	58	58/20 = 2.9*
[old X_L ÷ 10]	8	X_C	1/2	1	0	0	1/10	7/10	-7/10	9.6	9.6/(1/2) = 19.2
[old X_B - 0 new X_C]	7	X_B	0	0	1	0	0	-1	1	2	2/0 = ∞
		Sac.	4	8	7	0	.8	-1.4	1.4	90.8	
		Imp.	2	0	0	0	-.8	1.4	-M - 1.4	—	

[old X_W ÷ 20]	6	X_T ←	1	0	0	1/20	-1/10	⑪/⑳↓	-11/20	2.9	2.9/(11/20) = 5.27*
[old X_C - (1/2) new X_T]	8	X_C	0	1	0	-1/40	3/20	17/40	-17/40	8.15	8.15/(17/40) = 19.18
[old X_B - 0 new X_T]	7	X_B	0	0	1	0	0	-1	1	2	2/-1 = -2
		Sac.	6	8	7	.1	.6	-.3	.3	96.6	
		Imp.	0	0	0	-.1	-.6	.3	-M - .3	—	

[old X_T ÷ 11/20]	0	X_D	20/11	0	0	1/11	-2/11	1	-1	58/11	
[old X_C - (17/40) new X_D]	8	X_C	-17/22	1	0	-7/110	5/22	0	0	65/11	
[old X_B - (-1) new X_D]	7	X_B	20/11	0	1	1/11	-2/11	0	0	80/11	
		Sac.	72/11	8	7	7/55	6/11	0	0	1,080/11	
		Imp.	-6/11	0	0	-7/55	-6/11	0	-M	—	

The optimal solution obtained from the final simplex tableau is

$$X_T = 0 \qquad X_W = 0$$

$$X_C = 65/11 \qquad X_L = 0$$

$$X_B = 80/11 \qquad X_D = 58/11$$

$$P = 1,080/11 = 98.18 \text{ dollars}$$

Notice that when benches are included in Redwood's product line, it is no longer most profitable to make tables. We can also see that the surplus variable has a value greater than zero, indicating that $X_D = X_B - 2 = 58/11$ benches should be produced beyond the minimum level of 2. Finally, notice that the artificial variable is not in the final variable mix and has a value of zero. Since a_D has no economic meaning, we ordinarily do not include it when we report the optimal solution.

As a general rule, a *separate artificial variable should be used for every ≥ constraint, and each of these constraints must also have its own surplus variable.* The respective mix variable in the initial simplex tableau must always be that artificial variable introduced into the constraint equation for that row. An artificial variable must also ordinarily be used when there is an *equality con-straint* in the first formulation, as might be the case if Redwood were forced to make *exactly* 1 table for every 4 chairs. Since such a constraint begins in the form of an equality (=), neither a surplus nor a slack variable is required but an artificial variable is needed to begin the simplex procedure.

COST-MINIMIZATION PROBLEMS 12-2

Simplex can also be applied to solve cost-minimization problems. The procedural steps are the same as the ones we follow when maximizing P. The only major difference lies in the interpretation of the entry criterion. Since the per-unit improvement row consists of net changes in cost, *negative values* in that row indicate the improvement. The entering variable is therefore the variable having the largest negative entry (in absolute terms) in that row.

The Persian Sausage Problem

Suppose that a meat packer must determine the quantities of ingredients that should be used in making 100 pounds of Persian sausage. Table 12-3 provides the pertinent labeling requirements and cost data.

We will assume that spices and casings add an insignificant amount to the total sausage weight and that unlimited quantities of the main ingredients are available at the indicated costs. The total ingredient weight must equal 100 pounds. If we represent the number of pounds of beef by X_B, chicken by X_C, and lamb by X_L, the following linear program formulation applies:

TABLE 12-3

Labeling Requirements and Cost Data for the Persian Sausage Problem

Label Category	PERCENTAGE OF WEIGHT			Required Percentage
	Beef	Chicken	Lamb	
Fat	20	15	25	$\leq 24\%$
Protein	20	15	15	$\geq 12\%$
Water	60	70	60	$\leq 64\%$
Percentage of total weight	any	any	$\geq 30\%$	
Cost per pound	$1.00	$.50	$.70	

$$\text{Minimize} \quad C = 1X_B + .5X_C + .7X_L \quad \text{(objective)}$$

$$\text{Subject to} \quad .20X_B + .15X_C + .25X_L \leq 24 \quad \text{(fat)}$$

$$.20X_B + .15X_C + .15X_L \geq 12 \quad \text{(protein)}$$

$$.60X_B + .70X_C + .60X_L \leq 64 \quad \text{(water)}$$

$$1X_L \geq 30 \quad \text{(ingredient)}$$

$$1X_B + 1X_C + 1X_L = 100 \quad \text{(total weight)}$$

$$\text{where} \quad X_B, X_C, X_L \geq 0 \quad \text{(non-negativity)}.$$

An inspection of this program indicates that we must include two slack variables for the fat and water constraints and two surplus variables for the protein and ingredient constraints. These are respectively denoted by X_F, X_W, X_P, and X_I. Since they involve surplus variables, the protein and ingredient constraints must include the artificial variables a_P and a_I. Finally, we include an artificial variable a_T for the equality constraint for total weight.

The pre-simplex formulation of this linear program is

Minimize

$$C = 1X_B + .5X_C + .7X_L + 0X_F + 0X_P + 0X_W + 0X_I + Ma_P + Ma_I + Ma_T$$

Subject to

$$.20X_B + .15X_C + .25X_L + 1X_F + 0X_P + 0X_W + 0X_I + 0a_P + 0a_I + 0a_T = 24$$

$$.20X_B + .15X_C + .15X_L + 0X_F - 1X_P + 0X_W + 0X_I + 1a_P + 0a_I + 0a_T = 12$$

$$.60X_B + .70X_C + .60X_L + 0X_F + 0X_P + 1X_W + 0X_I + 0a_P + 0a_I + 0a_T = 64$$

$$0X_B + 0X_C + 1X_L + 0X_F + 0X_P + 0X_W - 1X_I + 0a_P + 1a_I + 0a_T = 30$$

$$1X_B + 1X_C + 1X_L + 0X_F + 0X_P + 0X_W + 0X_I + 0a_P + 0a_I + 1a_T = 100$$

where   all variables ≥ 0

Handling these artificial variables differs in one way from the handling of these variables in profit-maximization problems. In the objective function,

TABLE 12-4

The Initial Simplex Tableau for the Persian Sausage Problem

UNIT COST		1	.5	.7	0	0	0	0	M	M	M	
	Var. Mix	X_B	X_C	X_L	X_F	X_P	X_W	X_I	a_P	a_I	a_T	Sol.
0	X_F	.20	.15	.25↓	1	0	0	0	0	0	0	24
M	a_P	.20	.15	.15	0	−1	0	0	1	0	0	12
0	X_W	.60	.70	.60	0	0	1	0	0	0	0	64
M	a_I ←	0	0	①	0	0	0	−1	0	1	0	30
M	a_T	1	1	1	0	0	0	0	0	0	1	100
	Sac.	1.2M	1.15M	2.15M	0	−M	0	−M	M	M	M	142M
	Imp.	1 −1.2M	.5 −1.15M	.7 −2.15M	0	M	0	M	0	0	0	—

a_P, a_I, and a_T have positive unit costs of $+M$, making them terribly costly (and ensuring that these variables leave the variable mix early).

The initial simplex tableau is provided in Table 12-4. From the improvement row, we can see that X_L must be the entering variable, since the entry from its column is $.7 - 2.15M$, which exceeds the other negative entries of $1 - 1.2M$ and $.5 - 1.15M$ in absolute terms. To determine this, we look first at the M terms; the largest absolute values of the negative terms corresponds to the entering variable. For example, consider the following two sets of hypothetical improvement values (the numbers in parentheses represent the case when $M = 1,000,000$):

	Set 1		Set 2	
(4,997,000)	$-3,000 + 5M$		$50,000 - 1M$	$(-950,000)$
(−999,998)	$2 - 1M$		$20,000 - 1M$	$(-980,000)$
(−1,009,950)	$50 - 1.01M$	← choices →	$2,000 - 1M$	$(-998,000)$
(−499,980)	$20 - .5M$		$5,000 - 1M$	$(-995,000)$

In set 1, the third quantity locates the entering variable, because it has the largest absolute value of the negative coefficients of M. If more than one negative coefficient has the largest absolute value, then we choose the one with the lowest constant value (or the largest absolute negative value if there are negative terms). Thus, we choose the third value in set 2 to locate the entering variable.

The requirements for the exit criterion do not change in cost-minimization problems. We determine the ratios and select the smallest non-negative one, which establishes a_I as the exiting variable.

The remainder of the simplex procedure for the Persian sausage problem is provided in Table 12–5.

TABLE 12-5
The Remaining Iterations for the Persian Sausage Problem

UNIT COST		1	.5	.7	0	0	0	0	M	M	M	
	Var. Mix	X_B	X_C	X_L	X_F	X_P	X_W	X_I	a_P	a_I	a_T	Sol.
0	X_F	.20↓	.15	0	1	0	0	.25	0	−.25	0	16.5
M	a_P←	⟨.20⟩	.15	0	0	−1	0	.15	1	−.15	0	7.5
0	X_W	.60	.70	0	0	0	1	.60	0	−.60	0	46
.7	X_L	0	0	1	0	0	0	−1	0	1	0	30
M	a_T	1	1	0	0	0	0	1	0	−1	1	70
	Sac.	1.2M	1.15M	.7	0	−M	0	$-.7+1.15M$	M	$.7-1.15M$	M	$21+77.5M$
	Imp.	$1-1.2M$	$.5-1.15M$	0	0	M	0	$.7-1.15M$	0	$-.7+2.15M$	0	—
0	X_F	0	0	0	1	1↓	0	.10	−1	−.10	0	9
1	X_B	1	.75	0	0	−5	0	.75	5	−.75	0	37.5
0	X_W	0	.25	0	0	3	1	.15	−3	−.15	0	23.5
.7	X_L	0	0	1	0	0	0	−1	0	1	0	30
M	a_T←	0	.25	0	0	⟨5⟩	0	.25	−5	−.25	1	32.5
	Sac.	1	$.75+.25M$	.7	0	$-5+5M$	0	$.05+.25M$	$5-5M$	$-.05-.25M$	M	$58.5+32.5M$
	Imp.	0	$-.25-.25M$	0	0	$5-5M$	0	$-.05-.25M$	$-5+6M$	$.05+1.25M$	0	—

TABLE 12-5 (continued)

c	Basis										Sol.
0	X_F	-.05↓	0	1	0	0	.05	0	-.05	-.2	2.5
1	X_B	1	0	0	0	0	1	0	-1	1	70
0	X_W←	(.10)	0	0	1	0	0	0	0	-.6	4
.7	X_L	0	1	0	0	0	-1	0	1	0	30
0	X_P	.05	0	0	0	1	.05	-1	-.05	.2	6.5
	Sac.	1	.7	0	0	0	.3	0	-.3	1	91
	Imp.	-.5	0	0	0	0	-.3	M	$.3+M$	$-1+M$	—

c	Basis										Sol.
0	X_F	0	0	1	0	0	.5	.05↓	0	-.05	-.5	4.5
1	X_B←	0	0	0	0	0	-10	(1)	0	-1	7	30
.5	X_C	1	0	0	0	0	10	0	0	0	-6	40
.7	X_L	0	1	0	0	0	0	-1	0	1	0	30
0	X_P	0	0	0	0	1	-.5	.05	-1	-.05	-5	4.5
	Sac.	1	.7	0	0	0	-5	.3	0	-.3	4	71
	Imp.	0	0	0	0	0	5	-.3	M	$.3+M$	$-4+M$	—

c	Basis										Sol.
0	X_F	-.05	0	1	0	0	1	0	0	0	-.85	3
0	X_I	1	0	0	0	0	-10	1	0	-1	7	30
.5	X_C	0	1	0	0	0	10	0	0	0	-6	40
.7	X_L	1	0	0	1	0	-10	0	0	0	7	60
0	X_P	-.05	0	0	0	1	0	0	-1	0	.15	3
	Sac.	.7	0	0	0	0	-2	0	0	0	1.9	62
	Imp.	.3	0	0	0	0	2	0	M	M	$-1.9+M$	—

The optimal solution is

$$X_B = 0 \qquad X_F = 3$$
$$X_C = 40 \qquad X_I = 30$$
$$X_L = 60 \qquad X_P = 3$$
$$X_W = 0$$

$$C = 62 \text{ dollars}$$

Thus, no beef should be used in the Persian sausage, and the main ingredients should consist of 40 pounds of chicken and 60 pounds of lamb. The sausage will contain 3 pounds less fat than the maximum allowable amount, and 3 pounds of extra protein above the minimum requirement. Also, 30 pounds of lamb above the minimum required level of 30 pounds will be included.

12-3 A SUMMARY OF THE SIMPLEX FORMULATION REQUIREMENTS

We have seen that under various conditions the simplex procedure requires slack, surplus, or artificial variables in addition to the main problem variables. A summary of the simplex formulation requirements is provided in Table 12-6.

TABLE 12-6
A Summary of the Simplex Formulation Requirements

Type of Constraint	Constraint Relationship	Extra Variables Needed for Simplex	Objective Coefficient		Initial Variable Mix
			Max. P	Min. C	
Resource or maximum requirement	$\leq$	Slack (added)	0	0	Yes
		No artificial	—	—	—
Demand or minimum requirement	$\geq$	Surplus (subtracted)	0	0	No
		Artificial (added)	$-M$	$+M$	Yes
Mixture or exact requirement	$=$	No slack or surplus	—	—	—
		Artificial (added)	$-M$	$+M$	Yes

SPECIAL PROBLEMS IN LINEAR PROGRAMMING 12-4

At this point, we have substantially covered the simplex method. Only a few special problem areas remain to be discussed. First, we will consider two types of problems that have no practical solutions. Then we will describe the procedure to follow when there may be several optimal solutions (most attractive corners). Finally, we will consider two technical difficulties that are inherent in the simplex procedure.

Infeasible Problems

Thus far, we have encountered only problems that have solutions. It is possible, however, for constraints to be so restrictive that no solution exists. Such a linear program is called an *infeasible problem*. Consider the following linear program:

$$\text{Maximize} \quad P = 6X_1 + 4X_2$$

$$\text{Subject to} \quad X_1 + X_2 \le 5$$

$$X_2 \ge 8$$

$$\text{where} \quad X_1, X_2 \ge 0$$

This problem is graphed in Figure 12-1. Notice that there is no feasible solution region, since the constraints are mutually incompatible.

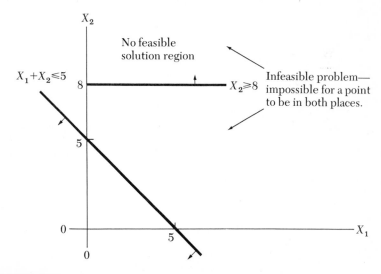

FIGURE 12-1
Graph for the infeasible problem.

It is not so easy to recognize that a problem is infeasible when several variables and constraints are involved. Fortunately, we can determine whether or not a problem is feasible when we begin to apply the simplex method. Table 12-7 shows the simplex tableaus for this infeasible problem using S_1 as the slack for the first constraint, S_2 as the surplus for the second, and a as the artificial variable. The final tableau includes the artificial variable in the variable mix, with a value of $a = 3$. We know that this makes no economic sense. *If one or more artificial variables remain in the final variable mix, the linear program must be infeasible.*

Ordinarily, an infeasible problem indicates that a mistake has been made in the initial formulation. The remedy is to check the constraint expressions to verify that they properly reflect the problem. One number may have been miscopied or assigned the wrong sign; or perhaps a $\leq$ should really be a $\geq$. Once the mistake has been remedied, the corrected linear program can be solved again. It is more perplexing when the formulation properly reflects the problem, indicating that the problem in itself represents contradictory requirements. Then unless the impasse is resolved, the decision maker will never be able to solve the problem. (No kind of answer—not even a poor one—is possible for an infeasible problem.)

TABLE 12-7
Simplex Tableaus for the Infeasible Problem

UNIT PROFIT		6	4	0	0	$-M$	
	Var. Mix	X_1	X_2	S_1	S_2	a	Sol.
0	S_1 ←	1	①↓	1	0	0	5
$-M$	a	0	1	0	-1	1	8
	Sac.	0	$-M$	0	M	$-M$	$5 - 8M$
	Imp.	6	$4 + M$	0	$-M$	0	—

4	X_2	1	1	1	0	0	5
$-M$	a	-1	0	-1	-1	1	3
	Sac.	$4 + M$	4	$4 + M$	M	$-M$	$20 - 3M$
	Imp.	$2 - M$	0	$-4 - M$	$-M$	0	—

Unbounded Problems

Another category of linear programs yields ridiculous solutions that place no effective limit on one or more variables. Thus, any level of profit is possible—even a profit level of trillions of dollars, or more. Such a linear program is called an *unbounded problem*. As an example consider the following linear program:

$$\text{Maximize} \quad P = \quad 3X_1 + 6X_2$$
$$\text{Subject to} \quad \quad 3X_1 + 4X_2 \geq 12$$
$$-2X_1 + \quad X_2 \leq \quad 4$$
$$\text{where} \quad \quad X_1, X_2 \geq \quad 0$$

The graph of this linear program in Figure 12-2 shows shows that the feasible solution region lies open and becomes wider in the direction of increasing P.

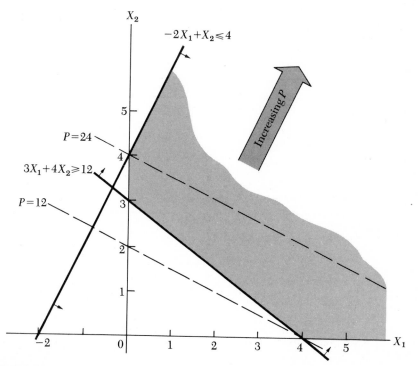

FIGURE 12-2
Graph for the unbounded problem.

There is no most attractive corner, and P can be as large as we want it to be. No matter how large a P is chosen, larger and larger P lines can be drawn through the feasible solution region. In essence, P can be infinite.

As in the case of infeasible problems, simplex can identify the unbounded problem for us. Table 12-8 shows the simplex iterations for this unbounded problem, using S_1 and a as the surplus and artificial variables for the first constraint and S_2 as the slack variable for the second. Notice that no exiting variable can be found in the third tableau, because no entry in the X_1 column is positive. In essence, there is no limit on the quantity X_1; it can replace either X_2 or S_1 in the variable mix at any level desired.

Whenever the exit criterion fails, the linear program is unbounded. *A linear programming problem is unbounded whenever none of the values in the entering variable's column is positive.*

TABLE 12-8
Simplex Tableaus for the Unbounded Problem

UNIT PROFIT		3	6	0	0	$-M$	
	Var. Mix	X_1	X_2	S_1	S_2	a	Sol.
$-M$	$a \leftarrow$	3	④↓	-1	0	1	12
0	S_2	-2	1	0	1	0	4
	Sac.	$-3M$	$-4M$	M	0	$-M$	$-12M$
	Imp.	$3 + 3M$	$6 + 4M$	$-M$	0	0	—
6	X_2	.75	1	$-.25$↓	0	.25	3
0	$S_2 \leftarrow$	-2.75	0	.25	1	$-.25$	1
	Sac.	4.5	6	-1.5	0	1.5	18
	Imp.	-1.5	0	1.5	0	$-M - 1.5$	—
6	X_2	-2↓	1	0	1	0	4
0	S_1	-11	0	1	4	-1	4
	Sac.	-12	6	0	6	0	24
	Imp.	15	0	0	-6	$-M$	—

There is no exiting variable.

In the real world, no economic situations are literally unbounded. Thus, when a linear program turns out to be unbounded, some essential restriction (plant capacity, initial inventory level, etc.) has been left out of the formulation. Once the missing constraint is determined, the properly formulated linear program should result in a realistic solution.

Ties for the Optimal Solution

In Chapter 9, we saw that whenever a most attractive corner lies on an edge parallel to the objective function, there is another equally attractive corner at the opposite end of that edge. All points on this edge correspond to optimal solutions.

In the higher dimensional problems encountered when simplex is used, similar ties for the most attractive corner apply. The simplex procedure can be used to evaluate every most attractive corner, finding all ties for the optimal solution. Such ties occur when the objective function coefficients are in constant ratio to the respective coefficients in the expression for one constraint (or some constraint that might result when two or more constraint equations are combined). Under some circumstances, there can be more than two most attractive corners, permitting a multitude of ties to occur. But there will ordinarily be no ties at all.

Suppose that we must amend our Persian sausage problem slightly because beef now sells for $.70 per pound instead of $1. The top tableau in Table 12-9 corresponds to the final simplex tableau in Table 12-5. (For simplicity, the artificial variable columns have been removed.) The first tableau provides the optimal solution

$$X_B = 0 \qquad X_F = 3$$
$$X_C = 40 \qquad X_P = 3$$
$$X_L = 60 \qquad X_W = 0$$
$$X_I = 30$$
$$C = 62 \text{ dollars}$$

which is identical to out prior optimal solution to the Persian sausage problem, except that *a zero improvement* exists for the nonmix variable X_B. This indicates that if some beef were used, so that X_B became part of the variable mix, there would be no change in total cost. In effect, a *simplex pivot* treating X_B as the entering variable would produce a new solution also having a cost of $C = 62$ dollars. In other words, a tie would exist for the optimal solution.

TABLE 12-9

A Further Simplex Iteration to Find the Tying Optimal Solution to the Persian Sausage Problem

UNIT COST		.7	.5	.7	0	0	0	0	
	Var. Mix	X_B	X_C	X_L	X_F	X_P	X_W	X_I	Sol.
0	X_F	−.05↓	0	0	1	0	1	0	3
0	X_I ←	①	0	0	0	0	−10	1	30
.5	X_C	0	1	0	0	0	10	0	40
.7	X_L	1	0	1	0	0	−10	0	60
0	X_P	−.05	0	0	0	1	0	0	3
	Sac.	.7	.5	.7	0	0	−2	0	62
	Imp.	0	0	0	0	0	2	0	—
0	X_F	0	0	0	1	0	.5	.05	4.5
.7	X_B	1	0	0	0	0	−10	1	30
.5	X_C	0	1	0	0	0	10	0	40
.7	X_L	0	0	1	0	0	0	−1	30
0	X_P	0	0	0	0	1	−.5	.05	4.5
	Sac.	.7	.5	.7	0	0	−2	0	62
	Imp.	0	0	0	0	0	2	1	—

Now suppose that we carry out one more iteration, treating X_B (beef) as the entering variable. In Table 12-9, we can see that X_I (surplus ingredient lamb) exits, and the solution is provided by the second tableau, where

$$X_B = 30 \qquad X_F = 4.5$$
$$X_C = 40 \qquad X_P = 4.5$$
$$X_L = 30 \qquad X_W = 0$$
$$X_I = 0$$
$$C = 62 \text{ dollars}$$

This solution is tied with the first optimal solution. In general, *a tie for optimal solution exists whenever a nonmix variable exhibits zero per-unit improvement in the final simplex tableau.* This is true whether that variable is a main, slack, or surplus variable. The tying solution can be found by a further simplex pivot

TABLE 12-10
Finding an Optimal Solution Lying on an Edge

Variable	VALUES FOR TYING OPTIMAL CORNER First	Second	Optimal Edge Point (40% First + 60% Second)
X_B	0	30	0 + 18 = 18
X_C	40	40	16 + 24 = 40
X_L	60	30	24 + 18 = 42
X_F	3	4.5	1.2 + 2.7 = 3.9
X_P	3	4.5	1.2 + 2.7 = 3.9
X_W	0	0	0 + 0 = 0
X_I	30	0	12 + 0 = 12
C	62	62	62

that treats this variable as the entering variable. (This feature is also present in the second tableau for X_I, which tells us that we could then enter X_I and exit X_B, bringing us back to where we started. The process is reversible.) Once an optimal solution has been found, it is a simple matter to employ further pivots successively to find all of the tying solutions.

We have found two optimal corner-point solutions. Any feasible linear combination of these solutions (any point on the connecting edge) will also be optimal. Whenever a fixed percentage of all the values of one corner is added to the complementary percentage of all the values of the other corner, such a combination will result. For example, Table 12-10 shows the optimal edge point when 40% of the first corner is combined with 60% of the second corner.

Redundant Constraints and Degeneracy

When the constraints of some linear programs are considered collectively, one or more of the problem constraints may be *redundant*. Ordinarily, no problem is caused by including a redundant constraint in a linear programming problem, although the simplex computations can be shortened if obviously redundant constraints are eliminated beforehand. For example, the second constraint provided below is less restrictive than the first one and is not needed:

$$2X_1 + 3X_2 \leq 6$$
$$2X_1 + 3X_2 \leq 7$$

It is often difficult to determine in advance whether a redundancy exists, however. Under some circumstances, simplex may therefore yield a *tie for the exiting variable.* The rules of simplex permit any tie (whether it is for an entering or an exiting variable) to be broken arbitrarily. But when this happens during the exit phase, the new tableau contains a zero value in the solution column, indicating that the variable for that row could lie outside the variable mix. In effect, a redundancy is present somewhere in the problem.

Whenever there is a zero in the solution column, the linear program is said to be *degenerate*. This is normally of no practical consequence. But on very rare occasions, degeneracy may cause the simplex procedure to *cycle* indefinitely, repeating an identical sequence of pivots and never reaching a conclusion. If this ever happens, the remedy is simple: Return to the tableau where the tie occurred, make the other variable the exiting variable, and proceed from there.

Variables That Are Unrestricted as to Sign

Simplex requires that every variable be non-negative. However, certain real-world problems involve variables that can be either positive or negative. In a security-investment problem, for example, the number of shares of a particular stock might be represented by a long position (a positive quantity), a short position (a negative quantity), or no shares (zero). Oil refining provides another example. Some byproducts can be created in one stage and consumed in a later one—in varying amounts in both cases. Thus, the net amount of the resulting byproduct could be either positive (more is created than is consumed) or negative (more is consumed than is created). In both applications *the sign of the variable is unrestricted.*

Simplex still requires non-negativity, even when it is applied to such a problem. One way to accommodate the non-negativity condition is to represent the unrestricted variable by the difference between two difference non-negative variables. For example

	Security Investment	Oil Refining
Unrestricted:	X_P = position in stock	X_B = net change in byproduct
New non-negative variables:	X_L = shares held long	X_C = byproduct created
	X_S = shares shorted	X_U = byproduct consumed
	$X_P = X_L - X_S$	$X_B = X_C - X_U$

The difference $X_L - X_S$ (or $X_C - X_U$) can be substituted everywhere X_P (or X_B) appears, and the respective linear programs will contain only non-negative variables. If the solution to the investment problem provides $X_L = 0$, $X_S = 100$, then $X_P = 0 - 100 = -100$. If the solution to the oil-refining problem is with $X_C = 10,000$, $X_U = 11,000$, then $X_B = 10,000 - 11,000 = -1,000$.

ROBLEMS

12-1 Consider the linear program

$$\text{Maximize} \quad P = 5X_1 + 6X_2$$

$$\begin{array}{lll}
\text{Subject to} & 3X_1 + 4X_2 \leq 12 & \text{(resource)} \\
& 2X_1 + 6X_2 \geq 12 & \text{(mixture)} \\
\text{where} & X_1, X_2 \geq 0 &
\end{array}$$

(a) Solve this problem graphically.
(b) Reformulate this problem in equation form suitable for simplex.
(c) Solve the problem again using the simplex procedure.

12-2 Consider the linear program

$$\text{Maximize} \quad P = 2X_1 - 3X_2$$

$$\begin{array}{lll}
\text{Subject to} & 4X_1 + 5X_2 \leq 40 & \text{(resource } A) \\
& 2X_1 - 6X_2 \leq 24 & \text{(resource } B) \\
& 3X_1 - 3X_2 \geq 6 & \text{(mixture)} \\
& X_1 \qquad\quad \geq 4 & \text{(demand)} \\
\text{where} & X_1, X_2 \geq 0 &
\end{array}$$

(a) Solve this problem graphically.
(b) Reformulate this problem in equation form suitable for simplex.
(c) Solve the problem again using the simplex procedure.

12-3 Consider the linear program

$$\text{Minimize} \quad C = .5X_A + .3X_B$$

$$\begin{array}{lll}
\text{Subject to} & X_A + 2X_B \geq 10 & \text{(restriction } Y) \\
& 2X_A + X_B \geq 8 & \text{(restriction } Z) \\
\text{where} & X_A, X_B \geq 0 &
\end{array}$$

(a) Solve this problem graphically.
(b) Reformulate this problem in equation form suitable for simplex.
(c) Solve the problem again using the simplex procedure.

12-4 For each of the following linear programs, an intermediate or final simplex tableau is presented. In each case, state whether the simplex procedure indicates (1) an optimal solution, (2) an unbounded problem, (3) an infeasible problem, (4) that further steps are required (in which case, find the entering and exiting variables), or (5) that a tie exists for the optimal solution and that the final tableau provides just one optimal solution.

$$\begin{array}{lll}
\text{(a) Maximize} & P = 14X_1 + 18X_2 + 16X_3 + 80X_4 \\
\text{Subject to} & 4\tfrac{1}{2}X_1 + 8\tfrac{1}{2}X_2 + 6X_3 + 20X_4 \leq 6,000 & \text{(resource } A) \\
& X_1 + X_2 + 4X_3 + 40X_4 \leq 4,000 & \text{(resource } B) \\
\text{where} & \text{all } Xs \geq 0 &
\end{array}$$

UNIT PROFIT	14	18	16	80	0	0	

	Var. Mix	X_1	X_2	X_3	X_4	X_A	X_B	Sol.
14	X_1	1	2	1	0	1/4	-1/8	1,000
80	X_4	0	-1/40	3/40	1	-1/160	9/320	75
	Sac.	14	26	20	80	3	1/2	20,000
	Imp.	0	-8	-4	0	-3	-1/2	—

(b) Maximize $P = 2X_1 + 2X_2$

Subject to
$$X_1 + X_2 \geq 3 \quad \text{(limitation)}$$
$$X_1 + X_2 \leq 2 \quad \text{(resource)}$$

where
$$X_1, X_2 \geq 0$$

UNIT PROFIT		2	2	0	0	$-M$	

	Var. Mix	X_1	X_2	X_L	X_R	a	Sol.
$-M$	a	0	0	-1	-1	1	1
2	X_1	1	1	0	1	0	2
	Sac.	2	2	M	M + 2	-M	4 - M
	Imp.	0	0	-M	-M - 2	0	—

(c) Maximize $P = X_1 + X_2$

Subject to
$$2X_1 + 2X_2 \leq 4 \quad \text{(resource } A\text{)}$$
$$X_1 \qquad\ \leq 3 \quad \text{(resource } B\text{)}$$

where
$$X_1, X_2 \geq 0$$

UNIT PROFIT		1	1	0	0	

	Var. Mix	X_1	X_2	X_A	X_B	Sol.
1	X_2	1	1	1/2	0	2
0	X_B	1	0	0	1	3
	Sac.	1	1	1/2	0	2
	Imp.	0	0	-1/2	0	—

(d) Maximize $\quad P = \quad 5X_1 + 6X_2$

Subject to $\qquad -4X_1 + 2X_2 \le 12 \quad$ (resource A)

$\qquad\qquad\quad -4X_1 + 3X_2 \le 12 \quad$ (resource B)

where $\qquad\qquad X_1, X_2 \ge 0$

UNIT PROFIT		5	6	0	0	
	Var. Mix	X_1	X_2	X_A	X_B	Sol.
0	X_A	$-4/3$	0	1	$-2/3$	4
6	X_2	$-4/3$	1	0	$1/3$	4
	Sac.	-8	6	0	2	24
	Imp.	13	0	0	-2	—

(e) Minimize $\quad C = 40X_1 + 60X_2$

Subject to $\qquad 3X_1 + 3X_2 \ge 3 \quad$ (restriction A)

$\qquad\qquad\quad 2X_1 + 3X_2 \ge 4 \quad$ (restriction B)

where $\qquad\qquad X_1, X_2 \ge 0$

UNIT COST		40	60	0	0	M	M	
	Var. Mix	X_1	X_2	X_A	X_B	a_A	a_B	Sol.
60	X_2	$2/3$	1	$-1/3$	0	$1/3$	0	1
M	a_B	1	0	1	-1	-1	1	1
	Sac.	$40 + M$	60	$-20 + M$	$-M$	$20 - M$	M	$60 + M$
	Imp.	$-M$	0	$20 - M$	M	$-20 + 2M$	0	—

12-5 Use the simplex procedure to solve Problem 10-2 (page 242) and determine how much Quicker Oats should spend on each advertising and promotional activity.

12-6 Use the simplex method to solve the Real Reels advertising budget problem (page 237).

12-7 Use simplex to solve Problem 10-4 (page 243) and determine how much the portfolio manager should invest in each financial instrument.

12-8 Use simplex to solve Problem 10-5 (page 243) and find the optimal solution for the sausage-ingredient problem.

12-9 Use simplex to solve problem 10-11 and determine the number of spot ads Blitz Beer should place with each radio station.

12-10 Use simplex to solve Problem 10-12 and find the optimal blending schedule for Horrible Harry's gasolines.

12-11 Use simplex to solve Problem 10-13 and find Geo-Pet's optimal dollar-investment levels in the proposed ventures.

12-12 Grubby Stakes Mining Company is establishing a production plan for the current week at its Bonstock Lode, which has three main veins of varying characteristics. The net yields per ton for each of the veins is provided below:

	Eastern	Northern	Tom's Lucky
Gold	.2 oz	.3 oz	.4 oz
Silver	30 oz	20 oz	30 oz
Copper	50 lb	20 lb	25 lb

Gold presently sells for $150 per ounce, silver sells for $5 per ounce, and copper sells for $2 per pound. Eastern is the most accessible vein, requiring 1 man-hour per ton of ore; Northern and Tom's Lucky veins are more remote and require 2 man-hours per ton. Only 300 man-hours are available, and all labor costs are fixed. At least 100 tons must be mined from the Northern vein this week, so that it can be reshored next week; there are no tonnage limitations for the other tunnels. The company must also yield at least 5,000 pounds of copper to meet contractual commitments.

Formulate Grubby's linear program to determine how many tons must be mined from each vein to maximize total revenue. Then use simplex to find the optimal solution.

12-13 The Flying Chef supplies in-flight dinners to airlines. On a particular run, the passengers are given their choice of beef, chicken, or fish entrees. The owner must decide how many meals of each type to prepare in order to minimize total cost. Historically, 55% of all passengers prefer beef, 30% prefer chicken, and 15% prefer fish. However, to compensate for varying tastes from flight to flight, the number of meals provided must be as great as the above percentages of total passengers. On the current flight, there are 200 passengers and 300 meals must be provided. Airline policy states that at least one-half the extra meals on any given flight must be beef. Costs are $2 for each beef entree, $1.50 for chicken, and $1 for fish.

Formulate the linear program for this problem. Then solve the problem using simplex. How many meals of each type should be provided?

12-14 Morrie's Thrift Shoppe sells three kinds of suits: used, seconds (rejects from large clothing manufacturers), and Hong Kong specials. Morrie is buying his stock for the coming season. The used suits yield an average profit of $30 per suit, each second nets $20, and the Hong Kong suits are the most profitable at $50 each. Since Morrie has a 100% markup policy, the preceding figures also represent his wholesale costs. Morrie can spend no more than $10,000 this year. To maintain his "quality" image, not more than one-fourth of his suits can be used suits. Morrie does not wish to be too exotic, so the Hong Kong suits must not outnumber the used and second suits combined. To maintain his factory contacts, Morrie must buy at least 100 seconds every year.

Morrie always sells his entire inventory every year, and he wishes to maximize his total suit profits. Formulate this problem as a linear program. Then identify any necessary slack and surplus variables separately and solve the problem using the simplex method.

12-15 For the linear program

$$\text{Maximize} \quad P = 6X_1 + 10X_2 + 2X_3$$
$$\text{Subject to} \quad 2X_1 + 4X_2 + 3X_3 \leq 40 \quad \text{(resource } A\text{)}$$
$$X_1 + X_2 \qquad \leq 10 \quad \text{(resource } B\text{)}$$
$$2X_2 + X_3 \leq 12 \quad \text{(resource } C\text{)}$$
$$\text{where} \qquad X_1, X_2, X_3 \geq 0$$

the slack variables are X_A, X_B, and X_C. The final simplex tableau is provided below:

UNIT PROFIT		6	10	2	0	0	0	
	Var. Mix	X_1	X_2	X_3	X_A	X_B	X_C	Sol.
0	X_A	0	0	2	1	−2	−1	8
6	X_1	1	0	−1/2	0	1	−1/2	4
10	X_2	0	1	1/2	0	0	1/2	6
	Sac.	6	10	2	0	6	2	84
	Imp.	0	0	0	0	−6	−2	—

A tie exists for the optimal solution.

(a) Identify the values of the solution variables. Then determine the tying optimal solution and provide the corresponding variable values.

(b) Determine the optimal edge-point solution lying halfway between the two tying optimal corner points.

12-16 For the following linear program

$$\text{Maximize} \quad P = 5X_1 + 2X_2 + 10X_3$$
$$\text{Subject to} \quad X_1 \quad - \quad X_3 \leq 10 \quad \text{(resource } A\text{)}$$
$$X_2 - X_3 \geq 10 \quad \text{(limitation } B\text{)}$$
$$\text{where} \qquad X_1, X_2, X_3 \geq 0$$

the extra variables are X_A (slack), X_B (surplus), and a (artificial). Consider the intermediate simplex tableau provided below:

UNIT PROFIT		5	2	10	0	0	−M	
	Var. Mix	X_1	X_2	X_3	X_A	X_B	a	Sol.
5	X_1	1	0	−1	1	0	0	10
2	X_2	0	1	−1	0	−1	1	10
	Sac.	5	2	−7	5	−2	2	70
	Imp.	0	0	3	−5	2	−M − 2	—

(a) Find the entering variable. Then determine the exiting variable. Do you notice anything unusual? Indicate your finding.

(b) The following constraint was missing from the earlier formulation:

$$X_1 + X_2 + X_3 \leq 10 \quad \text{(resource } C\text{)}$$

Use simplex to solve the new linear program from the beginning.

12-17 For the linear program

Maximize $\quad P = 20X_1 + 10X_2 + 2X_3$

Subject to

$$
\begin{aligned}
2X_1 + \quad X_2 + X_3 &\leq 9 \quad \text{(resource } A\text{)} \\
X_1 + \quad X_2 \quad\quad &\geq 10 \quad \text{(limitation } B\text{)}
\end{aligned}
$$

where $\quad\quad\quad\quad X_1, X_2, X_3 \geq 0$

the extra variables are X_A (slack), X_B (surplus), and a (artificial). The final simplex tableau is

UNIT PROFIT		20	10	2	0	0	$-M$	
	Var. Mix	X_1	X_2	X_3	X_A	X_B	a	Sol.
10	X_2	2	1	1	1	0	0	9
$-M$	a	-1	0	-1	-1	-1	1	1
	Sac.	$20 + M$	10	$10 + M$	$10 + M$	M	$-M$	$90 - M$
	Imp.	$-M$	0	$-8 - M$	$-10 - M$	$-M$	0	—

(a) What does the solution you obtained from this tableau tell you about the problem?

(b) Suppose this is corrected by changing the limitation level for B from 10 to 4. Using simplex, start from the beginning and find the optimal solution to this revised problem.

13

Duality in Linear Programming

We have seen how linear programming can be used to solve a variety of profit-maximization or cost-minimization problems. The variables in these applications are generally unknown quantities, such as number of tables, pounds of beef, or dollars spent on television advertising. In production-planning applications, the problem is to determine how much of each product type should be made. An entirely different way to represent the production decision as a linear program will be presented in this chapter.

We know that a linear program actually tells us how scarce resources should be allocated to maximize profits. Now suppose that our primary concern is to determine the most efficient application of the production resources themselves. Focusing on *resources*, rather than on products, requires a wholly different expression of the underlying problem. In effect, we must "cross through the looking glass" into a special mathematical environment that essentially mirrors our ordinary one. In this new linear programming environment, problems are formulated differently but have equivalent solutions. Every ordinary problem has its doppelgänger, which we refer to as the *dual linear program* or, for short, the *dual*.

13-1 THE DUAL LINEAR PROGRAM

Let's begin by returning to familiar territory and reconsidering the data for the Redwood Furniture problem in Table 13-1. The resource *costs* associated with wood and labor depend on how these factors are employed in production. In effect, we want to assign appropriate unit costs to the available wood and labor that somehow measure their worth in accomplishing an underlying production plan. Such costs will then express the increase in profit that can be achieved by acquiring one more unit of the respective resource. This provides us with the dual linear program.

Our problem is to assign unit wood and labor costs so that we

Minimize C = Total resource cost

= Total cost of wood + Total cost of labor

We want to do this in such a way that the end products—tables and chairs—are never more profitable than the true worth or cost of the resources used to produce them. Each product constraint takes the form

Cost of resources per product $\geq$ Profit per product

Such a requirement might seem peculiar at first. After all, how can any production plan be efficient if costs exceed profits? But remember that we are talking about a special kind of cost that *we set ourselves*—not the wholesale price of lumber or the labor wage scale. Our variables are not accounting costs and have nothing to do with payments to lumber mills or to workers. (Those costs are already reflected in the $6 per table and $8 per chair profit figures.)

Let's express our dual linear program in terms of the variables

$$U_W = \text{wood cost per board foot}$$

$$U_L = \text{labor cost per hour}$$

TABLE 13-1

Data for the Redwood Furniture Problem

Resource	UNIT REQUIREMENTS Table	Chair	Amount Available
Wood (board feet)	30	20	300
Labor (hours)	5	10	110
Unit profit	$6	$8	

Although any letter would suffice, our use of Us to designate the dual variables is traditional. The total resource costs may then be expressed as

Total cost of wood = Total board feet available × Cost per board foot

$$= 300U_W$$

Total cost of labor = Total hours available × Cost per hour

$$= 110U_L$$

The objective function may then be expressed as

$$\text{Minimize} \quad C = 300U_W + 110U_L \quad \text{(objective)}$$

Table 13-1 tells us that each table requires 30 board feet of wood and 5 hours of labor. In terms of the unknown cost variables

$$30U_W = \text{cost of wood per table}$$

$$5U_L = \text{cost of labor per table}$$

so that

$$30U_W + 5U_L = \text{cost of resources per table}$$

The table constraint

$$\text{Cost of resources per table} \geq \text{Profit per table}$$

is then

$$30U_W + 5U_L \geq 6 \quad \text{(table)}$$

Likewise, since a chair requires 20 board feet of wood and 10 hours of labor, the chair constraint is

$$\text{Cost of resources per chair} \geq \text{Profit per chair}$$

$$20U_W + 10U_L \geq 8 \quad \text{(chair)}$$

Since the worth of a resource can never be negative, non-negativity conditions apply to U_W and U_L.

The Primal and the Dual

Before we solve the dual and interpret it further let's see how it directly relates to the original Redwood Furniture problem, for which the variables were quantities of tables and chairs. The original linear program is called the *primal* to distinguish it from its dual. The primal and the dual programs for the Redwood Furniture problem are

Primal Program	Dual Program
X_T = number of tables	U_W = wood cost per board foot
X_C = number of chairs	U_L = labor cost per hour
Maximize	Minimize
$P = 6X_T + 8X_C$	$C = 300U_W + 110U_L$
Subject to	Subject to
$30X_T + 20X_C \leq 300$ (wood)	$30U_W + 5U_L \geq 6$ (table)
$5X_T + 10X_C \leq 110$ (labor)	$20U_W + 10U_L \geq 8$ (chair)
where $X_T, X_C \geq 0$	where $U_W, U_L \geq 0$

Notice that the two programs are arranged similarly. The exchange coefficients of the two problems arranged as matrices are

$$
\begin{array}{cc}
\text{Primal} & \text{Dual} \\
\begin{pmatrix} 30 & 20 \\ 5 & 10 \end{pmatrix} & \begin{pmatrix} 30 & 5 \\ 20 & 10 \end{pmatrix}
\end{array}
$$

Note that the rows of the dual coefficients are the columns of the primal coefficients and that the columns of the dual are the rows of the primal. We refer to one matrix as the *transpose* of the other. The coefficients of the objective of the primal linear program appear as the right-hand sides of the dual constraints, and the right-hand sides of the primal constraints provide the objective coefficients for the dual. In effect, the position of every constraint in the dual is exactly what we would obtain by rotating the primal 90° counterclockwise when the P equation is written last and then resequencing the inequalities.

The objective of the primal problem is to maximize P. The objective of the dual is the opposite—to minimize C. The primal constraints are $\leq$ inequalities; the dual constraints are $\geq$ inequalities. One linear program is the transpose of the other with totally opposite objective and constraint orientations. (In effect, the primal itself is the "dual" of the dual.)

A fundamental fact of linear programming is that for any feasible respective solutions to the dual and primal

$$C \geq P$$

Further, the objective value in both problems is identical for the respective optimal solutions. Thus

$$\text{Minimum } C = \text{Maximum } P$$

so that the smallest possible cost is equal to the maximum possible profit. We will learn the importance of this feature later.

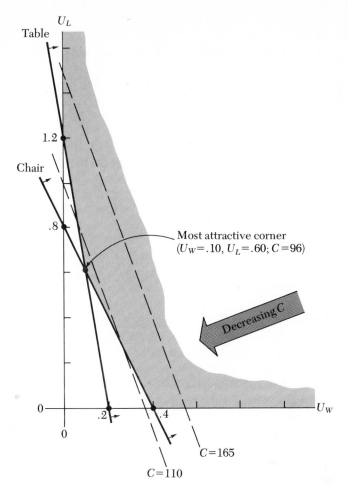

FIGURE 13-1
The graphical solution to the dual for the Redwood Furniture problem.

Solving the Dual Graphically

The dual linear program for the Redwood Furniture problem is solved graphically in Figure 13-1. Since the most attractive corner lies at the intersection of the table and chair constraint lines, the simultaneous solution of these equations provides

$$U_W = \$.10 \text{ per board foot}$$
$$U_L = \$.60 \text{ per hour}$$

and the minimum value of the objective function is

$$C = 300(.10) + 110(.60) = 96 \text{ dollars}$$

This is the figure that we originally obtained in Chapter 9 for the maximum profit of the primal linear program.

13-2 INTERPRETING THE DUAL LINEAR PROGRAM

Except as a mathematical curiosity, why are we interested in the dual at all? Our main reason for solving the dual is to obtain economic insight. We have seen that the optimal cost of 1 board foot of lumber is $.10. This cost indicates the actual worth of that much wood to Redwood's manufacturing operation. It tells us that one more unit of wood would provide an additional resource that could be used to produce more furniture that would be sold for a profit. In essence, we may view $.10 as the *opportunity cost* associated with not having an additional board foot of wood, since profit would be $.10 greater if 301 board feet of wood were used instead of the 300 board feet now available.

To verify that an additional board foot of wood would increase profit by $.10, we return to the graphical solution of the primal problem shown in Figure 13-2. There we can see that increasing the amount of available wood to 301 board feet results in a rightward shift of the wood line, making the feasible solution region wider than before. The intersection of the new wood line with the labor line provides the new most attractive corner, which shifts to the right and downward. This indicates that more tables and fewer chairs should be made than before. To determine the optimal solution exactly, we can simultaneously solve the new wood and labor constraint equations

$$30X_T + 20X_C = 301$$
$$5X_T + 10X_C = 110$$

which yields

$$X_T = 4.05$$
$$X_C = 8.975$$

The resulting profit is

$$P = 6(4.05) + 8(8.975)$$
$$= 96.10 \text{ dollars}$$

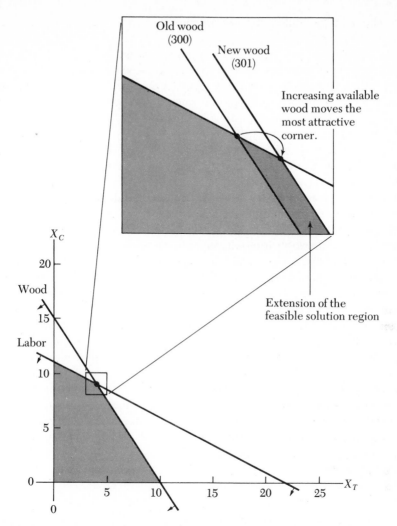

FIGURE 13-2
The graphical interpretation of the dual variable for the cost of wood.

which is exactly $.10 larger than the maximum profit when only 300 board feet of wood are available.

A similar conclusion applies to the optimal result $U_L = \$.60$ for labor. An additional hour of available labor will increase profit $.60. (You can verify this graphically with the primal, leaving available wood at the original amount of 300 board feet.)

Thus, the optimal dual variable values are really opportunity costs that indicate the potential profit that is lost by not having an additional unit of the respective resource, assuming that all resources are used optimally. These values are often referred to as *economic shadow prices*. It should be emphasized that $U_W = \$.10$ and $U_L = \$.60$ are not ordinary accounting or standard costs. These costs were already incorporated when the $6 per table and $8 per chair profits were originally set (before the linear program had been formulated the first time).

The opportunity costs of resources are valuable in that they tell us where it may be fruitful to modify existing policies. For example, suppose that Redwood can buy extra wood outside its regular supply channels for $.05 more per foot than the present price. It would be profitable to do so, since the premium paid would be smaller than the $.10 opportunity cost. Redwood would realize a net gain of $.05 for each additional foot of wood so acquired (up to a certain limit that we will establish in Chapter 14). Redwood would also improve its total profits by increasing available labor, as long as it could be obtained at a premium of less than $.60 per hour (for example, through overtime).

In one sense, the primal (original) linear program is concerned only with operational types of production decisions—determining what quantities of each product should be produced in a given time period. But the dual variables can point out areas that affect longer range decisions. For example, a host of constraints in manufacturing that arise from limited equipment availability or physical size pertain to capacities. The dual linear program for a production-planning decision establishes the opportunity cost of each extra hour of machine time or additional square foot of plant space. The solution to a tactical production problem can therefore provide attractive alternatives to consider in the strategical areas of capital investment. The dual values can indicate critical points where expansion may prove very profitable.

13-3 SOLVING THE DUAL LINEAR PROGRAM WITH SIMPLEX

Like any other linear program, the dual can be solved using simplex. Table 13-2 shows the iterations. The surplus variables are

$$U_T = \text{surplus table cost beyond unit profit}$$

$$U_C = \text{surplus chair cost beyond unit profit}$$

for the table and chair constraints, respectively. Two artificial variables a_T and a_C are also required in the initial variable mix. Simplex provides us with the same solution we found graphically in Chapter 9.

TABLE 13-2
Simplex Solution to the Dual for the Redwood Furniture Problem

OBJECTIVE COEFFICIENT		300	110	0	0	$+M$	$+M$	
	Var. Mix	U_W	U_L	U_T	U_C	a_T	a_C	Sol.
$+M$	$a_T \leftarrow$	㉚↓	5	-1	0	1	0	6
$+M$	a_C	20	10	0	-1	0	1	8
	Sac.	50M	15M	$-M$	$-M$	$+M$	$+M$	14M
	Imp.	300 $-50M$	110 $-15M$	$+M$	$+M$	0	0	—
300	U_W	1	1/6 ↓	$-1/30$	0	1/30	0	.2
$+M$	$a_C \leftarrow$	0	⑳/3	2/3	-1	$-2/3$	1	4
	Sac.	300	50 $+20/3M$	-10 $+2/3M$	$-M$	10 $-2/3M$	$+M$	$60 + 4M$
	Imp.	0	60 $-20/3M$	10 $-2/3M$	$+M$	-10 $+5/3M$	0	—
300	U_W	1	0	$-1/20$	1/40	1/20	$-1/40$	.10
110	U_L	0	1	1/10	$-3/20$	$-1/10$	3/20	.60
	Sac.	300	110	-4	-9	4	9	96
	Imp.	0	0	4	9	$M-4$	$M-9$	—

Let's compare the final simplex tableaus for the dual and for the primal, as shown in Table 13-3 (where, for clarity, the artificial variable columns have been removed). Remember that X_W represents unused wood and X_L represents unused labor. Looking at the per-unit improvement row in the primal tableau, we find improvements of $-1/10$ or $-\$.10$ for X_W and $-6/10$ or $-\$.60$ for X_L. These values indicate that a unit increase in unused wood decreases profits by $\$.10$ per board foot and that a unit increase in unused labor reduces profits by $\$.60$ per hour. But raising the level of an unused resource is tantamount to lowering the level of an available resource. If we reverse this, we can see that the same values imply a $\$.10$ or a $\$.60$ profit improvement for each additional board foot of wood or hour of labor that is made available. In effect, the final primal improvement row gives us the optimal values of the dual variables with their signs reversed. The optimal dual surplus variable values can be found in the same per-unit improvement row under X_T and X_C.

TABLE 13-3

**Final Primal and Duals Tableaus
for the Redwood Furniture Problem**

FINAL PRIMAL TABLEAU

UNIT PROFIT		6	8	0	0		
	Var. Mix	X_T	X_C	X_W	X_L	Sol.	
6	X_T	1	0	1/20	−1/10	4	Nonmix:
8	X_C	0	1	−1/40	3/20	9	$X_W = 0$
							$X_L = 0$
	Sac.	6	8	1/10	6/10	96	
	Imp.	0	0	−1/10	−6/10	—	
		$-U_T$	$-U_C$	$-U_W$	$-U_L$		

FINAL DUAL TABLEAU

OBJECTIVE COEFFICIENT		300	110	0	0		
	Var. Mix	U_W	U_L	U_T	U_C	Sol.	
300	U_W	1	0	−1/20	1/40	.10	Nonmix:
110	U_L	0	1	1/10	−3/20	.60	$U_T = 0$
							$U_C = 0$
	Sac.	300	110	−4	−9	96	
	Imp.	0	0	4	9	—	
		X_W	X_L	X_T	X_C		

We have illustrated an amazing fact. *Whenever simplex is used to solve the primal linear program, it simultaneously provides the solution to the dual.* Indeed, the simplex solution to the dual provides the optimal primal values as well. Looking at the per-unit improvement row in the dual tableau, we find a 4 under U_T and a 9 under U_C. These happen to be the optimal number of tables and chairs for the primal. Likewise, the zero improvements under U_W and U_L are the optimal values of the primal slacks for wood and labor, which have values of $X_W = 0$ and $X_L = 0$.

As a matter of fact, *the primal and the dual final simplex tableaus contain exactly the same information.* The same exchange coefficients for the nonmix variable columns are present in each tableau with reversed signs and in transposed positions (the columns of one are the rows of the other), reflecting the same kind of transposition in the initial formulations. This means that simplex can be used to solve either the dual or the primal linear programming problem first. Only a small amount of extra work is required to construct the final tableau to the other problem.

COMPUTATIONAL ADVANTAGES OF THE DUAL **13-4**

The fact that the solution to the primal provides the solution to the dual, and vice versa, is advantageous from a computational point of view. To illustrate, we will consider two extreme cases for the primal problem:

More variables than constraints

More constraints than variables

On the left we have a problem that involves more *main variables* (excluding slacks, surpluses, and artificials) than constraints. The reverse is true of the problem on the right. Simplex works much faster on short, squat problems like the one on the left, because the required number of iterations depends mainly on the number of rows involved. The tall skinny problem on the right will not only have many more rows but will also require more slack, surplus, and artificial variables. This tells us that computationally it would be much more efficient to solve the problem on the right in terms of its dual, thereby converting it into the short, squat form.

Whenever a primal linear program must be solved by hand, the dual solution can be read from the final simplex tableau and then used as a check for computational errors. This tableau provides the Us that can be plugged into the objective equation to determine if the resulting C is equal to the final profit. If this computed C is not equal to the maximum P, a computational error has been made and the solution should be completely rechecked.

COMPLEMENTARY SLACKNESS **13-5**

We have carefully chosen the variable subscripts in the Redwood Furniture problem so that it is immediately apparent what each variable represents. We have accomplished this by using the first letter in the word for the respective item as the subscript. Table 13-4 summarizes the optimal solution values for the primal and dual programs.

TABLE 13-4

Correspondence Between Primal and Dual Solutions

Item	VARIABLE TYPE			
	Primal Quantity		Dual Cost	
Product	Main		Surplus	
Table	$X_T = 4$	(tables)	$U_T = 0$	($/table)
Chair	$X_C = 9$	(chairs)	$U_C = 0$	($/chair)
Resource	Slack		Main	
Wood	$X_W = 0$	(board feet)	$U_W = .10$	($/board foot)
Labor	$X_L = 0$	(hours)	$U_L = .60$	($/hour)

One interesting feature is that the product of the optimal primal and dual variables is zero for each item:

$$X_T U_T = 4 \times 0 = 0$$
$$X_C U_C = 9 \times 0 = 0$$
$$X_W U_W = 0 \times .10 = 0$$
$$X_L U_L = 0 \times .60 = 0$$

This result illustrates the principle of *complementary slackness*.

As its name implies, complementary slackness relates the optimal value of slack or surplus variables to their counterpart main variables in the opposite problem. If one primal constraint involves positive slack, so that the constraint is *not binding* on the optimal solution, then all of the underlying resource is not being used and must have an opportunity cost of zero (making more of the resource will not improve profits). But if that constraint has zero slack, so that it is binding, then all of the resource is being used and should have a positive opportunity cost (more of the resource will improve profit by allowing greater production). Since resources are represented by slack variables in the primal and by main cost variables in the dual, this principle states that the following must hold for every resource:

$$\text{Primal slack} \times \text{Dual main} = 0$$

A similar argument applies for each product made. When no items are produced, this implies that the resources necessary to make these items can be better employed elsewhere; that is, the opportunity cost of those resources exceeds the unit profit of that product, so that there is surplus product opportunity cost. But if some of the product is made, then the opportunity costs of its resources must equal its unit profit (the resources are just as valuable when they are employed this way as they would be if they were used any other way), so that the surplus product cost is zero. Production quantities are primal main variables, and surplus product costs are dual surplus variables. Complementary slackness therefore indicates that for every product item

$$\text{Primal main} \times \text{Dual surplus} = 0$$

An important value of the complementary slackness principle is that it adds further meaning to duality. But it has practical application in linear programming algorithms other than simplex. For certain types of problems, these solution procedures are faster and more efficient than simplex. Complementary slackness can also be helpful in obtaining the primal linear programming solution when only the dual solution is known.

Solving the Primal from the Dual

Suppose that Redwood Furniture is considering the manufacture of two additional products—benches and planter boxes. We will assume that the benches yield a per-unit profit of $7 and the planter boxes yield a per-unit profit of only $2. We will further assume that a bench requires 25 board feet of wood and 7 hours of labor and a planter box only consumes 10 board feet of wood and 2 hours of labor.

We can use the dual values we found earlier for wood and labor to determine if it is even worthwhile to consider these new products. For the benches, the cost of the resources used is

$$\text{Cost of one bench} = 25U_W + 7U_L$$

$$= 25(\$.10) + 7(\$.60) = \$6.70$$

which is less than the profit of $7 per bench. Thus, benches should be made. A similar calculation shows that each planter box consumes resources at a cost of $2.20, which exceeds the per-unit profit of $2.00. Planter boxes should therefore not be made, since the resources that would be consumed to produce them can be used more profitably elsewhere.

But this analysis does not tell us how many benches to make. To determine this, we must solve the expanded linear program. Letting X_B represent the unknown quantity of benches to be produced, the primal linear program is

$$
\begin{array}{llll}
\text{Maximize} & P = & 6X_T + 8X_C + 7X_B \\
\text{Subject to} & U_W\text{: } 30X_T + 20X_C + 25X_B \le 300 & \text{(wood)} \\
& U_L\text{: } 5X_T + 10X_C + 7X_B \le 110 & \text{(labor)} \\
\text{where} & X_T, X_C, X_B \ge 0
\end{array}
$$

Since this program has three main variables, simplex is required. However, the dual for this problem has only two main variables and can be solved graphically. (Since the original linear program is expanded, the previous values $U_W = .10$ and $U_L = .60$ no longer apply.) The dual for the expanded problem is

$$\text{Minimize} \quad C = 300U_W + 110U_L$$

$$\text{Subject to} \quad 30U_W + 5U_L \geq 6 \quad \text{(table)}$$

$$20U_W + 10U_L \geq 8 \quad \text{(chair)}$$

$$25U_W + 7U_L \geq 7 \quad \text{(bench)}$$

$$\text{where} \quad U_W, U_L \geq 0$$

This dual is solved graphically in Figure 13-3. The optimal solution is represented by the intersection of the bench and chair lines. The simultaneous

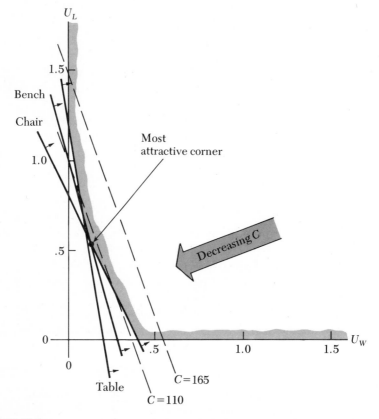

FIGURE 13-3
The graphical solution to the dual for the expanded Redwood Furniture problem.

solution of the respective constraint equations yields

$$U_W = 7/55$$

$$U_L = 30/55$$

and a cost of

$$C = 300\left(\frac{7}{55}\right) + 110\left(\frac{30}{55}\right) = \frac{1,080}{11}$$

In using the dual solution to find the primal solution, first we note that the chair and bench constraints are binding; they involve zero surplus cost in the dual. This means that the corresponding primal main variables are positive, or that $X_C > 0$, $X_B > 0$. Similarly, the table constraint is not binding, so that this product has a dual surplus cost and must not be produced in the optimal solution; thus, $X_T = 0$. Since U_W and U_L are nonzero values, there must be no corresponding primal slack for wood and labor.

These facts imply that we may treat the primal constraints just like equalities and may zero out X_T. This leaves us with

$$30(0) + 20X_C + 25X_B = 300 \quad \text{(wood)}$$

$$5(0) + 10X_C + 7X_B = 110 \quad \text{(labor)}$$

which can be solved simultaneously for X_C and X_B. The optimal quantities of chairs and benches are therefore

$$X_C = 65/11$$

$$X_B = 80/11$$

and the maximum profit is

$$P = 6(0) + 8\left(\frac{65}{11}\right) + 7\left(\frac{80}{11}\right) = \frac{1,080}{11}$$

which is identical to the minimum C we found for the dual.

PROBLEMS

13-1 Formulate the dual for the following primal linear program and then solve it graphically.

Maximize $\quad P = 12X_1 + 16X_2$

Subject to $\qquad 4X_1 + 4X_2 \le 16 \quad$ (resource A)

$\qquad\qquad\quad 6X_1 + 4X_2 \le 24 \quad$ (resource B)

where $\qquad\qquad X_1, X_2 \ge 0$

13-2 Reconsider Ace Widgets' problem of deciding how many regular and deluxe models to produce. The regular model requires 5 hours of finishing labor and 1 frame. The deluxe version requires 8 hours and 1 frame. Only 12 frames and 80 hours of labor are available. The per-unit profits are $10 for the regular model and $15 for the deluxe version.
(a) Formulate the primal linear program. Then solve it graphically.
(b) Formulate the dual linear program. State in words the meaning of your dual variables.
(c) Solve the dual graphically.

13-3 Now suppose that Ace Widgets in Problem 13-2 makes a third product—the super widget—at a per-unit profit of $25. Each super widget requires 10 hours of labor and 1 frame.
(a) Formulate Ace's new primal linear program.
(b) Formulate the dual linear program and then solve it graphically.
(c) Suppose that Ace can sell a fourth model—the cheap widget—at a per-unit profit of $6. This model requires 2 hours of labor and 1 frame. Should any cheap models be made?

13-4 For the linear program

$$\text{Maximize} \quad P = 100X_1 + 200X_2 + 150X_3$$
$$\text{Subject to} \quad 5X_1 + 20X_2 + 30X_3 \le 60 \quad \text{(resource } A\text{)}$$
$$10X_1 + 20X_2 + 50X_3 \le 100 \quad \text{(resource } B\text{)}$$
$$\text{where} \quad X_1, X_2, X_3 \ge 0$$

the following final simplex tableau applies (X_A and X_B are the slack variables for the first and second constraints, respectively):

UNIT PROFIT		100	200	150	0	0	
	Var. Mix	X_1	X_2	X_3	X_A	X_B	Sol.
100	X_1	1	0	4	−1/5	1/5	8
200	X_2	0	1	1/2	1/10	−1/20	1
	Sac.	100	200	500	0	10	1,000
	Imp.	0	0	−350	0	−10	—

(a) Formulate the dual linear program.
(b) Determine the solution to the dual from this tableau.

13-5 For the Piney Woods Furniture Company, which makes tables (T), chairs (C), and bookcases (B), the following linear program applies:

$$\text{Maximize} \quad P = 20X_T + 15X_C + 15X_B$$
$$\text{Subject to} \quad 10X_T + 3X_C + 10X_B \le 100 \quad \text{(wood)}$$
$$5X_T + 5X_C + 5X_B \le 60 \quad \text{(labor)}$$
$$\text{where} \quad X_T, X_C, X_B \ge 0$$

The dual linear program is

Minimize $C = 100U_W + 60U_L$

Subject to

$10U_W + 5U_L \geq 20$	(table)
$3U_W + 5U_L \geq 15$	(chair)
$10U_W + 5U_L \geq 15$	(bookcase)

where $U_W, U_L \geq 0$

and the solution to the dual is

$$U_W = 5/7 \quad U_L = 18/7 \quad C = 1580/7 \text{ dollars}$$

(a) What is the maximum premium that Piney Woods would pay for an additional unit of wood? For an additional unit of labor?

(b) Letting U_T, U_C, and U_B represent the dual's surplus variables for the respective constraints, determine the optimal values of these variables.

(c) Let X_W and X_L represent the primal slack variables. Use the principle of complementary slackness to determine which primal main and slack variables have nonzero values. Then algebraically determine the optimal solution to the primal linear program.

(d) Suppose that Piney Woods can sell desks at a per-unit profit of $50 and that each desk requires 30 board feet of wood and 10 hours of labor. Should any desks be made?

13-6 Pumpkin-Goblins must decide how many gallons of pumpkin (X_P) and licorice (X_L) ice cream to make for sale during Halloween week. All ingredients are in plentiful supply, except for artificial carbon black, vanilla extract, and orange food coloring. The following linear program applies.

Maximize $P = 2.00X_P + 1.50X_L$

Subject to

$.50X_L \leq 1,000$	(carbon black)
$.02X_P + .01X_L \leq 25$	(vanilla extract)
$.10X_P \leq 50$	(orange food coloring)

where $X_P, X_L \geq 0$

(a) Formulate the dual linear program.

(b) The solution to the primal linear program is $X_P = 250$, $X_L = 2,000$; $P = 3,500$. Assuming that these quantities are made, determine the amount of unused (slack) resource for each primal constraint.

(c) Identify the dual surplus variables. Then apply the principle of complementary slackness to determine the optimal solution to the dual linear program you found in (a).

13-7 A brewery president wishes to develop a monthly production schedule that will maximize gross profits. He sells three products: light beer, dark beer, and malt liquor. The respective production quantities (in gallons) are denoted by X_L, X_D, and X_M. The president is faced with three constraints pertaining to the respective usages and availabilities of hops-handling capacity (bushels), fermentation space (cubic feet), and bottling time (hours). The corresponding slack variables are X_H,

X_F, and X_B. The final simplex tableau is

UNIT PROFIT		1	2	1.5	0	0	0	
	Var. Mix	X_L	X_D	X_M	X_H	X_F	X_B	Sol.
1	X_L	1	0	0	−3	1	.5	100,000
1.5	X_M	0	0	1	−.6	0	1	10,000
2	X_D	0	1	0	2	1	−.75	20,000
	Sac.	1	2	1.5	.1	3	.5	155,000
	Imp.	0	0	0	−.1	−3	−.5	—

(a) What are the optimal production levels for the various products?

(b) For each constraint in the original primal problem, there is a variable in the dual problem with a minimization objective. Describe in words the meanings of these dual variables and indicate their respective values.

(c) A capital expansion is contemplated. The following incremental monthly costs of three alternatives are to be added to capacities:

> 1 bushel of hops-handling capacity, $.20
> 1 cubic foot of fermentation space, $1.00
> 1 hour of bottling time, $.10

Assuming that you can use the information in the final simplex tableau, what alternative investment would be most profitable if the capital expansion is very limited? Explain.

13-8 Referring to Sammy Love's candied-apple decision in Problem 11-12 (page 276):

(a) Formulate Sammy's linear program. Then identify separately any slack variables that would be needed to solve the problem with simplex.

(b) Formulate the dual linear program. Then separately identify any surplus variables that would be required to solve the problem using simplex.

(c) Solve the dual *graphically*. What are the optimal values of the dual main variables? Of the dual surplus variables?

(d) What is the greatest premium that Sammy should pay for extra cups of sugar? For extra ounces of gelatin?

(e) Using only your answer to part (c), find the solution to the primal linear program. How many candied apples of each type should Sammy make? What is his maximum profit? Which ingredients will not be totally used?

13-9 ChipMont manufactures three types of silicon chips for computers: central processing units (C), integrated circuits (I), and core memories (M). The following linear program applies:

Maximize $\quad P = .25X_C + .40X_I + .15X_M$

Subject to $\quad .005X_C + .02X_I + .01X_M \leq 10{,}000 \quad$ (silicon sheets)

$\quad\quad\quad\quad .2X_C + .5X_I + .1X_M \leq 200{,}000 \quad$ (labor in minutes)

where $\quad\quad\quad X_C, X_I, X_M \geq 0$

The dual linear program is

Minimize $C = 10,000U_S + 200,000U_L$
Subject to $.005U_S + .2U_L \geq .25$ (CPUs)
              $.02U_S + .5U_L \geq .40$ (integrated circuits)
              $.01U_S + .1U_L \geq .15$ (memories)
where $U_S, U_L \geq 0$

and the solution to the dual is

$$U_S = 10/3 \qquad U_L = 7/6 \qquad C = 800,000/3$$

(a) What is the maximum premium that ChipMont would pay for one additional silicon sheet? For one additional minute of labor?

(b) Letting U_C, U_I, and U_M represent the dual surplus variables for the respective constraints, find the optimal values of these variables.

(c) Letting X_S and X_L represent the primal slack variables, use the principle of complementary slackness to determine which primal main and slack variables have nonzero values. Then determine the optimal solution to the primal linear program algebraically.

(d) Suppose that ChipMont can manufacture an all-purpose video-game chip at a profit of $1 per chip. If each game chip requires .01 silicon sheet and .4 minute of labor, should any game chips be made?

13-10 Rott Irony makes three fancy door hinges: Baltic, chic, and Gothic. All of the materials used in making these hinges are plentiful, except that only 100 ft^2 of brass plate are on hand and a maximum of 200 hours of handcrafting labor can be spared. A set of heavy Baltic hinges requires 2 ft^2 of brass plate; a set of chic or Gothic hinges requires 1 ft^2. Handcrafting takes 1 hour for a set of Baltic hinges, 3 hours for a set of chics, and $1\frac{1}{4}$ hours for a set of Gothics. Rott can sell the entire production run at a profit of $10 for a set of Baltic or Gothics and $15 for a set of chics.

(a) Formulate Rott's linear program and separately identify any slack variables that would be required to solve the problem using simplex.

(b) Formulate the dual linear program and separately identify any surplus variables that would be required to solve the problem using simplex.

(c) Solve the dual *graphically*. What are the optimal values of the dual main variables? Of the dual surplus variables?

(d) What is the greatest premium that Rott should pay for each extra square foot of brass plate? For each extra hour of handcrafting?

(e) Solve the primal linear program using only your answer to (c). How many sets of each type of hinge should Rott make? What will Rott's maximum profit be?

14

Sensitivity Analysis in Linear Programming

No linear programming solution can be of a higher quality than the assumptions underlying the mathematical model itself. Often the basic parameters—unit profits or costs, exchange coefficients, requirement levels, and resource availabilities—are themselves only estimates or educated guesses. An unsureness about any of these parameters may cast doubt on the validity of the optimal solution itself. We can extend linear programming concepts to assess the effects of changes in the original parameter values. Such an extension is referred to as a *sensitivity analysis*.

The primary objective of sensitivity analysis is to determine exactly what effect minor variations in the assumed parameters have on the overall solution. When these variations make little difference, we say that the optimal solution is *insensitive* to a change in assumptions. The degree of sensitivity can range from no change at all to a considerable shift in the optimal solution and will vary with the parameter considered and with the magnitude of change in its value.

Related to sensitivity analysis are questions about the form of the model itself. For example, we may wonder how our solution will change if we incorporate a new resource constraint. Or, we may wish to evaluate how our answer will change if a new candidate product is included in the production plan. In this chapter, we will see how much of the work we have already accomplished can be preserved when the original problem is amended.

14-1 SENSITIVITY ANALYSIS FOR RIGHT-HAND-SIDE VALUES

For the purposes of illustration, we will reconsider the wood and labor constraints of the Redwood Furniture problem. What will happen to the optimal solution if a strike at the lumber mills makes less wood available? How will the new production plan be amended if one of the cabinetmakers goes on sick leave? We will answer these questions using the final simplex solution in Table 14-1 for our original linear program:

$$X_T = \text{number of tables}$$
$$X_C = \text{number of chairs}$$

Maximize $\quad P = 6X_T + 8X_C$

Subject to $\qquad 30X_T + 20X_C \le 300 \quad$ (wood)

$\qquad\qquad\quad 5X_T + 10X_C \le 110 \quad$ (labor)

where $\qquad\qquad\quad X_T, X_C \ge \quad 0$

Recall that the simplex procedure places us at the most attractive corner. A change in resource availability creates one of two effects. If the change is minor, the feasible solution region will expand or contract so that the most attractive corner is slightly repositioned and the mix variables simply assume different values. A major change may not only enlarge or reduce the feasible solution region, but it may also distort its basic shape to the extent that a new

TABLE 14-1

The Final Simplex Tableau for the Redwood Furniture Problem

UNIT PROFIT		6	8	0	0	
	Var. Mix.	X_T	X_C	X_W	X_L	Sol.
6	X_T	1	0	1/20	−1/10	4
8	X_C	0	1	−1/40	3/20	9
	Sac.	6	8	1/10	6/10	96
	Imp.	0	0	−1/10	−6/10	—

most attractive corner that is not analogous to the old one exists. Such a change creates a different optimal variable mix as well as new variable values.

The first question to be answered by sensitivity analysis is therefore: *Over what range of right-hand side values does the current variable mix apply?* Let's consider the amount of wood first. How small must the initial level of wood become before the simplex variable mix changes? To determine the level at which the variable mix will change, we only need to look at our unused wood slack variable X_W. If X_W is increased, then there will be less wood available to produce tables and chairs, and the production plan must be amended accordingly.

By what amounts can available wood be reduced? This is the same as asking how much can we increase X_W? We answer a similar question every time we apply the *entry criterion* in a simplex pivot. Treating X_W like an entering variable in Table 14-1, we can determine the maximum possible increase in unused wood before one of the mix variables, X_T or X_C, is reduced to zero and leaves the solution mix. An examination of the exchange coefficients for X_W shows that we must give up 1/20 of a table for each board foot of wood we increase X_W. This releases enough labor to make 1/40 of a chair more, since X_C has an exchange coefficient of $-1/40$ in the X_W column. As we enlarge X_W, Redwood will eventually run out of tables. Since the current optimal solution indicates that $X_T = 4$, we can trade all tables for 20 board feet of wood each, obtaining $4 \div 1/20 = 80$ board feet of unused wood. (Remember that Redwood cannot get back all of the 30 board feet required to produce each table, since it is profitable to divert some of this wood to making chairs.) Any increase in X_W smaller than 80 will still leave some wood for tables. This tells us that if the available wood is at least $300 - 80 = 220$ board feet, X_T will remain in the variable mix. If more than 80 board feet are removed Redwood cannot make any tables and will have to cut back on chairs as well.

Now what happens if we increase the amount of available wood? How large an increase can occur and still permit Redwood to manufacture both tables and chairs? Again, we can answer this by looking at X_W. In effect, adding more wood is analogous to borrowing wood, or obtaining surplus wood. Viewing surplus as negative slack, we can reduce X_W to a negative level. (Remember that this cannot actually be done, since all variables must be nonnegative. But let's pretend.) The interpretation of the exchange coefficients is reversed when an entering variable is decreased. The coefficients tell us that Redwood can *get back* 1/20 of a table and must get back $-1/40$ or give up 1/40 of a chair for each board-foot reduction in X_W. All 9 chairs can be exchanged for a deficit level of unused wood equal to $9 \div 1/40 = 360$ board feet. In other words, available wood can be increased up to 360 board feet beyond the original amount of 300 board feet, making the new total amount $300 + 360 = 660$, and it would still be more profitable for Redwood to make both tables and chairs. Any larger change would eliminate chairs from the production plan, so that X_C would be removed from the variable mix.

We can now see that the present variable mix will be optimal for all levels of available wood between the *lower limit* of 220 board feet and the *upper limit* of 660 board feet. This is verified graphically in Figure 14-1. Notice in part (a) that although the feasible solution region becomes narrower as the level of available wood is reduced, it maintains the same basic four-sided shape and that, until 220 board feet is reached, the most attractive corner is where the wood and labor constraint lines intersect. At 220 board feet and below, the feasible solution region is triangular and no tables are made while there is slack labor. In part (b), as the level of available wood is raised, the feasible region's shape remains the same and the intersection of the table and wood constraint lines provides the most attractive corner until 660 board feet is reached. Thereafter, the region is triangular, formed only by the labor constraint line and the axes, no chairs are made, and there is slack wood.

The Procedure When Slack Is Not in the Variable Mix

The Redwood Furniture final simplex tableau in Table 14-1 shows no slacks in the variable mix. We can summarize the procedure for finding the range in right-hand-side values over which the current variable mix will remain optimal. Using the final simplex tableau for the original problem, we treat the corresponding slack variable as if it were an entering variable and calculate the following exchange ratio for every row:

$$\text{Exchange ratio} = \frac{\text{Solution value}}{\text{Exchange coefficient in slack column}}$$

We then find the

> Lower limit = Original level − Smallest positive ratio
> or −∞   (if no ratio is positive)

and the

> Upper limit = Original level + Smallest absolute value of negative ratios
> or ∞   (if no ratio is negative)

If there is an exchange coefficient of zero, then the exchange ratio for that row will be +∞, even when the solution value is also zero. When only the solution value is zero, then the ratio is also zero, but it is treated as positive or negative (having the same sign as the exchange coefficient).

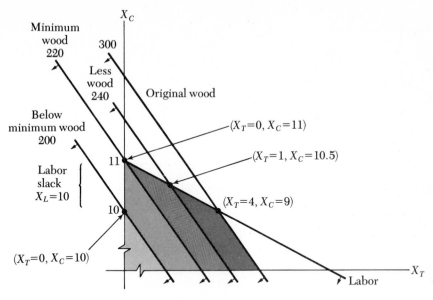

(a) Effect of lowering the wood level

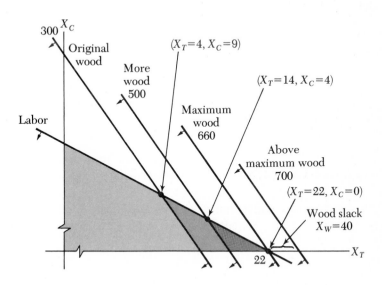

(b) Effect of raising the wood level

FIGURE 14-1

Graphical illustrations of how the feasible solution region changes for various levels of available wood.

TABLE 14-2

Range Calculations for the Right-Hand-Side Values

Variable Mix	WOOD RANGE FOR SAME OPTIMAL VARIABLE MIX		
	Exchange Coefficient in X_W Column	Solution Column	Exchange Ratio
X_T	1/20	4	$4 \div (1/20) = 80$
X_C	− 1/40	9	$9 \div (-1/40) = -360$
	Lower limit = 300 − 80 = 220 board feet		
	Upper limit = 300 + 360 = 660 board feet		

Variable Mix	LABOR RANGE FOR SAME OPTIMAL VARIABLE MIX		
	Exchange Coefficient in X_L Column	Solution Column	Exchange Ratio
X_T	− 1/10	4	$4 \div (-1/10) = -40$
X_C	3/20	9	$9 \div (3/20) = 60$
	Lower limit = 110 − 60 = 50 hours		
	Upper limit = 110 + 40 = 150 hours		

Table 14-2 shows how the range values are calculated for the right-hand sides of the wood and labor constraints. Since Redwood's problem only has two simplex rows, only two exchange ratios are calculated for each resource. We can see that X_T and X_C remain the optimal variable mix at any level of labor between 50 and 150 hours. (You can verify this graphically in a similar manner to the way we raised and lowered the level of wood in Figure 14-1.) *Each of the ranges we find in this manner applies only as long as the right-hand sides of all other constraint equations remain at their original levels.* Each range accommodates only one change at a time.

The Procedure for Slack in the Variable Mix

If the final simplex tableau has a slack variable in the variable mix, the applicable range for the corresponding right-hand side of the constraint must be determined differently. We have

Lower limit = Original level − Solution value of slack

Upper limit = ∞

The rationale for the lower limit is that not all of the available resource is used in the present optimal solution, so that we can eliminate some of the original resource and still have slack. Since the most slack we can eliminate is all of it, the reduction of the original right-hand-side level by any larger amount would change the variable mix. The upper limit is even easier to understand. Since not all of the present level of resource is being used, raising that level can only raise the slack. No other change is possible, and the variable mix must remain exactly the same.

The Right-Hand Sides of Other Types of Constraints

Thus, we have considered only the $\leq$ constraint usually associated with resource limitations. However, the same principles apply to the $\geq$ and $=$ constraints, which ordinarily pertain to minimum or exact requirements, respectively.

The surplus variable is the basis for determining the right-hand-side limits of the $\geq$ constraint. The exchange ratios must be interpreted in the reverse manner, however, since the surplus variable is originally subtracted (rather than added, as the slack is).

When the surplus is not in the variable mix

Lower limit = Original level − Smallest absolute value of negative ratios
   or $-\infty$ (if no ratio is negative)

Upper limit = Original level + Smallest positive ratio
   or ∞ (if no ratio is positive)

When the surplus is in the variable mix

Lower limit = $-\infty$

Upper limit = Original level + Solution value of surplus

For the strict equality constraint, the starting simplex formulation must include an artificial variable. The artificial variable here is analogous to the slack variable in sensitivity analysis. Everything remains exactly the same, except that the case of the artificial variable being in the final solution mix never needs to be considered. Why? As a practical matter, the artificial variables for the equality constraints are the only artificials ever used in sensitivity analysis. *The columns of all other artificial variables are best eliminated before starting.*

Sensitivity analysis of the right-hand side of constraints can be applied to the most general linear programming form, regardless of whether the underlying problem is profit maximization or cost minimization. Next, we will consider how to obtain the solution when the right-hand side of the constraint changes.

14-2 SOLVING FOR A RIGHT-HAND-SIDE CHANGE

If the right-hand side of one of the constraints changes, we could find the optimal solution to the revised problem by beginning the simplex procedure all over again. However, with just a little work, we can find the answer by slightly modifying the original solution. As long as the new right-hand side (r.h.s.) falls between the limits just described, the following rule applies to the revised solution value:

Revised value = Original value + Exchange coefficient × Net r.h.s. change

The net right-hand-side change is always found by subtracting the old level from the new one. For example, suppose that Redwood Furniture's wood supply is increased from 300 to 500 board feet. The revised production plan for tables and chairs would then be

$$X_T = 4 + (1/20)(500 - 300) \quad = 14 \text{ tables}$$

$$X_C = 9 + (-1/40)(500 - 300) = \quad 4 \text{ chairs}$$

where the exchange coefficients from the X_W column for slack wood in Table 14-1 apply. The new profit would therefore be

$$P = 6(14) + 8(4) = 116 \text{ dollars}$$

Or suppose that the available labor is decreased to 80 hours instead. The revised solution would then be obtained by using the exchange coefficients for slack labor X_L:

$$X_T = 4 + (-1/10)(80 - 110) = 7 \text{ tables}$$

$$X_C = 9 + (3/20)(80 - 110) \quad = 4.5 \text{ chairs}$$

and the profit would be

$$P = 6(7) + 8(4.5) = 78 \text{ dollars}$$

If the right-hand side of one of these revised constraints has a variable in the variable mix, then any new level within the applicable range will only cause the slack variable to increase or decrease by the net change. All other variable values and the profit will remain unchanged.

Matters become more complex when changing a right-hand-side value to a level outside the range for the present optimal variable mix. More elaborate sensitivity analysis can be used to solve such a changed problem. This analysis involves manipulating the original final simplex tableau and performing additional simplex pivots. Because this requires an extensive amount of work, it may be easier to solve the changed problem from scratch. Starting over again is also recommended when more than one constraint is revised.

Right-Hand-Side Changes for Other Types of Constraints

When the right-hand side of a strict equality constraint changes, the procedures are identical to those just described if we substitute the corresponding artificial variable for the slack. Analogous steps also apply to accommodating changes in the right-hand sides of $\geq$ constraints if we treat the corresponding surplus variable as we would a slack variable.

When the right-hand side of a $\geq$ constraint changes, the direction of change is reversed. (As we have seen before, this is because the surplus variable was originally subtracted on the left-hand side.) When the change falls within the prescribed limits, the following relationship applies whenever the surplus is not in the variable mix:

Revised value = Original value − Exchange coefficient × Net r.h.s. change

If the surplus is part of the variable mix, then it will simply increase or decrease by the amount of the change, and all the other variables and the profit will remain the same.

SENSITIVITY ANALYSIS FOR UNIT PROFIT 14-3

The other major area of sensitivity analysis arises from changes in unit profits. The underlying rationale is basically the same as it is for right-hand-side analysis (which can be applied to the dual problem, in which the right-hand sides are the primal unit profits). Like the foregoing analysis, the main consideration in evaluating changes in unit profits is finding *limits* over which the current variable mix applies.

Continuing with our original Redwood Furniture problem, let's see what happens if the profit per table is changed. As Figure 14-2(a) shows, an increase in table profit results in a new maximum P line. Increasing the profit per table from $6 to $10 yields a steeper profit line, but the most attractive corner remains the same. At a profit of $15 per table, it is no longer attractive to make

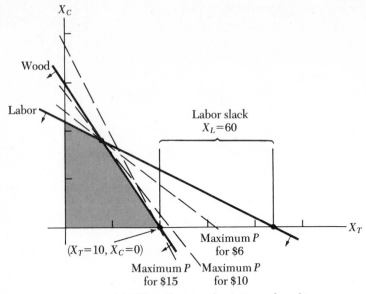

(a) Effect of raising the unit wood profit

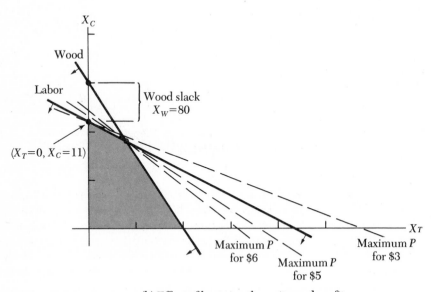

(b) Effect of lowering the unit wood profit

FIGURE 14-2
Graphical illustrations of how the most attractive corner (the optimal solution) changes with different unit profit levels for tables.

chairs, and the most attractive corner occurs where the wood line intersects the X_T axis; in effect, the resulting maximum P line is steeper than the wood constraint line. Figure 14-2(b) illustrates the reverse situation—when the unit table profit decreases. At a $5 profit, the maximum P line is flatter than before, and the original corner remains most attractive. At a $3 profit for each table, making tables is no longer attractive, and the most attractive corner occurs where the labor line intersects the X_C axis; the resulting maximum P line is flatter than the labor constraint line.

Figure 14-2 tells us that the same variable mix applies over a wide range of unit profits. Furthermore, exactly the same optimal variable values ($X_T = 4$, $X_C = 9$) apply over that range; only the level of P is affected. We may obtain the limits directly from the final simplex tableau given in Table 14-3 for the original problem. When the main variable being evaluated is in the final mix, first we calculate the following *improvement ratios*:

$$\text{Improvement ratio} = \frac{\text{Per-unit improvement value}}{\text{Exchange coefficient in variable row}}$$

These ratios are found only for the values in the columns of the nonmix variables.

The numerator is the per-unit improvement in total profit associated with an increase in the variable for that column. The per-unit improvement for X_W is $-1/10$, which indicates that profit will be reduced by $.10 for each additional board foot of unused wood. The denominator is the applicable exchange

TABLE 14-3
The Final Simplex Tableau for the Original Redwood Furniture Problem

UNIT PROFIT		6	8	0	0	
	Var. Mix.	X_T	X_C	X_W	X_L	Sol.
6	X_T	1	0	1/20	$-1/10$	4
8	X_C	0	1	$-1/40$	3/20	9
	Sac.	6	8	1/10	6/10	96
	Imp.	0	0	$-1/10$	$-6/10$	—

$$X_T \text{ improvement ratios:} \quad \frac{-1/10}{1/20} = -2 \qquad \frac{-6/10}{-1/10} = 6$$

$$X_C \text{ improvement ratios:} \quad \frac{-1/10}{-1/40} = 4 \qquad \frac{-6/10}{3/20} = -4$$

coefficient. In the X_T row and X_W column the exchange coefficient is $1/20$, which tells us that for every additional board foot of unused wood, we give up one-twentieth of a table. Dividing the profit lost from one more board foot of unused wood by the quantity of tables that must be sacrificed per board foot, we obtain our ratio for the X_T row and X_W column:

$$\frac{-1/10}{1/20} = -2 \text{ dollars}$$

This expresses the reduction in profit incurred by trading 1 table for 20 board feet of unused wood.

Now consider what happens if tables are sold at a lower price, so that they are less profitable. This should make the exchange of unused wood for a table less painful. If the profit per table is reduced by the $2 amount, to $6 − $2 = $4, then the unit sacrifice and improvement values of X_W will change to zero (verify this to your satisfaction). Trading tables for unused wood would not be harmful then. Any profit per table lower than $4 will make unused wood more attractive than any tables. In effect, a $2 drop in the profit per table establishes the lower limit of $4 for keeping X_T in the optimal variable mix. A similar argument can be made in terms of X_L to establish the upper limit of the profit per table.

The *unit-profit limits for main variables in the variable mix* are calculated from

Lower profit limit = Original level − Smallest absolute value of negative ratios
$\qquad\qquad$ or $-\infty$ (if no ratio is negative)

Upper profit limit = Original level + Smallest positive ratio
$\qquad\qquad$ or ∞ (if no ratio is positive)

where all the improvement ratios applicable to the variable being evaluated are used and entries in all nonmix variable columns (except artificials) are used. The improvement ratios for X_T and X_C are calculated in Table 14–3 and provide the following limits:

	Lower Limit	Upper Limit
Profit per table	$6 − 2 = $4	$6 + 6 = $12
Profit per chair	$8 − 4 = $4	$8 + 4 = $12

(It is simply coincidence that an identical range applies for tables and chairs.) As is true of right-hand-side ranges, the respective profit limits are valid only when all other unit profits are fixed at their original levels.

Thus, we have found that holding profit per chair at the original $8, the current optimal solution ($X_T = 4$, $X_C = 9$) will remain identical for any profit per table between $4 and $12. Only total profit itself can change, ranging from a low of $P = \$4(4) + \$8(9) = \$88$ to a high of $P = \$12(4) + \$8(9) = \$120$.

In performing a profit sensitivity analysis, the *artificial variable columns are ignored*. In effect, any exchange of quantities between mix variables and an artificial variable makes no sense, because the artificial variable itself has no economic interpretation. Thus, we would not compute ratios using the coefficients in the artificial columns.

As in right-hand-side analysis, we treat zero or a positive quantity divided by zero as ∞ and a negative quantity divided by zero as $-\infty$. Similarly, zero divided by -10 is included with the negative ratios (as the value zero) and zero divided by 100 yields a zero-valued positive ratio.

In Redwood Furniture problem, only finite positive values are profit limits, but these limits can be negative or infinite. Under some circumstances, for example, a variable with a *negative* unit profit can remain in the optimal variable mix (for example, a "loss leader").

Profit Range When the Main Variable Is Not in the Mix

If the main variable being evaluated is not in the final variable mix, a somewhat different procedure must be employed. Since simplex has determined that this variable is unattractive, its unit profit can be lowered to any level without causing the optimal variable mix to change. But raising its unit profit to some level should make the variable attractive enough to enter the mix. This level is the one at which the value of the unit improvement (in the bottom row of the simplex tableau) will no longer be negative. The *unit-profit limits for a main variable not in the mix* are therefore

Lower profit limit $= -\infty$

$$\text{Upper profit limit} = \text{Original level} + \frac{\text{Absolute size of per-unit}}{\text{improvement value}}$$

Changes in the Unit Profit Beyond Limits

Suppose that the profit per table is raised to $15—a value that exceeds the upper limit of $12 per table. What is the new optimal solution? As Table 14-4 shows, we simply change the unit profit for tables from $6 to $15, recalculate the sacrifice and improvement rows, and complete the simplex pivot. We obtain the new variable mix ($X_T = 10$, $X_L = 60$) with nonmix variables $X_C = 0$ and $X_W = 0$, and the revised total profit becomes $P = 150$ dollars. This result is confirmed graphically in Figure 14-2(a). You may verify that the new solution for a reduction below the limit to $3 per table will involve zero tables and 11 chairs, with $P = 88$. This is the solution indicated graphically in Figure 14-2(b).

TABLE 14-4

**A Simplex Iteration for a Change in the Unit Profit
for Tables Beyond the Upper Limit**

	UNIT PROFIT	15 X̶	8	0	0	
	Var. Mix	X_T	X_C	X_W	X_L	Sol.
15 X̶	X_T	1	0	1/20	−1/10 ↓	4
8	X_C ←	0	1	−1/40	(3/20)	9
Recomputed ⟨	Sac.	15	8	11/20	−3/10	132
	Imp.	0	0	−11/20	3/10	—
15	X_T	1	2/3	1/30	0	10
0	X_L	0	20/3	−1/6	1	60
	Sac.	15	10	1/2	0	150
	Imp.	0	−2	−1/2	0	—

TABLE 14-5

**A Simplex Iteration for a Change in per-Unit Chair Profit
Beyond the Upper Limit**

	UNIT PROFIT	15	13 X̶	0	0	
	Var. Mix	X_T	X_C	X_W	X_L	Sol.
15	X_T	1	2/3 ↓	1/30	0	10
0	X_L ←	0	(20/3)	−1/6	1	60
	Sac.	15	10	1/2	0	150
	Imp.	0	⤷2̶3	−1/2	0	—
15	X_T	1	0	1/20	−1/10	4
13	X_C	0	1	−1/40	3/20	9
	Sac.	15	13	17/40	9/20	177
	Imp.	0	0	−17/40	−9/20	—

To illustrate the treatment of a main variable that is not in the final variable mix, we will continue with our revised problem. The unit profits are now $15 per table and $8 per chair. In the final simplex tableau in Table 14-4, the per-unit improvement value of X_C is -2. Therefore, the following limits for profit per chair are applicable for the current variable mix:

$$\text{Lower profit limit} = -\infty$$

$$\text{Upper profit limit} = 8 + 2 = \$10$$

If the profit per chair is raised to a value greater than $10, the new optimal solution can be found by recomputing the per-unit improvement value accordingly and performing a simplex pivot. Such a change is shown in Table 14-5 for a $13 profit per chair.

Sensitivity Analysis for Unit Cost

The same sensitivity analysis procedures may be applied to a cost-minimization problem, where the objective coefficients are unit costs. When evaluating the unit cost of a main variable in the final optimal variable mix, the cost-limit calculations are identical to the profit analysis. If the main variable is not in the variable mix, the unit cost can be raised to any arbitrary level, and nothing will change. But the cost cannot be lowered by more than the per-unit improvement value without making it attractive to enter the variable mix. Thus, the *unit cost limits for a nonmix variable* are

Lower cost limit = Original level − Unit improvement value

Upper cost limit = ∞

ADDING A NEW VARIABLE TO THE PROBLEM 14-4

Sensitivity analysis may help us evaluate changes in a problem. When a revision is made, it is not necessary to solve the entire problem all over again from scratch. Instead, we can evaluate changes in the original problem's final simplex tableau. We are now ready to consider revisions in a linear program other than changes to right-hand sides or unit profits and costs. As before, a considerable, amount of work can be saved by beginning with the solution to the original problem.

One important revision must be made when a variable is added to the problem that was not included in the original variable mix. Such a situation may arise in production planning if a late order for a product not considered arrives after the linear program is solved originally. Or the linear program for a blending decision (whether it is for petroleum products, chemicals, cattle feed, or Persian sausages) may be solved before the arrival of an ingredient that was previously out of stock. To avoid the bother or expense of solving the new problem from the beginning, it is usually considerably easier to patch up the present solution to accommodate another variable (or even several variables).

For example, suppose that Redwood Furniture decides to produce benches in addition to tables and chairs and that the profit and resource requirements for each bench are

$$\text{Profit:} \quad \$7$$
$$\text{Wood:} \quad 25 \text{ board feet}$$
$$\text{Labor:} \quad 7 \text{ hours}$$

The final simplex tableau for the original Redwood Furniture problem, which involved only tables and chairs, is provided in Table 14-6.

It can be helpful to begin by formulating the dual linear program to see if it is even worthwhile to consider the new variable. The optimal dual variable values tell us the unit opportunity costs associated with each resource, which can be used to assess the attractiveness of the new variable. Recall that the primal simplex solution also provides the solution to the dual. From Table 14-6, we can readily see that $U_W = .10$ and $U_L = .60$. Since a bench can be made only by taking resources away from tables or chairs, we can obtain the total opportunity cost for making each bench by multiplying the dual variable values by the respective resource quantities and summing, or

$$.10(25) + .60(7) = 6.70 \text{ dollars}$$

This cost is smaller than the $7 profit for each bench. Thus, benches should be made, because each bench will increase total profit by $.30.

TABLE 14-6

The Final Simplex Tableau for the Original Redwood Furniture Problem

	UNIT PROFIT	6	8	0	0	
	Var. Mix	X_T	X_C	X_W	X_L	Sol.
6	X_T	1	0	1/20	−1/10	4
8	X_C	0	1	−1/40	3/20	9
	Sac.	6	8	1/10	6/10	96
	Imp.	0	0	−1/10	−6/10	—

TABLE 14-7

Calculations to Find the X_B Column for the Newly Added Bench Variable

| Mix Variable | SLACK OR SURPLUS EXCHANGE COEFFICIENTS | | QUANTITY SACRIFICED | | |
	Wood X_W	Labor X_L	Due to Wood $25 \times X_W$	Due to Labor $7 \times X_L$	Total X_B
X_T	1/20	$-1/10$	25/20	$-7/10$	11/20
X_C	$-1/40$	3/20	$-25/40$	21/20	17/40
Bench coefficient	25	7			
Type of variable	slack	slack			
Column multiplier	25	7			

To determine exactly how much of each product should now be made, we include the new variable for the number of benches X_B, which involves adding a column to the simplex tableau for X_B. We begin by establishing the appropriate exchange coefficients.

Recall that the exchange coefficient expresses how much of a mix variable must be given up to accommodate a per-unit increase in the variable for that column. Since each bench consumes wood and labor, building a bench has the same effect as raising the levels of the slack variables X_W and X_L. Using the appropriate values from the final simplex tableau in Table 14-6 and the bench requirements, we can make the calculations shown in Table 14-7. Multiplying the exchange coefficients in each row by the respective resource requirements for one bench, and summing, we see that we have to sacrifice 11/20 of a table and 17/40 of a chair to make each bench. These values serve as the exchange coefficients for X_B in the revised simplex tableau provided in Table 14-8.

After computing the per-unit sacrifice and improvement values of X_B, we proceed with the usual simplex steps. Entering X_B and exiting X_T from the variable mix, we obtain the second tableau in Table 14-8. No further improvement is possible, and the new optimal solution is

$$X_T = 0 \qquad\qquad X_C = 65/11$$
$$X_B = 80/11$$
$$P = 1{,}080/11 \text{ dollars}$$

When the original problem includes an $=$ constraint, the column of the corresponding artificial variable is used the same way any slack variable column is used to find the new exchange coefficients. If the problem contains a $\geq$ constraint, the sign of the cofficient for the new variable must be reversed before the products for the corresponding surplus variable column are obtained.

TABLE 14-8
Simplex Iterations to Add the New Main Variable

UNIT PROFIT		6	8	7	0	0	
	Var. Mix	X_T	X_C	X_B	X_W	X_L	Sol.
6	X_T ←	1	0	(11/20)	1/20	−1/10	4
8	X_C	0	1	17/40	−1/40	3/20	9
	Sac.	6	8	67/10	1/10	6/10	96
	Imp.	0	0	3/10	−1/10	−6/10	—
7	X_B	20/11	0	1	1/11	−2/11	80/11
8	X_C	−17/22	1	0	−7/110	5/22	65/11
	Sac.	72/11	8	7	7/55	6/11	1,080/11
	Imp.	−6/11	0	0	−7/55	−6/11	—

14-5 CASE ILLUSTRATION: THE PERSIAN SAUSAGE PROBLEM

To help assimilate the various procedures for the variety of sensitivity analyses and problem revision situations that can be encountered, we will now consider a comprehensive case illustration. We will successively analyze and modify the Persian sausage problem from Chapter 12. The problem objective is to establish the ingredient weights for making a 100-pound batch

TABLE 14-9
The Persian Sausage Requirements

Label Category	PERCENTAGE OF WEIGHT			Required Percentage
	Beef	Chicken	Lamb	
Fat	20%	15%	25%	≤24%
Protein	20	15	15	≥12%
Water and other	60	70	60	≤64%
Total weight (%)	any	any	≥30%	
Cost per pound	$1.00	$.50	$.70	

of sausage subject to the requirements in Table 14-9. Included is the restriction that all ingredients must sum to 100 pounds. The linear program is specified below, where the main variables are pounds of beef X_B, chicken X_C, and lamb X_L.

$$\text{Minimize} \quad C = 1X_B + .5X_C + .7X_L$$

$$\begin{aligned}
\text{Subject to} \quad & .20X_B + .15X_C + .25X_L \leq 24 \quad \text{(fat)} \\
& .20X_B + .15X_C + .15X_L \geq 12 \quad \text{(protein)} \\
& .60X_B + .70X_C + .60X_L \leq 64 \quad \text{(water)} \\
& 1X_L \geq 30 \quad \text{(ingredient)} \\
& 1X_B + 1X_C + 1X_L = 100 \quad \text{(total)}
\end{aligned}$$

$$\text{where} \quad X_B, X_C, X_L \geq 0$$

In the final simplex tableau in Table 14-10, X_F and X_W represent the slack weights for fat and water, X_P and X_I are surplus weights beyond the protein and ingredient minimums, and a_T is the artificial variable associated with the total weight requirement. (All other artificial variables originally used in conjunction with the $\geq$ constraints to begin the simplex procedure are no longer necessary and their columns do not appear in the table.)

The ranges for the respective right-hand sides of the original constraints are calculated in Table 14-11. Sample calculations of the new solutions for right-hand-side changes inside the respective limits are provided in Table 14-12.

TABLE 14-10

The Final Simplex Tableau for the Original Persian Sausage Problem Showing the Pivot for a Change in the Total Weight Requirement

UNIT PROFIT		1	.5	.7	0	0	0	0	M	
	Var. Mix	X_B	X_C	X_L	X_F	X_P	X_W	X_I	a_T	Sol.
0	X_F	−.05	0	0	1	0	1	0	−.85↓	3
0	X_I ←	1	0	0	0	0	−10	1	⑦	30
.5	X_C	0	1	0	0	0	10	0	−6	40
.7	X_L	1	0	1	0	0	−10	0	7	60
0	X_P	−.05	0	0	0	1	0	0	.15	3
	Sac.	.7	.5	.7	0	0	−2	0	1.9	62
	Imp.	.3	0	0	0	0	2	0	−1.9 + M	—

TABLE 14-11
Range Calculations for the Right-Hand Sides

Variable Mix	SLACK, SURPLUS, OR ARTIFICIAL VARIABLE: Not in Variable Mix		In Variable Mix			Solution
	Solution/X_W	Solution/a_T	X_F	X_P	X_I	
X_F	3	−3.53				3
X_I	−3	4.29				30
X_C	4	−6.67				40
X_L	−6	8.57				60
X_P		20.00				3
Smallest positive	3	4.29				
Smallest absolute negative	3	3.53				
Constraint type	≤ (water)	= (total)	≤ (fat)	≥ (protein)	≥ (ingredient)	
Original level	64	100	24	12	30	
Lower limit	$64-3=61$	$100-4.29$ $=95.71$	$24-3=21$	$-\infty$	$-\infty$	
Upper limit	$64+3=67$	$100+3.53$ $=103.53$	∞	$12+3=15$	$30+30=60$	

TABLE 14-12
Calculations for a Sample of the Right-Hand-Side Changes Within Their Respective Limits

Unit Cost	Variable Mix	SOLUTION FOR NEW RIGHT-HAND SIDES: Fat 25	Protein 5	Water 65	Ingredient 20	Total Weight 102
0	X_F	4	3	4	3	1.3
0	X_I	30	30	20	20	44
.5	X_C	40	40	50	40	28
.7	X_L	60	60	50	60	74
0	X_P	3	−4	3	3	3.3
Total Cost		$62	$62	$60	$62	$65.80
Net r.h.s. change		$25-24=1$	$5-12=-7$	$65-64=1$	$20-30=-10$	$102-100=2$

TABLE 14-13

Range Calculations for the Unit Ingredient Costs

Main Variables in Mix	NONMIX VARIABLES (NOT ARTIFICIAL) Improvement/X_B	Improvement/X_W	SMALLEST RATIO Positive	Absolute Negative
X_C	∞	.20	.20	none
X_L	.30	$-.20$	.30	.20
Improvement:	.30	2		

Main Variables in Mix	Original Level	Improvement	Lower Limit	Upper Limit
X_C	.50	0	$.50 - \infty = -\infty$	$.50 + .20 = .70$
X_L	.70	0	$.70 - .20 = .50$	$.70 + .30 = 1.00$
Main variable not in mix: X_B	1.00	.30	$1 - .30 = .70$	∞

Remember that the respective limits and the new solutions apply only as long as all other parameters are held constant at their original levels.

Continuing, we find the ranges in unit ingredient costs over which the present variable mix remains optimal. Table 14-13 shows how these cost limits are calculated. Each range applies only as long as all other parameters remain fixed. Remember that a change in unit cost will not change the variable values, as long as the new cost falls within the computed limits; only the total cost will change.

PROBLEMS

14-1 The following linear program applies for the Piney Woods Furniture Company, which makes tables (T), chairs (C), and bookcases (B):

$$\text{Maximize} \quad P = 20X_T + 15X_C + 15X_B$$
$$\text{Subject to} \quad 10X_T + 3X_C + 10X_B \leq 100 \quad \text{(wood)}$$
$$5X_T + 5X_C + 5X_B \leq 60 \quad \text{(labor)}$$
$$\text{where} \quad X_T, X_C, X_B \geq 0$$

Using X_W and X_L as the respective slack variables for unused wood and labor, the following final simplex tableau applies:

TABLE 14-14

UNIT PROFIT		20	15	15	0	0	
	Var. Mix	X_T	X_C	X_B	X_W	X_L	Sol.
20	X_T	1	0	1	1/7	−6/70	64/7
15	X_C	0	1	0	−1/7	2/7	20/7
	Sac.	20	15	20	5/7	18/7	1,580/7
	Imp.	0	0	−5	−5/7	−18/7	—

(a) Determine the ranges for available wood over which the present variable mix will remain optimal. Do the same for available labor.
(b) Find the new optimal solution when available wood is 90 board feet.
(c) Find the new optimal solution when available labor is 100 hours.

14-2 Referring to information contained in Problem 14-1:
(a) Determine the ranges for unit profits over which the current solution will remain optimal.
(b) What is the total profit when each table yields a profit of $18?
(c) What is the total profit when each chair yields a profit of $10?

14-3 Suppose that the bookcase profit in Problem 14-1 is raised to $25 per unit. Construct the final simplex tableau for this revised problem and indicate the optimal solution.

14-4 Suppose that the chair profit in Problem 14-1 is lowered to $5 per unit. Construct the final simplex tableau for this revised problem and indicate the optimal solution.

14-5 Piney Woods now wishes to expand its original linear program in Problem 14-1 to include a new product, desks, which yields a profit of $50 per unit. Each desk requires 30 board feet of wood and 10 hours of labor.
(a) Let X_D represent the number of desks to be made. Using the simplex tableau provided in Table 14-14, determine the values of the new X_D column. Then reconstruct the entire tableau to include this new column.
(b) Does your answer to (a) provide the optimal solution to the expanded problem? If not, continue to use simplex until you find the optimal solution.

14-6 Computer manufacturers presently buy ChipMont's entire production of the following types of silicon chips: central processing units (C), integrated circuits (I), and core memories (M). The following linear program applies:

$$\text{Maximize} \quad P = .25X_C + .40X_I + .15X_M$$

$$
\begin{aligned}
\text{Subject to} \quad & .005X_C + .02X_I + .01X_M \leq 10,000 && \text{(silicon sheets)} \\
& .2X_C + .5X_I + .1X_M \leq 200,000 && \text{(labor in minutes)} \\
& .10X_C + .40X_I + .15X_M \leq 400,000 && \text{(washing hours)} \\
& X_C - X_I + X_M \leq 0 && \text{(quantity limitation)} \\
\text{where} \quad & X_C, X_I, X_M \geq 0
\end{aligned}
$$

Using X_S, X_L, X_W, and X_Q as the respective slack variables, the following final simplex tableau has been obtained:

TABLE 4-15

UNIT PROFIT	.25	.40	.15	0	0	0	0	
Var. Mix.	X_C	X_I	X_M	X_S	X_L	X_W	X_Q	Sol.
0 X_S	0	0	6/700	1	−25/700	0	15/7,000	20,000/7
.40 X_I	0	1	−1/7	0	10/7	0	−2/7	2,000,000/7
0 X_W	0	0	85/700	0	−5/7	1	3/70	1,800,000/7
.25 X_C	1	0	6/7	0	10/7	0	5/7	2,000,000/7
Sol.	.25	.40	11/70	0	65/70	0	45/700	1,300,000/7
Imp.	0	0	−5/700	0	−65/70	0	−45/700	—

(a) Determine the range for available silicon sheets over which the present variable mix will remain optimal. Do the same for available labor and washing hours.
(b) Find the new optimal solution when 11,000 silicon sheets are available.
(c) Find the new optimal solution when 150,000 minutes of labor are available.
(d) Find the new optimal solution when 300,000 hours of washing time are available.

14-7 Referring to the data in Problem 14-6:
(a) Determine the ranges for unit profits over which the current solution will remain optimal.
(b) What is the total profit when each central processing unit yields a profit of $.30?
(c) What is the total profit when each integrated circuit yields a profit of $.10?
(d) What is the total profit when each core memory yields a profit of $.05?

14-8 Suppose the profit per memory chip in Problem 14-6 increases to $.20. Construct the final simplex tableau for this revised problem and indicate the optimal solution.

14-9 Suppose the profit per integrated circuit in Problem 14-6 increases to $.50. Construct the final simplex tableau for this revised problem and indicate the optimal solution.

14-10 Suppose the profit per central processing unit in Problem 14-6 decreases to $.15. Construct the final simplex tableau for this revised problem and indicate the optimal solution.

14-11 ChipMont wishes to expand the original linear program in Problem 14-6 to include a new product—a video-game chip. The per-unit profit for these chips is $1. The new chip requires .01 silicon sheet, .4 minute of sorting labor, and .20 hour of chemical wash.
(a) Let X_V represent the number of video game chips. Using the simplex tableau provided in Table 14-15, determine the values of the new X_V column. Then reconstruct the entire tableau to include this new column.
(b) Does your answer to (a) provide the optimal solution to the expanded problem? If not, continue to use simplex until you find the optimal solution.

14-12 For the linear program

$$\text{Maximize} \quad P = 10X_1 + 15X_2 + 20X_3$$

Subject to

$$2X_1 + 3X_2 + 4X_3 \le 100 \quad \text{(constraint } A\text{)}$$
$$4X_1 \qquad\quad + 2X_3 \ge 50 \quad \text{(constraint } B\text{)}$$
$$- 5X_2 + 5X_3 \ge 20 \quad \text{(constraint } C\text{)}$$
$$X_1 + X_2 + X_3 = 20 \quad \text{(constraint } D\text{)}$$

where

$$X_1, X_2, X_3 \ge 0$$

the following final simplex tableau applies.

TABLE 14-16

UNIT PROFIT		10	15	20	0	0	0	$-M$	
	Var. Mix.	X_1	X_2	X_3	X_A	X_B	X_C	a_D	Sol.
10	X_1	1	-1	0	0	$-1/2$	0	-1	5
20	X_3	0	2	1	0	1/2	0	2	15
0	X_A	0	-3	0	1	-1	0	-6	30
0	X_C	0	15	0	0	5/2	1	10	55
	Sac.	10	30	20	0	5	0	30	350
	Imp.	0	-15	0	0	-5	0	$-M - 30$	—

(a) Determine the ranges for the right-hand sides over which the present variable mix remains optimal.

(b) What is the optimal solution when the right-hand side for constraint A is raised to 200?

(c) What is the optimal solution when the right-hand side for constraint B is raised to 60?

14-13 Referring to the information contained in Problem 14-12:

(a) For each main variable, determine the ranges for unit profit over which the current solution remains optimal.

(b) What is the total profit when the unit profit for X_1 is raised to $12?

14-14 Construct the final simplex tableau for Problem 14-12 when the unit profit for X_3 is reduced below its lower limit to $10.

14-15 Construct the final simplex tableau for Problem 14-12 when the unit profit for X_1 is raised above its upper limit to $25.

14-16 A new variable X_4 is added to Problem 14-12. Its constraint coefficients are 2 for A and C, 3 for B, and 1 for D. The unit profit is $20.

(a) Using Table 14-16, determine the values for the new X_4 column. Then reconstruct the entire tableau to include this new column.

(b) Does your answer to (a) provide the optimal solution for the expanded problem? If not, continue with simplex until you determine the optimal solution.

14-17 The Sound Shack, a chain of retail stereo stores, sells four models of record turn-tables, complete with magnetic cartridge and stylus: SS-4, SS-5, SS-6, and SS-8. The company-owned plant is planning next month's production. Depending on the model, a regular or a super motor is used. One of three cartridges is installed on any model: Ace, Bidwell, or Capstone. Only the motors and cartridges, which are long lead-time items, constrain the quantities produced. All other components can be readily purchased from suppliers. In addition, there is a limitation due to the amount of assembly labor time available at the plant. Because it has been heavily back-ordered, at least 100 units of model SS-4 must be made.

The following linear program applies, where X_4, X_5, X_6, and X_8 represent the quantities of the various turnables to be made:

Maximize $\quad P = 20X_4 + 25X_5 + 35X_6 + 45X_8$

Subject to

$$
\begin{array}{llll}
X_4 + X_5 + X_6 & \leq 250 & \text{(regular motor)} \\
X_8 \leq 60 & \text{(super motor)} \\
X_4 & \leq 120 & \text{(Ace cartridge)} \\
X_5 & \leq 60 & \text{(Bidwell cartridge)} \\
X_6 + X_8 \leq 80 & \text{(Capstone cartridge)} \\
2X_4 + 3X_5 + 4X_6 + 6X_8 \geq 1{,}000 & \text{(labor)} \\
X_4 & \geq 100 & \text{(demand)}
\end{array}
$$

where $\quad$ all $Xs \geq 0$

It is assumed that all units produced will be sold and will yield the unit profits (in dollars) indicated in the program. The following final simplex tableau applies. The slack variables for the respective resource availability constraints are X_R, X_S, X_A, X_B, X_C, and X_L. X_D represents the surplus production of the SS-4 model beyond the required minimum.

TABLE 14-17
The Final Simplex Tableau for the Sound Shack Problem

UNIT PROFIT		20	25	35	45	0	0	0	0	0	0	0	
	Var. Mix.	X_4	X_5	X_6	X_8	X_R	X_S	X_A	X_B	X_C	X_L	X_D	Sol.
0	X_R	0	0	0	0	1	1	−1	−1	−1	0	0	50
45	X_8	0	0	0	1	0	1	0	0	0	0	0	60
0	X_D	0	0	0	0	0	0	1	0	0	0	1	20
25	X_5	0	1	0	0	0	0	0	1	0	0	0	60
35	X_6	0	0	1	0	0	−1	0	0	1	0	0	20
0	X_L	0	0	0	0	0	−2	−2	−3	−4	1	0	140
20	X_4	1	0	0	0	0	0	1	0	0	0	0	120
	Sac.	20	25	35	45	0	10	20	25	35	0	0	7,300
	Imp.	0	0	0	0	0	−10	−20	−25	−35	0	0	—

(a) Determine the range for available Capstone cartridges over which the present variable mix remains optimal. Determine the new optimal solution if the supply of these cartridges is 110 instead of 80.

(b) Returning to the original problem, determine the range for available Bidwell cartridges over which the present variable mix remains optimal. Determine the new optimal solution if the supply of these cartridges is 70 instead of 60.

(c) Returning to the original problem, over what range in available labor does the present variable mix remain optimal? If available labor is lowered from 1,000 to 900 hours, what is the new optimal solution?

(d) Returning to the original problem, over what range in the minimum demand for model SS-4 does the present variable mix remain optimal? If minimum demand is raised from 100 to 110 SS-4 turntables, what is the new optimal solution?

14-18 Continuing with the Sound Shack problem:

(a) Determine the range for the SS-8 model profit over which the present optimal solution in Table 14-17 remains the same. Suppose that competitive factors lower the unit profit for the SS-8 to $25. Determine the new final simplex tableau. How many of each type of turntable should be made?

(b) Continuing with the final tableau you obtained in (a), suppose that the unit profit for the SS-4 is reduced to $10 and determine the new optimal solution.

14-19 Continuing with the Sound Shack problem, suppose that management is considering reviving the SS-7 model turntable. This model uses the super motor and the Bidwell cartridge and requires 5 hours of labor. Using the original problem data and Table 14-7:

(a) If the dual variable values are $10 for super motors, $25 for Bidwell cartridges, and $0 per hour of labor, and if the unit profit for the SS-7 is only $25, should this model be reintroduced into the product line?

(b) If each SS-7 will yield a $40 profit instead, should this model be made? If so, determine the optimal solution.

15

The Transportation and Assignment Problems

One of the most important and successful applications of quantitative analysis in solving business problems has been in the area of the physical distribution of products. Great cost savings have been achieved by the more efficient routing of freight from supply points to required destinations. In this chapter, we will consider the *transportation problem*, which serves as the framework for analyzing such decisions. The purpose of the transportation problem in its basic form is to minimize the total cost of shipping goods from plants to warehouse distribution centers in such a way that the needs of each warehouse are met and every factory operates within its capacity.

Ordinarily, it is convenient to express such a problem mathematically in terms of a linear program. All linear programs including the transportation problem, can be solved by means of the simplex algorithm. But simplex is a general procedure, and its universality has built-in limitations. The special strucutre of the transportation problem permits us to solve it by using a faster, more streamlined algorithm than simplex. In studying the transportation problem, we will therefore gain a new insight into quantitative analysis: *The judicious choice of the solution procedure itself can result in savings of both time and money.* This chapter illustrates another way to "skin a cat" that is better for certain kinds of cats. It is important to know that alternative procedures exist or can be developed to solve a variety of linear programming problems.

The transportation problem establishes a convenient format that has been adapted to a variety of applications that do not involve the physical distribution of goods. One of these applications that we will discuss here is the *assignment problem*, which is concerned with the efficient placement of specific individuals in particular jobs. In this chapter we will also examine a production scheduling application.

15-1 A SKI SHIPMENT SCHEDULING ILLUSTRATION

In this section, we will return to the shipment scheduling application concerning the operation of the sporting goods company first discussed in Chapter 10. To review, the company makes skis in three plants throughout the world. The plants supply four company-owned warehouses that distribute the skis directly to ski shops. Depending on which mode is cheaper, the product is air-freighted or trucked from the plants to the warehouses. Table 15-1 provides the various point-to-point shipping costs of shipping a pair of skis. The problem is to find how many pairs of skis should be shipped from each

TABLE 15-1
The Shipping Costs Per Pair of Skis

	TO WAREHOUSES			
From Plants	Frankfurt	New York	Phoenix	Yokohama
Juarez	$19	$ 7	$ 3	$21
Seoul	15	21	18	6
Tel Aviv	11	14	15	22

TABLE 15-2
Shipment Schedule for Skis

From Plants	TO WAREHOUSES				Plant Capacity
	F	N	P	Y	
J	X_{JF}	X_{JN}	X_{JP}	X_{JY}	100
S	X_{SF}	X_{SN}	X_{SP}	X_{SY}	300
T	X_{TF}	X_{TN}	X_{TP}	X_{TY}	200
Warehouse demand	150	100	200	150	600

plant to the various warehouses to minimize total cost. This is accomplished by determining the quantities for the shipment schedule shown in Table 15-2, where X_{ij} represents the quantity shipped from plant i to warehouse j.

In Chapter 10, we formulated this problem as

Minimize $\quad C = \quad 19X_{JF} + \quad 7X_{JN} + \quad 3X_{JP} + 21X_{JY}$

$$+ 15X_{SF} + 21X_{SN} + 18X_{SP} + \quad 6X_{SY}$$

$$+ 11X_{TF} + 14X_{TN} + 15X_{TP} + 22X_{TY}$$

Subject to $\quad X_{JF} + \quad X_{JN} + \quad X_{JP} + \quad X_{JY} = 100 \quad$ (Juarez capacity)

$$X_{SF} + \quad X_{SN} + \quad X_{SP} + \quad X_{SY} = 300 \quad \text{(Seoul capacity)}$$

$$X_{TF} + \quad X_{TN} + \quad X_{TP} + \quad X_{TY} = 200 \quad \text{(Tel Aviv capacity)}$$

$$X_{JF} + \quad X_{SF} + \quad X_{TF} = 150 \quad \text{(Frankfurt demand)}$$

$$X_{JN} + \quad X_{SN} + \quad X_{TN} = 100 \quad \text{(New York demand)}$$

$$X_{JP} + \quad X_{SP} + \quad X_{TP} = 200 \quad \text{(Phoenix demand)}$$

$$X_{JY} + \quad X_{SY} + \quad X_{TY} = 150 \quad \text{(Yokohama demand)}$$

where $\quad$ all X's $\geq \quad 0$

Special Requirements of Transportation Problems

The number of constraints is dictated by the number of plants (or rows in the shipment schedule) and the number of warehouses (or columns in the shipment schedule). Altogether, every transportation problem must have exactly the following number of equality constraints:

Number of constraints = Number of rows + Number of columns

As we can see in Table 15-2, each X is represented exactly once in the capacity constraints and exactly once in the demand constraints. This can happen if and only if the total quantity shipped is exactly equal to the total quantity received: *Total plant capacity must equal total warehouse demand.* In our example, the capacities sum to 600, which is also the sum of the demands:

$$600 = 100 + 300 + 200 = 150 + 100 + 200 + 150$$

Later, we will see that this fact plays an important role in solving a transportation problem.

You may be wondering why each plant must produce exactly at its capacity and each warehouse must receive precisely its demand. Isn't that unrealistic? These requirements are needed to solve the problem by the most efficient means. Of course they are unrealistic, but we will see that it will always be possible to formulate any transportation problem in this manner, even when true demands and capacities are not in exact balance.

15-2 GETTING STARTED: THE NORTHWEST CORNER RULE

We solve the transportation problem in iterations proceeding from solution to solution much like we do in simplex. We begin with an initial solution that satisfies all constraints. A convenient starting point is to apply the *northwest corner rule*. We begin with a blank shipment schedule, shown in Table 15-3. Each plant-warehouse route is represented by a cell. For convenience, the unit shipping costs are placed in the upper right-hand corners of each cell. The central portion of the cell is reserved for the quantity to be shipped.

The northwest corner rule begins in the cell in the upper left-hand corner of the schedule. (On a map, this would be called the "northwest corner.") In this cell, we place the largest possible quantity that satisfies the capacity and demand constraints. This means that we look in the row and column margins of Table 15-3 for the smallest demand or capacity applicable and write this number in the northwest corner cell. Further cell allocations are made by moving down or to the right in the direction of leftover demand or capacity

TABLE 15-3
A Blank Shipment Schedule

From \ To	F	N	P	Y	Capacity
J	19	7	3	21	100
S	15	21	18	6	300
T	11	14	15	22	200
Demand	150	100	200	150	600

and inserting the maximum feasible quantity at each step. We stop when the southeast corner has been allocated. The cell-to-cell movement in this procedure is analogous to the movement of chess pieces. Only horizontal and vertical movements, like those of the "rook," are allowed; no diagonal "bishop" moves are permitted.

The northwest corner solution for the ski-distribution problem is provided in Table 15-4. Our beginning corner receives an allocation of 100 pairs to be shipped from Juarez to Frankfurt. This is the largest possible number of pairs of skis that can be shipped over that route, since Juarez's capacity is 100 pairs; Frankfurt must receive 150 pairs, but we cannot ship more skis from Juarez that it can make. This leaves an unfilled demand of $150 - 100 = 50$ pairs for Frankfurt, so our next cell for skis shipped from Seoul to Frankfurt lies directly below. The largest possible allocation to that cell is 50 pairs, since the gap in Frankfurt's demand is exhausted before this warehouse takes up Seoul's capacity. This leaves us with an unused capacity for Seoul in the amount of $300 - 50 = 250$ pairs. We therefore move to the cell at the right, where we must allocate a shipment from Seoul to New York. There we fill New York's total demand of 100, leaving $300 - 50 - 100 = 150$ pairs under capacity at Seoul. We move to the right again, where we allocate 150 pairs from Seoul to Phoenix. This does not exhaust that warehouse's demand, leaving $200 - 150 = 50$ pairs short at Phoenix. Moving down, we pick up 50 pairs from Tel Aviv to take care of Phoenix, and the move to the right, where we allocate the rest of Tel Aviv's capacity as a 150-pair shipment to Yokohama. At this point, all constraints are satisfied.

TABLE 15-4
The Shipment Schedule for Skis Found by the Northwest Corner Rule

From \ To	F	N	P	Y	Capacity
J	[19] (100)	[7]	[3]	[21]	100
S	[15] (50) →	[21] (100) →	[18] (150)	[6]	300
T	[11]	[14]	[15] (50) →	[22] (150)	200
Demand	150	100	200	150	600

The solution in Table 15-4 serves as the starting feasible solution. The cell entries are the values of the corresponding problem variables; empty cells correspond to zero quantities. The total cost of this shipment schedule is computed below to be $C = 11,500$ dollars.

Quantity	Unit Cost	Route Cost
$X_{JF} = 100$	$c_{JF} = 19$	$19 \times 100 = 1,900$
$X_{SF} = 50$	$c_{SF} = 15$	$15 \times 50 = 750$
$X_{SN} = 100$	$c_{SN} = 21$	$21 \times 100 = 2,100$
$X_{SP} = 150$	$c_{SP} = 18$	$18 \times 150 = 2,700$
$X_{TP} = 50$	$c_{TP} = 15$	$15 \times 50 = 750$
$X_{TY} = 150$	$c_{TY} = 22$	$22 \times 150 = 3,300$
		$C = 11,500$

15-3 SOLVING THE PROBLEM: THE TRANSPORTATION METHOD

We have just begun to solve this transportation problem. Our next task is to search for improvements We could try the trial-and-error approach, reallocating cell values until it becomes hard to find improvements. Not only would this procedure be inefficient, but there is no guarantee that the optimal solution would be found. We would probably give up in frustration, not knowing if more improvements were possible. Instead, we will take a systematic approach to the problem.

The Simplex Analogy

First, we will recall some important features of simplex that apply equally well here. We know that any feasible bounded problem has at least one optimal solution that is a corner point. Remember that a *corner point* can be defined as the solution to the underlying constraints when all so-called nonmix variables are fixed arbitrarily at zero. The free variables are called *mix variables*. Exactly the same principles apply to the transportation problem, which, after all, is just a special kind of linear program. The mix variables for any shipment-schedule solution correspond to the *nonempty cells* (cells containing a circled value); to the *empty cells* represent the nonmix variables.

The northwest corner rule provides us with a corner-point solution. (Here, we are referring to a corner in the higher dimensional space and *not* to the cell in a corner of the shipment-schedule table.) As in simplex, we seek a neighboring corner to evaluate next, choosing the one that improves cost at the greatest rate. And, as in simplex, we reach this corner by means of a pivot procedure in which the *status* of the cells is exchanged: A currently nonempty cell becomes empty, and a presently empty cell receives a quantity allocation. The new nonempty cell is referred to as the *entering cell*, and the cell it replaces is called the *exiting cell*. Such an exchange will result in a cheaper shipment schedule. We continue this procedure until we reach a most attractive corner that cannot be improved on. This is the optimal solution.

Finding the Entering Cell: Row and Column Numbers

The entering cell is found through economic analysis, as it is in simplex. In the transportation problem, we evaluate every empty cell by determining the per-unit cost improvement associated with allocating one unit to that cell. Our procedure for doing this may seem roundabout at first, but is it really quite efficient.

We begin by assigning special values to each row and column of the current shipment schedule. The unit shipping cost for a cell is denoted by c_{ij}. The *row numbers* are represented by r_i, and the *column numbers* are represented by k_j. These values are calculated so that the following relationship holds:

$$For\ nonempty\ cells: \quad c_{ij} = r_i + k_j$$

We begin by assigning zero as the row number for the first row. The pattern of the nonempty cells and their unit costs then dictate the values of the remaining row and column numbers. These are found algebraically by solving a sequence of equations, each with one unknown.

Returning to our ski-distribution example, consider the present solution shown in Table 15-5. The row and column numbers appear outside the shipment schedule in the respective margins. The letters indicate the *sequence* in which these values were obtained. The proper sequence is extremely important when computing the r and k values. A general rule in finding the row and column numbers is to work from the last number found until all nonempty cells in the present row or column have their two numbers. Then we move to the row or column containing the newest number(s) and repeat the procedure. We always use the newest r value to obtain the next k value, and vice versa. We stop when we have a full set of row and column numbers. A detailed explanation of how these values were obtained follows.

ⓐ We begin with the first row. It always receives a zero row number. Thus, $r_J = 0$.

ⓑ Looking at row J, we see that there is one nonempty cell JF that does not yet have a column number. For this cell

$$c_{JF} = r_J + k_F$$

TABLE 15-5
Row and Column Numbers for the Initial Solution to the Ski-Distribution Problem

From \ To	F	N	P	Y	Capacity	
J	[19] (100)	[7]	[3]	[21]	100	$r_J = \quad 0$ ⓐ
S	[15] (50)	[21] (100)	[18] (150)	[6]	300	$r_S = -4$ ⓒ
T	[11]	[14]	[15] (50)	[22] (150)	200	$r_T = -7$ ⓕ
Demand	150	100	200	150	600	
	$k_F = 19$ ⓑ	$k_N = 25$ ⓓ	$k_P = 22$ ⓔ	$k_Y = 29$ ⓖ		

must hold. We know that $c_{JF} = 19$, and we have just found $r_J = 0$. Plugging these numbers into this equation, we obtain

$$19 = 0 + k_F$$

and we find that $k_F = 19$.

ⓒ There are no other nonempty cells in row J. We now look in column F for any nonempty cell that does not have a row number. SF does not. We know that

$$c_{SF} = r_S + k_F$$

Plugging $c_{SF} = 15$ and $k_F = 19$ into this equation gives us

$$15 = r_S + 19$$

which yields

$$r_S = 15 - 19 = -4$$

ⓓ There are no other nonempty cells in column F. We then search row S, where we see that cell SN has no column number. Plugging $c_{SN} = 21$ and $r_S = -4$ into

$$c_{SN} = r_S + k_N$$

gives us

$$21 = -4 + k_N$$

so that $k_N = 21 - (-4) = 25$. There are no other nonempty cells in column N, so we don't use it further. But we are not finished with row S.

ⓔ Nonempty cell SP remains in row S without a column number. Substituting $c_{SP} = 18$ and $r_S = -4$ into

$$c_{SP} = r_S + k_P$$

yields

$$18 = -4 + k_P$$

so that $k_P = 18 - (-4) = 22$.

ⓕ We can see that column P contains nonempty cell TP, which has no row number. Plugging $c_{TP} = 15$ and $k_P = 22$ into

$$c_{TP} = r_T + k_P$$

we obtain

$$15 = r_T + 22$$

so that $r_T = 15 - 22 = -7$.

ⓖ One more nonempty cell, TY, remains in row T without a column number. Substituting $c_{TY} = 22$ and $r_T = -7$ into

$$c_{TY} = r_T + k_Y$$

gives us

$$22 = -7 + k_Y$$

and $k_Y = 22 - (-7) = 29$.

All rows and columns now have their numbers.

With practice, you can make these computations very rapidly in your head without having to use scratch paper.

The r and k values obtained in this way are now used in conjunction with the present shipment schedule to find the entering cell. To do this, we calculate the difference *for the empty cells*

$$c_{ij} - r_i - k_j$$

TABLE 15-6

**Improvement Values and Closed-Loop Path
for the Initial Solution to the Transportation Problem**

From \ To	F	N	P	Y	Capacity	
J	19 (100) (−)	7 −18	3 (+) −19	21 −8	100	$r_J = 0$
S	15 (50) (+)	21 (100)	18 (150) (−) −19	6	300	$r_S = -4$
T	11 −1	14 −4	15 (50)	22 (150)	200	$r_T = -7$
Demand	150	100	200	150	600	

$$k_F = 19 \qquad k_N = 25 \qquad k_P = 22 \qquad k_Y = 29$$

This difference indicates the per-unit *cost improvement* that can be achieved by raising the shipment allocation in the corresponding cell from its present level of zero. *The empty cell with the greatest absolute negative difference is the entering cell.*

Table 15-6 shows how the entering cell is found for our example. There, the differences have been entered in the lower left-hand corners of each empty cell. For example, the difference in cell JN is

$$c_{JN} - r_J - k_N = 7 - 0 - 25 = -18$$

This tells us that raising the quantity allocated to that cell will reduce costs by $18 per pair of skis. The other differences are calculated in the same way.

We can see that cells JP and SY in Table 15-6 are tied for the greatest cost improvement at $19 per pair. We will break this tie arbitrarily and choose JP as the entering cell. Our next step is to determine just how much we can allocate to that cell.

Finding the New Solution: The Closed-Loop Path

We begin by placing a $(+)$ in cell JP to indicate that its allocation (the shipment from Juarez to Phoenix) will be increased from zero quantity. Whatever change we make must be *balanced*, so that the new quantities in row J

and column P sum to the respective capacity of 100 for Juarez and demand of 200 for Phoenix. Thus, we must reduce cell JF by the amount of the change. We place a $(-)$ there to reflect this reduction. But if we reduce cell JF, we must make a compensating change in column F. Our rule is that *there can be only one increasing and one decreasing cell in any row or column. Except for the entering cell, all changes must involve nonempty cells.* Thus, we place a $(+)$ in cell SF, since it is the only nonempty cell in column F. This leaves us in row S, where a compensating $(-)$ change must be made. We can readily see that cell SN must be skipped because it is the only nonempty cell in its column, so we place the $(-)$ in cell SP. All of our changes now balance.

Connecting the $(+)$ and $(-)$s with line segments, we can see that they provide a *closed-loop path*. This path highlights the changes involved in reallocating the shipments. For *any entering cell, the closed-loop path is unique.* Its corners are alternating $(+)$ and $(-)$ cells, and only the entering cell is empty. *Only the corner cells on the path will be changed.* (Those cells that a line segment passes through are not involved.) We can find the close-loop path by proceeding either clockwise or counter-clockwise and starting up, down, right, or left (but never moving diagonally). We proceed, turning at each new $(+)$ or $(-)$, until our path closes. If we reach an impass, ending up in a cell where we cannot turn (because all other cells in its column or row are empty), then we backtrack to the last turning point and go the other way or move forward to another nonempty cell in the same row or column.

The closed-loop path verifies that we will indeed save $19 by increasing the quantity allocated to cell JP. Tracing its trajectory counter-clockwise, we have

$$\text{Change:} \quad (+) \quad (-) \quad (+) \quad (-)$$
$$\text{Cell:} \quad JP \quad JF \quad SF \quad SP$$

Each unit shifted along this path will produce a cost increase in the $(+)$ cells and a cost reduction in the $(-)$ cells, so that the net unit cost change is

$$3 - 19 + 15 - 18 = -19$$

The fact that we obtain -19 by using the r and k values is not coincidental. (The $c_{ij} - r_i - k_j$ differences are analogous to the entries in per-unit improvement row of a simplex tableau.)

We must now make our change in the shipment schedule. The shift in quantities will occur only in the cells at the corners of the closed-loop path. *The amount shifted each time is equal to the smallest quantity in the losing cells.* The smallest $(-)$ quantity is selected because all affected cells will change by plus or minus the same amount, and the resulting quantities cannot be negative. The smallest losing-cell shipment quantity occurs in cell JF, where 100 pairs can be taken away. Cell JF is therefore the exiting cell.

TABLE 15-7

The Second Solution to the Transportation Problem

$$C = 9,600$$

From \ To	F	N	P	Y	Capacity	
J	19	7	3 (100)	21	100	$r_J = 0$ ⓐ
	19	1	11			
S	15 (150)	21 (100)	18 (50) (−)	6 (+) −19	300	$r_S = 15$ ⓒ
T	11	14	15 (50) (+)	22 (150) (−)	200	$r_T = 12$ ⓕ
	−1	−4				
Demand	150	100	200	150	600	
	$k_F = 0$ ⓓ	$k_N = 6$ ⓔ	$k_P = 3$ ⓑ	$k_Y = 10$ ⓖ		

Table 15-7 shows the new shipment schedule that results from the allocation to cell JP. The total cost savings is

$$100 \times 19 = 1,900 \text{ dollars}$$

so that the total route cost is now $C = 11,500 - 1,900 = 9,600$ dollars.

Our example involves rectangular closed-loop paths. But *closed-loop paths may assume unusual shapes*, such as Ls, figure-8s, and even loops inside loops.

Further Iterations to Find the Optimal Solution

Now we begin again, using the new row and column numbers. Notice that except for $r_J = 0$, all of the r and k values in Table 15-7 are different than before. This is because the set of nonempty cells has changed. The sequence in which these numbers are obtained is different as well. There are no shortcuts; the r and k values must be recomputed from scratch for each new shipment schedule.

Next, we find the differences for the empty cells. We can see that cell SY is the entering cell, where costs are reduced by $19 per unit (coincidentally,

TABLE 15-8

The Third Solution to the Transportation Problem

$$C = 8,650$$

From \ To	F	N	P	Y	Capacity	
J	19	7	3 (100)	21	100	$r_J = \;$ 0 ⓐ
	0	−18	11			
S	15 (150)	21 (100)	18	6 (50)	300	$r_S = −4$ ⓔ
		(−)	19	(+)		
T	11	14	15 (100)	22 (100)	200	$r_T = \;$ 12 ⓒ
	−20	(+) −23		(−)		
Demand	150	100	200	150	600	

$$k_F = 19 \qquad k_N = 25 \qquad k_P = 3 \qquad k_Y = 10$$
$$\text{ⓖ} \qquad\qquad \text{ⓕ} \qquad\qquad \text{ⓑ} \qquad\qquad \text{ⓓ}$$

the same amount as before). The closed-loop path is indicated in Table 15-7, and the smallest quantity in the losing cells is 50 pairs.

Table 15-8 provides the next shipment schedule, where total cost has been reduced by $19 \times 50 = 950$ dollars to $C = 9,600 − 950 = 8,650$ dollars. Recomputing the row and column numbers and the empty-cell differences, we find that cell TN is the entering cell. Increasing its allocation will save \$23 per unit.

The smallest quantity in the losing cells is 100 pairs, which happens to be the same for cells SN and TY. Whenever there is a tie for the exiting cell, more than one cell will be reduced to zero. This presents a problem we have not encountered previously. Before we proceed, a few more observations must be made regarding the nature of our solution procedure.

The Required Number of Nonempty Cells

In our illustration, there have always been exactly six nonempty cells. All of the successive changes made in the shipment schedules guarantee this. This number is one less than the number of rows and columns. In general

Number of nonempty cells = Number of rows + Number of columns − 1

This condition results from the fundamental linear programming solution procedure. To have a corner-point solution, there must be as many mix variables (here, nonempty cells) as there are nonredundant constraints in the formulation of the linear program.

Every transportation problem has as many constraints as there are rows and columns in the shipment schedule. But together these constraints are redundant, because when the constraints are combined with the underlying condition that total capacity must be equal to total demand, any one constraint can be eliminated without affecting the problem solution. Our illustration involves three plant-capacity requirements (rows) and four warehouse-demand limitations (columns), or seven constraints in all. But both total capacity and demand must equal 600. If we left out the Yokohama demand constraint, for example, the other six constraints combined with this condition would still ensure that the Yokohama warehouse received its required 150 pairs of skis. Only six constraints are nonredundant. This is why the number of nonempty cells is one less than the number of rows and columns in the shipment schedule.

If there were less than the necessary number of nonempty cells, it would be impossible to obtain a unique set of row and column numbers and, in some cases, to form closed-loop paths. (Too many nonempty cells cause similar problems.) This does not mean that our example cannot have a solution with only five nonzero cells, but it does mean that a total of six cells must be treated as nonempty.

Ties for the Exiting Cell

Whenever there is a tie for the exiting cell, both cells will lose all of their allocation and be reduced to zero. To meet the required number of nonempty cells, exactly one of these tying cells must thereafter be treated as nonempty. Referring to Table 15-8, we can see that both cell SN and cell TY will be reduced to zero by reallocating 100 units along the closed-loop path. Either cell SN or cell TY must, however, continue to be treated as if it were nonempty. It does not matter which cell we choose, since ties can almost always be broken arbitrarily in linear programming.

Table 15-9 provides the new shipment schedule. The cost savings are $23 \times 100 = 2,300$ dollars, and the new total cost is $C = 8,650 - 2,300 = 6,350$ dollars. We place a circled zero in cell TY and treat it as nonempty, even though the shipping quantity is zero.

We can see that increasing the allocation into cell TF will save \$20 per unit. However, one of the losing cells is TY, which involves a zero quantity. Shifting zero around the closed-loop path gives us the new schedule in Table 15-10. The total cost for this schedule is exactly the same as before, but the zero shipping quantity now appears in cell TF. Although no quantities have changed, the new pattern for the nonempty cells is an improvement.

TABLE 15-9

The Fourth Solution to the Transportation Problem

$$C = 6,350$$

From \ To	F	N	P	Y	Capacity	
J	19 ⟨0⟩	7 ⟨5⟩	3 (100) ⟨11⟩	21	100	$r_J =$ 0 (a)
S	15 (150) (−)	21 ⟨23⟩	18 ⟨19⟩	6 (150) (+)	300	$r_S = -4$ (f)
T	11 ⟨−20⟩ (+)	14 (100)	15 (100)	22 (0) (−)	200	$r_T = 12$ (c)
Demand	150	100	200	150	600	

$$k_F = 19 \;\text{(g)} \qquad k_N = 2 \;\text{(d)} \qquad k_P = 3 \;\text{(b)} \qquad k_Y = 10 \;\text{(e)}$$

TABLE 15-10

The Fifth Solution to the Transportation Problem

$$C = 6,350$$

From \ To	F	N	P	Y	Capacity	
J	19 ⟨20⟩	7 ⟨5⟩	3 (100)	21 ⟨31⟩	100	$r_J =$ 0 (a)
S	15 (150) (−)	21 ⟨3⟩	18 (+) −1	6 (150)	300	$r_S = 16$ (e)
T	11 (0) (+)	14 (100)	15 (100) (−)	22 ⟨20⟩	200	$r_T = 12$ (c)
Demand	150	100	200	150	600	

$$k_F = -1 \;\text{(d)} \qquad k_N = 2 \;\text{(g)} \qquad k_P = 3 \;\text{(b)} \qquad k_Y = -10 \;\text{(f)}$$

TABLE 15-11

The Optimal Solution to the Transportation Problem

$C = 6,250$

From \ To	F	N	P	Y	Capacity	
J	19	7	3	21	100	$r_J = 0$ (a)
			(100)			
	19	4		30		
S	15	21	18	6	300	$r_S = 15$ (c)
	(50)		(100)	(150)		
		3				
T	11	14	15	22	200	$r_T = 11$ (e)
	(100)	(100)				
			1	20		
Demand	150	100	200	150	600	

$k_F = 0$ $k_N = 3$ $k_P = 3$ $k_Y = -9$
(d) (f) (b) (g)

Determining the Optimal Solution

Cell *SP* in Table 15-10 provides a $1 cost improvement. The smallest quantity in the losing cells is 100 pairs in cell *TP*. Reallocating this amount along the closed-loop path, we obtain the new shipment schedule in Table 15-11, where the cost saving is $1 \times 100 = 100$ and $C = 6,350 - 100 = 6,250$ dollars.

The schedule in Table 15-11 is optimal. No empty cells yield potential cost reductions, so that *further improvements are impossible.*

15-4 DUMMY PLANTS AND WAREHOUSES

We began our ski-distribution example with total demand and total capacity in balance. Ordinarily, distributions are not so perfectly balanced. There is usually excess system capacity or more demand than can possibly be filled. In such cases, the shipment schedule must include an additional plant or warehouse to take up the slack. We refer to these fictional distribution points as *dummy plants or warehouses.*

Consider the following example, involving two plants and three warehouses:

Plant Capacity		Warehouse Demand	
A	500	W	250
B	300	X	400
	800	Y	300
			950

Total demand is for 950 units, which exceeds the total capacity of 800 units by 150 units. The shortage in total capacity is made up by including a dummy plant with a 150-unit capacity. Table 15-12 provides the optimal shipment schedule for this expanded problem. All shipments from the dummy plant have zero cost, since they represent product items that are not being made and not being sent. Notice that 150 units from the dummy plant are allocated to warehouse X. This means that warehouse X is shorted 150 units. In effect, X is the most costly warehouse to service, so it receives less units than its capacity.

Now consider the following example:

Plant Capacity		Warehouse Demand	
A	300	W	200
B	400	X	350
C	200	Y	250
	900		800

TABLE 15-12
The Optimal Shipment Schedule for the Problem
Requiring a Dummy Plant

From \ To	W	X	Y	Capacity
A	(250) [2]	(250) [4]	[6]	500
B	[3]	[3]	(300) [1]	300
Dummy	[0]	(150) [0]	(0) [0]	150
Demand	250	400	300	950

TABLE 15-13

The Optimal Schedule for the Problem Requiring a Dummy Plant

To / From	W	X	Y	Dummy	Capacity
A	13	14	10 (250)	0 (50)	300
B	12	8 (350)	11	0 (50)	400
C	6 (200)	10	13	0	200
Demand	200	350	250	100	900

Here, the total plant capacity of 900 units exceeds the total demand for 800 units by 100 units. The surplus capacity is handled by including a dummy warehouse with a demand equal to the difference of 100. Table 15-13 provides the optimal solution to this problem. We use zero unit shipping costs to the dummy warehouse, reflecting the fact that allocations to those cells represent product items that are not being made and not being sent. We can see that 50 units apiece are allocated to the dummy warehouse from plant A and plant B. These amounts represent the unused surplus capacities of these plants. In terms of distribution costs, plants A and B are less efficient than plant C, which is operating at full capacity.

15-5 NORTHWEST CORNER RULE DIFFICULTIES

The northwest corner rule is used to find a starting solution to the transportation problem. Recall that its allocations progress rightward and downward, always to an adjacent cell, and that diagonal jumps are not allowed. In certain problem situations, the northwest corner rule leads us to a point where no further movement is possible. This difficulty is easily remedied by a slight modification of the rule.

Consider the shipment schedule in Table 15-14. Applying the northwest corner rule, we place 100 units in cell AW. Moving in the direction of surplus capacity, we then allocate 150 units to cell AX. This exhausts the capacity of plant A, and the remaining 50 units of warehouse X demand are filled by plant

TABLE 15-14

An Impass in Getting Started Using the Northwest Corner Rule

From \ To	W	X	Y	Z	Capacity
A	(100)------→(150)				250
B		(50)------→No surplus capacity			50
C		No unfilled demand			150
D					50
E					400
F					100
Demand	100	200	300	400	1,000

B. At this point, an impasse is reached: No further allocation can be made in row *B* or column *X*, and no horizontal or vertical movement is possible. We could bend our rule by moving diagonally to cell *CY* and continuing from there. But by doing this, we would end up with one less nonempty cell than the transportation problem requires.

To avoid that pitfall, we will move to the cell at the right or below anyway. *The direction we choose is arbitrary.* Suppose that we move down to cell *CX* and place a zero shipping quantity there. Cell *CX* will be treated as a nonempty cell, even though no shipment will be scheduled from plant *C* to warehouse *X*. We then proceed as before. Table 15-15 shows the completed shipment schedule. Although this problem has only one, some problems may require two or more circled zeros.

In proceeding to solve the problem, one of three things can happen to cell *CX*: (1) it will not be a turning point on the closed-loop path and continue to have a zero shipping quantity; (2) it will be a gaining cell, receiving an allocation and joining the ranks of the other nonempty cells as a full-fledged member; or (3) it will be a losing cell, so that the zero will move to a presently empty cell location.

The northwest corner rule is concerned only with the positions of cells and ignores cost information. Although this makes it easy to understand and to apply, it usually provides a starting solution that is far from the optimal solution. Later in this chapter, *Vogel's approximation* will be introduced as an alternative starting procedure. Although it is more elaborate, Vogel's approximation makes use of cost data and enables us to find a starting solution that ordinarily is quite close to the optimal one. When large problems are encountered, Vogel's approximation is usually faster and involves less work overall than the northwest corner rule.

TABLE 15-15
A Northwest-Corner Starting Solution Involving a Zero Shipping Allocation

From \ To	W	X	Y	Z	Capacity
A	(100)- - - - - →(150)				250
B		(50)			50
C		(0)- - - - - →(150)			150
D			(50)		50
E			(100)- - - - →(300)		400
F				(100)	100
Demand	100	200	300	400	1,000

15-6 THE ASSIGNMENT PROBLEM

An important managerial decision is personnel assignment. People vary so widely in their skill and competence levels that it is challenging to determine which workers are best suited to perform specific jobs. A classical application of the *assignment problem* is provided by a small machine shop, where individual machinists are assigned to particular machines or jobs. This must be done so that every worker is assigned to exactly one job and every job is assigned to a worker. The assignments must minimize the combined time or cost for completing all of the required jobs.

As we saw in Chapter 10, the linear programming approach is well-suited to machine-shop personnel assignments, because each task is well-defined and the respective productivities (time required per item) of each worker can be accurately measured. Moreover, machine-shop jobs require similar skills, so that workers can easily be shifted to new assignments. The types of personnel situations to which the assignment problem can be applied are limited. As a linear program, the assignment problem is encountered much less frequently than the transportation problem.

A Machine-Shop Assignment Problem

We will expand the machine-shop example described in Chapter 10 to include six individual machinists who are to be assigned to six jobs, each to be performed on a different type of machine. Each of the six tasks is to be

TABLE 15-16
Average Times for Machine-Shop Assignments (in minutes)

Individual \ Job j	Drilling	Grinding	Lathe	Milling	Polishing	Routing
Ann	13	22	19	21	16	20
Bud	18	17	24	18	22	27
Chuck	20	22	23	24	17	31
Eduardo	14	19	13	30	23	22
Sam	21	14	17	25	15	23
Tom	17	23	18	20	16	24

TABLE 15-17
Machine-Shop Assignment Schedule

Individual i \ Job j	D	G	L	M	P	R	Availability
A	X_{AD} [13]	X_{AG} [22]	X_{AL} [19]	X_{AM} [21]	X_{AP} [16]	X_{AR} [20]	1
B	X_{BD} [18]	X_{BG} [17]	X_{BL} [24]	X_{BM} [18]	X_{BP} [22]	X_{BR} [27]	1
C	X_{CD} [20]	X_{CG} [22]	X_{CL} [23]	X_{CM} [24]	X_{CP} [17]	X_{CR} [31]	1
E	X_{ED} [14]	X_{EG} [19]	X_{EL} [13]	X_{EM} [30]	X_{EP} [23]	X_{ER} [22]	1
S	X_{SD} [21]	X_{SG} [14]	X_{SL} [17]	X_{SM} [25]	X_{SP} [15]	X_{SR} [23]	1
T	X_{TD} [17]	X_{TG} [23]	X_{TL} [18]	X_{TM} [20]	X_{TP} [16]	X_{TR} [24]	1
Requirement	1	1	1	1	1	1	6

completed successively on aluminum castings that will be shaped into a final product. Past records provide individual performance data for all six workers. Table 15-16 summarizes the average times (in minutes) that each worker takes to complete each job for one item.

Our objective is to assign the individuals to jobs in such a way that the total average labor time per item is minimized. The assignments are summarized in the assignment schedule in Table 15-17. The unknown cell quantities are represented by the variables

$$X_{ij} = \text{fraction of time individual } i \text{ is assigned to job } j$$

The marginal row and column totals are 1. Thus, every person must be fully occupied (so that the row Xs sum to 1) and every job must be completely assigned (so that the column Xs sum to 1). The average completion times for individual–job combinations serve the same function as the unit shipping costs in a transportation problem.

15-7   THE VOGEL'S APPROXIMATION STARTING PROCEDURE

Our present example illustrates another starting procedure for transportation-type problems. Although it would work here, the northwest corner rule is considerably slower than another starting procedure—*Vogel's approximation.*

Vogel's approximation is based on the difference between the two lowest costs in each row and column. The greatest difference is found first (ties are broken arbitrarily), and the cheapest cell in that row or column is assigned the maximum possible quantity. This procedure is repeated for the remaining rows and columns until a complete feasible solution is found.

Table 15-18 represents the initial stage of Vogel's approximation as it applies to our machine-shop assignment problem. The lowest costs in row A are 13 and 16, yielding a difference of $16 - 13 = 3$. The differences in the other rows and columns also appear in the table. The greatest difference is $17 - 13 = 4$, which occurs in column L. The first quantity is therefore assigned to column L by placing a ① in cell EL, which is the lowest cost cell in that column.

Table 15-19 illustrates the second stage of the procedure. Because the maximum possible quantity has been assigned to column L and row E, they have both been eliminated. It is convenient to label the results of each stage of the procedure with a Roman numeral. The row and column differences calculated earlier no longer apply and are also crossed out. New differences are now computed using only the cells that remain. In stage II, the greatest difference

TABLE 15-18

The Machine-Shop Assignment Schedule Showing the Initial Stage of Vogel's Approximation

Job j / Individual i	D	G	L	M	P	R	Availability	Row Differences Between Lowest c_{ij}s
A	13	22	19	21	16	20	1	16 − 13 = 3
B	18	17	24	18	22	27	1	18 − 17 = 1
C	20	22	23	24	17	31	1	20 − 17 = 3
E	14	19	13 ①	30	23	22	1	14 − 13 = 1
S	21	14	17	25	15	23	1	15 − 14 = 1
T	17	23	18	20	16	24	1	17 − 16 = 1
Requirement	1	1	1	1	1	1	6	
Column Differences Between Lowest c_{ij}s	= 1 14 − 13	= 3 17 − 14	= 4* 17 − 13	= 2 20 − 18	= 1 16 − 15	= 2 22 − 20		①

of 4 appears in column D. The cheapest cell in column D is cell AD, which receives an allocation of ①.

Stage III of Vogel's approximation is shown in Table 15-20. There, the greatest difference occurs in row C, where the cheapest cell is cell CP. The maximum allocation into this cell is ①.

Table 15-21 presents the remaining stages of the approximation. Allocations of ① are made successively into cells SG (in stage IV) and BM (in stage V). The final assignment is a ① in the only available cell, TR. The total average

TABLE 15-19

The Second Stage of Vogel's Approximation in the Machine-Stop Assignment Problem

i \ Job j / Indi-vidual	D	G	L	M	P	R	Avail-ability	Row Differences Between Lowest c_{ij}s
A	13 ①	22	19	21	16	20	1	3 $16 - 13$ $= 3$
B	18	17	24	18	22	27	1	1 $18 - 17$ $= 1$
C	20	22	23	24	17	31	1	3 $20 - 17$ $= 3$
E	14	19	13 ①	30	23	22	1	1
S	21	14	17	25	15	23	1	1 $15 - 14$ $= 1$
T	17	23	18	20	16	24	1	1 $17 - 16$ $= 1$
Require-ment	1	1	1	1	1	1	6	
Column Differences Between Lowest c_{ij}s	1 $= 4*$ $17 - 13$	3 $= 3$ $17 - 14$	4	2 $= 2$ $20 - 18$	1 $= 1$ $16 - 15$	2 $= 3$ $23 - 20$	(I)	(II)

TABLE 15-20

The Third Stage of Vogel's Approximation in the Machine-Shop Assignment Problem

i \ j Individual	D	G	L	M	P	R	Availability	Row Differences Between Lowest c_{ij}s
A	①13	22	19	21	16	20	1	3 3
B	18	17	24	18	22	27	1	1 1 $18 - 17 = 1$
C	20	22	23	24	①17	31	1	3 3 $22 - 17 = 5*$
E	14	19	①13	30	23	22	1	1
S	21	14	17	25	15	23	1	1 1 $15 - 14 = 1$
T	17	23	18	20	16	24	1	1 1 $20 - 16 = 4$
Requirement	1	1	1	1	1	1	6	
Column Differences	1	3	4	2	1	2		(I)
Between	4	3		2	1	3		(II)
Lowest c_{ij}s		$=3$		$=2$	$=1$	$=1$		(III)
		$17 - 14$		$20 - 18$	$16 - 15$	$24 - 23$		

TABLE 15-21

The Remaining Stages of Vogel's Approximation in the Machine-Shop Assignment Problem

i \ Job j — Individual	D	G	L	M	P	R	Availability	Row Differences Between Lowest c_{ij}s
A	13 ①	22	19	21	16	20	1	3 3
B	18	17	24	18 ①	22	27	1	1 1 1 1 9*
C	20	22	23	24	17 ①	31	1	3 3 5
E	14	19	13 ①	30	23	22	1	1
S	21	14 ①	17	25	15	23	1	1 1 1 9*
T	17	23	18	20	16	24 ①	1	1 1 4 7 4
Requirement	1	1	1	1	1	1	6	

Column Differences Between Lowest c_{ij}s

	D	G	L	M	P	R	
	1	3	4	2	1	2	(I)
	4	3		2	1	3	(II)
		3		2	1	1	(III)
		3		2	1	1	(IV)
				2		3	(V)

time for this solution is

$$13 + 13 + 17 + 14 + 18 + 24 = 99 \text{ minutes}$$

We do not know whether or not this solution is optimal. We must now apply the basic transportation method to determine if any improvements can be made.

Note that when Vogel's approximation method is applied to transportation problems, the maximum possible quantity assignment is made to the cheapest cell in the pertinent row or column. This often results in crossing out a *single* row *or* column, instead of both the row and the column (as shown here). This is usually due to the fact that some surplus capacity remains in the affected row or some unfilled demand remains in the affected column. It is necessary to recompute row differences only after a column is crossed out, and new column differences are required only after a row is crossed out. At the end of the procedure, a single cell often remains. This cell naturally receives the final quantity allocation.

Positioning Circled Zeroes

The assignment schedule in Table 15-21 does not contain enough non-empty cells. Unlike the northwest corner rule, Vogel's approximation does not guarantee that exactly the required number of nonempty cells will be obtained. To apply the transportation method to our 6×6 machine-shop assignment problem, we require exactly $6 + 6 - 1 = 11$ nonempty cells. Five circled zeroes must therefore be included in the assignment schedule. Where do we put them?

It is easiest to position the circled zeroes as we determine the row and column numbers. This procedure is illustrated in Table 15-22. We start with $r_A = 0$. From this and nonempty cell AD, we obtain $k_D = 13$. The only circled 1 in column D is in cell AD, so a circled zero must be placed in the cheapest cell in column D. This is cell ED, which is then used to find $r_E = 1$. Using this value and cell EL, we obtain $k_L = 12$. As before, column L requires a circled zero so that we can determine the next row number. The cheapest cell without a row number is cell SL, and we place the next circled zero there. We then find $r_S = 5$ and $k_G = 9$. The cheapest cell in column G that requires a row number is cell BG, where we place the next circled zero. We then find $r_B = 8$ and $k_M = 10$. The cheapest cell in column M without a row number is TM, so a circled zero is placed there. We then find $r_T = 10$ and $k_R = 14$. Column R requires a circled zero in cell CR. The values $r_C = 17$ and $k_P = 0$ are then obtained. This gives us circled zeroes in cells ED, SL, BG, TM, and CR. Numerous other

TABLE 15-22

Finding Row and Column Numbers and Positioning Circled Zeroes in Using the Transportation Method to Solve the Machine-Shop Assignment Problem

Individual i \ Job j	D	G	L	M	P	R	Availability	
A	13 ①	22	19	21	16	20	1	$r_A = 0$ ⓐ
B	18	17 ⓪	24	18 ①	22	27	1	$r_B = 8$ ⓖ
C	20	22	23	24	17 ①	31 ⓪	1	$r_C = 17$ ⓚ
E	14 ⓪	19	13 ①	30	23	22	1	$r_E = 1$ ⓒ
S	21	14 ①	17 ⓪	25	15	23	1	$r_S = 5$ ⓔ
T	17	23	18	20 ⓪	16	24 ①	1	$r_T = 10$ ⓘ
Requirement	1	1	1	1	1	1	6	
	$k_D = 13$ ⓑ	$k_G = 9$ ⓕ	$k_L = 12$ ⓓ	$k_M = 10$ ⓗ	$k_P = 0$ ⓘ	$k_R = 14$ ⓙ		

combinations of circled zeroes are possible, but we need only one set to proceed with the transportation method.

15-8 SOLVING THE ASSIGNMENT PROBLEM USING THE TRANSPORTATION METHOD

The machine-shop assignment problem can now be solved using the transportation method. Table 15-23 illustrates the first iteration. The row and column numbers we found in Table 15-22 have been used to compute the

TABLE 15-23

**The First Iteration of the Transportation Method
in Solving Machine-Shop Assignment Problem**

Job j / Indi-vidual i	D	G	L	M	P	R	Availability	
A	13 ① 13	22 7	19 11	21 16	16 6	20	1	$r_A = 0$
B	18 −3	17 ⓪ (−) 4	24	18 ① (+) 14	22 5	27	1	$r_B = 8$
C	20 (+) −10	22 −4	23 −6	24 −3	17 ①	31 ⓪ (−)	1	$r_C = 17$
E	14 ⓪ (−) 9	19	13 ① (+)	30 19	23 22	22 7	1	$r_E = 1$
S	21 3	14 ① (+)	17 ⓪ (−)	25 10	15 10	23 4	1	$r_S = 5$
T	17 −6	23 4	18 −4	20 ⓪ (−) 6	16 6	24 ① (+)	1	$r_T = 10$
Requirement	1	1	1	1	1	1	6	

$$k_D = 13 \quad k_G = 9 \quad k_L = 12 \quad k_M = 10 \quad k_P = 0 \quad k_R = 14$$

empty cell differences. Cell CD is the entering cell, which has an improvement value of -10. The closed-loop path turns out to be a double figure-8. Notice that the losing cells all contain circled zeroes. The maximum quantity to be reallocated along the closed-loop path is zero, and exactly one of the losing cells will go blank in the next solution. We break the tie by choosing the most expensive losing cell, and the circled zero from cell CR moves to cell CD. The total time savings is $10 \times 0 = 0$.

After several more interations that involve only the movement of circled zeroes, we can establish that the present assignment of workers to jobs is in fact optimal. Actually, there is a tie for the optimal solution. Either of the following assignments will minimize total average time:

	OPTIMUM		ALTERNATIVE OPTIMUM	
Worker	Job	Time	Job	Time
Ann	Drilling	13 min	Routing	20 min
Bud	Milling	18	Milling	18
Chuck	Polishing	17	Polishing	17
Eduardo	Lathe	13	Lathe	13
Sam	Grinding	14	Grinding	14
Tom	Routing	24	Drilling	17
		99 min		99 min

And any solution in which Ann and Tom split the drilling and routing jobs—say, spending one-half of their time on each job—would also be optimal.

15-9 OTHER APPLICATIONS OF THE TRANSPORTATION PROBLEM

The scope of the transportation problem can be expanded to consider production costs as well as freight charges. For example, suppose that the three plants in the ski-distribution illustration all operated at different unit costs—say, $60 for Juarez, $50 for Seoul, and $65 for Tel Aviv. Cost differentials are just as important in choosing which plants will service which warehouses as the physical distances separating the production and consumption centers. By adding 60 to row J costs, 50 to row S costs, and 65 to row T costs, the ski-distribution transportation problem can be solved so that all distribution costs—instead of just the freight costs—can be optimized. Indeed, any formulation that does not reflect all cost differentials between plants is undesirable and generally leads to an inferior solution. (This revised problem will be left as an exercise.)

The transportation problem is so-named because it was originally used to determine shipment schedules in distribution systems. However, its basic source–destination structure makes it suitable for solving many other types of problems that do not involve the physical distribution of items. For example, this format can be used to establish a plant's production schedule for several time periods.

As an illustration, we will suppose that the Juarez ski plant can actually operate at as much as 150% of its stated capacity during the August–November period by placing its work force on overtime. We will also assume that the company policy is to use this plant exclusively to service the Phoenix warehouse. Moreover, we will assume that Juarez can make up to 100 pairs of skis monthly at a cost of $60 per pair using regular labor; for an additional $20 per pair, Juarez can make 50 additional pairs of skis per month using overtime

TABLE 15-24

The Optimal Ski-Production Schedule

From Month \ To Month	A	S	O	N	Dummy	Capacity
AR	60 (100)	61 (0)	62	63	0	100
AO	80	81 (50)	82	83	0 (0)	50
SR	M	60 (100)	61 (0)	62	0	100
SO	M	80	81 (50)	82	0	50
OR	M	M	60 (100)	61	0	100
OO	M	M	80 (50)	81	0	50
NR	M	M	M	60 (100)	0	100
NO	M	M	M	80 (0)	0 (50)	50
Demand	100	150	200	100	50	600

labor. Finally, we will assume that the factory can store extra skis for later distribution at a cost of $1 per pair per month.

Now suppose that the following demands occur at the Phoenix warehouse:

August	100 pairs
September	150
October	200
November	100
	550 pairs

Table 15-24 provides the optimal ski-production schedule. There are eight "plants," each representing the month and type of production (R = regular, O = overtime). There are four "warehouses"—one for each monthly demand, plus one dummy warehouse (since total capacity exceeds total demand).

In constructing Table 15-24, we have omitted the unit freight charge, since it is the same for all cells. Notice that it is impossible to satisfy an earlier demand from later production. For the sake of completeness, however, the cells representing these situations appear in the table. Such allocations receive a very large unit cost of M dollars. Any starting solution that involved such a cell would exit early. Also notice that each cell in the dummy column has a unit cost of zero.

The transportation problem is also applicable when the objective is to maximize profit. The simplest procedure would be to use the *negative* per-unit profits in place of costs. The same steps would then be followed, and no rules would change.

15-10   ADVANTAGES OF THE TRANSPORTATION METHOD

Earlier in this chapter, we indicated that a transportation problem could be solved using the simplex method described in Chapters 11 and 12. But the special structure of the transportation problem allows us to use a more limited algorithm that is tailor-made for it. At this point, you have worked with simplex enough to know what is required. Each iteration involves time-consuming computations, and one mistake can ruin everything! To really appreciate the transportation method, you have to work a few problems to see just how much easier and faster it is to use than simplex.

One main advantage of the transportation problem is that it involves only the main variables. Artificial variables are not required, as they are in simplex. After applying the northwest corner rule or Vogel's approximation, we are at least as far as we would be after eliminating the artificial variables in simplex—and the simplex procedure would require a minimum of iterations (tableaus) equal to the number of rows plus columns minus 1.

Although both procedures involve iterations, it is much easier to obtain a new table using the transportation method than it is to construct a new simplex tableau. The r and k values can be found by simple arithmetic, and the empty-cell differences can be computed as fast as they can be written down. The pivot step is also much easier in the transportation problem; finding the closed-loop path takes longer. The most time-consuming step is copying a blank shipment schedule for each iteration—and even that time can be minimized by using a copier or carbon paper.

A final advantage of the transportation method is that it is not nearly as error-prone as simplex. A quick tally will indicate whether or not the shipment quantities sum to the respective row and column totals. A mistake in calculating the r and k values will only slow the process down. Such mistakes are not "fatal" errors, as they are in simplex.

ADDITIONAL REMARKS **15-11**

We have indicated that the transportation method is more efficient than the general-purpose simplex algorithm. The transportation method illustrated in this chapter is actually a variant form of simplex and is based on exactly the same concepts. The row and column numbers are really analogous to the dual variable values, and the $c_{ij} - r_i - k_j$ differences represent the values in the per-unit improvement row of the simplex tableau that would apply if the transportation problem had been solved that way instead.

Some problem situations are so specially structured that a refinement of the transportation method itself provides an even more efficient solution procedure. Special-purpose linear programming algorithms have been developed to solve assignment problems. One popular approach is the *Hungarian method*,* which is more streamlined than the more general transportation method. The assignment problem may also be treated as an *integer program* (to be described in Chapter 16) and solved using a procedure such as the *branch-and-bound method*. Another group of algorithms, based on the concepts of flows through networks, are often used in place of the transportation method

---

* This method requires much trial and error, which may actually make it harder to apply to large problems.

to solve similar problems. Further discussion of these and other linear programming algorithms is beyond the scope of this book. Many of the references at
the back of the book examine these procedures in detail.

PROBLEMS

15-1   A distribution system must meet the following requirements:

Plant Capacity		Warehouse Demand	
A	100	U	150
B	150	V	200
C	300	W	200

Unit shipping costs are

From \ To	U	V	W
A	$10	$7	$8
B	15	12	9
C	7	8	12

(a) Formulate this transportation problem as a linear program.
(b) Determine the optimal solution using the transportation method.

15-2   *Problem 15-1 continued.* Suppose that a new plant D is opened that has a capacity
of 200. It costs $8 per unit for this plant to service each warehouse. Use the trans-
portation method to determine the shipment schedule that minimizes total transportation cost.

15-3   *Problem 15-1 continued.* Suppose that a new warehouse X is opened that has a
demand of 100. It costs $15 to ship each unit to this warehouse, regardless of the
origin. Use the transportation method to determine the minimum-cost shipment
schedule.

15-4   Apply Vogel's approximation to find the starting solution to the ski manufacturer's
transportation problem having the structure given in Table 15-3.

15-5   Use the transportation method to determine the optimal tombstone shipment
schedule for Druid's Drayage in Problem 10-8 (page 244).

15-6   An alternative (tying) optimal solution exists for a transportation problem whenever
an empty cell in the final schedule has an improvement value of zero. Beginning
with your final table from Problem 15-5, find the alternative optimal solution for
shipping tombstones.

15-7   Consider the following intermediate table for a transportation problem.

From \ To	J	K	L	M	N	O	P	Capacity
A	2		8	8	5 (100)	6 (100)	7	200
B	21	15	14	24	7	14 (100)	9	100
C	10	8 (200)	8	14 (100)	10	9	9	300
D	10	11	11 (200)	10	14	16	10	200
E	3	3 (200)	2	8	1	4 (100)	5	3(
F	9 (200)	11	12	8 (200)	9	8	7	400
G	12	11 (200)	10	11	13	10	11 (100)	300
H	10	8	12	17	10 (200)	12	10 (100)	300
Demand	200	400	400	300	300	300	200	2,100

Determine the row and column numbers. Then find the closed-loop path. (Remember, the closed-loop path is defined only by the turning points.) *Do not solve the problem further.* Indicate the new solution by crossing out the numbers that have changed and by adding the new shipment quantities to the revised cells.

15-8 Use the transportation method to determine the optimal production and shipment schedule for Ace Widgets in Problem 10-14 (page 246).

15-9 Use the transportation method to solve CompuQuick's assignment decision in Problem 10-3 (page 242).

15-10 Use the transportation method to solve Conformity Systems' assignment decision in Problem 10-10 (page 245).

15-11 Hans and Fritz, and their cousins Gert and Zelda, wish to divide their chores to minimize total combined working time and to maximize their playing time. Each is faster at certain daily chores. The following times apply:

	Chase Hippos	Pen Ostriches	Retrieve the Captain's Pipe	Scare Cannibals
Fritz	15 min	30 min	10 min	15 min
Hans	10	20	15	10
Gert	20	15	15	20
Zelda	10	20	10	15

Each brat must do one chore, and all chores must be done. Solve this assignment problem using the transportation method.

15-12 A freight dispatcher must supply five stores with daily shipments from two warehouses. The following unit cost and quantity requirements apply:

To store From warehouse	J	K	L	M	N	Warehouse loading capacity
A	$5	$8	$6	$4	$13	1,000
B	6	9	4	5	6	500
Store requirement	400	300	200	300	300	1,500

In addition, store N is so far from warehouse A that it is possible to send only one truckload per day from A to N. Up to 100 units can be carried in one trip.

(a) Construct the shipment schedule for this problem and find the northwest corner solution. (*Hints*: The special constraint may be handled with an extra source and a dummy destination. Certain cell allocations are impossible and must therefore be assigned very high costs.)

(b) Continue to solve the problem until you find the optimal shipment schedule.

15-13 Suppose that the following demands apply instead for providing skis from the Juarez plant to the Phoenix warehouse in the problem discussed in Section 15-9:

August	25 pairs
September	175
October	150
November	150

Also suppose that now the regular production cost is $50 per pair, the overtime premium is $25 per pair, and the storage cost is $5 per pair. Solve this problem using the transportation method to determine the optimal plan for ski production at the Juarez plant.

15-14 Love and Peace Leather Works creates products from exotic skins obtained by the owner on hunting trips. After each hunt, the skins are cut into strips to make purse straps, belts, plant hangers, and hat bands. These items are sold to The Skin Boutique at an agreed price. On the latest trip, our hunter has obtained the following numbers of strips: 30 rattlesnakes, 100 crocodiles, 50 armadillos, and 20 Gila monsters. Each strip is of equal size, and any one type of skin can be used for each final product. The Skin Boutique will buy up to 50 purse straps, 100 belts, 50 plant hangers, and 100 hat bands—regardless of the material used to make them. The prices yield the following profits to Love and Peace:

| Skin | PRODUCT | | | |
	Purse Strap	Belt	Plant Hanger	Hat Band
Rattlesnake	$ 5	$12	$ 5	$10
Crocodile	10	15	5	10
Armadillo	8	10	10	5
Gila monster	10	20	20	15

Solve this problem using the transportation method to determine how Love and Peace can maximize its profits.

15-15 The transportation method can be used to make cash-management decisions. Suppose that a company in a highly seasonal business has the following cash flows:

Month	Cash Receipts	Cash Expenditures	Accounts Payable
January	$10,000	$ 5,000	$ 5,000
February	15,000	10,000	5,000
March	35,000	20,000	5,000
April	10,000	10,000	10,000
	$70,000	$45,000	$25,000

Accounts are payable under terms of "2% (10 days) net, 30 days." This means that there will be a 2% savings on accounts that are paid in the month they are due and that there will be no savings on accounts that are paid in the next month. Bank loans are available at the rate of 1% simple interest per month. Cash held from one month to a later month will be invested in certificates of deposit at the same interest rate. Thus, each cash dollar invested and later converted will cost −$.01 for each month it is held; if it is used to pay a current payable instead, its cost will be −$.02. There is no cost for using current cash receipts to fill current cash expenditures. The cost of borrowing $1 is $.01 for each month it is held, including the current month. Accounts payable must be paid no later than one month after they are due. The funds for these accounts may be derived from cash or loans obtained in the current or earlier months, in which case the 2% savings applies. Or the accounts payable can be met from funds received or borrowed in the next month (but no later), with no savings resulting from the discount. Cash requirements cannot be met with funds obtained in later months. The company has a $20,000 line of credit for each month. Assume that cash will be managed at minimum cost over the four months.

(a) Treating cash receipts and loans taken in any given month as separate sources and the monthly cash expenditures and accounts payable as destinations, set up a schedule suitable for solving this problem using the transportation method.

(b) Solve the problem to determine the optimal cash-management plan.

16

Integer Programming and the Branch-and-Bound Method

Integer programming is an extension of linear programming, with the additional restriction that the variables must be integers or whole numbers. In this chapter, we will investigate integer programs and focus on one solution technique that has been successfully used to solve them—the *branch-and-bound method*.

AN INTRODUCTION TO INTEGER PROGRAMMING 16-1

We have seen that linear programs permit fractional solutions, which is satisfactory for most applications. In manufacturing, the completion of one-half or one-third of a unit might merely signify that the production period is ending with unfinished goods or some work-in-progress inventory. Even at the end of a production run, when no unfinished goods are held over, one-third of an item may be inconsequential when quantities are in the hundreds or thousands.

But there is a significant class of situations for which the solution values must be whole numbers or *integers*. For example, an airline might use a linear program to determine what aircraft to buy. A linear programming solution involving $5\frac{2}{3}$ Boeing-747's and $9\frac{3}{8}$ DC-10's would not be very meaningful.

Furthermore, a rounded solution—with respective values of 6 and 9, in this case— might not even be feasible or might cost millions of dollars more than the truly optimal solution. Problems that might otherwise be solved by employing linear programming, except that there are integer restrictions on the variables involved, fall into the category of *integer programs.*

Difficulties in Solving Integer Programs

To the uninitiated, integer programs may appear to be easier to solve than linear programs. After all, linear programs usually have an infinite number of feasible solutions, and most integer programs should have a finite number of integer solutions. This is true. But procedures for solving linear programs such as simplex allow us to find the optimal solution by evaluating only a few corner points. We never have to enter the interior.

Simplex locates the treasure lying on one of the few mountain peaks on the edge of unexplored territory. Integer programming can require an extensive search of all corner and interior points. Even small integer programs with a handful of constraints and variables may have billions of feasible solutions. And no known procedure even approaches simplex in keeping the number of evaluations to a minimum. We must trudge through the rain forest until we trip over the prize.

Several algorithms can be used in solving integer programs. The most promising are the branch-and-bound techniques described in this chapter. New research is currently under way to find more effective ways to evaluate integer programs.

Graphical Solutions

As an example, consider the following integer program:

$$\text{Maximize} \quad P = 14X_1 + 16X_2$$

$$\text{Subject to} \quad 4X_1 + 3X_2 \leq 12 \quad (A)$$

$$6X_1 + 8X_2 \leq 24 \quad (B)$$

where X_1 and X_2 are non-negative integers

In place of the requirement that all Xs ≥ 0, we specify that X_1 and X_2 must be non-negative integers.

It is convenient to begin by treating the problem as a linear program, which is solved graphically in Figure 16-1. If this solution involves only integer

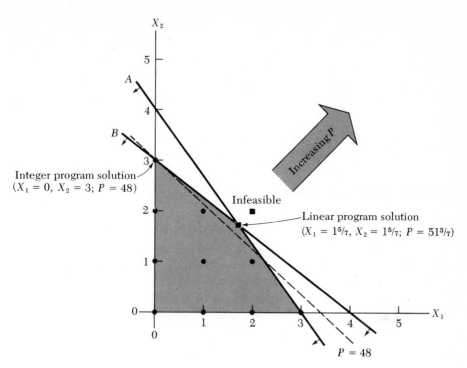

FIGURE 16-1

**Graphical solutions to a problem formulated as a linear program
and as an integer program.**

values, then it will be the solution to the integer program as well. But we obtain

$$X_1 = 1\tfrac{5}{7} \qquad X_2 = 1\tfrac{5}{7}$$
$$P = 51\tfrac{3}{7}$$

which does not meet the integer specifications. It is tempting to round this
solution off to ($X_1 = 2$, $X_2 = 2$), but our graph indicates that this is infeasible.
The dots in Figure 16-1, which are sometimes referred to as *lattice points*,
represent all of the integer solutions that lie within the feasible solution region
of the linear program. The optimal integer solution is

$$X_1 = 0 \qquad X_2 = 3$$
$$P = 48$$

Notice that its lattice point is not even adjacent to the most attractive linear programming corner.

Enumeration and Cutting-Plane Solutions

How do we solve integer programs? The most difficult approach would be to evaluate every lattice point to determine its P value and whether or not it is feasible. But even for a modest problem with only a few variables, this task could take years!

Figure 16-1 suggests that there is another way. First we can find a solution to the problem when it is formulated as a linear program (which, with luck, could contain integers). Notice that the optimal lattice point lies at the corner of the region obtained by cutting away the small triangle above the dashed line. This suggests a solution procedure that successively cuts down the feasible solution region until an integer-valued corner is found.

Cutting-plane methods, which are not limited to situations involving two variables, do just that. Each successive linear program is solved by simplex, and the feasible solution region for each linear program is smaller than its precursor. Eventually, one of the linear programs yields an all-integer solution.

Unfortunately, each cut can turn out to be a small whittling off a big log. Since even integer programs of modest size can involve thousands of iterations, the cutting-plane method could take even longer than complete enumeration. A more promising procedure called the *branch-and-bound method* will be described in the next section.

16-2 THE BRANCH-AND-BOUND METHOD

Branch-and-bound methods can be used to solve a variety of integer programs. All of these techniques are essentially enumerative in nature, but many obvious blind alleys are eliminated early in the search for the optimal solution. The number of necessary evaluations is usually (but not always) quite small relative to the size of the solution space.

This efficient search for the all-integer solution is accomplished by successively dividing the solution space into smaller *subsets*, each representing a class of solutions. These divisions are called *branching points*. Every new subset is eventually evaluated to determine whether it should be investigated further or discarded.

An evaluation is achieved by comparing objective function values to bounds. In cost-minimization problems, a *lower bound* is found for the objective values, or Cs, of the subset's feasible solutions. If this value is $\geq$ an *upper bound* on the optimal C, then the entire subset has been *fathomed* and can be eliminated from further consideration. The procedure is designed so that the upper bound can be revised after each evaluation. The gap between bounds becomes narrower as new and better solutions are found, and the later subsets involve fewer possibilities. Eventually, the optimal solution is uncovered.

Summary of the Branch-and-Bound Method

Every branch-and-bound *cost-minimization* problem involves the following steps:

(1) Initial Step: Identify the solution space, treating it as the first subset, and establish an upper bound of ∞ for the optimal C value.

(2) Branch Step: Apply an appropriate rule to select one of the remaining subsets, and partition it into two or more new solution subsets. (In cost-minimization problems, the usual rule is to partition the subset having the smallest lower bound.)

(3) Bound Step: For each new subset, determine the lower bound on the C values of the subset's feasible solutions.

(4) Fathoming Step: Determine if the best feasible integer solutions in any subsets have been uncovered and exclude them from further branching. If any of these subsets have a C value smaller than the current upper bound, revise the upper bound to equal the smallest value. The corresponding solution is the *best-solution-so-far*. Exclude from further consideration any subset that contains no feasible solution or that has a lower bound $\geq$ the upper bound on the optimal C. Return to the branch step until no unfathomed subsets remain. Then stop the procedure. The best-solution-so-far is the optimal solution.

The steps of the branch-and-bound method are slightly modified in *profit-maximization* problems. *Upper* bounds on the P values are found for each subset. When fathoming, these upper bounds are compared to a *lower* bound on the optimal P (zero may be used as a starting value). Subsets with upper bounds $\leq$ the lower bound are eliminated. The best-solution-so-far has the greatest P value of all of the evaluations yet made, and the current lower bound is equal to that value. Branching usually occurs in the unfathomed subset with the greatest upper bound.

16-3 SOLVING THE ASSIGNMENT PROBLEM USING INTEGER PROGRAMMING

We will illustrate the branch-and-bound method by applying it to the assignment problem, which we discussed as a linear program in earlier chapters. Here, each person i is to be assigned to exactly one job j. The integer programming formulation is

Minimize $\quad C = \sum_i \sum_j c_{ij} X_{ij}$

Subject to $\qquad \sum_j X_{ij} = 1 \quad$ for all $i \quad$ (personnel availabilities)

$\qquad\qquad \sum_i X_{ij} = 1 \quad$ for all $j \quad$ (job requirements)

where $\qquad\qquad X_{ij} = \begin{cases} 1 & \text{if person } i \text{ is assigned to job } j \\ 0 & \text{otherwise} \end{cases}$

We will use the branch-and-bound method to re-solve the machine-shop problem we discussed in Chapter 15. Recall that Ann, Bud, Chuck, Eduardo, Sam, and Tom must each be assigned to one of the following jobs: drilling, grinding, lathe, milling, polishing, or routing. The objective is to minimize the total average process time per completed item. Table 16-1 provides the average time c_{ij} (in minutes) that each worker takes to complete each job for one item.

We begin by finding the bounds within which the optimal objective must fall. The total cost (time) can be no smaller than the sum of the smallest cs in each column. Thus

$$\text{Lower bound} = 13 + 14 + 13 + 18 + 15 + 20 = 93$$

In setting bounds, we are not concerned with the feasibility of the corresponding assignments. (In this lower bound, both Ann and Sam are assigned two jobs,

TABLE 16-1
Average Times for Machine-Shop Assignments (in minutes)

Indi-^{i} vidual $\quad$ Job ^{j}	Drilling	Grinding	Lathe	Milling	Polishing	Routing
Ann	13	22	19	21	16	20
Bud	18	17	24	18	22	27
Chuck	20	22	23	24	17	31
Eduardo	14	19	13	30	23	22
Sam	21	14	17	25	15	23
Tom	17	23	18	20	16	24

while Chuck and Tom have none, so that 93 is not a feasible total.) The upper bound on C is not as easy to find, so we arbitrarily set it at any large value, such as infinity:

$$\text{Upper bound} = \infty$$

We begin to partition the solution space by separately considering each worker assigned to the first job (drilling). Each of these assignments is represented by a branch in the tree diagram in Figure 16-2. Each initial assignment defines a separate subset of the solution space.

For instance, the top branch represents all of the solutions for which Ann does the drilling. The cost of this AD assignment is 13 minutes. The 95 in the terminal node represents the lower bound placed on C by all the complete assignments (feasible and infeasible) involving $X_{AD} = 1$. To find this bound, we cross out row A and column D in Table 16-1 and add the minimum cs in the remainder of the columns to 13, so that

$$13 + 14 + 13 + 18 + 15 + 22 = 95$$

(This total is not feasible, since both 14 and 15 were obtained from row S.)

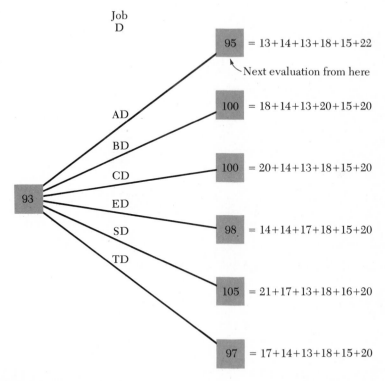

FIGURE 16-2
First branch-and-bound evaluation of the machine-shop assignment problem.

Similar lower bounds are obtained for the other five worker–drilling assignments and entered in the respective nodes of the tree. No feasible solutions are uncovered in any of the respective subsets. The upper bound on the optimal C remains at ∞, and no subsets can yet be fathomed.

We are ready for another evaluation. Since the AD assignment has the smallest lower bound, this subset is partitioned by branching out from AD. The tree for the second evaluation is shown in Figure 16-3. The SG assignment provides the lowest bound of 96, which is found by adding 13 minutes for AD and 14 minutes for SG and the column minimums in Table 16-1 that remain

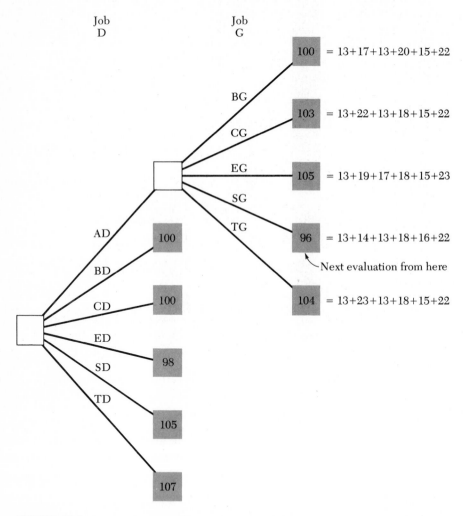

FIGURE 16-3
Second branch-and-bound evaluation of the machine-shop assignment problem.

after rows A and S and columns D and G are crossed out, or

$$13 + 14 + 13 + 18 + 16 + 22 = 96$$

Again, no new feasible solutions are uncovered (some rows in the assignment matrix are represented twice in each of the summations in Figure 16-3). The upper limit on the optimal objective value remains at $C = \infty$, and all of the remaining subsets are unfathomed.

Our third evaluation begins from the node with the smallest lower bound of 96, and we branch out from the subset of the AD and SG assignments (with $X_{AD} = 1$ and $X_{SG} = 1$). This is summarized in Figure 16-4. For the first time, the branch-and-bound method leads to feasible solutions: The CL assignment

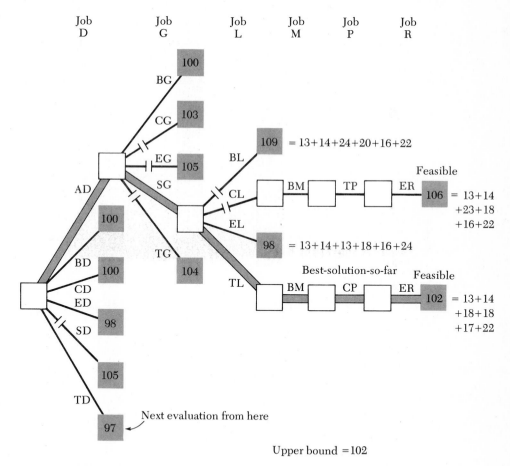

FIGURE 16-4
Third branch-and-bound evaluation of the machine-shop assignment problem.

yields a total cost of 106, and the *TL* assignment yields a total cost of 102. The latter is the value of the best-solution-so-far, and we have a new upper bound of 102 minutes for the optimal *C* value.

We can now eliminate some subsets. Any subset with a lower bound ≥ 102 obviously cannot contain the optimal solution, so we prune these from the tree in Figure 16-4. This eliminates the feasible solution with a total time of *C* = 106.

The next evaluation involves subsets branching from the node corresponding to the unfathomed subset with the smallest lower bound of 97. This evaluation is shown in Figure 16-5, where the previously pruned branches no longer appear. A new feasible solution with a total cost of 105 is uncovered, but its cost exceeds the upper bound of 102 and it must be pruned. The best-solution-so-far and the upper bound do not change. The branches leading to

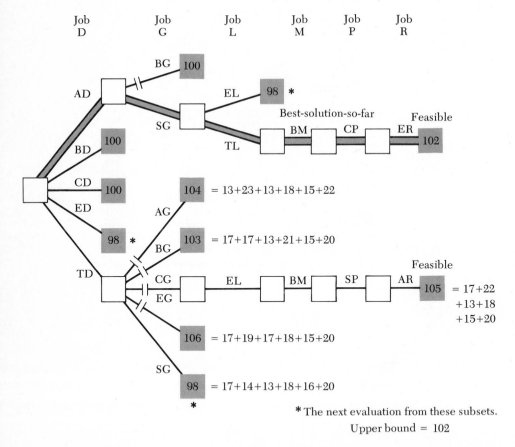

FIGURE 16-5
Fourth branch-and-bound evaluation of the machine-shop assignment problem.

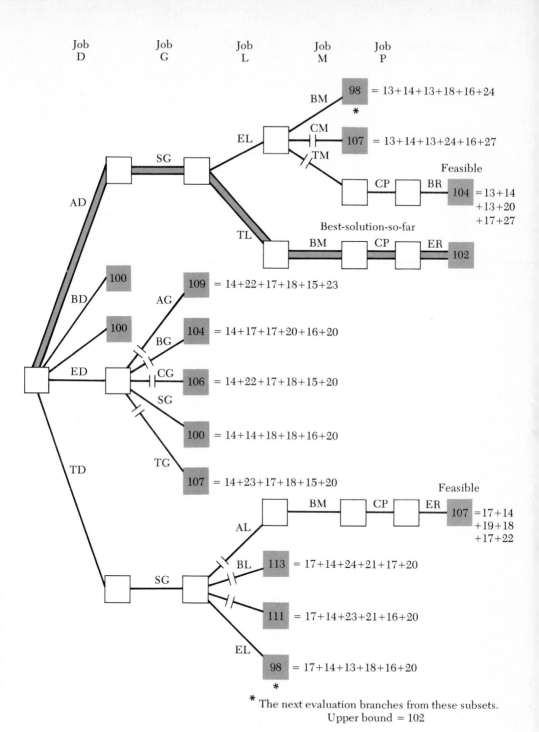

FIGURE 16-6
Fifth branch-and-bound evaluation of the machine-shop assignment problem.

subsets with lower bounds of 106, 104 and 103 are also pruned, since they all exceed the upper bound of 102.

Until now, we have always begun our next evaluation from the subset with the smallest lower bound. But three nodes share the smallest value of 98 in Figure 16-5. Ordinarily, we would break this tie arbitrarily. But since our problem is small in size, we can construct branches from all three nodes at the same time.

This fifth evaluation is presented in Figure 16-6, where two obviously nonoptimal feasible solutions branching from nodes AL and TM are uncovered. These and all of the branches leading to nodes ≥ 102 are pruned.

The sixth evaluation is shown in Figure 16-7, where a new upper bound of 99 corresponding to a new best-solution-so-far is found. The previous best-solution-so-far is pruned, as are several new feasible solutions and subsets having lower bounds ≥ 99.

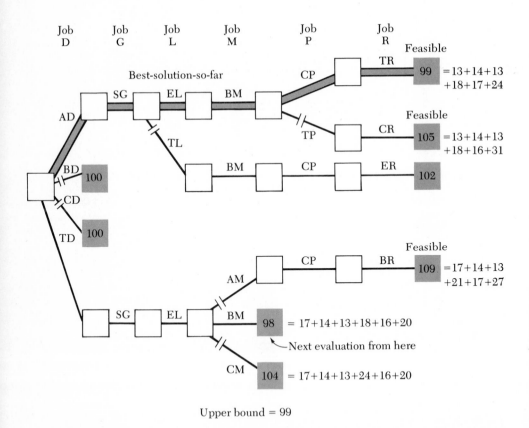

FIGURE 16-7
Sixth branch-and-bound evaluation of the machine-shop assignment problem.

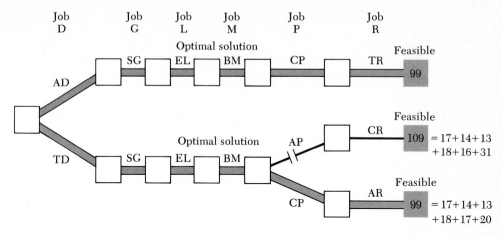

FIGURE 16-8
Final branch-and-bound evaluation of the machine-shop assignment problem.

The final evaluation in Figure 16-8 provides three feasible solutions, one of which is pruned because its C exceeds the upper limit. The two remaining solutions are optimal, since there are no more nodes to evaluate. These solutions are summarized below:

Worker	OPTIMUM		ALTERNATIVE OPTIMUM	
	Job	Time	Job	Time
Ann	Drilling	13 min	Routing	20 min
Bud	Milling	18	Milling	18
Chuck	Polishing	17	Polishing	17
Eduardo	Lathe	13	Lathe	13
Sam	Grinding	14	Grinding	14
Tom	Routing	24	Drilling	17
		99 min		99 min

Additional Remarks

Our integer programming solution to the assignment problem illustrates the advantages of using the branch-and-bound method instead of straight enumeration. There are a total of $6^6 = 46,656$ possible assignments in this problem alone. Of these, $6! = 720$ are feasible solutions. We only had to evaluate a tiny fraction of them here, but in a large assignment problem (involving, say, 20 persons and 20 jobs), even the branch-and-bound method may require a huge number of evaluations. The procedure has been programmed on digital computers, which has enhanced the applicability of the branch-and-bound method.

But larger problems may be impossible to solve in a reasonable amount of time, even with computer assistance. The potential for excessive evaluation is inherent in integer programming problems. For this reason, it may be preferable to solve large assignment problems as ordinary linear programming problems (which coincidentally provide integer solutions anyway).

The branch-and-bound method can be modified to reduce the number of evaluations by stopping the procedure after some affordable effort has been expended. The best-solution-so-far can then be considered satisfactory. It may be very close to the optimal solution, but a century or more of computer time could be needed to establish this fact for a large problem.

16-4 THE BRANCH-AND-BOUND METHOD FOR GENERAL INTEGER PROGRAMS

The branch-and-bound method can be extended to solve integer programs of a more general form. This is accomplished by ignoring the integer restrictions in the initial evaluation, so that the original constraints describe a *linear* program. The solution to this linear program establishes a lower limit on the objective of the integer program, and the solution space comprises all of the integer points that lie inside the feasible solution region defined by the linear program.

The original linear program is then partitioned into two linear programs by arbitrarily selecting one of the variables X_i that has a non-integer solution. We refer to X_i as the *branching variable*. Each of the *descendent* linear programs contains the original constraints. One of the new programs has an additional constraint of the form

$$X_i \leq L_i$$

and the other descendent linear program has the new constraint

$$X_i \geq L_i + 1$$

The constant L_i is the largest integer < the current solution value found for X_i by solving the *parent* linear program. The integer solution (if one exists at all) to the original parent problem will be the optimal solution (having all integer values) to one of these descendents, which may be found by solving a later-generation linear program.

Each of the linear programs encountered will describe a distinct subset of the original linear programming problem. The optimal C value (P value) of any linear program establishes a lower bound (an upper bound) on both the noninteger and integer solutions of its descendent linear programs. But no subset (unless it is infeasible) can be fathomed until the first integer solution is found. The respective C value establishes an upper bound on all integer solutions, and any subset with a lower bound $\geq$ that amount can be eliminated from further consideration. (When the objective is profit maximization, the lower bound on the optimal solution is established by the P value in the best integer solution found, and any subset with an upper bound $\leq$ that amount can be eliminated.) As in the assignment problem, branching in a cost-minimization problem occurs within the subset linear program with the most promising (the smallest) lower bound. (And in a profit-maximization problem, the subset with the greatest upper bound is partitioned.)

An Illustration of the Method

As an illustration, consider the following integer program:

$$\text{Minimize} \quad C = 4X_1 + 3X_2 + 5X_3$$
$$\text{Subject to} \quad 2X_1 - 2X_2 + 4X_3 \geq 7$$
$$2X_1 + 4X_2 - 2X_3 \geq 5$$

where X_1, X_2, and X_3 are non-negative integers

We will temporarily ignore the integer restriction and refer to the resulting linear program as Problem 1. The simplex method provides the following linear programming solution:

$$\text{Problem 1:} \quad X_1 = 2\tfrac{5}{6} \qquad X_3 = \tfrac{1}{3}$$
$$X_2 = 0$$
$$C = 13$$

Since two of the variables have non-integer values, further steps are required to uncover the integer solution. As our branching variable, we may use X_1 or X_3, both of which have non-integer values. We arbitrarily choose X_1.

The solution provides $X_1 = 2\tfrac{5}{6}$, so that 2 is the highest integer not exceeding this value. Thus, $L_1 = 2$, and the descendent linear programs include the original constraints, plus one of the following:

$$\text{Problem 2:} \quad X_1 \leq 2$$
$$\text{Problem 3:} \quad X_1 \geq 3$$

The respective solutions to these linear programs obtained using simplex are shown in Figure 16-9, which provides a tree summary of the entire procedure. Neither linear program has an integer solution, so further branching will be the next step.

Problem 3 has the smallest minimum cost of $C = 13\frac{1}{4}$, so it becomes the new parent linear program and the subset problems are partitioned from it. The only non-integer solution value is $X_3 = \frac{1}{4}$, which makes X_3 the branching variable. Using $L_3 = 0$ (the largest integer $< \frac{1}{4}$), the following descendent linear programs are obtained by adding the respective constraint to the parent problem. Thus

$$Problem\ 4: \quad X_3 \le 0 \quad or \quad X_3 = 0$$

$$Problem\ 5: \quad X_3 \ge 1$$

Both of these linear programs involve the original constraint and the restriction in Problem 3 that $X_1 \ge 3$.

The solutions are provided in Figure 16-9. Of all the unfathomed subsets, Problem 4 has the smallest objective of $C = 14$. This linear program is then partitioned, again using X_1 as the branching variable. This time $L_1 = 3$, which is the largest integer $< 3\frac{1}{2}$ (the solution value). The descendents include

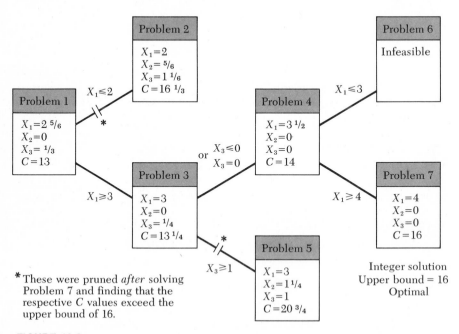

* These were pruned *after* solving Problem 7 and finding that the respective C values exceed the upper bound of 16.

FIGURE 16-9
The branch-and-bound method applied to a general integer program.

the earlier constraints for Problem 4 plus

$$Problem\ 6: \quad X_1 \le 3$$

$$Problem\ 7: \quad X_1 \ge 4$$

In Problem 6, we include $X_1 \ge 3$ (the earlier constraint for Problem 3). This constraint together with the new constraint yields the restriction that $X_1 = 3$ exactly.

Problem 6 is infeasible. Problem 7 yields the following solution:

$$Problem\ 7: \quad X_1 = 4 \quad\quad X_3 = 0$$

$$X_2 = 0$$

$$C = 16$$

Since all of the variables have integer values, this is a solution to the original integer program. This is the best-solution-so-far. The objective establishes an upper bound of 16 on the C values of any further integer solutions to be evaluated.

Referring to Figure 16-9, we can see that Problems 2 and 5 remain unfathomed. Since the respective C values (lower bounds) of these subsets exceed the upper bound of 16, these linear programs can be eliminated and the branches leading to them can be pruned. This leaves no subsets unfathomed, and our solution to Problem 7 is the *optimal integer solution*.

INTEGER PROGRAMMING APPLICATIONS 16-5

Integer programming has been applied to a wide variety of decision-making situations. Although it is not used as extensively as linear programming, integer programming is suited to almost as wide a range of applications. As we noted earlier, solving an integer programming problem requires a lot of computer time. Integer programming procedures are often used to solve problems involving a large number of variables, although computations are usually terminated before the optimal solution can be firmly established. The best-solution-so-far is then used in place of the optimal solution.

One popular application of integer programming is *facility location*. For instance, the problem of locating warehouses can be a significant decision for a manufacturer of bulky items, such as a chemical company. Literally hundreds of candidate cities could accommodate warehouses, but only a few cities will be chosen. These sites must be selected to minimize total distribution costs. If the warehouse locations were already fixed, the problem could be solved as a linear program, using the transportation method to determine the quantities to be shipped from source to destination. But when the warehouse locations are variables, an entire set of integer-value, zero–one, variables must be considered—one for each possible site. The fixed cost of operating a warehouse site applies only when a facility is built there. (Its variable is equal to *one*, and the fixed cost is charged in the objective function.) Otherwise, there is no fixed cost and the site variable has a value of *zero*.

The use of zero–one variables can be extended to other applications. Production runs usually involve fixed set-up costs, regardless of what quantities are eventually made. In any planning period, each product is assigned a zero–one variable indicating whether or not it will be produced in that period. The concepts encountered in warehouse location also apply to a variety of capital-budgeting decisions that involve not only physical facilities but also the introduction of new products and research and development projects, among others.

A fractional item may make no practical sense in a product-mix decision. A production run may be practical only in batches of a particular size—say, 1,000 items at a time. Integer requirements must be met in these cases.

Integer programming is applied in virtually all functional areas of business. New applications are being reported almost daily, verifying the importance of the procedure in business decision making.

PROBLEMS

16-1 Consider the following integer program:

$$\text{Maximize} \quad P = 3X_1 + 4X_2$$
$$\text{Subject to} \quad X_1 + 2X_2 \le 8$$
$$3X_1 + X_2 \le 10$$

where X_1 and X_2 are non-negative integers

(a) Ignoring the integer constraints, solve this problem graphically as a linear program.

(b) Identify all of the lattice points on your graph that lie inside the feasible solution region of the linear program.

(c) Find the most profitable feasible lattice point and the optimal solution to the original integer program.

16-2 Solve the following integer program graphically:

$$\text{Minimize} \quad C = 6X_1 + 8X_2$$
$$\text{Subject to} \quad 6X_1 + 7X_2 \ge 84$$
$$2X_1 \ge 11$$
$$3X_2 \ge 14$$

where X_1 and X_2 are non-negative integers

16-3 Solve the following integer program graphically:

Maximize $P = 5X_1 + 7X_2$

Subject to $12X_1 + 7X_2 \leq 84$

$5X_1 + 7X_2 \geq 35$

$2X_2 \leq 7$

where X_1 and X_2 are non-negative integers

16-4 Assume that Ace Widgets in Problem 9-8 (page 229) must produce only whole items. Formulate the problem as an integer program and solve it graphically.

16-5 Apply the branch-and-bound method to Problem 10-3 (page 242) to determine which of CompuQuick's computer facilities should be assigned to process each payroll.

16-6 Apply the branch-and-bound method to Problem 10-10 (page 245) to construct Conformity Systems' optimal employee–job assignment schedule.

16-7 Apply the branch-and-bound method to Problem 15-10 (page 381) and solve the brat-to-chore assignment problem.

16-8 The following costs apply to an assignment problem:

Individual i	Job j				
	J	K	L	M	N
A	3	17	5	21	13
B	10	4	14	24	7
C	10	15	26	8	20
D	23	6	9	19	25
E	11	18	27	12	22

Determine the optimal assignment, using the branch-and-bound method.

16-9 A six-person team is entered in the World Greased-Pig Wrestling Championship. The following wrestler-task assignments, along with the average penalty points assessed in preliminary contests, are possible:

Wrestler	Task					
	Grabbing	Holding	Identifying	Jerking	Kicking	Loading
Anastasia	0	18	7	2	21	14
Basil	9	1	15	24	31	6
Carlos	19	28	10	20	34	12
Daphne	4	16	16	3	13	32
Elsie	17	23	8	26	15	29
Fred	5	25	22	11	35	27

An assignment is to be made that will minimize the total average penalty points for the entire team. Apply the branch-and-bound method to determine the optimal assignment.

16-10 The solutions to several linear programs appearing in the table below have been obtained in the process of solving the following integer program:

Minimize $C = 5X_1 + 2X_2 + 3X_3$

Subject to $3X_1 - 2X_2 + 4X_3 \geq 8$

$3X_1 + 4X_2 - 2X_3 \geq 6$

where X_1, X_2, and X_3 are non-negative integers

Problem	Latest Branching Variable	X_1	X_2	X_3	C
1	none	$2\frac{2}{9}$	0	$\frac{1}{3}$	$12\frac{1}{9}$
2	X_1	2	$\frac{1}{3}$	$\frac{2}{3}$	$12\frac{2}{3}$
3	X_1	3	0	0	15
4	X_2	—	—	—	— (infeasible)
5	X_2	$1\frac{5}{9}$	1	$1\frac{1}{3}$	$13\frac{7}{9}$
6	X_1	1	$1\frac{5}{6}$	$2\frac{1}{6}$	$15\frac{1}{6}$
7	X_1	2	1	1	15

Construct a tree diagram summarizing the problem solution. Indicate the optimal solution(s).

16-11 Solve the following integer program:

Minimize $C = 2X_1 + 3X_2 + 4X_3$

Subject to $2X_1 - 3X_2 + 3X_3 \geq 7$

$-3X_1 + 2X_2 + 4X_3 \geq 5$

where X_1, X_2, and X_3 are non-negative integers

16-12 Find the integer programming solution to the Piney Woods Furniture problem originally stated as a linear program in Problem 11-11 (page 276).

17

Decision Making Using Experimental Information

We usually associate the term "experiment" with a test or an investigation. All experiments have one feature in common: *They provide information.* This information may serve to realign uncertainty. Information obtained by observing a solar eclipse can support hypotheses regarding the effect of the sun's gravity on stellar light rays. The way in which a person responds to your questions can help you decide whether you want him or her for a friend. *An experiment can help us make better decisions under uncertainty.*

However, most experiments are not conclusive. Any test can camouflage the truth. For instance, some potentially good employees will flunk well-designed employment screening tests, and some incompetents will pass them. Another good example is the seismic survey, which provides geological information about deep underground rock structures and is used to explore for oil deposits. Unfortunately, a seismic survey can deny the presence of oil in a field that is already producing oil and confirm the presence of oil under a site that has already proved to be dry. Still, such imperfect experiments can be valuable. An unfavorable test result can increase the chance of rejecting a poor prospect—a job applicant or a drilling site—and a favorable test result can enhance the likelihood of selecting a good prospect.

In this chapter, we will incorporate experimentation into the framework of our decision-making analysis. The information we obtain will affect the probabilities of the events that determine the consequences of each act. We can revise the probabilities of these events upward or downward, depending on the evidence we obtain. Thus, a geologist will increase the subjective probability of oil if the seismic survey analysis is favorable and will lower this probability if the survey is unfavorable.

The seismic survey epitomizes the role of experimental information in decision making. In business situations, several other classic sources of such information are commonly employed. A marketing research study serves to realign uncertainty regarding the degree of success that a new product will achieve in the marketplace. An aptitude test is often used to help predict a job applicant's future success or failure if he or she is hired—a decision that involves considerable uncertainty. A sampling study is frequently employed to facilitate quality-control decisions related to how satisfactorily items are produced or the amount of defective items arriving from a supplier.

First, we will investigate how to revise probabilities in accordance with experimental results by applying the probability concepts associated with Bayes' Theorem, which we discussed in Chapter 2. We will meld this probability information with all of the decision elements by means of a decision tree diagram. How much information is to be incorporated into the decision serves as a prelude to a more general analysis of the initial choice to experiment. For example, would an oil wildcatter use a seismic survey if it cost $50,000?

17-1 REVISING PROBABILITIES

The decision maker can usually make some kind of judgment about the uncertain events, which may be expressed as a set of *prior probabilities* for the respective events. Occasionally, such a judgment must be quantified in terms of *subjective probabilities*, because the events in question frequently arise from nonrepeatable circumstances. At other times, the prior probabilities may be *objective* in nature. In accordance with the information obtained from the experiment, the event uncertainties are realigned to obtain *posterior probabilities*. Figure 17-1 presents the sequence of steps in this procedure—exactly the one originally proposed by Thomas Bayes.

The Oil Wildcatter: A Case Illustration

For the purpose of illustration, we will suppose that an oil wildcatter must decide whether to drill for oil on a leased site. The wildcatter is contemplating hiring a geologist to conduct a detailed seismic survey of the area. At present, we are concerned only with the probability portion of this problem.

As a first step, the wildcatter must *exercise judgment* regarding the likelihood of striking oil. Since no two unproved drilling sites are very similar,

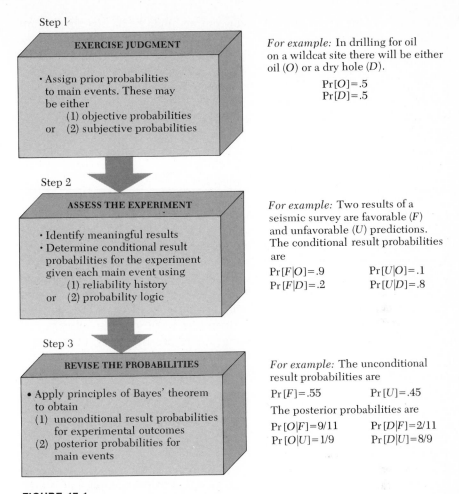

Step 1

EXERCISE JUDGMENT

· Assign prior probabilities
to main events. These may
be either
    (1) objective probabilities
or (2) subjective probabilities

For example: In drilling for oil
on a wildcat site there will be either
oil (O) or a dry hole (D).

$$\Pr[O]=.5$$
$$\Pr[D]=.5$$

Step 2

ASSESS THE EXPERIMENT

· Identify meaningful results
· Determine conditional result
probabilities for the experiment
given each main event using
    (1) reliability history
or (2) probability logic

For example: Two results of a
seismic survey are favorable (F)
and unfavorable (U) predictions.
The conditional result probabilities
are

$\Pr[F|O]=.9$ $\Pr[U|O]=.1$
$\Pr[F|D]=.2$ $\Pr[U|D]=.8$

Step 3

REVISE THE PROBABILITIES

• Apply principles of Bayes' theorem
to obtain
(1) unconditional result probabilities
    for experimental outcomes
(2) posterior probabilities for
    main events

For example: The unconditional
result probabilities are

$\Pr[F]=.55$ $\Pr[U]=.45$

The posterior probabilities are

$\Pr[O|F]=9/11$ $\Pr[D|F]=2/11$
$\Pr[O|U]=1/9$ $\Pr[D|U]=8/9$

FIGURE 17-1
**Steps in performing the probability portion of the decision-making analysis
when experimental information is used.**

no historical frequency is available. The wildcatter must therefore rely on a
subjective probability value. Suppose that he believes there is a 50–50 chance
of striking oil. Letting O represent oil and D represent a dry hole, the prior
probabilities of the basic events are

$$\Pr[O] = .5$$
$$\Pr[D] = .5$$

The next step the wildcatter takes is to *assess the experiment*—the
seismic survey, in this case. He begins by contemplating what results would be

meaningful to him. Although the seismic output might be highly complex and varied, we will assume, for simplicity, that the geologist's analysis can lead to only two meaningful results: a favorable (F) prediction for oil or an unfavorable one (U). It is necessary to obtain *conditional result probabilities* for the respective seismic outcomes given each possible basic event. Ordinarily, the conditional result probabilities for the experiment can be obtained objectively, either by estimation based on historical frequencies or by application of the underlying logic of probability. Thus, we may refer to these values as "logical-historical" probabilities to distinguish them from the several other types of probabilities we will encounter.

In our present example, the geologist has recorded the "batting average" for the procedure. Historical records show that on 90% of all fields known to produce oil, the wildcatter's prediction of oil has proved favorable; that is, 90% of all similar seismic survey data have provided favorable oil predictions when oil did exist. In other words, the seismic survey method is 90% reliable in arriving at a favorable forecast when oil is actually present. (Of course, such a percentage should not be biased by the fact that the seismic survey result may have affected the earlier decisions to drill on those sites. It is best to obtain a reliability figure by conducting a special test of the tester itself, which might be done by taking special seismic measurements on sites that are already producing oil). By taking simulated readings on known dry holes, the geologist has also determined that the survey is only 80% reliable in making an unfavorable prediction when no oil is present. The appropriate conditional result probabilities are

$$\Pr[F|O] = .90 \quad \text{and} \quad \Pr[U|O] = .10$$
$$\Pr[F|D] = .20 \quad \text{and} \quad \Pr[U|D] = .80$$

These are *historical probabilities* and can be regarded as statistical estimates of the underlying values, since they are based on limited samples of drilling sites. (Note that the conditional probability for a favorable result given oil is greater than the probability for an unfavorable prediction given a dry hole. There is no reason why a test must be equally discerning in both directions.)

In other situations, conditional result probabilities for an informational experiment can be obtained more directly without relying on historical frequencies. This would be true, for example, in assessing a quality-control sample. The precise probability distribution for the sample result can be determined through logical deduction, based only on the principles of probability and the type of events that characterize the sampled population. In Chapter 18, we will see how such *logical probabilities* can be determined using the binomial distribution.

The final step toward incorporating experimental information into the probability portion of decision analysis is to *revise the probabilities*. This revision ordinarily results in two kinds of probability values that are applicable at different stages of uncertainty. The *posterior probabilities* apply to the main events and the *unconditional result probabilities* apply to the experimental outcomes themselves. Although the underlying concepts of Bayes' Theorem are used to arrive at these values, the somewhat more streamlined procedure illustrated in Figure 17-2 proves more convenient when using tree diagrams to analyze a decision.

Using Probability Trees

The probability tree diagram in Figure 17-2(a) depicts the *actual chronology* of events in our illustration. The first fork represents the events for the site status: oil or dry. The second stage is represented by a fork for the seismic survey results. This particular arrangement represents the sequence in which the events actually occur: first, nature determined (several million years ago) whether this site would cover an oil field; second, our geologist conducts a seismic test today. The actual chronology also adheres to the manner in which the probability data were initially obtained. The wildcatter has directly assessed the probabilities for the site-status events, and the geologist has indicated the reliabilities for the survey. Thus, the values given earlier for the prior probabilities of oil and dry and the conditional result probabilities are placed on the corresponding branches in the probability tree in (a).

The probability tree diagram in Figure 17-2(b) represents the *informational chronology*. This is the sequence in which the decision maker finds out what events occur. First, the wildcatter obtains the result for the seismic survey, which is portrayed by the initial event fork. Then, if he chooses to drill, he ultimately determines whether or not the site covers an oil field. This is the sequence of events as they would appear on a decision tree (which will be discussed later). But this particular chronology does not correspond directly to the initial probability data. Additional work is required to obtain the probability values shown on the tree diagram in (b).

We begin by multiplying the branch probabilities together on each path in the tree diagram in Figure 17-2(a) to obtain the corresponding joint probability values. The same numbers apply regardless of the chronology, so the joint probabilities can be transferred to tree diagram (b). This must be done with care, since the in-between joint outcomes are not listed in the same order in (b) as they are in (a) because the analogous paths (event sequences) differ between the diagrams. For example, in diagram (a) we obtain the joint probability for oil and an unfavorable seismic result

$$\Pr[O \text{ and } U] = \Pr[O] \times \Pr[U|O] = .5 \times .1 = .05$$

This is the second joint probability in diagram (a) and corresponds to the third end position in diagram (b).

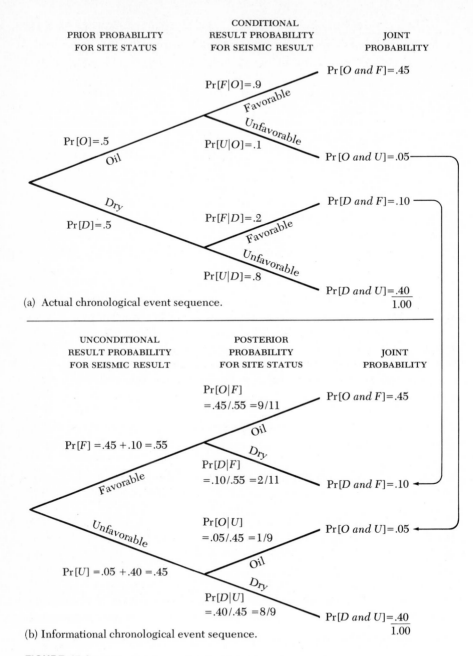

(a) Actual chronological event sequence.

(b) Informational chronological event sequence.

FIGURE 17-2
Probability tree diagrams showing the event chronologies
for drilling a wildcat well and using a seismic survey.

Next, we work entirely in diagram (b). First, we compute the unconditional result probabilities at the first stage. Here we use the addition law to obtain

$$\Pr[F] = \Pr[O \text{ and } F] + \Pr[D \text{ and } F] = .45 + .10 = .55$$

$$\Pr[U] = \Pr[O \text{ and } U] + \Pr[D \text{ and } U] = .05 + .40 = .45$$

These values are placed on the applicable branches at the first stage. Finally, the posterior probabilities for the second-stage events are computed using the basic property of conditional probability that

$$\Pr[A|B] = \frac{\Pr[A \text{ and } B]}{\Pr[B]}$$

Thus, we determine the posterior probability for oil, given a favorable seismic survey result, to be

$$\Pr[O|F] = \frac{\Pr[O \text{ and } F]}{\Pr[F]} = \frac{.45}{.55} = \frac{9}{11}$$

This value is placed on the second-stage branch for oil that is preceded by the earlier branch for a favorable result. Each of the other posterior probabilities shown in diagram (b) is found by dividing the respective end-position joint probability by the probability on the preceding branch.

Probabilities must be revised in this manner whenever experimental information is used in decision making. This happens because we ordinarily obtain our probabilities in the reverse chronology from the chronology required to analyze the problem.

POSTERIOR ANALYSIS 17-2

Figure 17-3 is a decision tree diagram of the wildcatter's choices after the seismic results are known. Here, we have assumed that (1) the lease will be sold for $250,000 on striking oil; (2) the cost of drilling will be $100,000; and (3) the seismic survey will cost $25,000. The decision to drill or to abandon the lease follows the seismic survey result, since the wildcatter obviously would not reach a decision before finding out the geologist's prediction. The revised probabilities found earlier for the informational chronology are used. Since the posterior probabilities for the site status events apply at the two decision points, using this decision tree as the basis for decision making is called *posterior analysis*.

Note that there is no event fork following the act to abandon the lease, because the oil wildcatter will never find out if there is oil unless he drills for it. (The uncertainty still exists, nevertheless; it would do no harm to have event

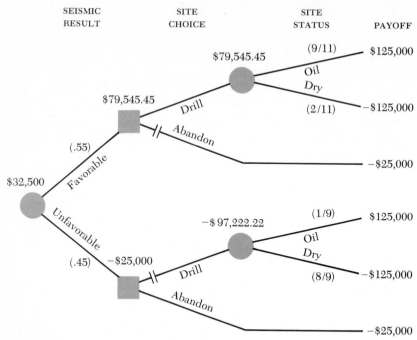

FIGURE 17-3
The wildcatter's decision tree diagram after the seismic survey is taken.

forks for oil versus dry at those points, but the payoff would be −$25,000 in either case, and an identical conclusion would be reached.)

Performing backward induction, we see that the wildcatter would prune the abandon branch and drill if a favorable seismic result were obtained and would do the opposite in the case of an unfavorable prediction. Even though drilling will lead to identical payoffs for either seismic result, the posterior probabilities of oil and dry are different for the favorable and unfavorable predictions. The expected payoff from drilling is $79,545.45 for a favorable seismic result, but it is a negative value (−$97,222.22) for an unfavorable result. The wildcatter's expected payoff for the optimal strategy is $32,500. As we see later, this amount will be helpful in determining whether the seismic survey should be used at all.

Obviously Nonoptimal Strategies

In the simpler decision structures, it may be convenient to streamline the decision tree diagram. We can conclude that the wildcatter would prune the same branches, regardless of the numbers involved. Since he is paying $25,000 for the seismic survey and this experiment provides fairly reliable predictions, the wildcatter should choose acts that are consistent with the

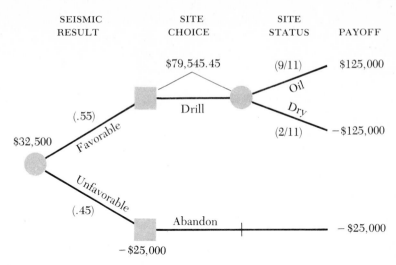

FIGURE 17-4
The simplified wildcatter's decision tree diagram
with obviously nonoptimal strategies excluded.

information obtained. But the tree in Figure 17-3 allows for three other strategies: (1) drill regardless of the result (prune both abandon branches); (2) abandon in either case (prune the two drill branches; or (3) do the opposite of what is predicted (prune the drill branch if the seismic result is favorable, and prune the abandon branch if it is unfavorable). The last strategy is ridiculous and would never be considered. The other two strategies are inferior to drilling or to abandoning without benefit of seismic results, since the $25,000 cost could be saved in either case. Such inferior strategies are *obviously nonoptimal strategies*.

Figure 17-4 illustrates how the wildcatter's decision tree diagram could have been drawn to exclude the obviously nonoptimal strategies. This representation can help to simplify an otherwise complex decision tree. However, for expository convenience, we will always use the complete decision tree diagram. When more than two acts or experimental results are involved, it is not easy to determine which strategies are obviously nonoptimal.

THE DECISION TO EXPERIMENT: PREPOSTERIOR ANALYSIS 17-3

In section 17-2, we illustrated the use of experimental information and described posterior analysis, which tells us what act we should select for each experimental outcome. Now we will incorporate into our analysis the additional choice of whether or not to obtain experimental information in the first place. The decision-making process is therefore expanded to include an initial stage involving the selection of acts concerning experimentation. The procedure employed to evaluate this expanded decision is sometimes referred to as *preposterior analysis.*

To illustrate how to incorporate the decision to use experimental information, we expand the oil wildcatter's decision. The expanded decision tree is presented in Figure 17-5. The additional decision of whether or not to make

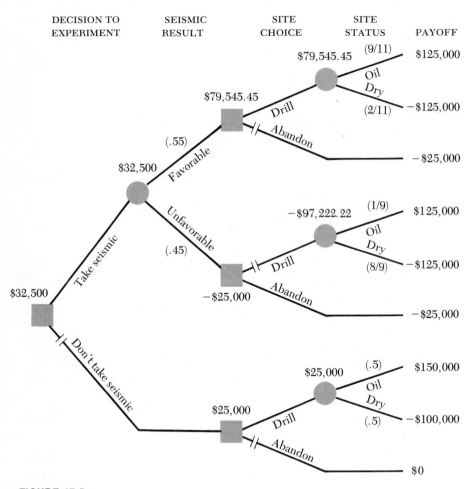

FIGURE 17-5

The wildcatter's decision tree diagram incorporating the initial decision regarding the seismic test.

the seismic test is treated as an initial decision point and becomes the initial act fork with branches for making and not making the seismic test. If the seismic test is made, an event fork follows that is related to the seismic result to be achieved; here, the unconditional result probabilities apply. These events are followed by the final decision to drill or to abandon the site. If the wildcatter drills, the last set of event forks represent the oil and dry events and the posterior probabilities apply. If the wildcatter initially decides not to make the seismic survey, then the choice to drill or to abandon the site must be made without any information; this is represented as the act fork at the bottom of the tree. In this case, drilling leads to a final event fork for the site status events. Here, the original prior probabilities apply for the oil and dry events. The payoffs in this bottom portion of the tree are $25,000 greater than their counterparts directly above, since the cost of the seismic survey is saved.

We now have a two-stage decision problem to analyze. Performing backward induction on the top portion of Figure 17-5, we obtain the result that we found earlier: Using the seismic survey yields an expected payoff of $32,500. We find that not using the survey leads to a smaller expected payoff of only $25,000. Thus, the branch "don't make seismic survey" is pruned at the first decision point. The course of action that will maximize the expected payoff is to make the seismic survey, and drill if it is favorable but abandon the site if it is unfavorable.

The Role of EVPI

In some decision-making situations, the foregoing procedure can be shortened considerably. Recall that the *expected value of perfect information*, or EVPI, indicates the worth of the best possible or ideal information about the events in the main decision. Information that is obtained through experiment is far from perfect in its predictive powers. If experimental evidence costs more than it can be worth at best, then it should obviously not be obtained.

In Table 17-1, the wildcatter's EVPI is calculated to be $50,000. (Here, the prior probabilities are used, since the seismic survey does not apply.) If the cost of the seismic survey were higher—say, $60,000—then it would be more profitable for the oil wildcatter not to bother to make the test, regardless of its reliability. In effect, the seismic branch would be pruned from the tree and there would be no need to calculate posterior probabilities or to conduct any preposterior analysis. Of course, this shortcut applies only when the cost of the information exceeds the EVPI. Since the wildcatter has to spend only $25,000, which is a smaller amount than the $50,000 EVPI, the complete preposterior analysis is required in this case.

TABLE 17-1

Calculation of the Wildcatter's EVPI

Event	Probability	Payoff Drill	Payoff Abandon	Row Maximum	Row Maximum × Probability
Oil	.5	$150,000	$0	$150,000	$75,000
Dry	.5	− 100,000	0	0	0
	1.0				$75,000

Expected payoff with perfect information = $75,000

Maximum expected payoff (with no information) = .5($150,000) + .5(− $100,000)

$$= \$25,000$$

EVPI = $75,000 − $25,000 = $50,000

PROBLEMS

17-1 An oil wildcatter has assigned a .40 probability to striking oil on his property. He orders a seismic survey that has proved only 80% reliable in the past. Given oil, it predicts favorably 80% of the time; given no oil, it augurs unfavorably with a frequency of .8.

Construct probability trees for the actual and informational chronologies, and indicate the appropriate probability values for each branch and end position.

17-2 Your friend places two coins in a box. The coins are identical in all respects, except that one is two-headed. Without looking, you select one coin from the box and lay it on the table.

(a) What is the prior probability that you will select the two-headed coin?

(b) As a source of predictive information about the selected coin, you may examine the showing face. Construct the probability tree diagram for the actual chronology of events.

(c) After you have examined the showing face of the coin, you may then turn it over to see what is on the other side. Construct the probability tree diagram for the informational chronology.

(d) If a head shows before you turn the coin over, what is the posterior probability that you selected the two-headed coin?

17-3 Solve the weather-forecasting problem originally posed in Problem 2-20 (page 45) by constructing probability trees for the actual and informational chronologies.

17-4 Solve the toothpaste-marketing problem posed in Problem 2-21 (page 46) by constructing probability trees for the actual and informational chronologies.

17-5 A box contains two pairs of dice. One pair is a fair one. The other pair consists of one die cube with a three on every side and one die cube with a four on every side. A pair is to be selected at random and tossed. You will only be able to see the top showing faces and not the sides. The main events of interest pertain to the crookedness or fairness of the tossed dice. (Both dice in the tossed pair will fall into the same category.) In each of the following cases, construct probability trees for the actual and informational chronologies.

(a) The experimental result is finding out whether or not a seven-sum (three and four, two and five, one and six) occurs.

(b) The experimental result is finding out whether or not a three-four combination occurs, which has a greater predictive worth than the result in (a).

17-6 The exploration manager for a small oil company must decide whether to drill on a parcel of leased land or to abandon the lease. As an aid in making this choice, the manager can first decide whether to pay $30,000 for a seismic survey, which will confirm or deny the presence of the anticlinal structure necessary for oil. She has judged the prior probability of oil to be .30. For oil-producing fields of similar geology, her experience has shown that the chance of a confirming seismic is .9; but for dry holes with approximately the same characteristics, the probability that a seismic survey will deny oil has been established at only .7. Drilling costs have been firmly established at $200,000. If oil is struck, the manager's company plans to sell the lease for $500,000.

(a) What is the manager's EVPI for the basic decision, using profit as the payoff measure? Comparing this value to the cost of the seismic survey, can you conclude definitely that no survey should be made?

(b) Construct the manager's decision tree diagram and determine the appropriate payoffs.

(c) Find the revised probabilities for the informational chronology and place these values on the corresponding branches of your decision tree diagram.

(d) Perform backward induction analysis to determine the course of action that will provide the maximum expected profit.

17-7 The following payoff table of marketing choices for a new film has been determined by the management of a motion picture studio:

Box Office Result Events	Distribute as "A" Feature	Sell to TV Network	Distribute as "B" Feature
Success	$5,000,000	$1,000,000	$3,000,000
Failure	−2,000,000	1,000,000	−1,000,000

The prior probability for a box office success has been judged to be .3. The studio plans a series of sneak previews. Historically, 70% of all of the studio's successful films have received favorable previews and 80% of all of the studio's box office failures have received unfavorable previews.

(a) Construct the probability tree diagrams for the actual and informational chronologies.

(b) Construct a table indicating all of the studio's possible strategies contingent on results of the sneak preview.

(c) Construct a tree diagram for the studio's decision, assuming that the film will definitely be previewed.

(d) Perform backward induction analysis. What is the optimal course of action? To which strategy in (b) does this correspond?

17-8 The makers of Quicker Oats oatmeal have packaged this product in cylindrical containers for 50 years. Management believes that the cylindrical container is inseparable from the product's image. But consumer tastes change, and the new marketing vice-president wonders if younger people will regard the round box as old-fashioned and unappealing. The vice-president wishes to analyze whether or not to package Quicker Oats in a rectangular box that will save significantly on transportation costs by eliminating dead space in the packing cartons. It is also believed that the change can actually expand Quicker Oats' market by uplifting the product's image. But previous study has shown that a small segment of the existing market buys the oatmeal primarily for the round box; these customers would be lost if the package were changed. The following payoff table has been established for the present net worth of retaining the old box versus using the new box.

National Market Response to New Box Events	Act	
	Retain Old Box	Use New Box
W: Weak	$0	− $2,000,000
M: Moderate	0	0
S: Strong	0	3,000,000

As prior probabilities for the new box response events, the marketing vice-president has estimated: $Pr[W] = .20$, $Pr[M] = .30$, $Pr[S] = .50$. The new box is to be test marketed for six months in a "barometer" city. Three outcomes are possible: decreased sales (D), unchanged sales (U), and increased sales (I). Historical experience with other products has established the following conditional result probabilities:

$$Pr[D|W] = .8 \qquad Pr[D|M] = .2 \qquad Pr[D|S] = 0$$
$$Pr[U|W] = .2 \qquad Pr[U|M] = .4 \qquad Pr[U|S] = .1$$
$$Pr[I|W] = 0 \qquad Pr[I|M] = .4 \qquad Pr[I|S] = .9$$

(a) Construct the probability tree diagrams for the actual and informational chronologies.
(b) Construct the Quicker Oats decision tree diagram, assuming that the new box will be test marketed.
(c) Perform backward induction. Then, indicate the maximum expected payoff act for each test outcome. What is the optimal strategy?

17-9 A gas prospector must decide how to dispose of a particular lease, which may be sold now for $20,000 or drilled on at a cost of $100,000. The drilling events and their prior probabilities are dry at .6 (D), low-pressure gas at .3 (L), and high-pressure gas at .1 (H). The lease will be abandoned for no receipts if D, it will be sold for $300,000 if L, and it will be sold for $500,000 if H.
(a) Which act—sell or drill—will maximize expected profit?
(b) What is the prospector's EVPI?
(c) For a cost of $10,000 a 90% reliable seismic survey can predict gas favorably (F) with a probability of .90 if there is gas or unfavorably (U) with a probability of .90 if the site is dry, but it cannot measure pressure. Construct probability tree diagrams for the actual and informational chronologies, using three gas events.
(d) Perform a decision tree analysis to determine what course of action will maximize the prospector's expected profit.

17-10 Lucky Jones must decide whether to participate in a card game offered by Inscrutable Smith. For the price of $5, Jones will draw a card from an ordinary deck of playing cards. If the card is a king, Smith is to pay Jones $60 (so that Jones wins

$55). But if the card is not a king, Jones will receive nothing for the $5. Smith, eager for action, offers Jones an additional enticement. For $3, Jones can draw a card without looking at it. Smith will then tell Jones whether or not the card is a face card. If Jones wishes to continue, an additional payment of $5 must be made for the game to proceed.

(a) Construct a decision tree diagram showing the structure of Jones' decision.

(b) Determine the probabilities for the events and the total profit for the end position.

(c) What course of action will provide Jones with the greatest expected payoff?

17-11 The decision tree diagram in Figure 17-6 has been constructed by a marketing manager who wishes to determine how to introduce a new product. The manager judges that the prior probability for marketing success is .40.

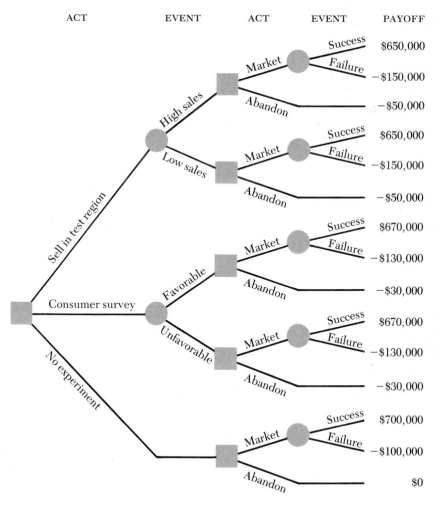

FIGURE 17-6

(a) From a consumer survey costing $30,000, the manager can obtain an 80% reliable indication of the product's impact in the marketplace. Thus, the probability for a favorable survey result given market success is .80, and the probability for an unfavorable result given market failure is .80. Find the posterior probabilities for the market events and the unconditional result probabilities for the survey events.

(b) A sales program costing $50,000 might be conducted in a test region. The results are judged to be 95% reliable. Find the posterior and unconditional result probabilities.

(c) Using the information given in the problem statement and your answers to (a) and (b), perform backward induction to find the manager's optimal course of action. (The payoffs in Figure 17-6 include the cost of experimenting.)

18

Decision Making Using Sample Information

In Chapter 17, we considered the general problem of using experimental information in decision making. We will now consider a decision commonly encountered in business situations that involves just *two acts*. The experiment is taking a *random sample* from a population whose characteristics will affect the ultimate payoffs. The decision maker's choice depends on the particular sample result obtained.

Two types of populations are encountered in these sampling experiments. The *qualitative population* is comprised of units that can be classified into categories. Examples are persons who can be categorized by occupation (blue-collar, professional, etc.), sex (male, female), or preferences (preferring a product, disliking a product); and production items that can be classified in terms of quality (satisfactory, unsatisfactory), weight (below the limit, above the limit), or color (light, medium, dark). The *quantitative population* associates a numerical value with each unit. For example, people can be measured in terms of income levels, aptitude test scores, or years of experience; or items can be assigned numerical values to indicate weight, volume, quantity of an ingredient, etc.

A sample from a qualitative population tells us how many sample units fall into a particular category, and this number reflects the prevalence of that attribute in the population, which in turn affects the payoff associated with the incidence of the attribute. For example, in deciding how to dispose of a supplier's shipment, a receiving inspector may discover that 12 of the items out of a random sample of 100 are defective, indicating that there is a high probability that the entire shipment is bad and that returning it might maximize expected payoff. The payoffs in such a problem are often expressed in terms of the proportion P of the population having the key attribute (for example, the proportion of defective items in the entire shipment). As in most decision making using experiments, the value of P itself and the number of defectives that will turn up in the sample are both uncertain. Probabilities for the number of defectives can be determined by using the binomial distribution.

A sample taken from a quantitative population provides a similar basis for action, such as accepting or rejecting a machine setting in a chemical process. Here, the mean quantity of a particular ingredient in each gallon may be the determining factor in establishing the payoff. The population mean μ measures the central quantity of the ingredient in all gallons made under that setting. The true value of μ is uncertain. A second area of uncertainty involves the quantities in the sample itself; here, the sample mean $\bar{X}$ may serve as the basis for decision making.

In this chapter, we will consider how to integrate sample information into the basic decision-making structure. As in Chapter 17, the procedure involves prior probabilities for P or μ, which must be revised to coincide with possible sample results to provide posterior probabilities for these population parameters. Backward induction with revised probabilities then provides the optimal decision rule, based on the sample statistic that is obtained. The analysis may be expanded to consider how many sample observations must be made.

18-1   DECISION MAKING WITH BINOMIAL PROBABILITIES

Charles Stereo: An Acceptance Sampling Illustration

Charles Stereo is a chain of retail outlets specializing in sound equipment. Because of its high volume, Charles stocks its inventory of stereo pickup cartridges by ordering lots of 100 units from various manufacturers. Bertrand Charles, the owner, wishes to decide whether to accept or reject a particular lot from one supplier, DICO. Each cartridge in a rejected lot is thoroughly inspected by Charles, and cartridges that are actually found to be defective are replaced by the supplier. An accepted lot is parceled without inspection to the retail stores for sale to customers, who are relied on to find the defective cartridges, which Charles replaces without charge from its inventory. DICO will not give

Charles credit for cartridges that have been used by retail customers, even if they were originally defective.

One of the Charles employees has suggested that the company sample incoming lots, using the information thereby obtained as a basis for deciding whether a lot should be accepted or rejected. Charles is skeptical about the advantages of sampling, since even after an inspection of randomly chosen items he cannot be certain of the value of the lot proportion defective P. An employee volunteers to analyze the decision and chooses the gross profit from a 100-item lot as the payoff measure.

Detailed records of all DICO cartridges received by Charles have been maintained, and the frequencies of lot proportions defective have been found. These frequencies serve as estimates of the following prior probabilities for values of P of .10, .20, and .30:

Possible Lot Proportion Defective P	Prior Probability
.10	.4
.20	.3
.30	.3
	1.0

To simplify our analysis, we will consider values of P only to the nearest whole 10%. (The same procedures would apply if we considered $P = .05, .06, \ldots, .35$).

Structuring the Decision

As an example, consider a sample of size $n = 2$ for the Charles decision problem diagrammed in Figure 18-1. An immediate choice, represented by the act fork at decision point a, is to determine whether or not to sample. If the choice is made to inspect the two randomly chosen items, the possible outcomes for the number of defectives are $R = 0$, $R = 1$, or $R = 2$, which are shown as events on the event fork at b. The choices to accept or reject the lot are represented by act branches in the forks at decision points c, d, e, and f. After the acts to accept or reject, the lot proportion defective P is determined either by a 100% inspection in the case of rejection or by a tally of returned cartridges if the lot is accepted. The various possible values of P are shown as events on forks g through n.

The payoffs for each end position are determined by adjusting a $1,000 lot markup downward to account for inspection costs and losses incurred when customers return used defective cartridges.

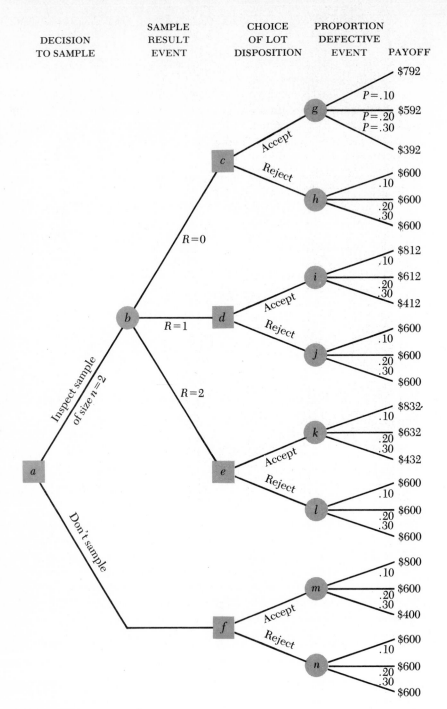

FIGURE 18-1
The decision tree for the Charles Stereo sampling decision.

Determining the Event Probabilities

The actual event chronology is provided in Figure 18-2. There, the first stage represents the prior probabilities for the proportion of defective cartridges in the shipment, and the second stage provides the conditional result probabilities for the number of defectives in the sample. The latter probabilities are

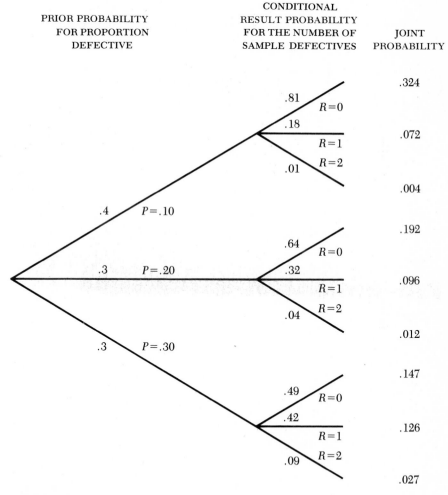

PRIOR PROBABILITY
FOR PROPORTION
DEFECTIVE

CONDITIONAL
RESULT PROBABILITY
FOR THE NUMBER OF
SAMPLE DEFECTIVES

JOINT
PROBABILITY

FIGURE 18-2
The actual chronology of events for the stereo-cartridge shipment decision.

TABLE 18-1

Binomial Conditional Result Probabilities

for the Number of Defectives in the Stereo-Cartridge Sample

P	r	$Pr[R = r] = \dfrac{n!}{r!(n - r)!} P^r(1 - P)^{n-r}$
.10	0	$1(.10)^0(.90)^2 =$ .81
.10	1	$2(.10)^1(.90)^1 =$ .18
.10	2	$1(.10)^2(.90)^0 =$ .01
		1.00
.20	0	$1(.20)^0(.80)^2 =$ .64
.20	1	$2(.20)^1(.80)^1 =$ .32
.20	2	$1(.20)^2(.80)^0 =$ .04
		1.00
.30	0	$1(.30)^0(.70)^2 =$ .49
.30	1	$2(.30)^1(.70)^1 =$ .42
.30	2	$1(.30)^2(.70)^0 =$ .09
		1.00

calculated in Table 18-1 using the binomial distribution.* (When n is large, it may be more convenient to obtain the binomial probabilities from Appendix Table A.) We can categorize these as logical probabilities, since they are based entirely on probability concepts rather than on past frequencies.

Each level of P corresponds to a *different population* and therefore requires a separate set of binomial probabilities. In calculating these values, *it is important not to confuse the level of P with its prior probability*. For example, in calculating the conditional result probabilities for the number of defectives in the sample when $P = .10$, we use .10 as the trial success probability P; we do not use .4, which is the prior probability for the event and is applied in a later step of the analysis.

After they have been determined, the binomial probabilities are placed on the corresponding second-stage branches of the actual chronology probability tree. The joint probabilities are then found by multiplying the probabilities on the respective branches. In doing this, *the events should not be confused with their probabilities*. Remember that $P = .10$, $P = .20$, and $P = .30$ are the *events* analogous to low, moderate, or high numbers of defectives in the population. (As events, it makes no sense to combine the values of P arithmetically. So since they should not be added together, they certainly do not have to sum

---

* Here, the population of cartridges is fixed in size. Unless the sampling is done with replacement, some error result from using binomial probabilities. But when the population is large in relation to n, such errors are negligible.

to 1!) The prior probabilities .4, .3, and .3 are the multipliers. Thus, the top joint probability in Figure 18-2 is

$$\Pr[P = .10 \ and \ R = 0] = .4 \times .81 = .324$$

and the other joint probabilities are calculated in the same way.

Figure 18-3 presents the informational chronology of events for the sampling experiment. The first stage provides the unconditional result probabilities for the number of sample items defective. This is in accordance with the

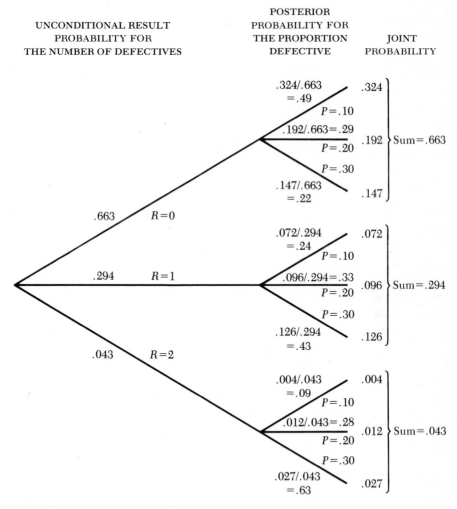

FIGURE 18-3
The informational chronology of events for the stereo-cartridge shipment decision.

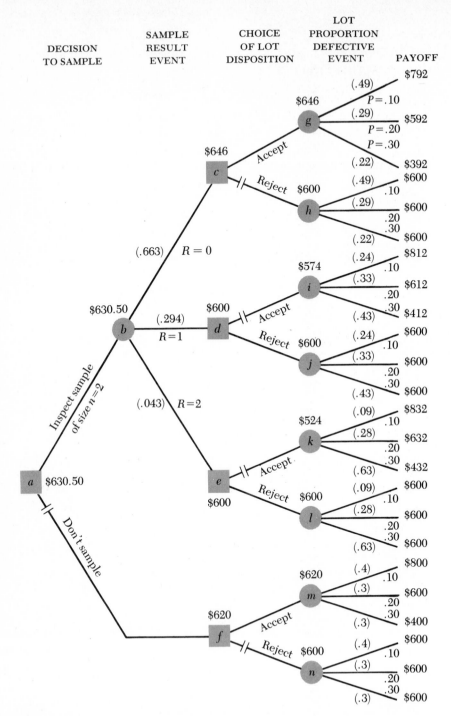

FIGURE 18-4

The Charles Stereo decision tree diagram showing the results of backward induction.

sequence in which Charles Stereo discovers the applicable outcomes. The posterior probabilities for the population proportion of defective cartridges are next given. This informational chronology provides the revised probabilities that are used in the complete decision tree diagram in Figure 18-4.

The Decision Rule

The results of the backward induction analysis are shown in Figure 18-4. Observe that when the number of defectives is $R = 1$ or more, rejection yields a higher expected payoff. This demonstrates the principle that as the number of defective items in the sample becomes larger, the evidence favors larger P values. We refer to the largest value of R for which the lot will be accepted as the decision maker's *acceptance number*, which we denote by C. In this example, the acceptance number is $C = 0$. With a sample size of $n = 2$, our decision maker will therefore apply the following *decision rule*:

Accept the lot if $R \leq C$

Reject the lot if $R > C$

The objective in two-action decision problems involving sampling is to select a decision rule. The optimal strategy is therefore equivalent to finding the value of C that maximizes expected payoff.

In Section 18-3, we will consider whether or not a different sample size can provide an even greater expected payoff than the one we obtained here for $n = 2$.

DECISION RULES BASED ON THE SAMPLE MEAN   18-2

A completely analogous procedure to decision making using binomial probabilities applies when samples are taken from quantitative populations.

A Computer Memory Device Decision

To illustrate decision making based on the sample mean, we will consider a computer center's decision regarding the kind of peripheral memory storage device to use in its computer system. The two proposed units are based on laser technology, and both units will operate more efficiently than the current memory storage device. One alternative is based on photographic principles and requires special film for storing the data. The other alternative employs holography—a process in which a three-dimensional image is retrieved from a special wafer. A photographic memory unit costs less to lease than a holographic unit but is slower and therefore more costly to operate. The storage capacities and reliabilities of the two units are identical.

The annual savings from using either alternative unit depends on the daily volume of peripheral memory access. Although the actual number of bits stored or retrieved varies daily, the mean daily access level can be used to establish an average annual access savings for each alternative. When this savings is added to the fixed lease cost, the resulting mean total annual savings serves as the payoff measure for this decision. This payoff depends on the mean daily gigabits (billion bits) accessed μ, which represents the average volume over all days.

The computer center manager is uncertain about the value of μ, since historical data on the density of peripheral memory traffic are incomplete.

Figure 18-5 presents the manager's decision structure when no sample information is available. Notice that different payoff values for mean annual savings are obtained for each type of unit and μ combination. Using prior

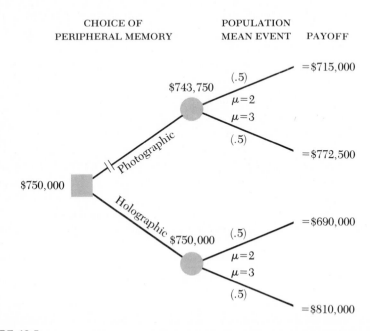

FIGURE 18-5

The computer center manager's decision structure when no sample is used.

probabilities of .5 for $\mu = 2$ and .5 for $\mu = 3$, we find that the holographic memory unit provides the greatest expected payoff of $750,000 in mean annual savings.

Decision Making with Sample Information

We will now consider the manager's analysis using sample data. The manager believes that for an extra few hundred dollars per day she can determine the precise level of peripheral memory access on sample days by adding a special accounting program to the software system. Any sampling cost arises from the slower processing that will result. Suppose that a sample of $n = 9$ days is to be used.

Since the sample data will be used to predict mean daily access levels, it is appropriate to summarize the sampling results in terms of the sample mean memory access level, which is computed from

$$\bar{X} = \frac{X_1 + X_2 + \cdots + X_n}{n}$$

where $X_1, X_2, \cdots, X_n$ are the observed levels for individual sample days. A large $\bar{X}$ will lend credence to the greater population mean value of $\mu = 3$ gigabits per day, and a small $\bar{X}$ will support $\mu = 2$. But since the sample results are not yet known, the actual value of $\bar{X}$ is uncertain. In Chapter 3, we investigated the properties of the sample mean. For large n, the sample mean is approximately normally distributed (under appropriate conditions that are assumed to apply here) with a mean of μ. In our discussion, we will use the *approximate* conditional result probabilities for $\bar{X}$ given in Table 18-2.

The manager's decision tree diagram using sample information is provided in Figure 18-6. The revised probabilities used there are obtained from Figure 18-7. Backward induction in Figure 18-6 indicates that the maximum expected annual savings will be achieved by selecting the photographic memory unit for $\bar{X} = 1$ and the holographic peripheral storage unit for $\bar{X} = 2$, $\bar{X} = 3$, or

TABLE 18-2
Approximate Conditional Result Probabilities for $\bar{X}$

Possible Mean	Conditional Probability Given $\mu = 2$	Conditional Probability Given $\mu = 3$
$\bar{X} = 1$	.35	.05
$\bar{X} = 2$	.35	.25
$\bar{X} = 3$	.25	.35
$\bar{X} = 4$	.05	.35

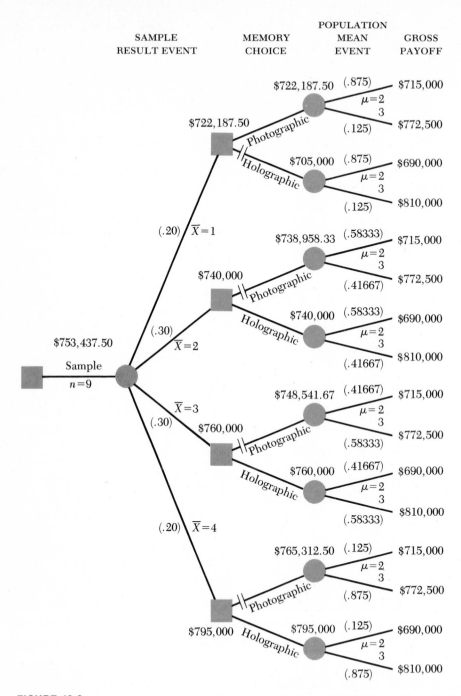

FIGURE 18-6
The computer center manager's decision structure using a sample of size *n* = 9.

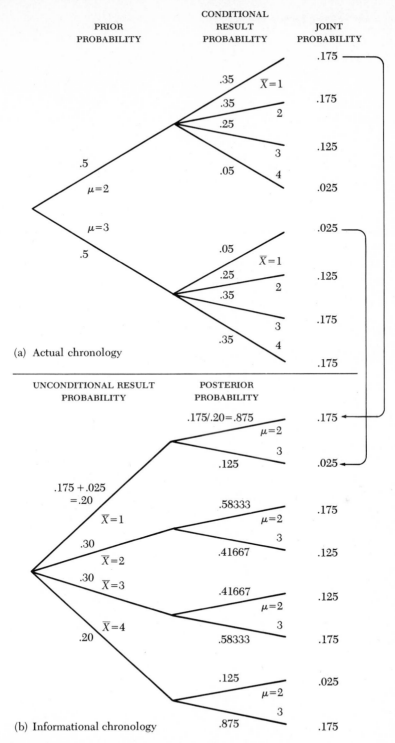

FIGURE 18-7
Revised probabilities for the computer memory device decision.

$\bar{X} = 4$. We can express this result in terms of the decision rule

$$\text{Select photographic unit if } \bar{X} \leq C$$

$$\text{Select holographic unit if } \bar{X} > C$$

where $C = 1$ gigabit per day.

The expected payoff is \$753,437.50 when the optimal decision rule is applied to a sample of size $n = 9$. We refer to this quantity as the *expected payoff with sample information*. It is based on gross payoffs and *does not reflect the cost of collecting the sample.*

Of course, sampling costs must ultimately be considered. Thus far, our analysis can be classified as *posterior*. We still have to consider the more basic decision of whether or not to sample in the first place, and if we sample, how large a sample to take. To answer these questions, we must move into the area of *preposterior analysis.*

18-3 DECIDING ABOUT THE SAMPLE: PREPOSTERIOR ANALYSIS

In our first example of decision making using sample information, we found that rather than accepting each lot of stereo cartridges, it was preferable to take a sample of size $n = 2$ first and to accept only the lots in which no sample defectives were found. But we did not investigate the possibility that selecting a different sample size might have been an even greater improvement. Although more observations will add to the sampling costs, the increased sample reliability should provide a net gain in expected payoff. An analysis of various sample sizes helps to determine exactly what kind of information to acquire.

Determining the Optimal Sample Size

How large a sample should be taken? We can investigate the choice of sample size in the same way that we determined whether or not to sample. By explicitly considering each possible level of n as an act in the decision structure, we can use the principles we have developed thus far to analyze the fully generalized decision. This decision involves not only the choice of whether or not to use experimental evidence but also the selection of the evidence to be obtained.

We can accomplish this for our acceptance sampling illustration (Charles Stereo) by augmenting the decision structure as shown in Figure 18-8, where four possible sample sizes $n = 1$, $n = 2$, $n = 3$, and $n = 4$ are considered. Each sample size is a separate choice in an initial act fork. A sample of size n has

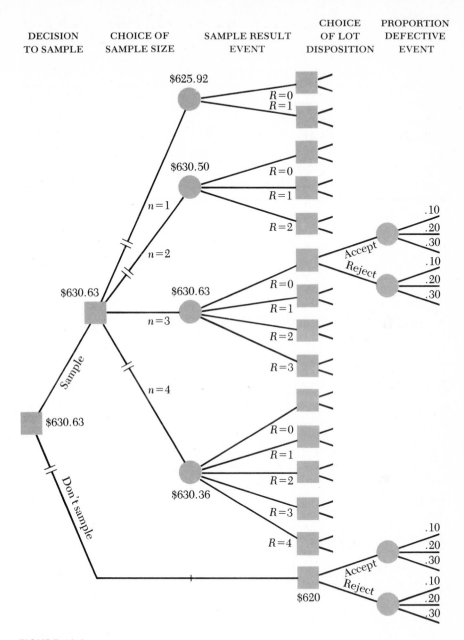

DECISION TO SAMPLE	CHOICE OF SAMPLE SIZE	SAMPLE RESULT EVENT	CHOICE OF LOT DISPOSITION	PROPORTION DEFECTIVE EVENT

FIGURE 18-8
The Charles Stereo decision tree diagram, incorporating the choice of sample size.

$n + 1$ possible sample outcomes, since the number of defectives may be $R = 0$, $R = 1, \ldots$, or $R = n$. Thus, the number of events in the sample outcome forks varies with the size of n, and there are $n + 1$ branches for each sample size.

The posterior probabilities for the possible values of P will differ, depending on n and the sample outcome, and must be recalculated for each sample size being considered. The end position payoffs for the paths of the decision tree depend on both the losses from returned defective cartridges and the sampling costs and must also be calculated separately. Once the payoffs have been determined, the sample size yielding the maximum expected payoff can then be arrived at by backward induction.

The following expected payoffs have been determined for the other values of n, as they were for $n = 2$:

Act	Expected Payoff
$n = 1$	$625.92
$n = 2$	630.50
$n = 3$	630.63 maximum
$n = 4$	630.36

Of the four sample sizes being considered, $n = 3$ has the maximum expected payoff of $630.63. The expected payoff rises when the sample size is increased from $n = 2$ to $n = 3$ and then declines for larger values of n. Thus, $n = 3$ is the *optimal sample size* for Charles Stereo to use in establishing an acceptance plan, and the branches of the decision tree in Figure 18-8 representing the other sizes of n are pruned. The expected payoff from the decision to sample is $630.63.

In a more general acceptance sampling problem, a large number of possible values of n may have to be evaluated before the optimal sample size can be determined. This can involve a staggering amount of calculation and require the use of a digital computer to find the n that yields the maximum expected payoff.*

Valuing Sample Information

The EVPI establishes the worth of perfect information and represents the difference in payoffs expected with perfect information and with no information at all, or

$$\text{EVPI} = \text{Expected payoff with perfect information} - \text{Maximum expected payoff (with no information)}$$

* In his book *Analysis of Decisions Under Uncertainty* (New York: McGraw-Hill, 1969), Robert Schlaifer describes a program developed at Harvard University to determine the optimal sample size for binomial or hypergeometric sampling.

For the computer center manager's decision discussed in Section 18-2, we have established that the best course of action when there is no information is to use the holographic unit, for which

Maximum expected payoff (with no information) = $750,000

If a perfect hypothetical predictor were available for the unknown value of the population mean daily access level, the manager would select the photographic memory, which has a payoff of $715,000, when $\mu = 2$ and the holographic memory, which has a payoff of $810,000, when $\mu = 3$. Thus, we have

Expected payoff with perfect information = .5($715,000) + .5($810,000)

$$= \$762,500$$

The expected value of perfect information is therefore

$$\text{EVPI} = \$762,500 - \$750,000 = \$12,500$$

The EVPI sets a limit on how much the manager is willing to pay for any kind of experimental information that will help to predict the value of μ.

We have seen that the EVPI can be useful as a rough gauge for deciding whether or not it is worthwhile to pursue further information. If the EVPI is very small, then sample information will not be worth its cost, and an immediate decision should be made solely from prior knowledge.

The Expected Value of Sample Information

Another measure similar to the EVPI expresses the worth of the information contained in the sample. The *expected value of sample information is calculated*

EVSI = Expected payoff with sample information
        − Maximum expected payoff (with no information)

To illustrate, we will continue with the computer center manager's decision. In Figure 18-6, we obtained the expected payoff of $753,437.50 using a sample of size $n = 9$ and applying the indicated decision rule for $\bar{X}$. Thus, for the memory device decision

$$\text{EVSI} = \$753,437.50 - \$750,000 = \$3,437.50$$

This amount represents how much better off the computer center manager would be on the average if she had the $n = 9$ sample result instead of no information at all. The EVSI is totally analogous to the EVPI, but applies to less reliable information gleaned from the sample. Like the EVPI, the EVSI establishes an upper limit on the amount a decision maker should pay to obtain the sample results.

The Expected Net Gain of Sampling

Preposterior analysis often begins with gross payoffs rather than net payoffs, and sampling costs must therefore be integrated at a later stage. (One reason for waiting to include the sampling costs is that it is sometimes easier to minimize expected opportunity loss than it is to maximize expected payoff. It is more convenient to include sampling costs at the end when such an approach is used.

In terms of gross annual savings, the manager is better off by the EVSI of $3,437.50 if she obtains the sample results and then applies the optimal decision rule with $C = 1$. Thus, the manager should be willing to pay up to $3,437.50 for the sample but should not sample at a higher cost. *As long as the cost of sampling is less than the EVSI, the decision maker is better off with the sample than without it.*

To obtain the peripheral memory access levels for the sample days, a special program must be added to the operating system that will slow down the processing of each job. As a result, the computer must operate for a longer period of time, which creates an added expense. We will assume that this additional cost is $100 per day. The total cost of sampling for $n = 9$ days is therefore $900. Since this figure is smaller than the EVSI, the computer center manager should prefer sampling to making a decision without the information sampling provides.

How large should n be? As a practical matter, n can be no larger in this example than the number of days that remain before the peripheral unit must be ordered. However, this question is ordinarily a matter of economics. We could compute the EVSI for several levels of n, subtracting the sampling costs in each case. Each resulting value would then represent the *expected net gain of sampling*, or ENGS. Treating n as a variable, the expected net gain of sampling is expressed

$$\text{ENGS}(n) = \text{EVSI}(n) - \text{Cost}(n)$$

Thus, when $n = 9$

$$\begin{aligned}\text{ENGS}(9) &= \text{EVSI}(9) - \text{Cost}(9)\\ &= \$3,437.50 - \$900\\ &= \$2,537.50\end{aligned}$$

Comparable figures could be obtained for other sizes of n, and the optimal sample size would be the one with the greatest expected net gain.

TABLE 18-3
EVSI and ENGS Values for the Charles Stereo Decision

Sample Size n	(1) Expected Payoff (Net)	(2) Expected Payoff (Gross)	(3) Maximum Expected Payoff (with No Information)	(4) EVSI(n) [(2)−(3)]	(5) Cost (n)	(6) ENGS(n) [(4)−(5)]
1	$625.92	$629.92	$620	$ 9.92	$ 4	$ 5.92
2	630.50	638.50	620	18.50	8	10.50
3*	630.63	642.63	620	22.63	12	10.63
4	630.36	646.36	620	26.36	16	10.36

* Optimal n.

The EVSI and ENGS results for the Charles Stereo decision appear in Table 18-3. The optimal sample size of $n = 3$ (identified earlier in Figure 18-8) has the greatest ENGS at $10.63. Note that EVSI increases as n increases, reflecting the greater reliability of larger samples. But sampling costs increase by $4 per observation, and we can see in the table that ENGS peaks at $n = 3$ and drops thereafter. Similar results will be found for most sampling situations. Ordinarily, our search for the optimal n ends when we find an ENGS that is smaller than the preceding one.

DECISION THEORY AND TRADITIONAL STATISTICS 18-4

To complete our discussion of decision making using sample information, a few comments should be made about the procedure presented here and the traditional statistical approach. In our two examples, we obtained the following optimal decision rules for the chosen sample sizes:

$$\text{Accept the lot if } R \le C \, (=0)$$
$$\text{Reject the lot if } R > C$$

and

$$\text{Select photographic unit if } \bar{X} \le C \, (=1)$$
$$\text{Select holographic unit if } \bar{X} > C$$

This type of result is usually obtained in a statistical testing procedure. However, the process for determing C is totally different.

Hypothesis-Testing Concepts Reviewed

In traditional statistics, the basic uncertainty is couched in special terminology. The main events are expressed as *hypotheses*. Each decision has two kinds of hypotheses. One is referred to as the *null hypothesis* (originally used to represent "no change"), and the other is the complementary *alternative hypothesis*. In the language of classical statistics, the following hypotheses would apply to the quality-control inspection problem:

Null hypothesis: Lot is good ($P = .10$)

Alternative hypothesis: Lot is poor ($P > .10$)

The hypotheses for the computer memory decision would be

Null hypothesis: Photographic unit is best ($\mu = 2$)

Alternative hypothesis: Holographic unit is best ($\mu = 3$)

The decision rules we formulated earlier can be expressed in terms of the respective hypotheses pairs. For the inspection decision, they would take the form

Accept the null hypothesis if $R \leq C$

Reject the null hypothesis if $R > C$

and for the computer memory decision, they would take the form

Accept the null hypothesis if $\bar{X} \leq C$

Reject the null hypothesis if $\bar{X} > C$

(Rejecting the null hypothesis is the same as accepting the alternative hypothesis.)

Traditional statistics focuses on the worst outcomes of the decision. These are called *errors* and are of two types. The *Type I error* occurs when the null hypothesis is rejected when it is actually true; the *Type II error* occurs when the null hypothesis is accepted when it is actually false. In the quality-control inspection problem, these errors are

Type I error: Reject lot when it is good

Type II error: Accept lot when it is poor

In the computer memory decision, the Type I error would be to use the holographic memory when the photographic memory is better, and the Type II error would be to select the photographic memory when the holographic memory is superior. (In either case, there are two correct choices: accepting the null hypothesis when it is true, and rejecting the null hypothesis when it is false.)

The decision structure for traditional statistical analysis is presented in Table 18-4. The main events themselves are not assigned probabilities. Rather, the controlling factors in establishing the decision rule (the value of C) are the probabilities for the two kinds of errors:

$$\alpha = \Pr[\text{Type I error}] = \Pr[\text{rejecting the null hypothesis when it is true}]$$

$$\beta = \Pr[\text{Type II error}] = \Pr[\text{accepting the null hypothesis when it is false}]$$

These probabilities are usually established in advance of sampling and are actually conditional probabilities (for which the status of the null hypothesis—true or false—is the given event). Conventionally, the Greek letters α (alpha) and β (beta) are used to represent the error probabilities. In the quality-control inspection decision, α represents the probability for rejecting a good lot, which is sometimes referred to as the *producer's risk*, and β is the probability for accepting a poor lot, or the *consumer's risk*.

Both types of errors are undesirable, but obviously neither error can be avoided entirely. Traditional statistics is concerned with selecting the sample

TABLE 18-4
Decision Table for the Traditional Statistical Decision

	Act	
Event	*Accept Null Hypothesis.* (Accept lot; select photographic.)	*Reject Null Hypothesis.* (Reject lot; select holographic.)
Null hypothesis is true. (Lot good; photographic best.)	*Correct decision*	*Type I error* (Return good lot; select holographic when photographic is best.) α = Target probability
Null hypothesis is false. (Lot poor; holographic best.)	*Type II error* (Accept poor lot; select photographic when holographic is best.) β = Target probability	*Correct decision*

size n and the decision rule (the value of C) that will achieve an acceptable balance between α and β. If n is fixed, one error probability can be reduced only by increasing the probability for the other error. Because the sample size itself is often dictated by economic or other considerations, it is usually possible to control only one error completely.

Generally, the null and alternative hypotheses are formulated in such a way that the Type I error is more serious. The tolerable probability for this error is specified at a level such as $\alpha = .01$, $\alpha = .05$, or $\alpha = .10$. The value of C is then chosen that guarantees that this level of α is not exceeded.

To illustrate, we will return to our quality-control inspection problem. Suppose that the $\alpha = .05$, so that C must be the smallest value such that

$$Pr[\text{rejecting the null hypothesis when it is true}] \leq \alpha$$

or

$$Pr[R > C|P = .10] \leq .05$$

For $C = 0$, the probability for incorrectly rejecting a good lot (from Table 18-1) is

$$Pr[R > 0] = 1 - Pr[R = 0] = 1 - .81 = .19$$

which is greater than the targeted Type I error probability of $\alpha = .05$. Trying $C = 1$, we obtain

$$Pr[R > 1] = Pr[R = 2] = .01$$

which is smaller than $\alpha = .05$. The optimal decision rule using the traditional procedure is therefore $C = 1$.

This value of C differs from the one we found previously ($C = 0$). *The optimal rule using decision-theory analysis will often differ from the optimal rule obtained using the traditional statistical hypothesis test.*

Contrasting the Two Approaches

Why do decision theory and traditional statistical analysis lead to different decision rules? The differences between these two procedures are:

(1) The decision-theory procedure considers the payoffs from every possible outcome. Payoffs are not explicitly considered in hypothesis testing, although they may influence the choice of α.

(2) Prior probabilities are applied directly in the decision-theory approach. Like payoffs, prior probabilities ought to play some role in establishing α.

(3) Hypothesis testing proceeds directly from the prescribed α to the decision rule. Decision-theory analysis arrives at the optimal decision rule by means of the Bayes decision rule, using the appropriate posterior probabilities and

the payoffs for each outcome. The resulting decision maximizes expected payoff.

Which procedure is preferable? Decision theory is plagued by subjective prior probabilities, which are considered by many to be the weakest link in its analytical chain. Many statisticians deny the existence of subjective probabilities, thereby relegating much of statistical decision theory to the ash heap. A major feature that makes traditional hypothesis-testing procedures more universally accepted is that no prior probabilities are required at all. *But the uncertainties regarding the population parameter still exist,* and traditional statistical procedures must also involve some sort of subjective assessment of these uncertainties when desired error probabilities are being established. In hypothesis testing, everything hinges on the prescribed significance level α (and also on β when there is the freedom or the capability to prescribe β). Unless α is carefully determined, inferior decisions are bound to occur. Decision theory permits the consistent and systematic treatment of chance and payoffs as well as attitude toward risk. Decision theory does not place the burden on the decision maker of requiring him or her to do everything at once by choosing a single number—"an α for all seasons."

When the outcomes do not have a natural numerical payoff measure or when the decision maker is risk-seeking or risk-averse, then the strengths of decision-theory analysis rest on a foundation of utility values. As we will see in Chapter 20, obtaining utilities requires a set of assumptions about attitudes, which are obtained by means of an elaborate procedure. Although any difficulties involved in employing utilities can be avoided by traditional statistics, α embodies everything, so that even more care must be exercised in choosing the appropriate target value.

The final and perhaps the most significant advantage of decision theory is that *it considers whether or not a sample should even be used.* We have seen that a greater expected payoff may be achieved by deciding what to do immediately, without incurring the expense of a sample. Traditional statistics never satisfactorily copes with this question. In addition, the choice of proper sample size is too often an *ad hoc* process in traditional statistics. (A sample size of 30 may be used, for example, because the Student t table stops at 30 degrees of freedom.) Decision theory explicitly considers the costs of the various sample sizes.

ADDITIONAL REMARKS 18-5

In this chapter, we have learned to analyze decision making using sampling. By employing the procedures described here, we can exercise judgment about the population characteristics by assigning prior probabilities to the possible values of the decision parameter P or μ. The benefits and costs of sampling can be systematically evaluated in a way that explicitly accounts for the payoffs for every outcome. This makes it possible even to consider the question of whether or not to sample in the first place. The principles of decision theory permit a more thorough analysis to be made than traditional statistics provides.

The procedures presented in this chapter have drawbacks. The main difficulties arise from the nature of decision tree analysis itself. Because the possible number of sample results and population parameters can be huge, many problems are too large to fit conveniently on a tree. Some problems require such a large amount of computational effort that a computer is needed to evaluate them.

But decision tree analysis presents a more fundamental problem. It is an inherently *discrete* procedure, since each event must be represented by a separate branch. Many problems involve continuous random variables. For example, P and μ may range over a continuous spectrum of possible values. Also, the sample mean $\bar{X}$ is often a continuous variable that is generally represented by the normal distribution. In Chapter 19, we will consider the case in which the normal curve serves as the prior distribution for μ. Nevertheless, it is still possible to apply decision tree analysis to these problem situations by approximating the continuous distributions. Methods for doing this with a few typical values representing the entire range of the continuous variable will be described in Chapter 21.

PROBLEMS

18-1   The president of Admiral Mills believes that the proportion of children P who will like Crunchy Munchy has the following probability distribution:

Possible Proportion P	Probability
1/4	1/3
1/2	1/3
3/4	1/3
	1

The president wishes to revise these probabilities to devise a strategy for later test marketing. Three children have been chosen at random, given Crunchy Munchy, and then asked if they like it.

(a) Construct the actual chronological probability tree diagram for the outcomes of this experiment, letting the values of P represent the events of the branches in the first-stage fork and the number of children found to like Crunchy Munchy represent the events of the second-stage branches.

(b) Enter the above probabilities for the possible P values on the appropriate branches. Then use the binomial formula to find the probabilities for the branches in the remaining forks and enter them on your diagram.

(c) Calculate the joint probabilities for each end position.

(d) Construct the probability tree diagram for the informational chronology, reversing the event sequences so that the branches of the first fork represent the number of children who like Crunchy Munchy, followed by forks for the values of P. Determine the probabilities for the events represented by each branch.

(e) If all three children like Crunchy Munchy, what are the posterior probabilities for P?

18-2 High Crock, the brewmaster and part owner of High & Higher Distilleries, has discovered a new fermentation process for malt ale that reclaims corn mash from whiskey vats to begin fermentation. Get, the marketing manager and joint owner of High & Higher, is excited about the revolutionary ale and has assigned the prior probabilities of $\Pr[P = .10] = .20$, $\Pr[P = .20] = .50$, and $\Pr[P = .30] = .30$ to the proportion P of the market segment he feels will buy the new beer. Get feels the probabilities should be revised before a final product decision is made. A random sample of $n = 3$ connoisseurs has been selected to test the new ale.

(a) Construct the actual chronological probability tree diagram, using the prior probabilities assigned by the marketing manager and the applicable binomial, conditional result probabilities obtained from Appendix Table A.

(b) From the probabilities generated in the actual chronology, construct the informational chronology, indicating the unconditional result, posterior, and joint probabilities.

18-3 A presidential campaign manager asks two politicians what they believe to be the true proportion P of voters favoring their party's candidate. The respective replies are .40 and .50. The manager's judgment leads her to assign equal chances that either politician is correct. A random sample of $n = 100$ registered voters will be chosen, and the number R preferring the candidate will be found. The following results are of interest: $R < 40$; $40 \le R \le 50$; $R > 50$.

(a) Construct the actual chronological probability tree diagram, using the sample results in the second stage. (Appendix Table A provides the conditional result probabilities.)

(b) Determine the probability tree diagram for the informational chronology.

(c) What is the posterior probability that $P = .40$, (1) given $R < 40$? (2) Given $40 \le R \le 50$? (3) Given $R > 50$?

18-4 Consider a slight modification in the computer memory device decision discussed in this chapter. Suppose that the following prior probabilities for the mean memory access levels apply:

$$\mu = 2 \text{ gigabits per day: } .6$$

$$\mu = 3 \text{ gigabits per day: } .4$$

Compute the new probabilities for the actual and informational chronologies in Figure 18-7 (page 433), assuming that the same conditional result probabilities apply.

18-5 The marketing manager of Blitz Beer must determine whether or not to sponsor Blitz Day with the Gotham City Hellcats. She is uncertain what the effect of the promotion will be in terms of the mean increase in daily sales volume that would result during the 100-day baseball season. The cost of sponsorship is $10,000, and each can of Blitz has a marginal cost of $.20 and sells for $.40. Two levels are judged equally likely for the mean increase in sales for the season: $\mu = 490$ and $\mu = 530$ cans per day.

(a) Construct the manager's payoff table.

(b) If the manager wishes to maximize expected payoff, what action should she take?

(c) Further experimental information may be desired before making a final decision. Calculate the EVPI. Can a sample from the underlying population—assuming it is cheap enough—be helpful in reaching this decision? Explain.

18-6 The decision tree diagram in Figure 18-9 has been constructed to determine whether or not to accept shipments from a particular supplier.

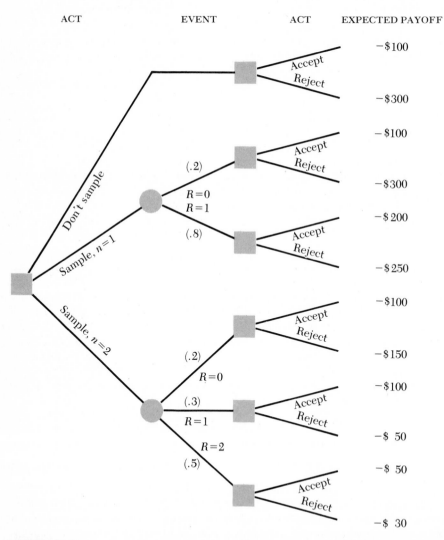

ACT	EVENT	ACT	EXPECTED PAYOFF

- $100
- $300
- $100
- $300
- $200
- $250
- $100
- $150
- $100
- $50
- $50
- $30

FIGURE 18-9

(a) Perform backward induction. Which choice—not to sample, to sample with $n = 1$, or to sample with $n = 2$—should be made?

(b) What is the optimal value of the acceptance number C if $n = 1$ is used? If $n = 2$ is used?

18-7 Suppose that the prior probabilities for the proportion P of CornChox buyers favoring a new package design are $\Pr[P = .4] = .5$ and $\Pr[P = .6] = .5$. Also suppose that if the new design is used, the present value of future profits will decrease by \$10,000 when $P = .4$ and increase by \$10,000 when $P = .6$. Sampling is very expensive, costing \$500 per observation.

(a) Which act provides the greatest expected payoff—not to sample or to sample with $n = 1$?

(b) Does sampling with $n = 1$ or $n = 2$ provide the greatest expected payoff? What can you conclude about the optimal sample size?

18-8 Suppose that the peripheral memory device decision problem in this chapter is modified so that the following prior probabilities for the mean memory access levels apply:

$$\mu = 2 \text{ gigabits per day:}\quad .3$$

$$\mu = 3 \text{ gigabits per day:}\quad .7$$

The decision tree diagram in Figure 18-10 (page 448) now applies.

(a) Perform backward induction.

(b) What is the value of C that will maximize expected payoff? Formulate the optimal decision rule.

(c) Calculate the EVSI.

(d) Determine the expected net gain of sampling for a sample costing \$900.

18-9 A quality control inspector must select the optimal sample size to use to determine whether to accept or reject incoming shipments. The following payoffs apply to the various assumed levels of the proportion defective:

Proportion Defective	Prior Probability	Accept	Reject
$P = .05$	.3	\$100	$-\$100$
$P = .10$	.4	0	0
$P = .20$	.3	-100	100

The following expected payoffs with sample information (ignoring the cost of sampling have been obtained):

Sample Size	Expected Payoff
$n = 1$	\$ 9.00
$n = 2$	15.70
$n = 3$	20.50
$n = 4$	24.22

(a) Find the expected payoff using sample information when $n = 5$. What acceptance number applies to the number of sample defectives R?

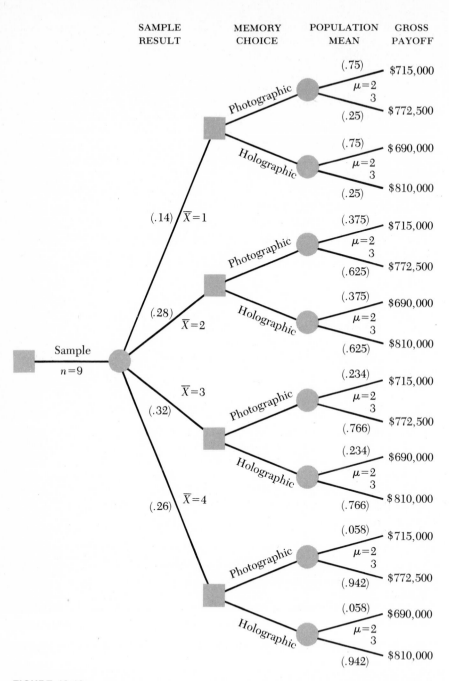

SAMPLE RESULT	MEMORY CHOICE	POPULATION MEAN	GROSS PAYOFF

FIGURE 18-10

(b) Assuming that each sample observation costs $3, determine ENGS(n) for n = 1 through n = 5. What is the optimal sample size?

18-10 A chemical process yields a mean of μ grams of active ingredient for every liter of raw material processed. Due to variations in the raw material and in the control settings, the true population mean for any particular batch is unknown until processing is complete. From past history, the plant superintendent judges that the following prior probabilities for μ apply:

Possible Mean μ	Probability
25 g	.3
30	.4
35	.3

Early in the processing of the current batch, the superintendent plans to select a random sample of n = 3 liters and precisely determine the amount of active ingredient each liter contains. The sample mean will then be calculated from these readings. Suppose that the following approximate conditional result probabilities apply:

	PROBABILITIES FOR X̄		
X̄	μ = 25 g	μ = 30 g	μ = 35 g
25 g	.7	.2	.2
30	.2	.6	.3
35	.1	.2	.5

Construct the actual chronological probability tree diagram. Then use this tree to find the tree for the informational chronology and to compute the unconditional result probabilities and the posterior probabilities for μ.

18-11 Referring to Problem 18-10, the plant superintendent must decide whether or not to adjust the control settings in processing a chemical batch. Suppose that the following payoff table applies:

Population Mean	Acts	
μ	Adjust	Leave Alone
25 g	$ 500	− $500
30	0	0
35	− 1,000	500

(a) Assuming that no sample is taken, what course of action will maximize the expected payoff?
(b) Find the plant superintendent's EVPI. Would he use a sample to facilitate his decision if it cost $400? (Answer yes, no, or maybe.) If it cost $200? Explain.

18-12 Referring to Problems 18-10 and 18-11 and to your answers to those exercises:
  (a) Construct the plant superintendent's decision tree diagram, assuming that he is committed to taking a sample. Use gross payoff figures.
  (b) Perform backward induction to determine the value of C (for accepting the need for adjustment) that will maximize expected gross payoff. Formulate the optimal decision rule that the superintendent should apply.
  (c) Calculate the EVSI.
  (d) Suppose that a sample of $n = 3$ liters costs $50. Calculate the superintendent's expected net gain of sampling.

18-13 A market researcher wishes to determine whether to accept the null hypothesis regarding the proportion P of Appleton smokers who will switch to a new mentholated version, Mapleton. Her null hypothesis is that $P = .1$. She takes a random sample of 100 current Appleton smokers, who will be contracted in six months to see if they have switched. The researcher wishes to protect against the Type I error with a probability of $\alpha = .005$. Using Appendix Table A, determine the smallest acceptance number C such that the probability that the number of switchers will exceed this number is less than or equal to the desired α. Then formulate the researcher's decision rule.

18-14 Referring to Problem 18-13, suppose that the following prior probabilities are obtained for P:

P	Probability
.05	1/3
.10	1/3
.15	1/3
	1

The following conditional result probabilities for the number of switchers R apply:

	$P = .05$	$P = .10$	$P = .15$
$R \leq 17$	1.0000	.9900	.7633
$R = 18$	0	.0054	.0739
$R \geq 19$	0	.0046	.1628

The decision maker's payoffs, including the cost of sampling, are

	Accept Null Hypothesis	Reject Null Hypothesis
$P = .05$	$ 10,000	− $2,000
$P = .10$	5,000	0
$P = .15$	− 2,000	4,000

(a) Calculate the posterior probability distribution for P, given each of the sample result events above. Then find the unconditional result probabilities.
(b) Construct the market researcher's decision tree diagram. Enter the appropriate probabilities you found in (a) on the branches and place the payoffs along the respective end positions.
(c) Should the decision maker accept or reject the null hypothesis if $R = 18$? Compare this result with your result in Problem 18-13.

19

Decision Making Using the Normal Distribution

I n Chapter 18, we saw how sampling can be used to obtain experimental information to facilitate decision making. There, we applied sampling to situations involving two acts with payoffs determined by the value of an uncertain population parameter, such as the mean μ or the proportion P. Our earlier discussion of decision making using the mean considered only discrete probability distributions, which apply when the number of possible values for the population mean or the sample mean is limited. But in most situations, both μ and $\bar{X}$ may be any point in a continuous range of values. In such cases, it is more realistic to analyze the decision in terms of continuous probability distributions.

In describing the procedures for doing this, we will expand the computer center manager's decision described in Chapter 18. Recall that a choice must be made between two peripheral memory storage units based on laser technology. One alternative is photographic in nature; the other employs the principles of holographic imagery. Our earlier analysis was based on only two values of the population mean of memory access levels μ, expressed in gigabits per day. There, we used prior probabilities of .5 for $\mu = 2$ and .5 for $\mu = 3$. We will now treat the unknown μ as a random variable with a *continuous prior probability distribution*, reflecting the possibility that μ can assume many other levels. For any given level of μ, we will also assume that there is a *continuous conditional probability distribution* for the possible values of $\bar{X}$, instead of the four whole numbers used earlier.

In both cases, the particular distributions are members of the *normal distribution* family. Although a variety of other prior distributions might be used for μ, we know from the central limit theorem (discussed in Chapter 3) that $\bar{X}$ tends to be normally distributed and that this is the only appropriate distribution to use.* Although different normal curves apply to μ and $\bar{X}$, we will establish that the true shape of the prior distribution for μ makes little difference.

19-1 DECISION MAKING USING OPPORTUNITY LOSSES

Until this point, we have been able to analyze decisions by maximizing expected payoff—a procedure sometimes referred to as the *Bayes decision rule*. We have established that an equivalent criterion is to minimize expected opportunity loss. For two-action problems involving continuous probability distributions, it is more convenient to focus on opportunity losses as a basis for decision making.

Figure 19-1 shows the essential relationship between payoff and opportunity loss for the computer memory device decision. The gross payoffs for the two memory units may be expressed in terms of the unknown mean daily access level as

$$\text{Gross payoff} = \begin{cases} \$600,000 + \$\ 57,500\ \mu & \text{for photographic} \\ \$450,000 + \$120,000\ \mu & \text{for holographic} \end{cases}$$

These payoffs are plotted as two lines in the top graph in Figure 19-1. The height of the respective lines at any level μ may be determined from the preceding equations. The slope of the photographic-unit payoff line is \$57,500, and the slope of the steeper holographic-unit payoff line is \$120,000. The two lines cross at that value of μ where the gross payoff is identical under each act. This value is referred to as the *breakeven mean* and is denoted as μ_b. The breakeven mean is found by setting the two payoff expressions equal to each other and solving for μ_b. In this case

$$\$600,000 + \$57,500\ \mu_b = \$450,000 + \$120,000\ \mu_b$$

so that

$$(\$120,000 - \$57,500)\ \mu_b = \$600,000 - \$450,000$$
$$\$62,500\ \mu_b = \$150,000$$

---

* The necessary conditions are that the population variance be finite and known and that the samples be large and independently selected.

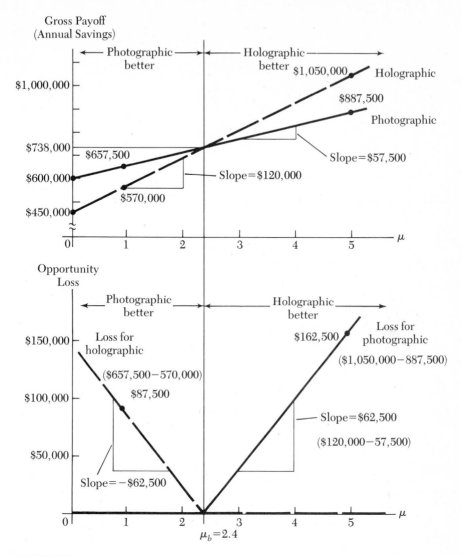

FIGURE 19-1
Payoff and opportunity loss graphs for the computer memory device decision.

and

$$\mu_b = \$150,000/\$62,500 = 2.4 \text{ gigabits per day}$$

For values of μ less than $\mu_b = 2.4$, the photographic memory yields the greatest annual savings; for means greater than μ_b, the holographic unit is preferable. At $\mu = \mu_b$, the annual savings is $738,000 using either alternative.

The bottom graph in Figure 19-1 represents the *opportunity losses* for the same alternatives. We can see that the photographic unit is the better choice when the true population mean lies below the breakeven level μ_b. Thus, whenever $\mu \leq \mu_b$, choosing the photographic unit will result in zero opportunity loss, which is represented by the horizontal line segment to the left of μ_b. If the true mean exceeds the breakeven level, the opportunity losses for the photographic unit rise, as represented by the upward-sloping line segment beginning at μ_b. The reverse holds for the holographic unit. For true population means above μ_b, the holographic alternative is better and its opportunity losses must be zero, as represented by the dashed horizontal line segment to the right of μ_b. To the left of μ_b, the opportunity losses for the holographic unit rise, as represented by the downward-sloping dashed line segment falling toward μ_b. The heights of points lying on the V-shaped portion represent the difference in savings between the best and worst acts at each level of μ. The "V" is symmetrical, and the two rising line segments have identical slopes (with opposite signs) of a magnitude equal to the difference between the slopes of the two payoff lines: $\$120,000 - \$57,500 = \$62,500$.

19-2 PRIOR ANALYSIS WITHOUT SAMPLE INFORMATION

In this chapter, we will assume that μ is a random variable having prior probabilities obtainable from the normal curve. Recall from Chapter 3 that any particular normal curve may be specified entirely by its mean and standard deviation (or variance). These parameters are denoted by μ_0 and σ_0, where the subscript zeros indicate that these are the initial, prior values and are not based on sampling information. Here, μ_0 is the expected value of the unknown population mean. This is the central value, and we will refer to μ_0 as the *expected mean*. The standard deviation σ_0 summarizes the variability in possible levels of μ.

Minimum Expected Opportunity Loss Acts

The values of μ_0 and σ_0 must be based largely on judgment, because the computer center in our example has no historical data that are directly related to μ. In other applications, however, μ_0 and σ_0 might be obtained from previous experience. For example, μ might represent the mean ingredient yield in several successive batches of a raw material used in chemical processing, and records might have been kept of the mean yield that each batch achieved. In Chapter 21,

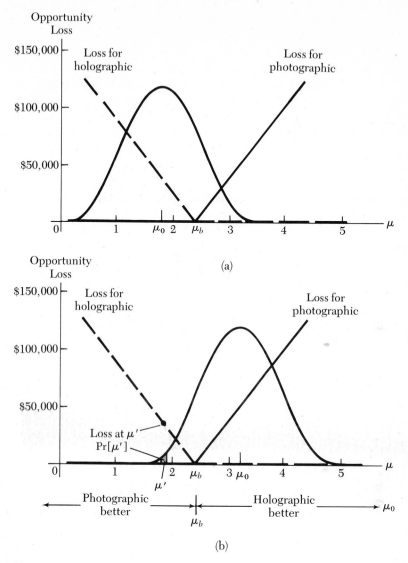

FIGURE 19-2
The applicable normal curves and opportunity losses when no sample is taken.

we will consider in detail the question of how subjective prior probability distributions can be obtained.

When no sample is taken, the decision is easy to make. Figure 19-2 relates the opportunity losses to the probabilities for μ by superimposing the normal curve for μ on the respective opportunity loss graphs for the two acts involved in the computer memory device decision. Figure 19-2(a) shows a possible arrangement when the expected mean μ_0 lies below the breakeven level. If $\mu_0 < \mu_b$, it is easy to see that the expected opportunity loss for the photographic unit will be smaller than the expected opportunity loss for the holographic unit, since most of the area under the normal curve is concentrated in the range of μ where the photographic opportunity loss is zero. (Remember that the *area* under the normal curve provides the probability.) The positive opportunity losses for the photographic unit, represented by the rising solid line segment, occur for unlikely levels of μ that are covered by the upper tail of the normal curve. On the other hand, the falling portion of the line for the holographic unit occurs over the most likely range of μ values, so the expected opportunity loss is greater for that act.

The reverse situation is shown in Figure 19-2(b), where $\mu_0 > \mu_b$ and the expected opportunity loss for the holographic unit is smaller.

From these graphs, we can conclude that *the optimal act having the minimum expected opportunity loss is the one with zero opportunity losses that lie on the same side of the breakeven level as the expected mean.* In our present example, the photographic unit is optimal when $\mu_0 < \mu_b$, whereas the holographic unit is optimal when $\mu_0 > \mu_b$. *If the expected mean coincides with the breakeven level, then the two alternatives are equally attractive.*

Suppose that the computer center manager determines that $\mu_0 = 2.5$ gigabits per day. Since this value is greater than $\mu_0 = 2.4$ and is at a level where the holographic unit has a zero opportunity loss, the manager would maximize expected savings and minimize expected opportunity loss by choosing that peripheral memory unit.

If no sample were to be taken, the decision could be made right now. But it may be better to take a sample before choosing the memory unit. Before this decision is made, the manager must quantitatively measure the act of choosing a holographic unit right now, which seems to be the best act. The actual expected opportunity loss for this act must be determined. The resulting number is the EVPI for the decision. (Recall that the expected value of perfect information is equal to the expected opportunity loss for the best act.)

Determining the EVPI: The Normal Loss Function

Unlike the situations we have encountered in earlier chapters, μ is a continuous variable here. Instead of a table of payoffs or losses for a few possible values of μ, we are now confronted with an infinite number of μs. One way out of this dilemma would be to approximate the continuous distribution for μ by a table involving a few typical values having probabilities that can be obtained from the normal curve. We could then compute an approximate expected opportunity loss in the usual manner.

For example, consider one possible mean μ' in Figure 19-2(b). All possible values in an interval about μ' can be represented by this typical value, and the shaded area shown under the normal curve is the probability that any one of those values will occur. By considering several such intervals, the expected opportunity loss can be approximated by multiplying the respective area by the loss for the typical value and summing the products. The more intervals that are used, the better this approximation becomes. Fortunately, this has already been done for us.

The expected opportunity loss for the optimal act, or the expected value of perfect information, can be calculated as

$$\text{EVPI} = |\text{slope}|\sigma_0 L(D_0)$$

where $L(D_0)$ is the *normal loss function* provided in Appendix Table C. Three constants applicable to the particular problem are used: (1) the absolute value of the slope of the opportunity loss line; (2) the standard deviation of the prior probability distribution for μ; and (3) the *standardized distance*

$$D_0 = \frac{|\mu_b - \mu_0|}{\sigma_0}$$

which expresses the separation between μ_b and μ_0 in units of standard deviation. (The numerator must always be positive, so absolute values are used.)

Now suppose that the computer center manager selects $\mu_0 = 2.5$ gigabits per day, with $\sigma_0 = 1$ gigabit per day. We have established that the holographic unit is better for this μ_0. Referring to Figure 19-1(b), we can see that the holographic loss line has a slope of $-\$62,500$, so that $|\text{slope}| = \$62,500$. The standardized distance separating the expected mean from the breakeven level is

$$D_0 = \frac{|\mu_b - \mu_0|}{\sigma_0} = \frac{|2.4 - 2.5|}{1} = .1$$

Referring to Appendix Table C, we find that for $D_0 = .1$

$$L(D_0) = L(.1) = .3509$$

and the minimum expected opportunity loss for using the holographic memory is

$$
\begin{aligned}
\text{EVPI} &= \$62,500(1)L(.1) \\
&= \$62,500(1)(.3509) \\
&= \$21,931
\end{aligned}
$$

This tells us that a perfect prediction for μ is worth only $21,931. This is the upper limit on the amount the decision maker might be willing to pay for less-than-perfect sample information. (This value differs from the EVPI of $12,500 calculated in Chapter 18. The discrepancy is due to the change in the prior probability distribution; our earlier example involved only two levels of μ, each with a probability of .5.)

In Chapter 18, we saw that the EVPI can be useful in deciding what and how much sample information to gather. We are now ready to consider this question.

19-3 DECISION STRUCTURE WHEN SAMPLING IS CONSIDERED

The structure for the computer memory device decision using sample information is provided by the decision tree diagram in Figure 19-3. Here, the initial choice of whether or not to use sample information is made. If no sample is taken, the prior probability distribution for μ applies. If sampling is chosen, the sample size must be selected, the sample data collected, and the sample mean calculated. Based on the value achieved for $\bar{X}$, either the photographic or the holographic memory unit is chosen. With sampling, the posterior probability distribution applies to the population mean μ. The event forks for the values of $\bar{X}$ and μ have many branches, since each variable is continuous. In each case, probability values can be obtained only by finding the appropriate areas under the respective normal curves.

The probability distributions provided in the upper portion of the decision tree represent the informational chronology. This event sequence is the reverse of the order in which probability information is generally presented. Figure 19-4 provides the probability trees for the two chronologies. The actual chronology in (a) begins with the value of μ (which must come first) followed by the event fork for $\bar{X}$. The prior normal probability distribution for μ is centered at a presumed value of the population mean denoted by μ_0 (the subscript zero indicates initial value). The mean of the conditional normal distribution for $\bar{X}$ has an uncertain center μ. The informational chronology in Figure 19-4(b) provides two curves with different centers. The unconditional distribution for $\bar{X}$ has a mean of μ_0, whereas the posterior probability distribution for the population mean is centered at a *revised value of μ_1*.

Since our probability distributions are continuous, it is not easy to obtain the revised versions needed to construct the decision tree. The backward

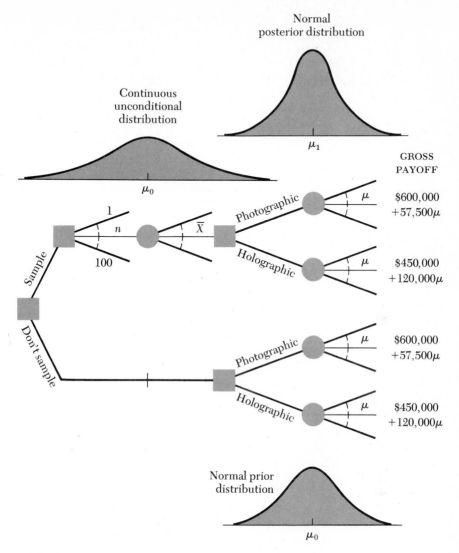

FIGURE 19-3
The structure of the computer memory device decision
when a prior normal probability distribution applies to the population mean.

induction required to determine the optimal decision rule, which specifies the action to take for each possible sample result, is also complicated. We must therefore depart from decision tree analysis and revert to *normal form analysis*, which itself must now be dressed in unfamiliar clothing.

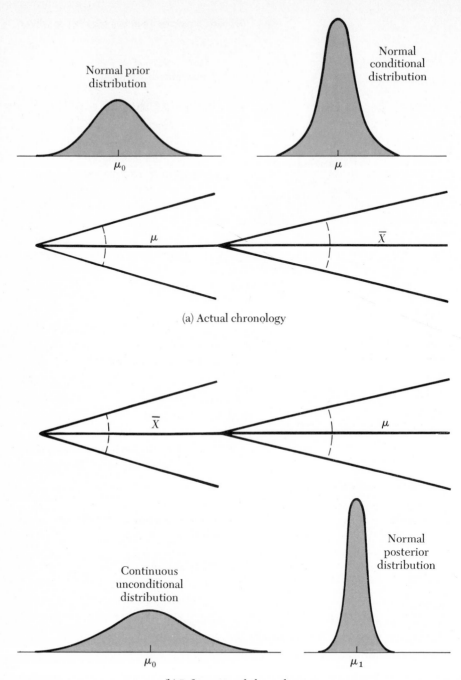

(a) Actual chronology

(b) Informational chronology

FIGURE 19-4
The representation of revising probabilities for the computer memory device decision.

POSTERIOR ANALYSIS FOR A GIVEN SAMPLE SIZE 19-4

We will begin our analysis of the sampling decision by arbitrarily choosing a sample size n. Later, we will consider just how large n should be.

Recall from Chapter 18 that for a given sample size, the Bayes criterion leads to the choice of a decision rule indicating what act to take for each possible value of the sample mean $\bar{X}$. Such a rule takes the form

Choose act 1 if $\bar{X} \leq C$

Choose act 2 if $\bar{X} > C$

where C is the critical value that minimizes expected opportunity loss and maximizes expected gross payoff. When we are dealing with a normal prior distribution for μ, our procedure for finding C is less direct than before. First, we must consider the characteristics of the posterior probability distribution for μ that corresponds to a given sample result.

The Posterior Probability Distribution for μ

Let's summarize certain essential features of the problem we intend to analyze. A random sample of size n is *to be* selected from the population of daily peripheral memory access levels, and a replacement memory unit will be chosen in accordance with the value achieved for the sample mean. The population itself has a frequency distribution of unspecified shape (it might be normal but need not be). This population has an uncertain mean μ, and we have a prior probability distribution for μ. Treating this unknown mean as a random variable, we assume that it has an expected value of μ_0 and a standard deviation of σ_0 and that its distribution is provided by the normal curve with these parameters.

The central limit theorem tells us that $\bar{X}$ has a probability distribution that is closely approximated by a normal curve when n is large. This curve is centered on μ and has a standard deviation of

$$\sigma_{\bar{X}} = \frac{\sigma_I}{\sqrt{n}}$$

where σ_I denotes the standard deviation of the population. The quantity σ_I summarizes the variability in *individual* daily access levels (and is not to be confused with σ_0, which summarizes the variability in the possible values of the *mean* daily access levels μ). Thus, there are two normal curves with different shapes and centers—one for μ and another for $\bar{X}$. The normal curve for $\bar{X}$ depends on the particular value that happens to be the true μ and therefore represents the conditional probability distribution for $\bar{X}$ given μ.

To obtain the *posterior* probability distribution for μ given the level of $\bar{X}$, we must apply the concepts of Bayes' Theorem using the normal curves for μ and for $\bar{X}$. The mathematics required to accomplish this is beyond the scope of this book, but it can be established that *the posterior probability distribution for μ is also a normal distribution with a mean of μ_1 and a standard deviation of σ_1*. The values for these parameters are

$$\mu_1 = \frac{\mu_0(1/\sigma_0^2) + \bar{X}(1/\sigma_{\bar{X}}^2)}{1/\sigma_0^2 + 1/\sigma_{\bar{X}}^2}$$

$$\sigma_1^2 = \sigma_0^2 \frac{\sigma_{\bar{X}}^2}{\sigma_0^2 + \sigma_{\bar{X}}^2}$$

with

$$1/\sigma_1^2 = 1/\sigma_0^2 + 1/\sigma_{\bar{X}}^2$$

The rationale for these results can be explained in terms of the information contained in the prior probability distribution and in the sample. If the informational content of a finding is summarized by the reciprocal of the variance, then the third expression above tells us that

Posterior information = Prior information + Sample information

where $1/\sigma_1^2$, $1/\sigma_0^2$, and $1/\sigma_{\bar{X}}^2$ measure the informational content of the posterior probability distribution, the prior probability distribution, and the sample, respectively. Thus, we can view μ_1 as the *weighted average* of μ_0 and $\bar{X}$, where the weights are the proportions of the posterior information derived prior to sampling and from sampling, respectively.

To illustrate these concepts, we return to our computer memory device decision, where $\mu_0 = 2.5$ gigabits per day and $\sigma_0 = 1$. Suppose that a sample of $n = 25$ days is to be monitored by a special program and that the individual daily access levels are to be determined precisely. The sample mean of these levels may be computed to be a value such as $\bar{X} = 2.65$ gigabits per day. Suppose that by examining the records of a similar facility, the manager has determined that $\sigma_I = 3$ gigabits per day for the center. Then

$$\sigma_{\bar{X}} = \frac{3}{\sqrt{25}} = .6$$

These values give us

$$1/\sigma_0^2 = 1/(1)^2 = 1$$
$$1/\sigma_{\bar{X}}^2 = 1/(.6)^2 = 2.78$$

and

$$\mu_1 = \frac{2.5(1) + 2.65(2.78)}{1 + 2.78} = 2.61$$

$$\sigma_1^2 = (1)^2 \frac{(.6)^2}{(1)^2 + (.6)^2} = .265$$

$$\sigma_1 = \sqrt{.265} = .51$$

The new expected mean of $\mu_1 = 2.61$ lies between the prior value of $\mu_0 = 2.5$ and the sample mean of $\bar{X} = 2.65$. It lies closer to $\bar{X}$ than to μ_0, reflecting the fact that the informational content of sampling in this situation is greater than the informational content available prior to sampling ($1/\sigma_{\bar{X}}^2 = 2.78$ versus $1/\sigma_0^2 = 1$). Thus, greater weight is attached to the sample mean.

The quantity of posterior information is

$$1/\sigma_1^2 = 1/.265 = 3.77$$

which exceeds both the informational contents before and after sampling. Notice that the new standard deviation of $\sigma_1 = .51$ is smaller than either σ_0 or $\sigma_{\bar{X}}$. This must always be true, since the posterior informational content is greater than the informational contents of both the prior probability distribution and the sample.

Figure 19-5 helps to explain this process. The non-normal population of individual daily access levels is provided at the top of the figure. Although the standard deviation of individual daily access levels is presumed to be $\sigma_1 = 3$, the population center is unknown. This unknown mean μ is the entire focus of our analysis. The sample mean of n random daily observations $\bar{X}$ is to be computed. Since its value is presently unknown, statistical theory tells us that the tall, solid normal curve in the lower portion of Figure 19-5 provides the probabilities for $\bar{X}$. This is a conditional curve, since it is presumed to be centered on the prior expected mean μ_0. The flatter, solid normal curve represents the prior probabilities for the value of the unknown μ and is also centered on μ_0.

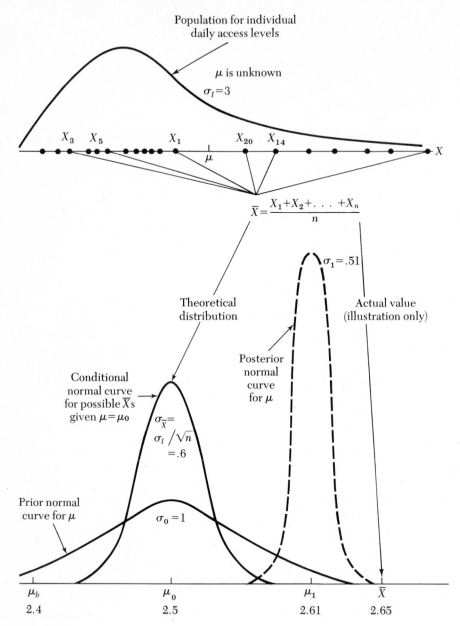

FIGURE 19-5
Distributions involved in posterior analysis with sampling (not drawn to scale).

When it is actually computed, the sample mean value may fall anywhere in the vicinity of μ_0. Depending on the location of the sample mean, the appropriate posterior normal curve for μ (represented here by the dashed curve centered on μ_1) is obtained. The center of the posterior normal curve will always lie between μ_0 and the computed $\bar{X}$.

Finding the Critical Value

We can now return to our earlier problem of finding the appropriate decision rule to apply to the posterior analysis. This involves selecting the critical value of C that minimizes the expected opportunity loss according to the decision rule

$$\text{Select photographic unit if } \bar{X} \leq C$$

$$\text{Select holographic unit if } \bar{X} > C$$

The best choice for C is the point of demarcation between those levels of $\bar{X}$ where the photographic unit is the better choice and those levels of $\bar{X}$ where the holographic unit is better. This is the level of $\bar{X}$ where the expected opportunity losses are identical under either act.

Earlier, we established that both acts are equally attractive when the expected mean is equal to the breakeven level. After sampling, the posterior expected mean applies, so that the point of demarcation must be the value of $\bar{X}$ that provides a posterior expected mean where

$$\mu_1 = \mu_b$$

Thus, we can substitute C for $\bar{X}$ in the earlier expression for μ_1 and set this expression equal to μ_b.

Solving for C, we then obtain

$$C = \frac{\mu_b[1/\sigma_0^2 + 1/\sigma_{\bar{X}}^2] - \mu_0(1/\sigma_0^2)}{1/\sigma_{\bar{X}}^2}$$

Substituting $\mu_b = 2.4$, $\sigma_0 = 1$, $\sigma_{\bar{X}} = .6$, and $\mu_0 = 2.5$ into this equation, we obtain

$$C = \frac{2.4[1/(1)^2 + 1/(.6)^2] - 2.5[1/(1)^2]}{1/(.6)^2}$$

$$= 2.36$$

The optimal decision rule for a sample of size $n = 25$ is therefore

Select photographic unit if $\bar{X} \le 2.36$

Select holographic unit if $\bar{X} > 2.36$

Thus, if the manager decides to sample with $n = 25$ and $\bar{X}$ turns out to be larger than $C = 2.36$ (say, $\bar{X} = 2.65$), then the holographic memory unit should be chosen. But if a smaller mean is found (say, $\bar{X} = 2.2$), then the photographic unit is optimal.

19-5 DECISIONS REGARDING THE SAMPLE: PREPOSTERIOR ANALYSIS

We are now ready to consider the decision of whether or not to sample at all, and if we sample, what size n to use.

In a sense, our previous discussion regarding the posterior probability distribution for μ may have been misleading. *The final normal curve for μ depends on the actual computed value of the sample mean.* Since we have yet to decide whether or not to sample at all (or how many sample observations to make if we do), we cannot use some future value of $\bar{X}$ to make a present decision about the sampling procedure itself. Until we know the actual $\bar{X}$ exactly, we do not know the center of the posterior probability distribution for μ.

We must therefore treat μ_1 itself as a random variable having a normal curve centered on μ_0 and a standard deviation of σ_{μ_1}. Although the underlying concepts are beyond the scope of this book, it has been established that

$$\sigma_{\mu_1}^2 = \sigma_0^2 \cdot \frac{\sigma_0^2}{\sigma_0^2 + \sigma_{\bar{X}}^2}$$

Although the expressions are superficially similar, keep in mind that σ_1 and σ_{μ_1} are different values and represent different variabilities. The former applies to the posterior probability distribution that is found after we know $\bar{X}$; the latter applies before the actual sample result is obtained and pertains to the variability in the center of the posterior probability distribution, which is still to be determined. In using the expression for $\sigma_{\mu_1}^2$, remember that σ_0 must be specified in advance and that $\sigma_{\bar{X}}$ may be calculated before sampling, using the known value of σ_I and the sample size n, as

$$\sigma_{\bar{X}} = \frac{\sigma_I}{\sqrt{n}}$$

The Expected Value of Sample Information

In Chapter 18, we introduced the expected value of sample information EVSI, which represents the predictive worth of sampling. In our present context, the EVSI is based on our expectations about the center of the posterior probability distribution for μ and, in particular, on the value of σ_{μ_1}. Since the standard deviation of μ_1 depends on $\sigma_{\bar{x}}$, which itself depends on the still-to-be-decided n, the EVSI will depend partly on the value eventually chosen for n. In keeping with our earlier notation, we will represent this dependence by using the expression EVSI(n) for the expected value of sample information.

We can calculate the expected value of sample information by employing a method similar to the one we used to find the EVPI earlier (when no sample applies). Only the constants used change from the EVPI calculation. Here

$$\text{EVSI}(n) = |\text{slope}|\sigma_{\mu_1}L(D_E)$$

where

$$D_E = \frac{|\mu_b - \mu_0|}{\sigma_{\mu_1}}$$

expresses the distance between μ_0 (the expected value of μ_1) and the breakeven level in units of standard deviation.

For the computer memory device decision, $\mu_b = 2.4$, $\mu_0 = 2.5$, $|\text{slope}| = \$62,500$, and $\sigma_{\bar{x}} = .6$ for $n = 25$. The variance of μ_1 is

$$\sigma^2_{\mu_1} = (1)^2\, \frac{(1)^2}{(1)^2 + (.6)^2} = .74$$

so that the standard deviation is

$$\sigma_{\mu_1} = \sqrt{.74} = .86$$

The standardized distance is

$$D_E = \frac{|2.4 - 2.5|}{.86} = .12$$

so that, from Appendix Table C

$$L(D_E) = L(.12) = .3418$$

and

$$\text{EVSI}(n) = \$62,500(.86).3418 = \$18,372$$

The result EVSI(25) = $18,372 tells us the true worth of a sample of $n = 25$ to the decision maker. As long as the sampling cost is less than this amount, the computer center manager will be better off with the sample information than without it. As we have already seen, the manager will determine the act to choose by formulating a decision rule for $\bar{X}$ based on the critical value $C = 2.36$.

The Decision to Sample

Now suppose that the computer center manager could determine the precise access level on each sample day at a cost of $100 per day. For a sample size of $n = 25$, the cost of sampling would then be $2,500. Since this amount is smaller than EVSI(25), *the manager should definitely make a decision based on a sample of some size* rather than choose an act without any information at all. The question remaining is: How large should n be?

Determining the Optimal Sample Size

We can answer this question by finding the expected net gain from sampling for various sample sizes, which is computed

$$\text{ENGS}(n) = \text{EVSI}(n) - \text{Cost}(n)$$

The optimal sample size is the one with the greatest ENGS(n) value. By trial and error, trying various values of n, we can determine the appropriate sample

TABLE 19-1
The Expected Net Gain of Sampling Computed for Several Sample Sizes

n	$\sigma_{\bar{X}} = 3/\sqrt{n}$	σ_{μ_1}	D_E	$L(D_E)$	EVSI(n)	Cost(n)	ENGS(n)
10	.95	.73	.14	.3328	$15,184	$1,000	$14,184
25	.60	.86	.12	.3418	18,372	2,500	15,872
29	.56	.87	.11	.3464	18,836	2,900	15,936
30	.55	.88	.11	.3464	19,052	3,000	16,052
31	.54	.88	.11	.3464	19,052	3,100	15,952
35	.51	.89	.11	.3464	19,269	3,500	15,769
40	.47	.90	.11	.3464	19,485	4,000	15,485

size. Table 19-1 provides the ENGS(n) values for a few sample sizes. Notice that the expected net gain increases until $n = 30$, after which it decreases. Thus, $n = 30$, for which ENGS(30) = \$16,052, is the optimal sample size.

The Optimal Decision Rule

We have now determined the computer center manager's optimal course of action. Sampling should be chosen, since this will provide a positive expected net gain. Furthermore, a sample size of $n = 30$ will result in the greatest expected net gain from sampling. The manager should therefore take a sample each day for 30 days, determine the precise memory access levels for these samples, and compute $\bar{X}$.

The standard deviation of $\bar{X}$ is

$$\sigma_{\bar{X}} = \frac{\sigma_I}{\sqrt{n}} = \frac{3}{\sqrt{30}} = .55$$

and, by using the appropriate constants for this problem, the critical value of $\bar{X}$ is

$$C = \frac{2.4[1/(1)^2 + 1/(.55)^2] - 2.5[1/(1)^2]}{1/(.55)^2}$$

$$= 2.37$$

A SUMMARY OF THE PROCEDURES   19-6

Before concluding, it will be helpful to summarize the concepts and procedures examined in this chapter. The various time frames involved are shown in Figure 19-6, where decision making using the normal distribution is separated into four stages.

We begin with *prior analysis*, during which the prior distribution for the unknown μ is obtained, generally through judgment. During this stage, payoffs are determined as linear functions of μ, leading directly to a breakeven analysis. The main decision might be made in this stage by comparing the mean μ_0 of the prior distribution to the breakeven level μ_b. Whether or not we stop at this stage depends on how worthwhile any further information about μ happens to be. This is roughly gauged by the EVPI, and further investigation is warranted only if the EVPI is great enough to justify the extra bother of evaluating the sample information. (Clearly, an EVPI of only \$10 would not justify any further

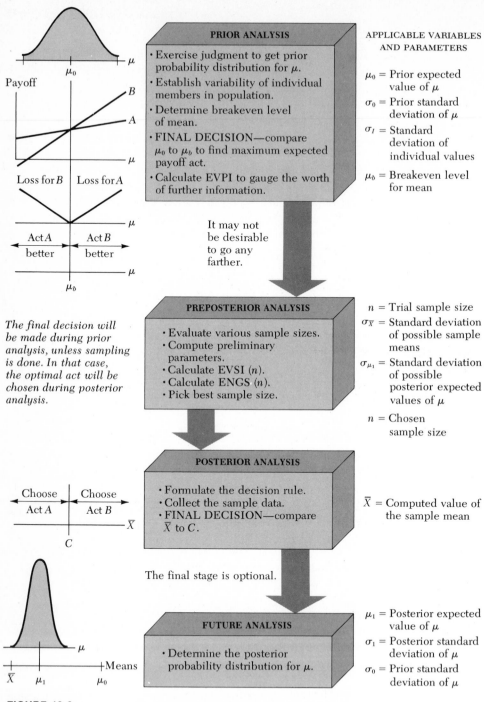

FIGURE 19-6

A summary of the relationship between the concepts and procedures for decision making using the normal distribution.

analysis; even an EVPI of $100 is apt to be smaller than the cost of a modest sampling study.)

If it might be worthwhile to obtain further information, then *preposterior analysis* follows. Here, the question is primarily whether or not to sample, and if sampling is chosen, what sample size n to take. The evaluation is computationally lengthy, involving calculations of various EVSIs and sampling costs for several values of n, so that the size with the greatest expected net gain from sampling can be determined.

The next stage involves *posterior analysis*. Here, the decision rule is established, the sample is collected, and the actual sample mean $\bar{X}$ is calculated. Depending on the value obtained for $\bar{X}$, the choice of the act for the main decision is indicated.

An *optional* fourth stage completes the procedure. Here, *future analysis* is concerned with the posterior probability distribution for μ. *This distribution is not required to make the main decision*, although it can serve as the starting point for future decisions involving μ. (This fact was not obvious in our earlier discussions, where we had to investigate the characteristics of the posterior distribution for μ to explain the procedures involved in posterior and preposterior analyses.)

Most students of this material suffer from a mild form of "symbol shock"— and for good reason! We have introduced five different standard deviations and an equal number of means. Moreover, $\bar{X}$ and μ_1 appear as subscripts to other symbols. Unfortunately, this Greek "alphabet soup" is unavoidable. Table 19-2 on page 475 provides a glossary to help you keep track of these symbols. It may also help to mention a few of the pitfalls commonly encountered in applying the various analyses.

(1) **Try not to confuse σ_1 with σ_{μ_1}.** The former expresses the variability in μ after the procedure is complete and is usually only calculated for future analysis. More essential is σ_{μ_1}, which expresses variability in the center μ_1 of the posterior distribution and is only used during preposterior analysis, when μ_1 is uncertain. (After sampling, μ_1 can be calculated and is certain, so there is no variability.) To make matters worse, σ_1^2 and $\sigma_{\mu_1}^2$ are calculated from expressions that are similar in appearance. Make sure you are using the right one.

(2) **Remember that some expressions involve the standard deviation σ and that others involve the variance σ^2.** Be sure to take the square root of the variance to obtain the corresponding standard deviation when it is needed, and to square the standard deviation to obtain the variance.

(3) **Prior analysis compares μ_b and μ_0, whereas posterior analysis compares $\bar{X}$ and C. Only one of these comparisons is ultimately used in making the main decision.**

(4) **Do not confuse σ_0 with σ_I.** The former expresses variability in μ itself and gauges how close to μ_0 we judge that μ lies. The standard deviation σ_I

pertains to individual population values. Ordinarily, σ_0 and σ_I are not equal. (In a decision involving human heights, σ_0 might be $\frac{1}{4}$ in., reflecting our lack of precision in predicting the population mean, and σ_I might be $2\frac{1}{2}$ in., expressing variability from person to person.)

(5) **Keep in mind that μ remains unknown.**   There will be no population census, and the value of μ will be uncertain throughout the entire analysis. On the other hand, μ_0 and μ_1 are the expected values of μ at the beginning and the end of the analysis, respectively. The value of μ_0 is known throughout, but μ_1 is uncertain throughout most of the analysis and can only be calculated last. The value of $\overline{X}$ is also uncertain until after the sample has been collected.

19-7   ADDITIONAL REMARKS

The special difficulties encountered when dealing with several different normal curves have forced us to depart from our usual decision tree analysis. If we approximated the various continuous probability distributions by discrete tables (using typical values for μ and $\overline{X}$), then we could apply the methods presented in Chapter 18 to reach nearly identical conclusions to those we achieved using the procedures discussed in this chapter. But it is more convenient to focus on opportunity losses and to use normal form analysis when the prior probability distribution for μ can be represented by the normal curve and the sample observations themselves range over a continuous scale (so that the probabilities for $\overline{X}$ are represented by another normal curve).

But what do we do if the prior probability distribution for μ is not a normal curve? An amazing fact, established by Robert Schlaifer, who originally proposed the procedures examined in this chapter,* is that *for practically any other type of prior probability distribution, the posterior probability distribution for μ will still very closely approximate a normal curve.* Thus, what form applies to the prior distribution for μ really makes very little difference.

Another nice feature of the present approach to decision making using sample information is that it is simpler than applying decision tree analysis with approximate probability distributions, which involves a tremendous number of computations that are unnecessary here. The present procedure entirely avoids the problem of finding the unconditional result probabilities for $\overline{X}$. The nature of the opportunity loss lines permits us to evaluate the two-action problem through a breakeven analysis that considers only the central value of μ and the nature of its prior probability distribution.

---

* Much of the material in Schlaifer's books, *Probability and Statistics for Business Decisions* (New York: McGraw-Hill, 1959) and *Introduction to Statistics for Business Decisions* (New York McGraw–Hill, 1961), carefully develops the concepts discussed in this chapter.

TABLE 19-2

Symbolic Glossary for Decision Making Using the Normal Curve

<table>
<tr><td colspan="2" align="center">**Means**</td></tr>
<tr><td>μ</td><td>*The mean of the underlying population.* The value of μ is the main uncertainty. Payoffs depend on the level of μ. Although probabilities for μ may be revised, we will never know the true value of μ.</td></tr>
<tr><td>μ_b</td><td>*The breakeven level for* μ. This is a known value, representing the level of μ where the payoff lines cross.</td></tr>
<tr><td>μ_0</td><td>*The expected or central value of the* prior *normal probability distribution for* μ. Largely *a matter of judgment,* this quantity is the decision analyst's 50–50 point for where μ might fall.</td></tr>
<tr><td>μ_1</td><td>*The expected or central value of the* posterior *normal probability distribution for* μ. This quantity is a weighted average of μ_0 and the computed sample mean $\bar{X}$, and it can be calculated only after obtaining sample results. This quantity provides the decision analyst with a revised 50–50 point for μ.</td></tr>
<tr><td>$\bar{X}$</td><td>*The sample mean.* The computed value of $\bar{X}$ determines which act will be chosen.</td></tr>
<tr><td colspan="2" align="center">**Standard Deviations**</td></tr>
<tr><td>σ_0</td><td>*The standard deviation of the* prior *normal probability distribution for* μ. Largely *judgmental,* this value summarizes (or indexes) the magnitude of the decision analyst's uncertainty about the value of μ.</td></tr>
<tr><td>σ_1</td><td>*The standard deviation of the* posterior *normal probability distribution for* μ. Based on both earlier judgment and actual sample results, this value also expresses the magnitude of uncertainty about the value of μ (but after revision in accordance with sample results).</td></tr>
<tr><td>σ_I</td><td>*The standard deviation of the population of individual values.* This is an index of the extent of individual differences. Like μ itself, σ_I is ordinarily unknown, and we must make an "educated guess" or use a "ballpark figure" for its value.</td></tr>
<tr><td>$\sigma_{\bar{X}}$</td><td>*The standard error (deviation) of* $\bar{X}$. This tells us how tightly $\bar{X}$ values will cluster about μ. It is computed by dividing the population standard deviation σ_I by $\sqrt{n}$.</td></tr>
<tr><td>σ_{μ_1}</td><td>*The standard deviation of the center* μ_1 *of the posterior normal probability distribution for* μ. Before sample data are collected, μ_1 is uncertain. This parameter summarizes the degree of that uncertainty. It is used only in calculating the EVSI levels that are used to select the best sample size n.</td></tr>
</table>

There are limitations to the procedures presented here, however. For instance, they cannot be used when the payoffs cannot be graphed as straight lines or when more than two basic actions are contemplated. We have presented a special-purpose tool that applies only to limited situations. Fortunately, many practical business decision-making applications fall into this category.

PROBLEMS

19-1 In each of the following situations, the prior probability distribution for the population mean is represented by the normal curve:

	(a)	(b)	(c)	(d)
Mean:	50	100	60	40
Standard deviation:	10	10	20	10
Breakeven level:	55	90	62	38
Slope:	$1,000	$5,000	$5,000	$10,000

Below the breakeven level for the mean, alternative A is more profitable; beyond the breakeven level, alternative B is better. In each case: (1) indicate which act is better and (2) calculate the EVPI.

19-2 Sonic Phonics specializes in stereo headphones. It is considering adding a new stereo helmet receiver for motorcyclists, but the owner is uncertain about the mean annual sales volume per outlet in the retail chain it supplies. He believes that the mean is normally distributed, with a mean of 60 and a standard deviation of 10 helmets per store. Altogether, 100 stores are involved. The helmet will have a product life of about one year, after which it is believed that the novelty will wear off. Production set-up costs will be $50,000. Each helmet will have a variable cost of $30 and will sell for a retail price of $40.

(a) Assume that the total increase in profits is to be maximized. In terms of the mean number of helmets sold per store, determine an expression for the payoff for making the helmet. For not making the helmet. What is the breakeven level?
(b) Should Sonic Phonics make the helmet?
(c) Calculate the EVPI.

19-3 The marketing manager of Blitz Beer must determine whether or not to sponsor Blitz Day with the Gotham City Hellcats. She is uncertain what the effect of the promotion will be in terms of the mean increase in daily sales volume that would result during the 100-day baseball season. The cost of sponsorship is $10,000, and each can of Blitz has a marginal cost of $.20 and sells for $.40.

(a) Assuming that change in profit is to be maximized, express the payoff function for the two alternatives in terms of the mean daily increase in cans sold.
(b) Suppose that Blitz Day will result in a mean increase that is judged to be normally distributed with a mean of 600 and a standard deviation of 50 cans per day. Should the brewer sponsor the event?
(c) What is the EVPI? Do you think it is worthwhile to obtain further information? Can a sample from the underlying population even be helpful in making this decision? Explain.

19-4 Reconsider the illustration in Chapter 19 of choosing between photographic and holographic peripheral memory storage units. Suppose that the following annual savings payoff function applies, where the access portion depends on the unknown mean access level of μ gigabits per day:

$$\text{Payoff} = \begin{cases} \$500,000 + \$\ 65,000\mu & \text{for photographic} \\ \$330,000 + \$150,000\mu & \text{for holographic} \end{cases}$$

(a) Find the breakeven level for the population mean.
(b) Which unit maximizes annual savings when the prior expected mean is $\mu_0 = 2.5$ gigabits per day?

19-5 *Problem 19-4 continued.* Suppose that the prior probability distribution for the population mean access level has an expected value of 2.3 gigabits per day and a standard deviation of .75 and that the population of individual daily access levels has a standard deviation of 3.5 gigabits per day.

(a) Calculate the EVPI.

(b) If a random sample of $n = 16$ days is chosen, find the optimal value of C that will maximize expected annual savings.

(c) Suppose that the sample mean turns out to be 1.75 gigabits per day. Determine the mean and the standard deviation of the posterior probability distribution for μ. Which memory unit will be chosen?

(d) Use your results from (c) to find the probability that the mean daily access level lies above the breakeven level.

19-6 *Problem 19-4 continued.* The sample size has not been chosen, but the cost of each daily observation is now $500. Use the constants provided earlier to calculate the expected net gain from sampling for the indicated sample sizes.

(a) 4

(b) 9

(c) 100

(d) Which one of the above sample sizes is best? Formulate the optimal decision rule for the corresponding sample mean.

19-7 A facilities planner for Waysafe Markets is evaluating a new electronic-scanning cash register. The planner is uncertain about the mean time μ that the new equipment will take to check out a typical customer with 2 sacks of groceries. Experience with present automatic registers yields a standard deviation for individual checkout times of $\sigma_I = 1$ minute, and this value is assumed to apply to the new system. It is the planner's judgment that μ has a prior normal probability distribution with a mean of $\mu_0 = 3$ minutes and a standard deviation of $\sigma_0 = .20$ minute.

(a) Find the probability that (1) $\mu \geq 3.5$; (2) $\mu \leq 2.75$.

A random sample of new system checkout times is to be obtained for further study.

(b) Assuming that $n = 100$ typical customers' checkout times will be obtained, calculate $\sigma_{\bar{X}}$ and find the conditional result probabilities that:

(1) $\bar{X} \leq 2.75$ minutes, given $\mu = 2.90$.

(2) $\bar{X} > 3.25$ minutes, given $\mu = 3.10$.

(3) $\bar{X}$ lies between 2.85 and 3.15 minutes, given $\mu = 3.00$.

(c) Calculate the standard deviation σ_1 of the posterior probability distribution for μ. This should be smaller than its prior probability distribution counterpart.

(d) Suppose that the sample results yield a computed value of $\bar{X} = 3.20$ minutes. Compute the expected value μ_1 of the posterior probability distribution for μ. In revising the probability distribution for μ, which source of information— prior judgment or the sample results—has been given the greater weight?

(e) According to the prior probability distribution for μ, there is a .50 probability that the true population mean checkout time will be $\mu \leq 3.00$ minutes. For future study, the posterior probability distribution will apply. Calculate the new probability that μ will fall at or below 3 minutes.

19-8 Yokum University's president knows that the population standard deviation in height of his male students is 2.5 in. He is uncertain about the mean height, which he characterizes as having a prior normal probability distribution with a mean of 69.5 in. and a standard deviation of .25 in. He wishes to decide whether or not to gamble with the president of Near Miss, whose men are known to be an average of 69 in. tall. The terms are that Yokum will get (give up) 100,000 druthers or fraction for each inch or fraction that the mean height of Yokum men exceeds (lies below) the Near Miss mean.

(a) Calculate the EVSI when a sample of $n = 100$ Yokum men are measured.

(b) Suppose that $n = 25$ Yokum men are measured in the sample. Find the level of $\bar{X}$ (C) that would make Yokum's president indifferent between gambling and not gambling.

(c) A sample of $n = 25$ Yokum men has a mean of $\bar{X} = 69.2$ in. Find the mean and the standard deviation of the posterior probability distribution for the mean height of Yokum men. Then find the probability that Yokum men are actually shorter than Near Miss men on the average.

19-9 A decision is to be made between act 1 and act 2. Act 1 will be chosen if $\bar{X} \leq C$. The applicable constants are $\mu_0 = 5$, $\sigma_0 = 2$, $\sigma_I = 24$, and $\mu_b = 4.5$. Each sample observation costs $.50, and the absolute value of the slope of the opportunity loss lines in $200.

(a) Determine the applicable EVPI when no sample is to be taken.

(b) Calculate the EVSI for: (1) $n = 4$; (2) $n = 9$; (3) $n = 25$; (4) $n = 100$.

(c) Calculate the ENGS(n) for your results in (b). Which sample size is the best?

(d) Suppose a sample size of $n = 100$ is used. Formulate the optimal decision rule. Which act should be chosen if: (1) $\bar{X} = 3.6$? (2) $\bar{X} = 3.9$?

19-10 The first stage of a chemical process yields a mean of μ grams of active ingredient for every liter of raw material processed. Due to variations in the raw material and in the control settings, the true population mean for any particular batch is unknown until processing is complete. The plant superintendent believes that μ is normally distributed with a mean of 30 g and a standard deviation of 2 g. The amount of variation in individual liters within a batch is summarized by a standard deviation of 6 g.

The plant superintendent will use the active ingredient in either a high-pressure or a low-pressure final-stage process. Each process provides an identical final product. The ultimate profit from each alternative is partly determined by μ. The following payoff function applies:

$$\text{Payoff} = \begin{cases} \$10,000 + \$300\mu & \text{for high-pressure process} \\ \$13,100 + \$200\mu & \text{for low-pressure process} \end{cases}$$

(a) Determine the breakeven level of μ. Will the high-pressure or the low-pressure process yield the greater expected profit?

(b) Calculate the value of the slope of the opportunity loss lines and the superintendent's EVPI.

19-11 *Problem 19-10 continued.* For a cost of $1 per liter, the superintendent can determine the actual yield of active ingredient per liter.

(a) Calculate the EVSI for: (1) $n = 4$; (2) $n = 9$; (3) $n = 16$.

(b) Calculate ENGS(n) for each of the sample sizes in (a). Which sample size is the best?

(c) Determine the optimal decision rule for the optimal sample size you found in (b). Which process should be used if: (1) $\bar{X} = 30$ g? (2) $\bar{X} = 32$ g? (3) $\bar{X} = 33$ g?

20

Decision Making with Utility

The goal of this chapter is to broaden the scope of decision theory through the introduction of a new payoff measure. We have seen that a good payoff measure should rank all possible outcomes in terms of how well they meet the decision maker's goals. This is often an easy task when there is no uncertainty. But the presence of uncertainty can severely complicate the issue when the possible outcomes to a decision are extreme. Such decisions contain elements of *risk*. Because people usually have different attitudes toward risk, two persons faced with an identical decision may actually prefer different courses of action.

The crucial role that attitude plays in any decision is illustrated by the divergent behavior of different persons faced with the same decision. The *umbrella situation* nicely demonstrates this point. *How can we explain why everyone does not carry an umbrella when we do?* To a certain extent, we can say that all individuals are not equally adept at selecting and exercising appropriate decision criteria. But this is only one possible explanation. With much justification, however, we can conclude that the difference in behavior can also be explained by differing attitudes toward the consequences. Some people may enjoy getting wet, but others may view it as an invitation to pneumonia and possibly the first step to a premature grave. Some people think it is chic to carry rain paraphernalia when it's not raining; others would rather lug around a ball and chain. Even if we can find two persons who have identical attitudes toward the decision consequences, they may still make opposite decisions because they may not have made identical *judgments* regarding the chance of rain. One person may rely on weather service prediction as a source of information, judging these subjective probabilities to be adequate. Another person may depend on lumbago pain as a fairly reliable measure of the probability of rain. (The role of judgment in establishing probabilities will be discussed further in Chapter 21.)

In this chapter, we will discuss utility as an alternative expression of payoff that reflects a person's attitudes. We will begin by examining the rationale for buying insurance. A brief historical discussion of utility and the underlying assumptions of a theory of utility will then be presented. Finally, a procedure will be introduced that can be used to determine utility values. The utility function so obtained provides a basis for our discussion of some basic attitudes toward risk.

20-1 ATTITUDES, PREFERENCES, AND UTILITY

In Chapter 6, we examined several procedures and criteria that help decision makers to make choices in the presence of uncertainty. In all cases, the payoff value of each outcome is required to analyze the decision. As we have seen, not all outcomes have an obvious numerical payoff. In this section, we will see how payoffs may be determined in such cases. Later in the chapter, we will develop methods of quantifying such consequences as reduced share of the market, loss of corporate control, and antitrust suits. Even when numerical payoffs can be naturally determined, we have seen that it may be unrealistic to select the act with the maximum expected payoff. In some cases, an extremely risky act fares better under the Bayes decision rule than an obviously preferred act. As noted in Chapter 6, this difficulty is not the fault of the Bayes criterion, but is caused by payoff values that do not reflect their true worth to the decision maker.

The Decision to Buy Insurance

The inadequacy of using such obvious measures as dollar cost or profit to indicate payoffs can be vividly illustrated by evaluating an individual's decision of whether or not to buy fire insurance. Spiro Pyrophobis wishes to decide whether to buy a fire insurance policy for his home. Our decision maker's payoffs will be expressed in terms of his out-of-pocket costs, which we will represent by negative numbers. Our question is: Will the Bayes decision rule lead to the choice of the act that is actually preferred?

TABLE 20-1
Payoff Table for the Decision to Buy Fire Insurance

		Act			
		Buy Insurance		Don't Buy Insurance	
Event	Probability	Payoff	Payoff × Probability	Payoff	Payoff × Probability
Fire	.002	−$100	−$ .20	−$40,000	−$80.00
No fire	.998	−100	−99.80	0	0
Expected payoff:			−$100.00		−$80.00

In answering this question, we will use the hypothetical payoff table provided in Table 20-1. Here, we have greatly simplified the decision. The acts are to buy or not to buy an annual policy with a $100 premium charge. If there is a fire, we will assume that Spiro's home and all its contents, valued at $40,000, will be completely destroyed.

Insurance actuaries have established that historically 2 out of every 1,000 homes in the category of Spiro's home burn down each year. The probability that Spiro's home will burn down is therefore set at 2/1,000 = .002. Thus, the complementary event—no fire—has a probability of 1 − .002 = .998. We can use these probability values to calculate the expected payoffs for each act in Table 20-1. The maximum expected payoff is − $80, which corresponds to the act "don't buy insurance" and is larger than the − $100 payoff from buying fire insurance.

In this example, the *Bayes decision rule indicates that it is optimal to buy no insurance.* Yet most persons faced with this decision choose to buy fire insurance. Loss of a home, which comprises the major portion of a lifetime's savings for many people, is a dreadful prospect. The expenditure of an annual premium, although not exactly appealing, buys a feeling of security that seems to outweigh the difference between the expected payoffs. Moreover, insurance policy premiums are higher than the expected claim size which is equivalent to the policyholder's expected dollar loss, so that the insurance company can pay wages and achieve profits. Thus, buying insurance can be considered an unfair gamble, where the payoff is not in the buyer's favor. Individuals can expect to pay more in insurance premiums than they will collect in claims.* Most persons feel fortunate if they never have to file a claim.

The Bayes decision rule selects the *less preferred act.* Does this mean that it is an invalid criterion? Rather than answer no immediately, let us consider the payoffs used. The true worth of the outcomes is not reflected by the dollar payoffs. A policyholder is willing to pay more than the expected dollar loss to achieve "peace of mind." We can say that the policyholder derives greater

---

* This is not true of life insurance, which is ordinarily a form of savings.

utility from having insurance. If dollar losses are valued on a scale of true worth or utility, then each additional dollar loss will make our decision maker feel disproportionately worse off. Thus, a 10% reduction in wealth may be more than twice as bad as a 5% reduction. The same is usually true for gains in dollar wealth; the second increase may not increase the decision maker's sense of well being as much as the first. In the parlance of economics, *the policyholder's marginal utility for money is decreasing.* Each successive dollar gain buys a smaller increase in utility; each additional dollar loss reduces utility by a greater amount than before.

Thus, we may question the validity of using dollars as our payoff measure. Instead, it might be preferable to measure the payoff of an outcome in terms of its worth or utility.

20-2 NUMERICAL UTILITY VALUES

We wish to obtain *numerical utility values* that express the true worth of the payoffs that correspond to decision outcomes. We refer to such numbers as *utilities.* Much investigation has been made of the true worth of monetary payoffs. The early eighteenth-century mathematician Daniel Bernoulli—a pioneer in developing a measure of utility—proposed that *the true worth of an individual's wealth is the logarithm of the amount of money possessed.* Thus, a graphical relationship between utility and money would have the basic shape of the curve in Figure 20-1. Note that although the slope of this curve is always positive, it decreases as the amount of money increases, reflecting the assumption of decreasing marginal utility for money.

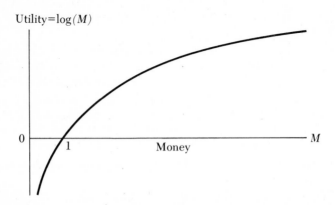

FIGURE 20-1
Bernoulli's utility function for money.

The Saint Petersburg Paradox

A gambling game called the *Saint Petersburg Paradox* led Bernoulli to his conclusion. In the game, a balanced coin is fairly tossed until the first head appears. The gambler's winnings are based on the number of tosses that are made before the game ends. If a head appears on the first toss, the player wins $2. If not, the "kitty" is doubled to $4—the reward if a head appears on the second toss. If a tail occurs on the second toss, the kitty is doubled again. The pot is doubled after every coin toss that results in a tail. The winnings are $2 raised to the power of the number of tosses until and including the first head. This procedure will be more interesting if you pause to think about what amount you would be willing to pay for the privilege of playing this game.

The probability that $n + 1$ tosses will occur before payment is the probability that there is a run of n tails and that the $(n + 1)$st toss is a head, or $(1/2)^{n+1}$. The payoff for $n + 1$ tosses is 2^{n+1}. We can therefore calculate the player's expected receipts from the sum

$$\$2(1/2) + \$2^2(1/2)^2 + \$2^3(1/2)^3 + \cdots = \$1 + \$1 + \$1 + \cdots = \$\infty$$

Since the number of $1s in this sum is unlimited, the *expected receipts from a play of this game are infinite*! Whatever amount you were willing to pay to play must have been a finite amount and therefore less than the expected receipts. Thus, the expected payoff for this gamble is also infinite, no matter what price is paid to play.

Few people are willing to pay more than $10 to play this game, and even at this price, a player would win only 1 out of 8 games on the average. A player paying $500 would show a profit in only 1 out of every 256 gambles on the average. The natural reticence of players to pay very much for this gamble led Bernoulli to his conclusion about the utility for money. In general, we say that a person who prefers not to participate in a gamble in which the expected receipts exceed the price to play has a *decreasing marginal utility for money*.

The Validity of Logarithmic Values

Via different paths of reasoning, other early mathematicians arrived at conclusions similar to Bernoulli's—that the marginal utility for money is decreasing—and proposed other utility curves with the same basic shape. A major fault of these early works is that they do not account for individual differences in the assignment of worth. A more modern treatment of utility in the abstract sense was advanced by John Von Neumann and Oskar Morgenstern in 1947 in their book *Theory of Games and Economic Behavior*. There, they proposed that a utility curve can be tailored for any individual, provided certain assumptions about the individual's preferences hold. These assumptions provide several valid, basic shapes for the utility curve, including curves similar to Bernoulli's. We will investigate some of these utility curves later in the chapter.

Outcomes Without a Natural Payoff Measure

Until now, the outcomes of our examples have had a *natural* numerical payoff measure, such as dollar profits, gasoline gallons saved, or time. But we have noted that some decisions have no numerical outcomes. As decision makers, we should be able to assess the relative worth of such an outcome.

In the case of most decisions, it is possible to determine preferences, although this is not always an easy task. Indeed, value judgments may be the most difficult step in analyzing a decision. Consider the student selecting a school from several top universities, the child choosing a candy bar, the bachelor contemplating getting married and forgoing the carefree life, the tired corporate founder pondering merger and retirement versus retaining control and delegating operating responsibility, or the innocent person choosing between pleading guilty to manslaughter or facing trial for murder. If we assume that we have the capability to rank the consequences in order of preference, we can extend the notion of utility so that numerical payoffs can be made for the most intangible outcomes.

20-3 UTILITY THEORY

The fundamental proposition of the modern treatment of utility is that it is possible to obtain a numerical expression of an individual's preferences. We can rank a set of outcomes by preference and then assign utility values that convey these preferences. The largest utility number is assigned to the most preferred outcome, the next largest number is assigned to the second most preferred outcome, and so forth. Suppose, for instance, that you are contemplating a menu. If you prefer New York steak to baked halibut and you wish to assign utility values to the entrees in accordance with your preferences, the utility of steak will be 5, or u(steak) $= 5$, and u(halibut) will be some number smaller than 5.

Before we describe how specific utility numbers can be obtained, we will discuss some of the assumptions underlying the theory of utility.

The Assumptions of Utility Theory

Various assumptions have been made about the determination of utilities.* All of them have one feature in common—that the values obtained pertain only to a *single individual* who behaves *consistently* in accordance with his or her own tastes.

Preference Ranking   The first assumption of utility theory is that a person can determine for any pair of outcomes O_1 and O_2 whether he or she prefers O_1 to O_2, prefers O_2 to O_1, or regards both equally. This assumption is particularly advantageous when we consider monetary values, because then we can assume that more money is always better than less. But we have seen that it can be very difficult to rank preferences when qualitative alternatives are considered. Can a person always determine a preference for or establish an indifference toward outcomes? If not, then utilities cannot be found for these outcomes.

Transitivity of Preference   The second assumption of utility theory is that if A is preferred to B and B is preferred to C, then A must be preferred to C. This property is called *transitivity of preference* and reflects an individual's consistency. Again, when we are dealing with monetary outcomes, we can usually assume transitivity.

Before we examine the assumptions of utility further, we will introduce gambles between outcomes so that uncertainty can be incorporated into the determination of utility.

Gambles and Expected Utility

We are presently concerned with making choices under uncertainty. Thus, the payoffs for decison acts are unknown, and each act can be viewed as a *gamble* with uncertain rewards. To evaluate such decisions, we must extend the concept of utility to gambles.

Recall that the Bayes decision rule involves comparisons between the expected payoffs of acts or strategies, so that the "optimal" choice has the maximum expected payoff. But the major difficulty with this criterion, as we have seen, is that the indicated course of action can be less attractive than some other action. For example, the Bayes decision rule tells us not to buy fire insurance when most people feel that insurance is desirable. We wish to overcome this obstacle by using utilities in place of dollar payoffs. We therefore

* Those discussed in this book are simplifications of the original axioms postulated by Von Neumann and Morgenstern.

require that the expected utility payoffs provide a valid means of comparing actions so that the action having the greatest expected utility is actually preferred to the alternative actions. Thus, buying fire insurance should have greater expected utility than not buying it.

But we can go one step further. Suppose that the most preferred action has the greatest expected utility, the next most preferred action has the next greatest utility, and so forth. Then expected utility would express preference ranking, and the *expected utility values would themselves be utilities*. Each utility value would express the worth of a *gamble* between outcomes obtained by averaging the utility values of the outcomes, using their respective probabilities as weights. This may be stated more precisely as a property of utility theory: In any gamble between outcome A and outcome B, with probabilities of q for A and $1 - q$ for B

$$u(\text{gamble}) = qu(A) + (1 - q)u(B)$$

Thus, the utility of a gamble between two outcomes is equal to the expected utility of the gamble. When acts having uncertain outcomes are viewed as gambles, the utility of an act is equal to the expected utility of its outcomes. *When payoffs are measured in terms of utilities, the Bayes decision rule will indicate that the act having the maximum expected utility is optimal*, so that this criterion can always be used to select the most preferred act or strategy.

Determining Expected Utilities

To illustrate, we will return to our fire-insurance example. Suppose that Spiro Pyrophobis values the dollar changes in his assets according to the utility function

$$u(M) = \sqrt{M + 40{,}000} - 200$$

where M expresses the change in cash position associated with each outcome.

Table 20-2 provides the utility calculations and the expected utility calculations for the acts "buy insurance" and "don't buy insurance." For instance, if no insurance is bought and there is a fire, a loss results, so that $M = -\$40{,}000$ (a negative change in cash position). The utility for this outcome is obtained from the calculation

$$u(-\$40{,}000) = \sqrt{-40{,}000 + 40{,}000} - 200$$
$$= \sqrt{0} - 200 = -200$$

The utilities for the other outcomes are calculated in a similar manner; $u(0) = 0$, and $u(-\$100) = -.25$.

TABLE 20-2
Determination of Utilities for Outcomes of the Fire-Insurance Decision and Calculation of Expected Utilities

(1)	(2)	(3)	(4)	(5)
		Cash Change	Utility	
Event	Probability	M	$\sqrt{M + 40,000} - 200$	Utility × Probability
		Buy Insurance		
Fire	.002	−$100	−.25	−.0005
No fire	.998	−100	−.25	−.2495
			Expected utility =	−.2500
		Don't Buy Insurance		
Fire	.002	−$40,000	−200	−.40
No fire	.998	0	0	0
			Expected utility =	−.40

Each act is a gamble. Buying insurance is a gamble having two identical outcomes in terms of dollar expenditure of −$100, since the same amount applies whether or not there is a fire. Buying no insurance is a gamble having cash outlays of −$40,000 if there is a fire and $0 if there is no fire. The utilities for the respective acts are therefore the expected utilities of the corresponding gambles. We can see from Table 20-2 that the expected utilities are −.25 for buying insurance and −.4 for not buying insurance. Since buying insurance has the higher utility, it must be preferred by the decision maker. Stated differently, the act "buy insurance" has the maximum expected utility payoff, so that the Bayes decision rule indicates that this act is the optimal choice.

Thus, when we use utilities as payoff values, the Bayes decision rule indicates the "proper" result. However, this does not permit us to conclude that whenever utilities are used as payoffs, this criterion will lead to a decision to buy insurance. The choice depends on the relationship between the chance of fire and the price of the insurance policy. Suppose, for example, that the price of Spiro's policy is raised to $200, so that the utility for the dollar payoffs for buying insurance is

$$u(-\$200) = \sqrt{-200 + 40,000} - 200$$
$$= \sqrt{39,800} - 200 = -.50$$

The expected utility for buying insurance is −.50, so that if the probability of fire remains the same, the act "don't buy insurance" will have a utility of −.4, which is greater than −.50, making "don't buy insurance" the preferred act. This is the opposite outcome from our earlier decision. The insurance has become too expensive to be attractive.

Many people faced with the same circumstances would buy insurance even if the premium were raised to $1,000 or more. *Their tastes would be different and this would be reflected by the different utility values they would assign to each outcome.* Premium prices may partly explain the prevalence of fire-insurance coverage and paucity of protection against natural disasters, such as earthquakes, tornados, and floods. One reason why people do not generally buy insurance policies to cover natural disasters might be the high premium required by insurance companies for such coverage (if it is offered at all) in relation to the probabilities of occurrence (which are difficult to obtain actuarily for such rare phenomena).

Further Assumptions of Utility Theory

The Assumption of Continuity.   The third assumption of utility theory is that of *continuity*, which tells us that the individual considers some gamble having the best and worst outcomes as rewards to be equally preferable to some middle or in-between outcome. To illustrate continuity, we will consider the following example.

Homer Briant owns a small hardware store in a deteriorating neighborhood and is contemplating a move. Because Homer is still young and has no special skills, he will not consider leaving the hardware business. A move cannot be guaranteed to be successful, since relocating will involve the maximum extension of his credit and there will be no time for a gradual buildup of business. Therefore, moving will either improve Homer's present business or be disastrous. Thus, Homer is faced with one of the following outcomes:

$$\text{Most preferred } O_3: \quad \text{increasing sales (if move is a success)}$$
$$O_2: \quad \text{decreasing sales (if Homer stays)}$$
$$\text{Least preferred } O_1: \quad \text{imminent bankruptcy (if move is a failure)}$$

Whether a move will be a success depends largely on luck or chance. Our assumptions of continuity presumes that there is some probability value q for a successful move that will make Homer indifferent between staying and moving. Figure 20-2 presents the decision tree diagram for this decision. The fork at node b represents a gamble between O_3 and O_1 resulting from the act "move." Continuity may be justified by observing that if the value of q is close to 1, so that a move will almost certainly be a success, Homer will prefer the gamble of moving to staying. But if q is close to 0, making bankruptcy a near certainty, Homer will prefer to stay in his present location. Thus, there must be a value of q somewhere between 0 and 1 beyond which Homer's preference will pass from O_2 to the gamble. This value of q makes the gamble as equally attractive as O_2.

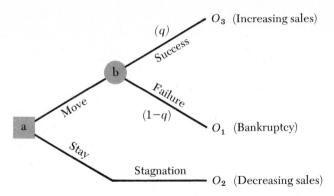

FIGURE 20-2
Homer's decision tree diagram for possible business relocation.

Continuity is a crucial assumption of utility theory, but it may be hard to accept, especially if the outcomes include the ultimate one—death. Suppose that you are allowed to participate in a lottery that offers you $100 if you win and death if you lose. Is there any probability for winning that would make you indifferent between the status quo and playing? A natural response is that this is not a very meaningful gamble, so we will recast the situation. Suppose that you are informed by a reliable source that you can drive your car one mile down the road and someone will be passing out $100 bills, one to a person. There are no gimmicks, and you will not be inconvenienced by a mob of people Would you go? If you answer yes, then consider your chances of getting killed in an automobile accident on your journey. For the past several years, approximately 50,000 persons have been killed in such accidents in the United States annually. So although it is quite small, the probability that your rather untimely death will occur while you are collecting your $100 is not zero. Going to get your $100 is a gamble having death as a possibile outcome, and you prefer the gamble to the status quo. Now suppose that we increase the chance of death. To reach your benefactor, you must cross a condemned bridge. Would you still go? Probably not, because the chance of death would be significantly higher. Somewhere in between these two extremes lies a probability for safely getting your $100 and a complementary probability for death that would make you indifferent between the status quo and the gamble.

The Assumption of Substitutability.   A fourth assumption of utility theory allows us to revise a gamble by *substituting* one outcome for another outcome that is equally well regarded. The premise is that the individual will be indifferent between the original and the revised gambles. The substitutability assumption can be illustrated by means of an example.

A husband and wife cannot agree about how to spend Saturday night. In desperation, they decide to gamble by tossing a coin to determine the kind of entertainment they will select. If a head occurs, they will spend the evening at the opera (her preference), and if a tail occurs, they will go to a basketball game. Suppose that the wife changes her mind and wants to go to a dance instead. The husband dislikes dancing just as much as the opera, so he would be indifferent between tossing for the opera or basketball and a revised gamble between dancing and basketball. This will hold regardless of the odds, providing the chance of going to the basketball game remains the same for the original and the revised gambles.

The principle of substitutability also holds if we treat a gamble as an outcome. For any outcome, we can substitute an *equivalent gamble* with two other outcomes as rewards that is equally as well regarded as the outcome the gamble replaces. For example, suppose that the wife insists on a movie instead. She wants to see a romance story, but he feels that as compensation for being dragged to a movie, they should see an adventure film. Suppose that the husband is indifferent between an opera or a coin toss to determine which of the two

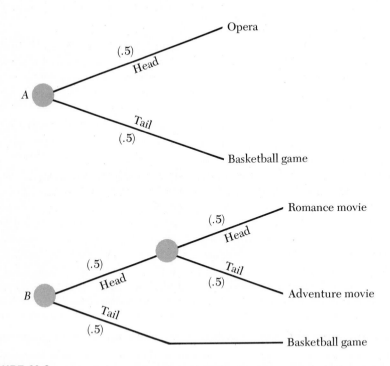

FIGURE 20-3

An illustration of the assumption of substitutability. The single-stage gamble at *A* and the two-stage gamble at *B* are equally well regarded.

movies to see. The second coin toss is an equivalent gamble to the opera outcome. Thus, the husband should be indifferent between the single- and the two-stage gambles in Figure 20-3.

The Assumption of Increasing Preference.   The final assumption of utility theory concerns any pair of gambles with identical outcomes. The gamble that has the greater probability for the more desirable outcome must be preferred. Thus, the preference for gambles between the same two outcomes *increases* as the probability for attaining the better outcome increases. That this is plausible should be apparent. Suppose that when a coin is tossed, you are paid $100 if a head occurs and nothing if a tail occurs. The probability of winning $100 is 1/2. It should be obvious that this gamble would be decidedly inferior to a gamble with the same outcomes and a probability of winning greater than 1/2.

Determining Utility Values **20-4**

We are now ready to assign utility values to outcomes. Figure 20-4 outlines this procedure. The numbers are obtained from a series of gambles between a pair of outcomes.

The Reference Lottery

The process begins with a preference ranking of all the outcomes to be considered. The most preferred and the least preferred outcomes are determined, and a gamble between these outcomes establishes the individual's utilities. We call this a *reference lottery*. It has two events: "win," which corresponds to achieving the best outcome, and "lose," which corresponds to attaining the worst outcome. Such a gamble is purely *hypothetical* and only provides a framework for assessing utility. The events "win" and "lose" do not relate to any events in the actual decision structure and are used to divorce the reference lottery from actual similar gambles. *The probability of winning the hypothetical reference lottery is a variable*, denoted by q, which changes according to the attitudes of the decision maker.

The initial assignment of utility values to the best and worst outcomes is *completely arbitrary*. It does not matter what values are chosen; assigning different values to these arbitrary utilities will result in different utility scales. This is similar to temperature measurement, in which two different and quite arbitrary values are used to define the Fahrenheit and Celsius scales. The choices

(1) All outcomes are ranked. A convenient designation is to let a subscript denote the order of preference:

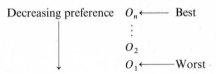

(2) Utilities for best and worst outcomes are arbitrarily assigned:

$u(O_n)$

$\vdots$ Utilities for intermediate outcomes are to be found.

$u(O_2)$
$u(O_1)$

(3) A reference lottery is formulated. This is a gamble having rewards O_n if won and O_1 if lost. The probability q for winning the reference lottery is treated as a variable, which can be changed at the will of the decision maker. The reference lottery is strictly hypothetical.

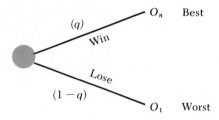

(4) For each intermediate outcome, the decision maker establishes the value of q that serves as a point of indifference between the outcome itself and the reference lottery.

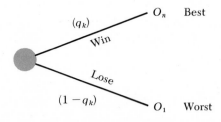

Thus, for intermediate outcome O_k, a win probability q_k is determined that results in a reference lottery that is equally as well regarded as O_k.

(5) The utility of O_k can now be determined. It is equal to the expected utility for the reference lottery with a win probability of q_k:

$$u(O_k) = q_k u(O_n) + (1 - q_k)u(O_1)$$

FIGURE 20-4

The procedure for assigning values to a set of outcomes.

of 32° Fahrenheit and 0° Celsius for the freezing point and of 212°F and 100°C for the boiling point of water result in quite different values on the these two scales for any particular temperature.

Obtaining Utility Values

Once the extreme utility values are determined, the decision maker can use the reference lottery to obtain utilities for the intermediate outcomes. This is accomplished by varying the "win" probability q until the decision maker establishes a value of q that serves as a *point of indifference* between achieving that outcome for certain and letting the reward be determined by the reference lottery. That particular value of q makes the reference lottery a gamble that is equivalent to the intermediate outcome so evaluated. We have seen that the assumption of continuity makes this possible. Again, we can add meaning to this procedure by considering its similarities to temperature measurement. The decision maker's subjective evaluation is analogous to designing a thermometer. A thermometer is designed by determining a core diameter that will permit a substance such as mercury to rise to various levels within its tubular cavity. For each level of heat, there is a corresponding height to which the mercury must rise. On the Celsius scale, the 100° mark corresponds to the mercury's height when the thermometer is placed in boiling water. Various levels of heat between the freezing and boiling points of water correspond to marks at prescribed heights above the zero mark, allowing heat to be measured in relative degrees. Similarly, the values of q established to make the decision maker indifferent between respective intermediate outcomes and the reference lottery serve to measure his or her relative preferences. The indifference values of q are like the markings on a thermometer, and the different outcome preferences are analogous to different levels of heat. These values of q are established through introspection and have no more to do with the actual chance of winning than the design of a thermometer is related to tomorrow's temperature.

Once an indifference value of q has been established for an outcome, its utility value can be determined by calculating the expected value of the reference lottery using that value of q. Letting O_1 and O_n represent the least and the most preferred outcomes, we can then find the utility of an outcome O_k of intermediate preference from

$$u(O_k) = q_k u(O_n) + (1 - q_k)u(O_1)$$

Here, q_k is the value of q that makes the decision maker *indifferent* between the certain achievement of O_k and taking a chance with the reference lottery. The

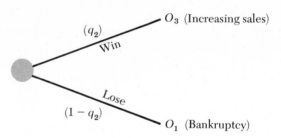

FIGURE 20-5
The reference lottery for Homer Briant's decision.

utility value $u(O_k)$ is analogous to a numerical degree value beside a marking on a thermometer.

To illustrate, we will continue with Homer Briant's contemplated business relocation. Homer has ranked his preferences for the outcomes of increasing sales (O_3), decreasing sales (O_2), and bankruptcy (O_1), and the reference lottery is shown in Figure 20-5. Suppose that the utility values of the extreme outcomes are arbitrarily set at 10 and -5, so that

$$u(O_3) = 10 \qquad u(O_1) = -5$$

Now assume that Homer contemplates the reference lottery in terms of 100 marbles in a box, some labeled W for "win" and the rest labeled L for "lose." A marble is to be selected at random. If it is a W, then Homer will be guaranteed outcome O_3 (increasing sales), but if it is an L, he will go bankrupt for certain, achieving outcome O_1. Homer is then asked what number of W marbles would make him indifferent between facing declining sales (outcome O_2) or taking his chances with the lottery. After considerable thought, Homer replies that 75 W marbles would make him regard O_2 and the reference lottery equally well. This establishes a reference lottery win probability of q_2 that makes it an equivalent gamble to outcome O_2:

$$q_2 = 75/100 = .75$$

This probability can then be used to calculate the utility of declining sales:

$$
\begin{aligned}
u(O_2) &= q_2 u(O_3) + (1 - q_2) u(O_1) \\
&= .75(10) + .25(-5) \\
&= 6.25
\end{aligned}
$$

Attitude Versus Judgment

It must be emphasized that the value $q_2 = .75$ is merely a device used to establish indifference. *The selected probability for winning the lottery has nothing to do with the chance that the most favorable outcome will occur.* In setting $q_2 = .75$, the decision maker is expressing an *attitude* toward one outcome in terms of the rewards of a hypothetical gamble. This value was obtained through introspection in an attempt to balance tastes and aspirations between remaining in a declining business or gambling to improve it. Homer is assumed to be capable of switching from introspection to dispassionate *judgment* when asked later what he thinks the actual chance is that moving his business will be a success. To arrive at the probability of success, our decision maker must use his experience and knowledge of such factors as the history of failures by relocated businesses, prevailing economic conditions, and possible competitor reactions.

Suppose that Homer judges his chance of success after moving to be 1/2. We can now analyze his decision problem by applying the Bayes decision rule, using utilities as payoff values. The decision tree diagram is shown in Figure 20-6. The expected utility payoff for the event fork at b is 2.5, which is the utility achieved by moving. Since this value is smaller than the 6.25 utility achieved by remaining in his present location, Homer Briant should not move. Thus, we prune the branch corresponding to the act "move" and bring the 6.25 utility payoff back to node a.

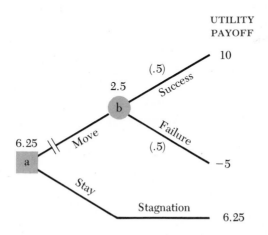

FIGURE 20-6
Homer Briant's decision tree diagram showing backward induction analysis with utility payoffs.

Utility and the Bayes Decision Rule

This example illustrates why the Bayes decision rule is valid when utility payoffs are used. The utility of a gamble is the expected value of the utilities assigned to its rewards. Since any act with uncertain outcomes may be viewed as a gamble, the act that provides the greatest utility—and therefore the one that must be preferred—is the act with the maximum expected utility payoff. The Bayes decision rule can therefore be viewed as an extension of utility theory, and the criterion serves only to translate the decision maker's preferences into a choice of act. Homer Briant decides to stay because this act provides the greater utility—which can only be the case, our theory states, if remaining in the present location is the preferred act. *In arriving at a choice, both the decision maker's attitudes toward the consequences and judgment regarding the chances of the events are considered and integrated.* The choice indicated by the Bayes criterion is optimal because it is preferred above all others.

If some other success probability (say, .90), had been determined, Homer would relocate, because doing so would have the higher utility: $.9(10) + .1(-5) = 8.5$. This might be the case, for example, if Homer learned that his major would-be competitor had just been taken over by his incompetent son. Changing event probabilities reflects only the decision maker's judgement regarding the factors that influence their occurrence. Only the *expected* utilities of uncertain *acts* can be affected by the revision of event probabilities. Regardless of the chance of the success of the relocation, the decision maker's utilities for the ultimate *outcomes* must remain unchanged. Only a change of taste or attitude, which might be caused by a death in the family or a change in personal finances, can justify revising the ultimate outcome utilities.

20-5   THE UTILITY FOR MONEY AND ATTITUDES TOWARD RISK

Applying the Utility Function in Decision Analysis

The reference lottery can be used to construct a utility function for money. To do this, the best outcome is selected so that it is no smaller than the greatest possible payoff, and the worst outcome is selected so that it is no larger than the lowest possible payoff. Monetary outcomes offer some special advantages. A monetary amount can be measured on a continuous scale, so that the utility function itself will be continuous. This suggests that it may be determined by finding an appropriate smoothed curve relating money values to their utilities. To do this, only a few key dollar amounts and some knowledge of the curve's general shape are required. The curve obtained by connecting the points can then serve as an approximation of the utility function.

Such a curve is shown in Figure 20-7 for the Ponderosa Record Company decision in Chapter 5. This utility curve has been derived according to the procedures just described by applying a reference lottery and using a few key monetary amounts as the outcomes. The reference lottery used ranges from +$100,000 (for win) to −$75,000 (for lose), which are more extreme than any possible payoff for ease of evaluation. Arbitrary utility values of $u(+\$100,000) = 1$ and $u(-\$75,000) = 0$ have been set for simplicity.

In practice, a utility function is found empirically by personally interviewing the decision maker. Ordinarily, the function will be described graphically by reading the utilities directly from the curve rather than by a mathematical equation.

We can use the utility curve in Figure 20-7 to analyze the Ponderosa president's decision problem. The original decision tree diagram is reconstructed in Figure 20-8. The utilities corresponding to each monetary payoff have been obtained from the utility curve and added to the tree. For instance, the utilities for the monetary payoffs $35,000 and −$55,000 are .84 and .32, respectively.

Backward induction is then performed using utilities instead of dollars. Here, we find that the optimal choice is "don't test market" and "abort." The two alternatives that involve marketing the record are too risky. Recall that

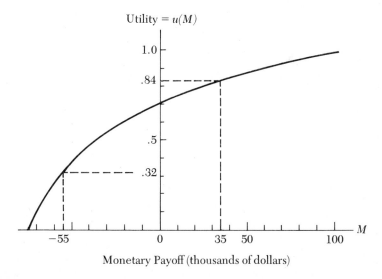

FIGURE 20-7
The utility function for the president of the Ponderosa Record Company.

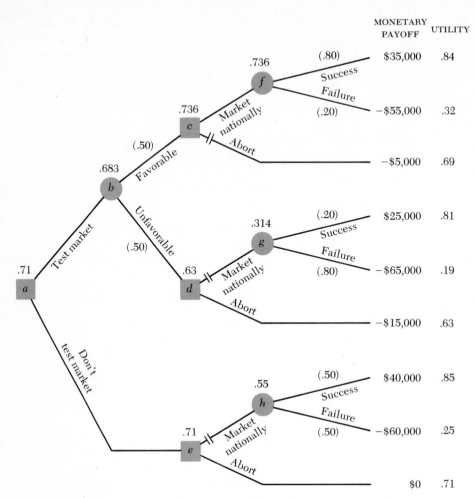

FIGURE 20-8

The Ponderosa decision tree diagram showing backward induction analysis with utility payoffs.

we reached a different conclusion in Chapter 5 when expected monetary values were used. But since utility values express the true worth of monetary outcomes, our latest solution is the valid one.

Attitudes Toward Risk and the Shape of the Utility Curve

The utility function for money can be used as the basis for describing an individual's attitudes toward risk. Three basic attitudes have been characterized. The polar cases are the *risk averter*, who will accept only favorable gambles, and the *risk seeker*, who will pay a premium for the privilege of participating in a gamble. Between these two extremes lies the *risk-neutral individual,* who considers the face value of money to be its true worth. The utility functions for each basic attitude appear in Figure 20-9. Each function has a particular shape, corresponding to the decision maker's fundamental outlook. All three utility functions show that utility increases with monetary gains. This reflects the underlying assumption of utility theory that utility increases with preference, which is combined with the additional assumption that more money will always increase an individual's well-being, so that the outcomes with greater payoffs are preferred. (This assumption may not be strictly true, but with the exception of eccentrics, most people behave in a manner that supports it.)

Throughout most of their lives, people are typically risk averters. These individuals buy plenty of casualty insurance. They avoid actions that involve high risks (chances of large monetary losses). Only gambles with high expected payoffs will be attractive to them. A risk averter's utility drops more and more severely as losses become larger, and the utilities for positive amounts do not grow as fast with monetary gains. The risk averter's marginal utility for money diminishes as the rewards increase, so that the risk averter's utility curve, shown in Figure 20-9(a), exhibits a decreasing positive slope as the level of monetary payoff becomes larger. Such a curve is *concave* when viewed from below.

The risk seeker's behavior is the opposite of the risk averter's behavior. Many of us are risk seekers at some stage of our lives. This attitude is epitomized by the "high roller," who may behave recklessly and who is motivated by the possibility of achieving the maximum reward in any gamble. This risk seeker will prefer *some* gambles with negative expected monetary payoffs to maintaining the status quo. The greater the maximum reward, the more the risk seeker's behavior will diverge from the risk averter's behavior. The risk seeker is typically self-insured, believing that the risk is superior to forgoing money spent on premiums. The risk seeker's marginal utility for money is increasing: Each additional dollar provides a disproportionately greater sense of well-being. The loss of one more dollar is felt only slightly more severely for large absolute levels of loss than for small ones. Thus, the slope of the risk seeker's utility curve, shown in Figure 20-9(b), increases as the monetary change improves. This curve is *convex* when viewed from below.

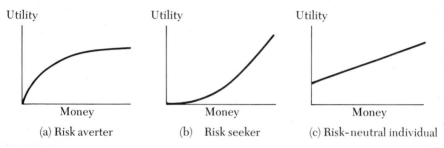

FIGURE 20-9

A graphical portrayal of utility functions for basic attitudes toward risk.

Our third characterization of attitude toward risk is the risk-neutral individual, who prizes money at its face value. The utility function for such an individual is a straight line, as shown in Figure 20-9(c). His or her utility for a gamble is equal to the utility of the expected monetary payoff. Risk-neutral individuals buy no casualty insurance, since the premium charge is greater than the expected loss. Risk-neutral behavior is epitomized by individuals who are enormously wealthy. The decisions of large corporations are often based on the Bayes decision rule applied directly to monetary payoffs, reflecting that increments in dollar assets are valued at their face amount.

In general, risk neutrality holds only over a limited range of money values. For example, many large firms do not carry casualty insurance, but almost all giant corporations will insure against extremely large losses—airlines buy hijacking insurance, for example. The same holds for individuals. Many risk-averse persons are risk-neutral when the stakes are small. The player in the World Series office pool falls into this category; losses are hardly noticeable and winnings permit the individual to indulge in some luxury. (Small gambles may add spice to a person's life—they are a form of entertainment. Thus, a person might play poker with more skillful players, where the expected payoff would be negative, just for the fun of it.) That people are risk-neutral for small risks is illustrated by their car-insurance purchases. Many generally risk-averse people carry deductible comprehensive coverage when they first purchase an automobile, and usually keep only the liability coverage when their car gets old. Again, this reflects risk neutrality over a limited range of monetary outcomes. This behavior does not contradict the curve shapes in Figure 20-9(a) and (b) because each curve can be approximated by a straight line segment throughout a narrow monetary interval.

Many people can be both risk averters and risk seekers, depending on the range of monetary values being considered. To an entrepreneur founding a business, the risks are very high—a lifetime's savings, plenty of hard work, burnt career bridges, a heavy burden of debt, and a significant chance of bankruptcy. Those who embark on the hard road of self-employment may often be viewed as risk seekers. They are motivated primarily by the rewards—monetary and otherwise—of being their own boss. Once entrepreneurs become established and are viewed by peers as future pillars of the community, their attitude toward risk will have evolved to a point where they can be characterized as risk averters. They are much more conservative (now there is something to conserve), and probably no venture imaginable could persuade them to risk everything they own to further their wealth.

We can conceive of an individual's attitudes varying between risk seeking and risk aversion over time. Usually a risk seeker has some definite goal or *aspiration level*, which can be achieved by obtaining a specific amount of money. A young sports enthusiast might be willing to participate in an unfair gamble if winning would provide sufficient cash for a down payment on his or her first motorcycle. The young professional may speculate in volatile stocks until he or she earns enough money to make a down payment on a fashionable home. To these risk seekers, losing is not much worse than maintaining the status quo. But once the goal is achieved, the risk seeker's outlook changes, and with a sated appetite, the risk seeker becomes a risk averter until some new goal enters his or her horizon.

A utility curve for such an individual appears in Figure 20-10. The horizontal axis measures total wealth in monetary units, rather than changes in current cash position. Here, the utility function is convex until an aspiration level is reached. Until that goal is achieved, the individual is a risk seeker. When this goal is reached, the individual becomes a conservative risk averter until more wealth permits the germination of a newer goal of a higher order. Then the

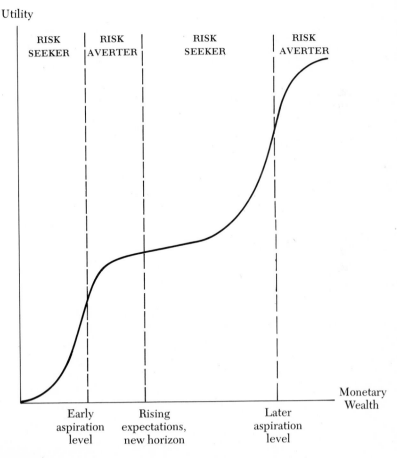

FIGURE 20-10

A graphical portrayal of the evolving utility function for an individual over a long time period.

cycle begins all over again with risk seeking, followed by another period of risk aversion.

Such a curve portrays behavior over a long period of time and is only an idealization of a long-run utility function. A great many factors can cause an individual's attitudes to change over time, and it may not be possible to obtain meaningful measures of the influence of remote goals. In general, the validity of a utility curve is very short-lived and is affected by changes in such factors as age, life style, family size, and total wealth. To be successfully employed, the utility function should to be updated prior to each decision.

PROBLEMS

20-1 Suppose that you are offered a gamble by Ms. I.M. Honest, a representative of a foundation studying human behavior. A fair coin is to be tossed. If a head occurs, you will receive $10,000 from Ms. Honest. But if a tail results, you must pay her foundation $5,000. If you do *not* have $5,000, a loan will be arranged, which must be repaid over a five-year period at $150 per month but can be deferred until you have graduated from school.
(a) Calculate your expected profit from participating in this gamble.
(b) Would you be willing to accept Ms. Honest's offer? Does your answer indicate that your marginal utility for money is decreasing?

20-2 Mr. Smith has offered you a gamble similar to that of Ms. Honest in Problem 20-1. If a head occurs, he will hand you $1.00. But if a tail results you must pay Mr. Smith $.50.
(a) Calculate your expected profit from participating in this gamble.
(b) Would you be willing to accept Mr. Smith's offer?

20-3 A homeowner whose house is valued at $40,000 is offered tornado insurance at an annual premium of $500. Suppose that there are just two mutually exclusive out-comes—complete damage or no damage from a tornado—and that the probability of damage from a tornado is .0001.
(a) Construct the homeowner's payoff table for the decision of whether or not to buy tornado insurance.
(b) Calculate the decision maker's expected monetary payoff for each act. Which act has the maximum expected payoff?
(c) Suppose that the homeowner decides not to buy tornado insurance. Does this contradict the decreasing marginal utility for money? Explain.

20-4 Actor Nathan Summers enjoys wearing costumes in front of audiences. Nathan likes dressing up like a little old lady the most and hates to dress up like an animal. Some-where in between lies his preference for wearing a cowboy suit. Assigning a utility of 10 to being a lady and a utility of −5 to being an animal, what is Nathan's utility for playing a cowboy if he is indifferent between this outcome and a coin toss determining which of the other two roles he will play?

20-5 A contractor must determine whether to buy or rent the equipment required to do a job up for bid. Because of lead-time requirements, he must decide whether to obtain the equipment before he knows if he has been awarded the contract. If he buys the equipment, the contract will result in $120,000 net profit after equipment resale returns, but if he loses the job, then the equipment will have to be sold at a $40,000 loss. By renting, his profit from the contract (if he wins it) will be only $50,000, but there will be no loss of money if the job is not won. The contractor's chance of winning are 50–50, and his utility function is $u(M) = \sqrt{M + 40,000}$.

(a) Construct the contractor's payoff table using profit as the payoff measure.

(b) Calculate the expected profit payoff for each act. According to the Bayes decision rule, what act should the contractor select?

(c) Construct the contractor's payoff table using utilities as the payoff measure.

(d) Calculate the expected utility payoff for each act. Which act provides the maximum expected utility?

(e) Which act should the decision maker choose? Explain.

20-6 An insurance policy would cost Hermie Hawks $1,000 per year to protect his home from tornado damage. Assume that any actual tornado damage to Hermie's house, valued at $100,000, would be totally destructive and that the probability that a tornado will hit his house during the year is .0025.

(a) If Hermie is risk-neutral, what would his optimal decision be regarding buying tornado insurance? Show your computations.

(b) How much above its expected claim size is the insurance company charging Hermie for its combined overhead and profit on the proposed policy?

(c) Hermie's utility function for any change in his monetary position for any amount M is

$$u(M) = 10,000 - (M/1,000)^2$$

What action should Hermie take to maximize his expected utility?

(d) What annual insurance premium charge would make Hermie indifferent between buying or not buying tornado insurance?

20-7 Suppose that the Ponderosa Record Company's utility function for money is $u(M) = [(M + 65,000)/10,000]^2$.

(a) Redraw Figure 20-8 (page 498), and calculate the utility for each end position.

(b) Perform backward induction analysis using the new utilities you have calculated. What strategy is optimal?

(c) On a piece of graph paper, plot the utilities you calculated in (a) as a function of monetary payoffs M. Sketch a curve through the points. Of what attitude toward risk is the shape of your curve indicative?

20-8 You may achieve the following outcomes (no rights are transferable):
  • 100 new records of your choice
  • A grade of C on the next examination covering utility
  • A year's assignment to Timbuktu, Mali
  • Confinement to an airport during a three-day storm
  • A month of free telephone calls to anywhere

(a) Rank these outcomes in descending order of preference, designating them O_5, O_4, O_3, O_2, and O_1.

(b) Let the utilities be $u(O_5) = 100$ for the best outcome and $u(O_1) = 0$ for the worst outcome. Consider a box containing 1,000 marbles, some of which are labeled "win" and the remainder of which are labeled "lose." If a "win" marble is selected at random from the box, you will achieve O_5. If a "lose" marble is chosen, you will attain O_1. Determine how many marbles of each type would make you indifferent between gambling or achieving O_2. Determine the same for O_3 and O_4.

(c) The corresponding probabilities for winning q_k can be determined by dividing the respective number of "win" marbles by 1,000. Use these probabilities to calculate $u(O_4)$, $u(O_3)$, and $u(O_2)$.

20-9 Suppose that Alvin Black's attitude toward risk is generally averse. For each of the following 50–50 gambling propositions, indicate whether Alvin (1) would be willing, (2) might desire, or (3) would be unwilling to participate. Explain the reasons for your choices.

(a) $10,000 versus $0. (b) $10,000 versus −$1,000.
(c) $15,000 versus −$10,000. (d) $500 versus −$600.
(e) $20,000 versus $10,000.

20-10 Lucille Brown is risk-neutral. Would she buy comprehensive coverage for her automobile if she agreed with company actuaries regarding the probability distribution for future claim sizes? Explain.

20-11 Victor White is a risk seeker. Does this necessarily imply that he will never buy casualty insurance? Explain.

20-12 J.P. Tidewasser has just undergone the first traumatic phase of determining his utility function for a range of money values. By his response to a series of gambles, it has been established that he is indifferent between making the 50–50 gambles on the left and receiving the certain amounts of money shown on the right:

Rewards of Gamble		Equivalent Amount
+$30,000	−$10,000	$ 0
+ 30,000	0	+ 10,000
0	− 10,000	− 7,000
+ 10,000	− 7,000	1,000

(a) If J.P. sets $u(\$30,000) = 1$ and $u(-\$10,000) = 0$, determine his utility for $0.
(b) Calculate J.P.'s utilities for +$10,000 and −$7,000.
(c) Calculate J.P.'s utility for +$1,000. What, if any, inconsistencies do you notice between this and your previous answers?

20-13 Hoopla Hoops is a retail boutique catering to current crazes. The owner must decide whether or not to stock a batch of Water Wheelies. Each item costs $2 and sells for $4. Unsold items cannot be returned to the supplier, who sells them in batches of 500. The following probability distribution is assumed to apply for the anticipated demand for Water Wheelies:

Demand	Probability
100	.05
200	.10
300	.15
400	.20
500	.20
600	.15
700	.10
800	.05
	1.00

Consider demand to mean the potential for sales. No more than what is demanded can be sold; but if demand exceeds on-hand inventory, then not all of the demand can be fulfilled.

(a) Calculate the expected demand. If you assume that the expected demand will actually occur, what profit corresponds to this amount? Use the utility curve shown in Figure 20-11 to determine the corresponding utility value.
(b) Calculate the expected profit from stocking 500 Water Wheelies. Does this differ from the amount you found in (a)? Explain this. Then determine the utility for the expected profit.

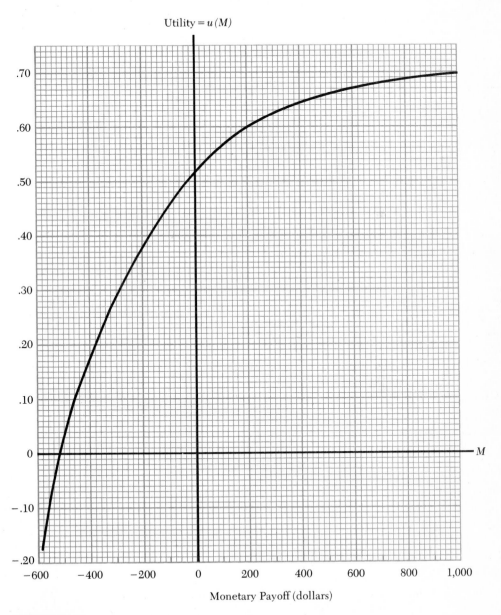

Utility $= u(M)$

Monetary Payoff (dollars)

FIGURE 20-11

(c) Calculate the expected utility for stocking 500 Water Wheelies. (First, calculate the profit for each level of possible demand; then find the utility for each level; finally, apply the probability weights.) Which act—stocking or not stocking Water Wheelies—provides the greatest expected utility?

20-14 Consider the plight of the decision maker in Problem 5-8 (page 125). She must interview dozens of candidates annually for keypunching jobs. Losses of her recoverable training expenses can therefore be significant. Suppose that she has constructed the utility function shown in Figure 20-11.

(a) Redraw Figure 5-5 (page 125).

(b) For the monetary payoff value for each end position, determine the decision maker's approximate utility value from the curve in Figure 20-11.

(c) Perform backward induction analysis using utilities as payoffs. Which strategy is optimal?

21

Assessing Probabilities Through Judgment

Although probability concepts have been extensively used in earlier chapters, little discussion has been devoted to *subjective probabilities*. Subjective probabilities are applicable to nonrepeatable circumstances, such as introducing a new product or drilling a wildcat oil well, and must be arrived at through *judgment*. This is in contrast to the long-run frequencies used to establish *objective probabilities*, which are valid only when elements of repeatability are present. Because so many business decisions involve one-shot situations that never recur exactly, there is a strong need for subjective probabilities when analyzing decision making under uncertainty. In this chapter, we will examine the procedures for translating judgment into the subjective probability values that are required to implement Bayesian analysis to help solve decision problems in the real world.

PROBABILITIES OBTAINED FROM HISTORY 21-1

Historical experience can be a convenient starting point for assigning probabilities. To calculate the historical frequency of an event, we need to know only two things: how many times the event has occurred in the past and the number of opportunities when it could have occurred. This is how fire-insurance underwriters obtain probabilities for determining the expected claim sizes that are used to establish policy charges. With tens of thousands of buildings involved, *the event frequencies themselves define the probabilities*, because in the traditional sense, probability fundamentally expresses long-run frequency of occurrence.

There are inherent difficulties in using historical frequencies as probabilities. One is the limited extent of history—the available data may only provide a crude frequency estimate. Unless the number of similar past circumstances is large, statistical estimates of event frequencies can be unreliable. Past history may be suitable for setting fire-insurance rates. But past frequencies cannot be wholly adequate—indeed, are unavailable—to determine the probability distributions for a great many variables encountered in business, such as the demand for a new product.

Another serious difficulty is that conditions change over time. The recent experience of automobile casualty insurance firms serves as an example of how changing conditions can make historical frequencies unsuitable for obtaining probabilities. Car insurers, who have consistently complained about losing money on collision and comprehensive coverage, have found that past experience has proved to be a poor predictor of future levels of damage claims. This is due not to sampling error, which is virtually nonexistent because the data obtained constitute a census, but rather to changing circumstances. Cars are becoming less and less sturdy, so that minor impacts that would hardly dent an older car can seriously damage a new one. Repair costs have also been rising in a pronounced inflationary spiral. More cars are sharing roads that are not increasing at the same rate, and driving habits are changing accordingly, affecting the accident rate. Automobile thefts have also been increasing as the result of new social pressures.

Using historical frequencies to estimate the probabilities of future automobile insurance claims may be compared to tossing a die, some side of which is shaved before each toss. We do not know which side has been shaved or by how much. Under these circumstances, we can never obtain a reasonable probability distribution for the respective sides from historical frequencies alone.

21-2 SUBJECTIVE PROBABILITIES

To apply basic decison-making models based on expected payoffs or utilities, we must employ probabilities. Past history can sometimes provide probability values that fit into the mold of long-run frequencies. But the applicability of such data is limited to events with a rich history, such as insurance claims. And even when they are available, these data can be misleading owing to the forces of change.

In many business decisions, the only recourse is to use subjective probabilities, which are not tied to a long-run frequency of occurrence, because so many decisions involve one-shot situations that may be characterized by essentially nonrepeatable uncertainties. Good *judgment* may be the only method available to transform such uncertainties into a set of probabilities for the various events involved.

We have seen that decision making under uncertainty is analogous to gambling. Unlike card games, lotteries, dice, or roulette, most real-life gambles can be analyzed only with the help of subjective probabilities, which reflect the decision maker's judgment and experience. But, how do we obtain a subjective probability?

Betting Odds

Subjective probabilities can be considered betting odds; that is, they can be treated just like the probabilities that the decision maker would desire in a lottery situation of his or her own design in which the payoffs are identical in every respect to the possible payoffs from the actual decision being evaluated. For example, suppose that a contractor assigns a subjective probability of .5 to the event of winning a contract that will increase profits by $50,000 and that losing the contract will cost $10,000. This contractor ought to be indifferent between preparing a bid for the contract and gambling on a coin toss where a head provides a $50,000 win and a tail results in a $10,000 loss. The subjective probability for winning the contract can therefore be transformed directly into an "objective" .5 probability of obtaining a head from a coin toss. Assuming indifference between the real-life gamble and a hypothetical coin toss, we can then substitute the latter into the decision analysis.

One practical benefit of substituting a hypothetical gamble for an actual uncertainty is that subjective probabilities can be used in conjunction with the traditional long-run frequencies of occurrence. In effect, apples and oranges may be mixed, permitting wider acceptance of decision-theory analysis. More significantly, a hypothetical gamble or lottery can provide a convenient means of obtaining the subjective probability value itself. Consider the following example.

Substituting a Hypothetical Lottery for the Real Gamble

A project engineer must choose between two technologies in designing a prototype sonar system. She may use Doppler shift or acoustic ranging. If the Doppler shift is used, time becomes a crucial factor. To analyze this decision, the engineer must determine the probability for completing the project on time. If she is late, the project will be canceled and she will be out of a job. But if she is early or on time, her contract will be extended for two more years. The event fork of concern appears in Figure 21-1(a).

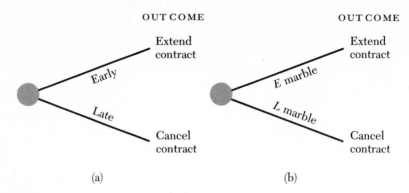

FIGURE 21-1
A project engineer's actual gamble (a) and a hypothetical lottery (b) yielding identical outcomes.

Suppose that the engineer considers the hypothetical lottery shown in Figure 21-1(b), in which one marble is to be randomly selected from a box of 100. Some marbles are labeled *E* (for early); the rest are marked *L* (for late). In this hypothetical gamble, selecting an *E* marble will result in an extended contract, but drawing an *L* marble will result in a canceled contract. Our engineer can determine the mix of *L* and *E* marble. She is asked what mixture will make her *indifferent* between letting her future be decided by trying the Doppler shift design or by selecting a marble from the box.

Suppose that the engineer determines that 70 *E* marbles and 30 *L* marbles would make her indifferent. This means that the probability for selecting an *E* marble is .70. This value can be considered the engineer's *judgmental assessment* that the project will be early or on time if the Doppler shift is used. Thus, our decision maker can let .70 represent the probability for being early or on time in analyzing her decision and place .70 on the early event branch of the fork in Figure 21-1(a).

Arriving at subjective probabilities by substituting the real-life gamble for an equally preferred lottery is a useful procedure when the number of possible events is small. But this method can be quite cumbersome when the situation involves more than a handful of events. In business applications, we are often faced with variables, such as product demand, which can be measured on many possible levels. It is best to use an entire *probability distribution* to represent such uncertain quantities.

Subjective Probability Distributions

We have seen that probability distributions can be divided into two categories. *Discrete probability distributions* apply to variables, such as the demand for cars, that must be a whole number. *Continuous probability distri-*

butions represent variables, such as time, that can be expressed on a continuous scale and measured to any degree of precision desired. When the number of possibilities is great, discrete variables are often treated as if they are approximately continuous. For this reason, we focus on finding continuous probability distributions.

Next we will consider using judgment to determine the normal distribution, which constitues perhaps the most common distribution family encountered in business decision making with continuous variables. We will then discuss the more general problem of establishing a probability distribution for *any* uncertain quantity.

DETERMINING A NORMAL CURVE JUDGMENTALLY 21-3

The normal distribution plays an important role in decision making. This is largely due to the fact that the probabilities for sample means can usually be characterized by a normal curve. But the normal curve can be applied in many applications other than sampling. The frequency patterns of physical measurements often approximate the normal curve. This feature makes it especially important in production applications, where natural fluctuations in size, density, concentration, etc., cause individual units to vary according to the normal distribution. Test scores used to determine personal aptitude or achievement are also often characterized by the normal curve. Questions of facility design as it relates to waiting lines in manufacturing, retailing, or data-processing situations must take into account the time needed to produce units, service customers, or complete jobs; these service times are often normally distributed.

Since the normal distribution is prevalent in such a broad spectrum of decision-making situations, we will give it special emphasis in this chapter. We have seen that any normal distribution is uniquely defined in terms of two parameters—the mean μ and standard deviation σ. Except in the rare circumstances when these parameters are known precisely, it is impossible to measure their values directly without expensive sampling procedures. It may be more convenient to exercise judgment in determining μ and σ. With these two quantities, we can specify the entire normal distribution. (In fact, it may be optimal not to take samples at all—a question we considered in Chapter 18. Often sampling itself is impossible because no population currently exists from which observations can be taken.)

Finding the Mean

The mean of the subjective normal curve for any quantity X believed to have a normal distribution can be established by selecting the *midpoint* of all possible values. *The subjective mean μ is that point judged to have a 50–50 chance* *that any value X will lie at or above this point versus below it.* This value is actually the *median* level, since it is just as likely that X will fall below or above the identified point. Because the normal curve is symmetrical, this central value must also equal the mean.

For example, suppose that an engineer is evaluating a new teleprocessing terminal design to determine if a prototype should be fabricated. Based on the physical characteristics of the unit compared to existing equipment of similar scope, the engineer concludes that messages could be printed at a rate of between 30 and 70 lines per second, depending on the type of message. Because the unit has never been built, the true rate X for a typical message is uncertain. The engineer assumes that this quantity is normally distributed, because similar data in related applications have been found to fit well to the normal curve.

To determine the mean printing rate, the engineer is asked to establish a level such that it is equally likely for X to fall above or below it. This decision can be phrased in terms of a coin toss: "Suppose that you had to find a middle value of X such that it would be difficult for you to choose whether an actual printing rate lies above or below it. If your professional reputation depended on being correct and you had to make a prediction for X, you would be willing to select one side or the other of that value by tossing a coin. Where would your midpoint lie?" After some thought the engineer might reply, "I think it is a coin-tossing proposition that the printing rate experienced in actual testing may fall above or below 50 lines per second." This establishes the desired midpoint and therefore the mean of the subjective probability distribution, so that $\mu = 50$ lines per second.

Relating the judgmental evaluation to coin tossing makes the problem easy for a person who is not used to dealing with probability. The 50–50 gamble is the easiest to envision. We may extend this concept to finding the standard deviation as well. *The subjective standard deviation σ can be found by establishing a middle range of values centered at μ such that X is judged to have an equal chance of lying inside or outside that interval.* To see how this works, let's review some properties of the normal curve.

Finding the Standard Deviation

In Chapter 3, we saw that the area under the normal curve between any two points is established by the distances separating each point from the mean, which are expressed in units of standard deviation. This standardized distance can be represented by a value of the normal deviate z, where for any particular point x, the corresponding normal deviate can be computed from

$$z = \frac{x - \mu}{\sigma}$$

We seek two possible values of X that are equally distant from μ such that the area between them is .50. This means that the area between μ and the upper limit must be one-half this value, or .25. From the normal curve areas in Appendix Table B, the normal deviate value of $z = .67$ provides the closest area, .2486. We can use $z = .67$ to find σ.

Figure 21-2 illustrates the underlying principles involved. The area between μ and $\mu + .67\sigma$ is about .25, so that the area in the interval $\mu \pm .67\sigma$ is about .50. If we know the distance separating the upper limit $\mu + 67\sigma$ and the mean μ, or the *half-width* of the interval, we can determine the corresponding value of σ by setting .67σ equal to that distance:

$$.67\sigma = \text{Upper limit} - \mu$$

Dividing both sides by .67, we obtain the expression for the *judgmental standard deviation*

$$\sigma = \frac{\text{Upper limit} - \mu}{.67} = \frac{\text{Half-width}}{.67}$$

Thus, to find σ, we need to establish only the width of the middle range (covered by the shaded area in Figure 21-2). This quantity is sometimes called the *interquartile range*. This evaluation is tantamount to establishing the half-width such that there is a 50–50 chance that any particular value of X will fall within μ plus or minus this quantity.

The engineer in our example is now asked to establish the half-width of the central interval. This problem might be formulated: "Select the range of

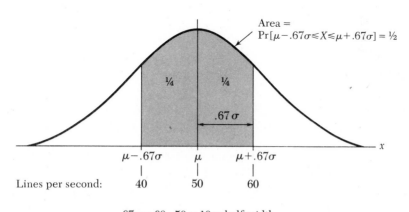

$$.67\sigma = 60 - 50 = 10 = \text{half-width}$$
$$\sigma = 10/.67 = 14.9$$

FIGURE 21-2
Finding the standard deviation of a subjective normal distribution.

values centered at $\mu = 50$ lines per second so that the actual printing rate will be just as likely to fall inside or outside of it. To find the interval, determine an amount such that μ plus or minus that quantity establishes the range." The engineer might respond: "I would guess that ± 10 lines per second is suitable for this purpose. This means that it is a coin-tossing proposition that the actual printing rate will fall somewhere between $50 - 10 = 40$ and $50 + 10 = 60$ lines per second." This establishes the half-width of 10 lines per second for the middle range, and the standard deviation can be calculated:

$$\sigma = \frac{10}{.67} = 14.9 \; lines \; per \; second$$

The subjective probability distribution for the actual printing time of the proposed terminal is now specified. Combining this with economic data, the decision maker can then apply decision-theory concepts to evaluate various alternatives regarding the manufacturing or marketing of the proposed unit.

21-4 THE JUDGMENTAL PROBABILITY DISTRIBUTION: THE INTERVIEW METHOD

The procedure we have just examined is a limited one. Although the normal distribution is very common, it is the exception. We will now consider how judgment can be exercised to determine probability distributions. Our procedure applies to any variable with a large number of possible values, such as product demand.

A natural and fairly simple procedure for obtaining a probability distribution judgmentally is to use cumulative probabilities. By posing a series of 50–50 gambles, it is quite simple to make a judgmental determination of the cumulative probability distribution for a random variable. Each response provides a point that can be plotted on a graph; a smoothed curve can then be drawn through the points. This curve completely specifies the underlying probability distribution. The following illustration shows how this procedure may be carried out.

The president of a food-manufacturing concern wishes to obtain the probability distribution for the demand for a brand new snack product. This will be used to help the president decide whether or not to market the product. A statistical analyst asks the president a series of questions to obtain answers that will be used to formulate later questions. The interview follows.*

---

* This procedure was inspired by Howard Raiffa, *Decision Analysis: Introductory Lectures on Choices Under Uncertainty* (Reading, Mass.: Addison-Wesley, 1968).

Q. What do you think the largest and smallest possible levels of demand are?

A. Certainly demand will exceed 500,000 units. But I would set an upper limit of 3,000,000 units. I don't think that under the most favorable circumstances we could sell more than this amount.

Q. Okay, we have determined the range of possible demand. Now I want you to tell me what level of demand divides the possibilities into two equally likely ranges. For example, do you think demand will be just as likely to fall above 2,000,000 as below?

A. No. I'd rather pick 1,500,000 units as the 50–50 point.

Q. Very good. Now let's consider the demand levels below 1,500,000. If demand were to fall somewhere between 500,000 and 1,500,000 units, would you bet that it lies above or below 1,000,000?

A. Above. I would say that a demand of 1,250,000 units would be a realistic dividing point.

Q. We will use that amount as our 50–50 point. Let's do the same thing for the upper range of demand.

A. If I were to pick a number, I would choose 2,000,000 units. I feel that demand is just as likely to fall into the 1.5 to 2 million range as into the 2 to 3 million range.

Q. Excellent. We're making good progress. To get a finer fix on the points obtained so far, now I want you to tell me whether you think demand is just as likely to fall between 1.25 and 2 million units as it is to fall outside that range.

A. Inside. I suppose this means I am being inconsistent.

Q. Yes, it does. Let's remedy this. Do you think that we ought to raise the 1,250,000 dividing point or lower the 2 million unit figure?

A. Lower the 2 million figure to 1.9 million.

Q. Let's check to see if this disturbs our other answers. Do you think that 1,500,000 splits demand over the range from 1,250,000 to 1,900,000 into two equally likely regions?

A. Yes, I am satisfied that it does.

Q. Just a few more questions. Suppose demand is above 1,900,000. What level splits this demand range into two equally likely regions?

A. I'd say 2,200,000.

Q. Good. Now if demand is between 2,200,000 and 3,000,000, where would you split?

A. I would guess that 2,450,000 units would be the 50–50 point.

Q. How about when demand is below 1,250,000?

A. Try 1,100,000 units.

Q. And when demand is between 500,000 and 1,100,000 units?

A. I think demand is far more likely to be close to the higher figure. I would bet on 950,000 units.

Table 21-1 shows the information obtained from this interview. The initial decision to divide demand at 1,500,000 units makes this level the 50% point or median. Since .5 has been judged the probability that demand will be below 1,500,000, we will refer to this as the .5 *fractile*. This means that the probability is .5 that the actual demand will be 1,500,000 units *or less*. Our

TABLE 21-1
A Food Manufacturer's Judgmental
Assessment of Fractiles for the
Demand for a New Snack Food

Fractile	Amount
0	500,000
.0625	950,000
.125	1,100,000
.25	1,250,000
.50	1,500,000
.75	1,900,000
.875	2,200,000
.9375	2,450,000
1.000	3,000,000

decision maker has chosen to divide the range from 500,000 to 1,500,000 units at a demand level of 1,250,000. Believing that the chance of demand falling into this range is .5, the president has judged the chance that demand will be at or below 1,250,000 units to be .5(.5) = .25; thus, we refer to 1,250,000 units as the .25 fractile. Again, this establishes a .25 probability that demand will be less than or equal to 1,250,000. The median of the range from 1,500,000 to 3,000,000 units is 1,900,000, which becomes the .75 fractile, since the probability is .5 + .5(.5) = .75 that demand will fall somewhere below 1,900,000 units. The analyst has proceeded to find the medians of the regions by working outward from previously determined 50% points. Thus, the .125 fractile of 1,100,000 units is the median demand for possible levels below the .25 fractile (1,250,000 units), which had to be determined first. The median of demands above 1,900,000 units is the .875 fractile of 2,200,000 units. Similarly, the median of the demands below 1,100,000 is the .0625 fractile of 950,000 units, while the median demand level above 2,200,000 is the .9375 fractile of 2,450,000.

The fractiles and the corresponding demands are plotted as points in Figure 21-3. The vertical axis represents the cumulative probability for demand. A curve has been smoothed through these points, which serves as an approximation of the cumulative probability distribution for the first-year demand for the snack product. The curve has an S shape; its slope increases initially and then decreases over higher levels of demand. The slope changes most rapidly for large and small demands, so that more points in these regions provide greater accuracy. This is why we work outward from the median in assessing the demand fractiles.

This example illustrates how we can obtain a very detailed measurement of judgment by posing a few 50–50 gambles. As a rule of thumb, the seven fractile values ranging from .0625 to .9375 in Table 21-1 are adequate for this

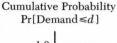

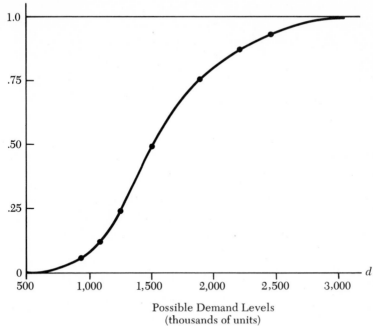

Possible Demand Levels
(thousands of units)

FIGURE 21-3
The cumulative probability distribution function for a new snack product
obtained by judgmental assessment.

purpose. Little can be gained from obtaining more fractiles, since further
gambles might result in a lumpy curve and would probably not alter the basic
shape anyway. Besides, there is no reason to "gild the lily" or to try the decision
maker's patience. A curve obtained by following this procedure provides about
as accurate a judgmental assessment as is humanly possible.

Common Shapes of Subjective Probability Curves

Ordinarily, subjective probability distributions obtained by judgmental
assessment provide S-shaped graphs that are elongated at either the top or the
bottom. Such graphs represent underlying probability distributions that are
skewed to the left or to the right, as the corresponding frequency curves in
Figure 21-4(a) and (b) show. Although skewed distributions are most common
for business and economic variables, a symmetrical distribution, shown in
Figure 21-4(c), is also possible.

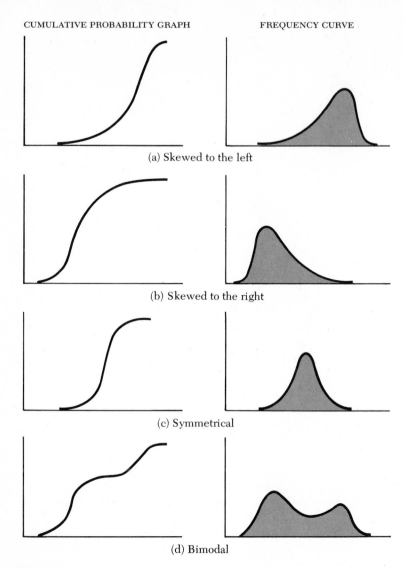

FIGURE 21-4

Possible shapes of subjective probability distributions.

Lumpy cumulative probability graphs with two stacked S-shaped curves, like the one in Figure 21-4(d), are to be avoided. The corresponding frequency curve has the two-humped shape that typifies a *bimodal distribution*. Such distributions reflect some underlying nonhomogeneous influence that operates differently for the lower-valued possibilities than it does for the higher-valued possibilities. In statistical applications, the bimodal distribution is epitomized by combining the heights of men and women. In statistics, it is more meaningful to portray male and female heights in terms of two separate curves.

A similar treatment applies to subjective probability distributions. If such a result occurs, for example, in assessing the demand for automobiles in the next model year, some identifiable factor in the decision maker's mind might explain the bimodality. A good example would be the possibility of an oil embargo like the one we experienced in 1973–1974, or the energy crisis of 1978. In such cases, the assessment should be broken down into greater detail: (1) Find a subjective probability for a gasoline shortage; (2) determine the subjective probability distribution for automobile demand assuming a shortage occurs; and (3) establish a second separate distribution for demand given that no shortage occurs.

If there is no identifiable explanation, lumpiness in the cumulative probability graph can be due to inconsistencies in expressing judgment, which may be resolved by moving one or more points to the left or right and reposing the succeeding 50–50 gambles. One easy consistency check is to see if there is actually a 50–50 chance of falling inside or outside the interquartile range, from the .25 fractile (1,250,000 units in our example) to the .75 fractile (1,900,000 units). If the decision maker judges the inside to be more likely, then the middle range should be narrowed, either by raising the .25 fractile (perhaps to 1,300,000 units) or by reducing the .75 fractile (perhaps to 1,800,000 units). Conversely, if the outside is more likely, then one of the fractiles should be changed in the opposite direction.

Approximating the Subjective Probability Distribution

It is difficult to employ the cumulative S curve directly in decision analysis, where expected values must be determined. Expected values are ordinarily calculated from a table that lists the possible variable values and their probabilities. To obtain such a table, it is necessary to approximate the cumulative probability curve by following the series of steps shown in Figure 21-5.

Each possible variable value is represented by an interval. A fairly accurate approximation is obtained with 10 intervals of equal width. The probabilities for each interval are shown as the step sizes at the upper limit for the respective interval. The probabilities for individual intervals are determined by the difference between successive cumulative probability values. All values in an interval are represented by a typical value. For this purpose, the midpoint is used.

To see how this is done, suppose that the decision maker now wishes to establish subjective probabilities for intervals of demand from 500,000 to 3,000,000 units in increments of 250,000. Table 21-2 shows how these demand probabilities have been obtained by reading values from the cumulative probability curve in Figure 21-3. We can use the probabilities we obtain to determine the approximate expected demand. A representative value is used for this

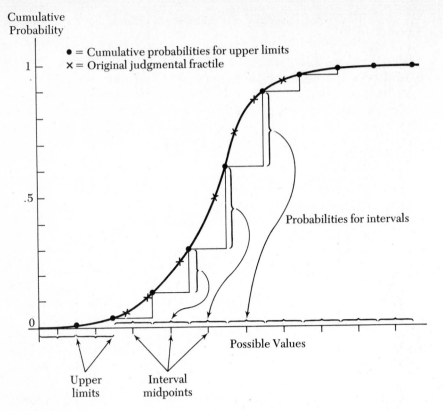

Cumulative Probability

● = Cumulative probabilities for upper limits
✕ = Original judgmental fractile

1

.5

0

Probabilities for intervals

Possible Values

Upper limits

Interval midpoints

FIGURE 21-5

An illustration of how to approximate a continuous distribution using 10 intervals.

TABLE 21-2

Subjective Probabilities for Intervals of Demand and an Approximate Calculation of the Expected Demand

(1) Demand Interval (thousands)	(2) Interval Midpoint (thousands)	(3) Probability for Demands at or Below Upper Limit (obtained from curve)	(4) Probability for Demand Interval	(5) Demand × Probability (2) × (4)
500– 750	625	.02	.02	12.50
750–1,000	875	.08	.06	52.50
1,000–1,250	1,125	.25	.17	191.25
1,250–1,500	1,375	.50	.25	343.75
1,500–1,750	1,625	.68	.18	292.50
1,750–2,000	1,875	.80	.12	225.00
2,000–2,250	2,125	.89	.09	191.25
2,250–2,500	2,375	.95	.06	142.50
2,500–2,750	2,625	.98	.03	78.75
2,750–3,000	2,875	1.00	.02	57.50

Approximate expected demand = 1,587.50

purpose. We have used the interval midpoints to arrive at 1,587,500 units as the expected demand. The same probability values and representative demands can be used to find the expected payoff from marketing the new snack. The total payoff can be determined for each representative level of demand. The weighted average of these payoffs, using the probabilities in Table 21-2, would then yield the expected payoff, which could be used in the total analysis.

The interval probabilities can be used to plot this histogram for demand shown in Figure 21-6. The height of .25 for the bar covering the interval from 1,250,000 to 1,500,000 units represents the probability that demand will fall somewhere between these amounts. Superimposed onto this histogram is a smoothed curve representing the judgmental frequency curve for demand. Note that the curve is positively skewed.

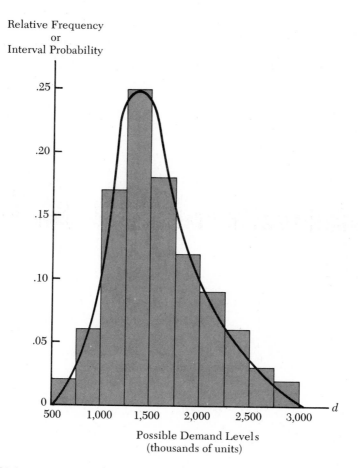

FIGURE 21-6

The frequency curve and the individual interval probabilities for the demand for a new snack product obtained by judgmental assessment.

21-5   FINDING A PROBABILITY DISTRIBUTION FROM ACTUAL/FORECAST RATIOS

The interview method is most suitable for use on a one-time basis when uncertain circumstances are involved that may never be encountered again. When judgmental forecasts of a single value are made more often, they provide a history that can be used to determine the underlying probability distribution.

We will illustrate this procedure with an example involving weekly sales forecasts for Blitz Beer made by the company's sales manager. The relevant data over a 10-month period are provided in Table 21-3. We will assume that the forecasts have been made solely from judgment. The actual sales values are divided by the respective forecast sales figures to provide *actual/forecast ratios*.

Actual sales of Blitz Beer for the first week were 1,133 barrels. The manager had forecast 1,200 barrels. Thus

$$\frac{\text{Actual sales}}{\text{Forecast sales}} = \frac{1,133}{1,200} = .94 \quad \text{(actual/forecast ratio)}$$

The sales manager's forecasting record is summarized in the cumulative probability graph in Figure 21-7. To plot this, the actual/forecast ratios are arranged in increasing value. There are 10 ratios, so each ratio is assigned a probability of 1/10. Thus, a .10 step in cumulative probability occurs at each value. A smoothed curve is then drawn freehand through the resulting cumu-

TABLE 21-3

Blitz Beer Weekly Sales (in Barrels) Showing Judgment Forecasts and Actual/Forecast Ratios

Actual	Forecast	Actual/Forecast
1,133	1,200	.94
1,422	1,150	1.24
1,288	1,300	.99
1,317	1,370	.96
1,080	1,410	.77
1,344	1,580	.85
1,506	1,650	.91
1,752	1,650	1.06
1,924	1,750	1.10
1,783	2,000	.89

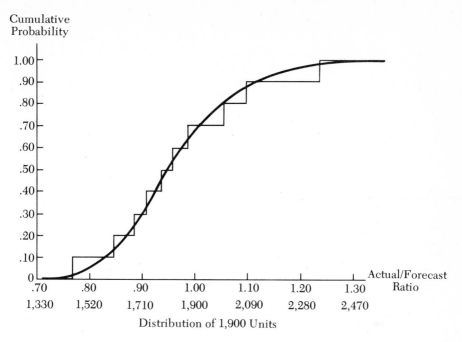

FIGURE 21-7
Subjective probability distribution of Blitz Beer sales based on actual/forecast ratios.

lative probability stairway. This curve can be combined with the sales manager's next forecast to obtain the cumulative probability distribution of beer sales for that week. The cumulative probability graph in Figure 21-7 provides the probability distribution when the sales forecast is 1,900 barrels. There, the horizonal axis has been found by multiplying the actual/forecast ratios by 1,900.

ADDITIONAL REMARKS 21-6

We have seen that probability values for decision making may sometimes be obtained from past history, but that past history is of limited use in business situations and may not exist at all for nonrepeatable circumstances. We have emphasized the direct assessment of a decision maker's judgment rather than traditional statistical techniques. But it should be noted that traditional techniques also rely heavily on judgmental inputs (usually of an indirect nature).

It is not necessary for a decision maker to obtain subjective probabilities personally. Such judgments can be delegated. For example, the chairman of

General Motors might rely on various officers within the corporation to determine some or all of the probabilities to be used in analyzing a decision. After all, this is an area in which expert opinion should be relied on whenever possible. Although exercising judgment to find subjective probabilities is similar to assessing attitudes toward decision outcomes (constructing and then using a utility curve), it is dangerous for any decision maker to delegate that role to others. Attitudes are highly personal and express unique tastes, whereas judgment can be shared. (The collective assessment of attitudes is prohibited by the axioms of utility theory. However, there is no reason why a committee cannot determine the subjective probabilities to be used.)

PROBLEMS

21-1 Discuss whether historical frequencies can be meaningful in estimating the probabilities for each of the following cases:
(a) The first-year salary levels of business-school graduates.
(b) The faces obtained by tossing an asymmetrical die.
(c) The deaths during the next year of people in various age, health, sex, and occupational categories.

21-2 Use your judgment to assess the probability that you will receive an A on your next examination. Imagine that your instructor will let you obtain your grade by lottery, so that 100 slips of paper (some labeled A; the rest, not A) will be put into a hat and mixed. You will draw one of these slips at random, and the letter obtained will be the grade you receive. How many A slips must there be to make you indifferent between letting your grade be determined by lottery or by earning it?

21-3 An automobile production manager believes that the time taken to install a new car bumper is normally distributed. He has established that it is a 50–50 proposition that this task will take more than 60 seconds and that it is "even money" that the required time for any particular car will be between 45 and 75 seconds.
(a) Determine the mean and the standard deviation of the subjective probability distribution.
(b) Find the probabilities that the installation for a particular car will take:
(1) between 50 and 70 seconds.
(2) less than 25 seconds.
(3) more than 1 minute.
(4) between 20 and 90 seconds.

21-4 The dean of The Dover School of Business is assessing the probability distribution for next term's grade point average (GPA) for the entire school. It is "even money" that the GPA will fall at or below 2.75. The dean assigns a 50–50 probability that the low side will be at or below 2.70 and that the high side will be at or above 2.80. If the GPA is lower than 2.70, it is a coin-tossing proposition that it will fall at or below 2.60; similarly, the odds are even that the GPA will fall at or above 2.95, given that it lies above 2.80. Find the subjective probability that the GPA will lie within the following limits:

(a) 2.60 and 2.95   (b) 2.70 and 2.80
(c) 2.60 and 2.75   (d) 2.75 and 2.95

21-5 Establish your own subjective probability distribution for the heights of adult males residing within 50 miles of your campus. Use the normal curve you obtain to establish the following probabilities that a randomly chosen man is
(a) less than 6′2″.   (b) taller than 5′6″.
(c) taller than your father.

21-6 Use the cumulative probability distribution function in Figure 21-8 to determine the following probabilities:
(a) $\Pr[D > 500]$ (b) $\Pr[D \le 150]$
(c) $\Pr[D \ge 300]$ (d) $\Pr[200 \le D \le 800]$

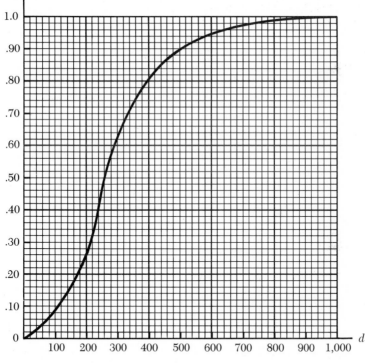

Cumulative
Probability
$\Pr[D \le d]$

Possible Demand Levels

FIGURE 21-8

21-7 Use the cumulative probability distribution graph in Figure 21-8 to determine the following fractiles:
(a) .10   (b) .50   (c) .125   (d) .75   (e) .37

21-8 The following fractiles apply to the subjective probability distribution for the demand for a new product:

Fractile	Quantity
.0625	10,000
.125	25,000
.25	35,000
.50	40,000
.75	45,000
.875	55,000
.9375	75,000

Establish the probabilities that demand will fall within the following limits:
(a) 10,000 to 40,000   (b) 35,000 to 75,000
(c) 25,000 to 55,000   (d) 25,000 to 45,000

21-9 A real estate investor has established the following judgmental results regarding the rate of return on a proposed project. No value less than -20% or greater than 40% is possible.

Rate of Return	50–50 Point
all	15%
below 15%	7
above 15%	20
below 7%	3
above 20%	24
below 3%	−4
above 24%	28

(a) Complete the following table for the investor:

Fractile	Rate of Return
0	
.0625	
.125	
.25	
.50	
.75	
.875	
.9375	
1.000	

(b) Plot the cumulative probability distribution for the investor's rate of return.
(c) From your graph, find the investor's subjective probability that the rate of return is between 20% and 40%.

21-10 Envision your income during the first full calendar year after graduation. Establish your own subjective probability distribution for the adjusted gross income figure that you will report to the IRS. (If applicable, include your spouse's earnings, interest, dividends, etc.) If your graph has an unusual shape, try to eliminate any inconsistencies or to identify the nonhomogeneous factors (pregnancy, unemployment, divorce, etc.) that might explain the shape. Remember, you are the expert about yourself.

21-11 Use the cumulative probability distribution for demand in Figure 21-8 to construct the probability distribution for demand, using five intervals in increments of 200. Select the midpoints of these intervals as representative values and determine the approximate expected demand.

21-12 The following approximation has been obtained for the subjective probability distribution for a product's demand:

Demand D	Probability
1,000	.08
2,000	.18
3,000	.36
4,000	.18
5,000	.10
6,000	.04
7,000	.03
8,000	.02
9,000	.01

(a) Determine the expected demand.
(b) Suppose that the payoff for each level of demand is determined by

$$\text{Payoff} = \begin{cases} -\$500 + .3D & \text{if } D \le 5,000 \\ \$1,000 & \text{if } D > 5,000 \end{cases}$$

Calculate the expected payoff.

21-13 A sports writer has forecast Rod Carew's seasonal batting average for a 10-year period. The following values apply:

Actual	Forecast	Actual	Forecast
.273	.250	.350	.278
.332	.315	.364	.340
.366	.320	.359	.355
.307	.365	.331	.360
.318	.330	.388	.373

(a) Compute the actual/forecast ratios. Plot the cumulative probability graph and then sketch a smoothed curve through the stairway.
(b) Suppose that the forecast batting average is .350 for the next baseball season. Read your graph to find the sports writer's subjective probability that Carew's batting average will be (1) $\le.300$; (2) $\le.360$; (3) $\le.375$.

22

Games and Interactive Decisions

ntil now, we have discussed decision-making situations in which choices are made by only one person. Such decision problems fall into two broad categories, depending on whether conditions are certain or uncertain. We have seen that when decisions are made under uncertainty, the ultimate outcome is determined jointly by the particular act that is chosen and by whatever uncertain event occurs. Uncertain events are generated randomly and could be called *nature's choices*. We could therefore view decision making under uncertainty as an *interactive* process with two participants—the decision maker and nature.

INTERACTIVE DECISION MAKING AND GAME THEORY 22-1

In this chapter, we will be concerned with *interactive decision making* involving more than one person. The outcomes of such decision problems are determined by whatever combination of actions results from the independent choices of several individual decision makers. Many important business decisions involve the interaction between two or more participants. Interaction often occurs in the pricing of products, where a firm's ultimate sales are determined not only by the price levels it selects but also by the prices its competitors set. The interaction between several decision makers is also necessary in operational applications. Television provides a good example. In recent years, TV networks have found that program success is largely dependent on what the competition presents in the same time slot; the outcomes of one network's programming decisions have therefore been increasingly influenced by the corresponding decisions made by other networks. Even financial planning involves interactive decision making. The success of a business tax strategy depends greatly on the position taken by the Internal Revenue Service regarding the expenses that may be disallowed.

When two or more persons collectively determine the outcomes, decision-making analysis takes on an added complexity. Good decision making requires not only the evaluation of personal alternatives but also the investigation of the opponent's or competitor's possible choices. A certain amount of second-guessing and role playing is required. Interactive decision making can be compared to a parlor game, such as chess, *Monopoly*, or bridge. To establish a winning strategy, successful players must be able to put themselves in their opponents' positions and try to anticipate their actions. The need to consider another person's goals and choices distinguishes interactive decision making from ordinary decisions under uncertainty, in which the only opponent is nature, who chooses randomly. It is obviously pointless to rationalize why nature chooses a particular event or how the occurrence of that event might be influenced by our actions. (We exclude decisions about how to influence the environment or weather.)

Within the past 40 years, an analytical framework for interactive decision making based on investigations of game situations has been developed. This effort was pioneered by John von Neumann and Oskar Morgenstern and culminated in 1947 with the publication of their book *Theory of Games and Economic Behavior*. As an area of academic study, *game theory* provides a series of mathematical models that can be quite useful in explaining interactive decision-making concepts. But as a practical tool, game theory is severely limited in scope. As we will see, the situations that may be analyzed by game theory must be extremely simple. For instance, most parlor games, such as chess, have not yet been thoroughly analyzed mathematically and may never be; even computerized systems cannot beat a competent human in chess, much less Bobby Fischer. And chess is orders of magnitude less complex than many interactive decisions encountered in business. Although game-theory principles can be applied directly to make optimal decisions in certain special situations, the primary value of game theory is the conceptual framework it provides that permits us to explain interactive decision making.

The simplest game to analyze involves two players, each of whom must make exactly one choice from his or her own set of alternatives. The game's outcome depends only on the particular pair of acts selected. Each player receives a numerical payoff, depending on the outcome that the players determine collectively.

An Example from the Battle of the Bismarck Sea

A vivid illustration of such a game situation may be taken from the Battle of the Bismarck Sea during World War II.

> In the critical stages of the struggle for New Guinea, intelligence reports indicated that the Japanese would move a troop and supply convoy from the port of Rabaul at the eastern tip of New Britain to Lae, which lies just west of New Britain on New Guinea. It could travel either north of New Britain, where poor visibility was almost certain, or south of the island, where the weather would be clear; in either case, the trip would take three days. General Kenney had the choice of concentrating the bulk of his reconnaissance aircraft on one route or the other. Once sighted, the convoy could be bombed until its arrival at Lae. In days of bombing time, Kenney's staff estimated the following outcomes for the various choices:*

TABLE 22-1

KENNEY'S STRATEGIES	JAPANESE STRATEGIES	
	Northern Route	Southern Route
Northern Route	2	2
Southern Route	1	3

Which routes should the two opponents have chosen? By going north, the Japanese commander would be no worse off than if he took the southern route; the northern route also provided the best of the worst possible exposures to bombing. General Kenney's choice was also clear; by concentrating his forces in the north, he could guarantee having two full bombing days. As it turned out, both commanders selected the northern alternative. As we shall see, their choices were consistent with the principles of game theory.

TWO-PERSON ZERO-SUM GAMES 22-2

Another detailed example will help to clarify the principles of game theory. Consider the case of Ms. Gray and Mr. Flannel—two bored rail commuters who while-away the mind-numbing hours by playing several games

---

* This example was developed by O.G. Haywood, Jr., and is quoted from R. Duncan Luce and Howard Raiffa, *Games and Decisions* (New York: John Wiley & Sons, 1958) pp. 64–65.

TABLE 22-2

Gray's Color-Bland Payoff Table (amounts in cents)

		FLANNEL'S ACTS		
		Red	White	Blue
GRAY'S ACTS	Red	−3	2	5
	White	−2	1	6
	Blue	−3	−3	−7

of Color-Bland daily. To play this game each player writes a color on a slip of paper. Patriotically, each participant may choose red, white, or blue. Depending on the colors chosen, varying numbers of pennies are exchanged. The payoff amounts used by Gray and Flannel are determined before playing each game of Color-Bland by a formula based on how many cars of the respective colors are seen by each person between stations (Gray looks out the left side; Flannel, the right). Between Dullstone and Blahsburg, Table 22-2 is constructed. The amounts shown are what Gray receives from Flannel (a negative figure represents a payment to Flannel).

Color-Bland is the simplest type of game we could encounter. One player's gain is matched by a corresponding loss to the opponent. Flannel's payoff table would contain the same amounts in Gray's payoff table with the signs reversed. For instance, if both players select red, Gray's payoff is −3 and Flannel's is +3, because Gray pays Flannel 3 cents; if both players choose white, Flannel pays Gray 1 cent, so that Gray's payoff is +1 and Flannel's is −1. Since the payoffs for either player provide all the essential information, only one player's payoff table is required to evaluate the decisions. By convention, the payoff table for the player listed at the left is constructed. Regardless of the outcome, Flannel's payoff will always be the negative of Gray's, so that the respective payoffs of the two players sum to zero. For this reason, Color-Bland is referred to as a *two-person zero-sum game.*

Analyzing the Decision: The Minimax Principle

Now we will consider the respective acts that Gray and Flannel should choose. Our clue as to how these choices should be made may be taken from the Battle of the Bismarck Sea example, in which each opposing commander selected the act for which the worst outcome was best. Such a decision-making criterion is referred to as the *minimax principle.* In two-person zero-sum games, the minimax principle always leads to the most preferred choices for both players.

Returning to the Color-Bland game, consider Flannel's choices. His losses or payments to Gray are represented in Table 22-3 by the quantities in the respective *column* for each of Flannel's color-choice acts. We will assume that

TABLE 22-3
Gray's Color-Bland Payoff Table Showing Minimax Analysis

FLANNEL'S ACTS

		Red	White	Blue	Row minimum
GRAY'S ACTS	Red	$\boxed{-3}$	②	5	−3
	White	$\boxed{-2}$	1	⑥	−2 ← Maximin payoff
	Blue	−3	−3	$\boxed{-7}$	−7

Column maximum: −2 (Minimax loss), 2, 6

Flannel wants to minimize his long-run losses from playing the game and keep his payments to Gray as small as possible. Flannel should therefore focus on the *circled* numbers in Table 22-3. These are the *column maximums* that represent the greatest payments Flannel might have to make to Gray. The smallest of these losses is −2, which occurs when Flannel chooses red and Gray picks white. Regardless of what color Gray selects, Flannel can do no worse than lose −2 cents (receive 2 cents) by choosing red. Flannel's choice of red is his *minimax loss act*, since this column amount is the minimum of the maximum possible payments that might be made to his opponent.

The possible payoffs to Gray for each of her color-choice acts are provided in the corresponding *rows* of the payoff table. We will assume that Gray views the game similarly and wishes to maximize her receipts from Flannel. Since the payoffs given in Table 22-3 are what Gray receives, she is concerned with the *boxed* quantities, which represent the *row minimums*. Gray can do no worse than receive one of these values, and the best of them occurs when she chooses white; this choice provides a payoff of −2 when Flannel chooses red. We refer to Gray's choice of white as her *maximin payoff act*, because this row contains the maximum of Gray's minimum possible payoffs from her opponent.

If the payoffs had originally been given from Flannel's point of view, all of the signs in Table 22-3 would be reversed and the numbers would represent payments to Flannel. A choice of white by Gray would then be the act resulting in the smallest of her greatest possible payments to Flannel, so that Gray's choice of white would also be her minimax loss act. Because one player's loss is always another player's gain, a feature of zero-sum games is that *one player's minimax loss act must be identical to the same player's maximin payoff act.* Thus, Flannel's choice of red is the same act that maximizes his own minimum potential gains.

For this particular Color-Bland game, Gray should choose white and Flannel should select red. Both participants would thereby be acting in accordance with the minimax principle of minimizing their maximum losses to the other player. It is easy to see why no other criterion should be used for this game.

By choosing his minimax loss act (red), Flannel guarantees himself a gain of at least 2 cents (a loss of -2 cents), regardless of the color that Gray picks. There is no advantage in Flannel choosing another color such as blue, which has a potentially larger gain of 7 cents (a loss of -7 cents) when Gray also chooses blue. That amount cannot be guaranteed, since Gray could reverse the take by picking red or white. Similarly, Gray can guarantee herself a payoff of at least -2 cents by choosing her maximin payoff act (white). Flannel can make her outcome worse if she chooses any other color. In following the minimax principle, neither player can sabotage the plans of the opponent without placing himself or herself in a worse position unnecessarily.

Saddle Points and the Value of the Game

Notice that in Table 22-3 the quantity -2 in the white row and red column is both boxed and circled. It is both the minimum of the column maximums and the maximum of the row minimums. We refer to this value as a *saddle point*, since it is the minimum value in its row and the maximum quantity in its column. Games with saddle points exhibit special features.

Even if the game is played repeatedly, no participant can advantageously deviate from the minimax principle for very long. Each player will always choose the same act—the one that provides the minimax loss to the other player and, at the same time, the maximin payoff to himself or herself. The two acts so obtained are referred to as the *equilibrium act-pair*. As long as either player continues to choose one of these acts, it is of no advantage to the other player to choose any other act.

When a saddle point is present, it is easy to find the *value of the game*. This quantity is the payoff amount in the saddle-point position. For the preceding Color-Bland game,

$$\text{Value of the game} = -2 \text{ cents} \quad \text{(to Gray)}$$

The value of the game is always expressed from the point of view of the participant whose receipts appear in the payoff table (and whose acts are listed on the left). In this example, the value to Gray is -2 cents, since that would be her payoff when both Gray and Flannel observe the minimax criterion.

Other Features of Two-Person Zero-Sum Games

The game-theory examples we have considered thus far have involved competitive situations in which each player has the same kind and number of acts to choose from. This may not always be the case, however. One player

TABLE 22-4

A Payoff Table for a Game Involving More Choices for One Player

PLAYER B'S ACTS

		B_1	B_2	B_3	B_4	B_5
	A_1	1	2	4	5	0
PLAYER A'S ACTS	A_2	3	3	4	5	4
	A_3	4	③	5	5	6

can have more acts than the other, as the payoff table in Table 22-4 indicates. There, player A has only three possible choices, and player B has five. Opponents may also have different types of choices. In Color-Bland, one player might pick green, yellow, or orange, and the other might select red, white, or blue. In some competitive situations, the opponents' alternatives are not remotely similar. For example, a firm in a regulated industry may be considering alternative *price levels* for a particular product at the same time government officials are determining *allowable rates of return* on invested capital. The company's future financial position obviously depends on its pricing choice and the rate of return selected by the government. Although it would be hard to put such a situation into a game framework, analogous disparities in types of player choices exist in simple games, too.

The game in Table 22-4 exhibits a saddle point, when player A chooses act A_3 and player B selects act B_2. This game has another saddle point, which is left as an exercise for the reader to find. When a game has several saddle points, all of the corresponding payoff quantities must be identical and each payoff must equal the value of the game.

More perplexing are games *without a saddle point*. We will now consider how such a game should be played.

MIXED STRATEGIES IN GAMES WITHOUT A SADDLE POINT 22-3

Suppose that the bored commuters continue to play from Blahsburg to Gotham City and that en route their car counts result in the new game of Color-Bland summarized in Table 22-5. This game does not have a saddle point, since no payoff is both largest in its column and smallest in its row. Gray's maximin payoff act is to choose red, and Flannel's minimax loss act is also to select red.

Should each player apply the minimax criterion? First consider Gray, who thinks that Flannel will pick red and may choose to play white instead,

TABLE 22-5
Gray's New Payoff Table

FLANNEL'S ACTS

		Red	White	Blue	Row minimum
	Red	$\boxed{-2}$	$\textcircled{4}$	5	$-2 \leftarrow$ Maximin payoff
GRAY'S ACTS	White	$\textcircled{0}$	$\boxed{-3}$	$\textcircled{6}$	-3
	Blue	-5	1	$\boxed{-6}$	-6
Column maximum		0	4	6	

↑
Minimax
loss

thereby achieving the better payoff of zero for herself. Anticipating Gray's plan, Flannel will switch to white to give Gray a worse payoff. But Gray knows what Flannel is guessing, and can choose red to his white, dramatically improving her outcome. However, Flannel (no dummy) knows that Gray knows what he should be guessing, and he can choose red to her red. Knowing all of this, Gray could pick white instead of red, in which case the second-guessing will begin all over again.

There is no single act that one player can choose that will guarantee either player the best of the worst outcomes. Since this game does not have a saddle point, there is no equilibrium act-pair.

The Mixed Strategy

The goal of game theory is to remove all guesswork on the part of the players by indicating an optimal course of action for each player. When there is a saddle point, a player can choose an act based on the predictability of his or her opponent. In games without saddle points, paradoxically, the guesswork can be eliminated only by *removing* all elements of predictability. And the only way for a player to confuse an opponent is to not know himself what act he will choose. This can be accomplished if each player selects his or her act randomly. Even if such a game is played the same way repeatedly, the random selection of acts will provide no pattern for prediction and there will be no way for either player to take undue advantage of the other.

Thus, in the latest version of Color-Bland, Gray and Flannel each roll a six-sided die to select their colors. For instance, Gray chooses red if the die toss results in a 1 or a 2, white if she rolls a 3 or a 4, and blue if she rolls a 5 or a 6.

Since each die has six equally likely faces, each potential color act will have a probability of 1/3, so that the following decision rule applies for Gray's mixed strategy:

Gray Chooses Act	With Probability
Red	$P_R = 1/3$
White	$P_W = 1/3$
Blue	$P_B = 1/3$

Such a rule is referred to as a *mixed strategy*, because any one of several acts may be chosen.

In games with a saddle point, each player will choose only one act. When a single act is selected, it is sometimes referred to as a *pure strategy*. This is a special case of mixed strategy in which the selected act has a probability of 1 and all other acts have a probability of zero.

Similarly, Flannel can apply his decision rule so that he picks red if his die toss results in a 1, white if a 2, 3, 4, or 5 is rolled, and blue if a 6 is rolled. Flannel's mixed strategy would then be

Flannel Chooses Act	With Probability
Red	$Q_R = 1/6$
White	$Q_W = 4/6$
Blue	$Q_B = 1/6$

Notice that Flannel's probabilities differ from Gray's probabilities. By convention, we will use subscripted Ps to denote the probabilities for the player whose payoffs appear in the payoff table (and whose acts are listed on the left) and subscripted Qs to represent the probabilities for the other player. The symbols are necessary because each player must select an optimal mixed strategy and the P and Q values must therefore be treated as variables.

Since uncertainty is now present, each player must evaluate his or her strategy in terms of expected payoff or expected loss. The calculations for obtaining Gray's expected payoff appear in Table 22-6.

First, the original amounts in each row of the payoff table are multiplied by the probability that Gray will choose the act in that row. The products are then summed one column at a time, so that the resulting subtotals provide Gray's expected payoffs *given* Flannel's color choice. Since Flannel's act are also chosen randomly, the final step is to multiply each subtotal by Flannel's corresponding probability Q for that color-choice act and then to sum the resulting products. Under the initial strategies, Gray's expected payoff is 1/3

TABLE 22-6

Gray's Expected Payoff Calculations When
Both Players Use Initial Mixed Strategies

Gray's Acts	Gray's Probabilities	$P \times$ Payoff Flannel's Acts		
		Red	White	Blue
Red	$P_R = 1/3$	$-2/3$	$4/3$	$5/3$
White	$P_W = 1/3$	0	$-3/3$	$6/3$
Blue	$P_B = 1/3$	$-5/3$	$1/3$	$-6/3$
Subtotals		$-7/3$	$2/3$	$5/3$
Flannel's Probabilities		$Q_R = 1/6$	$Q_W = 4/6$	$Q_B = 1/6$
$Q \times$ Subtotal		$-7/18$	$8/18$	$5/18$
		Expected payoff $= -7/18 + 8/18 + 5/18$		
		$= 6/18 = 1/3$		

cent. This means that after repeatedly playing this version of Color-Bland, Gray would expect to achieve an average payoff of 1/3 cent.

But this amount is deceptive, because it reflects Gray's expected winnings if and only if Flannel plays this particular mixed strategy. However, Flannel can dramatically worsen Gray's situation by simply changing his strategy. For instance, if Flannel makes a color-choice of red, Gray's expected payoff becomes $-7/3$ cents (a worse payoff by nearly 3 cents). As we have seen in earlier games, a player should assume the worst from an opponent. Gray might be able to improve her situation by changing strategies. What is her best mixed strategy? We will suppose that *Gray's goal is to maximize her expected payoff, regardless of the strategy Flannel chooses*. The **minimax theorem,** proved by von Neumann, tells us that it is possible for Gray to achieve this goal. An identical conclusion applies to Flannel as well, who may minimize his maximum expected loss (payment) to Gray through the judicious selection of his own strategy—again, regardless of how Gray plays the game.

Before we see how the players can determine their optimal strategies, we will introduce a shortcut procedure that permits us to simplify the required mathematics considerably.

The Elimination of Inadmissible Acts

In Chapter 5, we saw how some acts in a decision problem can be eliminated at the outset before any further analysis is required. This simplifies the decision structure because it permits a smaller number of acts to be considered.

TABLE 22-7
Gray's Payoff Table with the Inadmissible Acts Eliminated

FLANNEL'S ACTS

GRAY'S ACTS		Red	White	Blue	
	Red	−2	4	5	
	White	0	−3	6	
	Blue	−5	1	−6	Inadmissible

Inadmissible

Acts that are eliminated at the outset of a decision problem are called *inadmissible acts*, because they will never be chosen. We can extend this concept to games. *If a player has an act that is inferior to another act, regardless of what choice the opponent makes, then that act is inadmissible.*

Consider the latest Color-Bland game. For convenience, the payoffs are repeated in Table 22-7. It is easy to see that Gray would never choose blue, since that act provides smaller payoffs than red does for each of Flannel's color choices. Gray's red act *dominates* her blue act, making blue inadmissible. Gray would never choose blue under any circumstances, and its row can be crossed out of the payoff table. Ignoring Gray's blue row, we can see that Flannel's blue color-choice act provides greater payoffs to Gray than a choice of either red or white does, no matter what action Gray takes. Flannel's red and white both dominate his blue, which is therefore inadmissible. Flannel's blue column can also be crossed out of the payoff table. The remaining rows and columns are all admissible, so that the reduced payoff table must be analyzed further.

Notice that the blue column does not become inadmissible until the blue row is eliminated, because the −6 in the blue–blue position is smaller than either the blue–white payoff of 1 or the blue–red payoff of −5, making blue a better choice for Flannel than red or white if Gray actually makes a blunder and picks blue. Thus, we see that whenever a row (or column) is crossed out, all columns (or rows) remaining in the payoff table must be reevaluated.

In games with saddle points, the successive elimination of inadmissible acts eventually enables us to cross out all rows and columns except those representing equilibrium act-pairs. In some games, it is possible for an entry to be both the minimum value in its row *and* the maximum value in its column and still lie in the row or column of an inadmissible act. Although such an entry is technically a saddle point, it cannot correspond to an equilibrium act-pair. In a game with several saddle points, there may be ties (but not necessarily so) for equilibrium act-pairs. Before concluding that ties exist, *be sure to check all saddle points to see if any of them lie in inadmissible rows or columns.*

22-4 OPTIMAL MIXED STRATEGIES FOR ZERO-SUM GAMES

We are now left with the 2×2 Color-Bland game in Table 22-8, where each player can choose from only two acts. We must now find the act probabilities for each player. To simplify this procedure, we observe that all P and all Q values must sum to 1 and that P_B and Q_B are now zero. It therefore follows that

$$P_W = 1 - P_R$$
$$Q_W = 1 - Q_R$$

so that only two quantities, P_R and Q_R, are unknown.

We begin by evaluating Gray's possible strategies. Her expected payoff depends on Flannel's color choices and may be calculated for any value of P_R using the payoffs in the applicable column of the payoff table. Gray's expected payoffs may be expressed as

$$-2P_R + 0(1 - P_R) = -2P_R \qquad \text{(if Flannel picks red)}$$
$$4P_R - 3(1 - P_R) = -3 + 7P_R \qquad \text{(if Flannel picks white)}$$

The Graphical Solution

The procedure and rationale for finding the respective optimal mixed strategies for Gray and Flannel is easy to explain graphically. Figure 22-1 shows how Gray's expected payoffs vary for each possible level of P_R, which can range from zero to 1.

First, we will consider the case in which Flannel picks red, so that only the first column of the payoff table applies. If Gray applies $P_R = 0$, she will be certain to choose white and her expected payoff of 0 will be obtained from the

TABLE 22-8
Gray's Color-Bland Payoffs Reduced to a 2 × 2 Game

			FLANNEL'S ACTS	
			Q_R	$1 - Q_R$
			Red	White
GRAY'S	P_R	Red	-2	4
ACTS	$1 - P_R$	White	0	-3

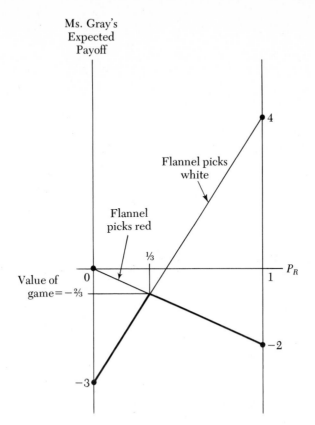

FIGURE 22-1
A graphical representation of Gray's optimal mixed strategy.

bottom cell in the red column of Table 22-8; this provides the point on the origin in the graph. At the other extreme, Gray might apply $P_R = 1$, in which case her expected payoff will be -2, which appears in the top cell in the red column of her payoff table; this corresponds to a second point at the bottom of the graph on the right side. The straight line connecting these two points provides Gray's expected payoffs for all levels of P_R between zero and 1, assuming that Flannel chooses red.

If Flannel chooses white instead, then the expected payoffs of -3 when $P_R = 0$ and 4 when $P_R = 1$ appear in the white column of Gray's payoff table. The line connecting the two corresponding points on the graph provides Gray's expected payoffs for all levels of P_R between zero and 1.

What value of P_R should Gray select? Remember that she wants to guarantee herself the largest expected payoff, regardless of what action her opponent takes. We must therefore consider how Flannel would behave if he knew Gray's P_R value. Notice that the two expected payoff lines in Figure 22-1 cross at $P_R = 1/3$. Suppose that Gray picks a smaller red probability, such as 1/4. Knowing this, Flannel will choose white, because that act will provide Gray with the lower expected payoff line. On the other hand, if Gray applies a P_R value greater than 1/3, such as 2/3, then Flannel will select red, which corresponds to the lower expected payoff line in this case. Flannel can effectively limit Gray's expected payoffs to those points on the heavy line segments meeting at $P_R = 1/3$. Gray receives her greatest expected payoff where these lines cross. Applying $P_R = 1/3$, Gray will receive the same expected payoff, regardless of the act Flannel chooses:

$$-2P_R = -2(1/3) = -2/3 \quad \text{(if Flannel picks red)}$$

$$-3 + 7P_R = -3 + 7(1/3) = -2/3 \quad \text{(if Flannel picks white)}$$

Unfortunately for Gray, this particular Color-Bland game is not in her favor. But by employing a mixed strategy with $P_R = 1/3$ and $P_W = 1 - P_R = 2/3$, she can make the best of a bad situation. This is Gray's optimal mixed strategy.

We must still determine Flannel's optimal mixed strategy. This is tantamount to finding the best level of Q_R. Using the applicable rows in the payoff table, we can express Flannel's expected payoffs in terms of this unknown quantity as

$$-2Q_R + 4(1 - Q_R) = 4 - 6Q_R \quad \text{(if Gray picks red)}$$

$$0Q_R - 3(1 - Q_R) = -3 + 3Q_R \quad \text{(if Gray picks white)}$$

Figure 22-2 presents the corresponding graph, in which separate lines are plotted (as before) for each of Gray's possible color choices. Flannel wants to minimize Gray's expected payoff (his expected loss). By knowing Flannel's level of Q_R, Gray can effectively limit the game's outcome to the points on the heavy line segments. The minimum expected payoff that Flannel can obtain occurs when $Q_R = 7/9$, where the two lines cross.

Flannel's optimal mixed strategy is to apply $Q_R = 7/9$ and $Q_W = 1 - Q_R = 2/9$, which leads to the same expected payoff regardless of Gray's choice:

$$4 - 6(7/9) = -2/3 \quad \text{(if Gray picks red)}$$

$$-3 + 3(7/9) = -2/3 \quad \text{(if Gray picks white)}$$

Notice that by following this strategy, Flannel is guaranteed a minimum expected payoff that is equal to Gray's maximum expected payoff.

For any zero-sum game involving mixed strategies, the value of the game is the maximum expected payoff than can be guaranteed, and this amount is also the minimum expected loss that can be assured. For the present Color-Bland game

$$\text{Value of the game} = -2/3 \text{ cents}$$

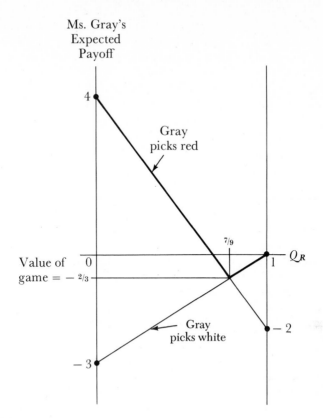

FIGURE 22-2
A graphical representation of Flannel's optimal mixed strategy.

The Algebraic Solution

The graphical analysis provides the key for finding a player's mixed strategy in a 2×2 game. It always corresponds to the point at which the two payoff lines cross—and that happens to be the point where the expected payoff is identical for both opponents' acts. We may solve the game algebraically by setting the two expected value equations equal to each other and solving for the unknown probability.

For Gray, the expected payoffs are $-2P_R$ (if Flannel picks red) and $-3 + 7P_R$ (if Flannel picks white). Thus, the optimal level of P_R occurs when

$$-2P_R = -3 + 7P_R$$

$$-9P_R = -3$$

and

$$P_R = 3/9 = 1/3$$

As before, $P_W = 1 - P_R = 2/3$, and the value of the game is $-2/3$.

For Flannel, the expected payoffs are $4 - 6Q_R$ (if Gray picks red) and $-3 + 3Q_R$ (if Gray picks white), so that Q_R must satisfy

$$4 - 6Q_R = -3 + 3Q_R$$
$$-9Q_R = -7$$

and thus

$$Q_R = 7/9$$

and $Q_W = 1 - Q_R = 2/9$.

Solving 3 × 2 and Larger Games: Salary Negotiations

The procedures just discussed can be applied to games in which one of the players has more than two acts from which to choose. An algebraic solution to such a game is more complex than the solution to the 2×2 game. However, we can easily extend the graphical method to find the optimal mixed strategy for each player as long as one of the players selects only two acts.

As a change of pace, we will consider an illustration of a conflict in which one party's gain is the other party's loss. Union and management bargaining over a labor contract, where each side can adopt a variety of stances and ploys, provides a good example of such a conflict. We will consider the case of a star baseball player who is seeking a salary increase from the owner of the Gotham City Robins. He is considering one of the three negotiating approaches shown in Table 22-9 which also indicates the assumed percentage salary increases.

TABLE 22-9
Baseball Star's Negotiation for a Percentage Salary Increase

			OWNER'S ACTS	
			Q_1	$Q_2 = 1 - Q_1$
			O_1 Benevolent	O_2 Stingy
	P_1	S_1 Go fishing	30	10
BASEBALL STAR'S ACTS	P_2	S_2 Firm stand	25	15
	P_3	S_3 Hat in hand	10	25

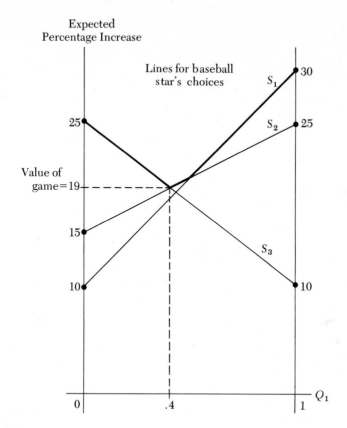

FIGURE 22-3
A graphical representation of the baseball team owner's optimal mixed strategy.

These payoffs are partly determined by the stance chosen by the owner.

Investigation of the payoff table does not show a saddle point, so mixed strategies must be determined. Since there are no inadmissible acts, we must find three probabilities, P_1, P_2, and P_3 for the baseball star's acts and two probabilities, Q_1 and Q_2, for the owner's choices.

First, we consider the owner's problem. She has only two acts and only one variable Q_1, since the probability for her second act is $Q_2 = 1 - Q_1$. The owner wants to pick a level of Q_1 that will keep the star's expected percentage increase as small as possible. The graph in Figure 22-3 shows the expected payoff lines for each of the ballplayer's choices; the heavy segments indicate the largest levels he can achieve for various levels of Q_1. The lowest point on these line segments occurs at the intersection of the S_2 and S_3 lines, which corresponds to the Q_1 level the owner should use.

To find Q_1, first we determine the expected payoff expressions, assuming that one of these acts will be chosen by the ballplayer. Using only the payoffs in the S_2 and S_3 rows of Table 22-9, we find that the following expressions apply:

$$25Q_1 + 15(1 - Q_1) = 15 + 10Q_1 \quad \text{(if ballplayer picks } S_2)$$
$$10Q_1 + 25(1 - Q_1) = 25 - 15Q_1 \quad \text{(if ballplayer picks } S_3)$$

Since these expressions represent the equations for the S_2 and S_3 lines in the graph, the Q_1 value where the lines intersect is found by setting the equations equal to each other and solving for the unknown value:

$$15 + 10Q_1 = 25 - 15Q_1$$
$$25Q_1 = 10$$
$$Q_1 = 10/25 = .4$$

The value of the game can then be found by substituting $Q_1 = .4$ into either expected payoff expression. Choosing the expression for S_2

$$\text{Value of the game} = 15 + 10(.4) = 19\%$$

Thus, the owner of the Robins can guarantee a minimum expected salary increase of 19% to her star by following a mixed strategy of assigning a probability of $Q_1 = .4$ to being benevolent (O_1) and a probability of $Q_2 = 1 - Q_1 = .6$ to being stingy (O_2).

But we have yet to establish the ballplayer's mixed strategy. Figure 22-3 shows that he would never choose S_1, since the owner could then guarantee a lower expected payoff when using $Q_1 = .4$. Thus, the player must consider a mixed strategy between S_2 and S_3 only and set $P_1 = 0$. This means that $P_2 + P_3 = 1$, so that $P_3 = 1 - P_2$. Using the S_2 and S_3 rows of the payoff table, we can determine the ballplayer's expected payoffs for each the owner's possible acts:

$$25P_2 + 10P_3 = 25P_2 + 10(1 - P_2)$$
$$= 10 + 15P_2 \quad \text{(if owner picks } O_1)$$

and

$$15P_2 + 25P_3 = 15P_2 + 25(1 - P_2)$$
$$= 25 - 10P_2 \quad \text{(if owner picks } O_2)$$

Setting these expressions equal to each other, we can solve for the unknown P_2:

$$10 + 15P_2 = 25 - 10P_2$$

$$25P_2 = 15$$

$$P_2 = 15/25 = .6$$

Thus, the ballplayer's optimal mixed strategy is not to go fishing by choosing S_1 ($P_1 = 0$), to take a firm stand (S_2) with a probability of $P_2 = .6$, and to plead with "hat in hand" (S_3) with a probability of $P_3 = 1 - P_2 = .4$. To verify this, we compute his expected payoff using either of the above expressions to see if his expected percentage increase is identical to the minimum expected value found earlier for the owner's strategy. Plugging $P_2 = .6$ into the first expression gives us

$$10 + 15(.6) = 19\%$$

which is identical to the value of the game established earlier.

When both players of a game have a choice of more than two acts, a more involved procedure based on linear programming principles is required to find the mixed strategies. This procedure will be described later in the chapter.

NON-ZERO-SUM AND OTHER GAMES   22-5

The two-person zero-sum game is easiest to analyze. A wide variety of other games have been studied, but unlike two-person zero-sum games, these more complex situations often have no pat solutions that are acceptable to all players.

Two-Person Non-Zero-Sum Games

A two-person *non-zero-sum game* occurs when one player's gain does not necessarily equal the other player's loss. This may be the case in games similar to those described earlier in this chapter when the particular payoff measure does not reflect the true worth of an outcome. In playing Color-Bland for example, Gray may derive much greater satisfaction from beating Flannel than the payoffs indicate, and losing a little bit may be just as undesirable to Gray as losing a lot. Flannel may have analogous feelings as well. A player's ego might be the dominant factor in evaluating a simple parlor game. Rather than points or monetary values, personal utility values would therefore serve as a more accurate way of ranking outcomes in such cases.

The essential feature of non-zero-sum games is not the way in which the true payoff values are determined but the requirement that the respective payoffs achieved by the two players do not sum to zero for at least one act-pair. This feature can severely complicate the analysis.

The Prisoner's Dilemma

A classical example of a non-zero-sum game is provided by the following "prisoner's dilemma."

> Two suspects are taken into custody and separated. The district attorney is certain that they are guilty of a specific crime, but he does not have adequate evidence to convict them at a trial. He points out to each prisoner that each has two alternatives: to confess to the crime the police are sure they have done, or not to confess. If they both do not confess, then the district attorney states he will book them on some very minor, trumped-up charge, such as petty larceny and illegal possession of a weapon, and they will both receive minor punishments. If they confess, they will be prosecuted, but he will recommend less than the most severe sentence. But if one confesses and the other does not, then the confessor will receive lenient treatment for turning state's evidence, whereas the latter will get "the book" slapped at him.*

The outcomes in Table 22-10 might apply to this example. Regardless of the numerical utility payoff values assigned to the various outcomes, the essential characteristic is that when one suspect confesses and the other does not, materially different payoffs result. Consider just the outcomes for prisoner A:

	B Does Not Confess	B Confesses
A Does Not Confess	1 year	10 years
A Confesses	3 months	8 years

It is easy to see that confessing is superior to not confessing for A, regardless of what B does. Not confessing is therefore an inadmissible act for A, and it would not be rational to choose it. A similar conclusion applies to prisoner B.

Thus, if both prisoners behave rationally, both of them will confess and receive eight-year sentences as their reward. The paradox here is that *if both prisoners behave irrationally instead, the positions of both prisoners will be significantly improved.* If neither prisoner confesses, then each will receive a light sentence of one year apiece.

The joint confessions can be regarded as an equilibrium act-pair, just as in a zero-sum game. As long as the prisoners are not allowed to cooperate, confessing is the minimax loss act for both suspects. If they are allowed to

* R. Duncan Luce and Howard Raiffa, *Games and Decisions* (New York: John Wiley & Sons, 1958) p. 95.

TABLE 22-10
Possible Outcomes for the Prisoner's Dilemma

		PRISONER B'S ACTS	
		Not Confess	Confess
PRISONER A'S ACTS	Not Confess	1 year each	10 years for A and 3 months for B
	Confess	3 months for A and 10 years for B	8 years each

cooperate and enter a binding agreement, then it is clearly in the best interests for both prisoners not to confess and for each to receive a one-year sentence.

Similar interactive decision-making situations are sometimes encountered in business. For instance, two small firms, each dominant in a separate region, might consider whether or not a market in each other's territory. As long as neither firm invades the other's region, both firms will continue to earn satisfactory profits. But if one firm begins to invade the other's territory when the second firm has not planned to expand also, then the second firm could be eliminated. If both firms try to expand simultaneously, each firm may survive but achieve a lower profit level than before. If the companies are not allowed to cooperate, the only rational outcome is for both firms to engage in damaging expansion—just like the joint confessions in the prisoner's dilemma. Clearly, if they are allowed to cooperate, both firms will choose to maintain the status quo.

Unlike the simpler zero-sum games in which it is never advantageous for a player to disclose his or her planned action, different solutions may arise in non-zero-sum games when disclosure and cooperation is allowed than when the game is strictly competitive. A variety of special situations arise in the study of non-zero-sum games. The prisoner's dilemma provides us with just one example. These other forms have been analyzed with varying degrees of success. In general, the non-zero-sum game is much more difficult to solve, and even when solutions are obtained, they are often not completely satisfactory.

Games with Several Players

In this chapter, we have considered games that involve only two persons. When three or more parties participate in a game, the situation may be too complex to be solved satisfactorily. The variety added by a third or a fourth person is staggering. Two or more players may gang up on the others, making collusions and partnerships of varying kinds and degrees possible. Multiplayer games are even less amenable to solution than the two-person non-zero-sum game.

22-6 ADDITIONAL REMARKS

Game theory, as we have seen, serves primarily as a model for explaining interactive decision making. In simpler situations, it may even be used to determine the best course of action. Its applicability to real-world problems is therefore quite limited. Even when it can be applied, the practicality of its results are criticized. It is hard to imagine a board chairman or an army general letting the final decision to a problem be determined by a role of the dice. Nor would we expect two bored commuters to solve a linear program to determine the probabilities to three decimal places for choosing a color to play—just to win a few pennies.

But successful and meaningful results can sometimes be achieved by exercising game-theory principles. Interactive decision making is highly complex, and game theory may provide good approximations for analyzing an otherwise intractable problem. For instance, the prisoner's dilemma can be used as a model to explain oligopolistic behavior or a farmer's crop-planting decision. Another approximation is provided by the mixed strategy. Although game theory presumes that one player knows the other player's acts and outcomes precisely, this is rarely true in the real world. Paradoxically, this fact makes the concept of mixed strategies more relevant. We do not actually have to toss a pair of dice to give an action the element of unpredictability that is required in a formal mixed strategy.

Game analysis serves as a microcosm for all quantitative methods, which share its strengths and imperfections to varying degrees. Almost all mathematical models developed to solve practical problems are imperfect approximations to reality, but even the simplest models may help to organize problem evaluation and to cull out myriads of poor solutions. At the very least, game theory provides us with a point of departure from which to investigate the most difficult type of decision making, and, as such, it is a very valuable management-science tool.

APPENDIX 22-1: GAMES AND LINEAR PROGRAMMING*

When a two-person zero-sum game involves more than two admissible acts for each player, linear programming can be used to establish the opposing players' strategies. As an illustration, consider the payoff table in Table 22-11

* Optional section.

TABLE 22-11

Gray's Payoff Table for the Final Color-Bland Game

			FLANNEL'S ACTS		
			Q_R	Q_W	Q_B
			Red	White	Blue
GRAY'S ACTS	P_R	Red	5	-2	4
	P_W	White	2	3	-1
	P_B	Blue	1	2	3

for the final version of Color-Bland that our bored commuters might play between Parsimony and Penumbra stations. Each player must choose the optimal levels of probabilities that apply to the various acts.

First, we will consider Gray's problem. She wants to choose P_R, P_W, and P_B so that she receives as large an expected payoff as possible, no matter what Flannel does. We have seen that the resulting monetary amount is the value of the game, which we will denote by V. Gray's objective is to

$$\text{Maximize } V = \text{Expected payoff} \quad \text{(objective)}$$

Gray's expected payoff under each of Flannel's acts must be at least as large as V. For instance, if Flannel chooses red, then using the values in the red column of the payoff table, Gray's expected payoff can be expressed

$$5P_R + 2P_W + 1P_B$$

Setting this expression $\geq V$ provides the constraint

$$5P_R + 2P_W + 1P_B \geq V \quad \text{(if Flannel picks red)}$$

Because V is also a variable, this expression can be written

$$5P_R + 2P_W + 1P_B - V \geq 0 \quad \text{(red constraint)}$$

Of course, the P values must be non-negative and must sum to 1. (And the sign of V is unrestricted. In Chapter 12, we described a procedure for handling such a variable, but it is unnecessary to employ here, since V turns out to be positive anyway.)

TABLE 22-12
The Final Simplex Tableau for the Color-Bland Game

UNIT PROFIT		0	0	0	1	0	0	0	$-M$	
	Var. Mix	P_R	P_W	P_B	V	X_R	X_W	X_B	a_P	Sol.
1	V	0	0	0	1	.375	.425	.200	1.825	1.825
0	P_R	1	0	0	0	$-.125$	.125	0	.125	.125
0	P_W	0	1	0	0	$-.125$	$-.075$	.200	.325	.325
0	P_B	0	0	1	0	.250	$-.050$	$-.200$	.550	.550
	Sac.	0	0	0	1	.375	.425	.200	1.825	1.825
	Imp.	0	0	0	0	$-.375$	$-.425$	$-.200$	$-M$ -1.825	—

$$-Q_R \qquad -Q_W \qquad -Q_B$$

Gray's complete linear program is formulated

Maximize $V = $ Expected payoff

Subject to $5P_R + 2P_W + 1P_B - V \geq 0$ (red constraint)

$-2P_R + 3P_W + 2P_B - V \geq 0$ (white constraint)

$4P_R - 1P_W + 3P_B - V \geq 0$ (blue constraint)

$P_R + P_W + P_B \quad = 1$ (probability constraint)

where $P_R, P_W, P_B \geq 0$

and can be solved using the simplex method. Table 22-12 shows the final simplex tableau. This result is obtained by reversing the signs and directions of the first three constraints, thereby eliminating the need for three artificial variables. The slack variables are X_R, X_W, and X_B, and the artificial a_P represents the probability constraint. Gray's optimal mixed strategy is

Gray Chooses Act	With Probability
Red	$P_R = .125$
White	$P_W = .325$
Blue	$P_B = .550$

and the

Value of the game $= V = 1.825$ cents

We will now consider Flannel's problem. Flannel wants to choose Q_R, Q_W, and Q_B so that his expected loss to Gray (her expected payoff) is as small as possible, no matter what color she picks. Flannel's objective is therefore to

Minimize $V =$ Expected loss   (objective)

Flannel's problem has the opposite orientation of the previous linear program. Gray's expected payoff must be no larger than V (the value of which we already know, but which we will still treat as a variable here for the sake of explanation.) For instance, suppose that Gray chooses red. Using the values in the red row of the payoff table, Gray's expected payoff is then expressed

$$5Q_R - 2Q_W + 4Q_B$$

Setting this expression $\leq V$ provides the constraint

$$5Q_R - 2Q_W + 4Q_B \leq V \quad \text{(if Gray picks red)}$$

which can be more conveniently expressed

$$5Q_R - 2Q_W + 4Q_B - V \leq 0 \quad \text{(red constraint)}$$

Like the P values, the Q values must be non-negative and must sum to 1. Mr. Flannel's complete linear program is formulated

Minimize	$V =$ Expected loss	
Subject to	$5Q_R - 2Q_W + 4Q_B - V \leq 0$	(red constraint)
	$2Q_R + 3Q_W - 1Q_B - V \leq 0$	(white constraint)
	$1Q_R + 2Q_W + 3Q_B - V \leq 0$	(blue constraint)
	$Q_R + Q_W + Q_B \quad = 1$	(probability constraint)
where	$Q_R, Q_W, Q_E \geq 0$	

and can also be solved using simplex. However, it is interesting to note that Flannel's linear program is the *dual* of Gray's linear program. (Recall that simplex automatically solves the dual while evaluating the primal.) The solution indicates that Flannel's optimal mixed strategy is

Flannel Chooses Act	With Probability
Red	$Q_R = .375$
White	$Q_W = .425$
Blue	$Q_B = .200$

and, as before

$$\text{Value of the game} = V = 1.825 \text{ cents}$$

PROBLEMS

22-1   Find the saddle point (or points) in each of the following two-person zero-sum games:

(a)

	B_1	B_2
A_1	3	-1
A_2	4	3

(b)

	B_1	B_2	B_3
A_1	4	4	10
A_2	2	3	1
A_3	6	5	7

(c)

	B_1	B_2
A_1	0	8
A_2	0	6
A_3	-2	4

(d)

	B_1	B_2	B_3
A_1	5	3	3
A_2	6	2	4

22-2   Find the inadmissible acts in the following game:

	B_1	B_2	B_3	B_4	B_5
A_1	3	2	4	3	4
A_2	2	3	3	2	3
A_3	2	3	-5	4	1
A_4	3	0	4	3	5

22-3   For the following game, determine the minimax course of action for player X. For player Y. What is the value of the game?

	Y_1	Y_2
X_1	2	0
X_2	3	2

22-4 Consider the following game (payoffs are profits to player A). P is the probability that player A will choose act A_1 and Q is the probability that player B will choose act B_1.

		Q	$1 - Q$
		B_1	B_2
P	A_1	5	-4
$1 - P$	A_2	-4	3

(a) Construct a graph that locates the optimal P that player A should apply, regardless of the action B takes.

(b) Determine the optimal P for player A algebraically. Then find the value of the game.

(c) Find player B's optimal mixed strategy.

(d) Find player A's expected payoff from the P you determined in (b) if player B chooses probability $Q = 1/5$ instead of applying his or her optimal mixed strategy. Is this different from the value of the game you found in (b)? Explain.

(e) Find player A's expected payoff when B chooses the Q you determined in (c) and A selects $P = 1/4$. Is this different from the value of the game you found in (b)? Explain.

(f) Find player A's expected payoff when B chooses the Q given in (d) and A selects $P = 1/4$. Is this different from the value of the game you found in (b)? Explain.

22-5 Consider the following game:

	B_1	B_2	B_3
A_1	2	7	4
A_2	5	1	5
A_3	3	4	4

(a) Eliminate any inadmissible acts.

(b) Determine player B's optimal mixed strategy.

(c) What act would player A never choose?

(d) Find player A's optimal mixed strategy and the value of the game.

22-6 Compass Point is a game played by two people. Each player has a small wheel with a pointer that must be set a north, east, south, or west. One player is designated "northeast-adjacent" and receives 2 points if two adjacent compass points (for example, north and west) are chosen. The other player is designated "southwest-opposite" and receives 4 points when two opposite directions (north–south or east–west) are chosen. If both players pick the same direction, then 5 points are awarded to the player whose designation includes that direction (that is, 5 points to the northeast-adjacent player if both players choose north or both pick east).

(a) Construct the payoff table representing the points awarded to the northeast-adjacent player.

(b) Eliminate any inadmissible acts.

(c) Does this game have an equilibrium act-pair? If so, identify it.

(d) Determine the optimal course of action for each player and the value of the game.

22-7   The Amalgamated Coffin Workers of Transylvania are negotiating with Dracula Enterprises over how many new converts must be housed in the coming year. The union wishes to make as few coffins as possible, whereas Dracula wants to maximize the number of coffins. The following payoff table represents the number of coffins expected to be made for the various combinations of union and management acts:

UNION'S ACTS

		Tranquil	Strike	Wooden Stake Sabotage
DRACULA'S ACTS	Tranquil	15	8	10
	Lock-in	10	12	15
	Bite Union Leaders	10	10	15

Find the optimal course of action for each of the participants and the value of the game.

22-8* Consider a game that offers the following payoffs to player A:

	B_1	B_2	B_3
A_1	-2	5	1
A_2	3	1	2
A_3	-1	6	-3

(a) Formulate a *linear program* that specifies the requirements for finding player A's optimal mixed strategy and the value of the game.

(b) Use the simplex method to solve the linear program.

(c) What is the optimal mixed strategy for A? For B? What is the value of the game?

22-9   The tennis coaches for Old Ivy College and Slipper Rock University must each determine which of their leading men and women players to pair in a mixed-doubles match. Although men and women have never played together before at either school, a record has been kept of the number of sets won in previous all-male and all-female matches at both schools. Both coaches feel that the difference in past sets won represents a player's relative advantage or disadvantage against a particular

---

* This problem involves material from the chapter appendix.

opponent. The following tables represent the net number of sets won by the Old Ivy players:

<table>
<tr><td colspan="3" align="center">SLIPPERY
ROCK
WOMEN</td></tr>
<tr><td></td><td>Ann</td><td>Belva</td></tr>
<tr><td>Cheryl</td><td>5</td><td>−3</td></tr>
<tr><td>Sandra</td><td>−4</td><td>2</td></tr>
</table>

OLD IVY WOMEN

<table>
<tr><td colspan="3" align="center">SLIPPERY
ROCK
MEN</td></tr>
<tr><td></td><td>Harry</td><td>Larry</td></tr>
<tr><td>Fred</td><td>−3</td><td>8</td></tr>
<tr><td>Ted</td><td>0</td><td>4</td></tr>
</table>

OLD IVY MEN

(a) Assuming that the relative advantage a particular mixed-doubles team has over its opponents can be expressed by adding the respective historical net winnings of the corresponding all-male and all-female matches, determine the net advantages to Old Ivy of each possible combination of mixed-doubles teams.

(b) Suppose that each coach must determine who will play before finding out who the opponents will be. Assuming that the net advantage of each possible team combination expresses the payoff for a zero-sum game, eliminate the inadmissible teams.

(c) Using the reduced payoff table you constructed in (b), determine the minimax action for each coach. Which school has the advantage? How many sets of tennis does it equal?

22-10 Avery's is a small chain of neighborhood department stores located in a suburban county. C.P. Blomberg is a similar establishment situated in an adjacent county. Both chains are financially strong enough to expand, and the only viable manner in which this can be accomplished is for each chain to open stores in the other's county. The following expected payoff tables provide the anticipated average profit levels over the next five years for the various courses of action:

AVERY'S PROFITS

	Blomberg Doesn't Expand	Blomberg Expands
Avery's Doesn't Expand	$300,000	−$100,000
Avery's Expands	500,000	100,000

BLOMBERG'S PROFITS

	Blomberg Doesn't Expand	Blomberg Expands
Avery's Doesn't Expand	$200,000	$400,000
Avery's Expands	−200,000	50,000

(a) Is this situation a zero-sum game? Explain.

(b) Find the equilibrium act-pair, if there is one.

(c) If the two chains are prohibited by state antitrust laws from cooperating, what course of action would each store take?

(d) If the two stores can cooperate, what course of action would each prefer?

22-11 It is possible to treat single-person decision making under uncertainty as a game with nature as the second participant and the uncertain events as nature's choices. Consider the following payoff table regarding a new product that may be produced in-house or whose patent may be sold to another manufacturer for a fixed fee plus a royalty on future sales:

	PRODUCT EVENTS	
ACTS	Success	Failure
Make	$100,000	$-$50,000
Sell Patent	15,000	10,000

(a) Using the minimax principle of game theory, determine the manufacturer's optimal course of action. What is the corresponding payoff level?

(b) Suppose the manufacturer judges that there is a 50–50 chance of product success. According to the Bayes decision rule, which course of action should the manufacturer take? What is the corresponding expected payoff?

(c) Using the probability information given in (b), calculate the manufacturer's expected payoff for the action indicated in (a).

(d) Does the minimax principle maximize the manufacturer's expected payoff as it would in a two-person game? Explain.

22-12 Two opposing political parties are nominating candidates for governor in separate conventions that are being held simultaneously. The following probabilities apply for the respective party winning the election for the indicated nominee pair:

Democratic Nominee	Republican Nominee	Probability for Democrat Winning	Probability for Republican Winning
Muck	Raker	.75	.25
Muck	Slinger	.25	.75
Mudd	Raker	.30	.70
Mudd	Slinger	.60	.40

Assume that each party wishes to maximize its probability for winning the election.

(a) If the Republican's win probability is subtracted from the Democrat's, the resulting difference can be used as the Democrat's payoff measure, so that a zero-sum game applies. Construct the appropriate payoff table.

(b) Apply the minimax criterion to determine the optimal action for each party.

22-13 The zero-sum game is a special case of the *constant-sum game*, and the same principles may be used to analyze both games. For example, in playing Color-Bland against Ms. Gray, the chauvinistic but chivalrous Mr. Flannel may give her a handicap by increasing each of her regular payoffs by 5 cents. Consider the following game without a handicap:

FLANNEL'S ACTS

		Red	White	Blue
	Red	−2	4	−3
GRAY'S	White	1	2	−4
ACTS	Blue	1	1	1

(a) Solve this game to find the minimax courses of action for the two players. What is the value of the game?
(b) Construct Gray's payoff table with the 5-cent handicap included. Then solve the game. Are the optimal courses of action the same? Compare the value of the handicapped game to the value of the game in (a). What is the difference in these amounts?

23

Waiting Lines (Queues)

Quantitative methods have been very successfully applied to waiting line situations. Although it may seem that no one cares how long you have to wait in line to cash a check or to buy groceries, most businesses pay a great deal of attention to customer waiting times. Many large retail establishments have actually been designed to achieve an optimal balance between customer inconvenience and operational efficiency. This explains why a supermarket may have ten checkout counters, even though only two or three are in operation most of the time; during Saturday afternoon rush hours, all of these counters may be open. Retailers do not dare to make their customers wait in line for very long, because people value their time highly and would rather switch to a competing store than wait for a few extra minutes.

In management science or operations research, a waiting line is called a *queue*. As a field of study, *queuing theory* is one of the richest areas of operations research methodology. The number of models representing specific situations has grown steadily over the years, and new ones are being reported even now. Queuing theory is one of the earliest quantitative methods. Its origins were published in a 1909 paper by a Danish telephone engineer, A.K. Erlang, whose name is associated with a large class of probability distributions used in conjunction with mathematical queuing models. Since then, thousands of articles and numerous books have been written on the subject.

The usual objective of a queuing model is to determine how to provide service to customers in such a way that an efficient operation is achieved. Unlike the inventory or linear programming models encountered earlier in this book, a minimum-cost or a maximum-profit solution is not always sought. Rather, the aim of these models is to determine various characteristics of the queuing system, such as the mean waiting time and the mean length of the waiting line. These mean values can then be used in a later cost analysis. Or a targeted level of satisfactory customer service is established, and facilities and operations are planned to meet this goal.

To the uninitiated, it may seem that any waiting line is a sign of inefficiency and that good management should eliminate the nuisance of waiting entirely. This viewpoint probably results from the fact that we are all somebody's customers, but relatively few of us operate public establishments. If we reflect on this problem, we can see that eliminating waiting lines entirely would be prohibitively costly for banks, stores, or gas stations. The main reason we have to wait in line at the bank is that customers arrive unpredictably (sometimes creating congestion) and seek a variety of services, each requiring a varying amount of a teller's time. Several times the usual number of tellers might be required to completely eliminate waiting lines, and many tellers would then be idle almost all the time. No bank has fewer tellers than are needed to service its customers within a reasonable time span, and these employees still spend many idle minutes. We never remember the days when we didn't have to wait in a line at all!

23-1   BASIC QUEUING SITUATIONS

All queuing situations involve customer arrivals at a *service facility*, where some time may be spent waiting for and then receiving the desired service. We usually think of customers as people, but customers may also be objects, such as cars being repaired in a garage, unfinished items proceeding to the next stage of production, aircraft waiting to land, or jobs being processed on a computer. A service facility can be a single person, such as a barber or a hairdresser, or several persons, such as a surgical team. A server can also be a machine that dispenses candy bars, stamps parts, or processes data, or a complex entity, such as an airport runway or an oil refinery port facility.

Structures of Queuing Systems

The simplest queing system involves a single-service facility that handles one customer at a time, so that any customer arriving while an earlier customer is being serviced must wait in line. Such a system is represented schematically

Arrival stream   Customers   Service
                        in queue   facility

FIGURE 23-1
Schematic of a single-server single-stage queue.

in Figure 23-1. In this *single-server single-stage queue*, all the required services are performed before each customer leaves. The waiting line itself is not necessarily a physical string of customers, like the line that forms at a theater ticket window. The waiting line can simply be some identifiable grouping of customers whose sequence of service may or may not be designated (perhaps by a number, as is often the case in a retail store where physical lines are inconvenient). The customers do not even have to comingle physically. For example, several inquiries (customers) might stack up in a central computer system, even though they have been processed by remote terminals scattered across a huge geographical expanse, or planes attempting to land at New York's Kennedy Airport might be spread over tens of thousands of square miles of air space.

Somewhat more complicated is the queuing system depicted in Figure 23-2, which is a *multiple-server single-stage queue* with several service facilities. In the simplest case, each facility provides identical service, a single waiting line forms, and the leading customer proceeds to the first free server. Many banks, employ such a system, where a single line feeds customers to the teller windows. Slightly different characteristics apply when arriving customers must select one server and wait in separate server lines, as is still the case when checking out of a large self-service market.

Another way of viewing queues is in terms of the number of service points or stages a customer must pass through before leaving the system. The simplest of these queuing systems is represented by the *single-server multiple-stage queue* shown in Figure 23-3. Before leaving the system, each customer must receive two or more kinds of service. This situation can arise when buying a bulky item, such as a tent, at a department store. First, you must wait for a clerk to

FIGURE 23-2
Schematic of a multiple-server single-stage queue.

FIGURE 23-3
Schematic of a single-server multiple-stage queue.

begin processing your order; second, the clerk checks out your credit by telephoning a central office, which may also have to run quick credit checks on several other customers; finally, a third queue may form when you pick up your tent at the loading dock. Such a queue might also apply in manufacturing, where semifinished items await further processing at various stages of production.

The most complex queuing system is the *multiple-server multiple-stage queue* shown in Figure 23-4. Such a system might apply when getting a driver's license. You line up at one of several windows to pay the fee and to receive a written test; then you take the exam and wait for it to be graded; next, your eyes are examined; this is followed by a behind-the-wheel test administered by one of several possible examiners; finally, you may then wait to be photographed and to obtain a temporary license.

Queue Disciplines

An important aspect of any queuing situation is the *order* in which customers receive service. We refer to the manner of customer sequencing as the *queue discipline*. The mathematical models developed for essentially the same queuing structure can differ, depending on the discipline that applies.

The most common queue discipline is a physical *FIFO* (*first in, first out*) *discipline*, where customers receive service in the order of their arrival. Retail establishments and public service agencies usually employ this system. Indeed,

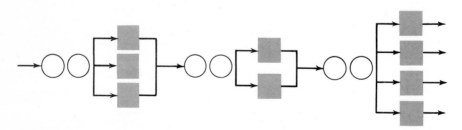

FIGURE 23-4
Schematic of a multiple-server multiple-stage queue.

FIFO has become almost a basic human right—like freedom of speech. In our generally calm modern society, few actions evoke as strong emotions as line cutting.* Many successful establishments rigidly enforce FIFO by issuing numbers to arriving customers. FIFO applies to all of the queuing models discussed in this chapter.

Much less common is the *LIFO* (*last in, first out*) *discipline*. There are some obvious circumstances, such as using elevators, in which LIFO may apply. In most cargo-handling situations, the last item loaded is the first one removed. The queuing aspects of these situations are not of great interest, but the following application of the LIFO discipline is well worth noting.

> Steel ingots arrive at a rolling-mill from open-hearth shops. They are still hot, but there are still temperature gradients within them. They must therefore be placed in reheating furnaces ("soaking pits") before being rolled into slabs or billets, as a more even heat distribution and a higher temperature are required by the rolling operation. If the soaking pits are full when the ingots arrive, they must wait. . . . While they wait, they become cooler. The longer they wait, the longer they must eventually remain in the soaking pits.[†]

To minimize energy costs the last (hottest) ingot in line should be the first one placed in a soaking pit, so that the LIFO discipline applies there.

Another interesting queue discipline is *SIRO* (*service in random order*). A theater refreshment counter during intermission is one of the most exasperating examples of SIRO. Perhaps the most important waiting-line situation involving SIRO occurs at a telephone switchboard. The telephone call that arrives just after a free line is open is the one that is placed. We can view this waiting line as being comprised of all calls that have encountered the "busy" signal. However, no record has been kept of these calls, so that there is no way to determine which call was placed first, and the only way for a call to connect is for the caller to redial it. The order of service may therefore be considered random. Modern telephone equipment places all calls on hold until they can be connected; in such systems, the FIFO discipline generally applies.

A variety of other queue disciplines exist. Situations in which customers have *priority* over others are very common. In a hospital emergency room, for example, the patients who have more serious problems are seen first. Computer systems often function according to priorities, so that the highest priority jobs are processed before all others, regardless of waiting times (and in elaborate systems, jobs may be automatically bumped into successively higher priorities the longer they wait). *Preemptive priority* queues arise when service on a lower priority customer is interrupted when a higher priority customer arrives. An example is the flat-tire job at a service station; the attendant stops working on the tire when a higher priority gasoline customer arrives.

---

* Prior to Christmas 1973, a man was killed in an altercation that resulted when a family crowded into a line of people waiting to see Santa Claus.

[†] Lee, A.M. *Applied Queuing Theory* (New York: St. Martin's Press, 1966), p. 16.

Arrival and Service Patterns

Arrival and service patterns are very important aspects of waiting-line situations. Customers typically arrive at the queuing system randomly. Various probability distributions can be used to represent the time between arrivals; the most common of these is the *exponential distribution*, which will be described later in this chapter. Service time also usually varies (although it may be *constant*), and a variety of probability distributions can be used to characterize service patterns as well. Queuing models can differ considerably for various combinations of arrival and service patterns.

Queuing models usually assume that customers arrive singly, although some models do allow for the batching of arrivals. The latter type of model might apply when a cross-country bus stops at a roadside restaurant. Most models assume that the same interarrival time distribution applies to all customers throughout the period studied. Obviously, this cannot always be true, since busy periods arise in nearly all waiting-line situations. Thus, a particular model may be appropriate only during peak hours, and another model may be required for slack periods. The service pattern is usually presumed to be independent of how customers arrive, which may not be strictly true for some types of service facilities. For example, a supermarket checker may work faster when several persons are waiting in line than when no one is.

23-2   THE EXPONENTIAL AND THE POISSON DISTRIBUTIONS

The most commonly used probability distribution for interarrival times is the exponential distribution, which historically closely fits the data actually observed for many queuing systems. The assumptions underlying this distribution are very simple. The central consideration is that *the exponential distribution applies to situations in which events occur randomly over time*. As an illustration, consider cars arriving at a toll-collection station. Figure 23-5 illustrates this concept. Each dot represents a car and is positioned so that its horizontal distance from the origin (at 9:00 A.M.) indicates when it arrives at the station. Such a graph could be constructed from an aerial photograph taken at 9:00 A.M. of the two miles of highway leading to the station. Assuming that all cars are traveling at the speed limit, we could then directly translate each car's distance from the station into its arrival time. Notice that the dots in Figure 23-5 are scattered across the page with no apparent pattern, as if they were placed there at random.

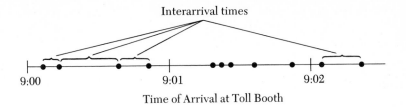

FIGURE 23-5
Random arrival times for cars at a toll station.

The Poisson Process

Even though the cars arrive randomly over time, much detailed information can be gleaned from one key characteristic of the arrival stream (of which our graph is only a small sample). Seemingly without pattern, such an arrival stream is an example of a *Poisson process*, named after the eighteenth-century mathematician and physicist Siméon Poisson. It is the randomness of this pattern that provides the basis for the information it yields. What distinguishes one arrival stream from another—and the only thing that can make any two Poisson processes differ—is the *mean arrival rate*. This parameter, denoted by λ (lower-case Greek lambda), tells us the mean number of arrivals occurring per minute (or some other unit of time, such as per second or per hour). A busy toll station may experience an arrival rate of $\lambda = 100$ cars per minute, whereas an out-of-the-way station may register a rate of $\lambda = 1/2$ cars per minute.

A Poisson process must meet the following conditions:

(1) A Poisson process has *no memory*. The number of events occurring in one interval of time is *independent* of what happened in previous time periods.
(2) The process rate λ *must remain constant* for the entire time period being considered.
(3) It is extremely *rare for more than one event to occur* in a small interval of time. The shorter the duration of the interval, the rarer the occurrence of two or more events becomes. And the probability that exactly one event will occur in such an interval is approximately λ times its duration.

The Poisson process provides two very important probability distributions. The one that is most important in queuing applications is the *exponential distribution*, which provides probabilities for the times between arrivals and, because time is the random variable, is *continuous* (like the normal distribution). The second distribution is the *Poisson distribution*, which provides probabilities for the number of arrivals in any specific interval of time. The Poisson distribution is *discrete* (like the binomial distribution), since the number of cars arriving in any particular unit of time must be a whole number. As we will see, *both the exponential and the Poisson distributions express the same process in different ways.*

The Exponential Distribution

The gaps between the dots in Figure 23-5 represent the interarrival times, or the times between successive arrivals of cars. The exponential distribution is concerned with the *size* of the gap, measured in units of time, that separates successive cars. Although the dots are scattered randomly over time, the relative frequency of interarrival times of various sizes is predictable. Suppose that the cars arriving at the toll station were observed for several minutes and that the time of each car's arrival was noted. These data would provide a histogram similar to the one in Figure 23-6(a), which approximates the shape of the underlying frequency curve in Figure 23-6(b), the height of which may be determined for any interarrival time t from

$$f(t) = \lambda e^{-\lambda t}$$

This expression is the probability density function for the exponential distribution and is based on the constant e, which is equal to 2.7183 and serves as the base for natural logarithms. The particular distribution applicable to a specific situation depends only on the level of λ. In our toll-station illustration, a mean arrival rate of $\lambda = 4$ cars per minute applies. Notice that the frequency curve intersects the vertical axis at a height of $\lambda = 4$ in Figure 23-6(b). The mean and the standard deviation of the exponential distribution are identical and may be expressed in terms of λ as

$$\text{Mean} = 1/\lambda$$

$$\text{Standard deviation} = 1/\lambda$$

Also notice that the mean time between arrivals is the reciprocal of the mean rate of arrivals. Thus, if $\lambda = 4$ *cars per minute*, then the mean time between arrivals is $1/\lambda = 1/4 = .25$ *minutes per car.* Another feature of the exponential distribution is that *shorter durations are more likely than longer ones,* so that the curve in Figure 23-6(b) decreases in height and the slope becomes less pronounced as t becomes larger. The tail of the exponential curve, like the tails of the normal curve, never touches the horizontal axis, indicating that there is no limit to how large the interarrival time t can conceivably be.

As is true of the normal curve, probabilities for the exponential random variable can be found by determining the area under the frequency curve. The cumulative probability that the time T between two successive arrivals is t or less may be obtained from

$$\Pr[T \le t] = 1 - e^{-\lambda t}$$

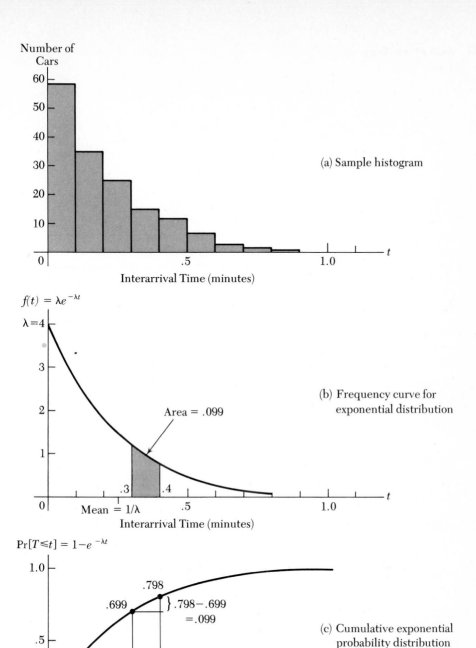

FIGURE 23-6
The exponential distribution for the interarrival times of cars at a toll station.

Figure 23-6(c) shows the applicable cumulative probability graph when $\lambda = 4$. Appendix Table D may be used to find values for $e^{-\lambda t}$.

For example, using $\lambda = 4$ cars per minute, we find that the probability that the interarrival time between any two cars is $t = .4$ minutes or less is

$$\Pr[T \le .4] = 1 - e^{-4(.4)} = 1 - e^{-1.6}$$

$$= 1 - .202$$

$$= .798$$

and the probability that this time is $t = .3$ minutes or less is

$$\Pr[T \le .3] = 1 - e^{-4(.3)} = 1 - e^{-1.2}$$

$$= 1 - .301$$

$$= .699$$

The probability that an interarrival time between .3 and .4 minutes will be achieved is therefore

$$\Pr[.3 \le T \le .4] = .798 - .699$$

$$= .099$$

This value is the area under the exponential frequency curve in Figure 23-6(b) between the interarrival times of .3 and .4 minutes.

The Poisson Distribution

The Poisson distribution expresses the probabilities for the number of arrivals in any given time period, such as the 1 minute between 9:08 and 9:09, the 5 minutes between 9:09 and 9:14, or the 1 hour between 10 A.M. and 11 A.M. Letting X represent the actual number of arrivals in a period of duration t, we can compute the probability that X is equal to one of the possible levels x from

$$\Pr[X = x] = \frac{e^{-\lambda t}(\lambda t)^x}{x!}$$

where

$$x = 0, 1, 2, \ldots$$

Continuing with our illustration, consider any 1-minute interval, so that $t = 1$ minute. Again, given $\lambda = 4$ cars per minute, we find that $\lambda t = 4$ cars. Appendix Table D provides $e^{-4} = .018316$. The probability that exactly 2 cars will arrive is therefore

$$Pr[X = 2] = \frac{e^{-4}(4)^2}{2!}$$

$$= \frac{.018316(4)^2}{2}$$

$$= .1465$$

The probability values for other numbers of cars are calculated in Table 23-1. Notice that the probabilities for arrivals between 0 and 14 sum to only .9999, reflecting the fact that the number of arrivals might be 15, 16, or some larger number, but that these unlisted quantities would have miniscule probabilities that round to zero at four decimal places. Indeed, the Poisson distribution assigns some small probability to any integer value, no matter how large.

The Poisson distribution is completely specified by the process rate λ and the period of duration t. Its mean and variance are identical and are expressed in terms of the parameters

$$\text{Mean} = \lambda t$$

$$\text{Variance} = \lambda t$$

TABLE 23-1

The Poisson Probability Distribution for the Number of Arrivals at a Toll Station in 1 Minute ($\lambda = 4$, $t = 1$)

Number of Arrivals x	Probability $Pr[X = x]$
0	.0183
1	.0733
2	.1465
3	.1953
4	.1953
5	.1563
6	.1042
7	.0596
8	.0297
9	.0133
10	.0053
11	.0019
12	.0006
13	.0002
14	.0001
	.9999

(Here, the mean is equal to the variance, rather than the standard deviation.) In this example, $\lambda = 4$ cars are expected to arrive in any given minute, and the variance in the number of arrivals is also 4. And because results for any two time periods are independent, the number of arrivals in any given minute has no effect on the probabilities for arrivals in the next minute. Thus, if 14 or more cars arrive between 9:05 and 9:06, (a rare event when $\lambda = 4$), the probability for the reoccurrence of that event between 9:06 and 9:07 remains unchanged.

Using Poisson Probability Tables

Like binomial probabilities, computing Poisson probabilities by hand can be an onerous chore. Cumulative values of the Poisson probabilities are computed in Appendix Table E for levels of λt ranging from 1 to 20. A table of individual probability terms is not provided because, like the binomial probabilities, the Poisson probabilities can be easily obtained from the respective cumulative values.

The table provides values of $\Pr[X \le x]$. For example, to find the cumulative probability values of the number of cars arriving at a toll booth during an interval of $t = 10$ minutes when the arrival rate is $\lambda = 2$ per minute, we consult Appendix Table E where $\lambda t = 2(10) = 20$.

The probability that the number of arriving cars is ≤ 15 is

$$\Pr[X \le 15] = .1565$$

whereas the probability that ≤ 20 cars will arrive during the 10-minute interval is

$$\Pr[X \le 20] = .5591$$

Like the cumulative binomial tables discussed in Chapter 3, it is possible to obtain the individual term, the $>$, $<$, $\ge$, and interval Poisson probability values from Appendix Table E. For example, the probability that exactly 15 cars will arrive in 10 minutes is

$$\Pr[X = 15] = \Pr[X \le 15] - \Pr[X \le 14] = .1565 - .1049 = .0516$$

Similarly, we can obtain the probability that the number of cars arriving lies between two values. Thus, the probability that between 16 and 20 cars will arrive in 10 minutes is

$$\Pr[16 \le X \le 20] = \Pr[X \le 20] - \Pr[X \le 15] = .5591 - .1565 = .4026$$

And the probability that > 20 cars will arrive is

$$\Pr[X > 20] = 1 - \Pr[X \le 20] = 1 - .5591 = .4409$$

Other Instances of Poisson Processes

The Poisson process is used in queuing analysis mainly to represent arrivals. As we will see, this process can also be used to represent completions of customer service when the server is busy. A multitude of applications other than queuing exist. The Poisson distribution can be used to represent inventory demands, for example. The exponential distribution can also apply to times between equipment failures and be used in reliability analyses of alternative engineering designs. A Poisson process may even be appropriate in some rather bizarre instances; historically, it fits well to the number of U.S. Supreme Court vacancies in any year, deaths of Prussian recruits kicked by horses, and freeze-ups of Lake Zurich.

Although our present application of the Poisson process treats events that occur randomly over *time*, the respective probability distributions may apply when time is not a factor. The Poisson process may appropriately characterize events that occur in *space* as well. If we consider the locations of objects spread randomly over a space (such as misspelled names in a telephone directory) to be events, then encountering objects while the space (in this case, the pages of the directory) is searched may also be viewed as a Poisson process. This particular application has proved fruitful in quality control and in such esoteric areas as developing radar search techniques, establishing tactics for ships transiting minefields, and hunting for submarines. Here, λ represents the mean number of events *per unit distance* (such as an inch), *area* (a square mile), or *space* (a cubic centimeter). More generally, λ may be the mean number of a particular kind of event per observation made of the phenomena in question. Thus, λ could be 3 errors per page or 5 bad debts per 1,000 installment contracts. The "durations" would be analogous—the space searched, the number of pages scanned, the number of contracts written, and so on.

Practical Limitations of the Poisson Process

A very serious mistake in applying one of the distributions associated with the Poisson process is to assume that the mean event occurrence rate λ holds over an extended duration when it does not. Many queuing situations involve random arrivals with rates that change depending on the time of day, the day of the week, the season of the year, or some other circumstance. The mean rate of vehicle arrivals at a metropolitan toll plaza will differ at 9 A.M. from the rate at 3 A.M., it will be different on Fridays than on Mondays, and it will be greater in the fall than in the summer, when many drivers are on vacation. It is still proper to treat a variety of such situations as a Poisson process, but care must be taken to keep the durations under consideration short and to apply the appropriate value of λ. Thus, a bank may find it best to keep only one-third of its teller windows open at 10:30 A.M. on Tuesday when λ is small, but optimal to open all of its windows when transaction traffic proves heaviest at, say, 5 P.M. on Friday.

23-3 THE SINGLE-SERVER QUEUING MODEL WITH EXPONENTIAL SERVICE TIMES

Basic queuing models are concerned with the state of the system. Under various assumptions regarding the queue discipline and service, a probability distribution may be obtained for the number of customers in the system (either waiting or receiving service) at any future point in time. This probability information can then be used to derive certain useful results mathematically, such as the amount of time that a customer can expect to wait in line.

Our initial model represents the single-server single-stage queuing system. We assume "first come, first served," so that the FIFO discipline applies. Arrivals are assumed to be a Poisson process, so that the arrivals are events that occur randomly over time and meet the other necessary conditions of that process. Thus, the interarrival times have an exponential distribution, and the number of customers arriving in any specified time interval has a Poisson distribution. Due to the resulting mathematical convenience, our basic model further assumes that *the service times are exponentially distributed*. The *mean service rate* (customers per minute, second, or hour) is represented by μ (lower-case Greek mu). It follows that the mean service time is $1/\mu$. Moreover, we assume that *the mean service rate must exceed the mean arrival rate*, or $\mu > \lambda$, so that the queuing system must have more than enough capacity to service all customers. (Without this last restriction, a queuing system would be unstable and the waiting line would grow indefinitely.)

Some Important Queuing Results

The queuing model provides the following important results:

(1) **The probability distribution for the number of customers in the system.** This distribution is the basis for establishing all the other results listed here. It can also be useful in designing facilities that can physically hold waiting customers.

(2) **The mean number of customers in the system.** This quantity accounts for the number of customers either waiting in line or receiving service. It is useful primarily as an intermediate device for finding the mean customer time spent in the system.

(3) **The mean customer time spent in the system.**   This is an average amount representing the total time spent by a customer in the system. When a cost can be associated with each unit of a customer's time, it can be used to make economic comparisons of alternative queuing systems.

(4) **Mean number of customers waiting (length of line).**   This quantity is similar to the mean number of customers in the system, but only involves the customers who are actually waiting in line and not being serviced. Knowing the average number of customers waiting in line can help to establish the size of holding facilities, such as the size of hospital waiting rooms, and is also used in an intermediate step to establish the mean customer waiting time.

(5) **The mean customer waiting time.**   This is an average value that can be used to evaluate the quality of service. Like the mean customer time spent in the system, this quantity may sometimes be used in economic analysis, but it is unsatisfactory for this purpose if alternative queuing systems involve different service-time distributions.

(6) **The server utilization factor.**   This is the proportion of time that the server actually spends with customers—the time during which the server is busy. It provides an estimate of the expected amount of server idle time that can be devoted to secondary tasks not directly involved with service.

Although a discussion of them is beyond the scope of this book, other important results, such as complete probability distributions for a customer's waiting time and the duration of the server's busy period, may be obtained from queuing models.

Basic Queuing Formulas

Although many of the mathematical details are beyond the scope of this book, algebraic expressions have been derived for all of the results provided by the present queuing model. We expressed all results in terms of two parameters:

$$\lambda = \text{mean customer arrival rate}$$

$$\mu = \text{mean service rate}$$

We will begin with the probability distribution for the number of customers in the system. This distribution can be found by considering each possible number of customers either waiting or receiving service as a distinct *state* that can be entered by the arrival of a new customer or left by the completion of the leading customer's service. The schematic representation in Figure 23-7 will help to explain this process. Consider a barbershop with a single barber. There are two ways in which there can be exactly one customer in the shop. There may be no customers in the shop and then one arrives; or there may be two customers in the shop and the first customer's service is completed. These

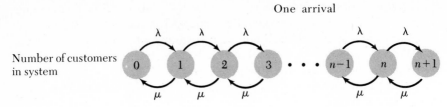

FIGURE 23-7
Schematic of single-server queuing system states.

two cases are represented by the two arrows pointing to 1 in Figure 23-7—one at the top leaving 0 and one at the bottom leaving 2. Likewise, the barbershop can leave the one-customer state either by the arrival of a new customer or by finishing with the present one. Again, these possibilities are shown as two arrows leaving 1—the top one pointing to 2 and the bottom one to 0. This same feature is exhibited for any number of customers n in the system. Beside each arrow, the mean rate is indicated for the possible change in state—λ for an arrival and μ for a departure.

For any given instant of time, we define

$$P_n = \Pr[n \text{ customers in system}]$$

Under the assumption of exponentially distributed arrival and service times, the probability for leaving a state must be equal to the probability of entering that state, and, in short time intervals, movement is possible only between neighboring states (two to three customers, five to four, six to seven, etc.). There are two ways to enter and two ways to leave any state except zero, depending on the preceding number of customers and on whether a departure or an arrival occurs first. The probability for one movement (arrival or service completion) is approximately the product of the corresponding rate (λ or μ) with the duration of time considered between changes. These facts lead to the following *balance equations*:

$$\lambda P_0 = \mu P_1$$
$$\lambda P_1 + \mu P_1 = \lambda P_0 + \mu P_2$$
$$\lambda P_2 + \mu P_2 = \lambda P_1 + \mu P_3$$

A solution of the balance equations provides the following result:

$$P_n = \left(\frac{\lambda}{\mu}\right)^n P_0$$

for

$$n = 1, 2, 3, \ldots$$

implying that

$$P_0 = 1 - \frac{\lambda}{\mu}$$

These expressions can then be used to derive the remaining queuing formulas, which follow.

Mean number of customers in the system:

$$L = \frac{\lambda}{\mu - \lambda}$$

Mean customer time spent in the system:

$$W = \frac{L}{\lambda} = \frac{1}{\mu - \lambda}$$

Mean number of customers waiting (length of line):

$$L_q = \frac{\lambda^2}{\mu(\mu - \lambda)}$$

Mean customer waiting time:

$$W_q = \frac{L_q}{\lambda} = \frac{\lambda}{\mu(\mu - \lambda)}$$

We define the

Server utilization factor:

$$\rho = \frac{\lambda}{\mu}$$

which is represented by ρ (lower-case Greek rho).

A Supply Room Example

Consider the queuing system involved in the operation of a central supply room for a large office. Employees can pick up needed supplies there, just like customers who make purchases at a stationery store. An average of 25 employee customers withdraw supplies during each hour of normal operation. A full-time clerk is required to check persons out of central supply, primarily to assure proper accounting control of requisitioned items. Each requisition takes an average of 2 minutes, so the clerk can check out 30 customers per hour. We will assume that the pattern of arrivals at the checkout counter is a close approximation to a Poisson process and that the checkout times are exponentially distributed. Thus

$$\lambda = 25 \text{ customers per hour}$$

$$\mu = 30 \text{ customers per hour}$$

The mean number of customers either waiting in line or being checked out is

$$L = \frac{\lambda}{\mu - \lambda} = \frac{25}{30 - 25} = 5 \text{ customers}$$

and the mean time spent by customers in the system is

$$W = \frac{1}{\mu - \lambda} = \frac{1}{30 - 25} = \frac{1}{5} \text{ hour}$$

or 12 minutes, which could also have been calculated $W = L/\lambda = 5/25 = 1/5$. The mean number of customers in the waiting line (or its length) is

$$L_q = \frac{\lambda^2}{\mu(\mu - \lambda)} = \frac{(25)^2}{30(30 - 25)}$$

$$= \frac{25}{6} = 4\frac{1}{6} \text{ customers}$$

and the mean customer waiting time is

$$W_q = \frac{\lambda}{\mu(\mu - \lambda)} = \frac{25}{30(30 - 25)} = \frac{1}{6} \text{ hour}$$

or 10 minutes, which could also have been calculated $W_q = L_q/\lambda = (25/6) \div 25 = 1/6$.

The server utilization factor is

$$\rho = \frac{\lambda}{\mu} = \frac{25}{30} = \frac{5}{6}$$

so that the supply room clerk is busy five-sixths of the time.

A Queuing System Cost Analysis

These results may be used to determine the average daily cost of the waiting-line situation. Suppose that the cost of the supply room clerk's labor is $5 per hour, whereas the unproductive time of employee customers is valued at an average hourly payroll figure of $7. The daily cost for the clerk is then

$$\$5 \times 8 = \$40$$

Each customer spends an average of $W = 1/5$ hour checking out of the supply room, so that the average queuing cost per customer is

$$\$7 \times 1/5 = \$1.40$$

An average of $25 \times 8 = 200$ customers request supplies daily, so that the average daily queuing cost is

$$\$1.40 \times 200 = \$280$$

The average total daily cost of checking out of the supply room is therefore

$$\$280 \text{ (queuing cost)} + \$40 \text{ (clerk's cost)} = \$320$$

This amount does not include the time that each employee spends selecting supplies off the shelves—time that is independent of the queuing system itself, which encompasses only the checkout process.

Management should consider this daily cost figure highly excessive, especially since the average cost of the labor lost checking out of the supply room is seven times as great as the cost of the clerk. Two remedies are possible. The checkout process itself could be speeded up by hiring a faster clerk, by making the customers do some of the bookkeeping, or by partially automating the system. Or one or more extra clerks could be hired to assist the first clerk. The latter alternative would involve a *multiple-channel queue*, which will be described later in the chapter.

Now we will consider a partially automated system that enables the clerk to double his service rate, so that $\mu = 60$ customers per hour. The mean customer time spent in the system then becomes

$$W = \frac{1}{\mu - \lambda} = \frac{1}{60 - 25} = \frac{1}{35} \text{ hour, or 1.7 minutes}$$

The considerably reduces the average total daily cost of the labor lost in checking out to

$$200 \times \$7 \times 1/35 = \$40$$

Suppose that the special equipment and handling required for automation costs $50 per day in addition to the clerk's wages. The average total daily cost would then be

$40 (queuing cost) + $50 (equipment cost) + $40 (clerk's cost) = $130

Partial automation would yield an average savings of $190 per day over manual operation with one clerk.

A Queuing System Probability Analysis

Management might also be concerned with the amount of traffic through the supply room. If too many people congregate there, it might become too attractive to persons wishing to socialize on company time. Using the partially automated system, the following probabilities apply for the number of persons being checked out:

$$P_0 = 1 - \frac{\lambda}{\mu} = 1 - \frac{25}{60} = \frac{7}{12} = .583$$

$$P_1 = \left(\frac{\lambda}{\mu}\right)^1 P_0 = \frac{25}{60}\left(\frac{7}{12}\right) = \frac{35}{144} = .243$$

$$P_2 = \left(\frac{\lambda}{\mu}\right)^2 P_0 = \left(\frac{25}{60}\right)^2\left(\frac{7}{12}\right) = \frac{175}{1728} = .101$$

TABLE 23-2
System State Probabilities for Number of Customers in Checkout Process ($\lambda = 25$, $\mu = 60$)

Number of Customers n	P_n	Cumulative Probability for $\leq n$	Probability for $> n$
0	.583	.583	.417
1	.243	.826	.174
2	.101	.927	.073
3	.042	.969	.031
4	.018	.987	.013
5	.007	.994	.006
6	.003	.997	.003
7	.001	.998	.002
8	.001	.999	.001
9	.000	.999	.001

Table 23-2 provides the system state probabilities for $n = 0$ through $n = 9$. We can see from the table that there is less than a 10% chance that more then two persons will ever be checking out of the supply room at the same time.

INTERPRETING QUEUING FORMULAS AND ALTERNATIVE EXPRESSIONS 23-4

An interpretation of the basic queuing formulas may prove helpful at this point. We might view λ as a measurement of the "demand" for service and μ as an expression of the "capacity" of the service facility. The difference $\mu - \lambda$ then represents the "excess capacity" of the system to fill demand. Thus, the mean number of customers in the system is the ratio of demand to excess capacity, or

$$L = \frac{\text{Demand}}{\text{Excess capacity}} = \frac{\lambda}{\mu - \lambda}$$

When excess capacity is small in relation to demand, congestion is heavy and a large number of customers can be expected in the system. In the supply room operated manually by one clerk, demand is $\lambda = 25$ customers per hour, which is five times the excess capacity of $\mu - \lambda = 5$ customers per hour, so that $L = 5$ customers.

The mean customer time spent in the system can be determined by multiplying the mean time between customer arrivals $1/\lambda$ and the mean number of customers L, or

$$W = \left(\frac{1}{\lambda}\right)L = \frac{L}{\lambda}$$

When the supply room is operated manually with one clerk, we find an average of 5 customers in the system, who arrive once every $1/\lambda = 1/25$ hour. Each customer can therefore expect to spend $1/25 \times 5 = 1/5$ hour checking out of the supply room. (It may seem perplexing that to obtain W from L, we multiply by the mean time between arrivals $1/\lambda$ instead of the mean service time $1/\mu$. But remember that $L = 5$ is only a mean figure—not the actual number in the system, which at any given time might be more or less than 5. If it is known in advance that exactly 5 customers are in the system, then the fifth customer would indeed expect to spend $(1/\mu)(5) = (1/30)(5) = 1/6$ hour being checked out. But that result is not W, which applies only when the number of customers is unspecified.)

A customer's mean waiting time is simply the difference between the mean time that customer spends in the system and the mean service time for that customer, or

$$W_q = W - \frac{1}{\mu}$$

This is algebraically equivalent to $\lambda/[\mu(\mu - \lambda)]$. The mean customer waiting time is also equal to the product of the mean time between arrivals and the mean number of customers in the waiting line, or

$$W_q = \left(\frac{1}{\lambda}\right) L_q = \frac{L_q}{\lambda}$$

Multiplying both sides of this equation by λ, we obtain the expression for the mean number of customers in the waiting line

$$L_q = \lambda W_q$$

We can see that all of the queuing results can be obtained by beginning with L, which we may view as the ratio of "demand" (λ) to "excess capacity" ($\mu - \lambda$). We could start with W, L_q, or W_q instead and obtain the other results without memorizing all four basic formulas. And, some of the relationships described here apply to other queuing situations, where one result may be easier to obtain directly than the others. Alternative expressions for the queuing results using the server utilization factor are described below.

It is easy to see that when the checkout clerk operates the supply room manually, he will only be busy an average of 5 minutes out of every 6. In an eight-hour day, the clerk will check out $8 \times 25 = 200$ customers. This will take an average of 2 minutes (1/30 hour), so that a total of 400 minutes will be spent checking out customers. Each working day is comprised of $60 \times 8 = 480$ minutes. The proportion of busy minutes is therefore $400/480 = 5/6$.

The expression for W_q can be obtained from the expression for W by multiplying by the server utilization factor, so that

$$W_q = \left(\frac{\lambda}{\mu}\right) W$$

This same fact applies to L_q and to L, so that

$$L_q = \left(\frac{\lambda}{\mu}\right) L$$

Thus, we can see why the values of L_q and W_q, which do not consider that customer receiving service, are both smaller than L and W, which do. Since the clerk is only busy $\lambda/\mu = 5/6$ of the time under manual operation, L_q and

W_q are only five-sixths as large as L and W. The expression for L_q may also be arrived at by subtracting the server utilization factor from the mean number of customers in the system:

$$L_q = L - \frac{\lambda}{\mu}$$

This is algebraically equivalent to $\lambda^2/[\mu(\mu - \lambda)]$. One rationale for this result is that L_q does not include the one customer who may be receiving service. Since the server is only busy λ/μ of the time, then on the average, we can expect that fraction of a customer to be receiving service at any time. Thus, the fraction λ/μ of a customer must be subtracted to provide the expected number of customers who are waiting only.

THE MULTIPLE-SERVER QUEUING MODEL 23-5

We can now extend the basic queuing model for a one-service facility to the case of several facilities. We will assume that each facility is identical in all respects and that each is capable of performing service at the rate of μ customers per unit of time. As before, the pattern of arrivals is assumed to be a Poisson process and the service times are presumed to be exponentially distributed. The queuing formulas given here are based on the FIFO discipline, and we will assume that the customer at the head of the line proceeds to the first free server.

Queuing Formulas

The queuing formulas for a multiple-channel system are based on principles similar to those used for a single server, but a new parameter is needed to represent the number of channels:

$$S = \text{number of service channels}$$

Figure 23-8 shows how movement occurs between customer states. As in the single-server model, the arrows represent changes and the quantity beside an arrow corresponds to the applicable rate for that particular change.

Notice that when all servers are not busy—that is, when the number of customers n is less than S—no customers are waiting in line and the combined rate of service is $n\mu$. For example, consider a bank that has 5 tellers, so that $S = 5$. When $n = 3$ customers are present, each is being served and the combined rate at which service is being performed is 3μ. For any increment of time, it is

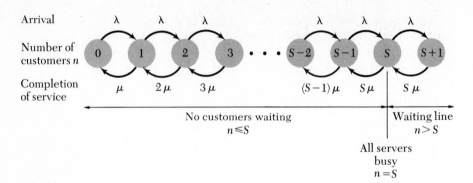

FIGURE 23-8
Schematic of multiple-server queuing system states.

therefore three times as likely that service will be completed for any one of these three customers as a group as it is that service will be completed individually for any specific customer. When the number of customers is at least as large as the number of servers, so that $n \geq S$, all servers are busy and the combined rate of service is $S\mu$. If the bank has $n = 7$ customers, then two customers are waiting in line and the combined service rate is 5μ. As in our earlier model, we assume that total service capacity must exceed customer requirements, so that $S\mu > \lambda$.

The queuing formulas that result with S service channels are a little more complex than those that apply to the single-channel case. When there are S service channels, queuing formulas are based on *the probability that no customers are in the system*:

$$P_0 = 1 \Bigg/ \left[\sum_{n=0}^{S-1} \frac{(\lambda/\mu)^n}{n!} + \frac{(\lambda/\mu)^S}{S!} \left(\frac{1}{1 - \lambda/S\mu} \right) \right]$$

Also important is *the probability that n persons are in the system*:

$$P_n = \begin{cases} \dfrac{(\lambda/\mu)^n}{n!} P_0 & \text{if } 0 \leq n \leq S \\[3mm] \dfrac{(\lambda/\mu)^n}{S! S^{n-S}} P_0 & \text{if } n \geq S \end{cases}$$

The remaining expressions, all based on first calculating L_q, follow.

Mean number of customers waiting (length of line):

$$L_q = \frac{(\lambda/\mu)^S (\lambda/S\mu)}{S!(1 - \lambda/S\mu)^2} P_0$$

Mean customer waiting time:

$$W_q = \frac{L_q}{\lambda}$$

Mean customer time spent in the system:

$$W = W_q + \frac{1}{\mu}$$

Mean number of customers in the system:

$$L = L_q + \frac{\lambda}{\mu}$$

Server utilization factor:

$$\rho = \frac{\lambda}{S\mu}$$

Notice that the server utilization factor differs from that of a single-server system. In a multiple-server system, it is not possible to express the mean customer waiting time as the product of λ/μ and the mean customer time in the system. Thus

$$W_q \neq \left(\frac{\lambda}{\mu}\right)W \quad \text{and} \quad L_q \neq \left(\frac{\lambda}{\mu}\right)L$$

One reason for this is that λ/μ does not represent the same thing in a multiple-server queuing system.

Example—Two Copying Machines

A company is considering renting office copying machines. One alternative is to lease two model A machines that can make 100 copies per minute. However because items must be manually placed on the machine to be copied, the effective copying rate is quite a bit slower. The actual machine time will also vary from user to user, depending on the number of copies required and the originals used. Based on the manufacturer's historical experience for offices with similar workloads, the total time per user is approximately exponentially distributed with a mean of 2 minutes per job. The effective service rate is therefore .5 jobs per minute. The demand for copying by company employees occurs at the rate of three jobs every 5 minutes, or an average of .6 jobs per minute. Historical experience shows that the need for copying occurs randomly over time and that a Poisson process applies to jobs arriving at the copying center. The parameters of this problem are

$$S = 2 \text{ service channels}$$

$$\mu = .5 \text{ jobs per minute}$$

$$\lambda = .6 \text{ jobs per minute}$$

The probability that no jobs are in the copying system is

$$
P_0 = 1 \Big/ \left[\frac{(\lambda/\mu)^0}{0!} + \frac{(\lambda/\mu)^1}{1!} + \frac{(\lambda/\mu)^2}{2!} \left(\frac{1}{1 - \lambda/2\mu} \right) \right]
$$

$$
= 1 \Big/ \left[\frac{(.6/.5)^0}{0!} + \frac{(.6/.5)^1}{1!} + \frac{(.6/.5)^2}{2!} \left(\frac{1}{1 - .6/2(.5)} \right) \right]
$$

$$
= 1 \Big/ \left[1 + 1.2 + \frac{(1.2)^2}{2} \left(\frac{1}{1 - .6} \right) \right]
$$

$$
= 1/[1 + 1.2 + 1.8] = 1/4 = .25
$$

The mean number of jobs waiting to be copied is therefore

$$
L_q = \frac{(.6/.5)^2[.6/2(.5)]}{2![1 - .6/2(.5)]^2} (.25) = .68 \text{ job}
$$

and the mean waiting time per job is

$$
W_q = \frac{L_q}{\lambda} = \frac{.68}{.6} = 1.13 \text{ minutes}
$$

The mean time each job spends in the copying center is

$$
W = W_q + \frac{1}{\mu} = 1.13 + \frac{1}{.5} = 3.13 \text{ minutes}
$$

and the mean number of jobs at the copying center at any given time is

$$
L = L_q + \frac{\lambda}{\mu} = .68 + \frac{.6}{.5} = 1.88 \text{ jobs}
$$

Management is concerned about the average hourly cost of operating two model A machines. Each job is personally processed by the user, whose average hourly payroll cost is $10. Machine rental is a straight $.05 per copy, and an average job involves 12 copies.

The average number of jobs per hour is

$$.6 \times 60 = 36 \text{ jobs}$$

and each employee using the machine spends an average of $W = 3.13$ minutes, or

$$\frac{3.13}{60} = .0522 \text{ hour}$$

in the copying center. The average hourly cost of the labor lost in making copies is therefore

$$\$10 \times 36 \times .0522 = \$18.79$$

The hourly rental cost for the two machines is

$$\$.05 \times 12 \times 36 = \$21.60$$

The total hourly average cost of operating two model A machines is therefore

$$\$18.79 \text{ (labor lost)} + \$21.60 \text{ (equipment rental)} = \$40.39$$

Two Servers Compared to One Server Who Is Twice As Fast

An interesting result arises from queuing theory. To the uninitiated, it may seem that one server who is twice as fast will produce results identical to two separate facilities, each servicing customers at the regular rate. *This is not true.* (If it were, we would not need a separate model for multiple-channel queues; the single-channel system with twice as large a value of μ could be used instead.)

Suppose that the effective service rate of the model T copying machine is twice as fast as that of the model A. If $\mu = 1$ job per minute, the single-server model provides a mean number of jobs waiting of

$$L_q = \frac{\lambda^2}{\mu(\mu - \lambda)} = \frac{(.6)^2}{1(1 - .6)} = .9 \text{ job} \qquad \text{(one model T)}$$

which is more than three times as large as the comparable number when two model A machines are used. The mean waiting time per job using one model T would be

$$W_q = \frac{L_q}{\lambda} = \frac{.9}{.6} = 1.5 \text{ minutes} \qquad \text{(one model T)}$$

which is considerably longer than before. Of course, the service rate of the model T is twice as fast, so the average time a job spends in the system is smaller than it would be if two model A machines were used or

$$W = \frac{1}{\mu - \lambda} = \frac{1}{1 - .6} = 2.5 \text{ minutes} \quad \text{(one model T)}$$

This results in a smaller hourly lost labor cost of

$$\$10 \times 36 \times \frac{2.5}{60} = \$15.00$$

Even if the faster model T rents for a little more per copy than the slower model A does, it would still be cheaper for management to rent one model T instead of two model A machines.

23-6 ADDITIONAL REMARKS

In this chapter, we have described only two queuing models in detail. Both models presume the FIFO discipline and exponential distributions for interarrival and service times. Many other queuing situations exist and have been studied in detail. Several additional queuing models are described in the appendix to this chapter.

Arrivals that occur *singly* over time often historically fit the Poisson distribution. It is inappropriate to use this distribution when customers arrive in groups—for example, when customers pick up their baggage after a flight. Generally, a Poisson process is of limited duration, so that the basic queuing formulas are really only applicable for short periods of time. As we have seen, a bank or a toll station will exhibit different characteristics at different times of the day or on different days of the week. Thus, a different value of λ may be appropriate for any particular period, and different mean waiting times and queuing results would apply to each.

For mathematical simplicity, the two queuing models discussed in this chapter are based on exponential service times. This assumption is tenuous and may cause the queuing models to lack credibility. Recall that the exponential distribution assigns the greatest probability to very short time periods (and a service time of zero is the most likely); theoretically, there is no upper limit on how long service can take under this distribution pattern. But few service patterns fit the exponential distribution well. The normal distribution or some other two-tailed, nonsymmetrical distribution would provide more realistic representations in the majority of cases. This raises some serious questions about the usefulness of basic queuing models, except to explain underlying queuing concepts. However, although the assumption of exponential service may not be strictly true, the queuing formulas provided in this chapter may often yield satisfactory approximations to the actual results that would be derived using more accurate models.

As is true of certain other applications of quantitative methods, various mathematical queuing models have limited scope and often only approximate reality. This is due to the many simplifying assumptions that must ordinarily be made to accommodate the mathematical analysis. To avoid erroneous results, numerical solution procedures are often used instead of standard queuing formulas to evaluate complex queuing situations. One useful procedure—*Monte Carlo simulation*—will be discussed in Chapter 25.

APPENDIX 23-1:
SOME FURTHER QUEUING MODELS*

A tremendous variety of queuing models exists. Each model applies to a particular situation in which any one or a combination of differences occurs in the underlying structure, queue discipline, or arrival or service pattern. This appendix provides four additional queuing models that are widely applicable. All of these models are based on the FIFO discipline and assume a Poisson process for arrivals. The first two models also assume that service times are exponentially distributed.

A Single-Server Model for a Finite Queue

Often the number of customers that a queuing system can handle at any given time is limited. For example, a hospital emergency room only has enough beds to accommodate a specific number of patients waiting to see the attending doctors, and any additional patients must be diverted to other hospitals. A waiting line of limited length is called a *finite queue*. A finite queue might arise due to a physical constraint, such as the emergency room. Or customers might simply give up when the waiting line becomes too long. In either case, a customer who is turned away does not return to the system. Systems involving finite queues differ from the queuing systems discussed in the chapter, where no limits were placed on the number of customers waiting for service. The underlying queuing formulas must be modified to reflect this structural difference. The resulting model can be expressed in terms of the constant

$$M = \text{maximum number of customers in the system}$$

* Optional section.

The probabilities for the number of customers in the system are

$$P_0 = \frac{1 - \lambda/\mu}{1 - (\lambda/\mu)^{M+1}}$$

$$P_n = (\lambda/\mu)^n P_0 \quad \text{for } 0 \leq n \leq M$$

The mean number of customers in the system is

$$L = \frac{\lambda/\mu}{1 - \lambda/\mu} - \frac{(M+1)(\lambda/\mu)^{M+1}}{1 - (\lambda/\mu)^{M+1}}$$

The remaining queuing results may be found from this expression. The mean length of the waiting line is found by subtracting the proportion of time the server is busy, which is $1 - P_0$ here:

$$L_q = L - (1 - P_0)$$

The respective mean customer times are

$$W_q = \frac{L_q}{\lambda(1 - P_M)} \qquad W = \frac{L}{\lambda(1 - P_M)}$$

A Single-Server Model for a Limited Population

A related queuing model arises when the customers arriving at the system represent a small population. Although this case resembles the model for a finite queue, here the potential customers (rather than the line itself) are limited. Such a situation may arise in a plant that contains several machines that need to be serviced when they break down. Each malfunctioning machine is treated as an arriving customer, and the breakdowns can be assumed to be a Poisson process. The model involves the constant

M = maximum number of customers that may need service

The probabilities for the number of customers either waiting or receiving service are

$$P_0 = 1 \left/ \sum_{n=0}^{M} \left[\frac{M!}{(M-n)!} \left(\frac{\lambda}{\mu}\right)^n \right] \right.$$

$$P_n = \frac{M!}{(M-n)!} \left(\frac{\lambda}{\mu}\right)^n P_0 \quad \text{for } 1 \leq n \leq M$$

The remaining results are

$$L_q = M - \frac{\lambda + \mu}{\lambda}(1 - P_0) \qquad L = L_q + (1 - P_0)$$

$$W_q = \frac{L_q}{\lambda(M - L)} \qquad W = \frac{L}{\lambda(M - L)}$$

A Single-Server Model with Poisson Arrivals and Any Service-Time Distribution

The assumption of exponentially distributed service times disagrees with the actual service pattern ordinarily found in many queuing systems. Fortunately, the basic queuing results can be extended to apply to any distribution for service times; the only values that must be specified are the mean $1/\mu$ and the variance σ^2. The results differ only slightly from the basic model described in the chapter:

$$P_0 = 1 - \lambda/\mu \qquad P_n = (\lambda/\mu)^n P_0$$

$$L_q = \frac{\lambda^2 \sigma^2 + (\lambda/\mu)^2}{2(1 - \lambda/\mu)} \qquad L = L_q + \frac{\lambda}{\mu}$$

$$W_q = \frac{L_q}{\lambda} \qquad W = W_q + \frac{1}{\mu}$$

The state probabilities are the same as in the basic model. Notice that L_q—and therefore all the other queuing results—depend on the variance σ^2 of the service-time distribution. L_q, L, W_q, and W all become larger as σ^2 increases. Thus, greater variability in service time will result in longer lines and longer waiting times. This indicates that consistency in service times is very important to the overall quality of the service provided.

A Single-Server Model with Constant Service Times

As a special case, suppose that service times are constant, so that it takes time $1/\mu$ to serve each customer. Since successive customers will all require the same amount of time, the variance is zero. Substituting $\sigma^2 = 0$ into the preceding model, we find

$$L_q = \frac{(\lambda/\mu)^2}{2(1 - \lambda/\mu)}$$

The results for L, W_q, and W can then be calculated as before, using this level for L_q.

PROBLEMS

23-1 On Tuesday mornings, customers arrive at the Central Valley National Bank at a rate of $\lambda = 1$ per minute. What is the probability that the time between the next two successive arrivals will be (a) shorter than 1 minute; (b) longer than 5 minutes; (c) between 2 and 5 minutes?

23-2 During the late Friday rush at the Central bank in Problem 23-1, an average of $\lambda = 5$ customers arrive per minute. What is the probability that no customers will arrive during a specified 1-minute interval?

23-3 A telephone switchboard receives calls between 9 and 10 A.M. during weekdays at the rate of $\lambda = 3$ per minute. Find the probabilities that the number of calls received in any interval of
(a) $t = 2$ minutes will be equal to 3.   (b) $t = 1$ minute will be equal to zero.
(c) $t = 1.5$ minutes will be equal to 4.   (d) $t = 1$ minute will be at least 1.

23-4 For each of the following single-server queuing systems, determine the values of L, W, L_q, W_q, and ρ:

	(a)	(b)	(c)	(d)
	$\lambda = 20$	$\lambda = 8$	$\lambda = 2$	$\lambda = .4$
	$\mu = 25$	$\mu = 12$	$\mu = 5$	$\mu = .7$

23-5 Patrons arrive at a small post office at the rate of 30 per hour. There is one clerk on duty, who takes an average of 1 minute to serve each customer.
(a) Calculate the mean customer time: (1) spent waiting in line and (2) spent receiving or waiting for service. Also find the mean number of customers: (3) in line and (4) receiving or waiting for service.
(b) Construct the probability distribution for the number of customers inside the post office (stopping at that n where the probability rounds to zero to two decimal places).

23-6 For each of the following waiting-line situations, give at least one reason why the models provided in this chapter might be inappropriate for determining the mean customer waiting time.
(a) Telephone calls being placed through a manually operated switchboard.
(b) Customers arriving at a restaurant for dinner.
(c) Patients visiting a dermatologist, who sees patients only by appointment.
(d) A bottling machine filling empties with ingredients.
(e) Plant workers showing their badges to a security guard while passing through the corridor into the main building.

23-7 Sammy Lee is the sole operator of a barbershop. Between noon and 6 P.M. on Saturday afternoons, 1 customer arrives every 15 minutes on the average. Sammy takes an average of 10 minutes to trim each customer. His little shop has chairs for only 2 waiting customers in addition to the customer getting a haircut.
(a) What is the probability that any particular customer will have to spend part of his waiting time standing up?
(b) What percentage of an average Saturday afternoon is Sammy busy? How many hours is he idle on an average Saturday afternoon?

23-8 Between 9 and 10 A.M. on Saturday—his peak business period—customers arrive at Sammy Lee's barbershop at a mean rate of $\lambda = 5$ per hour. During the Thursday slump between 2 and 3 P.M., customers arrive at the rate of $\lambda = 1$ per hour. In either case, the arrivals can be represented as a Poisson process.

(a) Does this mean that more customers will always arrive during the peak period than during the slump? Explain.

(b) Compare the probability that exactly 2 customers will arrive during Sammy's slump to the probability that the same number will arrive during his peak period.

(c) If the mean rate of arrivals for the week as a whole is 3 customers per hour, can Sammy use the Poisson distribution with $\lambda = 3$ to find the probability that next week's arrivals will be between 100 and 150? Explain.

23-9 Ace Airlines has one reservations clerk on duty at a time to handle information about flight times and make reservations. All calls to Ace Airlines are answered by an operator. If a caller requests information or reservations, the operator transfers the call to the reservations clerk. If the clerk is busy, the operator asks the caller to wait. When the clerk becomes free, the operator transfers the call of the person who has been waiting the longest. Assume that arrivals and services can be approximated by a Poisson process. Calls arrive at a rate of 10 per hour, and the reservations clerk can service a call in an average of 4 minutes.

(a) What is the average number of calls waiting to be connected to the reservations clerk?

(b) What is the average time that a caller must wait before reaching the reservations clerk?

(c) What is the average time it takes for a caller to complete a call?

23-10 Suppose that the management of Ace Airlines in Problem 23-9 is considering installing some visual display equipment and a new reservations system. One of the benefits of this system is that it will reduce the average time required to service a call from 4 to 3 minutes.

(a) Under the new system, what would be the average number of calls waiting to be connected?

(b) Under the new system, what would be the average waiting time for a caller?

Suppose that instead of installing the new system, a second reservations clerk is added. Calls could then be referred to whichever clerk was free.

(c) What would be the average number of calls waiting?

(d) What would then be the average waiting time for a caller?

23-11 Mildred's Tool and Die Shop has a central tool cage manned by a single clerk, who takes an average of 5 minutes to check and carry parts to each machinist who requests them. The machinists arrive once every 8 minutes on the average. A machinist's time is valued at $15 per hour; a clerk's time is valued at $9 per hour. What are the average hourly queuing system costs associated with the tool cage operation?

23-12 Mildred wishes to improve the costs for the tool cage operation in Problem 23-11. Two alternatives are:

(1) Use two clerks who are equally fast.

(2) Have a machinist instead of a clerk operate the tool cage. (Special knowledge enables the machinist to provide service twice as fast as the clerk.)

(a) Determine the mean machinist time spent checking out tools for both alternatives.

(b) Find the average hourly queuing system costs for both alternatives. Which one would be cheaper?

(c) Discuss any advantages of each alternative that cannot be measured by applying queuing models.

23-13 C.A. Gopher & Sons is to excavate a site from which 100,000 cubic yards of dirt must be removed. Gopher has the choice of using a scoop loader or a shovel crane. He has leased 10 trucks at $20 per hour. A scoop loader costs $40 per hour, and a shovel crane costs $60 per hour. Once work has been started, the trucks will arrive according to a Poisson process at a mean rate of $\lambda = 7$ trucks per hour. Truck-filling times are exponentially distributed. A scoop loader can fill an average of 10 trucks per hour. The shovel crane is faster and is capable of filling 15 trucks per hour on the average. (For simplicity, we will assume that the truck arrival rate is the same, regardless of the equipment used.)

Since the number of truck arrivals required to excavate the site is fixed by the amount of dirt to be removed, the optimal choice of filling equipment will be the one that minimizes the combined average hourly costs of unproductive truck time plus the cost of the filling equipment. Determine the optimal choice.

23-14 The manager of a WaySafe market with 10 checkout counters wishes to determine how many counters to operate on Saturday morning. His decision will be determined in part by the costs assigned to each additional minute that a customer spends checking out of the store. In a special experiment in obsolete stores about to be closed, customers were forced to wait in line for an abnormally long time. The study concluded that an average of $.05 in future profits is lost for every minute that a customer spends waiting.

Assume that WaySafe customer arrivals at the checkout area are approximated by a Poisson process with a mean rate of $\lambda = 2$ per minute, that each attendant can check out customers at a mean rate of .5 per minute, and that the service time is exponentially distributed.

(a) What is the minimum number of checkers required for the service capacity to *exceed* the demand for service? Determine the mean customer waiting time when that many checkers are providing service.

(b) What is the mean customer waiting time if one more checker is added?

(c) The salary expense for each checker is $10 per hour. What number of checkers will minimize the total hourly queuing system cost—the number in (a) or in (b)? (Ignore service time, since no penalty applies for actual checkout time spent.)

23-15 Another WaySafe supermarket manager is analyzing her operations on Saturday mornings, when 6 full-service checkout stands are currently in operation. The arrival rate (Poisson process) to the stands is 1 customer per minute. The mean checkout time is 5 minutes per customer (assuming an exponential distribution) and is the same for all checkers. By analyzing the records used to obtain these data, the manager has determined that one-half of the customers buy 5 items or less. This group can be serviced in an average of 1 minute each (again, assuming an exponential distribution); it takes a mean of 9 minutes to serve the longer customers. The manager wants to know if she should convert one full-service checkout stand to serve customers who buy only 5 items or less. Answer the following questions when $P_0 = .005$, regardless of whether $S = 5$ or 6.

(a) What is the expected waiting time per customer for the present operational setup?

(b) For the proposed operational setup, what is the expected waiting time for customers buying (1) 6 or more items and (2) 5 or less items, assuming that the latter customers can only go through the small-item checkout stand.

(c) If you were buying more than 5 items, which system would you prefer? Why?

(d) Which system would be more efficient if the cost of a (1) customer's waiting time is $.05 per minute and the cost of a (2) customer's waiting time is $.20 per minute?

23-16 In each of the following situations, use Appendix Table E to find the probabilities that the stated number of events approximate a Poisson process with $\lambda = 8$ per hour when the duration considered is:

(a) $t = 2$ hours, 10 or fewer events   (b) $t = 1.5$ hours, 6 or more events

(c) $t = 1$ hour, exactly 3 events   (d) $t = .125$ hour, between 1 and 5 events.

23-17 A typist commits errors at a rate of .01 per word. Assuming that a Poisson process applies, use Appendix Table E to find the probabilities that the number of errors committed in a 500-word letter will be:

(a) exactly 5   (b) zero

(c) more than 10   (d) between 3 and 7

*23-18 A hospital emergency room can accommodate at a maximum of $M = 5$ patients. The patients arrive at a rate of 4 per hour. The single staff physician can only treat 5 patients per hour. Any patient overflow is directed to another hospital.

(a) Determine the probability distribution for the number of patients either waiting for or receiving treatment at any given time.

(b) Determine the mean values of the number of patients in the emergency room; the number of patients waiting to see the doctor; the patient waiting time; and the patient time spent in the emergency room.

(c) Repeat the calculations in (b), assuming that there is no restriction on the number of patients to receive treatment.

*23-19 A machinist serves $M = 5$ machines as they break down. Machines fail at a rate of 1 per day, and the machinist fixes them at rate of 2 per day.

(a) Determine the probability distribution for the number of machines that will break down at any given time.

(b) Calculate L_q, L, W_q, and W.

(c) Repeat (b) for a machinist who services a population of thousands of machines. Assume that machine failures and service times occur at the given rates.

*23-20 Solve Problem 23-5(a) when the service time is normally distributed with a mean of $1/\mu = 1$ minute and a standard deviation of $\sigma = .30$ minutes.

*23-21 Solve Problem 23-5(a) when the service time is constant at a rate of $\lambda = 1$ customer per minute

* Problems marked with an asterisk involve material in the chapter appendix.

24

Network Planning with PERT

I mportant applications of quantitative methods can be made in the area of *project management*, where a great deal of effort is aimed at a specific accomplishment. Such a program might be the construction of a dam, the development of a new aircraft, the implementation of a new computer system, or the introduction of a new product. All of these examples require management that is oriented toward directing and coordinating the activities of disparate organizations and people. Each project is fraught with uncertainties and takes a great deal of time to complete.

THE IMPORTANCE OF TIME IN PLANNING 24-1

Time is often a paramount factor in selecting alternative ways of completing such projects. This is especially true of construction projects, which must generally be completed by the builder by the date the user plans to begin operating the facilities. A new headquarters building for a corporation illustrates the importance of timely completion.

Suppose that a company's present lease expires in June and that it is planning to move from New York to the San Francisco tower in July. The move itself requires planning to keep disruptions in company functions to a minimum. Hundreds of employees will also be selling their homes, buying new ones, and packing to move. If the new building isn't ready for occupancy until October, either a temporary San Francisco headquarters will have to be found or all moving plans must be delayed. In either case, much bother and expense will result. The builder must therefore be given every incentive to finish the job in June. Such an incentive might involve a bonus of thousands of dollars per day for early completion, with a substantial penalty imposed on each day's delay.

The builder will want to finish the job as quickly as possible and will have every expectation of achieving an acceptable profit. This too requires a lot of planning. The efforts of dozens of subcontractors, who will be separately responsible for such components as air-conditioning, excavation, glasswork, and carpeting, will have to be coordinated. Because the sequence of work is not very flexible (for instance, the framework must be completed before the plumbing or wiring can begin), this coordination must be achieved through the judicious *scheduling of activities*. All subcontractors must adhere to this overall schedule, since a delay on the part of any one of them could make the entire project late.

One procedure generally used to establish schedules for large projects is is the *Program Evaluation and Review Technique*, usually referred to by the acronym PERT. This procedure may also be referred to as the *Critical Path Method*, or CPM. In addition to helping establish schedules, PERT can serve as a management tool for controlling the progress of any large project when timely completion is important.

PERT was developed in the late 1950s, when it came into extensive use in military research and development. Its first important application was in the Polaris program for the first submarine-launched ballistic missiles. PERT has been credited with saving several months in completion time compared with the expected results if more traditional procedures had been used. Since then, PERT and other project management tools have been adopted by the Defense Department for most large research and development efforts. PERT has also been adopted by the construction industry, and to a lesser extent it has been successfully employed in other types of industrial applications.

24-2 THE BASIC CONCEPTS OF PERT

PERT builds on a foundation of basic work groupings called *activities*. In construction, an activity is usually a function, such as excavating or installing plumbing, that is the responsibility of a single subcontractor. In the development of an aircraft, designing the landing gear might be one activity; that same component might involve several more activities in successive stages: testing materials, establishing final specifications, fabricating test gears, ground testing, and flight testing. Regardless of how the activities are identified, they have one feature in common: *Activities take time.* Usually, activities also consume resources in the form of labor, material, or money.

The number of activities to be identified will vary with the scope of the project. There may be only a handful of activities involved in building a house, but the construction of a nuclear power plant or an oil refinery might involve several thousand activities. One ballistic-missile development program involved more than 2,000 activities at the top-management level, where the Air Force established schedules and directly monitored the progress of contractors. Several major contractors were responsible for separate systems of the missile, such as propulsion or guidance. Each organization had its own activities to control, so that each contractor monitored several thousand activities for internal PERT purposes. Altogether, tens of thousands of activities were involved in the development of this particular missile.

PERT involves structuring the various project activities in such a way that schedules are developed, alternative plans are investigated, and the project's status is continuously monitored. This is accomplished by employing a graphical procedure.

The PERT Network

The central focus of any PERT procedure is a logical representation of the project activities. This is accomplished by means of a *PERT network*, which graphically indicates the interrelationships between the activities in chronological order. Figure 24-1 provides the PERT network for constructing a small home. Each activity is represented by an *arrow*,* and each arrow is connected with another in such a way that the required sequence of activities is followed. Before a network can be constructed, all activities must be identified and the immediately preceding activities must be determined. This information is provided in Table 24-1 for the home construction illustration.

We see that the project starts with excavating, which is activity (*a*). The foundation (*b*) and the outside plumbing (*c*) follow immediately. Both the framing (*d*) and the brickwork (*h*) are preceded by the foundation (*b*), which must be completed before these activities can begin. The basic principle underlying a PERT network is that certain activities must be completed before others can begin, whereas some activities can be conducted simultaneously. The network must follow the basic chronological logic dictated by the characteristics of the project. In constructing a home, grading and excavation must be completed before the foundation can be poured. And the foundation must be present before the framework can be installed. The network in Figure 24-1 has been purposely simplified, and some necessary details may be missing. It does *not* represent every house—only a particular one.

---

* * CPM applications use a circle to represent an activity. Although graphically reversed, the basic concepts of either procedure are the same.

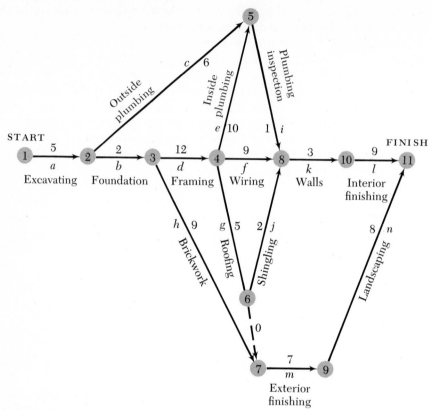

FIGURE 24-1
A PERT network for building a home.

Notice that the arrows for framing (*d*) and brickwork (*h*) activities begin at *circle* 3. This circle constitutes that *point in time* when the foundation (activity *b*) is completed. The PERT network for this project has 11 circles, which are called *events*. An event signals the completion or the starting point of one or more activities. Although any arbitrary system can be used, the events in this illustration have been numbered so that each activity arrow begins with a lower-numbered event than the event number at the end of the arrow. This system can be convenient when a PERT network is computerized, because each activity can then be defined by a beginning and terminating event pair. The events themselves consume neither time nor resources. They serve mainly as *project milestones* and provide the logical "glue" that connects the various activities.

The activities in any neighboring collection exhibit one of two basic relationships to each other. When activities must be completed in a strict sequence, they appear in a *series*, as shown in Figure 24-2. For example, excavating (*a*), pouring the foundation (*b*), and framing (*d*) must be performed in

TABLE 24-1

**Basic Data Used to Construct a PERT Network
for Building a Home**

Activity	Activity Immediately Preceding	Expected Completion Time
(a) Excavating	—	5 days
(b) Pour foundation	a	2
(c) Outside plumbing	a	6
(d) Framing	b	12
(e) Inside plumbing	d	10
(f) Wiring	d	9
(g) Roofing	d	5
(h) Brickwork	b	9
(i) Plumbing Inspection	c, e	1
(j) Shingling	g	2
(k) Cover walls	f, i, j	3
(l) Interior finishing	k	9
(m) Exterior finishing	h, g	7
(n) Landscaping	m	8

that order. The activity sequence *a-b-d* must be represented by a succession of arrows, each following the other, indicating that an activity cannot begin until the preceding activity has been completed. Such a sequence of activities forms a portion of a particular *path* through the network from start to finish. The sequence *a-b-d-f-k-l* in Figure 24-1 is one of several such paths.

Activities that may occur simultaneously can be stacked as shown in Figure 24-3. Any such arrangement involves *parallel* activities. Conceivably, plumbers, electricians, and roofers could all work on the house on the same day. Because parallel activities may be of varying durations, it is not necessary that they actually occur simultaneously, but we allow for that possibility in our PERT network. If for some reason electricians and plumbers cannot work together (perhaps because quarters are cramped), then the present portrayal becomes unrealistic and the project network should be restructured to reflect a series arrangement between inside plumbing and wiring. *But activities should not be placed in series unless it is absolutely necessary.* Whenever two or more jobs may be done at the same time, this possibility should be reflected in the

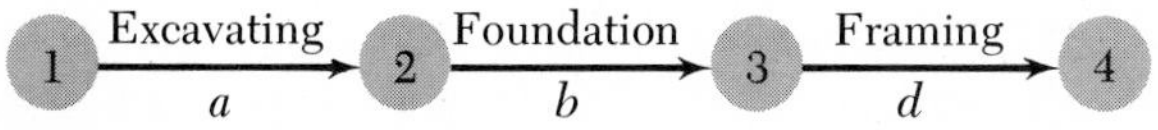

FIGURE 24-2
Activities in series.

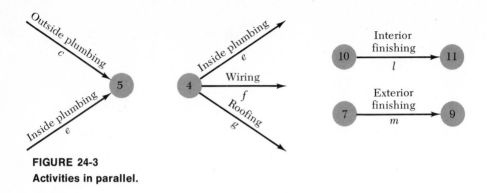

FIGURE 24-3
Activities in parallel.

network—even if it has never been done that way before. This approach allows greater flexibility in planning and may actually shorten the project's duration.

Once the required activity sequence has been specified, the construction of the PERT network can begin. It is best to use a very large sheet of paper for this and to begin with a rough draft. The network can then be copied and some events can be repositioned to keep the number of crossing arrows small. In some applications, the PERT network is drawn in successive revised versions as new activities or interrelationships come to mind.

Computer routines have been written as an aid in arriving at a final graphical display. It may be impractical to have any pictorial representation at all of very large projects. (If drawn, a PERT network with several thousand activities could completely cover the walls of a big room.) Such projects are usually processed entirely on a computer.

The arrow length and the duration of the corresponding activity are not related. In elaborate PERT systems, the network itself may be time-phased, so that *events* are positioned sequentially according to a master schedule (developed in an earlier PERT analysis) at distances from the start of one week (or day or month) to an inch or some other fixed interval. Although such graphical fine points can be helpful when communicating with managers, they are not essential to the successful application of PERT.

Dummy Activities

The broken arrow leading from event 6 to event 7 in Figure 24-1 is an example of a *dummy activity*. Such a portrayal is required to meet the underlying chronology of the work groupings without introducing spurious constraining relationships. The requirements in Table 24-1 indicate that shingling (*j*) is preceded by roofing (*g*) and that exterior finishing (*m*) is preceded by both brickwork (*h*) and roofing (*g*). All of these constraints are met by the network arrangement shown in Figure 24-4.

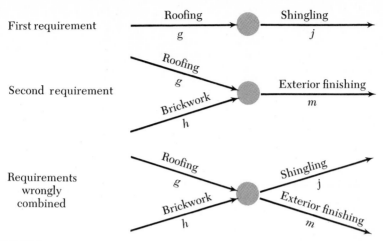

FIGURE 24-4
Incorrect network representation.

However, the final portion of Figure 24-4 is incorrect, since it improperly indicates that shingling (j) cannot start until brickwork (h) is completed (see Figure 24-5). No such requirement exists, and there is no apparent reason why shingling cannot commence while the bricklayers are still working (this particular house does not have a fireplace protruding through the roof). This means that the X formed by the activities in the bottom portion of Figure 24-4 does not apply; only the first three portions shown in Figure 24-6 are correct.

The graphical dilemma is solved by using two events in place of one and letting the precedence of activity g before activity m be represented by a broken arrow pointing downward. The resulting dummy activity explicitly disallows the spurious constraint indicated earlier. A dummy activity is necessary only to preserve the interactivity logic; it consumes neither time nor resources.

Activity Completion Times

The duration of an activity is usually uncertain. It is impossible to predict the exact number of working days it will take to frame a house, although reliable estimates accurate to plus or minus a few days can be made. Much less precision can be expected in estimating how long a research effort or a series of tests will take.

FIGURE 24-5
Spurious requirement induced by not employing a dummy activity.

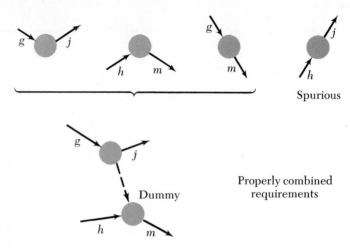

FIGURE 24-6
Correct network representation involving a dummy activity.

In its most general form, PERT treats activity completion times as random variables, each having a distinct probability distribution. To further simplify the analysis, each variable is usually represented by a mean value called the *expected activity completion time.* The numbers appearing above the arrows in the PERT network in Figure 24-1 are the expected completion times for the various activities. For instance, framing (activity *d*) has a mean completion time of 12 days. After the job is done, the builder's records may show that it actually took 11.50 or 13.25 days to erect the frame. But before building begins, the actual time is an unknown future value, and the expected time of 12 days is a convenient number to use in planning.

24-3 AN ANALYSIS OF THE PERT NETWORK

Thus far, we have seen what a PERT network represents and how such a network may be constructed. We will soon see how PERT may be used in project planning and control. A major advantage of PERT is that *the network provides a basis for establishing a compatible activity schedule that permits project completion in a minimum amount of time.* Additional PERT concepts will be discussed when the steps leading to a final schedule are described.

Keep in mind that much of the following discussion is essentially *deterministic,* since the expected activity times are treated as if they were the actual durations. Later in the chapter, we will investigate some of the implications of this approach.

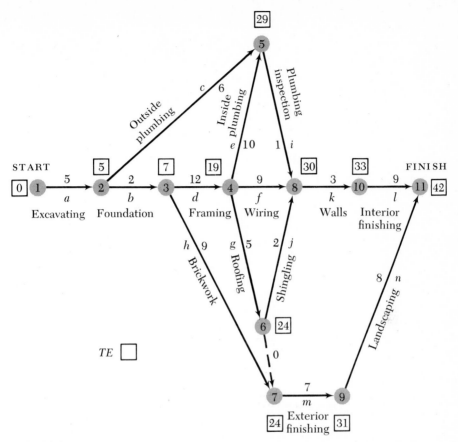

FIGURE 24-7
PERT network for building a home, showing the earliest possible event times (*TE*s).

The Earliest Possible Event Times

PERT analysis begins by focusing on events. Recall that an event is simply a point in time that represents either the completion of one activity or a group of parallel activities or the start of one or more activities. An event is therefore a milestone that must be reached by all activities that directly precede it before future activities can begin. For example, event 4 in the home-building network, redrawn for convenience in Figure 24-7, must occur just after framing is finished and before inside plumbing, wiring, or roofing can begin.

Our first step is to find the *event times* when the respective events occur. If we want to schedule each activity so that it begins as soon as possible, the permissible starting time for a particular activity can be no later than the *earliest possible event time* for the event preceding that activity.

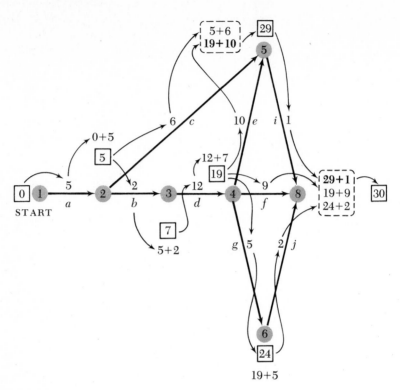

FIGURE 24-8
Illustration of how to find event *TE* values.

For convenience, we use the letters *TE* to represent the earliest possible event times that can be expected. We begin at the start of the project, designated as time zero (so that it can represent any calendar time desired, such as 8 A.M. on Friday, November 16, 1984). A *TE* value of 0 applies to event 1 in Figure 24-7. For ease of identification, each *TE* is placed in the *square* alongside its corresponding event. The *TE* for any event is based on the sum of preceding events *TE* plus the expected completion time for the connecting activity.

Figure 24-8 shows how to apply this principle. There, event 2 is connected to event 1 by excavating (activity *a*), which takes a mean of 5 days to complete. Thus, the *TE* for event 2 is 0 + 5 = 5 days, and the earliest that event 2 can be expected to occur is at the *end* of the fifth working day of the project. Likewise, the *TE* for event 3 is obtained by adding the *TE* for event 2 to the 2-day expected completion time for the foundation (activity *b*, which connects events 2 and 3) to obtain 5 + 2 = 7 days. At event 4, we add this time to the mean framing (activity *d*) time of 12 days to obtain a *TE* of 7 + 12 = 19 days.

When two or more activities terminate at a single event, that event cannot occur until all those activities are completed. Thus, its *TE* is equal to the earliest point in time when the last activity is expected to be complete. Consider event 5, where both outside and inside plumbing (*c* and *e*) terminate. We find the respective expected numbers of working days for the earliest completion of these activities to be

$$5 + 6 = 11 \text{ days for outside plumbing } (c)$$

$$19 + 10 = 29 \text{ days for inside plumbing } (e)$$

The largest sum of 29 days is required for inside plumbing (*e*), which is expected to be the last of the two activities to be completed. Thus, a *TE* of 29 is the earliest possible time for event 5. In general, the *TE* for an event must be the largest sum applicable to those activities that terminate there.

Now consider event 8, where three activities terminate. The earliest possible completion times for these activities are

$$29 + 1 = 30 \text{ days for plumbing inspection } (i)$$

$$19 + 9 = 28 \text{ days for wiring } (f)$$

$$24 + 2 = 26 \text{ days for shingling } (j)$$

As before, the *TE* for event 8 must be the largest of these values, or 30.

TE values are found by making a *forward pass* through the network to establish the earliest possible times expected for the respective events. By adding successive activity completion times together, we can see that *an event's earliest possible time (TE) is equal to the longest duration of all activity paths leading to it from the start*. For instance, paths *a-c* and *a-b-d-e* lead to event 5; the durations of these paths are

$$5 + 6 = 11 \text{ days for path } a\text{-}c$$

$$5 + 2 + 12 + 10 = 29 \text{ days for path } a\text{-}b\text{-}d\text{-}e$$

The longer duration path to event 5 takes 29 days—the same figure found for its *TE*. Likewise, there are four paths leading to event 8. The durations of these paths are

$$5 + 6 + 1 = 12 \text{ days for path } a\text{-}c\text{-}i$$

$$5 + 2 + 12 + 10 + 1 = 30 \text{ days for path } a\text{-}b\text{-}d\text{-}e\text{-}i$$

$$5 + 2 + 12 + 9 = 28 \text{ days for path } a\text{-}b\text{-}d\text{-}f$$

$$5 + 2 + 12 + 5 + 2 = 26 \text{ days for path } a\text{-}b\text{-}d\text{-}g\text{-}j$$

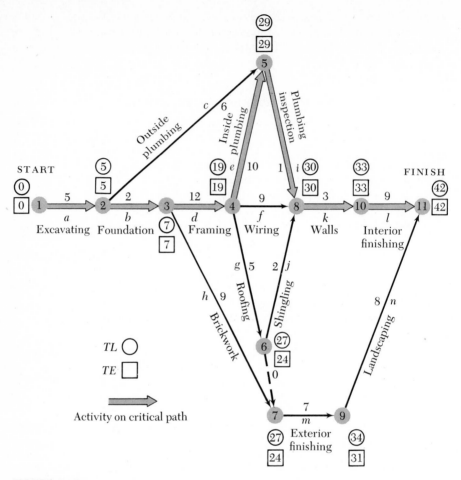

FIGURE 24-9
PERT network for building a home showing the critical path,
the earliest possible event times (*TE*s), and the latest allowable event times (*TL*s).

and the longest duration of 30 days is the *TE* for event 8.

The Critical Path

The path with the longest total time through the PERT network from start to finish is called the *critical path*. The shaded arrows in Figure 24-9 indicate this particular activity sequence for the home-construction project, giving us

Critical path = *a-b-d-e-i-k-l*

The following table represents the succession of activities on the critical path:

Activity Sequence	Expected Completion Time
START	
(a) Excavating	5 days
(b) Pour foundation	2
(d) Framing	12
(e) Inside plumbing	10
(i) Plumbing inspection	1
(k) Cover walls	3
(l) Interior finishing	9
FINISH	Total 42 days

Because they comprise the critical path, the tasks in this table are called *critical activities.*

The duration of the critical path is equal to the *TE* for the last event in the project, which is event 11 in our example. That final milestone can occur no sooner than 42 working days from the start. This is also the earliest time that all activities—and therefore the project itself—can be finished. Thus, *the duration of the critical path can serve as the expected completion time for the entire project.*

Although the critical path is *defined* by the particular activity sequence that takes the longest time, it is *sometimes identified* in terms of an event sequence. In our illustration

$$\text{Critical path} = 1\text{-}2\text{-}3\text{-}4\text{-}5\text{-}8\text{-}10\text{-}11$$
$$\text{START} \qquad \text{FINISH}$$

Several activity sequences may tie for the longest amount of time in a PERT network. In such cases, each sequence will be a critical path. There is no reason why a project can't have several critical paths.

The critical path has many ramifications. Before investigating these further, however, we will describe two additional preliminary PERT procedures.

Latest Allowable Event Times

By themselves, the earliest event times are insufficient to establish schedules because not all activities must start at the earliest opportunity. Many "harmless" or noncritical activities can actually be started later without delaying the entire project. A second set of numbers for the network events, called the *latest allowable event times,* serves to establish limits on the degree of scheduling flexibility.

The latest allowable event times, abbreviated *TL*, appear inside the *circles* beside the respective events in Figure 24-9. The *TL* value establishes the point in time by which an event must occur before an automatic delay can be expected in everything that follows, including the project itself.

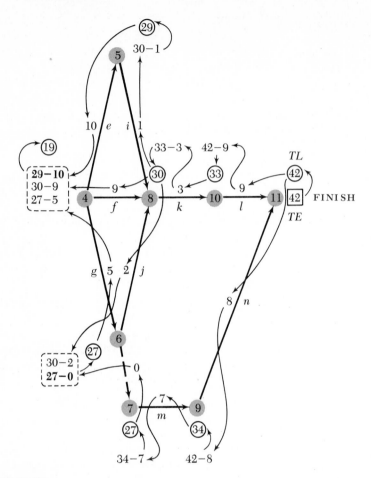

FIGURE 24-10
Illustration of how to find event *TL* values.

For example, consider event 9, which follows exterior finishing (*m*). If this milestone does not occur before its latest allowable time of $TL = 34$ days, the project cannot be expected to be completed in the shortest possible duration of 42 working days. To see why this is so, suppose that event 9 doesn't occur until the end of the 36th working day. Since 8 more days are expected for landscaping, the project could then be expected to take 44 days to complete.

The TL and the TE values are determined similarly, but the TL values are computed in a *backward pass* through the network, and expected activity completion times are *subtracted*. Figure 24-10 illustrates this procedure. We start at the project finish, assigning the same number to the TL value of the last event that we obtained earlier for its TE value. Thus, event 11 is assigned a latest allowable time of $TL = 42$ days. Subtracting the 9 days for completing interior finishing (l), we obtain a TL of $42 - 9 = 33$ days for event 10. Repeating this step for event 8, we start with the TL we just found for event 10 and subtract the activity time of 3 for covering the walls (k)—the connecting activity—to obtain $33 - 3 = 30$ days, which is the TL for event 8.

No special problems exist until an event is encountered that is the beginning point for more than one activity, so that two or more arrows point away from it. For example, event 4 signals the starting point for three activities:

> (e) inside plumbing, ending at event 5
>
> (f) wiring, ending at event 8
>
> (g) roofing, ending at event 6

To determine the TL for event 4, we find the *smallest difference* between the TL for the terminating event and the activity time:

> $29 - 10 = 19$ days for inside plumbing (e)
>
> $30 - 9 = 21$ days for wiring (f)
>
> $27 - 5 = 22$ days for roofing (g)

Thus, the latest allowable time for event 4 is 19 days.

Like the TE values, each TL value is related to an activity sequence—the longest duration path from the event to the project finish. The durations of these paths equal the sum of the applicable activity times as well as the earliest *project* completion time minus the TL value. (In our example, the longest path leading from event 4 to the finish is expected to take $42 - 19 = 23$ days).

The significance of the TL values in project scheduling will be discussed later. We will now examine the importance of the information that can be gleaned when the TE and TL values are considered together.

Event Slack Times: Finding the Critical Path

The TE value of an event establishes the earliest possible time within which it can be expected to occur; the TL value of that event is the latest allowable time that it can occur without causing expected delays in the entire project. The difference between these quantities tells the project manager how much leeway exists in achieving such an event. This duration, called the *event slack time*, is computed

$$\text{Event slack time} = TL - TE$$

As an example, consider event 9, which has a TL of 34 days and a TE of 31 days; its event slack time is therefore $34 - 31 = 3$ days. The slack times for the other home-construction events are computed similarly. These slack times appear in the triangles beside the respective events in Figure 24-11.

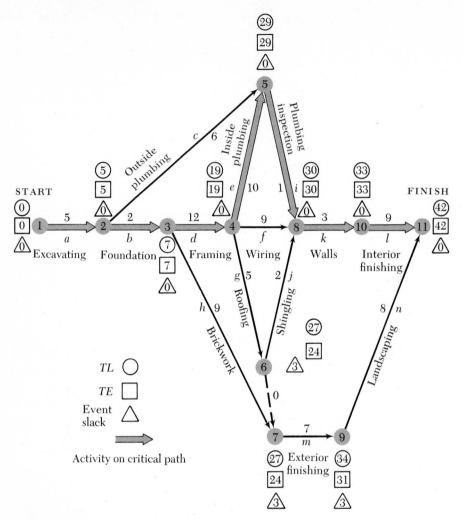

FIGURE 24-11
The complete PERT network for the home-building example.

The main advantage of event slack times in PERT analysis is that they help to identify the critical path. Although the *TE* for the terminal event tells us the length of the critical path, it can be hard to identify exactly which acts comprise that path without some guideline. In a network of several-hundred activities, there can be millions of distinct paths from start to finish, but there may be only one critical path. It would be an incredible waste of time, money, and human resources to attempt to locate it by trial and error.

Because the critical path is the longest activity sequence from start to finish, it should be readily apparent that *all connecting events in the critical path must have zero slack times*. This, limits our search to those paths connecting zero-slack events. In Figure 24-11, there are three such sequences:

$$1\text{-}2\text{-}5\text{-}8\text{-}10\text{-}11 \qquad (\text{or, } a\text{-}c\text{-}i\text{-}k\text{-}l)$$

$$1\text{-}2\text{-}3\text{-}4\text{-}5\text{-}8\text{-}10\text{-}11 \qquad (\text{or, } a\text{-}b\text{-}d\text{-}e\text{-}i\text{-}k\text{-}l)$$

$$1\text{-}2\text{-}3\text{-}4\text{-}8\text{-}10\text{-}11 \qquad (\text{or, } a\text{-}b\text{-}d\text{-}f\text{-}k\text{-}l)$$

Two of these paths are not critical because their activity times do not sum to the project duration of 42 days that we found earlier. The activity times in the first path sum to 24 days; in the last path, they total only 40 days. The middle sequence describes the critical path identified in the network in Figure 24-11.

PLANNING AND CONTROL USING THE PERT NETWORK 24-4

The PERT network information in Figure 24-11 can be used to establish project schedules and to aid in controlling activities so that delays can be avoided.

Activity Scheduling

Recall that the earliest possible event time *TE* sets a lower limit on when successive activities can be expected to start and that the latest allowable event time *TL* sets an upper limit on when preceding activities can end without causing expected delays in the project. Thus, considered together, the *TE* and *TL* values provide the basis for scheduling activities.

A schedule for an activity consists of a starting date and a completion date. The PERT network establishes limits for these dates. An activity can be expected to begin on any date between its *early starting time ES* and its *late starting time LS*. By adding the estimated activity completion time, these dates determine the *early finishing time EF* and the *late finishing time LF*.

An activity's early starting time is equal to the earliest possible time *TE* in which the immediately preceding event can be attained, or

$$ES = TE \text{ for preceding event}$$

By adding the expected activity completion time, represented by the letter *t*, we can then compute the early finishing time for each activity, or

$$EF = ES + t$$

The late finishing time for an activity is equal to the TL for the event at the point when it ends, or

$$LF = TL \text{ for succeeding event}$$

Subtracting the expected activity completion time, we can calculate the late starting time as

$$LS = LF - t$$

Table 24-2 shows these quantities for the home-building project. Consider, for example, wiring (activity f). From Figure 24-11, we see that this activity is preceded by event 4 (with an earliest possible time of $TE = 19$) and succeeded by event 8 (with a latest allowable time of $TL = 30$). Thus, the early starting time for wiring is $ES = 19$ days from the project start. Adding the expected completion time of $t = 9$ days for this activity, the early finishing time for wiring is $EF = 19 + 9 = 28$ days from time zero. The late finishing time for wiring is $LF = 30$ days, and the late starting time is $LS = 30 - 9 = 21$ days.

In scheduling the project, the builder can start wiring anytime between the early starting time of $ES = 19$ days and the late starting time of $LS = 21$ days. Thus, if the project is to start at 8 A.M. on Wednesday, August 1, 1984, wiring may be scheduled to begin sometime just after 19 working days, or at 8 A.M. on August 28 (the beginning of the 20th day) but not later than after 21 working

TABLE 24-2
Limits for Scheduling Home-Building Activities

Activity	t	STARTING TIMES		FINISHING TIMES	
		ES Preceding TE	LS $LF - t$	EF $ES + t$	LF Succeeding TL
(a) Excavating	5	0	0	5	5
(b) Pour foundation	2	5	5	7	7
(c) Outside plumbing	6	5	23	11	29
(d) Framing	12	7	7	19	19
(e) Inside plumbing	10	19	19	29	29
(f) Wiring	9	19	21	28	30
(g) Roofing	5	19	22	24	27
(h) Brickwork	9	7	18	16	27
(i) Plumbing inspection	1	29	29	30	30
(j) Shingling	2	24	28	26	30
(k) Cover walls	3	30	30	33	33
(l) Interior finishing	9	33	33	42	42
(m) Exterior finishing	7	24	27	31	34
(n) Landscaping	8	31	34	39	42

days (8 A.M. on August 30). If the early starting time is chosen, wiring can be scheduled for completion at any time between the two corresponding finishing dates. But if a late starting time is chosen, wiring must be scheduled for completion exactly at the late finishing time (the end of the 30th working day, or 5 P.M. on September 11—assuming that Labor Day is a working day).

Activity Slack Times

We have now identified the points in time that are associated with the activities themselves. These points provide another set of measures, called *activity slack times*, that are useful in project planning. Like their event counterparts discussed earlier, these values indicate how much leeway exists in completing an activity before project delays can be expected. For any particular activity, the activity slack time is computed from the difference between the late and early finishing times, or

$$\text{Activity slack time} = LF - EF$$

(The same results can be obtained from the difference $LS - ES$.)

The activity slack times for our home-building example are computed in Table 24-3. Notice that some activities have zero slack. *A critical path connects only zero-slack activities, and all such activities lie on at least one critical path.* Our example has only one critical path, *a-b-d-e-i-k-l*.

TABLE 24-3
Activity Slack Times for the Home-Building Project

| | | FINISHING TIME | | Activity |
Activity		LF	EF	Slack Time
(a)	Excavating	5	5	0
(b)	Pour foundation	7	7	0
(c)	Outside plumbing	29	11	18
(d)	Framing	19	19	0
(e)	Inside plumbing	29	29	0
(f)	Wiring	30	28	2
(g)	Roofing	27	24	3
(h)	Brickwork	27	16	11
(i)	Plumbing inspection	30	30	0
(j)	Shingling	30	26	4
(k)	Cover walls	33	33	0
(l)	Interior finishing	42	42	0
(m)	Exterior finishing	34	31	3
(n)	Landscaping	42	39	3

Although they are very similar, activity slack measures something different than event slack does, and one set of values cannot generally be computed directly from the other set.

Milestone Scheduling

Sometimes it is necessary to establish milestone schedules for project events rather than for activities. When PERT is applied to military development programs in which the Defense Department specifies important dates in contractual work statements, event scheduling is a convenient device. Although a PERT network may serve as a basis, the actual schedule times are negotiated between the government agency and the contractor. To avoid potential delays in meeting these dates, the contractor must schedule each finishing time for each activity so that it occurs no later than the applicable milestone date for the succeeding event.

An example from a major weapon system project demonstrates how important PERT planning is in establishing milestone schedule dates. One contractor was responsible for designing and building hardware, which was then to be tested by another contractor. The second contractor was scheduled to provide the Air Force with its testing results on a certain date. But the first contractor's schedule called for delivery of the necessary hardware *after* the testing had to be performed. This obvious inconsistency in contractor schedules went unnoticed for several months, until a PERT network was developed and its critical path was determined.

Managing with PERT

The preceding example illustrates an important feature of PERT: It can provide a structure for controlling the multitude of activities in a complex project. When separate organizations are responsible for work that must be done in small pieces over a long period of time at widely separated locations, good coordination of these efforts is a prerequisite for success. Strict adherence to mutually compatible schedules almost assures this. Although it is by no means a panacea, PERT accomplishes this function well.

Management through PERT doesn't stop with the publication of schedules. Remember, the PERT analysis we have examined so far is based on a single set of numbers—the *expected* activity completion times. The amount of time actually required for a particular activity is uncertain. Consider the framing of a house. Inclement weather, an accident on the job, poor workmanship, illness, or a variety of other circumstances might delay its completion. As we have seen in our home-building example, this particular activity is critical. A delay in framing will delay the project unless the lost time can be made up by speeding up the completion of one or more later activities on the critical path.

If the timely completion of the entire project is extremely important, the critical activities deserve special attention. This is an excellent application of the *management-by-exception principle*. Less attention should be paid to activities that are not on the critical path simply because small delays in completing them will not delay the entire project.

Again, it should be emphasized that the expected activity completion times themselves are only estimated values. If some activity that was not on the critical path were unduly delayed, the critical path from that point in time onward might actually shift and a new set of activities might become critical. Special managerial attention should therefore be given to the critical and near-critical (low slack time) activities.

REPLANNING AND ADJUSTMENT WITH PERT 24-5

As just indicated, PERT involves much more than setting schedules. If situations that cause unusual delays are encountered, PERT must somehow accommodate them. Also, our discussions until now have focused on time to the exclusion of resources that might be consumed in completing a project. This is natural, since PERT is essentially a time-minimizing procedure. But a project manager should also be concerned with minimizing the *cost* of the resources being used.

The Time–Cost Trade-off

The expected activity completion times used in the basic PERT analysis are predicated on some assumed level of resource commitment. Labor is the dominant resource in most projects that lend themselves to PERT analysis, and management has the greatest flexibility and control over this resource. For instance, it is possible to shorten the time it takes to complete an activity by concentrating more labor on it. This can be accomplished in framing a house simply by using a larger crew of carpenters than originally planned.

Ordinarily, an activity can be shortened only by increasing its cost. For example, adding a third carpenter to the original two will shorten the work completion time but will not necessarily increase overall crew output by 50%, which can happen only if the work of the original two carpenters is less than optimal (from a productivity point of view). Beyond the optimal crew size, the marginal productivity of each extra worker decreases so that the total framing cost will be higher if three carpenters are employed. Another way to get the job done faster is to permit overtime work, but any overtime wage premium would also raise the total cost of completing the job.

Figure 24-12 shows how project completion time and cost are related by a curve. Each point on this *time–cost trade-off curve* corresponds to a possible

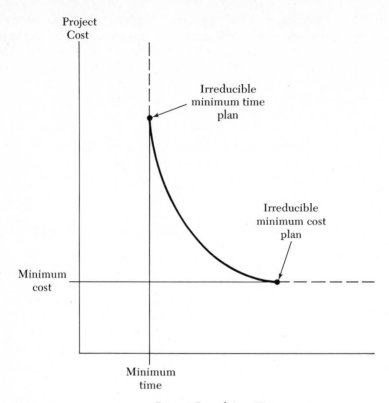

FIGURE 24-12
Time–cost trade-off curve for a project.

project plan. Note the dilemma faced by a project manager: It is possible to reduce the duration of a project only by increasing its cost and to reduce its cost only by increasing the duration of the project. Moreover, there are irreducible minimum plans with respect to time and cost. Only these plans and the ones lying in between, represented by the solid portion of the time–cost trade-off curve will ever be considered.

Unless time savings can be expressed in terms of a dollar return, quantitative analysis cannot identify the optimal point on the curve, because minimizing time and minimizing cost are competing objectives.

Regular and Crash Activity Plans

A good activity manager should be aware not only of how long a particular task might take under varying working conditions, but also of how much these various working arrangements should cost. When quantified, such

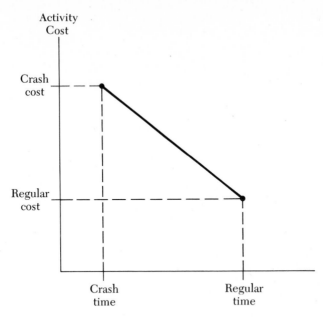

FIGURE 24-13
Time–cost trade-off line for an activity.

information provides a graph such as the one shown in Figure 24-13, where two planning extremes determine a time–cost trade-off for an activity. The *crash activity plan* brings the expected activity completion time to its irreducible minimum, regardless of cost. At the other extreme, the *regular activity plan* involves the most efficient working arrangement in terms of resource use; it is the minimum-cost plan. Either of these plans, or one between them, may be chosen.

Table 24-4 provides some potential data for regular and crash activity plans for our home-building project. We can see that excavating (activity *a*) is expected to take 5 days and to cost $1,000 in labor under the regular plan. On a crash basis, larger equipment can be rented to reduce the completion time of excavating by 1 day to a crash time of 4 days for a total direct crash cost of $1,300; the additional cost of shortening this activity's completion time is $300 per day reduced. Pouring the foundation (activity *b*) cannot be shortened. The expected regular time for outside plumbing (activity *c*) is 6 days and the regular cost is $900. But if the plumbers work overtime, an expected crash time of 4 days and a crash cost of $1,300 can be achieved; the added cost reflects the overtime pay, so that the crash program for outside plumbing costs $400 more and saves 2 days, and the daily cost of reducing that activity's completion time is $200. Altogether, the direct costs (nonmaterial) total $16,350 under the regular plans and $20,150 if all possible activities are crashed.

TABLE 24-4
Regular and Crash Programs for Building a Home

Activity	EXPECTED ACTIVITY TIMES Regular	Crash	DIRECT COST Regular	Crash	Added Cost Per Day Reduced
(a) Excavating	5 days	4 days	$1,000	$1,300	$300 per day
(b) Pour foundation	2	2	500	500	—
(c) Outside plumbing	6	4	900	1,300	200
(d) Framing	12	8	2,400	2,800	100
(e) Inside plumbing	10	7	1,500	2,100	200
(f) Wiring	9	6	1,800	2,250	150
(g) Roofing	5	3	1,000	1,400	200
(h) Brickwork	9	7	1,800	2,150	175
(i) Plumbing inspection	1	1	50	50	—
(j) Shingling	2	2	400	400	—
(k) Cover walls	3	2	300	425	125
(l) Interior finishing	9	8	1,500	1,725	225
(m) Exterior finishing	7	5	1,200	1,650	225
(n) Landscaping	8	4	2,000	2,100	25
			$16,350	$20,150	

Constructing the Time–Cost Trade-off Curve

The time–cost trade-off curve can help the manager select a master plan for the project. To start, we consider the plan by which all activities are to be conducted on a regular basis, so that the first set of activity times in Table 24-4 apply. These times were used in the original PERT network constructed earlier. The final version of this network is repeated in Figure 24-14. This plan has a completion time of 42 days and total direct costs of $16,350.

Since the duration of the project is dictated by the longest activity sequence through the PERT network, it can only be shortened by reducing the completion times of activities on the critical path. For the initial plan, the critical path is a-b-d-e-i-k-l. As long as this path remains critical, any reduction in the expected completion time of one of the critical activities will reduce the project completion time by the same amount.

From the initial regular project plan, a succession of faster plans will be developed by crashing various activities in such a way that each new plan is the cheapest possible one for the indicated project completion time. Table 24-5 shows the plans that result.

The procedure is started by crashing the cheapest critical activity, which happens to be framing (activity d), since this increases the direct costs by the smallest amount (only $100 per day saved). A maximum reduction of 4 days is possible. This faster plan yields a project completion time of 38 days and a larger total direct cost of $16,750.

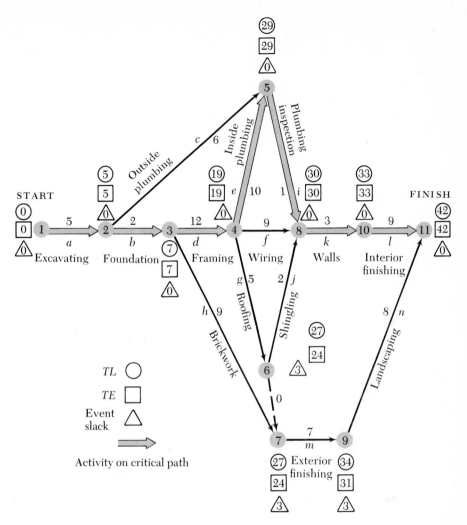

FIGURE 24-14
PERT network for the home-building example
when all activities have regular expected completion times (plan 1).

The third plan is to crash activity k (walls), the next cheapest critical activity at \$125, for a reduction of 1 day in completion time. This plan takes 37 days and costs \$16,875.

The cheapest critical activity remaining to be crashed is inside plumbing (e), which costs \$200 extra for each day's reduction. Although activity e can be crashed from 10 to 7 days to save 3 days, just 2 days of this reduced completion time will be felt by the project as a whole. This is because two other paths

TABLE 24-5

Potential Home-Building Project Plans, Listed in Increasing Order of Additional Cost per Day Saved

Project Plan	Project Completion Time	Total Direct Cost	Last Activity Crashed	Additional Cost per Day Saved	Critical Path
1	42 days	$16,350	none	—	a-b-d-e-i-k-l
2	38	16,750	d by 4 days	$100	a-b-d-e-i-k-l
3	37	16,875	k by 1 day	125	a-b-d-e-i-k-l
4	35	17,275	e by 2 days	200	a-b-d-e-i-k-l
					a-b-d-f-k-l
					a-b-d-g-m-n
5	34	17,525	l by 1 day	225	a-b-d-e-i-k-l
			n by 1 day	25	a-b-d-f-k-l
				250	a-b-d-g-m-n
6	33	17,825	a by 1 day	300	a-b-d-e-i-k-l
					a-b-d-f-k-l
					a-b-d-g-m-n
7	32	18,200	e by 1 day	200	a-b-d-e-i-k-l
			f by 1 day	150	a-b-d-f-k-l
			n by 1 day	25	a-b-d-g-m-n
				375	

(a-b-d-f-k-l- and a-b-d-g-m-n) also become critical when the time for activity e is reduced by 2 days. Thus, the fourth plan incorporates a 2-day reduction (a partial crash) in the expected completion time for activity e to 8 days. This lowers the project time to 35 days and increases the cost to $17,275. This plan, reflecting all of the time changes made so far, has the PERT network shown in Figure 24-15. Each of the *three* critical paths takes 35 days. (If activity e were completely crashed all the way to 7 days, the project would still take 35 days, since that activity does not lie on the two new critical paths.)

The next time reduction is complicated by the fact that there are several critical paths. The durations of all three paths must be reduced in order to shorten the project further. This could be accomplished in a variety of ways. By trial and error, we can find the cheapest method. This is to crash interior finishing (l) and to partially crash landscaping (n), saving 1 day on each activity at a combined cost of $250. This fifth plan allows the project to be completed in 34 days at a cost of $17,525.

All three critical paths involve excavating (a). Crashing this activity is the next cheapest change, costing $300 for a 1-day reduction in completion time.

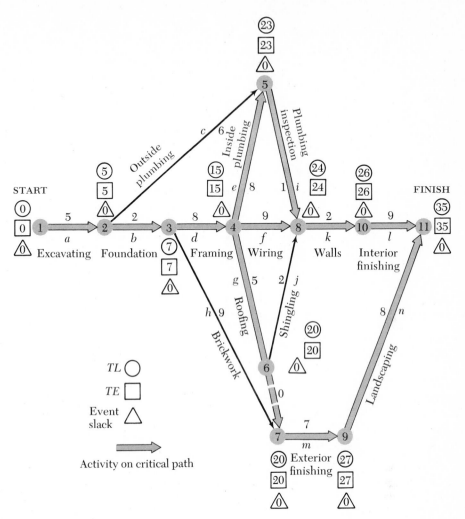

FIGURE 24-15
PERT network for plan 4.

This results in plan 6, which reduces the project completion time to 33 days and increases total direct costs to $17,825.

The seventh plan must involve a 1-day reduction in activity *e*, since this is the only activity remaining in the original critical path that has not been completely crashed. In the other two critical paths, a 1-day partial crash reduction combination for activities *f* and *n* provides the least costly change. Altogether, these time reductions raise total direct cost by $375 to $18,200 and reduce project completion time to 32 days. The PERT network for plan 7 is provided

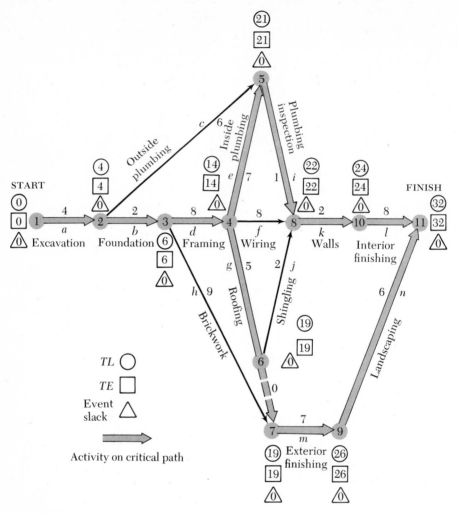

FIGURE 24-16
PERT network for plan 7.

in Figure 24-16. No further time reductions are possible, because every activity in the critical path *a-b-d-e-i-k-l* is completely crashed. Since that critical path cannot be shortened, any further crashing of critical activities will only increase total direct cost without providing a compensatory time savings for the project as a whole.

The procedure just outlined for finding each new plan is strictly a matter of trial and error. It will be helpful to begin with several blank copies of the basic PERT network. The project time for new plans should be reduced in *one-day increments* to avoid making large time reductions that might not be valid for the project as a whole due to the unnoticed emergence of new critical paths. (Two or more successive plans involving identical activity changes can be combined later.) For each new plan, start with a fresh network, change the activity times on the arrows, and recompute the TE, TL, and slack values. Then clearly mark the critical paths. As you go along, put an × on the arrows of those activities on your latest diagram that cannot be crashed further and cross the respective activities off your original list (like the one in Table 24-4). Ignoring earlier networks, study your latest diagram to find further time-reduction alternatives. Changes will become more complex as the number of critical paths grows. Fortunately, fewer possibilities are left to be considered after each new plan.

The time–cost trade-off curve for the home-building project appears in Figure 24-17. This curve provides the builder with a comprehensive summary of possible master plans and indicates the most efficient plan for successive

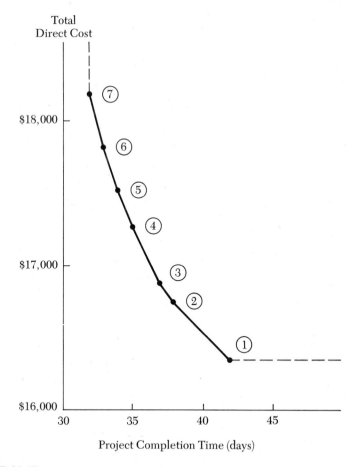

FIGURE 24-17

Time–cost trade-off curve for the home-building example.

reductions in project completion time. For example, if there is some advantage in shaving 5 days off the original completion time, then plan 3 should be adopted if the gain outweighs the added cost. (In-between plans are also possible, such as a 2-day reduction in expected project completion time by only partially crashing activity d by 2 days instead of the full 4 days possible.)

Updating the PERT Network

Once a plan has been established, the appropriate schedules can be determined and the project can be started. PERT can still be used as the project progresses. The actual completion times of the early activities can deviate, perhaps considerably, from the expected values identified at the outset due to such factors as strikes, poor weather, illness, or chance. Or the expected completion times for some future activities may have to be revised in the light of new information. Or a subcontractor may simply not be able to start work on the scheduled date. Such discrepancies may necessitate revising the PERT network, because much of the earlier analysis is no longer applicable. For example, a delay of several days in the completion of the brickwork could effectively shift the critical path in our home-building example to a portion of the network never considered critical before.

When the project is well underway, PERT procedures are the same as before, except that completed activities will have actual rather than expected completion times. New time–cost trade-offs can be made (completed activities, of course, cannot be changed), and a new master plan can be developed that involves revised schedules.

The ability to update PERT networks is especially important in long projects with considerable uncertainties, such as those encountered in weapon system development. Such projects can take more than five years to complete and often involve major technological breakthroughs. In such cases, all of the activities cannot even be identified in detail before the project starts. Initial PERT planning often begins with educated guesses about the specific tasks that will be required three or four years into the project. As planning becomes more precise, the PERT network can grow and be based on more sophisticated time estimates. As the PERT network is modified, revised schedules reflecting current planning can be periodically published.

24-6 ADDITIONAL REMARKS

In this chapter, we have reviewed the essential concepts of PERT, but we have barely scratched the surface of this method of analysis. For instance, we have not considered how to deal explicitly with the uncertainties about activity completion times or how to obtain the expected values. Appendix 24-1 discusses a traditional procedure for probability analysis using PERT. A further treatment involving simulation will be presented in Chapter 25.

Although it may not readily appear to be so, the mathematical properties of PERT place it in an area of linear programming. Establishing *TE* values is a linear programming problem in which the objective is to minimize time. A whole class of linear programming problems involving network flows can be analyzed in a manner similar to the PERT network.

Large PERT systems are generally computerized. A variety of programs have been developed to perform various portions of PERT analysis. These programs often integrate PERT into the structure of broader management information systems. A precursor was the Defense Department's PERT/Cost System, which linked cost control and scheduling of activities. The success of that system was limited due to conflicts with contractors' internal accounting systems. But despite problems with some of the systems associated with PERT, its time-minimization and scheduling aspects are generally accepted as a very valuable management tool.

APPENDIX 24-1:
TRADITIONAL PERT ANALYSIS WITH THREE TIME ESTIMATES*

In the body of this chapter, we did not consider how we arrive at expected activity completion times. Although the techniques presented in Chapter 21 can be used for this purpose, in traditional PERT analysis, they are obtained from a special procedure that involves three time estimates:

$$a = \text{optimistic time}$$

$$m = \text{most likely time}$$

$$b = \text{pessimistic time}$$

These estimates are fairly easy for activity line managers to provide.

The activity duration will almost certainly exceed the optimistic time *a*, and the actual completion time will almost certainly be below the pessimistic time *b*. The most likely time *m* is analogous to the *mode* in statistics. These three time estimates specify a particular continuous probability distribution that is a member of the *modified beta distribution* family. Such a distribution can be symmetrical or skewed (positively or negatively), depending on the relative positions of *a*, *m*, and *b*. The frequency curves for each case appear in

* Optional section.

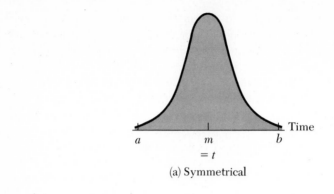

(a) Symmetrical

(b) Negatively skewed   (c) Positively skewed

FIGURE 24-18
Three basic shapes of frequency curves for the PERT modified beta distribution.

Figure 24-18. The expected activity completion time may be computed from these three estimates:

$$t = \frac{a + 4m + b}{6}$$

The values calculated from this equation can then be used in the main PERT analysis.

It may also be useful to know the variance in completion time, which is computed

$$\text{Variance} = \left(\frac{b - a}{6}\right)^2$$

Suppose that the expected regular activity completion times t for each activity used in the home-building example are obtained in this manner from the three time-estimate sets provided in Table 24-6.

TABLE 24-6
Three Time Estimates Used to Compute the Expected Values and Variances of Activity Completion Times for the Home-Building Example

Activity	Optimistic Time a	Most Likely Time m	Pessimistic Time b	Expected Time $\mu = \dfrac{a + 4m + b}{6}$	Variance $\left(\dfrac{b - a}{6}\right)^2$
a	3	5	7	5	.444
b	1	1.5	5	2	.444
c	4	5	12	6	1.778
d	8	10	24	12	7.111
e	7	10	13	10	1.000
f	5	9.5	11	9	1.000
g	3.5	5	6.5	5	.250
h	6	8	16	9	2.778
i	1	1	1	1	0
j	1	2	3	2	.111
k	1.5	3.0	4.5	3	.250
l	7	9	11	9	.444
m	6	6.5	10	7	.444
n	5	7.5	13	8	1.778

Notice that the possible times for each activity vary considerably. Thus, any of the various events in the PERT network could occur at a wide variety of points in time, and the project completion time could be considerably shorter or longer than the 42 days originally anticipated.

As a result, the duration T of the original critical path a-b-d-e-i-k-l cannot be predicted precisely. We do know that its expected value, represented by μ, is the sum of the expected completion times for the component activities, or

$$\mu = 5 + 2 + 12 + 10 + 1 + 3 + 9 = 42 \text{ days}$$

If we assume that the activity times are *independent*, we can closely approximate the complete probability distribution for the length T of this particular path. Its variance σ^2 is then the sum of the variances of the individual completion times for the critical activities, or

$$\sigma^2 = .444 + .444 + 7.111 + 1.000 + 0 + .250 + .444 = 9.693$$

And the standard deviation for T is

$$\sigma = \sqrt{9.693} = 3.11 \text{ days}$$

A general form of the central limit theorem, discussed in Chapter 3, indicates that T is approximately normally distributed with a mean of μ and a variance of σ. Thus, we can establish the probability that 50 days or less will be required to complete path a-b-d-e-i-k-l as

$$z = \frac{50 - 42}{3.11} = 2.57$$

$$\Pr[T \le 50] = .5 + .4949 = .9949$$

and the probability that it will take more than 40 days as

$$z = \frac{40 - 42}{3.11} = -.64$$

$$\Pr[T > 40] = .5 + .2389 = .7389$$

There is one major fallacy in this analysis. *T is the duration for a particular path—not for the project itself.* This point has been widely misunderstood. There is a considerable chance that some path other than the one we identify as the critical path will actually take longer. Thus, $\mu = 42$ days is not really a measure of how long the *project* may be expected to take, and it can considerably understate the true value of the project's expected length.

A complete probability analysis of project completion time is beyond the scope of this book. In Chapter 25, Monte Carlo simulation will be used to estimate the mean project completion time.

APPENDIX 24-2: THE CPM NETWORK*

A different graphical representation than the PERT network depicted in this chapter is frequently used in some applications. The alternative portrayal is the *CPM (critical path method) network*, in which each activity is represented by a *circle*. The circles are connected with arrows in accordance with the required logical sequence to form a network like the one shown in Figure 24-19 for the home-building example. The expected activity completion times appear inside the respective circles. (For convenience, circles are also used to represent the project's start and finish.)

* Optional section.

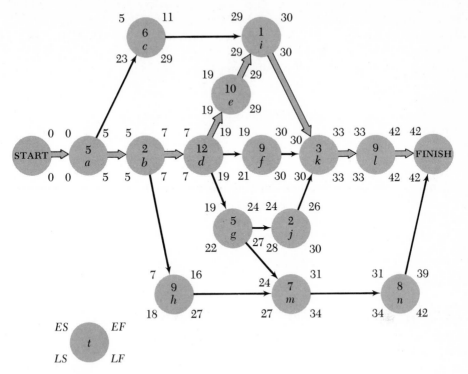

FIGURE 24-19
CPM network for the home-building example.

The critical path is located by a similar procedure. First, a forward pass is made to obtain the *ES* and the *EF* values. A value of zero is used for the start; the *ES* value is the largest *EF* value of the immediately preceding activities. An activity's *ES* value represents the longest path of activities that must be completed before that activity can be started. The *LS* and *LF* values are found in a backward pass. The *LS* value that is used to start this process is equal to the *ES* value of the project finish; the *LF* value is always the smallest *LS* value of the immediately succeeding activities. An activity's *LF* is the longest duration from its completion to the project finish. The following relationships apply

$$EF = ES + t$$

$$LS = LF - t$$

$$\text{Activity slack} = LF - EF = LS - ES$$

The critical path is one connecting zero-slack activities.

One distinct disadvantage of the CPM network is that it is clumsy to use to identify events, which makes it less desirable for milestone scheduling. Each divergence or convergence of arrows corresponds to the standard PERT network event. The earliest possible and latest allowable event times may be obtained from

$$TE = \text{largest } EF \text{ for the preceding activity}$$

$$TL = \text{smallest } LS \text{ for the succeeding activity}$$

Another disadvantage of the CPM network is that it is harder to identify activities for computer processing. In standard PERT analysis, each activity can be defined in terms of preceding or succeeding events. The main advantage of the CPM network is that it is easier to graph than the PERT network because dummy activities are not required.

PROBLEMS

24-1 Find the critical path for the PERT network in Figure 24-20.

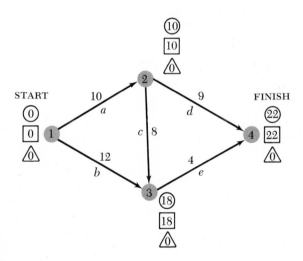

FIGURE 24-20

24-2 Copy the PERT network given in Figure 24-21 on a piece of paper.
  (a) Determine the *TE, TL*, and slack values for each event.
  (b) Identify the critical path(s). What project duration is indicated?
  (c) Find the *ES, EF, LS, LF*, and slack values for each activity.

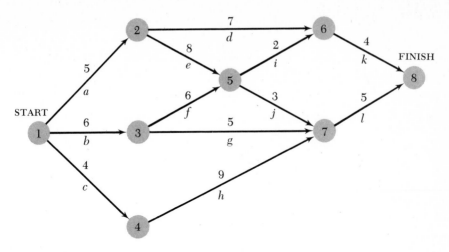

FIGURE 24-21

24-3 Construct a PERT network and identify the critical path(s) for the following activity sequence for a project:

Activity	Immediately Preceding Activity	Expected Completion Time
a	—	2 days
b	—	3
c	—	2
d	b	4
e	a, b	3
f	b	2
g	f, c	5
h	g	4
i	f	3
j	i, d	2
k	j	1
l	e	6

24-4 Consider the PERT network in Figure 24-20, where the expected completion times are in eight-hour working days. Assuming that the project will start at 8 A.M. on Monday, September 1, determine a set of mutually compatible schedule dates for starting and finishing each activity that will permit the project to be completed in a minimum amount of time. (No work is to be done on weekends or holidays, and activities must start at 8 A.M. and end at 5 P.M. on the scheduled dates.)

24-5 The following activities apply to the computerization of a company's accounting system, which is presently operated manually:

Activity	Expected Completion Time
(a) Select computer	2 months
(b) Assemble and install computer	6
(c) Design data input forms	2
(d) Design output report forms	2
(e) Write main processing programs	6
(f) Write input routines	4
(g) Write output routines	3
(h) Generate accounting data bank	3
(i) Test and revise system	2

All of the program routines can be written independently before the computer is installed and can be debugged using computer time rented from another company. No programs or routines can be written until the particular computer model has been selected, although forms and reports can be designed while alternative computers are being evaluated. No input or output routines can be written until the corresponding forms have been designed. The main processing programs and input routines are required to establish the accounting data bank, which can be created on rental equipment. The final activity before implementation is complete is to test and revise the system.

(a) Construct a PERT network for converting the accounting system.
(b) What is the earliest time that the conversion can be finished, assuming that the completion times are certain?
(c) Establish the early and late starting and finishing times for each activity. Which times are critical?

24-6 Consider the PERT network in Figure 24-21. Suppose that the following regular and crash data apply:

| Activity | EXPECTED TIME | | DIRECT COST | |
	Regular	Crash	Regular	Crash
a	5 days	4 days	$100	$ 120
b	6	4	200	260
c	4	4	300	300
d	7	5	500	580
e	8	6	700	800
f	6	5	500	560
g	5	5	400	400
h	9	8	950	1020
i	2	2	200	200
j	3	2	250	325
k	4	3	350	440
l	5	3	500	700

(a) Construct the time–cost trade-off curve for this project. (*Hint:* Before starting, make several copies of the PERT network, omitting the activity times; use a new network for each plan.

(b) Suppose that the project manager values each day of the project completion time saved at $85. Which point your curve is optimal? What direct cost and project completion time apply?

24-7 In publishing a textbook, the following simplified sequence of activities applies:

Activity	Preceding Activity	Expected Completion Time
(a) Write book	—	12 months
(b) Design book	a	1
(c) Edit manuscript	a	6
(d) Check editing	c	2
(e) Accept design	b	1
(f) Copyedit	d, e	2
(g) Prepare artwork	d, e	4
(h) Accept and correct artwork	g	$\frac{1}{2}$
(i) Set galleys	f	4
(j) Check and correct galleys	i	1
(k) Pull page proofs	h, j	2
(l) Check and correct pages	k	1
(m) Prepare index	k	1
(n) Set and correct index	m	$\frac{1}{2}$
(o) Check camera-ready copy	l, n	$\frac{1}{2}$
(p) Print and bind book	o	1

(a) Construct the PERT network and determine the critical path for this activity sequence. How long should the project take from start to finish?

(b) If the project is well-managed, it is possible to produce a book in 18 months or less without crashing any activities. This contradicts your findings in (a). Discuss each of the following:

(1) How do you think publishers get the job done so quickly?

(2) Does this mean that PERT is not applicable to book publishing?

(3) Publishers usually require an author's complete manuscript before they begin to work on the book. In light of your answer to (2), suggest how PERT might be used to shorten the publication time of a book even further.

24-8 *Probability Analysis.* Consider the PERT network in Figure 24-22. Suppose that the following probabilities (in parentheses) apply to the completion times for the various activities:

a	b	c	d	e
8 (1)	5 $(\frac{1}{2})$	2 $(\frac{1}{2})$	5 $(\frac{1}{4})$	8 $(\frac{3}{4})$
	6 $(\frac{1}{2})$	3 $(\frac{1}{2})$	6 $(\frac{3}{4})$	9 $(\frac{1}{4})$

(a) Use these data to compute the expected activity completion times. Then determine the critical path and its duration based on the expected values.

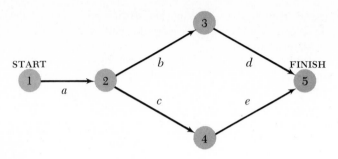

FIGURE 24-22

(b) What actual durations are possible for the critical path you found in (a)? Assuming that activity times are independent events, find the probability for each duration.

(c) Repeat (b) for the other (noncritical) path.

(d) Use your answers to (b) and (c) and the multiplication law to construct the joint probability table for the durations of the two paths.

(e) From your joint probability table, identify the situations in which the "critical" path is actually of shorter duration than the "noncritical" path. What is the probability that any one of these situations will occur?

(f) Use your joint probability table to determine the probability distribution for the length of the longest path(s) from START to FINISH. This distribution represents the *project* completion time. What is its expected value? Is this the same as the duration you found in (a)? Explain.

*24-9 *PERT with Three Time Estimates.* Consider a small project that involves the following activities:

Activity	Preceding Activity	COMPLETION TIMES (days)		
		Optimistic	Most Likely	Pessimistic
a	—	5	6	7
b	—	4	5	18
c	a	4	15	20
d	b, c	3	4	5
e	a	16	17	18

(a) Determine the expected value and the variance of the completion time for each activity.

(b) Use the expected times from (a) to find the critical path.

(c) Assuming that the normal distribution applies, find the probability that the critical path will take between 18 and 26 days to complete.

* This problem involves material in Appendix 24-1 to the chapter.

25

Simulation

In the analytic procedures we have examined thus far, an algorithm provides a problem solution that can be mathematically proved to be optimal. In decision making under uncertainty, a solution obtained in this manner generally provides a maximum expected payoff or a minimum expected cost. All of these problems therefore involve variables whose values are determined by chance, so that probability distributions must be specified in advance.

We will now consider a *numerical solution procedure* that seeks optimal alternatives essentially through a trial-and-error process. This *simulation* technique may be applied to practically any decision problem that involves uncertainty. It is a problem-solving approach that offers several advantages over traditional analytic methods. The most significant advantage of simulation is that it can provide answers for problems that are difficult, or even impossible, to solve in a purely mathematical way.

Simulation thoroughly evaluates each alternative by generating a series of values for each random variable at the frequencies indicated by their probability distributions. This is done by sampling from populations of possible values of the variables. The resulting quantities are combined in accordance with an underlying mathematical model to provide a particular value for the payoff measure. After a number of repetitions, a statistical pattern in the results can be discerned. Simulation is therefore a procedure that tries out each alternative "on paper" over and over again; in effect, it represents a sample from the future. As in most random sampling procedures, random numbers are used to generate the events and quantities involved, as if they were determined by spins of a roulette wheel. For this reason, the procedure has become known as *Monte Carlo simulation.*

25-1 THE NATURE OF SIMULATION

A simulation only *represents* reality and can be used in decision-making situations, training, or a variety of other applications. Monte Carlo procedures employ very special kinds of simulations that must be distinguished from the simulations that are most familiar to us.

Other Kinds of Simulation

A simulation is often physical in nature, as epitomized by ground flight simulators. These modern pilot-training devices duplicate flying conditions as closely as possible. There are several advantages to simulated flight. It exposes pilots to a multitude of conditions over a short period of time—experiences that would be extremely costly to duplicate in an actual aircraft. Hazardous situations that would never be created intentionally with real planes can be routinely duplicated in simulated flights. Such exposure has proved valuable in training pilots to cope with real emergencies.

Training applications involving nonphysical simulations of a similar nature are encountered with increasing frequency. For instance, the case method used by many business schools asks the student to simulate the decision process of an actual manager. Like the errors of the airline pilot trainees, mistakes on such cases are not damaging (except to the gradepoint average), and these cases provide a concentrated exposure to problems that few managers would otherwise experience in their careers. Game-type simulations in which students run hypothetical businesses in competition with one another are also becoming popular. The interaction of individual decisions in a simulated marketplace produces results that are useful in making later choices and that represent improvements in the decision-making process itself.

Physical simulations are helpful when decisions must be made about the design of buildings, cities, waterways, or aircraft. An architect's three-dimensional model of a design is a simulation; the simulated building provides insights that are impossible to glean from sketches alone. The U.S. Army Corps of Engineers has constructed a physical model of the San Francisco Bay that is helpful in evaluating proposals for such activities as dredging and filling in terms of their overall impact on tides and navigation. The flight characteristics of a proposed aircraft can be determined in advance through the simulated flight of a model inside a wind tunnel; the model's aerodynamic properties can lead to refinements in the final design itself.

The Features of Monte Carlo Simulation

Monte Carlo simulation differs from other kinds of simulation in that it is nonphysical in nature and often employs a mathematical model having optimization as the desired end. Thus, Monte Carlo simulation is concerned almost exclusively with decision making itself rather than with training decision makers. Since the procedure is applied to decisions made under uncertainty, the models are *stochastic* in nature. Because chance elements are involved, an alternative must be evaluated under a variety of randomly generated conditions. Although an architect usually makes just one mock-up of a design, a Monte Carlo simulation repeatedly reconstructs the situation in variant forms, according to the events and values that turn up each time. With a somewhat changed model, the same process must be begun again for every alternative. And, when the simulation is finished, all that remains is a history of what happened, which is best analyzed by statistical techniques.

Although Monte Carlo simulation is more widely used than other quantitative methods, it should not be confused with other types of simulation used in decision making that bear a superficial resemblance. For example, it is possible to simulate stock-market trading strategies by using past data to make hypothetical trades. Such a simulation involves a tremendous amount of data and may require a computer. In this respect, a stock-market simulation resembles a Monte Carlo simulation. However, a stock-market simulation is essentially *deterministic* in nature, since previous market conditions are known and *certain*. In contrast, Monte Carlo simulation is a special procedure that is ordinarily used in conjunction with *uncertain* situations.

A variety of problems have been analyzed using Monte Carlo simulation. The oil-tanker port facility study described in Chapter 1 was analyzed using this procedure. Each design alternative was evaluated by more than 1,000 years of simulated operation to arrive at a statistically reliable estimate of its expected rate of return. Monte Carlo simulation has been used to establish baseball batting orders, select rocket combinations to use in launching satellites, and evaluate starting-time policies at golf courses. It has served in planning restaurant menus, in choosing a car, and in estimating how many tellers a bank should hire. It has determined optimal inventory policies for small retailers and large conglomerates. It has proved useful in production control in the manufacture of automobiles, bicycles, and submarines. Monte Carlo simulation has been used to evaluate queuing systems of all kinds—even those without first-come, first-served policies or exponentially distributed service times.

25-2   CONCEPTS AND PROCEDURES: A WAITING-LINE SIMULATION

As an aid in our discussion of the concepts and procedures of Monte Carlo simulation, we will apply the technique to a simple waiting-line situation.

A One-Man Barbershop Illustration

Sammy Lee, owner of a one-man barbershop, is contemplating adding a part-time assistant on Saturdays—the busiest day of the week. His daughter Samantha, who is studying quantitative methods at a distant university, has offered to perform a study to help her father make his decision. As a first step, Samantha wants to evaluate the characteristics of the present operation.

Samantha knows that customers arrive at Sammy's more or less randomly over time and that the time Sammy spends with a particular customer can vary substantially. To help in performing her final analysis she wants to establish applicable Saturday values for the following:

(1) Mean arrival rate (λ)
(2) Mean time between arrivals ($1/\lambda$)
(3) Mean service rate (μ)
(4) Mean service time ($1/\mu$)
(5) Mean customer waiting time (W_q)
(6) Mean customer time in the system (shop) (W)
(7) Mean number of customers in the waiting line (L_q)
(8) Mean number of customers in the system (shop) (L)
(9) Server utilization factor (proportion of time the barber is busy with customers) (ρ)

Samantha knows the textbook formulas for computing these values, but she also knows that they depend on a series of crucial assumptions that may not apply in her father's case. Since she is too far away to observe what goes on at Sammy's shop directly, she will have to simulate the Saturday operations in order to estimate the preceding parameters.

Duplicating Reality

Any Monte Carlo simulation seeks to duplicate reality as closely as possible within practical limitations. Thus, Samantha wants to conduct a simulation that resembles in all important respects what she would find if she actually observed her father's shop in operation.

Customer	Clock Time at Arrival	Clock Time at Beginning of Service	Clock Time at End of Service
Mr. Jones	9:15	9:15	9:30
Mr. Smith	9:25	9:30	9:45
Mr. Green	9:30	9:45	10:00

FIGURE 25-1
Simple customer log for actual observations at a barbershop.

If Samantha were watching the true operation, what information would she need to find the desired parameter values and how should she arrange the data to obtain the target results?

The simplest solution is to maintain a log, as illustrated in Figure 25-1, identifying each customer and recording when he arrives, when he receives his haircut, and when he is finished. As we will see, such a log contains the minimum amount of information necessary to answer the questions.

However, by giving a little additional thought to the design of such a log, we can save some work later on. Items (2) and (4) on Samantha's list of parameters are the mean times between arrivals and for service, respectively. The data needed to compute these means exist in the original log, but, by adding two more columns, the bored log keeper can list the times between successive customer arrivals and the service time for each customer. Another new column can record how long each customer must wait before receiving service. Since a new customer's service cannot begin until the barber is finished with those ahead of him, waiting time is the elapsed clock time between his arrival and the end of service for the preceding customer (and thus the beginning of service for him). Figure 25-2 shows what this more detailed log might look like.

Of course, Samantha can't be there, so she must use fictional customers. Her simulated log, discussed later, will be similar to the one in Figure 25-2.

Customer	Time Between Arrivals	Clock Time at Arrival	Clock Time at Beginning of Service	Service Time	Clock Time at End of Service	Waiting Time
Mr. Jones		9:15	9:15	15	9:30	0
Mr. Smith	10	9:25	9:30	15	9:45	5
Mr. Green	5	9:30	9:45	15	10:00	15

FIGURE 25-2
Detailed customer log for actual observations at a barbershop.

Because she is only interested in the queuing aspects of the barbershop, it is important that the arrival and service patterns of her fictional customers match those of the real ones. In this way, the interactions between the timing of various events in her simulation will be representative of those occurring in real life.

Probability Distributions

The essential inputs for Samantha's simulation are probability data regarding the patterns of customer arrivals and service. Since much of her analysis involves time, two probability distributions are sought: one for the time between successive customer arrivals and another for the service times of individual customers. Although the basic data for generating these distributions can best be determined by clocking customers during the actual operation of the shop, Sammy can't afford to hire someone to do this. Samantha therefore has to apply the techniques presented in Chapter 21 to help her father establish subjective probabilities for these random variables.

Although both variables are continuous, Samantha determines the discrete approximations in Table 25-1 for the underlying probability distributions. Her hypothetical customers must therefore arrive randomly, and the frequency of interarrival times must be consistent with the probabilities given in Table 25-1. The amount of time taken to cut any customer's hair should also be unpredictable and vary according to the respective probabilities.

Generating Events Using Random Numbers

A Monte Carlo simulation generates events so that they occur with long-run frequencies that are identical to their probabilities. This process is very similar to a statistical study in which *random numbers* are used to select a sample from a population of values.

TABLE 25-1

Probability Distributions for Times Between Customer Arrivals and Customer Service Times

TIMES BETWEEN ARRIVALS		CUSTOMER SERVICE TIMES	
Time	Probability	Time	Probability
5 min	.10	5 min	.05
10	.15	10	.20
15	.25	15	.40
20	.25	20	.20
25	.15	25	.10
30	.10	30	.05
	1.00		1.00

You may recall from an earlier study of statistics that random numbers have no particular pattern and could record the outcomes from successive spins of a wheel of fortune, when any digit between 0 and 9 is equally likely to occur. Appendix Table F contains a list of random numbers created by the RAND Corporation. For convenience, we will use the following partial listings taken from the first two columns of that table:

*12*651	*61*646
*81*769	*74*436
*36*737	*98*863
*82*861	*54*371
*21*325	*15*732
*74*146	*47*887
*90*759	*64*410
*55*683	*98*078
*79*686	*17*969
*70*333	*00*201

Notice that the random numbers listed here contain five digits. Since the probability values for the barbershop simulation are accurate to only two places, we can therefore ignore all but the first two digits and use only the italicized portion of each number.

It really doesn't matter how random numbers are picked from the table, as long as the values of earlier numbers do not influence the choice of future ones.

In simulating the operations of Sammy Lee's barbershop, each hypothetical customer can be considered to be a sample observation taken from the population of all future clients seeking a Saturday haircut. In traditional statistics, sample customers are randomly selected from a master list. But in a simulation, the customers are imaginary ones with all the essential characteristics of real customers, so that they must be created in such a way that they could have come from a list like the log in Figure 25-2 that has not been and may never be constructed under actual operation. Although they are used differently in simulation than in an ordinary sampling study, random numbers serve this purpose.

In the actual operation of a barbershop, the chance events—each customer's arrival and service times—occur randomly. These events are simulated by translating successive entries on the list of random numbers. Thus, a random number of 67 for the tenth customer could mean that he arrives 20 minutes after the ninth. *A separate random number is used for each variable.* Thus, the next random number on the list might be 19, which could represent a service time of 10 minutes for this customer.

Before the actual simulation begins, exactly which random numbers are to correspond to each event or uncertain quantity must be determined. The barbershop study requires two random-number assignments—one for each of the time random variables. Consider the time between arrivals first.

TABLE 25-2
Random-Number Assignment for Times Between Arrivals
Using Cumulative Probabilities

Time Between Arrivals	Probability	Cumulative Probability	Random Numbers
5 min	.10	.10	01–10
10	.15	.25	11–25
15	.25	.50	26–50
20	.25	.75	51–75
25	.15	.90	76–90
30	.10	1.00	91–00

Table 25-1 indicates that an interarrival time of 5 minutes occurs with a probability of .10. This outcome should result 10% of the time in a simulation. Of course, there is no reason why more or less than 10% of these 5-minute outcomes can't occur, just as a sequence of coin tosses can result in more or less than 50% heads. But when a large number of cases are considered, the frequency of occurrence for any event should be very close to its probability. We can let random numbers determine when a 5-minute outcome will occur. Since any possible number is equally likely to appear in any position on a list of random numbers, we want to assign exactly 10% of these so that they correspond to an interarrival time of 5 minutes.

Any 10% of the random numbers will suffice, but these numbers must be identified in advance. It's easiest if we assign the smallest 10% of them to represent 5 minutes. Thus, we will set any two-digit random number between 01 and 10, inclusively, to correspond to a 5-minute interarrival time.

The next possible interarrival time is 10 minutes, which occurs with a probability of .15. Thus, the second 15% of the random numbers—those between 11 and 25—will be assigned to that event. To speed the process of assigning random numbers, it is helpful to construct a cumulative probability distribution like the one shown in Table 25-2. Each successive set of random numbers begins where the last set left off, ending with the value that is identical (except for the decimal point) to the respective cumulative probability. This approach guarantees that the proportion of random numbers assigned will always be identical to the probability for the outcome. In doing this, 00 is treated as 100.*

The same procedure is used to assign random numbers to service times in Table 25-3.

---

* An alternative procedure is to use 00 as the low value. The assignment would then be 00–09 for 5 minutes, 10–24 for 10 minutes, . . . , 90–99 for 30 minutes.

TABLE 25-3
Random-Number Assignment for Service Times

Service Time	Probability	Cumulative Probability	Random Numbers
5 min	.05	.05	01–05
10	.20	.25	06–25
15	.40	.65	26–65
20	.20	.85	66–85
25	.10	.95	86–95
30	.05	1.00	96–00

Setting Up the Simulation

Before starting her simulation, Samantha Lee must set it up so that she can create a hypothetical log. She begins by making up the *worksheet* in Figure 25-3. For convenience, each customer is given an identity number corresponding to the order of arrival. Notice that two additional columns [(1) and (5)] are required for the random numbers that determine the times between arrivals and the service times. The numbers in these columns may be entered in advance or one at a time as they are needed.

In general, a simulation is a series of *trials*, each of which is a repetition of the basic steps. In our example, the entries made in each customer row constitute a trial. The steps taken comprise a portion of the *simulation model*. In the barbershop simulation, the worksheet itself spells out that part of the overall model in which the trials are generated. Later, we will discuss the remaining parts of this particular model.

	(1)	(2)	(3)	(4)	(5)	(6)	(7)	(8)
Trial or Cust. No.	*Rand. No.*	*Time Betw. Arriv.*	*Clock Time at Arriv.* [last (3) + (2)]	*Clock Time at Beg. of Serv.* [(3) or last (7)]	*Rand. No.*	*Serv. Time*	*Clock Time at End of Serv.* [(4) + (6)]	*Waiting Time* [(4) − (3)]
1								
2								
3								

FIGURE 25-3
Worksheet for the one-man barbershop simulation.

The simulation model is basically mathematical and can be defined in terms of algebraic expressions. It is often more convenient, however, to indicate the procedures of the model in a worksheet that clearly delineates each step. In large-scale simulations that must be run on a digital computer, the model is generally imbedded in the programming instructions.

Conducting the Simulation

We are now ready to conduct the simulation. The worksheet entries for one customer at a time appear in Table 25-4.

TABLE 25-4
Worksheet Entries for the Barbershop Simulation

Trial or Cust. No.	(1) Rand. No.	(2) Time Betw. Arriv.	(3) Clock Time at Arriv. [last (3) + (2)]	(4) Clock Time at Beg. of Serv. [(3) or last (7)]	(5) Rand. No.	(6) Serv. Time	(7) Clock Time at End of Serv. [(4) + (6)]	(8) Waiting Time [(4) − (3)]
Open			9:00					
1	(12)	10	9:10	9:10	(61)	15	9:25	0
2	(81)	25	9:35	9:35	(74)	20	9:55	0
3	(36)	15	9:50	9:55	(98)	30	10:25	5
4	(82)	25	10:15	10:25	(54)	15	10:40	10
5	(21)	10	10:25	10:40	(15)	10	10:50	15
6	(74)	20	10:45	10:50	(47)	15	11:05	5
7	(90)	25	11:10	11:10	(64)	15	11:25	0
8	(55)	20	11:30	11:30	(98)	30	12:00	0
9	(79)	25	11:55	12:00	(17)	10	12:10	5
10	(70)	20	12:15	12:15	(00)	30	12:45	0
11	(14)	10	12:25	12:45	(53)	15	1:00	20
12	(59)	20	12:45	1:00	(08)	10	1:10	15
13	(62)	20	1:05	1:10	(62)	15	1:25	5
14	(57)	20	1:25	1:25	(97)	30	1:55	0
15	(15)	10	1:35	1:55	(90)	25	2:20	20
16	(18)	10	1:45	2:20	(23)	10	2:30	35
17	(74)	20	2:05	2:30	(68)	20	2:50	25
18	(11)	10	2:15	2:50	(16)	10	3:00	35
19	(41)	15	2:30	3:00	(17)	10	3:10	30
20	(32)	15	2:45	3:10	(91)	25	3:35	25
		345				360		250

Elapsed time = 3:35−9:00
= 6 hours and 35 minutes
= 395 minutes

Samantha begins with the first customer, obtaining the random number 12 from the first list provided earlier. This appears in column (1) and corresponds to a time between arrivals of 10 minutes, which is entered in column (2). Since there is no prior customer, these minutes are simply added to the shop's 9:00 opening time, providing 9:10 as the clock time at arrival for customer number 1. This time is entered in column (3) and also in column (4) for the clock time at beginning of service, since Sammy is free to serve that customer immediately on his arrival. The next random number, 61, is read from the second list and entered in column (5). This corresponds to the service time of 15 minutes, which is placed in column (6). Adding the values in columns (4) and (6) yields a clock time of 9:25 when service ends, which is entered in column (7). Because this customer is served immediately, there is no waiting time.

The second customer is assigned the random number 81 and arrives at 9:35, 25 minutes after the first. Sammy Lee has finished with the preceding customer at 9:25, so service begins immediately at 9:35 with no waiting. The next random number, 74, corresponds to a 20-minute service time, so customer 2 is finished at 9:55.

Meanwhile, the third customer arrives 15 minutes after the second, at 9:50. Sammy is busy with customer 2 until 9:55, so customer 3's service cannot begin until then and he must wait 5 minutes. In general, the clock time at beginning of service is the *greatest* of the entries in columns (3) and (7).

The simulation continues until 20 customers have been monitored. It is now possible for Samantha to estimate the various parameters. This procedure constitutes the remaining portion of the simulation model.

Summing the values in column (2) and dividing by the number of customers, we calculate the *estimated mean time between arrivals* to be

$$\frac{\text{Total time between arrivals}}{\text{Number of customers}} = \frac{345}{20} = 17.25 \text{ minutes per customer}$$

The reciprocal of this result, in units of customers per minute, is the *estimated mean arrival rate*, which is calculated

$$\frac{1}{\text{Mean time between arrivals}} = \frac{1}{17.25} = .058 \text{ customers per minute} \atop (3.48 \text{ customers per hour})$$

Summing the entries in column (6) and dividing by 20 customers, we calculate the *estimated mean service time* to be

$$\frac{\text{Total service time}}{\text{Number of customers}} = \frac{360}{20} = 18.00 \text{ minutes per customer}$$

And the reciprocal of this result provides the *estimated mean service rate* of

$$\frac{1}{\text{Mean service time}} = \frac{1}{18} = .056 \text{ customers per minute}$$
$$(3.36 \text{ customers per hour})$$

The true values of these parameters can be computed from the initial probability distributions, so that it is unnecessary to use these estimates. But some interesting points can be made by comparing the estimates to their true values (the expected values calculated in Table 25-5 using the initial probability distributions).

Notice that the true mean time between arrivals is 17.50 minutes per customer, which is quite close to the simulation result of 17.25. However, the true mean service time of 16.25 minutes per customer is considerably smaller than the simulated value of 18.00. We must keep in mind that a simulation is a sample result, and like any statistical estimate, it can be expected to contain sampling errors. In this particular simulation, the service times were longer than usual, reflecting the fact that abnormally large random numbers were used. This shouldn't detract from the value of the simulation, however, since the service times actually observed on any particular Saturday may also tend to be longer than usual.

As in any sampling situation, the only protection against sampling error is to increase the precision or the reliability of the simulation estimates by

TABLE 25-5
Expected Value Calculations to Determine True Parameter Values

Possible Times	Probability	Time × Probability
Between arrivals:		
5 min	.10	.50 min
10	.15	1.50
15	.25	3.75
20	.25	5.00
25	.15	3.75
30	.10	3.00
	$1/\lambda$ = mean time between arrivals =	17.50 min
For service:		
5 min	.05	.25 min
10	.20	2.00
15	.40	6.00
20	.20	4.00
25	.10	2.50
30	.05	1.50
	$1/\mu$ = mean service time =	16.25 min

conducting a sufficiently large number of trials. If 200 rather than 20 customers were evaluated, we would expect the estimated mean service time to be much closer to the true parameter value. Later we will consider the question of just how many trials ought to be used.

Samantha's other parameters must be estimated because they cannot be computed as easily as the simple expected values we just determined. Returning to Table 25-4, we divide the total of the column (8) values by the number of customers to determine the *estimated mean customer waiting time*, or

$$\frac{\text{Total waiting time}}{\text{Number of customers}} = \frac{250}{20} = 12.50 \text{ minutes}$$

Including the total of the column (6) service times in the numerator, we obtain the *estimated mean customer time spent in the system*:

$$\frac{\text{Total waiting time} + \text{Total service time}}{\text{Number of customers}} = \frac{250 + 360}{20}$$

$$= 30.50 \text{ minutes}$$

This calculation reflects that a customer's time in the barbershop must be spent waiting for and then receiving service. This result is therefore equivalent to the sum of the mean waiting and service times:

$$12.50 + 18.00 = 30.50$$

The remaining parameter estimates require some thought. Consider the problem of finding the average number of customers waiting at any given time. This could be accomplished by taking every five-minute time interval in the simulation and determining how many customers are waiting in each one. A relative frequency distribution indicating the proportion of times 0, 1, 2, 3, or 4 persons were waiting could then be found, and their weighted average would provide the desired result. Fortunately, all of this extra work is unnecessary. Instead, we divide the total waiting time in column (8) by the simulation's *elapsed time*, or its duration from start to finish (calculated in Table 25-4 to be 395 minutes) to obtain the *estimated mean number of customers waiting*:

$$\frac{\text{Total waiting time}}{\text{Elapsed time}} = \frac{250}{395} = .63 \text{ customers}$$

It may seem a bit odd that customers result when we divide minutes by minutes, but this computation is the mathematical equivalent of the weighted average approach. We may view total waiting time as the product of the times when customers wait and the number of customers waiting, so that the numerator is in units of customer-minutes.

Similarly, the totals for columns (6) and (8) can be added and divided by elapsed time to provide the *estimated mean number of customers in the system*:

$$\frac{\text{Total service time} + \text{Total waiting time}}{\text{Elapsed time}} = \frac{360 + 250}{395}$$

$$= 1.54 \text{ customers}$$

This represents the average number of customers either waiting or receiving service at any point in time.

To find the proportion of time the barber is busy with a customer, we divide the total from column (6) by the elapsed time to obtain the *estimated server utilization factor*:

$$\frac{\text{Total service time}}{\text{Elapsed time}} = \frac{360}{395} = .91$$

We can see that Sammy Lee spends about 91% of the time that the shop is in operation on Saturday actually cutting hair. Another interpretation of .91 is that it represents the fraction of a customer who may be receiving service at any point in time. By subtracting this value from the estimated mean number of customers in the barbershop, we obtain the estimated mean number of customers who are waiting, or

$$1.54 - .91 = .63$$

Transient Simulation States

You may have wondered why Samantha Lee stopped her simulation abruptly with the twentieth customer at 3:35, in the middle of a busy period that started about 2 P.M. Shouldn't she have continued her simulation until closing time?

All simulations must begin and end some time, and the number of trials is generally established in advance. In the barbershop example, this can lead to distortions near the beginning and the end of the simulation. Sammy Lee opened his shop at 9 A.M., and customers started trickling in at 9:10. No opening-time congestion, which might occur in reality, was possible. Also, no successful barber quits for the day when customers are still waiting. The middle of the simulation is the closest approximation of reality. Distortions encountered at the beginning and the end arise because the simulation is then in *transient states*. An analogy with the performance test on an automobile engine may be helpful. An engine exhibits different characteristics while warming up than it does when it has been running for a while. To realistically assess performance, only the results obtained after the engine has warmed up should be considered. Also, a slight sputtering or coughing the instant after the ignition switch is shut off should not be reflected in the performance rating.

The impact of transitional distortions can be minimized by conducting the simulation over a longer period of time. If Samantha uses 1,000 customers (so that 50 Saturdays are considered back-to-back), distortions at the beginning and the end can be safely ignored.

It is another matter entirely if the barbershop actually goes through transient states when it is in actual operation. This might happen if customers are lined up at the door when Sammy arrives or if he varies his closing time to accommodate stragglers. Also, arrivals may be more concentrated at 2 or 3 P.M. than at other times. And Sammy may slow down in the afternoon, thereby increasing the service times. The simulation model itself must be sufficiently complex to realistically reflect the varying characteristics of a system.

Decision Making with Simulation

Samantha Lee's simulation provides a variety of estimates for the key parameters that can be helpful in any further analysis. Remember that Sammy Lee's basic problem is deciding whether or not to hire a second barber to work on Saturdays. To evaluate this alternative, a second simulation must be performed that involves a somewhat more complex procedure (which is left as an exercise for the reader to determine). A similar set of estimated parameter values will be obtained in this later simulation and can then be compared with the initial ones.

The comparison of two or more simulations can be a demanding task, especially when several kinds of information are provided by each one. To a certain extent, such a comparison presents the same problems we encountered when we evaluated samples taken from several populations. The statistical aspects of simulation will be discussed in the next section.

THE STATISTICAL ASPECTS OF SIMULATION   25-3

A simulation is completely analogous to a sampling study. Consider the similarities between estimating the mean customer waiting time and estimating a city's mean disposable family income. Each simulation trial provides one randomly chosen waiting time, whereas a randomly selected family yields a sample observation of income. In either case, planning is involved in setting up the study and in deciding how many observations to make. Although the data are collected differently, the results are qualitatively equivalent. Whether we are reporting results or deciding what to do, we must acknowledge and contend with potential sampling error. Thus, conclusions in either situation are in the nature of *statistical inferences*.

Required Number of Trials

As indicated earlier, the number of simulation trials determines the precision and reliability of the resulting estimate. This number plays the same role as the sample size does in traditional statistics. In the planning stage of the simulation, the number of trials must be treated as a variable, which we denote by n. Samantha Lee used $n = 20$ in her simulation, but how large should n be in estimating mean waiting time? In determining the answer, we will assume that no simulation data are available.

To simplify our discussion and ease the transition from traditional statistics, we will adopt conventional notation. Each individual waiting time can be represented by an X with the appropriate subscript, so that X_1 represents customer 1's waiting time, X_2 represents customer 2's waiting time, and so on. The arithmetic mean of these X values is denoted by $\bar{X}$. The standard deviation for the population of all future Saturday waiting times is σ. The mean waiting time for the population is denoted by W_q (instead of μ, which represents the true mean service rate in standard queuing formulas). W_q is the quantity to be estimated. The expected value of $\bar{X}$ is W_q, and from the central limit theorem we know that $\bar{X}$ is approximately normally distributed with

$$\text{Mean} = W_q$$

$$\text{Standard deviation} = \frac{\sigma}{\sqrt{n}}$$

where σ is known in advance.

Of course, we don't know the value of σ. We must guess its value, and we use the subscript g to distinguish the guessed value of the standard deviation from its true value, so that

$$\sigma_g = \text{guessed value for standard deviation}$$

A rule of thumb for finding σ_g is that it should equal one-sixth the difference between the largest and smallest conceivable values:*

$$\sigma_g = \frac{\text{Largest value} - \text{Smallest value}}{6}$$

Suppose that Sammy Lee occasionally keeps a Saturday customer waiting up to 60 minutes, but never any longer. The smallest waiting time is obviously zero,

---

* If the individual waiting times were normally distributed, they would fall within $\pm 3\sigma$, or a range of 6σ, of the true mean about 99.7% of the time. Of course, some other distribution may apply, so the above procedure is not completely accurate.

so that

$$\sigma_g = \frac{60 - 0}{6} = 10 \text{ minutes}$$

Before finding n, it is necessary to establish target levels for precision and reliability. These are

d = target precision level (maximum deviation from the true value)

z = normal deviate for the target reliability level

It should be emphasized that both of these levels are essential, since precision and reliability are competing ends. An overly precise estimate, such as W_q = 2.343 min $\pm$ .0005, is almost totally unreliable. On the other hand, a very imprecise result, such as "W_q lies between 0 and 100 minutes," may be perfectly reliable—even if no simulation is conducted.

The target precision level d expresses the maximum deviation that can be tolerated between the estimate and its true value—either above or below it—in terms of the units involved (minutes, in the present example). The reliability expresses the probability that the target precision level will be met. Because such a probability is obtained from a normal curve centered at the true mean with standard deviation of $\sigma/\sqrt{n}$ (represented by $\sigma_g/\sqrt{n}$), for a specific d, z, and σ_g there is a unique n such that*

$$n = \frac{z^2 \sigma_g^2}{d^2}$$

Suppose that Samantha wishes to be precise to the nearest whole minute, so that $d = 1$, with a reliability of .95, so that the required normal deviate is $z = 1.96$. Plugging these values and $\sigma_g = 10$ into preceding equation, we find that her required sample size is

$$n = \frac{(1.96)^2 (10)^2}{(1)^2} = 384.16, \text{ or } 385$$

(Since n is always expressed in whole numbers, 384.16 is raised to 385.) By using only 20 customers, Samantha has *undersampled* and will not meet her target levels. Often, n values calculated in this manner are huge, so that hand simulations by necessity involve undersampling. (In computer simulations, the proper n can usually be applied at minimal cost.) Undersampling produces fuzzy results, which makes it difficult to compare the alternatives simulated.

---

* A complete explanation and deriviation of this equation is too lengthy to include here. See Lawrence L. Lapin, *Statistics for Modern Business Decisions*, 2nd ed. (New York: Harcourt Brace Jovanovich, 1978), pp. 261–66, for a complete discussion.

The Confidence Interval Estimate

An *interval estimate* is often used to report data from a simulation, just as it is used to report ordinary sample data. When estimating a mean, two values are used to construct such an interval—the sample mean $\bar{X}$ and the *sample standard deviation*

$$s = \sqrt{\frac{\sum (X - \bar{X})^2}{n - 1}}$$

The latter statistic can be calculated from simulation data and serves as the estimator of the unknown value of σ. The n used here—and in any other statistical calculation involving data—must be the *actual* number of trials. In the barbershop simulation, $n = 20$ (not the desired level of 385 found earlier).

Ordinarily, some *confidence level*, such as 95% or 99%, is used to report the results. A normal deviate value z, such as 1.96 or 2.57, corresponds to the level chosen. For the large samples generally used in simulations, the following expression determines the *confidence interval estimate*:

$$\text{True mean} = \bar{X} \pm z \frac{s}{\sqrt{n}}$$

Before computing the confidence interval for the mean customer waiting time, the sample standard deviation must be found. This is calculated in Table 25-6 to be $s = 12.7$ minutes. Samantha desires a 95% confidence level, so that $z = 1.96$. Plugging these values, along with $\bar{X} = 12.50$ and $n = 20$, into this equation we determine the confidence interval for the mean customer waiting time:

$$W_q = 12.50 \pm (1.96) \frac{12.7}{\sqrt{20}}$$

$$= 12.50 \pm 5.57 \text{ minutes}$$

or

$$6.93 \le W_q \le 18.07 \text{ minutes}$$

The proper interpretation of this result is: *If the 20 customer simulation were repeated over and over again, using different random numbers each time, then an interval constructed in this manner would contain the true mean waiting time in about 95 out of every 100 cases, but about 5 of such intervals would lie totally above or below the true value.*

Notice that this confidence interval is quite wide, reflecting the lack of precision due to undersampling.

TABLE 25-6

Calculations for the Sample Standard Deviation of Customer Waiting Times

Customer i	Waiting Time X_i	Deviation $(X_i - \bar{X})$	$(X_i - \bar{X})^2$
1	0	−12.50	156.25
2	0	−12.50	156.25
3	5	−7.50	56.25
4	10	−2.50	6.25
5	15	2.50	6.25
6	5	−7.50	56.25
7	0	−12.50	156.25
8	0	−12.50	156.25
9	5	−7.50	56.25
10	0	−12.50	156.25
11	20	7.50	56.25
12	15	2.50	6.25
13	5	−7.50	56.25
14	0	−12.50	156.25
15	20	7.50	56.25
16	35	22.50	506.25
17	25	12.50	156.25
18	35	22.50	506.25
19	30	17.50	306.25
20	25	17.50	306.25
	250	0.00	3,075.00

$$\bar{X} = \sum X/n = 250/20 = 12.50 \text{ min}$$
$$s = \sqrt{3{,}075.00/(20 - 1)} = \sqrt{161.84} = 12.7 \text{ min}$$

Further Statistical Considerations

We have barely scratched the statistical surface of simulation. Many other kinds of inferences can be made. For instance, Samantha Lee may want to compare the W values for one-man and two-man barbershops, which would bring another set of sample data into the picture. Various hypothesis testing procedures can be employed for this purpose. If several alternatives are to be simulated, an analysis of variance might be conducted. A detailed discussion of these procedures is beyond the scope of this book, but many good statistical references are provided in the bibliography at the back of the book.

However, there are further complications. Samantha wants to estimate nine parameters, and an elaborate report might consider inferences about them as well. Usually a simulation estimates only one parameter.

In some simulations, a probability or a proportion is estimated instead of a mean. For example, the optimal number of telephone information operators might be the smallest sized crew that provides a .95 probability of rendering service within 10 seconds. In simulating various alternatives, the true probability for a particular crew size could be estimated by the proportion of calls (trials) receiving service within 10 seconds. Although there is not enough space to describe them in this book, equivalent expressions can be used to find n and to compute confidence intervals for such quantities.

25-4 SIMULATION AND PERT

In our discussion of PERT (Program Evaluation and Review Technique) in Chapter 24, we saw that much of the analysis ignores the uncertainties about activity times. Using only expected times, we can provide the project manager with a time–cost trade-off curve for deciding which activities, if any, should be crashed. Unfortunately, the project completion times obtained in this manner can seriously understate the true expected project completion times.

Consider the PERT network in Figure 25-4, which illustrates a project with five activities. Each activity is represented by an arrow, and the regular activity completion times appear on the respective arrows. The times in boldface for activities b and d are *certain* and cannot vary; the times for activities a, c, and e are *expected* times. Traditional PERT analysis is based on the *critical path*, which is the longest duration activity sequence from start to finish. Given the times in this network, all paths (a-d, a-c-e, and b-e) are critical, and each path is expected to take 20 days.

The continuous probability distributions for the three expected activity completion times are represented in Figure 25-5 by cumulative probability graphs. The project will be simulated using random numbers to determine the times that will be obtained in each trial.

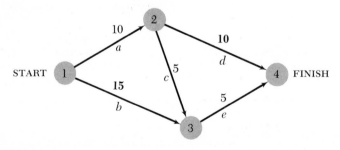

FIGURE 25-4
A PERT network illustrating a project with five activities.

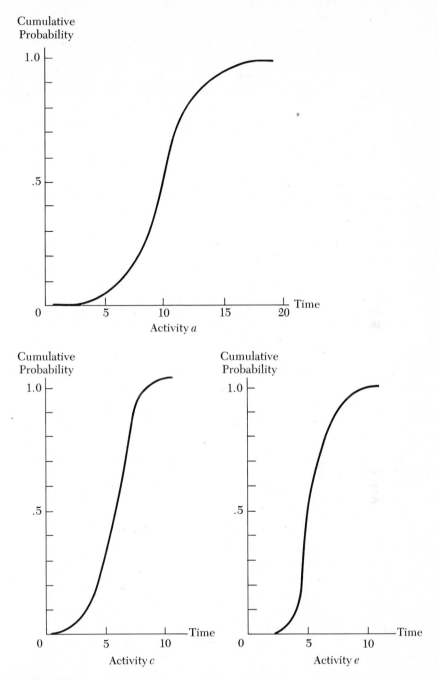

FIGURE 25-5
Cumulative probability distributions for PERT expected activity completion times.

Using Random Numbers with Continuous Distributions

When a cumulative probability graph has been constructed for a continuous random variable (see Chapter 21 to find out how this is done), the graph itself may be used to determine which quantities correspond to the random numbers. As we saw in the barbershop simulation, random numbers can be assigned to trial variable values by establishing the *range* for the random numbers. The upper limit of that range is identical to the cumulative probability for the value, except for the decimal point. When the variable is continuous, cumulative probability serves the same purpose, except that only single quantities—not ranges—are involved. Because fractional activity times are possible, it is convenient to use all of the digits in each random number.

Figure 25-6 illustrates the procedure for generating completion times for activity *a*. Consider 12651 as the first random number; this corresponds to a cumulative probability of .12651, representing a height on the graph slightly below .13. From the curve, we can see that the time corresponding to this cumulative probability is roughly 6.8 days. Similarly, we may locate the cumulative probability corresponding to a second random number, 81769. The curve at that height represents a time of approximately 12.3 days. Since any random number between 00000 and 99999 is equally likely, each possible height on the curve is just as likely in each trial. Notice that the steepest portion of the curve occurs around 10 days, indicating that more possible random numbers will yield times falling near 10 than any other time. The curve is flatter near 5 days, so that fewer random numbers will lead to times near that level. The graphical procedure therefore generates times more frequently for the more typical levels and less frequently for the rarer levels. For a large number of trials, the frequencies can be expected to match the underlying probabilities exactly, which is just what a simulation is supposed to do.

The Simulation

The results of $n = 20$ trials for the PERT simulation are provided in the worksheet shown in Table 25-7. Each trial involved reading three random numbers onto the respective cumulative probability graphs for activities *a*, *c*, and *e* to determine the corresponding activity completion times. The path with the longest total time through the network was then determined, and the duration of that critical path established the project completion time for the particular trial.

The simulation provides some interesting results. Notice that the simulated mean project completion time of 21.96 days is almost two days *longer* than

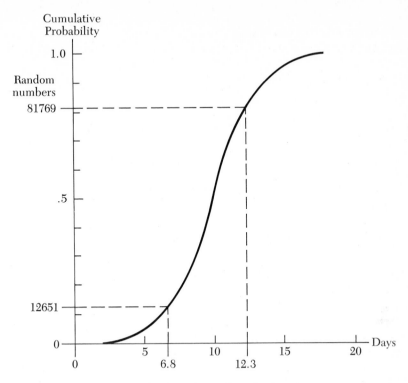

Regular Completion Time for Activity *a*

FIGURE 25-6
Using a cumulative probability curve to assign random numbers to quantities.

the 20-day completion time indicated using expected values alone. Since only 20 trials were used, we must rely on statistical analysis to tell us whether this difference is significant or the natural result of sampling error. However, studies have established that similar results are generally the case in PERT simulations with a larger number of trials. Also notice that if the mean simulation times for the various activities are considered, all three paths based on these averages are shorter than 21.96 days. This illustrates the tendency of traditional PERT procedures, which are based on average times and individual paths, to under-state the mean completion time for the project as a whole. One explanation for is that no particular path can really be considered singly, for there is some probability that any one of several paths will actually be the longest. Notice that all three paths turned out to be critical in at least one trial and that in no trial was there more than one critical path.

TABLE 25-7
Worksheet and Results for PERT Simulation

| | ACTIVITY TIMES (days) | | | | | | | | |
| | a | | b | c | | d | e | | Longest | |
Trial	Random Number	Time	Time	Random Number	Time	Time	Random Number	Time	(Critical) Path	Project Duration
1	(12651)	6.8	15	(61646)	6.3	10	(11769)	4.2	b-e	19.2
2	(81769)	12.3	15	(74436)	6.8	10	(02630)	2.7	a-d	22.3
3	(36737)	9.4	15	(98863)	8.5	10	(77240)	6.2	a-c-e	24.1
4	(82861)	12.6	15	(54371)	6.2	10	(76610)	6.2	a-c-e	25.0
5	(21325)	7.8	15	(15732)	4.0	10	(24127)	4.6	b-e	19.6
6	(74146)	11.3	15	(47887)	6.0	10	(62463)	5.4	a-c-e	22.7
7	(90759)	13.9	15	(64410)	6.5	10	(54179)	5.1	a-c-e	25.5
8	(55683)	10.2	15	(98078)	8.3	10	(02238)	2.7	a-c-e	21.2
9	(79686)	12.0	15	(17969)	4.2	10	(76061)	6.2	a-c-e	22.4
10	(70333)	11.0	15	(00201)	.5	10	(86201)	6.9	b-e	21.9
11	(14042)	7.0	15	(53536)	6.1	10	(07779)	3.8	b-e	18.8
12	(59911)	10.3	15	(08256)	3.1	10	(06596)	3.6	a-d	20.3
13	(62368)	10.4	15	(62623)	6.4	10	(62742)	6.0	a-c-e	22.8
14	(57529)	10.2	15	(97751)	8.2	10	(54976)	5.4	a-c-e	23.8
15	(15469)	7.1	15	(90574)	7.5	10	(78033)	6.3	b-e	21.3
16	(18625)	7.6	15	(23674)	4.6	10	(53850)	5.1	b-e	20.1
17	(74626)	11.3	15	(68394)	6.7	10	(88562)	7.2	a-c-e	25.2
18	(11119)	6.4	15	(16519)	4.1	10	(27384)	4.7	b-e	19.7
19	(41101)	9.6	15	(17336)	4.2	10	(48951)	4.9	b-e	19.9
20	(32123)	9.0	15	(91576)	7.6	10	(84221)	6.7	a-c-e	23.3
Totals		196.2	300		115.8	200		103.9		439.1
Averages		9.81	15		5.79	10		5.20		21.96

25-5 SIMULATING INVENTORY POLICIES

Simulation can be also used to evaluate alternative inventory policies. Figure 25-7 shows the log a retailer might use to record the actual operations of an inventory system for a single product. From this log format, a more detailed simulation worksheet might be developed to simulate various inventory policies, such as "order 500 items whenever any day starts with less than 60 units."

Daily demand is one random variable for which a probability distribution must be obtained. Some probability distribution would apply to the number of days until an order arrives, and another uncertainty might be reflected in the lead time it takes to receive the order. The values of both variables would apply

Day	Starting Inven- tory	Items Re- ceived	Items Demand- ed	Items Sold	Items Back- ordered	Items Ordered	Days for Order to Arrive	Holding and Shortage Costs	Order- ing Cost
6/7	150	0	100	100	0	0	—	$1.50	—
6/8	50	0	75	50	25	500	2	3.00	$5.00
6/9	0	0	85	0	85	0	—	8.50	—
6/10	0	500	55	55	0	0	—	0.00	—
6/11	335	0	60	60	0	0	—	3.35	—

FIGURE 25-7
Hypothetical log for the actual daily operation of an inventory system.

to the number of days until an order arrives and would be generated with random numbers.

The log picture in Figure 25-7 indicates that all items demanded will be sold unless the inventory is depleted, in which case short items will be back-ordered and supplied when the next shipment arrives. Inventory holding costs are presumed to be $.01 per item held at the start of each day, which represents a daily proration of annual holding costs (usually expressed as a monetary amount per dollar value). A straight penalty of $.10 is assumed to apply for each item short, and the ordering cost is $5.00, regardless of how many items are ordered.

The same approach may be taken for more elaborate problems that involve several products, each having different demand and lead-time distributions. These products may compete for space and working capital, and their costs will differ. Some items may receive quantity discounts from the supplier. Shortage penalties may be more elaborate and may include an additional cost for each day the shortage lasts.

SIMULATION VERSUS THE ANALYTIC SOLUTION 25-6

Whenever possible, management scientists use simulation as a last resort. An analytic solution is preferable if it is valid and can be obtained with less work. One reason is that simulation involves a great deal of effort and expense, even when it is performed with the assistance of a computer. A separate simulation is required for each alternative, and hundreds or thousands of these might have to be performed. And after the simulations are finished, only statistical estimates—not true values—are available. It is not surprising that an algebraic expression providing the exact answer would be more desirable.

Simulation should be viewed in its proper perspective and used sparingly. But no one has categorized the situations in which it should and should not be used. We must never force a problem to fit a particular analytic solution simply to avoid the tedium of simulation, unless the assumptions underlying the model closely fit the problem. We can illustrate the pitfalls of doing this by considering the barbershop example once again.

In Chapter 23, we saw that various formulas can be used to obtain the parameters of a single-channel queue. These formulas depend only on the mean arrival rate λ and the mean service rate μ. In the case of Sammy Lee's barbershop, the reciprocals of these values were computed earlier from the probability data:

$$1/\lambda = 17.50 \text{ minutes per customer}$$

$$1/\mu = 16.25 \text{ minutes per customer}$$

Thus

$$\lambda = 1/17.50 = .057 \text{ customers per minute}$$

$$\mu = 1/16.25 = .062 \text{ customers per minute}$$

Plugging these values into the formula for the mean customer waiting time gives us

$$W_q = \frac{\lambda}{\mu(\mu - \lambda)} = \frac{.057}{.062(.062 - .057)} = 184 \text{ minutes}$$

which is more than ten times the value obtained in the simulation. Another queuing formula tells us that the mean arrival rate multiplied by W_q equals the mean number of customers waiting. Thus

$$L_q = \lambda W_q = .057(184) = 10.5 \text{ customers}$$

which disagrees with the simulation results by the same factor.

Why are these discrepancies so great? The explanation is that the operation of Sammy Lee's barbershop does not agree with an underlying assumption of the queuing model—the often overlooked assumption that the arrival and service times must be *exponentially distributed*. The probability distributions used in the simulation do not even resemble the exponential distribution, which indicates that a time of zero is the most likely to occur.

The barbershop example was purposely picked to dramatize what can happen if an appropriate analytic solution procedure is blindly followed. Not all procedures work so poorly—even when their assumptions are not met exactly. The EOQ (Economic Order Quantity) formulas used to design inventory policies are generally very successful in finding answers that are close to optimal in such cases. They are said to be *robust* with regard to a variety of violations in the underlying assumptions. It may not be worth the extra work to simulate inventory policies when a very good answer can be found much more simply by working a 30-second calculation.

In the quest for analytic solutions, the model itself can so distort reality that the mathematically developed conclusions are not valid and can even be misleading. This happened with PERT. Appendix 24-1 describes in detail a popular procedure for obtaining the probability distribution for the duration of that particular path identified as the "critical" one. The label "critical path" is something of a misnomer, since expected (average) activity completion times are traditionally used to identify this activity sequence. Earlier in this chapter, we saw why such an analysis based on average times understates the true mean *project* completion time.

The traditional PERT model provides a probability analysis for a variable nobody really cares about—namely, the length of a particular path that may or may not turn out to be the longest one. Project managers are more appropriately concerned with the time it will take to finish the entire project, which is a totally different variable. Analytic procedures cannot provide a probability analysis of this variable, except in very small networks. In conjunction with the PERT network, simulation is the more viable procedure to use to determine the characteristics of project completion times.

SIMULATION AND THE COMPUTER 25-7

Monte Carlo simulation involves many repetitions of the same computational steps, which makes the digital computer an ideal tool for applying simulation. Once the computer program has been written, each alternative can be simulated and thousands of trials can be conducted at a relatively modest cost. Indeed, perhaps no other management science technique has been nurtured so dramatically by the advent of bigger and faster computers.

Simulation Programs and Languages

Simulation has become so integrated with the computer that special computer languages (similar to BASIC, COBOL, and FORTRAN) have been written just to perform simulations. One of these languages is SIMSCRIPT, which is based on FORTRAN. Instructions may be written in this language without a detailed knowledge of computers. A special program, called a *compiler*, then converts the SIMSCRIPT instructions into machine language. (Compilers exist for a variety of computers.)

Another popular simulation procedure applies the General Purpose System Simulator (GPSS), which is really a program developed by IBM for its computers. Versions are also available for use on computers from other manufacturers. GPSS is more efficient in some respects than SIMSCRIPT, but inferior in others. In choosing a simulation language, the overriding consideration is the system that happens to be available.

If no special simulation software is accessible, it is still possible to use ordinary programming languages, such as FORTRAN, to conduct a computer simulation. All the major languages are supplied with library routines that are useful in computer simulation. These routines are especially important in generating random numbers.

Random-Number Generation

It would be terribly impractical to prepare random numbers ahead of time and feed them into the computer during a simulation. This would not only slow down the processing, but it might consume too much core memory. Besides, consider the awful job of compiling and keypunching these numbers and the fact that computer simulations can involve billions of random numbers—far too many to be taken from published lists.

The random numbers in a computer simulation are invariably generated by the computer itself as they are needed. This is usually done by providing a seed number, which is multiplied by one constant and divided by another value; the remainder term is then used as the random number. The next number is always found in this way from the last number. Of course, all such numbers can be predicted in advance, so that they are not really random at all.

Values generated in this way are called *pseudo-random numbers*. They can be used in simulations because *they look like true random numbers*. The generation of pseudo-random numbers yields a stream of numbers that exhibit all essential properties—nearly equal frequencies for all possible values, little serial correlation, and no abnormally long or short runs of any particular type of number.

The Disadvantages of Computer Simulation

Computer simulation does have some disadvantages. Paramount among these is the programming effort. Unless statistical reliability is very critical or a large number of alternatives must be considered, it is often easier in the long run to "crank it out by hand." The inherent characteristics of the digital computer can create a lot of extra work. For example, computers don't read graphs, necessitating the approximation of continuous probability distributions by constructing a table of typical values and their associated probabilities. Also, some computer models are pictorial in nature (similar to a PERT network), and it is especially demanding to write a special program that duplicates the human capacity to make visual inspections.

PROBLEMS

25-1 Consider the following probability distribution for the times between arrivals of cars stopping at a toll booth:

Time	Probability
5 sec	.35
10	.23
15	.15
20	.11
25	.08
30	.05
35	.03

(a) Construct the cumulative probability distribution and determine a random-number assignment suitable for simulation. (Use the first two digits of the random numbers.)

(b) Simulate the arrival of 20 cars and calculate the estimated mean time between arrivals.

25-2 For the probability distribution in Problem 25-1, perform the expected value calculation to find the true mean time between arrivals.

25-3 As part of a simulation to determine advertising response, you must create trial persons who fall into one of the following categories:

Category	Probability
Urban	.36
Suburban	.47
Rural	.17

Prepare a two-digit random-number assignment to generate these events.

25-4 Consider the cumulative probability for demand provided in Figure 21-8 on page 525. Use the following random numbers to generate 20 demands:

99582	53390	46357	13244
18080	02321	05809	04898
30143	52687	19420	60061
46683	33761	47452	23551
48672	28736	84994	13071

What is the estimated mean demand?

25-5 A staff analyst for Big-E Corp. has developed a simulation model to estimate the mean annual rate of return for new projects. Separate simulations, each consisting of several investment lifetime trials, will be conducted for the various alternatives. The analyst wishes to determine how many trials to create for a particular case if the lifetime annual rate of return may fall between -20% and 40%. How many trials are required to estimate the mean rate of return to the nearest 1% when a reliability of 95% is desired?

25-6 The mean time required by automobile assemblers to hang a car door is to be estimated. Assuming that the guessed value of the standard deviation is 10 seconds, determine the required n under the following conditions:
(a) The desired reliability probability for being in error by no more than 1 second (in either direction) is .99.
(b) The desired reliability probability for being in error by no more, than 1 second is .95.
(c) A reliability of .99 is desired, with a target precision of 2 seconds. How does the n you obtain here compare with your answer to (a)?

25-7 Construct a 95% confidence interval for the true means, given the following simulation results:
(a) $n = 100$; $\bar{X} = 100.53$ min; $s = 25.3$ min.
(b) $n = 200$; $\bar{X} = 69.2$ in.; $s = 1.08$ in.
(c) $n = 350$; $\bar{X} = \$12.00$; $s = \$7.00$

25-8 Construct a 95% confidence interval estimate for the mean project completion time using the simulation results given in Table 25-7 (page 660) for the PERT illustration in the chapter.

25-9 Consider the alternative of adding a second barber to Sammy Lee's shop on Saturdays. This will attract more clients, so that customers will arrive closer together. Suppose that the following probabilities apply:

Time Between Arrivals	Probability
5 min	.35
10	.25
15	.20
20	.10
25	.10

Also suppose that the second barber has the same service time distribution as Sammy.

(a) Set up a worksheet for simulating the two-man barbershop. (*Hint:* Only one random number is needed for each customer's service time.)

(b) Assuming that a customer will pick Sammy if both barbers are free and the first free barber otherwise, conduct a 20-customer simulation with the random numbers used in Table 25-4 (page 646).

(c) Find the estimated mean customer waiting time.

25-10 Considering Sammy's barbershop again, suppose that enough simulations were conducted to determine the true mean waiting times of

$$W_q = 15 \text{ minutes for one barber}$$

$$W_q = 5 \text{ minutes for two barbers}$$

Also suppose that Sammy suffers a loss of goodwill of $.05 for each minute that *each* customer spends waiting. The shop is open for 8 hours on Saturdays. Each customer brings in an average revenue of $4.00, and the second barber costs Sammy $5.00 per hour.

Using the probability data in the chapter and in Problem 25-9, compute Sammy's average Saturday earnings for one barber and for two barbers. What should Sammy do?

25-11 Suppose that the retailer in Section 25-5 experiences a daily demand for items according to the following probability distribution:

Demand	Probability
40	.04
50	.08
60	.15
70	.23
80	.20
90	.15
100	.10
110	.05

and that the lead time distribution for filling an order is

Lead Time	Probability
1 day	.20
2	.25
3	.20
4	.15
5	.10
6	.10

(a) Simulate 25 days of operation to estimate the mean daily inventory cost, given an order quantity of 500, if an order is placed whenever a day's starting inventory falls below 60 items and the starting inventory is 150 items.

(b) Repeat your simulation given an order quantity of 1,000 and an order point of 100. Use the same random numbers you did in (a).

(c) Which of the two inventory policies appears to be less costly?

25-12 Although it is not an accepted practice, you can generate your own random numbers in a pinch by tossing a coin. For instance, a list of two-digit decimal numbers can be obtained by generating a list of seven-digit binary numbers from seven tosses of a coin. This is done by assigning a 0 to a tail and a 1 to a head and then converting the results of every seven tosses to a decimal number. For example, the sequence HTHHTTH yields the binary number 1011001. In decimals, this number can be expressed as the sum

$$
\begin{array}{rcl}
1 \times 2^6 &=& 64 \\
0 \times 2^5 &=& 0 \\
1 \times 2^4 &=& 16 \\
1 \times 2^3 &=& 8 \\
0 \times 2^2 &=& 0 \\
0 \times 2^1 &=& 0 \\
1 \times 2^0 &=& \underline{1} \\
& & 89
\end{array}
$$

Any decimal values greater than 99 can be thrown away. Generate a list of ten two-digit random decimal numbers this way.

25-13 The dice game of "Craps" provides an interesting example of when not to simulate. The outcome is based on the values achieved from tossing two six-sided dice. One way to place a bet is to "play the field." Here, the bettor indicates that he or she wishes to make a bet with a complicated payoff, depending on which faces of the dice show. If a "field" number (defined by a sum value of 2 through 4 or 9 through 12) occurs, the player wins. If the roll of the dice yields any other total, the player loses. A field gamble is further complicated by varying payoffs: 1 to 1 for all field numbers except 2 or 12, 2 to 1 on a 2, and 3 to 1 on a 12. Winning bettors keep their original bet and are also paid their winnings. Losing players forfeit their wagers.

(a) For a bet of $1, use this information and the basic concepts of probability to find the probability distribution for a gambler's net winnings.

(b) Suppose that a system player has an initial bankroll of $7. Beginning with a $1 bet, this player's strategy is to place successive field bets until winning once or losing the original $7. Either of these outcomes terminates the play. As long as money remains, the gambler will double the last wager lost.

Simulate 10 runs of this system to estimate the gambler's mean winnings per play. (To simplify things, you may roll dice rather than use random numbers.)

(c) Solve the problem in (b) analytically by determining the appropriate probability values and finding the gambler's expected winnings. Then compare this to the simulated value you found in (b). (*Hint:* A tree diagram might be helpful.)

25-14 A company's computer microwave transmission network, which connects five cities, is provided in Figure 25-8. Each line represents a channel, and transmissions between

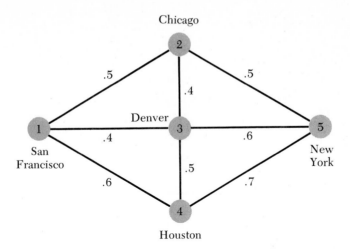

FIGURE 25-8

two cities may be routed over any sequence of clear channels. The number above
each line represents the probability for interference on that channel at any given
moment. Management is contemplating adding more channels and wants to
estimate the probability that San Francisco and New York communications will
be completely blocked by interference at any given time.

Estimate this probability by simulating this system for 20 trials. (*Hint:* You
may want to make 20 copies of the network before starting, so that the blocked
channels for each trial can be clearly identified.)

26

Dynamic Programming

Often decision making involves several choices that must be made at different times. For example, in automobile production planning, monthly decisions may be made regarding how many cars of various models should be produced in each assembly plant. Successful planning requires that enough cars be available to satisfy the highly seasonal and varying monthly demands, that this be achieved at a minimum cost, and that very few cars remain unsold at the start of the new model year. In meeting monthly demands while minimizing total annual production costs, more units will be produced in certain months than in others. But there should not be much variation in month-to-month production, since this might necessitate excessive overtime costs in some periods and inefficient use of labor in others.

We may view each month's production level as a separate decision. Each earlier choice, however, affects the freedom of choice in later months. And the annual profit or cost is determined collectively from the individual monthly decisions.

A variety of similar situations involving sequential decision making can be evaluated by *dynamic programming*—a quantitative method that is similar in scope to linear programming. The goal of both procedures is the efficient allocation of resources. Thus, either programming approach is designed to determine the variable values that minimize cost, maximize profit, or optimize any one of a variety of other kinds of payoffs. Dynamic programming differs from the other allocation models described in this book in that it considers decision making *over time*. We use the word *dynamic* because *time* is explicitly incorporated into the model.

This does not mean that decision making over time can only be evaluated by a dynamic programming model. In Chapter 15, we saw how the transportation method of linear programming can be used to establish several successive monthly production levels. But in automobile production planning, linear programming would simultaneously consider all 12 monthly production levels. Dynamic programming simplifies matters considerably, since it allows us to view each month *separately*. Unlike linear programming, dynamic programming may consider a variety of relationships between variables—including nonlinear ones.

The main advantage of dynamic programming is its *computational efficiency*. Suppose that we are faced with a situation involving a sequence of 4 decisions, each having 10 alternatives. Evaluating such a problem by a trial-and-error method would be an onerous chore, since $10^4 = 10,000$ possible choices would have to be considered in order to locate the optimal decision. Using dynamic programming, we can reduce the number of evaluations to $4 \times 10 = 40$. The savings in effort realized by using dynamic programming rather than complete enumeration can be extremely great when decision problems have many decision points.

A classic explanation of dynamic programming concepts is provided by the *stagecoach problem*.*

26-1 BASIC CONCEPTS: THE STAGECOACH PROBLEM

Following the advice of Horace Greeley to "go West, young man," Tom Wysaker is selecting a stagecoach route from New York to San Francisco. His possible choices are shown in Figure 26-1. Each westward leg of Tom's journey begins with a decision to take a particular stagecoach line (represented by an arrow). Successive decision points are therefore called *stages*. Regardless of the overall route chosen, a total of five stages are involved in the trip to California. Each stagecoach line begins in one state (or territory) and ends in another. Thus, each successive decision-point square represents a beginning *state* for the subsequent journey leg. Picking a stagecoach line in one state is tantamount to choosing the state from which the next stagecoach will depart. The stagecoach problem highlights the essential features of any dynamic programming problem. Each successive decision point is a stage, which is usually numbered 1, 2, 3, . . . ,

---

* This problem was originally described by Harvey M. Wagner. Our example differs in many ways from the version in his book, *Principles of Operations Research*, 2nd ed. (Englewood Cliffs, N.J.: Prentice-Hall, 1975).

STAGE 5   STAGE 4   STAGE 3   STAGE 2   STAGE 1

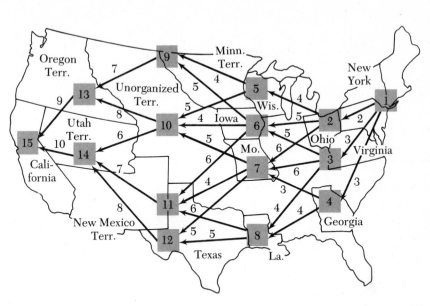

FIGURE 26-1
A routing network for the stagecoach problem.

for convenience. All stages begin in some kind of state, which instead of a place could be a set of circumstances, a number, or a collection of quantities. The state at any stage is determined by only two factors: the preceding state and the decision made at the prior state.

The Best Policy: The Principle of Optimality

A nineteenth-century stagecoach trip across North America is fraught with hazards ranging from Indians and robbers to floods, forest fires, and buffalo stampedes. Tom Wysaker's overriding goal is therefore to get to San Francisco in one piece. Since he is no expert in evaluating risks, Tom relies on life-insurance companies for help. They have provided rates for $10,000 of coverage for one trip on the various stagecoaches; these charges are indicated along the arrows in Figure 26-1. Assuming that the probability of being killed is directly proportional to the total premium charge, Tom wants to pick the route (the 5-stagecoach sequence) with the minimum life-insurance policy costs.

In a multistage decision problem analyzed by dynamic programming, a particular sequence of alternatives is called a *policy*. The optimal policy is the sequence of alternatives that achieves the decision maker's goal.

The fundamental precept of dynamic programming is the *principle of optimality*, which tells us that

The optimal policy must be one such that, regardless of how a particular state is reached, all later choices proceeding from that state must be optimal.

As we will see, the principle of optimality allows us to find the best policy by evaluating one stage at a time. Thus, dynamic programming procedures start with the *last* stage and work from stage to stage *backward* in time.

Mathematical Formulation of the Problem

In his final stage, Tom Wysaker will be in one of the two states, 13 or 14, preceding his destination. In either case, he has a single choice—to take the final stagecoach to San Francisco, which will bring him to state 15. His policy cost includes a charge of $9 if Tom ends his journey on stage 5 from state 13 and a cost of $10 if he ends his journey from state 14.

It is convenient to express mathematically the cost of or the payoff for the optimal policy of going from one stage to the end. This representation is provided by the *cost function*

$f_n(s)$ = cost, entering from state s, of using an optimal policy from stage n to the end

Since Tom Wysaker's last leg is stage 5, the following values of the cost function apply at that stage:

$$f_5(13) = \$ 9 \quad \text{(to state 15)}$$

$$f_5(14) = \$10 \quad \text{(to state 15)}$$

In applications with another objective, such as maximizing profit or optimizing some other payoff measure, $f_n(s)$ is the profit or the payoff function.

The objective of any dynamic program is to find the value of the cost function for the initial state at stage 1 and the corresponding optimal choices. To achieve this for the stagecoach problem, further notation is required. We represent the cost of taking a particular stagecoach line that connects two states by

$$c_{sj} = \text{cost of going from state } s \text{ to state } j$$

The cost at stage n of the optimal policy from any given state to the end is therefore

$$f_n(s) = \text{minimum} \left[c_{sj} + f_{n+1}(j) \right]$$

Notice that the cost function for an earlier stage is evaluated using the values from the succeeding stage, since the procedure works backward in time. This expression is called a *recursive relationship*. It provides the optimal choice at stage n for the given optimal policy at stage $n + 1$ and applies to every stage except the last one, for which the starting values are generally available directly.

In the stage coach problem, all possible values of $f_n(s)$ are found for successively smaller stages n, beginning with the f_5 values. The recursive relationship is last applied to determine $f_1(1)$. The minimum cost of the optimal policy is equal to $f_1(1)$. The optimal policy is identified by tracing back through the steps taken to determine the corresponding sequence of states. (Several policies might be optimal due to ties.)

Solving the Problem

We begin solving the problem in the final stage, using the values $f_5(13) = \$9$ and $f_5(14) = \$10$, and move backward to stage $n = 4$. Suppose that stage 4 begins in state 9; a stagecoach leaving from there only goes to state 13, where the insurance cost (from Figure 26-1) is $c_{9,13} = \$7$. Thus

$$f_4(9) = c_{9,13} + f_5(13)$$

$$= \$7 + \$9 = \$16 \quad \text{(to state 13)}$$

Stage 4 may also begin in state 10. Since this state is connected to two states, 13 and 14, we must evaluate two sums:

$$c_{10,13} + f_5(13) = \$8 + \$\ 9 = \$17 \quad \text{(to state 13)}$$

$$c_{10,14} + f_5(14) = \$6 + \$10 = \$16 \quad \text{(to state 14)}$$

The cost function for departing from state 10 is the smaller of these sums:

$$f_4(10) = \text{minimum } (\$17, \$16) = \$16 \quad \text{(to state 14)}$$

We can see that if stage 4 starts in state 10, it will be cheaper to go from there to state 14 rather than to state 13. Regardless of how state 10 is reached, it will always be better to go from there to state 14. This doesn't mean that Tom Wysaker must ever enter state 10. But if his optimal policy brings him there, then that same policy must lead him to state 14—not to state 13. This illustrates the principle of optimality. Since we are evaluating the problem backward, we cannot know the state that it will ultimately be best to start from at stage 4 until we are finished. It might be state 9, 10, 11, or 12. But we can determine the best course of action for each of these possibilities. Only when all the stages have been evaluated can the pieces be put together to form the final picture. To achieve the answer, it is necessary to save enough information to use in future evaluations of the earlier stages.

Two types of data must be stored. Since the recursive relationship determines the levels of $f_n(s)$, the values of this function must somehow be recorded so that they can be used in the evaluation of the next stage. It is also important

TABLE 26-1

Stagecoach Problem Evaluation of Stage 4

STAGE 4

Possible Choices

j	$c_{sj} + f_5(j)$			
s	13	14	Minimum $= f_4(s)$	Optimal Decision
Entering State — 9	$16	—	$16	to state 13
10	17	$16	16	to state 14
11	—	17	17	to state 14
12	—	18	18	to state 14

at any stage to note the corresponding optimal decisions, so that the complete optimal policy can be identified once the procedure is finished. Usually, this can all be accomplished by constructing a table for each of the earlier stages. The cost function for each possible entering state for stage 4 is computed and recorded for later use in Table 26-1. The final column indicates the optimal decision for each starting state.

Our evaluation of stage 4 is completed by considering the other two possible starting states, which have minimum costs to the journey's end of

$$f_4(11) = \$7 + \$10 = \$17 \quad \text{(to state 14)}$$

$$f_4(12) = \$8 + \$10 = \$18 \quad \text{(to state 14)}$$

The evaluations of stages 3, 2, and 1 are similar. The results are provided in Table 26-2.

We can see that stage 1 involves a minimum cost of $26 if Tom Wysaker's first choice is the optimal one of proceeding to state 2 on his first stagecoach trip. By following the optimal policy, the first leg of Tom's journey will take him from state 1 to state 2, where he will catch the second stagecoach. The evaluation of stage 2 indicates that Tom's optimal decision on leaving state 2 is to go to state 5. Taking the stagecoach on that line will bring Tom to the third leg of his trip. The evaluation of stage 3 indicates that Tom will minimize his overall life-insurance cost by proceeding from state 5 to state 9. Table 26-1 indicates that stage 4 proceeds from there to state 13 at the minimum cost for the remainder of the journey. The fifth stagecoach can then be taken from state 13 to Tom's final destination, state 15 (California).

This optimal policy is expressed by the sequence of states 1-2-5-9-13. It is easy to verify from Figure 26-1 that the total cost for a life-insurance policy over this route is indeed $26 (the sum of the costs on the corresponding arrows).

TABLE 26-2

Stagecoach Problem Evaluations of Earlier Stages

STAGE 3

Possible Choices

s \ j	$c_{sj} + f_4(j)$				Minimum $= f_3(s)$	Optimal Decision
	9	10	11	12		
Entering State 5	$20	$21	—	—	$20	to state 9
6	21	20	$23	—	20	to state 10
7	—	21	21	$23	21	to state 10 or 11
8	—	—	23	23	23	to state 11 or 12

STAGE 2

Possible Choices

s \ j	$c_{sj} + f_3(j)$				Minimum $= f_2(s)$	Optimal Decision
	5	6	7	8		
Entering State 2	$24	$25	$27	—	$24	to state 5
3	—	25	27	$27	25	to state 6
4	—	—	24	27	24	to state 7

STAGE 1

Possible Choices

s \ j	$c_{sj} + f_2(j)$			Minimum $= f_3(s)$	Optimal Decision
	2	3	4		
Entering State 1	$26	$28	$27	$26	to state 2

Alternative Solution Approaches

To the uninitiated, this procedure may seem overly elaborate. After all, there are only 27 possible routes (which can be verified by counting). Wouldn't it be simpler just to sum the costs along each route and then select the lowest one?

This naive approach might actually be a simpler way to solve a small problem. But imagine trying to evaluate a similar route-selection situation involving 10 stages, each having 10 states, which could result in $10^{10} = 10$ billion separate policies. The complete enumeration of all of these policies would involve about 100 million times as many evaluations as dynamic programming.

But can't dynamic programming be applied without employing all the elaborate mathematics? Yes, sometimes this is convenient, depending on the structure of the problem. For instance the required bookkeeping could be kept on the routing network itself by writing above each node the smallest cost expended to reach the destination from that state and somehow flagging the corresponding decision.

Figure 26-2 illustrates such a graphical *network analysis* for the stagecoach problem (which has been evaluated in a similar manner to the backward pass through a PERT network). The boldface numbers are the minimum policy costs for the remaining portion of the stagecoach trip. They are identical to the cost function values given in the earlier mathematical evaluation and were found in essentially the same way; working from left to right, the next boldface number is the smallest sum of the preceding one plus the policy cost between the two states. The little arrows indicate the optimal choice for each state by pointing in the direction in which the minimum cost was obtained. Starting in New York, these flag arrows indicate the optimal policy for the stagecoach journey.

For many small problems, a graphical approach may require the least amount of work to determine the solution. But a graphical analysis is not always possible due to either the sheer size or the complex nature of a problem.

Another approach to solving problems of modest size is to perform a *decision tree analysis*. Figure 26-3 provides the decision tree diagram for the

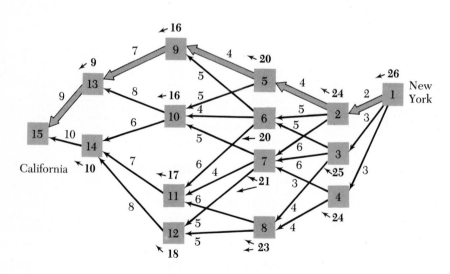

Optimal Policy: 1-2-5-9-13

FIGURE 26-2

A graphical network analysis of the stagecoach problem.

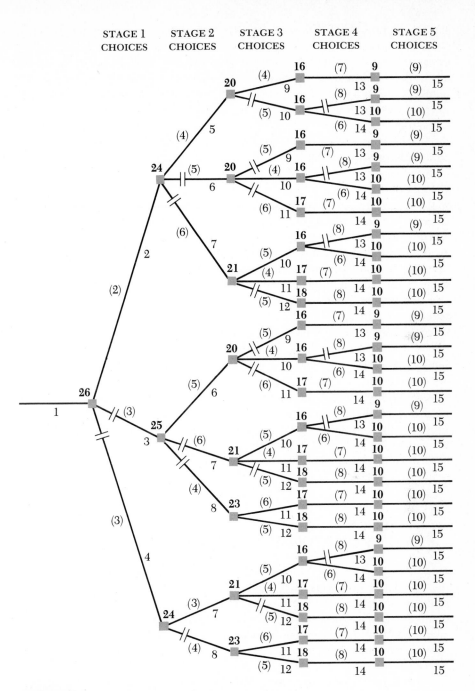

FIGURE 26-3
A decision tree analysis of the stagecoach problem.

stagecoach problem. Each box on the tree represents a decision point, and each possible choice is designated by a separate branch. There may be several possible decision points at each stage, depending on the choices made in earlier stages; all decision points at a common stage are aligned vertically. There are two numbers on each branch: the identity of the chosen state and (in parentheses) the policy cost of that particular leg of the journey. For instance, stage 1 departures from state 1 leave for states 2, 3, or 4. The costs of these legs are shown on the first three branches as (2), (3), and (3). Each possible policy is represented by a path, or sequence of branches, through the tree. Altogether, there are 27 such paths.

The analysis is performed through a process of *backward induction* similar to the one we used in Chapter 5. The process begins with the decision points in stage 5. The respective policy costs from a particular stage to the end of the journey are represented by the boldface numbers above the boxes. These values are found by adding the succeeding boldface value and the cost on the connecting branch. The minimum sum is then entered above the box for the decision point being evaluated. All branches with greater sums correspond to inferior choices and are pruned from the tree. The optimal solution is represented by the sequence of unpruned branches. Again, we can see that the path 1-2-5-9-13-15 represents the optimal policy, at a cost of $26.

Like network analysis, decision tree analysis involves essentially the same steps as the mathematical procedure. The cost function values of $f_n(s)$ are the boldface numbers in Figures 26-2 and 26-3. Although we can avoid expressing the underlying recursive relationship mathematically, it is still present regardless of how a dynamic programming problem is solved. Large problems may require an elaborate set of calculations and may best be solved with a computer. The tabular arrangement used in Tables 26-1 and 26-2 lends itself to computer applications.

26-2 TYPES OF DYNAMIC PROGRAMS

Dynamic programs exist in a variety of forms. The formulation of each problem is unique, but all problems are similar to the stagecoach problem in that only one stage needs to be evaluated at a time. The principle of optimality guarantees that the optimal policy will be found eventually after evaluating all possible entering states for each stage. Dynamic programs fall into several categories.

One classification is in terms of the problem objective and the corresponding recursive relationship. In the stagecoach problem, the objective is to minimize cost, and the cost function for a stage is obtained by adding the cost of a journey leg to the cost function value of the succeeding stage and selecting the minimum sum. In the next section, we will consider the objective of maximizing payoff, so that payoffs are added together and the greatest sum constitutes the value of the payoff function. A later example involves a problem in which the reliability of a system is maximized by finding the smallest failure probability; each evaluation involves the *product* of failure probabilities.

It is possible to treat a variety of constraints in a dynamic programming problem. The knapsack problem described in the next section involves choosing various items in amounts such that their collective weight does not exceed a specific limit. When several constraints exist, a multidimensional formulation exists. Advanced dynamic programming techniques allow such problems to be solved by a one-dimensional procedure.

All of the problems considered in this chapter fall into the discrete category, since the possible choices and states are limited to a finite number of values. It is possible to extend dynamic programming principles to analyze problems involving continuous variables, so that the number of states or variable values can be infinite. Another important dichotomy is deterministic (no uncertainty) versus stochastic problems. Stochastic problems deal with uncertainty about the state that will result from a particular choice and are analyzed by dynamic programming in a manner similar to decision tree analysis.

Unlike linear programming, this solution procedure is difficult to summarize in a concise way that will tell us how to solve all of the problems that are represented as dynamic programs. Each case is different. Our discussion of dynamic programming of necessity must be limited to a few examples. By studying them, we can learn how dynamic programming may be applied to other situations.

A KNAPSACK PROBLEM: MAXIMIZING PAYOFF   26-3

Our second example of dynamic programming involves deciding how many items of various types should be transported via a method with limited carrying capacity. Each item consumes a portion of this capacity and will yield a specific unit payoff when unloaded at the destination.

In our illustration, a smuggler is faced with the dilemma of determining which of the various items listed in Table 26-3—and how many of each—to carry in a knapsack. The smuggler plans a cross-country ski trip into Transylvania, where possession of these items is either forbidden or incurs large import duties. Past experience shows that a maximum of 10 pounds of contraband can safely be carried on any trip. The weight of each item and the payoff on reaching Transylvania are also given in Table 26-3.

TABLE 26-3

Items for the Smuggler's Knapsack

Type of Contraband Item n	Payoff v_n	Weight w_n
(1) Bundle of cigars	$104	2 lbs
(2) Gold ingot	42	1
(3) Bundle of ermine pelts	212	4
(4) Jug of perfume	270	5
(5) Radio transmitter	165	3

Formulation of the Problem

The smuggler's problem is to select numbers of the various items to carry in such a way that total payoff will be maximized. We let

$$x_n = \text{number of items of type } n \text{ to carry}$$

$$N = \text{number of item types considered}$$

$$v_n = \text{payoff of one type } n \text{ item}$$

$$w_n = \text{weight of one type } n \text{ item}$$

$$W = \text{total weight limitation}$$

The products $v_n x_n$ and $w_n x_n$ express the payoff and weight, respectively, for carrying x_n items of type n. The sum of these terms over all item types will provide the total payoff and weight. Thus, the objective is to find the values of x_n that

$$\text{Maximize} \quad \sum_{n=1}^{N} v_n x_n$$

$$\text{Subject to} \quad \sum_{n=1}^{N} w_n x_n \leq W$$

where x_n may be any integer between zero and the largest amount of item n that does not exceed the total weight limitation. In our illustration, $N = 5$ and $W = 10$ pounds.

Suppose that the smuggler tries to solve this problem without using dynamic programming. One approach is to identify the item type with the greatest return per pound, which happens to be item (5), radio transmitters, at $55 per pound. The smuggler can pack the greatest possible number of transmitters without exceeding the 10-pound limit. Since each transmitter weighs 3 pounds, the smuggler can pack 3 of them and 1 pound will still remain to be filled. All other items, with the exception of a single gold ingot, are too heavy to take up the remaining knapsack capacity. Thus, the smuggler may carry $x_5 = 3$ transmitters and $x_2 = 1$ gold ingot. The total payoff for this policy would be \$537. As we will see, the smuggler can actually improve the value of the items in the knapsack through a systematic evaluation.

The Dynamic Programming Solution

This problem can be solved as a dynamic program in a similar manner to the way in which we solved the stagecoach problem. A straightforward approach is to determine the number of items of each type by selecting them one at a time. We may treat each item type as a separate stage in which a decision must be made about the number of items to be included in the smuggler's knapsack. It is convenient to use the unassigned knapsack capacity as the starting state for each stage. As in the stagecoach analysis, we will begin our evaluation by working backward from item 5.

Analogous to the function in the stagecoach problem, the payoff function $f_n(s)$ will represent the payoff when starting in state s and using the optimal policy from stage n to the end. In other words, when s pounds remain in the knapsack for the inclusion of items of type n and beyond, $f_n(s)$ represents that portion of the total payoff obtained just from these items.

The payoff function for stage 5, representing the possible payoffs in radio transmitters, is expressed by

$$f_5(s) = \text{maximum } v_5 x_5$$

where

$$w_5 x_5 \leq s$$

Thus, $f_5(s)$ is the maximum possible payoff for the number of radio transmitters packed. That quantity is x_5, which cannot exceed the unassigned weight capacity of s pounds. The payoff value and the corresponding optimal decision for each possible state are listed in Table 26-4. Notice that x_5 can assume a value of at most 3, but that a smaller maximum level may apply, depending on the remaining knapsack capacity level s. At this stage, $v_5 = 165$ and the maximum level of s is 10.

The recursive relationship for this problem is

$$f_n(s) = \text{maximum } [v_n x_n + f_{n+1}(s - w_n x_n)]$$

The quantity x_n represents the amount of item n placed in the knapsack. This amount will add $v_n x_n$ to the total payoff and will take up $w_n x_n$ pounds of the weight remaining for assignment to later items. The payoff for the optimal policy from the later stage corresponds to this remaining capacity state in the amount of $s - w_n x_n$ pounds. Thus, x_n must be chosen to maximize the sum of the present item type payoff and the payoff function values for all future items.

Table 26-5 shows the payoff function values for the various stages. To see how these values were obtained, consider stage 4, where $s = 8$. This indicates

TABLE 26-4

Knapsack Problem: Last Stage Evaluation for the Number of Radio Transmitters

STAGE 5

Possible Choices

	x_5	$165x_5$				Maximum $= f_5(s)$	Optimal Decision
s		0	1	2	3		
Entering	0	$0	—	—	—	$ 0	$x_5 = 0$
State	1	0	—	—	—	0	$x_5 = 0$
	2	0	—	—	—	0	$x_5 = 0$
	3	0	$165	—	—	165	$x_5 = 1$
	4	0	165	—	—	165	$x_5 = 1$
	5	0	165	—	—	165	$x_5 = 1$
→6		0	165	$330	—	330	$x_5 = 2$*
	7	0	165	330	—	330	$x_5 = 2$
	8	0	165	330	—	330	$x_5 = 2$
	9	0	165	330	$495	495	$x_5 = 3$
	10	0	165	330	495	495	$x_5 = 3$

TABLE 26-5

Knapsack Problem: Evaluations for Earlier Stages

STAGE 4

Possible Choices

	x_4	$270x_4 + f_5(s - 5x_4)$			Maximum $= f_4(s)$	Optimal Decision
s		0	1	2		
Entering	0	$ 0	—	—	$ 0	$x_4 = 0$
State	1	0	—	—	0	$x_4 = 0$
	2	0	—	—	0	$x_4 = 0$
	3	165	—	—	165	$x_4 = 0$
	4	165	—	—	165	$x_4 = 0$
	5	165	$270	—	270	$x_4 = 1$
→6		330	270	—	330	$x_4 = 0$*
	7	330	270	—	330	$x_4 = 0$
	8	330	435	—	435	$x_4 = 1$
	9	495	435	—	495	$x_4 = 0$
	10	495	435	$540	540	$x_4 = 2$

TABLE 26-5 (continued)

STAGE 3

Possible Choices

s	x_3 0	1	2	Maximum $= f_3(s)$	Optimal Decision
		$212x_3 + f_4(s - 4x_3)$			
0	$ 0	—	—	$ 0	$x_3 = 0$
1	0	—	—	0	$x_3 = 0$
2	0	—	—	0	$x_3 = 0$
3	165	—	—	165	$x_3 = 0$
4	165	$212	—	212	$x_3 = 1$
5	270	212	—	270	$x_3 = 0$
6	330	212	—	330	$x_3 = 0$
7	330	377	—	377	$x_3 = 1$
8	435	377	$424	435	$x_3 = 0$
9	495	482	424	495	$x_3 = 0$
→10	540	542	424	542	$x_3 = 1^*$

Entering State (rows labelled at left)

STAGE 2

Possible Choices

s	x_2 0	1	2	3	4	5	6	7	8	9	10	Maximum $= f_2(s)$	Optimal Decision
					$42x_2 + f_3(s - 1x_2)$								
0	$ 0	—	—	—	—	—	—	—	—	—	—	$ 0	$x_2 = 0$
1	0	$ 42	—	—	—	—	—	—	—	—	—	42	$x_2 = 1$
2	0	42	$ 84	—	—	—	—	—	—	—	—	84	$x_2 = 2$
3	165	42	84	$126	—	—	—	—	—	—	—	165	$x_2 = 0$
4	212	207	84	126	$168	—	—	—	—	—	—	212	$x_2 = 0$
5	270	254	249	126	168	$210	—	—	—	—	—	270	$x_2 = 0$
6	330	312	296	291	168	210	$252	—	—	—	—	330	$x_2 = 0$
7	377	372	354	338	333	210	252	$294	—	—	—	377	$x_2 = 0$
8	435	419	414	396	380	375	252	294	$336	—	—	435	$x_2 = 0$
9	495	477	461	456	438	422	417	294	336	$378	—	495	$x_2 = 0$
→10	542	537	519	503	498	480	464	459	336	378	$420	542	$x_2 = 0^*$

Entering State (rows labelled at left)

STAGE 1

Possible Choices

s	x_1 0	1	2	3	4	5	Maximum $= f_1(s)$	Optimal Decision
			$104x_1 + f_2(s - 2x_1)$					
10	$542	$539	$538	$524	$500	$520	$542	$x_1 = 0^*$

Entering State

that there are 8 pounds of unfilled capacity at the start of stage 4, where the number of perfume jugs to include must be decided. The given values $v_4 = \$270$ and $w_4 = 5$ pounds apply to this item.

Suppose that no jug of perfume is packed, so that $x_4 = 0$. This leaves $8 - 0 = 8$ pounds for stage 5, radio transmitters. Table 26-4 indicates a payoff of $f_5(8) = \$330$ when 8 pounds remain at that stage. The applicable payoff at stage 4 when $s = 8$ and $x_4 = 0$ is

$$v_4 x_4 + f_5(8 - w_4 x_4) = 270 x_4 + f_5(8 - 5 x_4)$$
$$= 0 + f_5(8) = \$330 \quad \text{(when } x_4 = 0)$$

Now suppose that $x_4 = 1$ jug of perfume is packed. This leaves $8 - 5(1) = 3$ pounds of remaining knapsack capacity and, from Table 26-4, $f_5(3) = \$165$. Thus

$$270 x_4 + f_5(8 - 5 x_4) = \$270(1) + f_5(3)$$
$$= \$270 + \$165 = \$435 \quad \text{(when } x_4 = 1)$$

We do not consider the case when $x_5 = 2$ jugs are placed in the knapsack. This amount is infeasible, since it would take up more than the available 8 pounds.

The payoff function at stage 4 when $s = 8$ pounds is the maximum of the these two amounts, or

$$f_4(8) = \text{maximum } [\$330, \$435] = \$435 \quad \text{(when } x_4 = 1)$$

The optimal decision on reaching state $s = 8$ in stage 4 is to pack $x_4 = 1$ jug of perfume. The same procedure applies for other levels of s.

Similar evaluations were made successively at each of the earlier stages, as shown in Table 26-5. The last evaluation is for stage 1, where the maximum possible payoff is found to be

$$f_1(10) = \$542 \quad \text{(when } x_1 = 0)$$

(Only one state, $s = 10$, is considered for this stage, since the problem begins with an empty knapsack.) This amount corresponds to the following optimal policy:

$$x_1 = 0 \quad \text{(bundle of cigars)}$$
$$x_2 = 0 \quad \text{(gold ingot)}$$
$$x_3 = 1 \quad \text{(bundle of ermine pelts)}$$
$$x_4 = 0 \quad \text{(jug of perfume)}$$
$$x_5 = 2 \quad \text{(radio transmitters)}$$

This optimal policy was found by tracing back through the evaluation tables. The results of this procedure are shown in Table 26-4 and 26-5 by the arrow for the entering state and the asterisk for the optimal item amount. Starting in stage 1, we can see that $x_1 = 0$ is the optimal decision, so no cigars are packed. This leaves 10 pounds for the second item type, so that $s = 10$ is the starting state for stage 2. The optimal decision there is $x_2 = 0$, and no gold ingots are packed. Thus, 10 pounds remain for the third item type, and the $s = 10$ row for the stage-3 evaluation leads to the optimal choice of $x_3 = 1$ bundle of ermine pelts. Since each bundle weighs 4 pounds, only 6 pounds of knapsack capacity remain. Reading across the $s = 6$ row in the stage-4 evaluation, we can see that $x_4 = 0$ jug of perfume is the optimal choice, so that 6 pounds of knapsack capacity still remain. Finally, we proceed to the stage-5 evaluation in Table 26-4, where the $s = 6$ row indicates the optimal choice of $x_5 = 2$ radio transmitters.

Applications of the Knapsack Problem

The knapsack problem can be expanded to consider additional contraints. Thus, it might be applied to a variety of cargo-loading problems, where the volume of the items must be considered in addition to their weight. The same concepts could be extended to a multiproduct inventory decision involving floor space or budgetary restrictions. The problem of provisioning space parts to inaccessible places—for, say, oil exploration in Alaska or scientific expeditions in the Antarctic—is structured similarly to the smuggler's knapsack problem.

The knapsack problem has even been used to analyze capital budgeting decisions. For each alternative project, the projected rate of return on invested capital usually constitues the payoff measure. Since the actual return is generally subject to chance, the variation in possible returns provides a measure of risk. The objective in solving this type of problem is to select projects in such a way that the total return is maximized without exceeding tolerable limits on risk while remaining within the overall budget.

When several constraints are involved in a knapsack-type problem, special mathematical difficulties arise. A discussion of these difficulties is beyond the scope of this book. The detailed solutions to more advanced dynamic programming problems are provided in many of the references listed in the bibliography at the back of the book.

MAXIMIZING A SYSTEM RELIABILITY 26-4

Many important problems in area of reliability can be solved by using a variety of quantitative methods. Consider the decisions faced by the designers of an interplanetary space probe with a variety of component systems (guidance,

TABLE 26-6
Power-Failure Probabilities for a Space Probe System

Number of Power Cells	PROBABILITY OF SYSTEM POWER FAILURE		
	System 1	System 2	System 3
1	.50	.60	.40
2	.15	.20	.25
3	.04	.10	.10
4	.02	.05	.05
5	.01	.02	.01

propulsion, television, reception, transmission, and so on). Unless all systems function throughout the entire mission, it will be a complete failure. Various components must be carefully designed to satisfy overall payload constraints and still be capable of surviving in a hostile space environment. One interesting question concerns the power supply for the various system components.

Suppose that a particular probe is designed to carry exactly five power cells, each of which must be located physically within one of three electronic systems. If one system's power should fail, it will be powered on an auxiliary basis by the cells of the remaining systems. The probability that any particular system will experience a power failure depends on the number of cells originally assigned to it. Table 26-6 provide the estimated power-failure probabilities for a particular space probe.

Since almost any power failure would result from environmental factors rather than excessive use, any overloading effect on a cell due to auxiliary use can be ignored. The failure events for the respective systems can therefore be treated as if they were independent.

The design engineers must determine how many power cells should be assigned to each system to maximize overall system reliability. This can be accomplished by minimizing the probability that all systems will suffer a power failure.

The Dynamic Program

The dynamic programming formulation begins with the specification of the states and stages. We may view each decision about the number of power cells for a system as a stage. The number of power cells chosen for one system limits the amount of cells available for the next system, so that the entering state s for a particular stage must be the number of cells as yet unassigned. The decision variables can be expressed as x_1, x_2, and x_3 and represent the number of cells assigned at the respective stage to the corresponding system. It is convenient to denote the probability for a power failure in the nth system, or stage, symbolically in terms of the corresponding variable by $p_n(x_n)$.

Because system failures are independent, the multiplication law tells us that the product of these individual probabilities provides the probability that all systems will suffer a power failure. The problem is therefore to find the variable values that

$$\text{Minimize} \quad p_1(x_1)p_2(x_2)p_3(x_3)$$

$$\text{Subject to} \quad x_1 + x_2 + x_3 = 5$$

$$\text{where} \quad x_1, x_2, x_3 \geq 1$$

The constraint indicates that all five power cells must be assigned. No system may operate on auxiliary power at the outset, so that variable values of zero are impossible.

The function $f_n(s)$ for this problem expresses the smallest probability, entering with state s, that the nth and all higher systems will fail. In the case of system 3

$$f_3(s) = \text{minimum } p_3(x_3)$$

is the starting state, and the recursive relationship is

$$f_n(s) = \text{minimum } [p_n(x_n)f_{n+1}(s - x_n)]$$

Solving the Dynamic Program

The evaluations of the reliability problem are provided in Table 26-7. Notice that stage 3 cannot be entered from states $s = 4$ or $s = 5$, since at least one power cell a piece must be assigned in stage 1 and in stage 2. Likewise, the minimum cell requirements for each system do not permit stage 2 to be entered from states $s = 1$ or $s = 5$. Thus, no more than three cells can be assigned in any stage.

The stage-3 function values are obtained directly from the given data. It may be helpful to illustrate how the values are obtained for stage 2. Consider entering stage 2 with $s = 4$ power cells to be assigned. If $x_2 = 1$ power cell is assigned to system 2, then $s - x_2 = 4 - 1 = 3$ cells will be available for system 3. The failure probability for systems 1 and 2 combined will then be

$$p_2(x_2)f_3(s - x_2) = p_2(1)f_3(3)$$

$$= .60(.10) = .06 \quad \text{(when } x_2 = 1)$$

TABLE 26-7

Reliability Problem Evaluations

STAGE 3

Possible Choices

	x_3	$p_3(x_3)$				
s		1	2	3	Minimum $= f_3(s)$	Optimal Decision
Entering State →1		.40	—	—	.40	$x_3 = 1*$
2		.40	.25	—	.25	$x_3 = 2$
3		.40	.25	.10	.10	$x_3 = 3$

STAGE 2

Possible Choices

	x_2	$p_2(x_2)f_3(s - x_2)$				
s		1	2	3	Minimum $= f_2(s)$	Optimal Decision
Entering State →2		.24	—	—	.24	$x_2 = 1*$
3		.15	.08	—	.08	$x_2 = 2$
4		.06	.05	.04	.04	$x_2 = 3$

STAGE 1

Possible Choices

	x_1	$p_1(x_1)f_2(s - x_1)$				
s		1	2	3	Minimum $= f_1(s)$	Optimal Decision
Entering State 5		.02	.012	.0096	.0096	$x_1 = 3*$

since $p_2(1) = .60$ is the given failure probability for system 2 when only one cell is assigned to it. Likewise, when $x_2 = 2$, the failure probability is

$$p_2(x_2)f_3(s - x_2) = p_2(2)f_3(2)$$

$$= .20(.25) = .05 \quad \text{(when } x_2 = 2\text{)}$$

and when $x_2 = 3$, the failure probability is

$$p_2(x_2)f_3(s - x_2) = p_2(3)f_3(1)$$

$$= .10(.40) = .04 \quad \text{(when } x_2 = 3\text{)}$$

The minimum failure probability for systems 2 and 3, when stage 2 is entered with $s = 4$, is therefore

$$f_2(4) = \text{minimum } (.06, .05, .04) = .04 \quad (\text{when } x_2 = 3)$$

The values of $f_2(s)$ when $s = 2$ or $s = 3$ are calculated in a similar manner.

Notice that stage 1 has only one entering state of $s = 5$, since all of the cells are yet to be assigned when system 1 is considered.

We can see that $f_1(5) = .0096$ is the smallest probability for total power failure. The corresponding optimal policy is to make the following power cell assignments:

$$x_1 = 3 \text{ to system 1}$$

$$x_2 = 1 \text{ to system 2}$$

$$x_3 = 1 \text{ to system 3}$$

OPTIMIZING MULTI-PERIOD INVENTORIES AND PRODUCTION 26-5

In Chapter 15, we solved a problem about production and inventory decisions regarding skis made in a Juarez plant and sold from a Phoenix warehouse. That particular problem was expressed as a linear program and solved by using the transportation method. Recall that linear programs require that all underlying relationships be expressed mathematically by straight lines or planes in higher dimensions. We will now reconsider the ski manufacturing and distribution problem in a more general form, so that a linear programming formulation no longer applies. This new problem will be solved as a dynamic programming problem.

Table 26-8 provides the monthly demands d_n for skis during the winter season. Virtually all direct labor is casual and temporary, so that any number of skis up to the plant capacity of 400 pairs may be produced each month. The direct labor cost is \$40 per pair. The Juarez plant is completely shut down

TABLE 26-8
Demands for Pairs of Skis

Month n	Demand d_n
(1) August	100
(2) September	200
(3) October	300
(4) November	400

during months when there is no production, and supervisory personnel are given an unpaid holiday to save a further \$2,000 in monthly payroll costs. Demands may be filled either from current production or from inventory. Each ski held in inventory at the beginning of the month costs the company \$5. Our problem is to determine the monthly production levels x_1, x_2, x_3, and x_4 in such a way that total cost is minimized. The production quantities may be 0, 100, 200, 300, or 400 pairs. Each month is a separate problem stage with some beginning inventory level as its entering state. Stage 1 (August) has a beginning inventory level of $s = 0$. Since no skis can be saved until the next season, stage 4 (November) must end with zero inventory.

The Dynamic Program

The combined monthly production and inventory cost for the ski manufacturer depends on the beginning inventory s and on the production quantity x_n. This cost can be determined from

$$c(s, x_n) = \begin{cases} 5s + 2,000 + 40x_n & \text{if } x_n > 0 \\ 5s & \text{if } x_n = 0 \end{cases}$$

Regardless of the production level, there will be an inventory cost of $5s$ dollars. Since \$2,000 in supervisory costs are incurred only for nonzero production levels, two separate cost expressions apply, depending on whether or not $x_n = 0$.

Because the fixed supervisory cost is incurred for only some of the possible variable values, a linear program cannot be used to solve this problem.* The dynamic programming procedure applies when the variable cost of making skis changes with the level of production; in this case, a nonlinear relationship exists between costs and quantities.

In any given month, the beginning inventory plus the production level determines how many units are available to satisfy that month's demand. All demands must be met. A month's ending inventory serves as the beginning inventory for the next month and is the sum of the available quantities minus the demand. Beginning with s pairs of skis, the number of pairs on hand at the end of month n is

$$s + x_n - d_n$$

which is also the beginning inventory for month $n + 1$.

The last month must end with no inventory, so that

$$s + x_4 - d_4 = 0$$

---

* Our illustration could actually be formulated as an *integer program* involving a set of variables assigned a value of either zero or 1 to represent the presence or absence of the fixed monthly supervisory cost.

or

$$x_4 = d_4 - s$$

where s is that month's beginning inventory. Since $d_4 = 400$ and x_4 may fall anywhere between 0 and 400, then s may equal 0, 100, 200, 300, or 400 when $n = 4$.

The cost function $f_n(s)$ represents the minimum remaining cost of entering from state s and following an optimal policy from stage n to the end. For the last stage

$$f_4(s) = c(s, x_4) = c(s, d_4 - s)$$

so that when $s = d_4 = 400$ (so that $x_4 = 0$)

$$f_4(400) = 5(400) = \$2,000$$

If s is less than $d_4 = 400$, then the cost function is

$$f_4(s) = 5s + 2,000 + 40(400 - s)$$

For instance, when $s = 300$

$$
\begin{aligned}
f_4(300) &= 5(300) + 2,000 + 40(400 - 300) \\
&= 1,500 + 2,000 + 4,000 \\
&= \$7,500
\end{aligned}
$$

which corresponds to a production level of $x_4 = 100$ units.

The recursive relationship is

$$f_n(s) = \text{minimum} \left[c(s, x_n) + f_{n+1}(s + x_n - d_n) \right]$$

which represents the smallest sum of the month n cost and the minimum cost for beginning month $n + 1$ with a starting inventory of $s + x_n - d_n$.

Solving the Dynamic Program

Table 26-9 provides the evaluations for the four stages of this problem. Notice that in stage 3, the production level plus the starting inventory must be at least the 300 units demanded in the third month, so that x_3 must be at least 300 when $s = 0$ and 200 when $s = 100$. Also, no more than 400 units can be carried over to stage 4, so that x_3 cannot exceed 300 when $s = 400$ and 200 when $s = 500$. The maximum inventory level for entering stage 3 is $s = 500$, which reflects the maximum possible production of 400 each in stages 1 and 2,

TABLE 26-9
Evaluations for the Ski-Manufacturing Problem

STAGE 4

	s	$f_4(s)$	Optimal Choice
Entering	→0	$18,000	$x_4 = 400*$
State	100	14,500	$x_4 = 300$
	200	11,000	$x_4 = 200$
	300	7,500	$x_4 = 100$
	400	2,000	$x_4 = 0$

STAGE 3

Possible Choices

	x_3	$c(s, x_3) + f_4(s + x_3 - 300)$					Minimum	Optimal
	s	0	100	200	300	400	$= f_3(s)$	Choice
Entering	→0	—	—	—	$32,000	$32,500	$32,000	$x_3 = 300*$
State	100	—	—	$28,500	29,000	29,500	28,500	$x_3 = 200$
	200	—	$25,000	25,500	26,000	26,500	25,000	$x_3 = 100$
	300	$19,500	22,000	22,500	23,000	21,500	19,500	$x_3 = 0$
	400	16,500	19,000	19,500	18,000	—	16,500	$x_3 = 0$
	500	13,500	16,000	14,500	—	—	13,500	$x_3 = 0$

STAGE 2

Possible Choices

	x_2	$c(s, x_2) + f_3(s + x_2 - 200)$					Minimum	Optimal
	s	0	100	200	300	400	$= f_2(s)$	Choice
Entering	0	—	—	$42,000	$42,500	$43,000	$42,000	$x_2 = 200$
State	100	—	$38,500	39,000	39,500	38,000	38,000	$x_2 = 400$
	→200	$33,000	35,500	36,000	34,500	35,500	33,000	$x_2 = 0*$
	300	30,000	32,500	31,000	32,000	33,000	30,000	$x_2 = 0$

STAGE 1

Possible Choices

	x_1	$c(s, x_1) + f_2(s + x_1 - 100)$					Minimum	Optimal
	s	0	100	200	300	400	$= f_1(s)$	Choice
Entering	0	—	$48,000	$48,000	$47,000	$48,000	$47,000	$x_1 = 300*$
State								

less the demands of 100 and 200 pairs for those months. Similar restrictions apply at stage 2, where $s = 300$ is the largest possible beginning inventory.

The value of the cost function for stage 1, $f_1(0) = \$47,000$, corresponds to the optimal policy

$$x_1 = 300 \text{ pairs}$$

$$x_2 = 0$$

$$x_3 = 300$$

$$x_4 = 400$$

Thus, the Juarez plant will have a beginning inventory only at stage 2 (September), which is exactly enough to satisfy that month's demand of 200 units. The plant should be shut down in September and should produce in the other months.

PROBABILISTIC DYNAMIC PROGRAMMING 26-6

The examples we have considered so far are deterministic, since they do not involve uncertainty. Dynamic programming can also be used to solve problems in which the state resulting from a particular choice is uncertain. This uncertainty is expressed in terms of the probabilities that a particular state will occur. In Chapter 5, we saw that the usual decision criterion for making choices under uncertainty is the Bayes decision rule. Whether this leads to maximizing *expected* payoff or *minimizing* expected cost, the principle of optimality still applies, and a stage-by-stage evaluation of the decision as a dynamic programming problem will lead to the optimal policy. The procedure is very similar to the backward induction used in decision tree analysis that we encountered in earlier chapters. Further discussion of this topic is beyond the scope of this book, but additional information can be obtained from many of the references listed in the bibliography in the back of the book.

ADDITIONAL REMARKS 26-7

Dynamic programming is a very useful quantitative method that can be applied to a wide variety of multi-stage decision problems occurring over time or when choices may be made sequentially. At times, it can serve as an alternative to linear programming, although dynamic programming can also be used to solve integer and nonlinear programming problems. Situations suited to this procedure are similar in structure from stage to stage, so that a single recursive relationship holds for all stages. The principle of optimality indicates that the optimal policy can be found by evaluating a stage at a time and finding the best choice for every possible starting state.

The main advantage of dynamic programming is its computational efficiency. The procedure is often used in conjunction with a digital computer, and the simple mathematical formulation and tabular arrangement make it especially easy to write a computer program for conducting individual evaluations. Even when dynamic programming problems are moderately large, a computer solution is desirable—if only to eliminate computational errors, which magnify in impact as the earlier stages are reached.

PROBLEMS

26-1 Modify the stagecoach problem in Figure 26-1 by raising the insurance costs $2 for each journey leg beginning in an even-numbered state and reducing insurance costs $1 for each journey leg beginning in an odd-numbered state. Then solve the modified problem:
(a) by network analysis.
(b) by decision tree analysis.
(c) in the standard manner, providing a separate evaluation table for each stage.

26-2 The following evaluation results have been obtained for a knapsack problem involving a capacity of 10 pounds:

STATE	STAGE 1		STAGE 2		STAGE 3		STAGE 4	
s	$f_1(s)$	x_1	$f_2(s)$	x_2	$f_3(s)$	x_3	$f_4(s)$	x_4
0	—	—	$60	2	$26	0	$10	0
1	—	—	63	2	27	0	12	0
2	—	—	65	1	29	0	12	0
3	—	—	67	3	30	1	12	1
4	—	—	68	2	32	1	14	1
5	—	—	68	2	34	1	14	1
6	—	—	70	3	36	2	15	1
7	—	—	72	4	38	1	16	1
8	—	—	73	3	40	2	17	2
9	—	—	73	4	41	3	18	2
10	$100	2	75	4	41	3	20	2

Items 1 and 2 weigh 1 pound apiece, item 3 weighs 2 pounds, and item 4 weighs 3 pounds. Find the optimal policy. How many pounds will be carried in the knapsack?

26-3 Suppose that we modify the example in Section 26-3 slightly, so that the smuggler's knapsack can carry no more than 9 pounds.
(a) Use dynamic programming procedures to find $f_1(9)$.
(b) Trace through your evaluation tables to determine the optimal policy.

26-4 Modify the ski-manufacturing example in Section 26-5 by raising September demand to 300 and reducing November demand to 300. Find the optimal production quantities for each month.

26-5 The Ace Widget Company is planning its manufacturing operations for the next five months. The following demands apply:

January	200
February	300
March	300
April	200
May	400

Each item held in inventory from one month to the next incurs a $1 carrying charge. There are 200 unsold items remaining at the end of December. The widgets are to be redesigned for June, so that no ending inventory is desired. A maximum of 400 units may be manufactured in any given month. Total production costs are

0 units	$ 0
100 units	1,000
200 units	1,300
300 units	1,450
400 units	1,525

Determine the minimum-cost production plan.

26-6 A construction superintendent must assign additional dump trucks to various excavation sites so that total cost is minimized. Only five trucks are available. The following costs apply:

	Excavation Site		
Number of Trucks	1	2	3
0	$10,000	$15,000	$20,000
1	10,000	14,000	18,000
2	9,000	13,250	17,500
3	8,500	12,750	17,250
4	8,000	12,500	17,000
5	7,500	12,000	16,750

Determine the optimal number of additional trucks that should be assigned to each site.

26-7 Traveling salesman Hoppy Scott must visit five cities, making exactly one stop in each. The following airfares apply:

From \ To	A	B	C	D	E
A	—	$100	$ 60	$130	$ 70
B	$100	—	50	80	110
C	60	50	—	90	120
D	130	80	90	—	40
E	70	110	120	40	—

Hoppy must visit city A first, and can arrive in the remaining cities in any order. It does not matter in which city the trip ends.

Use dynamic programming to determine the sequence of cities that will minimize Hoppy's total airfare.

26-8 Re-solve the space probe power-cell assignment problem in Section 26-4, assuming that there is no longer a minimum requirement that one or more power cells must be located within each system.

26-9 Consider the assignment of brats to daily chores in Problem 15-11 (page 382). Use dynamic programming to solve that problem so that total working time is minimized.

26-10 Fly Me Airlines must determine how many planes of various types to order for next year. The following data apply:

Aircraft	Mean Profit per Passenger-Mile	Mean Number of Passengers Carried	Price
(1) CD-10	$.02	200	$20 million
(2) L-1111	.03	150	25
(3) B-7070	.01	100	10
(4) Tupolev 100	.02	150	15

The aircraft fleet expansion budget is $75 million. The company must spend some or all of these funds in such a way that the mean profit per 1,000-mile trip is maximized. How many planes of each type should Fly Me order?

26-11 Shirley Smart must take five final examinations. She has 60 hours of study time available, and her expected grade in each course will depend on how she allocates her time. The following data apply:

Course	Expected Grade for Hours of Study Time			
	5	10	15	20
Accounting	C	C	B	A
Finance	B	B	B	A
Marketing	B	A	A	A
Quantitative methods	D	C	B	A
Statistics	C	C	C	B

Shirley wishes to maximize her expected total grade points. For each course, 4 points are given for an A, 3 for a B, 2 for a C, and 1 for a D. Determine how Shirley should budget her study time.

27

Decision Making with Markov Processes

Much decision making is concerned with establishing continuing policies for the various operational aspects of a business or organization. Business functions such as marketing, production, and finance involve uncertainties of a recurring nature. In this chapter, we describe a procedure based on the structure of these uncertainties that can sometimes help to select an operating policy.

THE MARKOV PROCESS 27-1

The particular situations we will consider here are broadly categorized as *Markov processes*, after the Russian mathematician who helped to pioneer modern probability theory. Several features distinguish a Markov process from more general uncertain situations. The basic process structure is best described in terms of a *system*. Examples of such systems include the marketplace for a product and its competing brands, the machinery used to manufacture that product, and the billing, credit, and collection procedures involved in converting accounts receivable from the product's sales into cash. At any given time, the respective systems may be in one of several possible *states*. In marketing applications, these states can be expressed in terms of the brand that a customer is presently using. In production, that state of concern may be the number of machines in working order. A customer's financial transaction can fall into one of the following states: cash sale, credit sale, or uncollectable funds.

The Characteristics of a Markov Process

The main distinguishing feature of a Markov process is that it is concerned with the *probabilities* for being in various states at any given time and for moving from one state to another. A Markov process essentially has no memory, so that the probability for moving from one state to another state does not depend on previous occurrences. This feature is sometimes called the *Markovian property*. For example, consider a smoker who is a potential buyer of Lucky Strike cigarettes. Suppose that we view brand switching as a Markov process. If this assumption is valid, the Markovian property tells us that this person will change from Camel to Lucky Strike with a *constant probability*, such as 1/10 (determined by marketing research), when making a subsequent cigarette purchase—regardless of whether he or she has been a loyal Camel smoker for decades or has recently switched to Camel from Pall Mall. A further characteristic of a Markov process is that the *long-run probability* of being in a particular state will be constant over time and will hold regardless of the state probabilities that applied in the beginning. This tells us that the long-run probability that any particular smoker will buy Lucky Strike on the next purchase, which sales experience might show to be a value such as 1/20, must be *constant* over time.

The implications from assuming that a Markov process applies to cigarette purchases may seem a bit unrealistic. After all, brands come and go. Once Camel, Lucky Strike, Pall Mall, and Viceroy were leading sellers; today, none of them are leaders (and some may be gone forever). How can we realistically assume that today's favorite brand will not suffer the same fate? The answer is that we can't. What is ignored is that the various probabilities in a Markov process can be changed through *outside action*. For example, advertising and promotion can cause more or fewer persons than before to switch to or from a particular brand. The possibility of such action adds the element of decision making to a Markov process.

State and Transition Probabilities

To further illustrate the concepts of a Markov process, we will expand on the problem of brand switching. Suppose that three brands A, B, and C all satisfy the same need and can be readily substituted for each other. The product is a convenience item (such as toothpaste or cigarettes) that is bought frequently.

TABLE 27-1

Transition Matrix for the Buyers of Three Brands

From State \ To	State		
	A	B	C
A	.90	.05	.05
B	.10	.80	.10
C	.10	.15	.75

Any user is said to be in one of the states A, B, or C, depending on the brand he or she is presently using. Thus, each buyer will be faced from time to time with a buying decision that may result in a change from one state (brand) to another. We will assume that this decision will be made periodically, so that changes will occur over time. We will also assume that the number of states (brand choices) is finite. Our example therefore falls into the class of situations called *Markov chains*, which are distinguished from more general Markov processes in which states may be continuous (for example, a physical dimension or the level of bulk inventory).

A marketing research study based on detailed interviews with a sample of several hundred users has determined the frequency at which buyers as a whole have either remained with their present brand or changed brands. These data provide the *transition probabilities* given in Table 27-1. Such a table is sometimes referred to as the *transition matrix*.

The number in the top left-hand corner reflects the research result that 90% of the users of brand A were found to retain that brand on subsequent purchase. This led to the conclusion that the probability is .90 for moving from state A to state A on the next purchase. Likewise, the probability is .05 for moving from state A to state B, and the same value applies to switching from A to C. These transition probabilities are *conditional probabilities* for entering the state listed on the right given the starting state on the left. As such, the values in each row must sum to 1.

In establishing their advertising policies, the producers of the various brands are concerned not with the transition probabilities but with their relative shares of the market. More specifically, each producer wishes to determine the probability that any particular customer will purchase its brand. We refer to such a value as a *state probability*. Such a number is an unconditional probability, and its value may change over time. For convenience, we represent the state probability for state i at period n symbolically as

$$p_i(n) = \Pr[\text{state } i \text{ occurs in period } n]$$

Suppose that further marketing research data shows that brand A currently captures 45% of the market; brand B, 35%; and brand C, 20%. These values apply in the initial period of our investigation. Our interpretation of these numbers is that any particular randomly chosen user of the product will have the following state probabilities in the initial period $n = 0$:

$$p_A(0) = .45$$

$$p_B(0) = .35$$

$$p_C(0) = .20$$

How State Probabilities Change Over Time

The product manufacturers are concerned with how permanent these market shares are and how they might change from period to period. We can determine such changes by looking at the state probabilities in successive periods. As we have noted, a Markov process should have long-run probabilities that are constant over time. Before that equilibrium situation is reached, the process should be given some time to settle down.

Assuming that each customer will make the next brand choice in accordance with the transition probabilities given earlier, we can determine the state probabilities that apply in period $n = 1$ after the buyers have made their initial purchases.

Consider state A. To find the probability that brand A will be chosen, we assume that this choice will be made by retaining brand A or by switching from either brand B or C to A. The joint probabilities for these results may be determined by multiplying the respective transition probability in column A of the transition matrix by the corresponding state probability. Summing these products, we obtain the new state probability for A:

Old State Probability	$\times$	Transition Probability	$=$	New State Probability
.45	$\times$	.90	$=$	.4050
.35	$\times$	.10	$=$	.0350
.20	$\times$	.10	$=$	.0200
		$p_A(1)$	$=$	.4600

Similar calculations provide the other new state probabilities:

$$.45 \times .05 = .0225 \qquad .45 \times .05 = .0225$$

$$.35 \times .80 = .2800 \qquad .35 \times .10 = .0350$$

$$.20 \times .15 = .0300 \qquad .20 \times .75 = .1500$$

$$p_B(1) = .3325 \qquad p_C(1) = .2075$$

Notice that the state probabilities for period 1 have changed, indicating that more people will be buying brands A and C than before and that brand B's share of the market will drop. We can use the state probabilities for period 1 in the same manner as before to find the applicable state probabilities for period 2:

$.4600 \times .90 = .41400$	$.4600 \times .05 = .02300$	$.4600 \times .05 = .02300$
$.3325 \times .10 = .03325$	$.3325 \times .80 = .26600$	$.3325 \times .10 = .03325$
$.2075 \times .10 = .02075$	$.2075 \times .15 = .03113$	$.2075 \times .75 = .15563$
$p_A(2) = .46800$	$p_B(2) = .32013$	$p_C(2) = .21188$

We can see that the state probabilities have changed further, although not by as much as before. Using our latest results, we can find the state probabilities for period 3:

$.46800 \times .90 = .42120$	$.46800 \times .05 = .02340$	$.46800 \times .05 = .02340$
$.32013 \times .10 = .03201$	$.32013 \times .80 = .25610$	$.32013 \times .10 = .03201$
$.21188 \times .10 = .02119$	$.21188 \times .15 = .03178$	$.21188 \times .75 = .15891$
$p_A(3) = .47440$	$p_B(3) = .31128$	$p_C(3) = .21432$

Continuing in this manner, we find further changes in the state probabilities. Table 27-2 shows the results for increments of five periods. Notice that the successive changes are smaller. This suggests that the state probabilities may be converging toward a set of constants and that they will eventually remain unchanged. At that point, the process reaches a *steady state* and will remain the same until outside actions change the transition probabilities.

Once a steady state has been reached, the state probabilities for a Markov process are constant from period to period. These values are referred to as *steady-state probabilities*. From Table 27-2, we can see that in our illustration the steady-state probabilities are approximately .500 for brand A, .286 for brand B, and .214 for brand C. These probabilities represent the long-run shares of the market that each brand can be expected to capture.

TABLE 27-2
State Probabilities for Selected Periods

	$n = 0$	$n = 5$	$n = 10$	$n = 15$	$n = 20$	$n = 25$	$n = 30$
$p_A(n)$	.45	.48371	.49466	.49824	.49942	.49982	.49994
$p_B(n)$	.35	.30023	.28970	.28693	.28610	.28584	.28575
$p_C(n)$	.20	.21616	.21564	.21483	.21448	.21434	.21431

27-2   THE CALCULATION OF STEADY-STATE PROBABILITIES

A considerable amount of work was required to evaluate this problem for $n = 30$ time periods. It is possible to take a shortcut and to find the steady-state probabilities algebraically. In doing this, we use the fact that *when the process is in a steady state, the probability for leaving any particular state must equal the probability for entering that state.* We can therefore ignore the time period n and represent the steady-state probability for state i by p_i. As we have seen, the probability for entering a particular state is found by multiplying the state probability by the respective quantities in the applicable *column* of the transition matrix. In our example, the fact just stated provides the following relationships:

$$p_A = .90p_A + .10p_B + .10p_C$$

$$p_B = .05p_A + .80p_B + .15p_C$$

$$p_C = .05p_A + .10p_B + .75p_C$$

and the following restriction applies:

$$p_A + p_B + p_C = 1$$

The steady-state probabilities must satisfy these equations. (Although there are more equations than unknowns, any one of the first three equations is redundant, due to the fact that the transition probabilities for any starting state must sum to 1.)

We can solve these equations simultaneously to determine the steady-state probabilities exactly. Solving the first equation for p_A gives us

$$p_A - .9p_A = .1p_B + .1p_C$$

$$.1p_A = .1p_B + .1p_C$$

and

$$p_A = p_B + p_C$$

Since all of the probabilities must sum to 1, using $p_B + p_C$ for p_A gives us

$$(p_B + p_C) + p_B + p_C = 1$$

or

$$2p_B + 2p_C = 1$$

Thus

$$p_B = .5 - p_C$$

and

$$p_A = (.5 - p_C) + p_C = .5$$

Substituting $p_A = .5$ and $p_B = .5 - p_C$ into the second equation, we find

$$.5 - p_C = .05(.5) + .80(.5 - p_C) + .15p_C$$
$$-.35p_C = -.075$$

and

$$p_C = \frac{-.075}{-.35} = \frac{3}{14} = .21429$$

Thus

$$p_B = .5 - \frac{3}{14} = \frac{7}{14} - \frac{3}{14} = \frac{4}{14} = .28571$$

and the complete set of steady-state probabilities is

$$p_A = .50000 \qquad p_B = .28571 \qquad p_C = .21429$$

which agrees closely with the probabilities given in Table 27-2 for $n = 30$.

DECISION MAKING WITH A MARKOV PROCESS 27-3

We have now set the stage for a decision analysis. Suppose that the manufacturer of product A wishes to consider three different advertising and promotional policies. Policy 1 will increase brand A loyalty through a coupon-redemption plan. Policy 2 involves a series of ads aimed at capturing some of the brand B market, and policy 3 involves a series of ads aimed at capturing some of the brand C market. Each policy will modify the Markov process, and each change will result in a different transition matrix.

The transition matrices for these three policies are provided in Table 27-3. The transition probabilities in each matrix are determined by the policy itself, and they are assumed to apply only if the particular policy is actually put into operation. The applicable steady-state probabilities corresponding to the respective transition matrices are also provided in Table 27-3. These values

TABLE 27-3

Transition Matrices and Steady-State Probabilities for Alternative Advertising and Promotional Policies

POLICY 1

From State \ To	State		
	A	B	C
A	.95	.025	.025
B	.10	.800	.100
C	.10	.150	.750

$$p_A = 14/21 \qquad p_B = 4/21 \qquad p_C = 3/21$$
$$= .667 \qquad\quad = .190 \qquad\quad = .143$$

POLICY 2

From State \ To	State		
	A	B	C
A	.90	.05	.05
B	.15	.75	.10
C	.10	.15	.75

$$p_A = 19/34 \qquad p_B = 8/34 \qquad p_C = 7/34$$
$$= .559 \qquad\quad = .235 \qquad\quad = .206$$

POLICY 3

From State \ To	State		
	A	B	C
A	.90	.05	.05
B	.10	.80	.10
C	.15	.15	.70

$$p_A = 6/11 \qquad p_B = 3/11 \qquad p_C = 2/11$$
$$= .545 \qquad\quad = .273 \qquad\quad = .182$$

were obtained algebraically in the same manner as before, using the entries from the respective transition matrices.

Which policy is best? Altogether, 10,000,000 units of all brands are projected to be sold while the various campaigns are in effect. The manufacturer of brand A achieves a gross profit of $1 on each item sold. The expected total gross profit for brand A is therefore $10,000,000 \times p_A$. This is computed in Table 27-4 for each policy. We can now establish each policy's expected improvement over the status quo. Subtracting the costs of the various plans, we determine the

TABLE 27-4
Evaluation of Three Alternative Advertising and Promotional Policies for Brand A

	Market Share p_A	Expected Total Gross Profit $\$10,000,000p_A$	Expected Improvement	Added Cost of Policy	Expected Net Payoff
No change	.500	$5,000,000	—	—	—
Policy 1	14/21 (.667)	6,666,667	$1,666,667	$1,500,000	$166,667
Policy 2	19/34 (.559)	5,588,235	588,235	400,000	188,235
Policy 3	6/11 (.545)	5,454,540	454,540	300,000	154,540

expected net payoffs for the policies shown in Table 27-4. Policy 2 appears to be the best choice, even though it captures a smaller market share than policy 1.

A further illustration involving the establishment of an optimal maintenance policy will help us to understand how to analyze decision making using Markov processes.

<hr>

FINDING AN OPTIMAL MAINTENANCE POLICY   27-4

Questions of equipment maintenance occur in almost all businesses, including households. When should routine maintenance—such as cleaning a typewriter, lubricating a car, or replacing the bearings in a milling machine—be conducted? Most machines will function a long time without care, but as we well know from personal experience, such neglect can be costly in the end and may result in a major overhaul or even junking the equipment.

We can view the problem of establishing a maintenance policy in terms of a Markov process in which the various operating conditions are the states. An optimal decision rule or policy is sought that specifies the remedial action to be taken for each equipment state. Any difference between actions for a given state can be reflected in terms of the cost or payoff and the transition probabilities. Entire policies may be compared in terms of expected costs or payoffs calculated by using the applicable state probabilities obtained from the respective transition matrices.

As an illustration, consider a machine that is classified in one of the following states at the beginning of each day:

Operating Condition States
(1) Good operating condition
(2) Slightly out of adjustment
(3) Operating erratically
(4) Inoperable

Any one of the following actions can be taken to put the machine into operation at the corresponding cost:

Action	Cost	
(1) Do nothing	$ 0	(n)
(2) Do routine maintenance	100	(r)
(3) Adjust	300	(a)
(4) Adjust and do routine maintenance	350	(a & r)
(5) Overhaul	1,000	(o)

For each of the 4 states, any one of 5 actions may be taken, so that the number of possible distinct maintenance policies is $5^4 = 625$. Fortunately, management considers only a limited number of policies, since many of these policies are prohibitively costly or obviously unattractive. Further restrictions limit the possibilities. For instance, an inoperable machine must be overhauled before it can work again, and a machine that is in good operating condition or that only requires adjustment should not be overhauled.

The simplest policy is to do nothing until the machine is inoperable and then overhaul it. The transition matrix for this plan, referred to as policy 1, is given in Table 27-5. Remember that the policy itself establishes the transition probabilities, so that these probabilities apply only if the policy is adopted. The transition probabilities reflect the daily change in state. They are obtained from testing a variety of actions under all operating conditions. The data indicate that doing nothing when the machine is in good operating condition (state 1) results in a .90 probability that that same state will occur on the second day. Smaller probabilities apply in row 1 for ending up in the other states; these values become progressively smaller as the degree of disrepair increases. If the machine is out of adjustment (state 2), it cannot be restored to good operating condition without human intervention; the probability for moving from state

TABLE 27-5
Transition Matrix for Policy 1: Do Nothing Until Machine Is Inoperable

From State	1	2	3	4	Action	Cost	Steady-State Probability
1	.90	.06	.03	.01	n	$ 0	50/76 = .658
2	0	.80	.10	.10	n	0	15/76 = .197
3	0	0	.50	.50	n	0	6/76 = .079
4	1	0	0	0	o	1,000	5/76 = .066

2 to state 1 is therefore zero. The other row 2 probabilities indicate that it is most likely for the machine to remain out of adjustment (state 2) than to revert to erratic operation (state 3) or inoperability (state 4). Row 3 indicates that once the machine is operating erratically (state 3), there is a 50–50 chance that it will remain in that state or become inoperable (state 4). Finally, row 4 indicates that there is a probability of 1 moving from inoperability (state 4) to good operating condition (state 1), since the machine must then be overhauled.

The steady-state probabilities p_1, p_2, p_3, and p_4 can then be obtained for policy 1 in the usual manner by solving the following equations:

$$p_1 = .90p_1 + 1p_4$$
$$p_2 = .06p_1 + .80p_2$$
$$p_3 = .03p_1 + .10p_2 + .50p_3$$
$$p_4 = .01p_1 + .10p_2 + .50p_3$$
$$p_1 + p_2 + p_3 + p_4 = 1$$

The first equation tells us that

$$p_4 = .10p_1$$

and the second equation provides the result

$$p_2 = .30p_1$$

Substituting $.30p_1$ for p_2 in the third equation and solving for p_3, we obtain

$$p_3 = .03p_1 + .10(.30p_1) + .50p_3$$

or

$$.50p_3 = .03p_1 + .03p_1$$

so that

$$p_3 = .12p_1$$

Finally, substituting the preceding results into the last equation

$$p_1 + .30p_1 + .12p_1 + .10p_1 = 1$$

so that

$$1.52p_1 = 1$$

and

$$p_1 = 1/1.52 = 100/152 = 50/76$$

The other steady-state probability values follow from this result, so that

$$p_1 = 50/76 = .658$$
$$p_2 = 15/76 = .197$$
$$p_3 = 6/76 = .079$$
$$p_4 = 5/76 = .066$$

The applicable transition matrices for the four other policies to be considered by management are given in Table 27-6. The transition probabilities in the *rows* of these matrices reflect the particular action indicated.

Policy 2 involves routine maintenance for states 1, 2, and 3 and overhauling in state 4. The transition probabilities in rows 1, 2, and 3 differ from those for policy 1, reflecting the fact that routine maintenance reduces the chance of declining to a worse state of disrepair.

Policy 3 involves a different action for each state. Row 1 is the same as it is under policy 1, since the action taken from state 1 is doing nothing in either case. Row 2 applies when the machine is out of adjustment (state 2) and is adjusted under this policy, so that there is a .80 probability that the machine will return to good operating condition (state 1). The probabilities for achieving the inferior operating conditions from state 2 are substantially lower than before. Row 3, corresponding to an erratically operating machine, contains more favorable probabilities than it does under policy 2, since both adjustment and routine maintenance will be performed.

Policy 4 differs from Policy 3 only in row 1, where routine maintenance is done. This action is identical to what is done in state 1 under policy 2. Policy 5 is the same as policy 4 except that when the machine is operating erratically (state 3); then an overhaul is made, and the row 3 transition probabilities indicate a certain return to good operating condition (state 1).

The steady-state probabilities under each policy appear to the right of the respective transition matrices. These probabilities may be used to determine the expected daily operating cost of each policy. The computations in Table 27-7 indicate the surprising result that policy 1—do nothing until the machine is inoperable and then overhaul it—minimizes expected daily cost at a steady-state average of only $66 per day. One explanation for this is that the steady-state probability for the machine becoming inoperable is only .066, so that it is unworkable only 66 out of every 1,000 days on the average. Routine maintenance and adjustment costs are just too high to warrant those actions while the machine will still work.

TABLE 27-6

Transition Matrices for the Four Remaining Maintenance Policies

POLICY 2

To From State	State 1	2	3	4	Action	Cost	Steady-State Probability
1	.95	.03	.01	.01	r	$ 100	40/53 = .755
2	0	.85	.10	.05	r	100	8/53 = .151
3	0	0	.60	.40	r	100	3/53 = .057
4	1	0	0	0	o	1,000	2/53 = .038

POLICY 3

To From State	State 1	2	3	4			
1	.90	.06	.03	.01	n	$ 0	450/554 = .812
2	.80	.10	.08	.02	a	300	30/554 = .054
3	0	0	.70	.30	a & r	350	53/554 = .096
4	1	0	0	0	o	1,000	21/554 = .038

POLICY 4

To From State	State 1	2	3	4			
1	.95	.03	.01	.01	r	$ 100	900/989 = .910
2	.80	.10	.08	.02	a	300	30/989 = .030
3	0	0	.70	.30	a & r	350	38/989 = .038
4	1	0	0	0	o	1,000	21/989 = .021

POLICY 5

To From State	State 1	2	3	4			
1	.95	.03	.01	.01	r	$ 100	1,500/1,585 = .946
2	.80	.10	.08	.02	a	300	50/1,585 = .032
3	1	0	0	0	o	1,000	19/1,585 = .012
4	1	0	0	0	o	1,000	16/1,585 = .010

TABLE 27-7
Expected Daily Cost Calculations
for the Various Maintenance Policies

Policy	State	Steady-State Probability	Action	Cost	Cost × Probability
1	1	.658	n	$ 0	$ 0
	2	.197	n	0	0
	3	.079	n	0	0
	4	.066	o	1,000	66.00
					$66.00 = expected cost
2	1	.755	r	100	75.50
	2	.151	r	100	15.10
	3	.057	r	100	5.70
	4	.038	o	1,000	38.00
					$134.30 = expected cost
3	1	.812	n	0	0
	2	.054	a	300	16.20
	3	.096	a & r	350	33.60
	4	.038	o	1,000	38.00
					$87.80 = expected cost
4	1	.910	r	100	91.00
	2	.030	a	300	9.00
	3	.038	a & r	350	13.30
	4	.021	o	1,000	21.00
					$134.30 = expected cost
5	1	.946	r	100	94.60
	2	.032	a	300	9.60
	3	.012	o	1,000	12.00
	4	.010	o	1,000	10.00
					$126.20 = expected cost

This policy is similar to the one that many Americans apply to automobile maintenance. We generally abuse our vehicles and—except for oil changes, lubrications, tune-ups, and the replacement of batteries, worn tires, and brake linings—we make repairs only after the car stops running. One explanation is that mechanical work is very expensive, often costing more than a worn-out and depreciated car is worth. However, airlines go to the other extreme in maintaining planes, replacing engines after several hundred hours of operation and performing extensive preventive maintenance, whether or not it is visibly needed. In the latter case, the cost of failure is huge in comparison to the relatively trivial costs of routine maintenance.

ADDITIONAL REMARKS 27-5

In this chapter, we have illustrated the underlying concepts of a Markov process. A class of decisions may be analyzed using the appropriate transition matrix for each alternative policy to find the steady-state probabilities. These probabilities are then combined with economic data to calculate the expected costs or payoffs, which can then be compared to determine the optimal policy.

The validity of this analysis is based on the steady-state behavior of the system under the various policies. Although the adoption of a new operating policy can result in a new transition matrix immediately, it generally takes a while for any Markov process to settle into the steady state. This is because the individual state probabilities usually differ from their long-run values. Until the equilibrium condition is reached, the system as a whole is in a *transient state*.

Thus, a complete analysis should consider what conditions apply in the transient state and how long the revised system takes to reach a steady state. If the changes are greater under some alternatives than others or if the durations of the transient phases differ, then these differences should also be considered when selecting the optimal policy.

Analyzing a decision in terms of a Markov process may be more valid in some applications than in others. For instance, this approach has been criticized when applied to brand switching, because the transient state can be quite lengthy in relation to the duration of the alternative advertising policies being evaluated. There is some question of whether a steady state is ever reached before the marketplace is perturbed by further competitive forces. Obviously, an analysis based wholly on steady-state behavior would be invalid if this were true. A more fundamental criticism of brand-switching applications pertains to the transition matrix itself. Competitors and shifting customer tastes may cause unanticipated changes in the transition probabilities, so that these values may be uncertain and even short-lived regardless of the marketing policy that a particular manufacturer adopts. The transition matrix that actually results might be viewed as the outcome of a complex interactive decision process involving several parties.

In other applications where outside forces are minimal and where policies are expected to operate under stable conditions for a long time, an analysis based on the Markov process may be the proper procedure. This is often the case in establishing equipment maintenance policies. The same basic approach has been employed with varying degrees of success in a wide variety of applications, including designing port facilities, planning political strategies, and establishing policies for releasing water from dams.

We have barely covered the theoretical aspects of Markov processes here. The processes themselves are special cases of more general stochastic processes. When the Markov process is combined with decision making, the resulting mathematical procedure falls into the broad category of a *Markovian decision model*. These models, in turn, may fit into a variety of categories described in this book. For instance, decisions involving a Markov process can be solved as linear programming problems. Others can be expressed as dynamic programs. Thus, the simplex method or a variety of other solution procedures can be used to establish an optimal policy for a particular situation. Although a detailed discussion of the theory of Markov processes and the more advanced models and procedures used with them in decision making is beyond the scope of this book, several references provided in the bibliography provide opportunities for further study of this rich topic.

PROBLEMS

27-1   A system may be in state 1 or state 2. The following transition matrix applies:

From \ To	1	2
1	1/3	2/3
2	3/4	1/4

Determine the steady-state probabilities.

27-2   A system may be in one of three states. The following transition matrix applies:

From \ To	A	B	C
A..	1/2	0	1/2
B	1/4	1/4	1/2
C	1/3	1/3	1/3

(a) Suppose that in the initial period, the system will be in state A with certainty. Determine the value $p_A(5)$, $p_B(5)$, and $p_C(5)$.
(b) Compute the steady-state probabilities.

27-3   The following transition matrix applies to a system:

From \ To	1	2
1	.2	.8
2	.6	.4

(a) Compute the steady-state probabilities.

(b) Suppose that $p_1(0) = .4$ and $p_2(0) = .6$. Compute the successive state probabilities $p_1(n)$ and $p_2(n)$ for $n = 1, 2, 3,$ and 4. In what period does $p_1(n)$ lie within .001 of the steady-state probability for state 1?

27-4 Suppose that the brand A manufacturer discussed in Section 27-3 tries advertising policy 4, under which a 98% period-to-period retention applies to brand A, and there is only a 1% chance of switching either from A to B or from A to C. Under this policy, the transition probabilities for starting from the other brands remain at the original levels. Policy 4 will cost $3 million. If we assume that the goal of maximizing expected gross payoff is valid, would the manufacturer prefer this policy to the ones discussed in the chapter?

27-5 Reevaluate the maintenance decision discussed in Section 27-4 when the following costs apply:

$	0	(n)
	50	(r)
	150	(a)
	200	$(a \& r)$
	1,000	(o)

Which policy yields the minimum expected daily cost?

27-6 Consider a sixth possible policy for the machine maintenance decision described in Section 27-4. Under this policy, nothing is done until the machine begins to operate erratically (when it is adjusted and routine maintenance is performed) or until it is inoperable (when an overhaul is performed).

(a) Determine the applicable transition matrix (This can be obtained by using the pertinent rows from policy 1 and policy 3 in Tables 27-5 and 27-6.)

(b) Find the steady-state probabilities.

(c) What is the expected daily maintenance cost of this new policy? Is it better than all of the original five policies?

27-7 Whenever one state can be reached from another state sometime in a Markov process, the two states are said to *communicate*. If a state is never left, it is referred to as an *absorbing state*.

(a) What can be said regarding the steady-state probability for an absorbing state that communicates with all of the remaining states?

(b) A Hawaiian potato chip is reputed to have the following transition matrix for brand-switching in its market:

From \ To	Hawaiian Chip	Mainland Chip
Hawaiian Chip	1	0
Mainland Chip	.01	.99

If this matrix is valid, which chip will eventually have the entire market to itself? Verify your answer by computing the steady-state proportion of the market held by each chip. What kind of state is the buyer of the Hawaiian chip in?

27-8   Each sales transaction at Ace Widgets falls into one of the following states:
(1) Cash received
(2) Account receivable
(3) Uncollectable funds
Suppose the following transition matrix applies to each successive month after a sale:

From \ To	1	2	3
1	1	0	0
2	.80	.19	.01
3	0	0	1

(a) If $p_1(0) = .9$, $p_2(0) = 0$, and $p_3(0) = .1$, find $p_1(1)$, $p_2(1)$, and $p_3(1)$. Do you notice anything unusual?

(b) What can you conclude regarding the steady-state probabilities with respect to the values of the initial state probabilites?

27-9   Republican Senator Herman Angel is running for reelection against a Democratic challenger, Representative Sheila Saint. The 10,000 voters of Pearly Gates may be categorized in one of five ways:

State	Percentage Who Vote for Angel
(1) Rabid Republican	99%
(2) Liberal Republican	95
(3) Fence sitter	50
(4) Straying Democrat	40
(5) Indelible Democrat	10

Angel forces are running a special campaign to attempt to move the voters into the more favorable categories. Without these special efforts, the following transition matrix currently applies to a day-to-day switch in voter sentiment:

From \ To	1	2	3	4	5
1	.95	.05	0	0	0
2	.10	.80	.10	0	0
3	0	.15	.70	.15	0
4	0	0	.20	.70	.10
5	0	0	0	.25	.75

(a) Election day is a long way off. If no special campaign is conducted, how many Pearly Gaters can be expected to vote for Angel?

(b) The special campaign will focus on making fence sitters more favorable to Republican sentiment. This will result in an identical transition matrix except for new row 3 transition probabilities of

$$0 \quad .40 \quad .50 \quad .10 \quad 0$$

Now how many Pearly Gaters can be expected to vote for Angel?

27-10 An oil company is evaluating two alternative plans for supplying a remote off-shore drilling platform with drill bits. The first policy is to keep just one working bit at the site and air-drop a replacement in when it breaks. The alternative policy is to keep two bits at the site and to send a replacement by boat only when one of them breaks; the boat will replace all broken bits. There is only a 10% chance that a drill bit will break on any given day; a bit cannot be replaced on the same day that it breaks. An air-drop takes place the next day, so no lost production occurs. A sea delivery takes two days longer and only one boat can be dispatched at a time. Each day's lost production represents $10,000 in lost future profits, and the two delivery modes have identical costs. A production loss occurs whenever a bit breaks, which is assumed to happen near the beginning of a working day. When replacements are made or deliveries are received, they occur just before the day's drilling begins. Depending on the delivery policy chosen, some or all of the following states apply at the beginning of any particular scheduled drilling day:

> A: No good bits.
> B: One good bit; no break yesterday.
> C: One good bit; a break yesterday.
> D: Two good bits; last replacement was for one bit.
> E: Two good bits; last replacement was for two bits.

(a) Construct the transition matrices for the two policies.
(b) Find the steady-state probabilities for each policy.
(c) Consider the air-drop policy. Each transition may involve a production cost (a loss). Determine the expected cost of starting in each state by summing the products of these costs with the corresponding probabilities in the applicable row of the transition matrix. Then apply the steady-state probabilities to determine the expected daily policy cost.
(d) Repeat (c) for the sea-delivery policy.
(e) Which policy minimizes expected daily cost?

Bibliography

BASIC CONCEPTS AND SURVEY OF TOPICS

Ackoff, R. L. *Scientific Method: Optimizing Applied Research Decisions*. New York: John Wiley & Sons, 1962.

———, and P. Rivett. *A Manager's Guide to Operations Research*. New York: John Wiley & Sons, 1963.

———, and M. W. Sasieni. *Fundamentals of Operations Research*. New York: John Wiley & Sons, 1968.

Argyris, C., "Management Information Systems: The Challenge to Rationality and Emotionality," *Management Science*, February 1971, pp. B-275–B-292.

Baumol, W. J. *Economic Theory and Operations Analysis*. 4th ed. Englewood Cliffs, N.J.: Prentice-Hall, Inc., 1977.

Caywood, T. E., et al., "Guidelines for the Practice of Operations Research," *Operations Research*, September 1971, pp. 1127–48.

Churchman, C. W., R. L. Ackoff, and E. L. Arnoff. *Introduction to Operations Research*. New York: John Wiley & Sons, 1957.

Duckworth, W. E. et al. *A Guide to Operational Research*. 3rd ed. New York: Halsted Press, 1977.

Enrick, N. L. *Management Operations Research*. New York: Holt, Rinehart and Winston, 1965.

Hillier, F. S., and G. J. Lieberman. *Introduction to Operations Research*. 3rd ed. San Francisco: Holden-Day, 1980.

Miller, D. W., and M. K. Starr. *Executive Decisions and Operations Research*. 2nd. ed. Englewood Cliffs, N.J.: Prentice-Hall, Inc., 1969.

———, and M. K. Starr. *The Structure of Human Decisions*. Englewood Cliffs, N.J.: Prentice-Hall, Inc., 1967.

Rivett, P. *Model Building for Decision Analysis*. New York: John Wiley & Sons, 1979.

Sasieni, M., A. Yaspan, and L. Friedman. *Operations Research: Methods and Problems*. New York: John Wiley & Sons, 1959.

Teichrow, D. *An Introduction to Management Science: Deterministic Models*. New York: John Wiley & Sons, 1964.

Turban, E., "A Sample Survey of Operations-Research Activities at the Corporate Level," *Operations Research*, May–June 1972, pp. 708–721.

Wagner, H. M., *Principles of Operations Research*. 2nd ed. Englewood Cliffs, N.J.: Prentice-Hall, Inc., 1975.

———, "The ABC's of OR," *Operations Research*, October 1971, pp. 1259–81.

Woolsey, R. E. D., "Operations Research and Management Science Today," *Operations Research*, May–June 1972, pp. 729–37.

PROBABILITY CONCEPTS (Chapters 2–3)

Feller, W. *An Introduction to Probability Theory and Its Applications*, Vol. 1. 3rd ed. New York: John Wiley & Sons, 1968.

Hodges, J. L., Jr., and E. L. Lehmann. *Elements of Finite Probability*. San Francisco: Holden-Day, 1965.

Lapin, L. L. *Statistics for Modern Business Decisions*. 2nd ed. New York: Harcourt Brace Jovanovich, 1978.

Laplace, Pierre Simon, Marquis de. *A Philosophical Essay on Probabilities*. New York: Dover Publications, 1951.

Lindgren, B. W., and G. W. McElrath. *Introduction to Probability and Statistics*, 4th ed. New York: Macmillan, 1969.

Mosteller, F., R. Rourke, and G. Thomas, Jr. *Probability and Statistics*. Reading, Mass.: Addison-Wesley, 1978.

Parzen, Emmanuel. *Modern Probability Theory and Its Applications*. New York: John Wiley & Sons, 1960.

FORECASTING (Chapter 4)

Box, G. E. P., and G. M. Jenkins. *Time Series Analysis: Forecasting and Control*. rev. ed. San Francisco: Holden-Day, 1976.

Brown, R. G. *Smoothing, Forecasting, and Prediction*. Englewood Cliffs, N.J.: Prentice-Hall, Inc., 1963.

Chambers, J. C., S. K. Mullick, and D. D. Smith, "How to Choose the Right Forecasting Technique," *Harvard Business Review*, July–August 1971, pp. 45–74.

Gross, C., and R. Peterson. *Business Forecasting*. Boston: Houghton Mifflin, 1976.

Holt, C. C., F. Modigliani, J. F. Muth, and H. A. Simon. *Planning Production, Inventories, and Work Force*. Englewood Cliffs, N.J.: Prentice-Hall, Inc., 1960.

Lapin, L. L. *Statistics for Modern Business Decisions*. 2nd ed. New York: Harcourt Brace Jovanovich, 1978.

Makridakis, S., and S. C. Wheelwright. *Forecasting Methods and Applications*. New York: John Wiley & Sons, 1978.

———, *Interactive Forecasting*. 2nd ed. San Francisco: Holden-Day, 1978.

McLaughlin, R. L. *Time Series Forecasting*. Marketing Research Technique, Series No. 6, American Marketing Association, 1962.

Raiffa, H. *Decision Analysis: Introductory Lectures on Choices Under Uncertainty*. Reading, Mass.: Addison-Wesley, 1968.

Schlaifer, R. *Analysis of Decisions Under Uncertainty*. New York: McGraw-Hill Book Co., 1969.

Spencer, M. H., C. G. Clark, and P. W. Hoguet. *Business and Economic Forecasting: An Econometric Approach*. Homewood, Ill.: Richard D. Irwin, 1965.

DECISION THEORY AND UTILITY (Chapters 5–6, 17–22)

Aitchison, J. *Choice Against Chance: An Introduction to Statistical Decision Theory*. Reading, Mass.: Addison-Wesley, 1970.

Brown, R. V., A. S. Kahr, and C. Peterson. *Decision Analysis for the Manager*. New York: Holt, Rinehart and Winston, 1974.

Chernoff, H., and L. E. Moses. *Elementary Decision Theory*. New York: John Wiley & Sons, 1959.

Lapin, L. L. *Statistics for Modern Business Decisions*. 2nd ed. New York: Harcourt Brace Jovanovich, 1978.

Luce, R. D., and H. Raiffa. *Games and Decisions: Introduction and Critical Survey*. New York: John Wiley & Sons, 1957.

Miller, D. W., and M. K. Starr. *Executive Decisions and Operations Research*. 2nd ed. Englewood Cliffs, N. J.: Prentice-Hall, Inc. 1969.

Morris, W. T. *Management Science: A Bayesian Introduction*. Englewood Cliffs, N. J.: Prentice-Hall, 1968.

Pratt, J. W., H. Raiffa, and R. Schlaifer. *Introduction to Statistical Decision Theory*. New York: McGraw-Hill Book Co., 1965.

Raiffa, H. *Decision Analysis: Introductory Lectures on Choices Under Uncertainty*. Reading, Mass.: Addison-Wesley, 1968.

Schlaifer, R. *Analysis of Decisions Under Uncertainty*. New York: McGraw-Hill Book Co., 1969.

———. *Introduction to Statistics for Business Decisions*. New York: McGraw-Hill Book Co., 1961.

INVENTORY DECISIONS (Chapters 7–8)

Arrow, K. J., S. Karlin, and H. Scarf. *Studies in the Mathematical Theory of Inventory and Production*. Stanford, Ca.: Stanford University Press, 1958.

Buffa, E. S., and W. Taubert. *Production-Inventory Systems: Planning and Control*. 3rd ed. Homewood, Ill.: Richard D. Irwin, 1979.

Greene, J. H. *Production and Inventory Control Handbook*. New York: McGraw-Hill Book Co., 1970.

Hadley, G., and T. M. Whitin. *Analysis of Inventory Systems*. Englewood Cliffs, N. J.: Prentice-Hall, Inc., 1963.

Hillier, F. S., and G. J. Lieberman. *Introduction to Operations Research*. 3rd ed. San Francisco: Holden-Day, 1980.

Holt, C. C., F. Modigliani, J. F. Muth, and H. A. Simon. *Planning Production, Inventories, and Work Force*. Englewood Cliffs, N. J.: Prentice-Hall, Inc., 1960.

Magee, J. R., and D. M. Boodman, *Production Planning and Inventory Control*. 2nd ed. New York: McGraw-Hill Book Co., 1967.

Starr, M. K., and D. W. Miller. *Inventory Control: Theory and Practice*. Englewood Cliffs, N. J.: Prentice-Hall, Inc., 1962.

Wagner, H. M. *Principles of Operations Research*. 2nd ed. Englewood Cliffs, N. J.: Prentice-Hall, Inc., 1975.

––––––. *Statistical Management of Inventory Systems*. New York: John Wiley & Sons, 1962.

Whitin, T. M. *The Theory of Inventory Management*. Reprint of 1957 ed. Westport, CT: Greenwood Press, Inc.

LINEAR AND INTEGER PROGRAMMING (Chapters 9–16)

Dantzig, G. B. *Linear Programming and Extensions*. Princeton, N. J.: Princeton University Press, 1963.

Garvin, W. W. *Introduction to Linear Programming*. New York: McGraw-Hill Book Co., 1960.

Gass, S. I. *Linear Programming*. 4th ed. New York: McGraw-Hill Book Co., 1975.

Hadley, G. *Linear Programming*. Reading, Mass.: Addison-Wesley, 1962.

Hillier, F. S., and G. J. Lieberman. *Introduction to Operations Research*, 3rd ed. San Francisco: Holden-Day, Inc., 1980.

Kim, C. *Introduction to Linear Programming*. New York: Holt, Rinehart and Winston, Inc., 1971.

Kwak, N. K. *Mathematical Programming with Business Applications*. New York: McGraw-Hill Book Co., 1972.

Naylor, T. H., E. T. Byrne, and J. M. Vernon. *Introduction to Linear Programming: Methods and Cases*. Belmont, Ca.: Wadsworth Publishing Co., 1971.

Simonnard, M. *Linear Programming*. Englewood Cliffs, N. J.: Prentice-Hall, Inc., 1966.

Wagner, H. M. *Principles of Operations Research with Applications to Managerial Decisions*. Englewood Cliffs, N. J.: Prentice-Hall, Inc., 1975.

GAMES AND INTERACTIVE DECISIONS (Chapter 22)

Davis, M. D. *Game Theory: A Nontechnical Introduction*. New York: Basic Books, Inc., 1973.

Luce, R. D., and H. Raiffa. *Games and Decisions: Introduction and Critical Survey*. New York: John Wiley & Sons, 1957.

Karlin, S. *Mathematical Methods and Theory in Games, Programming and Economics.* Reading, Mass.: Addison-Wesley Publishing Co., Inc., 1959.

May, F. B. *Introduction to Games of Strategy.* Boston: Allyn and Bacon, 1970.

McKinsey, J. C. C. *Introduction to the Theory of Games.* New York: McGraw-Hill Book Co., 1952.

Owen, G. *Game Theory.* Philadelphia: W. B. Saunders Co., 1968.

Rapoport, A. *Two Person Game Theory.* Ann Arbor: University of Michigan Press, 1966.

Vajda, S. *The Theory of Games and Linear Programming.* New York: Halsted Press, 1967.

Von Neumann, J., and O. Morgenstern. *Theory of Games and Economic Behavior.* New York: John Wiley & Sons, 1953.

Williams, J. D. *The Compleat Strategist.* rev. ed. New York: McGraw-Hill Book Co., 1965.

QUEUES (Chapter 23)

Cooper, R. B. *Introduction to Queueing Theory.* New York: Macmillan, 1972.

Cox, D. R., and W. L. Smith. *Queues.* London: Methuen & Co., Ltd., 1961.

Gross, D., and C. M. Harris. *Fundamentals of Queueing Theory.* New York: Wiley-Interscience, 1974.

Hillier, F. S., and G. J. Lieberman. *Introduction to Operations Research.* 3rd ed. San Francisco: Holden-Day, Inc., 1980.

Lee, A. M. *Applied Queueing Theory.* New York: St. Martin's Press, 1966.

Morse, P. M. *Queues, Inventories, and Maintenance.* New York: John Wiley & Sons, 1958.

Newell, G. F. *Applications of Queueing Theory.* New York: Halsted Press, 1971.

Prabhu, N. U. *Queues and Inventories.* New York: John Wiley & Sons, 1965.

Saaty, T. L. *Elements of Queueing Theory.* New York: McGraw-Hill Book Co., 1961.

Wagner, H. M. *Principles of Operations Research.* Englewood Cliffs, N. J.: Prentice-Hall, Inc., 1975.

PERT (Chapter 24)

Baker, B. N., and R. L. Ellis. *An Introduction to PERT/CPM.* Homewood, Ill.: Richard D. Irwin, 1964.

Evarts, H. E. *Introduction to PERT.* Boston: Allyn and Bacon, 1964.

Levin, R. I., and C. A. Kirkpatrick. *Planning and Control with PERT/CPM.* New York: McGraw-Hill Book Co., 1966.

Lockyer, K. G. *An Introduction to Critical Path Analysis,* New York: Beckman Pubs. 1969.

MacCrimmon, K. R., and C. A. Ryavec, "Analytical Study of the PERT Assumptions," *Operations Research,* January 1964, pp. 16–37.

Moder, J. J., and C. R. Philips. *Project Management with CPM and PERT,* 2nd ed. New York: D. Van Nostrand, 1970.

Weist, J. D., and F. K. Levy. *A Management Guide to PERT/CPM: With Gert-PDM, DCPM and Other Networks.* 2nd ed. Englewood Cliffs, N. J.: Prentice-Hall, Inc., 1977.

SIMULATION (Chapter 25)

Bonini, C. P. *Simulation of Information and Decision Systems in the Firm.* Englewood Cliffs, N. J.: Prentice-Hall, Inc., 1963.

Emshoff, J. R., and R. L. Sisson. *Design and Use of Computer Simulation Models.* New York: MacMillan, 1970.

Evans, G. W., G. F. Wallace, and G. L. Sutherland. *Simulation Using Digital Computers.* Englewood Cliffs, N. J.: Prentice-Hall, Inc., 1967.

General Purpose Simulation System/360: Introductory User's Manual. White Plains, N. Y.: IBM Corporation, 1967.

Kleijnen, J. P. C. *Statistical Techniques in Simulation.* New York: Marcel Dekker, 1974.

Markowitz, H. M. "Simulating with SIMSCRIPT," *Management Science*, June 1966, pp. B-396–404.

Martin, F. F. *Computer Modeling and Simulation.* New York: John Wiley & Sons, 1968.

Meier, R. C., W. T. Newell, and H. J. Pazer. *Simulation in Business and Economics.* Englewood Cliffs, N. J.: Prentice-Hall, Inc., 1969.

Naylor, T. H., J. L. Balintfy, D. S. Burdick, and K. Hu. *Computer Simulation Techniques.* New York: John Wiley & Sons, 1968.

Pugh, A. L. *DYNAMO User's Manual*, 5th ed. Cambridge, Mass.: MIT Press, 1976.

Schmidt, J. W., and R. E. Taylor. *Simulation and Analysis of Industrial Systems.* Homewood, Ill.: Richard D. Irwin, 1970.

Tocher, K. D. *The Art of Simulation.* London: The English University Press, 1963.

DYNAMIC PROGRAMMING (Chapter 26)

Bellman, R. E. *Adaptive Control Processes: A Guided Tour.* Princeton, N. J.: Princeton University Press, 1961

———. *Dynamic Programming.* Princeton, N. J.: Princeton University Press, 1957.

———, and S. E. Dreyfus. *Applied Dynamic Programming.* Princeton, N. J.: Princeton University Press, 1962.

Hillier, F. S., and G. J. Lieberman. *Introduction to Operations Research*, 3rd ed. San Francisco: Holden-Day, 1980.

Howard, R. A. *Dynamic Programming and Markov Processes.* Cambridge, Mass.: MIT Press, 1960.

Kaufman, A., and R. Cruon. *Dynamic Programming: Sequential Scientific Management.* New York: Academic Press, 1967.

Nemhauser, G. L. *Introduction to Dynamic Programming.* New York: John Wiley & Sons, 1966.

Wagner, H. M. *Principles of Operations Research*, 2nd ed. Englewood Cliffs, N.J.: Prentice-Hall, Inc., 1975.

White, J. D. *Dynamic Programming.* San Francisco: Holden-Day, 1969.

MARKOV PROCESSES (Chapter 27)

Derman, C. *Finite State Markovian Decision Processes*. New York: Academic Press, 1970.

Freedman, D. *Markov Chains*. San Francisco: Holden-Day, 1971.

Hillier, F. S., and G. J. Lieberman. *Introduction to Operations Research*, 3rd ed. San Francisco: Holden-Day, 1980.

Howard, R. *Dynamic Programming and Markov Processes*. Cambridge, Mass.: MIT Press, 1960.

Kemeny, J. G., and J. L. Snell. *Finite Markov Chains*. New York: Springer-Verlag New York, Inc., 1976.

Martin, J. J. *Bayesian Decision Problems and Markov Chains*. Reprint of 1967 ed. New York: John Wiley & Sons, 1975.

Wagner, H. M. *Principles of Operations Research*, 2d ed. Englewood Cliffs, N. J.: Prentice-Hall, Inc., 1975.

Appendix
Tables

TABLE A
Cumulative Values for the Binomial Probability Distribution

$$\Pr[R \le r]$$

n = 1

P r	.01	.05	.10	.20	.30	.40	.50
0	0.9900	0.9500	0.9000	0.8000	0.7000	0.6000	0.5000
1	1.0000	1.0000	1.0000	1.0000	1.0000	1.0000	1.0000

n = 2

P r	.01	.05	.10	.20	.30	.40	.50
0	0.9801	0.9025	0.8100	0.6400	0.4900	0.3600	0.2500
1	0.9999	0.9975	0.9900	0.9600	0.9100	0.8400	0.7500
2	1.0000	1.0000	1.0000	1.0000	1.0000	1.0000	1.0000

n = 3

P r	.01	.05	.10	.20	.30	.40	.50
0	0.9703	0.8574	0.7290	0.5120	0.3430	0.2160	0.1250
1	0.9997	0.9927	0.9720	0.8960	0.7840	0.6480	0.5000
2	1.0000	0.9999	0.9990	0.9920	0.9730	0.9360	0.8750
3	1.0000	1.0000	1.0000	1.0000	1.0000	1.0000	1.0000

n = 4

P r	.01	.05.	.10	.20	.30	.40	.50
0	0.9606	0.8145	0.6561	0.4096	0.2401	0.1296	0.0625
1	0.9994	0.9860	0.9477	0.8192	0.6517	0.4752	0.3125
2	1.0000	0.9995	0.9963	0.9728	0.9163	0.8208	0.6875
3	1.0000	1.0000	0.9999	0.9984	0.9919	0.9744	0.9375
4	1.0000	1.0000	1.0000	1.0000	1.0000	1.0000	1.0000

n = 5

P r	.01	.05	.10	.20	.30	.40	.50
0	0.9510	0.7738	0.5905	0.3277	0.1681	0.0778	0.0313
1	0.9990	0.9774	0.9185	0.7373	0.5282	0.3370	0.1875
2	1.0000	0.9988	0.9914	0.9421	0.8369	0.6826	0.5000
3	1.0000	1.0000	0.9995	0.9933	0.9692	0.9130	0.8125
4	1.0000	1.0000	1.0000	0.9997	0.9976	0.9898	0.9688
5				1.0000	1.0000	1.0000	1.0000

TABLE A (*continued*)

$n = 10$

P \ r	.01	.05	.10	.20	.30	.40	.50
0	0.9044	0.5987	0.3487	0.1074	0.0282	0.0060	0.0010
1	0.9957	0.9139	0.7361	0.3758	0.1493	0.0464	0.0107
2	0.9999	0.9885	0.9298	0.6778	0.3828	0.1673	0.0547
3	1.0000	0.9990	0.9872	0.8791	0.6496	0.3823	0.1719
4	1.0000	0.9999	0.9984	0.9672	0.8497	0.6331	0.3770
5	1.0000	1.0000	0.9999	0.9936	0.9526	0.8338	0.6230
6	1.0000	1.0000	1.0000	0.9991	0.9894	0.9452	0.8281
7				0.9999	0.9999	0.9877	0.9453
8				1.0000	1.0000	0.9983	0.9893
9						0.9999	0.9990
10						1.0000	1.0000

$n = 20$

P \ r	.01	.05	.10	.20	.30	.40	.50
0	0.8179	0.3585	0.1216	0.0115	0.0008	0.0000	0.0000
1	0.9831	0.7358	0.3917	0.0692	0.0076	0.0005	0.0000
2	0.9990	0.9245	0.6769	0.2061	0.0355	0.0036	0.0002
3	1.0000	0.9841	0.8670	0.4114	0.1071	0.0160	0.0013
4	1.0000	0.9974	0.9568	0.6296	0.2375	0.0510	0.0059
5	1.0000	0.9997	0.9887	0.8042	0.4164	0.1256	0.0207
6	1.0000	1.0000	0.9976	0.9133	0.6080	0.2500	0.0577
7	1.0000	1.0000	0.9996	0.9679	0.7723	0.4159	0.1316
8	1.0000	1.0000	0.9999	0.9900	0.8867	0.5956	0.2517
9	1.0000	1.0000	1.0000	0.9974	0.9520	0.7553	0.4119
10				0.9994	0.9829	0.8725	0.5881
11				0.9999	0.9949	0.9435	0.7483
12				1.0000	0.9987	0.9790	0.8684
13					0.9997	0.9935	0.9423
14					1.0000	0.9984	0.9793
15						0.9997	0.9941
16						1.0000	0.9987
17							0.9998
18							1.0000

TABLE A (*continued*)

$n = 50$

P r	.01	.05	.10	.20	.30	.40	.50
0	0.6050	0.0769	0.0052	0.0000	0.0000	0.0000	0.0000
1	0.9106	0.2794	0.0338	0.0002	0.0000	0.0000	0.0000
2	0.9862	0.5405	0.1117	0.0013	0.0000	0.0000	0.0000
3	0.9984	0.7604	0.2503	0.0057	0.0000	0.0000	0.0000
4	0.9999	0.8964	0.4312	0.0185	0.0002	0.0000	0.0000
5	1.0000	0.9622	0.6161	0.0480	0.0007	0.0000	0.0000
6	1.0000	0.9882	0.7702	0.1034	0.0025	0.0000	0.0000
7	1.0000	0.9968	0.8779	0.1904	0.0073	0.0001	0.0000
8	1.0000	0.9992	0.9421	0.3073	0.0183	0.0002	0.0000
9	1.0000	0.9998	0.9755	0.4437	0.0402	0.0008	0.0000
10	1.0000	1.0000	0.9906	0.5836	0.0789	0.0022	0.0000
11	1.0000	1.0000	0.9968	0.7107	0.1390	0.0057	0.0000
12	1.0000	1.0000	0.9990	0.8139	0.2229	0.0133	0.0002
13	1.0000	1.0000	0.9997	0.8894	0.3279	0.0280	0.0005
14	1.0000	1.0000	0.9999	0.9393	0.4468	0.0540	0.0013
15	1.0000	1.0000	1.0000	0.9692	0.5692	0.0955	0.0033
16				0.9856	0.6839	0.1561	0.0077
17				0.9937	0.7822	0.2369	0.0164
18				0.9975	0.8594	0.3356	0.0325
19				0.9991	0.9152	0.4465	0.0595
20				0.9997	0.9522	0.5610	0.1013
21				0.9999	0.9749	0.6701	0.1611
22				1.0000	0.9877	0.7660	0.2399
23					0.9944	0.8438	0.3359
24					0.9976	0.9022	0.4439
25					0.9991	0.9427	0.5561
26					0.9997	0.9686	0.6641
27					0.9999	0.9840	0.7601
28					1.0000	0.9924	0.8389
29						0.9966	0.8987
30						0.9986	0.9405
31						0.9995	0.9675
32						0.9998	0.9836
33						0.9999	0.9923
34						1.0000	0.9967
35							0.9987
36							0.9995
37							0.9998
38							1.0000

TABLE A (*continued*)

$n = 100$

P	.01	.05	.10	.20	.30	.40	.50
r							
0	0.3660	0.0059	0.0000	0.0000	0.0000	0.0000	0.0000
1	0.7358	0.0371	0.0003	0.0000	0.0000	0.0000	0.0000
2	0.9206	0.1183	0.0019	0.0000	0.0000	0.0000	0.0000
3	0.9816	0.2578	0.0078	0.0000	0.0000	0.0000	0.0000
4	0.9966	0.4360	0.0237	0.0000	0.0000	0.0000	0.0000
5	0.9995	0.6160	0.0576	0.0000	0.0000	0.0000	0.0000
6	0.9999	0.7660	0.1172	0.0001	0.0000	0.0000	0.0000
7	1.0000	0.8720	0.2061	0.0003	0.0000	0.0000	0.0000
8	1.0000	0.9369	0.3209	0.0009	0.0000	0.0000	0.0000
9	1.0000	0.9718	0.4513	0.0023	0.0000	0.0000	0.0000
10	1.0000	0.9885	0.5832	0.0057	0.0000	0.0000	0.0000
11	1.0000	0.9957	0.7030	0.0126	0.0000	0.0000	0.0000
12	1.0000	0.9985	0.8018	0.0253	0.0000	0.0000	0.0000
13	1.0000	0.9995	0.8761	0.0469	0.0001	0.0000	0.0000
14	1.0000	0.9999	0.9274	0.0804	0.0002	0.0000	0.0000
15	1.0000	1.0000	0.9601	0.1285	0.0004	0.0000	0.0000
16	1.0000	1.0000	0.9794	0.1923	0.0010	0.0000	0.0000
17	1.0000	1.0000	0.9900	0.2712	0.0022	0.0000	0.0000
18	1.0000	1.0000	0.9954	0.3621	0.0045	0.0000	0.0000
19	1.0000	1.0000	0.9980	0.4602	0.0089	0.0000	0.0000
20	1.0000	1.0000	0.9992	0.5595	0.0165	0.0000	0.0000
21	1.0000	1.0000	0.9997	0.6540	0.0288	0.0000	0.0000
22	1.0000	1.0000	0.9999	0.7389	0.0479	0.0001	0.0000
23	1.0000	1.0000	1.0000	0.8109	0.0755	0.0003	0.0000
24				0.8686	0.1136	0.0006	0.0000
25				0.9125	0.1631	0.0012	0.0000
26				0.9442	0.2244	0.0024	0.0000
27				0.9658	0.2964	0.0046	0.0000
28				0.9800	0.3768	0.0084	0.0000
29				0.9888	0.4623	0.0148	0.0000
30				0.9939	0.5491	0.0248	0.0000
31				0.9969	0.6331	0.0398	0.0001
32				0.9984	0.7107	0.0615	0.0002
33				0.9993	0.7793	0.0913	0.0004
34				0.9997	0.8371	0.1303	0.0009
35				0.9999	0.8839	0.1795	0.0018

TABLE A (continued)

$n = 100$

P r	.01	.05	.10	.20	.30	.40	.50
36				0.9999	0.9201	0.2386	0.0033
37				1.0000	0.9470	0.3068	0.0060
38					0.9660	0.3822	0.0105
39					0.9790	0.4621	0.0176
40					0.9875	0.5433	0.0284
41					0.9928	0.6225	0.0443
42					0.9960	0.6967	0.0666
43					0.9979	0.7635	0.0967
44					0.9989	0.8211	0.1356
45					0.9995	0.8689	0.1841
46					0.9997	0.9070	0.2421
47					0.9999	0.9362	0.3086
48					0.9999	0.9577	0.3822
49					1.0000	0.9729	0.4602
50						0.9832	0.5398
51						0.9900	0.6178
52						0.9942	0.6914
53						0.9968	0.7579
54						0.9983	0.8159
55						0.9991	0.8644
56						0.9996	0.9033
57						0.9998	0.9334
58						0.9999	0.9557
59						1.0000	0.9716
60							0.9824
61							0.9895
62							0.9940
63							0.9967
64							0.9982
65							0.9991
66							0.9996
67							0.9998
68							0.9999
69							1.0000

SOURCE: © 1980 by Harcourt Brace Jovanovich, Inc., and reproduced with their permission from *Management Science* by Lawrence L. Lapin.

TABLE B
Areas Under the Standard Normal Curve

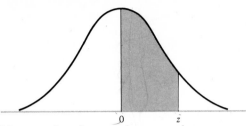

The following table provides the area between the mean and normal deviate value z.

Normal Deviate z	.00	.01	.02	.03	.04	.05	.06	.07	.08	.09
0.0	.0000	.0040	.0080	.0120	.0160	.0199	.0239	.0279	.0319	.0359
0.1	.0398	.0438	.0478	.0517	.0557	.0596	.0636	.0675	.0714	.0753
0.2	.0793	.0832	.0871	.0910	.0948	.0987	.1026	.1064	.1103	.1141
0.3	.1179	.1217	.1255	.1293	.1331	.1368	.1406	.1443	.1480	.1517
0.4	.1554	.1591	.1628	.1664	.1700	.1736	.1772	.1808	.1844	.1879
0.5	.1915	.1950	.1985	.2019	.2054	.2088	.2123	.2157	.2190	.2224
0.6	.2257	.2291	.2324	.2357	.2389	.2422	.2454	.2486	.2518	.2549
0.7	.2580	.2612	.2642	.2673	.2704	.2734	.2764	.2794	.2823	.2852
0.8	.2881	.2910	.2939	.2967	.2995	.3023	.3051	.3078	.3106	.3133
0.9	.3159	.3186	.3212	.3238	.3264	.3289	.3315	.3340	.3365	.3389
1.0	.3413	.3438	.3461	.3485	.3508	.3531	.3554	.3577	.3599	.3621
1.1	.3643	.3665	.3686	.3708	.3729	.3749	.3770	.3790	.3810	.3830
1.2	.3849	.3869	.3888	.3907	.3925	.3944	.3962	.3980	.3997	.4015
1.3	.4032	.4049	.4066	.4082	.4099	.4115	.4131	.4147	.4162	.4177
1.4	.4192	.4207	.4222	.4236	.4251	.4265	.4279	.4292	.4306	.4319
1.5	.4332	.4345	.4357	.4370	.4382	.4394	.4406	.4418	.4429	.4441
1.6	.4452	.4463	.4474	.4484	.4495	.4505	.4515	.4525	.4535	.4545
1.7	.4554	.4564	.4573	.4582	.4591	.4599	.4608	.4616	.4625	.4633
1.8	.4641	.4649	.4656	.4664	.4671	.4678	.4686	.4693	.4699	.4706
1.9	.4713	.4719	.4726	.4732	.4738	.4744	.4750	.4756	.4761	.4767
2.0	.4772	.4778	.4783	.4788	.4793	.4798	.4803	.4808	.4812	.4817
2.1	.4821	.4826	.4830	.4834	.4838	.4842	.4846	.4850	.4854	.4857
2.2	.4861	.4864	.4868	.4871	.4875	.4878	.4881	.4884	.4887	.4890
2.3	.4893	.4896	.4898	.4901	.4904	.4906	.4909	.4911	.4913	.4916
2.4	.4918	.4920	.4922	.4925	.4927	.4929	.4931	.4932	.4934	.4936
2.5	.4938	.4940	.4941	.4943	.4945	.4946	.4948	.4949	.4951	.4952
2.6	.4953	.4955	.4956	.4957	.4959	.4960	.4961	.4962	.4963	.4964
2.7	.4965	.4966	.4967	.4968	.4969	.4970	.4971	.4972	.4973	.4974
2.8	.4974	.4975	.4976	.4977	.4977	.4978	.4979	.4979	.4980	.4981
2.9	.4981	.4982	.4982	.4983	.4984	.4984	.4985	.4985	.4986	.4986
3.0	.49865	.4987	.4987	.4988	.4988	.4989	.4989	.4989	.4990	.4990
4.0	.49997									

SOURCE: © 1970 by Harcourt Brace Jovanovich, Inc., and reproduced with their permission from *Statistical Analysis for Decision Making* by Morris Hamburg.

TABLE C
Loss Function for Decision Making with the Normal Curve

$L(D)$

D	.00	.01	.02	.03	.04	.05	.06	.07	.08	.09
.0	.3989	.3940	.3890	.3841	.3793	.3744	.3697	.3649	.3602	.3556
.1	.3509	.3464	.3418	.3373	.3328	.3284	.3240	.3197	.3154	.3111
.2	.3069	.3027	.2986	.2944	.2904	.2863	.2824	.2784	.2745	.2706
.3	.2668	.2630	.2592	.2555	.2518	.2481	.2445	.2409	.2374	.2339
.4	.2304	.2270	.2236	.2203	.2169	.2137	.2104	.2072	.2040	.2009
.5	.1978	.1947	.1917	.1887	.1857	.1828	.1799	.1771	.1742	.1714
.6	.1687	.1659	.1633	.1606	.1580	.1554	.1528	.1503	.1478	.1453
.7	.1429	.1405	.1381	.1358	.1334	.1312	.1289	.1267	.1245	.1223
.8	.1202	.1181	.1160	.1140	.1120	.1100	.1080	.1061	.1042	.1023
.9	.1004	.09860	.09680	.09503	.09328	.09156	.08986	.08819	.08654	.08491
1.0	.08332	.08174	.08019	.07866	.07716	.07568	.07422	.07279	.07138	.06999
1.1	.06862	.06727	.06595	.06465	.06336	.06210	.06086	.05964	.05844	.05726
1.2	.05610	.05496	.05384	.05274	.05165	.05059	.04954	.04851	.04750	.04650
1.3	.04553	.04457	.04363	.04270	.04179	.04090	.04002	.03916	.03831	.03748
1.4	.03667	.03587	.03508	.03431	.03356	.03281	.03208	.03137	.03067	.02998
1.5	.02931	.02865	.02800	.02736	.02674	.02612	.02552	.02494	.02436	.02380
1.6	.02324	.02270	.02217	.02165	.02114	.02064	.02015	.01967	.01920	.01874
1.7	.01829	.01785	.01742	.01699	.01658	.01617	.01578	.01539	.01501	.01464
1.8	.01428	.01392	.01357	.01323	.01290	.01257	.01226	.01195	.01164	.01134
1.9	.01105	.01077	.01049	.01022	$.0^29957$	$.0^29698$	$.0^29445$	$.0^29198$	$.0^28957$	$.0^28721$
2.0	$.0^28491$	$.0^28266$	$.0^28046$	$.0^27832$	$.0^27623$	$.0^27418$	$.0^27219$	$.0^27024$	$.0^26835$	$.0^26649$
2.1	$.0^26468$	$.0^26292$	$.0^26120$	$.0^25952$	$.0^25788$	$.0^25628$	$.0^25472$	$.0^25320$	$.0^25172$	$.0^25028$
2.2	$.0^24887$	$.0^24750$	$.0^24616$	$.0^24486$	$.0^24358$	$.0^24235$	$.0^24114$	$.0^23996$	$.0^23882$	$.0^23770$
2.3	$.0^23662$	$.0^23556$	$.0^23453$	$.0^23352$	$.0^23255$	$.0^23159$	$.0^23067$	$.0^22977$	$.0^22889$	$.0^22804$
2.4	$.0^22720$	$.0^22640$	$.0^22561$	$.0^22484$	$.0^22410$	$.0^22337$	$.0^22267$	$.0^22199$	$.0^22132$	$.0^22067$

TABLE C (continued)

x										
2.5	$.0^{2}2004$	$.0^{2}1943$	$.0^{2}1883$	$.0^{2}1826$	$.0^{2}1769$	$.0^{2}1715$	$.0^{2}1662$	$.0^{2}1610$	$.0^{2}1560$	$.0^{2}1511$
2.6	$.0^{2}1464$	$.0^{2}1418$	$.0^{2}1373$	$.0^{2}1330$	$.0^{2}1288$	$.0^{2}1247$	$.0^{2}1207$	$.0^{2}1169$	$.0^{2}1132$	$.0^{2}1095$
2.7	$.0^{2}1060$	$.0^{2}1026$	$.0^{3}9928$	$.0^{3}9607$	$.0^{3}9295$	$.0^{3}8992$	$.0^{3}8699$	$.0^{3}8414$	$.0^{3}8138$	$.0^{3}7870$
2.8	$.0^{3}7611$	$.0^{3}7359$	$.0^{3}7115$	$.0^{3}6879$	$.0^{3}6650$	$.0^{3}6428$	$.0^{3}6213$	$.0^{3}6004$	$.0^{3}5802$	$.0^{3}5606$
2.9	$.0^{3}5417$	$.0^{3}5233$	$.0^{3}5055$	$.0^{3}4883$	$.0^{3}4716$	$.0^{3}4555$	$.0^{3}4398$	$.0^{3}4247$	$.0^{3}4101$	$.0^{3}3959$
3.0	$.0^{3}3822$	$.0^{3}3689$	$.0^{3}3560$	$.0^{3}3436$	$.0^{3}3316$	$.0^{3}3199$	$.0^{3}3087$	$.0^{3}2978$	$.0^{3}2873$	$.0^{3}2771$
3.1	$.0^{3}2673$	$.0^{3}2577$	$.0^{3}2485$	$.0^{3}2396$	$.0^{3}2311$	$.0^{3}2227$	$.0^{3}2147$	$.0^{3}2070$	$.0^{3}1995$	$.0^{3}1922$
3.2	$.0^{3}1852$	$.0^{3}1785$	$.0^{3}1720$	$.0^{3}1657$	$.0^{3}1596$	$.0^{3}1537$	$.0^{3}1480$	$.0^{3}1426$	$.0^{3}1373$	$.0^{3}1322$
3.3	$.0^{3}1273$	$.0^{3}1225$	$.0^{3}1179$	$.0^{3}1135$	$.0^{3}1093$	$.0^{3}1051$	$.0^{3}1012$	$.0^{4}9734$	$.0^{4}9365$	$.0^{4}9009$
3.4	$.0^{4}8666$	$.0^{4}8335$	$.0^{4}8016$	$.0^{4}7709$	$.0^{4}7413$	$.0^{4}7127$	$.0^{4}6852$	$.0^{4}6587$	$.0^{4}6331$	$.0^{4}6085$
3.5	$.0^{4}5848$	$.0^{4}5620$	$.0^{4}5400$	$.0^{4}5188$	$.0^{4}4984$	$.0^{4}4788$	$.0^{4}4599$	$.0^{4}4417$	$.0^{4}4242$	$.0^{4}4073$
3.6	$.0^{4}3911$	$.0^{4}3755$	$.0^{4}3605$	$.0^{4}3460$	$.0^{4}3321$	$.0^{4}3188$	$.0^{4}3059$	$.0^{4}2935$	$.0^{4}2816$	$.0^{4}2702$
3.7	$.0^{4}2592$	$.0^{4}2486$	$.0^{4}2385$	$.0^{4}2287$	$.0^{4}2193$	$.0^{4}2103$	$.0^{4}2016$	$.0^{4}1933$	$.0^{4}1853$	$.0^{4}1776$
3.8	$.0^{4}1702$	$.0^{4}1632$	$.0^{4}1563$	$.0^{4}1498$	$.0^{4}1435$	$.0^{4}1375$	$.0^{4}1317$	$.0^{4}1262$	$.0^{4}1208$	$.0^{4}1157$
3.9	$.0^{4}1108$	$.0^{4}1061$	$.0^{4}1016$	$.0^{5}9723$	$.0^{5}9307$	$.0^{5}8908$	$.0^{5}8525$	$.0^{5}8158$	$.0^{5}7806$	$.0^{5}7469$
4.0	$.0^{5}7145$	$.0^{5}6835$	$.0^{5}6538$	$.0^{5}6253$	$.0^{5}5980$	$.0^{5}5718$	$.0^{5}5468$	$.0^{5}5227$	$.0^{5}4997$	$.0^{5}4777$
4.1	$.0^{5}4566$	$.0^{5}4364$	$.0^{5}4170$	$.0^{5}3985$	$.0^{5}3807$	$.0^{5}3637$	$.0^{5}3475$	$.0^{5}3319$	$.0^{5}3170$	$.0^{5}3027$
4.2	$.0^{5}2891$	$.0^{5}2760$	$.0^{5}2635$	$.0^{5}2516$	$.0^{5}2402$	$.0^{5}2292$	$.0^{5}2188$	$.0^{5}2088$	$.0^{5}1992$	$.0^{5}1901$
4.3	$.0^{5}1814$	$.0^{5}1730$	$.0^{5}1650$	$.0^{5}1574$	$.0^{5}1501$	$.0^{5}1431$	$.0^{5}1365$	$.0^{5}1301$	$.0^{5}1241$	$.0^{5}1183$
4.4	$.0^{5}1127$	$.0^{5}1074$	$.0^{5}1024$	$.0^{6}9756$	$.0^{6}9296$	$.0^{6}8857$	$.0^{6}8437$	$.0^{6}8037$	$.0^{6}7655$	$.0^{6}7290$
4.5	$.0^{6}6942$	$.0^{6}6610$	$.0^{6}6294$	$.0^{6}5992$	$.0^{6}5704$	$.0^{6}5429$	$.0^{6}5167$	$.0^{6}4917$	$.0^{6}4679$	$.0^{6}4452$
4.6	$.0^{6}4236$	$.0^{6}4029$	$.0^{6}3833$	$.0^{6}3645$	$.0^{6}3467$	$.0^{6}3297$	$.0^{6}3135$	$.0^{6}2981$	$.0^{6}2834$	$.0^{6}2694$
4.7	$.0^{6}2560$	$.0^{6}2433$	$.0^{6}2313$	$.0^{6}2197$	$.0^{6}2088$	$.0^{6}1984$	$.0^{6}1884$	$.0^{6}1790$	$.0^{6}1700$	$.0^{6}1615$
4.8	$.0^{6}1533$	$.0^{6}1456$	$.0^{6}1382$	$.0^{6}1312$	$.0^{6}1246$	$.0^{6}1182$	$.0^{6}1122$	$.0^{6}1065$	$.0^{6}1011$	$.0^{7}9588$
4.9	$.0^{7}9096$	$.0^{7}8629$	$.0^{7}8185$	$.0^{7}7763$	$.0^{7}7362$	$.0^{7}6982$	$.0^{7}6620$	$.0^{7}6276$	$.0^{7}5950$	$.0^{7}5640$

SOURCE: Reproduced from Robert Schlaifer, *Introduction to Statistics for Business Decisions*, published by McGraw-Hill Book Company, 1961, by specific permission of the copyright holder, the President and Fellows of Harvard College.

TABLE D
Exponential Functions

y	e^y	e^{-y}	y	e^y	e^{-y}
0.00	1.0000	1.000000	3.00	20.086	.049787
0.10	1.1052	.904837	3.10	22.198	.045049
0.20	1.2214	.818731	3.20	24.533	.040762
0.30	1.3499	.740818	3.30	27.113	.036883
0.40	1.4918	.670320	3.40	29.964	.033373
0.50	1.6487	.606531	3.50	33.115	.030197
0.60	1.8221	.548812	3.60	36.598	.027324
0.70	2.0138	.496585	3.70	40.447	.024724
0.80	2.2255	.449329	3.80	44.701	.022371
0.90	2.4596	.406570	3.90	49.402	.020242
1.00	2.7183	.367879	4.00	54.598	.018316
1.10	3.0042	.332871	4.10	60.340	.016573
1.20	3.3201	.301194	4.20	66.686	.014996
1.30	3.6693	.272532	4.30	73.700	.013569
1.40	4.0552	.246597	4.40	81.451	.012277
1.50	4.4817	.223130	4.50	90.017	.011109
1.60	4.9530	.201897	4.60	99.484	.010052
1.70	5.4739	.182684	4.70	109.95	.009095
1.80	6.0496	.165299	4.80	121.51	.008230
1.90	6.6859	.149569	4.90	134.29	.007447
2.00	7.3891	.135335	5.00	148.41	.006738
2.10	8.1662	.122456	5.10	164.02	.006097
2.20	9.0250	.110803	5.20	181.27	.005517
2.30	9.9742	.100259	5.30	200.34	.004992
2.40	11.023	.090718	5.40	221.41	.004517
2.50	12.182	.082085	5.50	244.69	.004087
2.60	13.464	.074274	5.60	270.43	.003698
2.70	14.880	.067206	5.70	298.87	.003346
2.80	16.445	.060810	5.80	330.30	.003028
2.90	18.174	.055023	5.90	365.04	.002739
3.00	20.086	.049787	6.00	403.43	.002479

TABLE E
Cumulative Probability Values for the Poisson Distribution

$$\Pr[X \leq x]$$

λt	1.0	2.0	3.0	4.0	5.0	6.0	7.0	8.0	9.0	10.0
x										
0	0.3679	0.1353	0.0498	0.0183	0.0067	0.0025	0.0009	0.0003	0.0001	0.0000
1	0.7358	0.4060	0.1991	0.0916	0.0404	0.0174	0.0073	0.0030	0.0012	0.0005
2	0.9197	0.6767	0.4232	0.2381	0.1247	0.0620	0.0296	0.0138	0.0062	0.0028
3	0.9810	0.8571	0.6472	0.4335	0.2650	0.1512	0.0818	0.0424	0.0212	0.0103
4	0.9963	0.9473	0.8153	0.6288	0.4405	0.2851	0.1730	0.0996	0.0550	0.0293
5	0.9994	0.9834	0.9161	0.7851	0.6160	0.4457	0.3007	0.1912	0.1157	0.0671
6	0.9999	0.9955	0.9665	0.8893	0.7622	0.6063	0.4497	0.3134	0.2068	0.1301
7	1.0000	0.9989	0.9881	0.9489	0.8666	0.7440	0.5987	0.4530	0.3239	0.2202
8		0.9998	0.9962	0.9786	0.9319	0.8472	0.7291	0.5926	0.4557	0.3328
9		1.0000	0.9989	0.9919	0.9682	0.9161	0.8305	0.7166	0.5874	0.4579
10			0.9997	0.9972	0.9863	0.9574	0.9015	0.8159	0.7060	0.5830
11			0.9999	0.9991	0.9945	0.9799	0.9466	0.8881	0.8030	0.6968
12			1.0000	0.9997	0.9980	0.9912	0.9730	0.9362	0.8758	0.7916
13				0.9999	0.9993	0.9964	0.9872	0.9658	0.9262	0.8645
14				1.0000	0.9998	0.9986	0.9943	0.9827	0.9585	0.9165
15					0.9999	0.9995	0.9976	0.9918	0.9780	0.9513
16					1.0000	0.9998	0.9990	0.9963	0.9889	0.9730
17						0.9999	0.9996	0.9984	0.9947	0.9857
18						1.0000	0.9999	0.9993	0.9976	0.9928
19							0.9999	0.9997	0.9989	0.9965
20							1.0000	0.9999	0.9996	0.9984
21								1.0000	0.9998	0.9993
22									0.9999	0.9997
23									1.0000	0.9999
24										0.9999
25										1.0000

TABLE E (continued)

λt	11.0	12.0	13.0	14.0	15.0	16.0	17.0	18.0	19.0	20.0
x										
0	0.0000	0.0000	0.0000	0.0000	0.0000	0.0000	0.0	0.0	0.0	0.0
1	0.0002	0.0001	0.0000	0.0000	0.0000	0.0000	0.0000	0.0000	0.0000	0.0
2	0.0012	0.0005	0.0002	0.0001	0.0000	0.0000	0.0000	0.0000	0.0000	0.0000
3	0.0049	0.0023	0.0011	0.0005	0.0002	0.0001	0.0000	0.0000	0.0000	0.0000
4	0.0151	0.0076	0.0037	0.0018	0.0009	0.0004	0.0002	0.0001	0.0000	0.0000
5	0.0375	0.0203	0.0107	0.0055	0.0028	0.0014	0.0007	0.0003	0.0002	0.0001
6	0.0786	0.0458	0.0259	0.0142	0.0076	0.0040	0.0021	0.0010	0.0005	0.0003
7	0.1432	0.0895	0.0540	0.0316	0.0180	0.0100	0.0054	0.0029	0.0015	0.0008
8	0.2320	0.1550	0.0998	0.0621	0.0374	0.0220	0.0126	0.0071	0.0039	0.0021
9	0.3405	0.2424	0.1658	0.1094	0.0699	0.0433	0.0261	0.0154	0.0089	0.0050
10	0.4599	0.3472	0.2517	0.1757	0.1185	0.0774	0.0491	0.0304	0.0183	0.0108
11	0.5793	0.4616	0.3532	0.2600	0.1847	0.1270	0.0847	0.0549	0.0347	0.0214
12	0.6887	0.5760	0.4631	0.3585	0.2676	0.1931	0.1350	0.0917	0.0606	0.0390
13	0.7813	0.6815	0.5730	0.4644	0.3632	0.2745	0.2009	0.1426	0.0984	0.0661
14	0.8540	0.7720	0.6751	0.5704	0.4656	0.3675	0.2808	0.2081	0.1497	0.1049
15	0.9074	0.8444	0.7636	0.6694	0.5681	0.4667	0.3714	0.2866	0.2148	0.1565
16	0.9441	0.8987	0.8355	0.7559	0.6641	0.5660	0.4677	0.3750	0.2920	0.2211
17	0.9678	0.9370	0.8905	0.8272	0.7489	0.6593	0.5640	0.4686	0.3784	0.2970
18	0.9823	0.9626	0.9302	0.8826	0.8195	0.7423	0.6549	0.5622	0.4695	0.3814
19	0.9907	0.9787	0.9573	0.9235	0.8752	0.8122	0.7363	0.6509	0.5606	0.4703
20	0.9953	0.9884	0.9750	0.9521	0.9170	0.8682	0.8055	0.7307	0.6472	0.5591
21	0.9977	0.9939	0.9859	0.9711	0.9469	0.9108	0.8615	0.7991	0.7255	0.6437
22	0.9989	0.9969	0.9924	0.9833	0.9672	0.9418	0.9047	0.8551	0.7931	0.7206
23	0.9995	0.9985	0.9960	0.9907	0.9805	0.9633	0.9367	0.8989	0.8490	0.7875
24	0.9998	0.9993	0.9980	0.9950	0.9888	0.9777	0.9593	0.9317	0.8933	0.8432
25	0.9999	0.9997	0.9990	0.9974	0.9938	0.9869	0.9747	0.9554	0.9269	0.8878
26	1.0000	0.9999	0.9995	0.9987	0.9967	0.9925	0.9848	0.9718	0.9514	0.9221
27		0.9999	0.9998	0.9994	0.9983	0.9959	0.9912	0.9827	0.9687	0.9475
28		1.0000	0.9999	0.9997	0.9991	0.9978	0.9950	0.9897	0.9805	0.9657
29			1.0000	0.9999	0.9996	0.9989	0.9973	0.9940	0.9881	0.9782
30				0.9999	0.9998	0.9994	0.9985	0.9967	0.9930	0.9865
31				1.0000	0.9999	0.9997	0.9992	0.9982	0.9960	0.9919
32					0.9999	0.9999	0.9996	0.9990	0.9978	0.9953
33					1.0000	0.9999	0.9998	0.9995	0.9988	0.9973
34						1.0000	0.9999	0.9997	0.9994	0.9985
35							0.9999	0.9999	0.9997	0.9992
36							1.0000	0.9999	0.9998	0.9996
37								1.0000	0.9999	0.9998
38									1.0000	0.9999
39										0.9999
40										1.0000

SOURCE: © 1980 by Harcourt Brace Jovanovich, Inc., and reproduced with their permission from *Management Science* by Lawrence L. Lapin.

TABLE F
Random Numbers

12651	61646	11769	75109	86996	97669	25757	32535	07122	76763
81769	74436	02630	72310	45049	18029	07469	42341	98173	79260
36737	98863	77240	76251	00654	64688	09343	70278	67331	98729
82861	54371	76610	94934	72748	44124	05610	53750	95938	01485
21325	15732	24127	37431	09723	63529	73977	95218	96074	42138
74146	47887	62463	23045	41490	07954	22597	60012	98866	90959
90759	64410	54179	66075	61051	75385	51378	08360	95946	95547
55683	98078	02238	91540	21219	17720	87817	41705	95785	12563
79686	17969	76061	83748	55920	83612	41540	86492	06447	60568
70333	00201	86201	69716	78185	62154	77930	67663	29529	75116
14042	53536	07779	04157	41172	36473	42123	43929	50533	33437
59911	08256	06596	48416	69770	68797	56080	14223	59199	30162
62368	62623	62742	14891	39247	52242	98832	69533	91174	57979
57529	97751	54976	48957	74599	08759	78494	52785	68526	64618
15469	90574	78033	66885	13936	42117	71831	22961	94225	31816
18625	23674	53850	32827	81647	80820	00420	63555	74489	80141
74626	68394	88562	70745	23701	45630	65891	58220	35442	60414
11119	16519	27384	90199	79210	76965	99546	30323	31664	22845
41101	17336	48951	53674	17880	45260	08575	49321	36191	17095
32123	91576	84221	78902	82010	30847	62329	63898	23268	74283
26091	68409	69704	82267	14751	13151	93115	01437	56945	89661
67680	79790	48462	59278	44185	29616	76531	19589	83139	28454
15184	19260	14073	07026	25264	03388	27182	22557	61501	67481
58010	45039	57181	10238	36874	28546	37444	80824	63981	39942
56425	53996	86245	32623	78858	08143	60377	42925	42815	11159
82630	84066	13592	60642	17904	99718	63432	88642	37858	25431
14927	40909	23900	48761	44860	92467	31742	87142	03607	32059
23740	22505	07489	85986	74420	21744	97711	36648	35620	97949
32990	97446	03711	63824	07953	85965	87089	11687	92414	67257
05310	24058	91946	78437	34365	82469	12430	84754	19354	72745
21839	39937	27534	88913	49055	19218	47712	67677	51889	70926
08833	42549	93981	94051	28382	83725	72643	64233	97252	17133
58336	11139	47479	00931	91560	95372	97642	33856	54825	55680
62032	91144	75478	47431	52726	30289	42411	91886	51818	78292
45171	30557	53116	04118	58301	24375	65609	85810	18620	49198
91611	62656	60128	35609	63698	78356	50682	22505	01692	36291
55472	63819	86314	49174	93582	73604	78614	78849	23096	72825
18573	09729	74091	53994	10970	86557	65661	41854	26037	53296
60866	02955	90288	82136	83644	94455	06560	78029	98768	71296
45043	55608	82767	60890	74646	79485	13619	98868	40857	19415
17831	09737	79473	75945	28394	79334	70577	38048	03607	06932
40137	03981	07585	18128	11178	32601	27994	05641	22600	86064
77776	31343	14576	97706	16039	47517	43300	59080	80392	63189
69605	44104	40103	95635	05635	81673	68657	09559	23510	95875
19916	52934	26499	09821	87331	80993	61299	36979	73599	35055
02606	58552	07678	56619	65325	30705	99582	53390	46357	13244
65183	73160	87131	35530	47946	09854	18080	02321	05809	04898
10740	98914	44916	11322	89717	88189	30143	52687	19420	60061
98642	89822	71691	51573	83666	61642	46683	33761	47542	23551
60139	25601	93663	25547	02654	94829	48672	28736	84994	13071

SOURCE: The Rand Corporation, *A Million Random Digits with 100,000 Normal Deviates.* New York: The Free Press, 1955. Reproduced with permission of The Rand Corporation.

Answers to Selected Problems

2-1 1/4

2-3 (a) 1/5   (b) 1/10,000   (c) 1/4   (d) 2/3

2-6 (a) 2/3   (b) 2/3   (c) 1/3   (d) 1   (e) 0

2-11 (b) .75   (c) Not independent

2-12 (a) 1/13   (b) 1/26   (c) 1/2   (d) 3/13

2-15 (a) $\Pr[\text{reject}] = .15$; $\Pr[\text{bad}] = .10$; $\Pr[\text{reject}|\text{bad}] = .95$ (b) .095

2-18 (a) .72398   (b) .00051   (c) .25257

2-20 (a) .947   The greens should *not* be watered.   (b) .333

2-22 (a) .8   (b) .2

3-1

Proceeds	Probability
−$20,000	1/9
− 10,000	2/9
0	3/9
10,000	2/9
20,000	1/9

3-8 (a) Yes   (b) Yes   (c) No   (d) No   (e) No

3-11 (a) .25   (b) .50   (c) 5

3-14 (a) .0490   (b) .2262   (c) .6723   (d) .9687

3-16 (a) .0565   (b) .0710   (c) .8744   (d) .5956   (e) .2500   (f) .8534

3-19 (a) .4332 (b) .1915 (c) .2420 (d) .0062 (e) .0968 (f) .9861
(g) .97585 (h) .0606

3-21 .9544

4-1 Winter $ 72,000   Spring $ 84,700
Summer 121,000   Fall   179,685

4-3 (b) $\hat{Y} = 200.67 + 9.673X$ $(X = 0$ at 1970)
(c) 297.40

4-4 Winter   50.6   Spring   89.8
Summer 150.9   Fall   108.7

4-5

Quarter	(b) Moving Average	(c) Percentage of Moving Average	Seasonal Index	(d) Deseasonalized Data
1976 W			93.4	4.2
S			112.0	5.4
S	6.8	63.2	69.2	6.2
F	7.8	138.5	125.4	8.6
1977 W	8.7	89.7	93.4	8.4
S	9.4	112.8	112.0	9.5
S	10.3	67.0	69.2	10.0
F	11.6	116.4	125.4	10.8
1978 W	12.6	102.4	93.4	13.8
S	13.6	111.8	112.0	13.6
S	14.4	71.5	69.2	14.9
F	14.4	129.8	125.4	14.9
1979 W	14.3	97.2	93.4	14.9
S	14.1	102.1	112.0	12.9
S	13.9	73.4	69.2	14.7
F	14.3	121.0	125.4	13.8
1980 W	15.3	88.2	93.4	14.5
S	16.2	112.3	112.0	16.3
S			69.2	20.5
F			125.4	16.5

4-7

t	F_t	t	F_t
1	—	11	5,173.2
2	4,890	12	5,191.9
3	4,898.0	13	5,227.1
4	4,926.8	14	5,268.3
5	4,960.1	15	5,313.0
6	5,000.0	16	5,363.8
7	5,040.0	17	5,402.3
8	5,044.0	18	5,449.4
9	5,094.4	19	5,465.6
10	5,128.6	20	5,499.4

4-10 (b) $\hat{Y} = 22.405 + 3.619X$

4-11 (a) 1,100   (b) 900   (c) 700

4-14 $\hat{Y} = -.5595 + .0817X_1 + 1.1605X_2$

5-3 Choose either A_1 or A_3.

5-4 A_3 and A_5

5-5 Spring-action movement

5-7 Test market. If that is successful, market nationally; if it is unsuccessful, abort.

5-8 Use no test and hire each candidate.

5-11 Market nationally with no consumer testing.

5-13 Use the juvenile hormone.

6-2 (a) A_2 or A_3 (b) A_2 (c) A_2

6-5

		Act				
Event	Probability	A_1	A_2	A_3	A_4	A_5
E_1	.2	10	0	10	5	0
E_2	.2	15	0	15	0	15
E_3	.6	0	10	5	5	5
Expected Opportunity Losses:		5	6	8	4	6

Act A_4 has the lowest expected opportunity loss.

6-6 (a) 27 for A_1 (b) 39   (c) 12   (d) 12   (e) They are the same values.

6-8 (a)

Sales Event	Probability	Tire Act			Row Maximum
		A	B	C	
4,000	.30	$120,000	$130,000	$120,000	$130,000
7,000	.50	255,000	295,000	300,000	300,000
10,000	.20	390,000	460,000	480,000	480,000
Expected Payoffs:		241,500	278,500	282,000	285,000

(b) See above. Tire C is best.

(c) EVPI = $285,000 - 282,000 = \$3,000$

(d)

Sales Event	Probability	Tire Act		
		A	B	C
4,000	.30	$10,000	$ 0	$10,000
7,000	.50	45,000	5,000	0
10,000	.20	90,000	20,000	0
Expected Opportunity Losses:		43,500	6,500	3,000

7-1 $Q^* = 200$; order once every .2 year.

7-4 (a) $Q^* = 2,620$, $S^* = 2,544$, $T^* = .262$ year   Out of stock .029 of the time.
(b) \$763.23; smaller

7-9 (a) 158.1 tons   (b) .79 year   (c) .1581 year

7-11 (a) 632.5 acres   Fertilize every .127 year, or 7.9 times yearly.

8-1 Stock 150 boxes.

8-3 (a) 62   (b) \$3.247   (c) \$2.803

8-6 6,120 trees

8-8 (a) $\mu = 7.3$ pairs   (b) $r = 9$, $Q = 32$ (c) 1.7 pairs   (d) \$68.21

9-2 (a) $X_1 = 7.5$, $X_2 = 2.5$ (b) $X_1 = 1.5$, $X_2 = 1$ (c) $X_1 = -.5$, $X_2 = 2$
(d) $X_1 = -1.5$, $X_2 = 4.5$

9-3 $X_A = 2.4$, $X_B = 2.4$, $P = 26.4$

9-6 (b) There are two most attractive corners:
(1) $X_1 = 4$, $X_2 = 4$, $P = 24$ (2) $X_1 = 12$, $X_2 = 0$, $P = 24$
(c) $P = 24$ The point represents an optimal solution.

9-8 (a) Letting X_R = Quantity of regular models; X_D = Quantity of deluxe models

$$\text{Maximize} \quad P = 10X_R + 15X_D$$
$$\text{Subject to} \qquad 5X_R + \;\; 8X_D \le 80 \quad \text{(labor)}$$
$$X_R + \quad X_D \le 12 \quad \text{(frame)}$$
$$\text{where} \qquad X_R, X_D \ge 0$$

(b) $X_R = 5\frac{1}{3}$, $X_D = 6\frac{2}{3}$, $P = 153\frac{1}{3}$ dollars

9-10 4 forged bits, 6 machined bits, $P = 102$ dollars

10-1 Letting $\quad X_F$ = quantity of fancy lamps
X_O = quantity of ornate lamps
X_P = quantity of plain lamps
X_R = quantity of rococco lamps

$$\text{Maximize} \quad P = 100X_F + 150X_O + 200X_P + 200X_R$$

Subject to					
$10X_F +$	$8X_O +$	$10X_P +$	$20X_R \le 1,000$	(labor)
$2X_F +$	$3X_O +$	$1X_P +$	$1X_R \le 200$	(machine)
$10X_F +$	$20X_O +$	$15X_P +$	$30X_R \le 5,000$	(sheet metal)
		$- \quad X_P +$	$2X_R \le 0$	(quantity)

$$\text{where} \qquad X_F, X_O, X_P, X_R \ge 0$$

10-5 Letting $\quad X_H$ = pounds of hog bellies $\quad X_P$ = pounds of pork
X_T = pounds of tripe $\qquad X_C$ = pounds of chicken
X_B = pounds of beef

$$\text{Minimize} \quad C = .30X_H + .20X_T + .70X_B + .60X_P + .45X_C$$

Subject to						
$X_H +$	X_T				$\le .10$	(restriction)
				$X_C \le .25$		(chicken)
		X_B			$\ge .30$	(beef)
$3X_H +$	$5X_T +$	$4X_B +$	$3X_P +$	$3X_C \ge 3$		(protein)
$7X_H +$	$4X_T +$	$2X_B +$	$4X_P +$	$5X_C \le 4$		(fat)
$6X_H +$	$7X_T +$	$10X_B +$	$9X_B +$	$8X_C \le 8$		(water)

$$\text{where} \qquad \text{all } Xs \ge 0$$

10-6 Letting X_A = number of gallons of Ant Can't
X_B = number of gallons of Boll-Toll
X_C = number of gallons of Caterpillar-Chiller

Maximize $P = 5X_A + 6X_B + 7X_C$
Subject to

$$
\begin{aligned}
.1X_A + .1X_B + .1X_C &\le 1{,}000 &&\text{(catalyst)} \\
.1X_A \qquad\quad + .1X_C &\le 1{,}000 &&\text{(malathion)} \\
.2X_B + .2X_C &\le 2{,}000 &&\text{(parathion)} \\
X_A - X_B \qquad &\le 500 &&\text{(quantity mix)}
\end{aligned}
$$

where $X_A, X_B, X_C \ge 0$

10-8 Letting X_{ij} = Number of tombstones shipped from quarry i to mason j
$i = A$ or B
$j = C, D,$ or E

Minimize $C = 10X_{AC} + 15X_{AD} + 8X_{AE} + 12X_{BC} + 9X_{BD} + 10X_{BE}$
Subject to

$$
\begin{aligned}
X_{AC} + X_{AD} + X_{AE} &= 100 &&\text{(Abinger capacity)} \\
X_{BC} + X_{BD} + X_{BE} &= 200 &&\text{(Barnesly capacity)} \\
X_{AC} + X_{BC} &= 50 &&\text{(Cedrick's demand)} \\
X_{AD} + X_{BD} &= 150 &&\text{(Dunstan's demand)} \\
X_{AE} + X_{BE} &= 100 &&\text{(Eldred's demand)}
\end{aligned}
$$

where   all $Xs \ge 0$

10-11 Letting X_B = Number of spots on KBAT
X_J = Number of spots on WJOK
X_R = Number of spots on WROB
X_P = Number of spots on KPOW

Maximize $P = 300X_B + 120X_J + 150X_R + 400X_P$
Subject to

$$
\begin{aligned}
100X_B + 50X_J + 75X_R + 150X_P &\le 10{,}000 &&\text{(funds)} \\
X_B &\le 30 &&\text{(availability on KBAT)} \\
X_P &\le 40 &&\text{(availability on KPOW)} \\
.25X_B - .75X_J - .75X_R + .25X_P &\le 0 &&\text{(golden oldie)}
\end{aligned}
$$

where   all variables ≥ 0

10-12 Letting X_{ij} = quantity of ingredient i used in product j
with $i = U, E, M$ representing unleaded gasoline, ethyl alcohol, and methyl alcohol, respectively
and $j = G, P$ representing products gasohol and petrolmeth, respectively (No variable X_{MG} is used, since gasohol contains no methyl alcohol.)

Minimize $C = 1.00X_{UG} + 1.50X_{EG} + 1.00X_{UP} + 1.50X_{EP} + .5X_{MP}$
Subject to

Availability Constraints

$$
\begin{aligned}
X_{UG} + X_{UP} &\le 20{,}000 &&\text{(unleaded gas)} \\
X_{EG} + X_{EP} &\le 3{,}000 &&\text{(ethyl alcohol)} \\
X_{MP} &\le 5{,}000 &&\text{(methyl alcohol)}
\end{aligned}
$$

Demand Constraints

$$X_{UG} + X_{EG} \geq 10,000 \quad \text{(gasohol demand)}$$
$$X_{UP} + X_{EP} + X_{MP} \geq 5,000 \quad \text{(petrolmeth demand)}$$

Octane Constraints

Gasohol:
$$\frac{90X_{UG} + 120X_{EG}}{X_{UG} + X_{EG}} \geq 91$$

or $-1X_{UG} + 29X_{EG} \geq 0$ (gasohol octane)

Petrolmeth:
$$\frac{90X_{UP} + 120X_{EP} + 110X_{MP}}{X_{UP} + X_{EP} + X_{MP}} \geq 93$$

or $-3X_{UP} + 27X_{EP} + 17X_{MP} \geq 0$ (petrolmeth octane)

Volume Constraints

Gasohol:
$$\frac{X_{EG}}{X_{UG} + X_{EG}} \leq .10$$

$-.10X_{UG} + .90X_{EG} \leq 0$ (gasohol volume)

Petrolmeth:
$$\frac{X_{EP} + X_{MP}}{X_{UP} + X_{EP} + X_{MP}} \leq .30$$

$-.30X_{UP} + .70X_{EP} + .70X_{MP} \leq 0$ (petrolmeth volume)

where   all $Xs \geq 0$

10-15 (a) (1) 50   (2) 40   (3) 4,000   (4) 4,000
(b) $40 for each batch type

11-3 (a) *Sac.* 3 7 9 -3 23 75
    Imp. 2 0 0   10 -15 —
(b) X_4 is the entering variable; X_3 is the exiting variable.

11-5 (a, b)

UNIT
PROFIT   3   2   1   0   0

Var. Mix	X_1	X_2	X_3	X_4	X_5	Sol.
0	X_4	0	2	1 ↓	1	0	10
0	X_5←	0	-3	②	0	1	15
3	X_1	1	1	0	0	0	20
	Sac.	3	3	0	0	0	60
	Imp.	0	-1	1	0	0	—

(c)

UNIT
PROFIT   3   2   1   0   0

Var. Mix	X_1	X_2	X_3	X_4	X_5	Sol.
0 X_4	0	3.5	0	1	−.5	2.5
1 X_3	0	−1.5	1	0	.5	7.5
3 X_1	1	1	0	0	0	20
Sac.	3	1.5	1	0	.5	67.5
Imp.	0	.5	0	0	−.5	—

11-7   (a) $X_1 = 0$, $X_2 = 3$, $P = 9$

(b) Letting X_A, X_B, and X_C represent the respective slack variables.

Maximize $P = 2X_1 + 3X_2 + 0X_A + 0X_B + 0X_C$
Subject to $3X_1 + 2X_2 + 1X_A + 0X_B + 0X_C = 6$ (resource A)
          $1X_1 + 0X_2 + 0X_A + 1X_B + 0X_C = 5$ (resource B)
          $0X_1 + 1X_2 + 0X_A + 0X_B + 1X_C = 4$ (resource C)
where   all Xs ≥ 0

(c)

UNIT
PROFIT   2   3   0   0   0

Var. Mix	X_1	X_2	X_A	X_B	X_C	Sol.
0 X_A ←	3	②↓	1	0	0	6
0 X_B	1	0	0	1	0	5
0 X_C	0	1	0	0	1	4
Sac.	0	0	0	0	0	0
Imp.	2	3	0	0	0	—

3 X_2	3/2	1	1/2	0	0	3
0 X_B	1	0	0	1	0	5
0 X_C	−3/2	0	−1/2	0	1	1
Sac.	9/2	3	3/2	0	0	9
Imp.	−5/2	0	−3/2	0	0	—

11-11 Letting X_W = quantity of unused wood

X_L = quantity of unused labor

UNIT PROFIT		20	15	15	0	0	
	Var. Mix	X_T	X_C	X_B	X_W	X_L	Sol.
0	X_W ←	⑩ ↓	3	10	1	0	100
0	X_L	5	5	5	0	1	60
	Sac.	0	0	0	0	0	0
	Imp.	20	15	15	0	0	—

20	X_T	1	.3 ↓	1	.1	0	10
0	X_L ←	0	③.5	0	−.5	1	10
	Sac.	20	6	20	2	0	200
	Imp.	0	9	−5	−2	0	—

20	X_T	1	0	1	1/7	−3/35	64/7
15	X_C	0	1	0	−1/7	2/7	20/7
	Sac.	20	15	20	5/7	18/7	1,580/7
	Imp.	0	0	−5	−5/7	−18/7	—

$$X_T = 64/7 \qquad X_W = 0$$
$$X_C = 20/7 \qquad X_L = 0$$
$$X_B = 0$$
$$P = 1,580/7$$

11-12 (c) Sammy should make 150 butterscotch, 0 cinnamon, and 100 peppermint apples, at a profit of $35.

11-15 ChipMont should make 285,714.3 chips each of the CPU and integrated types and no memory chips, at a profit of $185,714.30.

12-1 (a) $X_1 = 2.4$, $X_2 = 1.2$; $P = 5(2.4) + 6(1.2) = 19.2$

(b) X_R = unused quantity of resource

X_M = surplus beyond minimum mixture requirement

a_M = artificial variable for mixture constraint

Maximize $P = 5X_1 + 6X_2 + 0X_R + 0X_M - Ma_D$

Subject to $3X_1 + 4X_2 + 1X_R + 0X_M + 0a_M = 12$ (resource)

$\qquad\qquad 2X_1 + 6X_2 + 0X_R - 1X_M + 1a_M = 12$ (mixture)

where all variables ≥ 0

(c)

UNIT PROFIT		5	6	0	0	$-M$	
	Var. Mix	X_1	X_2	X_R	X_M	a_M	Sol.
0	X_R	3	4↓	1	0	0	12
$-M$	a_M ←	2	⑥	0	-1	1	12
	Sac.	$-2M$	$-6M$	0	M	$-M$	$-12M$
	Imp.	$5 + 2M$	$6 + 6M$	0	$-M$	0	—
0	X_R ←	⑩/6 ↓	0	1	4/6	$-4/6$	4
6	X_2	2/6	1	0	$-1/6$	1/6	2
	Sac.	2	6	0	-1	1	12
	Imp.	3	0	0	1	$-M - 1$	—
5	X_1	1	0	6/10	4/10	$-4/10$	12/5
6	X_2	0	1	$-2/10$	$-9/30$	9/30	6/5
	Sac.	5	6	18/10	6/30	$-6/30$	96/5
	Imp.	0	0	$-18/10$	$-6/30$	$-M + 6/30$	—

$X_1 = 12/5 = 2.4 \qquad X_R = X_M = 0$

$X_2 = 6/5 = 1.2$

$P = 96/5 = 19.2$

12-3 (a) $X_A = 2$, $X_B = 4$; $P = 2.2$

(b) X_Y = surplus beyond restriction Y a_Y = artificial variable for restriction Y

X_Z = surplus beyond restriction Z a_Z = artificial variable for restriction Z

Minimize $C = .5X_A + .3X_B + 0X_Y + 0X_Z + Ma_Y + Ma_Z$

Subject to $1X_A + 2X_B - 1X_Y + 0X_Z + 1a_Y + 0a_Z = 10$ (Y)

$\qquad\qquad 2X_A + 1X_B + 0X_Y - 1X_Z + 0a_Y + 1a_Z = 8$ (Z)

where all variables ≥ 0

(c)

UNIT COST		.5	.3	0	0	M	M	
	Var. Mix	X_A	X_B	X_Y	X_Z	a_Y	a_Z	Sol.
M	$a_Y \leftarrow$	1	② ↓	−1	0	1	0	10
M	a_Z	2	1	0	−1	0	1	8
	Sac.	3M	3M	−M	−M	M	M	18M
	Imp.	.5 − 3M	.3 − 3M	M	M	0	0	—

.3	X_B	1/2 ↓	1	−1/2	0	1/2	0	5
M	$a_Z \leftarrow$	③/2	0	1/2	−1	−1/2	1	3
	Sac.	.15 +1.5M	.3	−.15 +.5M	−M	.15 −.5M	M	1.5 +3M
	Imp.	.35 −1.5M	0	.15 −.5M	M	−.15 +1.5M	0	—

.3	X_B	0	1	−8/12	2/6	8/12	−2/6	4
.5	X_A	1	0	2/6	−2/3	−2/6	2/3	2
	Sac.	.5	.3	−4/120	−7/30	1/30	7/30	2.2
	Imp.	0	0	1/30	7/30	M −1/30	M −7/30	—

$$X_A = 2 \quad X_B = 4 \quad X_Y = 0 \quad X_Z = 0 \quad P = 2.2$$

12-5 Quicker Oats should spend the following amounts:

$100,000 for television
55,000 for radio
20,000 for magazines
25,000 for prizes

12-10 The following quantities (in gallons) should be used by Horrible Harry's:

	Unleaded Gasoline	Ethyl Alcohol	Methyl Alcohol
Gasohol	29,000/3	1,000/3	—
Petrolmeth	3,500	0	1,500

12-12 Using the variables X_E = number of tons from Eastern, X_N = number of tons from Northern, X_T = number of tons from Tom's Lucky, with X_L representing unused labor, X_R and X_C as surplus variables for the Northern requirement and copper constraints, and a_R and a_C as the artificial variables, we obtain the following final simplex tableau:

UNIT PROFIT		280	185	260	0	0	0	$-M$	$-M$	
	Var. Mix	X_E	X_N	X_T	X_L	X_R	X_C	a_R	a_C	Sol.
0	X_C	0	0	75	50	80	1	-80	-1	2,000
185	X_N	0	1	0	0	-1	0	1	0	100
280	X_E	1	0	2	1	2	0	-2	0	100
	Sac.	280	185	560	280	375	0	-375	0	46,500
	Imp.	0	0	-300	-280	-375	0	$-M$ $+375$	$-M$	—

12-13 160 beef, 60 chicken, 80 fish; $C = 490$ dollars

12-16 (a) unbounded problem   (b) $X_1 = 0$, $X_2 = 10$, $X_3 = 0$; $P = 20$

13-1 Letting U_A = A cost per unit
$\qquad\quad U_B$ = B cost per unit

$\qquad$ Minimize $C = 16U_A + 24U_B$
$\qquad$ Subject to $4U_A + 6U_B \geq 12$ (variable 1)
$\qquad\qquad\qquad\quad 4U_A + 4U_B \geq 16$ (variable 2)
$\qquad$ where $U_A, U_B \geq 0$

$\qquad U_A = 4$, $U_B = 0$, $C = 64$

13-2 (b) Letting U_L = cost per hour of labor
$\qquad\qquad\qquad U_F$ = cost per frame
$\qquad$ (c) $U_L = 5/3$, $U_F = 5/3$, $C = 460/3$ dollars

13-5 (a) \$5/7; \$18/7   (b) $U_T = 0$, $U_C = 0$, $U_B = 5$ (c) $X_T = 64/7$, $X_C = 20/7$,
$\qquad X_B = 0$, $P = 1580/7$ dollars   (d) Yes

13-10 (e) Rott should make no Baltics, 400/7 Gothics, and 300/7 Chics, at a profit of \$8,500/7.

14-1 (a)

	Lower Limit	Upper Limit
Wood	36	120
Labor	50	$166\frac{2}{3}$

	(b)	(c)
X_T	54/7	40/7
X_C	30/7	100/7
X_B	0	0
P	1,530/7	2,300/7

14-2 (a)

	Lower Limit	Upper Limit
Table	15	50
Chair	6	20
Bookcase	$-\infty$	20

14-3 (a)

UNIT
PROFIT

				25			
		20	15	~~15~~	0	0	

	Var. Mix	X_T	X_C	X_B	X_W	X_L	Sol.
25	$X_B \leftarrow$	1	0	①$^{\downarrow}$	1/7	$-6/70$	64/7
15	X_C	0	1	0	$-1/7$	2/7	20/7
	Sac.	25	15	25	10/7	15/7	1,900/7
	Imp.	-5	0	0	$-10/7$	$-15/7$	—

$$X_T = 0 \qquad\qquad X_W = 0$$
$$X_C = 20/7 = 2.86 \qquad X_L = 0$$
$$X_B = 64/7 = 9.14$$
$$P = 1,900/7 = 271.43$$

14-5 (a)

UNIT
PROFIT

		20	15	15	50	0	0	

	Var. Mix	X_T	X_C	X_B	X_D	X_W	X_L	Sol.
20	$X_T \leftarrow$	1	0	1	(24/7)$^{\downarrow}$	1/7	$-6/70$	64/7
15	X_C	0	1	0	$-10/7$	$-1/7$	2/7	20/7
	Sac.	20	15	20	330/7	5/7	18/7	1,580/7
	Imp.	0	0	-5	20/7	$-5/7$	$-18/7$	—

50	X_D	9/8	0	7/24	1	1/24	$-1/40$	8/3
15	X_C	$-5/4$	1	5/12	0	$-1/12$	1/4	20/3
	Sac.	75/2	15	125/6	50	5/6	5/2	700/3
	Imp.	$-35/2$	0	$-35/6$	0	$-5/6$	$-5/2$	—

$$X_T = 0 \qquad\qquad X_D = 8/3$$
$$X_C = 20/3 \qquad\qquad X_W = 0$$
$$X_B = 0 \qquad\qquad X_L = 0$$
$$P = 700/3 = 233.33$$

14-12 (a)

Constraint	Lower Limit	Upper Limit
A	70	∞
B	40	72
C	− ∞	75
D	14.5	25

(b) Only X_A changes, to 130.

(c) $X_1 = 10$, $X_2 = 0$, $X_3 = 10$; $X_A = 40$, $X_B = 0$, $X_C = 30$; $P = 300$

14-13 (a)

Variable	Lower Limit	Upper Limit
X_1	− ∞	20
X_2	− ∞	30
X_3	12.5	∞

(b) 360

14-14

UNIT PROFIT		10	15	10	0	0	0	− M	
	Var. Mix	X_1	X_2	X_3	X_A	X_B	X_C	a_D	Sol.
10	X_1	1	0	0	0	− 1/3	1/15	− 1/3	26/3
10	X_3	0	0	1	0	1/6	− 2/15	2/3	23/3
0	X_A	0	0	0	1	− 1/2	1/5	− 4	41
15	X_2	0	1	0	0	1/6	1/15	2/3	11/3
	Sac.	10	15	10	0	5/6	1/3	40/3	655/3
	Imp.	0	0	0	0	− 5/6	− 1/3	− M − 40/3	—

14-16 (a) New X_4 Column   (b) New Solution

New X_4 Column	New Solution
1/2	$X_1 = 0$
1/2	$X_2 = 0$
− 1	$X_3 = 10$
1/2	$X_4 = 10$
	$P = 400$

15-1 (b)

From \ To	U	V	W
A	—	50	50
B	—	—	150
C	150	150	—

$C = 4,350$

15-4

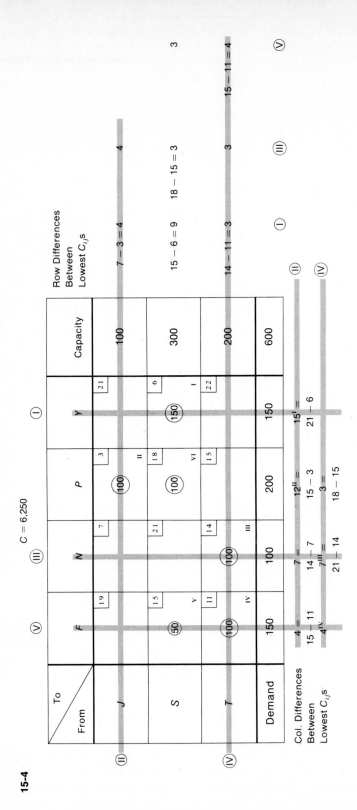

15-5 Ship 100 tombstones to Eldred from Abinger, and ship 50 tombstones to Cedrick and 150 tombstones to Dunstan from Barnesly.

15-11

Brat	Chore
Fritz	Retrieve the Captain's pipe
Hans	Scare cannibals
Gert	Pen ostriches
Zelda	Chase hippos

15-13

Production	Used for Demand
August regular—25	August—25
August overregular—75 ⎫	September—175
September regular—100 ⎭	
October regular—100 ⎫	October—150
October overtime—50 ⎭	
November regular—100 ⎫	November—150
November overtime—50 ⎭	
$C = \$27{,}875$	

16-1 (c) $X_1 = 2, X_2 = 3; P = 18$

16-4 $X_R = 6, X_D = 6; P = 150$

16-8

Person	Job	Cost
A	L	5
B	N	7
C	M	8
D	K	6
E	J	11
		37

16-12 $X_T = 9, X_C = 3, X_B = 0; P = 225$

17-2 (a) 1/2   (d) 2/3

17-5 (a)

Result	Unconditional Probability	Posterior Probability	
		Fair	Crooked
7	7/12	1/7	6/7
Not 7	5/12	1	0

17-7 (d) Distribute the film as an "A" feature if the results of the sneak preview are favorable, but sell to TV (T) if the results are unfavorable.

17-8 (c) The optimal strategy is to retain the old box if sales decrease and to use the new box otherwise.

18-1 (b)

Number of Children Liking	Proportion		
	$P = 1/4$	$P = 1/2$	$P = 3/4$
$R = 0$	.4219	.1250	.0156
$R = 1$	.4219	.3750	.1406
$R = 2$	.1406	.3750	.4219
$R = 3$	.0156	.1250	.4219
	1.0000	1.0000	1.0000

(e)

P	Posterior Probability
1/4	.0278
1/2	.2222
3/4	.7500
	1.0000

18-6 (a) Sample with $n = 2$.   (b) $C = 1$ for $n = 1$; $C = 0$ for $n = 2$.

18-8 (b) $C = 1$ (c) $1,317.30   (d) $417.30

18-11 (a) Leave alone.   (b) $300   He would not sample for a cost of $400, but he might sample if the cost is only $200.

18-12 (b) $C = 25g$ (c) $120.23   (d) $70.23

19-1

	(a)	(b)	(c)	(d)
(1)	A	B	A	B
(2)	$1,978	$4,166	$35,090	$30,690

19-2 (a) Payoff $= \begin{cases} -\$50,000 + \$1,000\,\mu & \text{for helmet} \\ \$\,0 & \text{for no helmet} \end{cases}$

$\mu_b = 50$ helmets per store

(b) Yes   (c) $833.20

19-5 (a) $14,688
(b) 1.59 gigabits per day
(c) $\mu_1 = 1.76$; $\sigma_1 = .57$ Choose the photographic unit.
(d) .3372

19-9 (a) $114.52

	(1)	(2)	(3)	(4)
(b)	$1.84	$7.63	$23.90	$59.88
(c)	$-$ .16	$3.13	$11.40	$ 9.88

$n = 25$ is best
(d) Choose A_1 if $\bar{X} = 3.6$ and A_2 if $\bar{X} = 3.9$.

20-3 (a)

Events	Acts	
	Policy	No Policy
Tornado	$-$500	$-$40,000
No tornado	$-$500	0

(b) $-\$500$ for a policy; $-\$4$ for no policy   (c) No

20-5 (a)

	Acts	
Events	Buy	Rent
Win contract	$120,000	$50,000
Lose contract	$-40,000$	0

(b) $40,000 for buying; $25,000 for renting

(c)

	Acts	
Events	Buy	Rent
Win contract	400	300
Lose contract	0	200

(d) 200 for buying; 250 for renting   (e) Rent

20-9 (a) Willing   (b,c) Might be willing   (d) Unwilling   (e) Willing

20-11 No

20-12 (a) 1/2   (b) 3/4; 1/4   (c) 1/2   Inconsistent

21-1 (a) No   (b) Yes   (c) Maybe

21-3 (a) 60 sec; 22.4 sec   (b) (1) .3472   (2) .0594   (3) .5000   (4) .8832

21-6 (a) .105   (b) .15   (c) .38   (d) .73

21-11 302

22-2 A_3, A_4, B_3, B_4, B_5

22-4 (b) $P = 7/16$; Value of game $= -1/16$ (c) $Q = 7/16$ (d) Unchanged
(e) Unchanged   (f) 13/20; Yes

22-7

DRACULA		UNION	
Act	Probability	Act	Probability
Tranquil	2/9	Tranquil	4/9
Lock-in	7/9	Strike	5/9
Bite union leaders	0	Wooden stake sabotage	0

$V = $ value of game $= 100/9$ coffins

22-8 (c)

PLAYER A		PLAYER B	
Act	Probability	Act	Probability
A_1	1/5	B_1	0
A_2	4/5	B_2	1/5
A_3	0	B_3	4/5

$V = $ value of game $= 9/5$

22-10 (a) No   (b,c) Expand (for both)   (d) Do not expand

22-13 (a) Both players should choose blue; 1 cent.   (b) Yes; 5 cents.

23-1 (a) .632121   (b) .006738   (c) .128597

23-4

	(a)	(b)	(c)	(d)
L	4	2	.67	1.33
W	.20	.25	.34	3.33
L_q	3.2	1.33	.27	.76
W_q	.16	.17	.13	1.90
	.8	.67	.4	.57

23-7 (a) .20   (b) 66.67%; 2 hours

23-11 $34

23-12 (a) (1) .0923 hour   (2) .0606 hour   (b) (1) $28.38   (2) $21.82
       One machinist clerk is cheapest.

23-14 (a) 5 checkers; 1.11 minutes   (b) .290 minute   (c) $56.66 for $S = 5$; $61.74
       for $S = 6$

23-16 (a) .0774   (b) .9797   (c) .0286   (d) .6315

23-18 (a)

n	P_n
0	.271
1	.217
2	.173
3	.139
4	.111
5	.089

     (b) $L = 1.868$, $L_q = 1.139$, $W_q = .31$ hour, $W = .51$ hour   (c) $L = 4$, $L_q = 3.2$,
     $W_q = .8$ hour, $W = 1$ hour

23-19 (a)

n	P_n
0	.0367
1	.0918
2	.1835
3	.2753
4	.2753
5	.1376

     (b) $L_q = 2.11$, $L = 3.07$, $W_q = 1.09$ days, $W = 1.59$ days   (c) $L_q = .5$, $L = 1$,
     $W_q = .5$ day, $W = 1$ day

23-20 $L_q = .1475$, $L = .6475$, $W_q = .295$ minute, $W = 1.295$ minutes

23-21 $L_q = .25$, $L = .75$, $W_q = .5$ minute, $W = 1.5$ minutes

24-1 a–c–e

24-3 b–f–g–h

24-7 (a) a–c–d–f–i–j–k–m–n–o–p 32 months

24-9 (a)

Activity	Expected Time	Variance
a	6	.11
b	7	5.44
c	14	7.11
d	4	.11
e	17	.11

(b) $a-c-d$ (c) .7568

25-2 $1/\lambda = 13.05$ seconds

25-5 385

25-7 (a) $95.57 \leq \mu \leq 105.49$ minutes   (b) $69.05 \leq \mu \leq 69.35$ inches
(c) $\$11.27 \leq \mu \leq \$12.73$

25-10 $89.142 for one barber; $113.191 for two barbers. Hire the helper.

25-13 (a)

Net Winnings	Probability
$-\$1$	20/36
1	14/36
2	1/36
3	1/36

(c) $-\$.09$

26-1 (a,b,c) $1-2-5-9-13$ cost = 24 dollars

26-3 (a) $495   (b) All items are zero except for radio transmitters, 3 of which will be carried.

26-5 Produce 400 units in February, March, and May, and make no units in the other months, at a cost of $5,075.

26-6 Assign two trucks to sites 1 and 2 and one truck to site 3, at a cost of $40,250.

26-10 The two best policies are: (1) to buy 3 CD-10s, 1 Tupolev 100, and none of the other models, or (2) to buy 5 Tupolev 100s.

27-1 $p_A = .5294$, $p_B = .4706$

27-3 (a) $p_1 = 3/7$, $p_2 = 4/7$ (b) In period 4

27-5 Policy 3

27-9 (a) 7,977   (b) 9,080.2

Index

S